Building the Kingdom:
Giannozzo Manetti on the Material and Spiritual Edifice

Medieval and Renaissance Texts and Studies

Volume 317

Arizona Studies in the Middle Ages and the Renaissance

Volume 20

Building the Kingdom:
Giannozzo Manetti on the Material and Spiritual Edifice

Christine Smith and Joseph F. O'Connor

ACMRS
(Arizona Center for Medieval and Renaissance Studies)
Tempe, Arizona
in collaboration with
BREPOLS
2006

ASMAR Volume 20: ISBN 978-2-503-52581-5 D/2007/0095/29

Library of Congress Cataloging-in-Publication Data

Smith, Christine (Christine Hunnikin)
Building the kingdom : Giannozzo Manetti on the material and spiritual edifice / Christine Smith and Joseph F. O'Connor.
p. cm. -- (Medieval and Renaissance texts and studies ; v 317)
Includes bibliographical references.
ISBN-13: 978-0-86698-362-4 (alk. paper)
ISBN-10: 0-86698-362-7 (alk. paper)
1. Manetti, Giannozzo, 1396-1459. Vita Nicolai V summi pontificis. 2. Manetti, Giannozzo, 1396-1459. De secularibus et pontificalibus pompis. 3. Nicholas V, Pope, 1397-1455--Art patronage--Early works to 1800. 4. Santa Maria del Fiore (Cathedral : Florence, Italy)--Early works to 1800. 5. Architectural criticism--Italy--Early works to 1800. I. Manetti, Giannozzo, 1396-1459. Vita Nicolai V summi pontificis. English & Latin. Selections. II. Manetti, Giannozzo, 1396-1459.a De secularibus et pontificalibus pompis. English & Latin. III. O'Connor, Joseph F., 1943- IV. Arizona Center for Medieval and Renaissance Studies. V. Title.

NA2599.8.M36S65 2006
720.945'09024--dc22

2006038856

∞
This book is made to last.
It is set in Adobe Caslon Pro,
smyth-sewn and printed on acid-free paper
to library specifications.
Printed in the United States of America

Table of Contents

Part Two

Acknowledgments

This book grew out of a larger project we embarked on over ten years ago. Both the project and the book advanced because of the encouragement of sponsors willing to entertain the idea that a collaboration between an art historian and a classicist might bear interesting fruit. Grants from the Research Division of the National Endowment for the Humanities and from the J. Paul Getty Trust enabled us to undertake the fundamental work upon which all our subsequent joint effort was based. Research across disciplines is notoriously time-consuming, and the wide-ranging nature of our study stretched us even further. As the book's scope enlarged beyond its original modest ambitions, the work was sustained by additional support from the Harvard Graduate School of Design, Georgetown University's Graduate School of Arts and Sciences, and the Mellon Fellowship Program of St. Louis University's Vatican Microfilm Library. We owe particular thanks to Dean Peter Rowe of Harvard, Dean Gerald Mara of Georgetown, and the late Dr. Charles Ermatinger of St. Louis University for their interest in our project.

Much of our work together was conducted in the Byzantine Library of Dumbarton Oaks in Washington, D.C., and at the American Academy in Rome; both extended to us not only the means to conduct our research, but a stimulating and hospitable welcome to the community of scholars resident there. The texts we edited and many unpublished source materials were accessible to us through the generosity of the Vatican Library, the Biblioteca Medicea Laurentiana in Florence, and the Vatican Film Library in St. Louis. In all of these places, the directors and staff provided access, help, and unfailing courtesy. Further work was advanced through the astonishing holdings of Harvard's Widener and Houghton Libraries and the library of Villa I Tatti, the Harvard Center for Renaissance Studies. These great libraries are treasures which we were privileged to enjoy.

In the final stages of the book, we were fortunate to draw on the expertise of others. Steven Wolf took our descriptions of the Vatican Palace's complicated history and plan and converted them into digital images. Christopher L. Celenza, reading for MRTS, provided us with lengthy, detailed, and perceptive comments and further bibliographical suggestions which we welcomed and found useful and stimulating, particularly in the area of Renaissance intellectual and institutional history. Julia Haig Gaisser of Bryn Mawr reviewed closely the texts, translations, and commentaries and made numerous invaluable suggestions. Leslie MacCoull edited the final manuscript with a thoroughness, scholarly erudition and intelligence for which we are grateful.

While our book was at press some important studies appeared which we were not able to incorporate, in particular Anna Modigliani's critical edition and Italian translation of the *Life of Nicholas V* (Rome, 2005); we did, however take into account her 1999 Italian translation of the same work. The new critical edition and translation of Leon Battista Alberti's *Momus* (Cambridge, MA, 2003) appeared too late for us to cite it as the standard work. We took account of Stefano Borsi's *Leon Battista Alberti e Roma* (Florence, 2003) in the notes to our text, but not of his *Leon Battista Alberti e l'antichità romana* (Florence, 2004). We were not able to consult Alessio Monciatti's *Il Palazzo Vaticano nel medioevo* (Florence, 2005).

An earlier version of Chapter 2 was published in *Atti del VII Centenario del Duomo di Firenze. II. La cattedrale come spazio sacro*, eds. T. Verdon and A. Innocenti (Florence, 2001) and of Chapter 4 in *Perspectives on Early Modern and Modern Intellectual History* (Rochester, 2000); a portion of Chapter 7 appeared in *Studia Humanitatis. Essays in Honor of Salvatore Camporeale* (Baltimore, 2004).

PREFACE

Great buildings were leading double lives well before the birth of Christ. The Tower of Babel represented human pride and ambition to the ancient Hebrews; the Jerusalem Temple, the locus of encounter between humanity and divinity; Hellenistic observers saw evidence of technological and cultural achievement in the Seven Wonders. As the largest objects conceived and made by humans, exceptional buildings were more, and other, than their materials, design, engineering, and ornament. Only with the advent of Christianity, however, did human beings become buildings, "built up" in faith as temples (Ephesians 2:20-21), and "living stones" (1 Peter 2:5) of the City of God. The metaphor once inverted, the lives of buildings and persons were inextricably intertwined: reference to one implied the other, and the "Last Judgment" about an edifice was of its moral character, not artistic merit.[1] Thus the great architectural ekphrases of religious structures in the Christian era—Paulus Silentiarus's on Hagia Sophia or Abbot Suger's on St. Denis, are good examples—evoke not only the material building but also an invisible double, the spiritual edifice. Such descriptions are not only repositories of factual information about buildings but also vehicles for expressing the values and ideas of their authors. It is the author who confers significance on the building by articulating the aspirations of its builder and reporting the spectators' response.

We study such accounts, two of which are our subject here, as intellectual history. Drawing on our respective expertises in architecture history and in classical languages and literatures, we go about this in a particular way. We first match the verbal description to the edifice to test its accuracy: a fully developed ekphrasis is literature, shaped by its author's knowledge and purposes. The ways in which an account is partial or misleading are clues to these. Establishing from where the author draws his ideas about buildings—these are almost never fresh inventions—is philological work of tracing technical terms, aesthetic criteria, and imagery. Then we relate the text to its contexts, above all to the author's intellectual profile, but also to historical and cultural circumstances. Although we are almost never sure whether the author's view is reliable evidence for that of the patron and audience or an accurate account of the physical building, we know what is probable through comparison with other contemporaneous testimony, both built and written. In the end, having clarified what the author says, we interpret what he means.

---

[1] J. Onians, "The Last Judgment of Renaissance Architecture," *Royal Society of Arts Journal* 128 (1980): 701-20.

Our conclusions primarily concern the author, who has certainly said what he has said, secondarily the building, and only tentatively the builder and audience.

This being our method, our study of Giannozzo Manetti's accounts of Florence Cathedral in *On the Secular and Pontifical Parades* (*De pompis*) and of Pope Nicholas V's architectural patronage in his *Life of Nicholas V, Supreme Pontiff* is bifocal, seeking to clarify both the physical reality described and Manetti's literary procedures and purposes. We offer here a close reading of these two texts. Though both focus on architecture, Manetti is not interested in buildings principally as artifacts, but as extensions of thought, values, and experience. Both descriptions privilege new religious structures as of the highest importance, and both connect a great church to a remarkable historical event that took place in it. These structures are religious both in function and in their larger purposes, and Manetti approaches them, not as a Christian scholar or a theologian, but as a Christian observer of his own world. Our challenge is to discern the ways in which Manetti situates these buildings within his culture and within his understanding of human and sacred history. We draw some general conclusions about the author, the author, that is, of these particular works and not Manetti in general: because it is in these texts, uniquely, that Manetti seeks to connect the materiality and particularity of a physical—indeed, his personal—experience of buildings with immaterial and general concepts.

The first text, little known before Eugenio Battisti published a transcription in 1960, is his *De secularibus et pontificalibus pompis*, a description of the events surrounding the consecration of Florence Cathedral on 25 March 1436; the work includes an ekphrasis of the church's ornamented interior. Since the building still stands and will be well known to most readers, it provides a firm standard against which to measure Manetti's account. The liturgy of consecration is also fixed, so we can be fairly certain about how the account relates to what actually took place. These "controls" are fundamental for evaluating the second text, Book 2 of his *Life of Nicholas V, Supreme Pontiff*. This contains one of the most famous architectural ekphrases of the early Renaissance, Nicholas's plan for extensive building and renovation in Rome: a reconfiguration of the Borgo and the Apostolic Palace and the construction of a new basilica of St. Peter. In this case what the projects exactly consisted of is controversial, and the physical and documentary evidence is fragmentary. In fact, they are known best through Manetti's account. Our commitment is to attain greater clarity about what he says: in some cases this also clarifies what was built. Manetti records an exceptionally pivotal pontificate, for the achievements of which the buildings are the main exemplar. Nicholas V was the first pope to reside uninterruptedly in Rome since the early fourteenth century, his predecessors having been obliged to live at Avignon or elsewhere because Rome was insecure. And Nicholas was the first to reside permanently at the Vatican rather than at Rome's cathedral, St. John Lateran, initiating the practice still followed today. Under Nicholas the last antipope abdicated, thus ending the

Western schism; some internal reform of the church was begun, and the great debate over church governance—indeed, over the nature of the church—was engaged by a pontiff and his Curia with adequate financial, physical, and political resources. The nature and significance of Nicholas's building projects are essential keys to the historic importance of this pontificate.

We provide here a critical edition of both texts, based on the principal manuscripts, together with English translations and commentaries. Since the architectural portion of the *Life of Nicholas* constitutes the organizing image of Manetti's assessment of his papacy, we present the entirety of Book 2 of the *Life* on the achievements of his reign. In addition, we include a brief excerpt from Book 3, the "Testament," where Manetti represents Nicholas on his deathbed explaining his motives for his building project; though it adds no new architectural information, it provides a different voice—if authentic, that of the patron himself—through which the project may be evaluated.

This study of Manetti's architectural ideas began as a translation project and was at the outset, of necessity, primarily concerned with his language. His Latin grammar is transparent; his meaning less so. As our study progressed, we realized that Manetti's descriptions are rooted in his knowledge, primarily philological, of the Greek and Latin classics and in the Scriptures and Christian Fathers. His library was substantial, his reading was wide, and he was part of the early Humanist movement that recovered and translated many hitherto unknown texts. He continually alludes to classical and Christian writers, none more so than Paul and Augustine, and his themes and images are generally drawn from them. To trace his thought, we examined primary sources: his other works, books we know him to have owned or to which he had access, classical works that were coming to light in the first half of the Quattocentro, and works of his contemporaries. We found that his use of his sources was eclectic, suited to the topic at hand, but that his thought was not eclectic in every subject. His logic, physics, and ethics mostly clearly correspond to the Scholastic understanding of Aristotle; his politics and concept of history are Augustinian; and his theology is Pauline. His concern for order, for instance, can certainly be associated with the ideas of pseudo-Dionysius the Areopagite, newly translated by his teacher Ambrogio Traversari. Yet he was attracted to that aspect of Dionysius's thought because of his even more pronounced attachment to Scholastic and Aristotelian dialectic, Augustine's understanding of the human condition, and Paul's spirituality. These, we suggest, are the foundations of Manetti's literary and intellectual personality. We believe that a faithful rendering of Manetti's thought will be consonant with these few privileged sources, even though his eclectic reading put at his disposal a diverse and disparate fund of facts and ideas, which he summoned at will.

In the light of this, we had to recover, as best we could, how he uses words, even commonplace words. We discovered that his vocabulary is often shaped by his reading, but not usually Paul and Augustine. He prefers a technically precise vocabulary often from Aristotle (whether directly or indirectly) or from biblical commentaries and glosses, both patristic and medieval. In many instances, his particular use of words, which had eluded many of his modern readers, dramatically affects and enriches his meaning. These discoveries became such an important component of our work that we devote two chapters to his use of words and his rhetorical practice; numerous entries in the commentaries further elucidate his use of language. We clarify the availability of drawings for Nicholas's projects; how Manetti understood mass and space and therefore architectural and urban form; and, in the case of the Vatican palace, a close study of his vocabulary has led to a new interpretation of Nicholas's planned renovations there.

In the course of this study, then, we came to approach Manetti in a way different from other interpreters. Much has been written by historians and art historians on the material fabric of these buildings and on their relation to political, institutional, and cultural history. We hope to shed new light from a different direction by examining how Manetti's words and arguments endow these buildings with meaning. Once we realized that his technical vocabulary derives from his reading and not from architectural practice, his underlying meaning clarifies; it is in dialogue with Augustine and Aristotle and other thinkers, past and contemporary, whose work he knew and had absorbed. Two contexts assume large importance. First, when his works are set beside his reading they become engaged in a set of values and ideas both traditional and new. Second, when they are read in the specific context of the work in which they are embedded, the architectural descriptions advance Manetti's literary purposes. In the case of *De pompis*, for example, Manetti's ekphrasis of Florence Cathedral is inseparable from its liturgical function: the action of consecration endows the place consecrated with profound historical and theological significance. So too, in our second text, the coronation of Frederick III illuminates the special nature of ceremonials that would take place in Nicholas's new St. Peter's and reinforces Manetti's view of the papacy within secular and sacred history. To show the relationship of the architectural narratives to Manetti's larger themes, we have looked at the overall organization of the texts, particularly the *Life*. Architecture functions both as a reality and as a metaphor within his work; this becomes clearer if we understand his aims and strategies in the whole text.

The result does not purport to be an even-handed assessment of Nicholas V, or an objective church history, or a systematic intellectual biography of Giannozzo Manetti, or even architectural history. It deals instead with architecture as it can be described and as a repository of ideas and arguments. These texts become eloquent witnesses to Manetti's response to, and construction of, his world. Our chapters deal with his rhetoric and descriptive vocabulary; his experiential approach to knowledge; the interaction of liturgy, architecture, and experience; the place of books and buildings in the Roman Church as an institutional entity; the moral issues of patronage; "wholeness" as a criterion of architectural excellence; the theology of building; and Manetti's historic view of Nicholas V's pontificate.

We carry further and amplify recent scholarship which acknowledges a criticism of papal policies that underlies the encomiastic praise dominating the surface of the narrative in the *Life of Nicholas V*, where architecture is the central paradigm for papal prestige and the authority of the church, that is, for the pope as a ruler and the church as a political institution. The liabilities of rulership are never more clear than in the Quattrocento debate over the issues of magnificence and tyranny, of which architecture is a visible and material extension. If buildings manifest, in Manetti's account, Nicholas's greatness as a ruler, they become for his detractors the main focus of their criticism. We understand not only the buildings account, but indeed the *Life* as a whole, to be apologetic and we examine it from this point of view in our chapters.

The commentaries which follow the texts and translations add further clarification and engage still other issues, sometimes at length; they are meant as complementary to the narratives of the chapters. In a sense, however, all that we have written is a kind of gloss on these two texts, with those topics requiring a lengthier, expository treatment or explication with much non-Manettian material in the form of chapters and shorter, more factual, or entirely internal material relegated to the commentaries. It was not our aim to provide a unified overall account of either work: there is abundant and excellent bibliography of this kind on both, to which we direct the reader. On the other hand, we comment knowing which aspects of the texts scholars have found most problematic: we concentrate our effort where we can further the state of knowledge, as on the description of the Vatican Palace; where a closer reading of the text does not, as in the vexed problem of Manetti's unit of measurement, we summarize the issue for colleagues who may have more luck. Again, if our discoveries advance scholarship on questions for which the text has been evoked as evidence—Early Renaissance architectural and urban theory or the role of Leon Battista Alberti, for instance—we give a fuller treatment.

What, then, do we conclude about our author? Manetti is deeply interested in both the secular and the sacred, or rather, discerning the sacred through the secular. In both the consecration description and the life of Nicholas V, he presents display and magnificence as manifestations of the Church Militant becoming the Church Triumphant. In so doing, he takes a particular stand on the relation of the supernatural to the natural, in which the former is manifest in the latter. Whether he describes this relation as a sketch in which the appearance of the finished painting can already be discerned, or as a mirror-image reflection, Manetti sees the life and works of his own time as holy and for that reason meaningful. We might liken his view to Augustine's idea of historical reality as the City of God in pilgrimage in this world, or to the pseudo-Dionysius the Areopagite's notion of mystical *theosis*, or to the ecclesiological concept of the sanctification of the Church Militant. But for Manetti, though familiar with these contexts, assumption of the presence of the supernatural in the natural is not an intellectual opinion but rather the particular mode of his religious understanding. It is different from apocalypticism or millennialism, for Manetti believes the reign of Christ to have begun and the Kingdom of God to be at hand.

Manetti is neither an abstract thinker nor a theologian. His experience is not the impetus for allegorical or symbolic discourse; he constructs no logical systems. His practical theology affirms the continuing value, utility, and authority of tradition, understood as the immediate past—which we call medieval or Scholastic—amplified by the remote past of pagan and Christian antiquity. Thus he takes his clarity of organization and precision of terminology from the Scholastics, but composes Ciceronian periodic sentences for attractiveness and eloquence. His linguistic practice is at one with his general view of culture: he sees the new Humanist library as a traditional Scholastic library to which classical and secular works are added; and in architecture, he understands that already existing buildings can be augmented and modified in order to create a perfect whole. Manetti's conservatism and eclecticism have disappointed those who believe that rejection of the past is the precondition for progress, that vision requires originality, and that the sacred and the secular are incompatible, the one holding the other back. Yet Manetti exemplifies a way of living not heroically, but thoughtfully, harmoniously connected to his world, appreciative of and appreciated by his contemporaries. He addresses a readership of different educational backgrounds, coming from different social classes, and exercising different professions: the dual dedication of the *Life*, to a rich merchant interested in art and to a trained theologian and prince of the church, is paradigmatic. A layman, he writes about religion and the church in the kind of language his readers understood.

If Manetti were not convinced of the value of the particular, the material, and the here-and-now, he would not have composed descriptions of buildings, related contemporary events, or recorded the biography of a contemporary person. Rooted firmly in the world of his own experience, he believes it to have significant intellectual and cultural as well as theological import. Moreover, he trusts that this can be articulated and shared through a detailed account. Though these two texts dwell on architecture, they are not primarily interested in architecture for its own sake, but in articulating for his readers how its experience fits in the great order of things, an order which he believes is divine. For human affairs this order is most clearly manifest in his view of government based on classical political theory and Christianized. This theory combines Augustine's *City of God* with Scholastic interpretations of Aristotle as advanced especially by Dominican expositors. To these are added new Humanist insights argued through the use of historical exemplars and applied to current events. In the end, Manetti believes that human dignity is fulfilled in the coming-into-being of God's reign. The material edifice advances on earth the building of the Kingdom.

Abbreviations

PG	Patrologia Graeca
PL	Patrologia Latina
RIS	*Rerum Italicarum Scriptores*
CAG	Commentaria in Aristotelem Graeca
CCSL	Corpus Christianorum, Series Latina
CCCM	Corpus Christianorum, Continuatio Mediaevalis

List of Illustrations

Part I

Introduction to the Author: "A Most Learned Man, A Man of the Highest Modesty and Prudence, A Man Who Deserves Our Affection"

So Poggio Bracciolini described Giannozzo Manetti to Pietro da Noceto, familiar of Pope Nicholas V, upon Manetti's appointment as papal secretary in 1451.[1] Besides his intellect and virtue, Vespasiano da Bisticci, his admiring biographer, remembers him as a man of great faith: "He used to say that our faith ought not to be called faith but certitude since all the articles of religion, written and approved by the Church, are as true as saying a triangle is a triangle" (*Vite*, 1:488). These qualities — learning, probity, and faith — are evidenced through his career and his writings. A friend of the leading intellectuals of his day, he was admired for his reading and retentive memory. His uprightness of character lent authority to the public duties he assumed for the Florentine Republic. Though a layman, he was a leading scripture scholar and deeply committed to Christian culture as embodied in the institution of the papacy.

Manetti was born in 1396 to a wealthy Florentine merchant family and seemed destined to a life of commerce. By 1425 he belonged to the Bankers and Money Changers Guild; by 1427 his family was the tenth richest in Florence. In 1421, however, at the age of twenty-five, he began an intensive course of study in grammar, rhetoric, philosophy, and especially theology under the tutelage of Girolamo da Napoli and Evangelista da Pisa, both later prominent in the Florentine Studio.[2] His further study was influenced throughout the 1430s by his association with Ambrogio Traversari, who guided his studies in Greek and at whose prompting he began the study of Hebrew. Vespasiano portrays him as a leader in an intellectual circle during the Florentine stay of Pope Eugenius IV, who personally honored him (*Vite*, 1:48). This circle, which included Leonardo

---

[1] "He is a most learned man, a man of the highest modesty and prudence, a man who deserves our affection. I am not displeased that he is my personal friend. His virtue and his authority bring a fuller dignity to that office": *Epistulae* 3, 64, quoted by A. Greco in *Vespasiano da Bisticci: Le Vite* (Florence, 1970), 1:491–92, n. 3.

[2] Vespasiano gives brief lives of both: *Vite*, 2:393–96.

Bruni, Poggio Bracciolini, and Carlo Marsuppini, also nourished the Humanist interests of the young Tommaso Parentucelli, the future Pope Nicholas V, whose authoritative biography Manetti would write (*Vitae* 1:42–43). During all this time, he continued to manage his business affairs, only later in his career gradually transferring the family interests to his sons.

The scope of his learning can be gauged by the depth of his library and by the range of his own writings. Enabled by his wealth, he amassed one of the largest collections of books in private hands in the early Quattrocentro.[3] His writings are everywhere informed by his broad reading; even in early works such as the *De illustribus longaevis* of 1436,[4] he could summon authors as diverse as Tertullian, Rhabanus Maurus, Homer, Livy, Plato, Plutarch, and Petrarch, as well as the Old and New Testaments. His works affirm the variety of his interests: translations of Greek and Hebrew Scripture and of Aristotle's ethical works;[5] a philosophical work on the nature and dignity of man;[6] lives of Socrates, Seneca, Dante, Petrarch, and Boccaccio;[7] a compilation of historical persons who lived long lives; another compilation, titled *Against the Jews and Gentiles*;[8] and various other works. In his own day, however, he was especially known for his eloquence

---

[3] For an enumeration of Manetti's books in Latin, see G. Cagni, "I codici Vaticani Palatino-Latini appartenuti alla biblioteca di Giannozzo Manetti," *La bibliofilia* 62 (1960): 1–43.

[4] *De illustribus longaevis*, Bib. Vat., MS. Pal. lat. 1603, fols.

[5] Manetti's Latin translations of the Psalms and the New Testament are preserved in Vatican MSS. Pal. Lat. 40–43 and 45 and Urb. Lat. 5 and 6. These were apparently completed in Naples between 1455 and 1457. See J. Bentley, *Humanists and Holy Writ: New Testament Scholarship in the Renaissance* (Princeton, 1983), 58.

[6] G. Manetti, *De dignitate et excellentia hominis*, ed. E. Leonard (Padua, 1975). Alfonso of Aragon asked Manetti to write this treatise during an embassy to Naples in 1452; the project was delayed by Manetti's participation in the Florentine embassy to the coronation of Frederick III in March of that year but then was completed sometime in 1452–1453. An earlier version dates to before 1449. See C. Trinkaus, *'In Our Image and Likeness': Humanity and Divinity in Italian Humanist Thought* (London, 1970), 231; O. Glaap, *Untersuchungen zu Giannozzo Manetti 'De Dignitate et excellentia hominis'. Ein Renaissance-Humanist und sein Menschenbild* (Stuttgart, 1994), 13 ff.; F. Lelli, "Jews, Humanists and the Reappraisal of Pagan Wisdom Associated with the Ideal of the *Dignitas hominis*," in *Hebraica Veritas?: Christian Hebraists and the Study of Judaism in Early Modern Europe*, ed. A. Coudert and J. Shoulson (Philadelphia, 2004), 49–70.

[7] *Biographical Writings*, ed. and trans. S. Baldassarri and R. Bagemihl (Cambridge, MA, 2003).

[8] The work, written 1454–1459, is known from a single manuscript, Vat. Urb. Lat. 154. See A. De Petris, "L'*adversus Iudeos et gentes* di Giannozzo Manetti," *Rinascimento* 16 (1976): 193–205.

as an orator. His speeches to the Genoese, Sienese, Venetians, and others were circulated and read.[9] The speeches, in contrast with his other works, were part of his public career as an ambassador for the Florentine Republic on some of its most important diplomatic and ceremonial missions. He represented Florence at the wedding of the Prince of Naples (1445) and delivered the official congratulations to Nicholas V on his accession to the papacy (1447)[10] and to Frederick III on his coronation (1452).[11]

Nicholas made Manetti a papal secretary in 1451, but only in 1453, because Cosimo de'Medici's ill-will made Florence unsafe, did Manetti relocate to Rome. There he intended to complete two projects, a new Latin translation of Hebrew and Greek Scriptures and an encyclopedic work called *Against the Jews and Gentiles*. Neither was complete when Nicholas died in 1455. Manetti seems to have remained in Rome early into the reign of Callixtus III, composing his monumental *Life of Nicholas V* and arguing in favor of the continuation of Nicholas's policies.[12] Of the two works which brought him to Rome, the latter, not really an attack on Jewish or pagan learning, but an enumeration of Hebrew and classical figures who contributed greatly to the emergence of Christian culture, was partially completed at the court of Alfonso of Aragon. The Old Testament translation project produced only the *Psalms*, which were widely criticized; this criticism led him to write his last work, *Apologeticus*, defending his undertaking and explaining the scholarly principles upon which it was based.[13] Of the New Testament, he translated the Gospels, letters of Paul, and the book of Revelation. He died in Naples in 1459.

At the end of the Quattrocento, Paolo Cortesi, reviewing the learned men whom the century had produced, singled out two as especially distinguished for learning: Giannozzo Manetti and Leon Battista Alberti (1404–1472).[14] Manetti he held to be "the most learned of all," possessing "a wonderful keenness for all branches of learning." Some eulogizing verses, probably dating from shortly after Manetti's death and found on the last page of a manuscript of Thomas Aquinas' *Summa Theologiae*, suggest the reasons for his status:

---

[9] G. Petti Balbi, *Giannozzo Manetti: Elogi dei Genovesi* (Milan, 1974); *Giannozzo Manetti. Das Corpus der Orationes*, ed. H.W. Wittschier (Cologne, 1968).

[10] Bib. Vat., MS. Urb. lat. 387, fols. 184v–188r.

[11] M. Freher, ed., *Germanicarum Rerum Scriptores* (Hanover, 1611), 3:5–14.

[12] For the entire *Life*, see *Vita Nicolai summi pontificis*, in Muratori, *RIS*, 3.2:907–60; and Giannozzo Manetti, *Vita di Nicolò V*, Italian trans., intro. and comm. A. Modigliani, pref. M. Miglio (Rome, 1999).

[13] *Giannozzo Manetti. Apologeticus*, ed. A. De Petris (Rome, 1981).

[14] P. Cortesi, *De hominibus doctis dialogus*, trans. and ed. M. Graziosi (Rome, 1973), 32. The work dates ca. 1490 and was dedicated to Lorenzo de'Medici.

The Hebrews augment the native Latins' tears
while the Greeks, Giannozzo, lament your loss.
So that there might remain before the eyes
an image of a better life, his survivors have painted
Giannozzo here. The Hebrew, Greek, and Latin Muses
have adorned him with laurel;his probity rendered the signs golden.[15]

The inscription stresses the three classical languages — Hebrew, Greek, and Latin — which Manetti had mastered and the probity of his life. Others also testify to the high esteem in which Manetti was held: Antonio da Barga, completing his history of Tuscany in 1449, included Manetti as one of the six most distinguished and highly regarded men of his time.[16] Vespasiano da Bisticci not only included Manetti in his *Vite* but also wrote a separate, extensive biography of him, the *Commentario*. Naldo Naldi also composed a biography.[17]

---

[15] In A. Bandini, *Catalogus codicum latinorum Bibliothecae Mediceae Laurentianae* (Florence, 1764), 2:36. The manuscript (III.36. Cod. LXXXIV) was once in the Medici collection at the Badia Fiesolana and preserves a caption to a painting of Manetti. The Latin text reads:

Hebraei patriis lacrymas auxere Latinis,
Et Graeci, dum te, Iannocte, queruntur ademptum;
Esset ut ante oculos vitae melioris imago,
 Iannoctum pinxit hic sua posteritas.
Hebraeae hunc lauro, Graiae Latinaeque Camoenae
 Ornarunt, probitas aurea signa dedit.

A similar poem was composed by Carlo Marsuppini for Leonardo Bruni's tomb in Sta. Croce (ca. 1445):

After Leonardo passed from life,
History mourned, Eloquence was silent,
And it is said the Muses, both Greek
And Latin, could not control their tears.

Manetti was buried in the church of the Olivetani in Naples, then brought to Florence where he was temporarily interred in the wall of the sacristy of Sto. Spirito, waiting for definitive burial in a family chapel in the same church that never became available. He was probably buried under the pavement in the church; a part of his tombstone is still in the cloister adjoining the sacristy.

[16] Trinkaus, *'In Our Image and Likeness'*, 413 n. 3: the other five men were Coluccio Salutati, Ambrogio Traversari, Leonardo Bruni, Accursius, and Poggio Bracciolini.

[17] Vespasiano's biography is the *Comentario della vita di Messer Giannozzo Manetti*, in *Vite*, 2:515–622; Naldo Naldi's "Vita Janotii de Manectis" is in Muratori, *RIS*, 20:527–608.

These testimonials indicate that Manetti's status among his contemporaries equaled that of his better known associates — Bruni, Poggio, Alberti. Yet the qualities praised by Manetti's admirers have often eluded modern assessments. For example, one quite typical summary of his best-known work, the *Life of Nicholas V*, criticizes "the near impenetrability of Manetti's text, written in an amalgam of medieval and corrupt Latin and couched in the worst forms of Ciceronian hyperbole."[18] Even the most recent, and sympathetic, scholarship judged Manetti's uncertain use of architectural terminology to be a sign of his technical incompetence.[19] If his language is not pure, his style too rhetorical, and the content of his writing untruthful, his contemporaries did not notice it. To these, "he seemed a Demosthenes," the Greek orator and model of classical eloquence (whose works Manetti owned).[20] A challenge of this study, then, is to listen closely to what Manetti says and how he says it in an attempt to recover some of the expressive force and intellectual content that so impressed his early audience. Much of the vitality of his language and thought will be discovered to derive from his appropriation of his vast reading and his allusions to scriptural, patristic, Scholastic, and classical ideas that were the shared intellectual property of his ambient culture.

Manetti experiences his world through the reading he has absorbed. Some of Manetti's scholarly work — from the *De Illustribus longaevis* early in his career to the *Contra Iudaeos et Gentes* at its end — is compilatory, information culled from myriad sources and organized categorically. The information contained in these is eminently retrievable, reading to be put into the service of an argument. Although even in Manetti's time such compilations were occasionally criticized, Manetti's contemporary, St. Antoninus, Archbishop of Florence, whose own *Summa* served a similar purpose, defended their utility.[21] St. Antoninus, like Manetti, associated ideas with his sermon theme by looking up an individual word in a concordance or collection of distinctions.[22] Most likely Manetti's scholarly writings were intended for this method of composition: reference works, that is, rather than independent essays. When he used architectural terminology, Manetti followed this method, consulting lexica, glosses, and similar aids, though

[18] E. MacDougall, review of T. Magnuson, *Studies in Roman Quattrocento Architecture* (Rome, 1958), *Art Bulletin* 44 (1962): 67–75, here 67.

[19] *Vita*, trans. Modigliani, intro., 56 n. 16.

[20] For Manetti's ability to speak like Demostheses, see Vespasiano in his *Comentario*, ed. Greco, 553; for the codex, *Giannozzo Manetti, Das Corpus der Orationes*, ed. Wittschier, 33; for an analysis of the influence of Demosthenes on Manetti's oratorical style and political ideals see *Orationes*, ed. Wittschier, 190–91.

[21] Discussed in P. Howard, *Beyond the Written Word: Preaching and Theology in the Florence of Archbishop Antoninus 1427–1459* (Florence, 1995), 45.

[22] Howard, *Beyond the Written Word*, 151.

these are more likely to be theological or literary rather than technical sources. Manetti worked within the accepted methods and sources of research for theologians, expanded to include sources favored by the Humanists. His vast reorganization of factual knowledge underlies the allusiveness of his rhetoric. These allusions might be as explicit as, for example, the armory of the Athenians or Solomon's Temple, or minimalist nods to Livy or St. Paul which must be read intertextually to yield the richness of their implicit thought. This does not mean merely that he carries around a great deal of information, but that he has the ability to use what he has read to make new observations and put things in new relationships. In fact, this is at the heart of his rhetorical practice in the two texts studied here, the *De secularibus et pontificalibus pompis* of 1436 and the *De gestis pontificalibus Nicolai quinti* of 1455. His ability to recall and rearrange commonly known classical, scriptural, and Scholastic sources led his contemporaries to call on him to interpret events they themselves had experienced.

Today, Manetti is principally studied by art historians for his account of the building projects of Pope Nicholas V. Yet Manetti had no special interest in architecture, nor did he, unlike Alberti, accord it high status. We can establish with some precision how Manetti understood architecture to be related to other branches of knowledge. In his treatise *On the Dignity of Man* (ca. 1452), Manetti acknowledged that human intelligence (one of three natural potencies of the rational soul) operates through human inventiveness and praised the "machinery which the wondrous and almost unbelievable acuteness and vigor of human, or rather, divine genius decided to engineer and fashion with singular and exceptional resourcefulness" (3.20). He used Brunelleschi's dome as example.[23] Yet Manetti's view of the branches of human knowledge was hierarchical. When he listed the civilizing works of man in ascending order — navigation, building, painting, sculpture, poetry, history, oratory and jurisprudence, philosophy, medicine, astronomy and theology — architecture was next to lowest in terms of status (*De dignitate*, 2.36–44). The power of human intelligence discernible in the first four areas is more admirable "as we ascend to the higher and more liberal monuments of the free arts" (2.41). The same hierarchical order of value determines Manetti's account of the books in Nicholas V's library. He begins with the "less serious" (grammarians and poets), rises to the historians and political philosophers, then to physics and metaphysics, and culminates in theology (*Life*, 14).

Manetti reiterated the inferior status of architecture in an oration preceding Sigismondo Malatesta's victory for Florence at Vada in 1453. The occasion

[23] *De dignitate*, 2.38: "First let us discuss human intelligence. . . . With what mental acumen did Filippo Brunelleschi, clearly the leading architect of our day, build the great, or rather the greatest dome, that amazing one on the Florentine Duomo, using — to say it is unbelievable! — no wood or iron supports."

required that he argue the precedence of the art of military leadership over all other arts, not only "painting, sculpture, architecture, and all other manual and physical activities" but also "intellectual activities that are praiseworthy and of better repute."[24] The list which followed of the intellectual arts — grammar, logic, rhetoric, poetry, geometry, music, astrology, medicine, law, civil order, natural philosophy, and ethics — gives additional insight into Manetti's cultural formation and values. Evidently he still saw knowledge structured by the medieval divisions of the trivium and quadrivium, onto which two subjects from the new curriculum of the *studia humanitatis* — poetry and ethics — had been grafted. History, central to the Humanist curriculum, is omitted, while some traditional subjects — logic, natural philosophy, and mathematics — absent from the Humanist curriculum are retained.[25] His inclusion of medicine, law, and political science reveals an affinity with the writings and interests of non-university intellectuals like Coluccio Salutati (*De lege et medicina*) and Leonardo Bruni (especially the *History of Florence*), as well as with the traditional strengths of the curriculum of the Studio of Florence.[26] Thus, although Manetti was willing to admire Brunelleschi's engineering for the dome, as did all eulogists at the death of the architect in 1446, he seems to have viewed architecture as one of the mechanical arts produced by manual labor and without intellectual content.

Given his apparent lack of interest in, or appreciation of, architecture, he was, surprisingly, one of the most prolific writers on buildings in the Quattrocento. His earliest architectural description, *De pompis*, is an eyewitness account of the consecration of the Cathedral of Florence (25 March 1436), written at the request of Agnolo Acciaiuoli. Almost two decades later in 1455, he composed his *Life of Nicholas V*, which at length presents as the pope's central achievement his vast building project at the Vatican. Both accounts describe their buildings in great detail and both comment on their spiritual and historical significance.

A close reading of these texts will show that Manetti's interest in architecture, or in any material or intellectual achievement such as book collecting, is grounded in a view of history, politics, and ecclesiology. In both texts, for example, the body of Christian believers is described as a militant church being

---

[24] "La pictura, la scholtura, l'architectura, [e] tutti gli altri exercitij manuali et corporei," and "exercitij intellectivi che sono e laudabili e più famosi," in P. Scapecchi, "*Victoris imago*. Problemi relativi al Tempio Malatestiano," *Arte Cristiana* 714 (1986): 155–64.

[25] For the Humanist curriculum see P. O. Kristeller, *Renaissance Thought and its Sources* (New York, 1979), 23.

[26] G. Brucker, "Florence and its University, 1348–1434," in *Action and Conviction in Early Modern Europe. Essays in Memory of E.H. Harbison*, ed. T. Rabb and J. Siegel (Princeton, 1969), 220–36; P. Grendler, *Schooling in Renaissance Italy. Literacy and Learning, 1300–1600* (Baltimore, 1989).

built up, edified, perfected. In both the position of the pope, whether Eugenius IV or Nicholas V, is central to understanding the proper relationship between the secular and the sacred. The enactment of ceremonial within secular (the parade through the streets of Florence, the Vatican palace) and sacred (Florence Cathedral, the new St. Peter's) spaces dramatizes what for Manetti is its underlying reality. In this sense, great and enduring buildings monumentalize human capacity to order this world rightly, that is, in harmony with God.

These ideas emerge from Manetti's words when they are examined in the light of his reading, his other writings, and the views of his contemporaries. This is not to say that Manetti's ideas were accepted by everyone or that they are normative for early Renaissance Humanism. But they were understood and admired if not necessarily shared. In the tempestuous years during and following the return from Avignon and the Council of Basle, the status of the papacy was argued among secular princes and churchmen. In these two texts, Manetti's position is never argued directly, but even through architecture, as he summons the fund of ideas and images supplied by his reading, he develops a coherent and self-sufficient sketch of the order of things and its connection to the unfolding of Christian history within his own times. In this, he is influenced by the politics of Aristotle, whose works he knew well, interpreted in the Thomistic, Scholastic sense. In essence, he shares the political theory developed by Dominicans like Juan de Torquemada.[27]

Manetti's approach to architecture is fundamentally different from Alberti's and, although Manetti has frequently been seen as Alberti's mouthpiece in the *Life*, this is most unlikely. Manetti does not share Alberti's appetite for architecture in its own right. He is not interested in engineering or the art of building. His architectural descriptions stand in service to arguments, lively in his ambient world, about the church, civil society, power, cultural inheritance, and human nature. The real and would-be architectural achievements in our two texts are illuminated by Manetti's understanding of his own times.

---

[27] Juan de Torquemada (1388–1468) was a Dominican who studied theology in Paris before being appointed by Eugenius IV in 1434 Master of the Sacred Palace, a position which involved oversight of preaching and studies at the papal court. In 1439 he was made Cardinal of San Sisto; in 1446, Cardinal of S. Maria in Trastevere. Under Nicholas, Torquemada wrote a commentary on Gratian's *Decretum* and (1449–1453) his *Summa de ecclesia*, much influenced by Aquinas. On him, see T. Izbicki, *Protector of the Faith. Cardinal Johannes de Turrecremata and the Defense of the Institutional Church* (Washington, DC, 1981), 6–18.

Chapter One

Manetti and the Art of Persuasion

Language and Figures

In works other than his formal orations, such as the *De pompis* and the *Life of Nicholas V*, Manetti's argumentation and language closely resemble his practice as an orator.[1] His writings present themselves more as orally delivered than as highly-wrought written prose. As a successful diplomat, Manetti sought to persuade. Though he was capable of Ciceronian concinnity and knew the techniques of ornamentation, his typical formula for convincing his audience was to be clear and orderly. He avoided originality and extremes, seeking instead the familiar and the conventional and allowing them to acquire meaning through context. Take, for example, the topos that a building is like the human body, an idea that occurs both in classical (Vitruvius) and Christian (Augustine) sources. Manetti uses this comparison in his descriptions both of Florence Cathedral (1436) and of St. Peter's (1455) in almost identical language (*De pompis* 7; *Life* 51–52).[2] While he sees no reason to produce a fresh version of the topos itself, its associative logic is different in each. Florence Cathedral exhibits, as does the human body, a visible shape that manifests its perfection of form. It becomes Christ's body, the church, through the rite of consecration, a transfiguration experienced internally by those in attendance and reported by Manetti. In contrast, the noble appearance of Nicholas's St. Peter's, like the human body, becomes a microcosm of the world and a figure of Noah's saving ark. This also is the church, but as a Roman and papal institution outside of which there is no salvation. In this and other instances, Manetti chose figures, similes, exempla, interpretations, or comparisons likely to be familiar to his audience. Their significance, however, varies with the background of ideas and values against which they resonate, and this can be easily

[1] As an orator of the Florentine Republic, from 1437 to 1453 he participated vigorously in the negotiations among the unsettled states of Italy. In addition to the grand ceremonials of papal and imperial coronations, he led delegations to Genoa, Venice, Naples, Rimini, Siena, and the Holy See. He addressed heads of state: Tommaso Campofregoso, Alfonso of Aragon, Sigismondo Malatesta, Francesco Foscari, Eugenius IV, and Nicholas V. For a detailed account of Manetti's diplomatic missions, see Vespasiano, *Vite*, 1:490–525.

[2] The image is discussed in Chapter 9.

overlooked. His sources are so numerous and culturally diverse that, absent direct reference, the connection between Manetti's thought and the classical, biblical, patristic, and Scholastic authors he is known to have read[3] is not always easy to detect. Yet Manetti employs even the most ordinary expressions so precisely that the commonplace can often be located within a certain intellectual culture, revealing the mentality within which this early Renaissance spectator understood buildings. Manetti brought the rich architectural associations available within a vast and specialized literature to a literate, but non-specialist, audience; and he applied it to works about which that audience cared deeply.

In one important respect, words in common use were inadequate to Manetti's task. The Latin terminology that Manetti needed to describe architecture had not yet been fixed.[4] Builders used vernacular terminology which must have served them in their work.[5] Intellectuals knew of this fully developed vernacular, as we learn from Lorenzo Valla (1455):

> If it is necessary for community of language to exist within those crafts which are achieved by hand, how much more must this be so in those which actually consist of language.[6]

But since educated people wrote in Latin, not the vernacular, they had to address the problem of how to describe post-classical architectural forms in a classical language. The lack of precise and generally accepted terms could result in the convoluted and redundant language, for example, of Flavio Biondo, referring to the apse of St. Peter's in 1461: "in the apse, or, to use the more popular expression, in the tribune chapel and vault of St. Peter's altar."[7] It may be that after Giovanni Tortelli's *De orthographia*, written for Nicholas in 1448–1449, people

---

[3] *Orationes*, ed. Wittschier, 27–33; G. Cagni, "Biblioteca di Giannozzo Manetti."

[4] J. O'Connor, "Architecture," in *Medieval Latin Studies: An Introduction and Bibliographical Guide*, ed. F.A.C. Mantello and A.G. Riggs (Washington, DC, 1996), 436–42.

[5] We know some of this vocabulary from written sources of various sorts. For example, the new statutes of the Roman *magistri aedificiorum et stratarum*, in 1452, empowered them to tear down anything blocking public space including: "tecto, banco, mignano, porticho, muro, tavolato, steccato, [e] cosse de muro": M. Miglio, "L'immagine del principe e l'immagine della città," in *Principi e città alla fine del medioevo,* ed. S. Gensini (Rome, 1996), 315–32, here 328.

[6] Translated in M. Baxandall, *Giotto and the Orators* (New York, 1986), 119, quoted from the "Oratio clarissimi viri d. Laurentii Vallae habita in principio sui studii die xviii Octobris MCCCCLV."

[7] B. Nogara, *Scritti inediti e rari di Flavio Biondo*, Studi e testi 48 (Rome, 1927), 207: letter of 20 September 1461.

were more sensitive to using new words for new things.[8] But it does not seem to have influenced Manetti's language, probably because he drew his architectural vocabulary primarily from literary sources. Even if Manetti had known the vernacular vocabulary for building, it is not clear he would have used it or that his readers would have preferred it. His architectural vocabulary does not become more technical in the twenty years that separate the *De pompis* from the *Life of Nicholas*, despite the fact that he was in a position to witness major building projects being undertaken. In general, he seems to have adopted the orator's distaste for the vernacular, non-classical usages, and loan words. For descriptive accuracy, however, he sometimes can find no alternative; hence *apothecae* (*Life* 29) and *dietas* (*De pompis* 9, 32), Greek loan words, or his use of *area*, which he glosses with the Greek *platea* (*Life* 40); or when he explains *magna cappella* with the vulgar *tribuna*, and then uses the vulgar term thereafter (46). In the cathedral ekphrasis of the *De pompis* (10) he defines the domed spaces of the three east-end arms as *fornices* "which they popularly call tribunes", each having *cameras* "which they term chapels."

What principally distinguishes Manetti's terminology from Alberti's is Manetti's activity as a translator of the Old and New Testaments, which obliged him to study medieval glosses on the architectural terminology he encountered there. In his 1456 *Apology against the Objectors to his New Translations of the Psalter*, he advised taking a middle ground between *ad verbum* and *ad sensum* translation, although translation of Scripture — the word of God — should be close to literal.[9] This accounts for why Manetti sometimes finds the Greek term, rather than the Latin, most directly equivalent to the vulgar. At least in the cases where his sources are known, the Greek words come not from contact with Byzantine emigré scholars in Florence and Rome, as might have been supposed, but from his scriptural studies. So, for example, *chirothecae* (*De pompis* 23) is the official term for episcopal gloves used in papal Bulla and by liturgists since the twelfth century.[10] Manetti's activity as a translator, and the heated debates about transla-

---

[8] This is O. Besomi's view: "Dai 'Gesta Ferdinandi Regis Aragonum' del Valla al 'De ortographia' del Tortelli," *Italia medioevale e umanistica* 9 (1966): 75–121. See also the discussion of neologisms in C. Smith, *Architecture in the Culture of Early Humanism: Ethics, Aesthetics and Eloquence 1400–1470* (New York, 1992), 69–76.

[9] *Apologeticus*, ed. De Petris, Book 5. Agnolo Manetti said that his father, Giannozzo, had decided to retranslate the *Nicomachean Ethics* because he thought Leonardo Bruni's version (1416–1417) was too free. See C. Celenza, "Renaissance Humanism and the New Testament: Lorenzo Valla's Annotations to the Vulgate," *Journal of Medieval and Renaissance Studies* 24 (1994): 33–52, here 46–48.

[10] J. Braun, *Die liturgische Gewandung in Occident und Orient* (Freiburg im Breisgau, 1907), 359.

tion in the first half of his century, are outside our subject.[11] But his preference for (what are to him) precise technical terms shaped the way we approached his texts both in translation (we stay close to the literal to preserve his meaning) and in interpretation: in more than a few instances we were able to identify the precise significance of his more obscure words by consulting his sources.

Alberti also worked with unfamiliar terminology, especially in Vitruvius. But his aim was never to translate these terms — both Vitruvius's *De architectura* and Alberti's *De re aedificatoria* are in Latin — and because he had a clear commitment to *ad sensum* rendering, he eliminated Vitruvius's obscure terms and substituted neologisms wherever appropriate. Alberti's primary concern was the development of a terminology which could be used by contemporary patrons and, perhaps, architects. He systematically combined reading with observing and compared the forms of Roman antiquity with those of medieval and early Renaissance Italy. Manetti the translator, by contrast, remained faithful to the historical tradition of words and their interpretation, even though this sometimes seems to make little architectural sense. Moreover, Manetti's mental storehouse of architectural types seems to have been formed by buildings described in Scripture: these serve as both formal and linguistic models against which the buildings he describes are defined.

The differences between Manetti and Alberti exemplify a general division between the classicism of some Humanists, who urged *imitatio* as the approach to ancient culture, and the historicism of others who saw *philologia* as an instrument for critical retrospection on that culture. Salvatore Camporeale has proposed as paradigmatic of this controversy the invectives exchanged between Poggio Bracciolini and Lorenzo Valla during 1452–1453.[12] Poggio, for instance, asserted that the Greco-Roman heritage possessed an *auctoritas* to which criteria of true and false could not be applied because, as the cultural memory of the West, it was valid in an absolute sense, having been held in the highest veneration for more than a millennium; Valla, on the other hand, viewed that same heritage as culturally relative.[13] Alberti's *De re aedificatoria* and Manetti's *Life*, then, are paradigms of opposed approaches to the formation of a modern vocabulary of

[11] We would want, for instance, to compare his translation of the *Nicomachean Ethics* with Bruni's and his approach to Bible translation with Valla's *Collatio novi testamenti*, contemporaneous with his own translation work in Rome. See Celenza, "Renaissance Humanism," 37; and Bentley, *Humanists and Holy Writ*, 35. Virtually all of Book 5 of the *Apologeticus* is about translation theory, and De Petris' excellent notes are themselves an introduction to the related controversies.

[12] S. I. Camporeale, "Il problema della *imitatio* nel primo Quattrocento. Differenze e controversia tra Bracciolini e Valla," *Annali di architettura* 9 (1997):149–54, here 149.

[13] Camporeale, "Il problema," 151.

architecture, the one concerned with contemporary usefulness and the other fitting present reality to Scriptural models as interpreted in patristic and medieval exegesis. While the first is serviceable in practice, the second connects buildings to a tradition of ideas and values.

Argumentation

To ask how Manetti constructed his arguments is to explore how his mind thought through his subject. Proper argumentation, what constitutes persuasion, was very much a topic of debate between the Humanists interested in the revival of classical texts and those connected to the ascendancy of Thomistic Scholasticism. While in retrospect these two intellectual strands seem distinct and sometimes opposed, they often coexisted to a common purpose, two different manners of expressing the same thought. The debate was grounded more in efficacy than in content. Indeed, Kristeller and others have argued that in the early Renaissance, Humanism and Scholasticism do not represent so much opposition between new and old modes of thinking as competing approaches to curriculum: grammar, rhetoric, poetry, and moral philosophy in contrast with logic and natural philosophy.[14] In fifteenth-century Italy, Scholastic argumentation was often simply the product of a traditional university education, and by the 1450s it was linked to the increasing importance of Aquinas as an authority. Scholasticism tended to value definitions of what things are, whereas the new approach to knowledge, associated with the Humanist curriculum, asked how things were seen, used, or exemplified. Poggio Bracciolini's *De varietate fortunae*, begun in the early 1430s and presented to Nicholas V in 1448, highlights these seemingly incompatible forms of argument.[15] In this dialogue, Antonio Loschi defines Fortune from the authorities, Aristotle and Aquinas, while Poggio asserts that one understands what Fortune is only from historical examples and visible evidence, above all the ruins of Rome. These two currents have also been observed in Quattrocento sermons in Rome, distinguished by O'Malley as thematic (Scholastic) or epideictic (classicizing) on the basis of their metaphysics: the former are

[14] P. O. Kristeller, "Humanism and Scholasticism in the Italian Renaissance," *Byzantion* 17 (1944–1945): 346–74, esp. 368–69; E. Rummel, *The Humanist-Scholastic Debate in the Renaissance and Reformation* (Cambridge, MA, 1995); L. Panizza, "Pico della Mirandola e il 'De genere dicendi philosophorum' del 1485. L'Encomio paradossale dei 'barbari' e la loro parodia," *I Tatti Studies* 8 (1999): 69–103; D. MacCulloch, *Reformation* (London, 2003), 86–87.

[15] This contrast is illustrated throughout Book 1: *De varietate fortunae*, ed. O. Merisalo (Helsinki, 1993), 91–100.

concerned with what God *is*, the latter, with what God *does*.[16] The Humanists demanded that sermons aid the listener in making moral choices: thus Poggio Bracciolini begins his dialogue on avarice by complaining about the Scholastic style of St. Bernardino's sermons in Rome and claiming they were not useful.[17] While Poggio saw a clear advantage in Humanist rhetoric's utility, the difference between a Humanist and Scholastic style of theology, in O'Malley's view, was probably not apparent to most in the fifteenth century, and both could co-exist in the same person.[18]

Manetti himself recognized and understood the distinction between the two but not the contradiction. Thus, in his *Life of Seneca*, he writes:

> The orator has one way of speaking, the philosopher must use another. Orators commonly amplify and embellish with five words what they have to say, while the proper and particular task of philosophers is to set out their meaning in plain and lucid speech.[19]

In his *On the Dignity of Man*, he tells us that he sometimes switches from the Humanist or rhetorical manner to the Scholastic or dialectical: "Still, for the sake of arguing and clarifying we sometimes tighten our arguments not just in the manner of orators but also in that of dialecticians" (3.23). With this statement, he moves from argument from example (drawing from Cicero) to argument from definition and from the authority of Aristotle. This mixed culture is especially evident in curial Rome at mid-century, when Manetti joined it. Indeed, it seems to have originated not as a difference between Humanism and Scholasticism, but as a distinction between the technical language and logic of the professional theologian and the freer, rhetorical usage of the preacher or teacher to a lay community: a difference, then, not of education or personal predilection but of audience.[20] Indeed, like that of the preacher St. Antoninus, Manetti's exegesis combines figures taken most often from Scripture with narrative *exempla*.[21] The two intellectual

---

[16] J. O'Malley, *Praise and Blame in Renaissance Rome. Rhetoric, Doctrine, and Reform in the Sacred Orators of the Papal Court, c. 1450–1521* (Durham, NC, 1979), 36–44.

[17] P. Bracciolini, "De Avaritia," in *The Earthly Republic. Italian Humanists on Government and Society*, ed. B. Kohl and R. Witt (University Park, PA, 1978), 243–45.

[18] J. O'Malley, "Some Renaissance Panegyrics of Aquinas," *Renaissance Quarterly* 27 (1974): 174–92, here 189.

[19] *Biographical Writings*, ed. and trans. Baldassarri and Bagemihl, 265.

[20] See Rummel, *The Humanist-Scholastic Debate*, 36, where she discusses this in relation to Jean Gerson (1363–1429); and Howard, *Beyond the Written Word*, 3, distinguishing the practical theology of the preacher from the speculative theology of the academician.

[21] This is St. Antoninus's recommendation in his *Summa*, 3.18.6 intro., col. 1039d, cited and discussed in Howard, *Beyond the Written Word*, 119.

currents are fundamentally distinguished by the relative importance of rhetoric and dialectic, as was recognized since the thirteenth century. In his commentary on Aristotle's *Rhetoric* (1270s) Giles of Rome distinguished rhetoric — concerned with moral issues and the practical intellect, aiming to arouse the emotions to persuade the will, suitable for a general and unlearned audience, persuading by examples, concerned with the particular, and seeking to secure belief that something is good — from dialectic — addressing the speculative intellect, intended for a refined and intelligent audience, demonstrating probability by syllogism and inductive logic, concerned with the universal, and aiming to secure opinion on what is true.[22] These differences were known to all educated people — Lapo da Castiglionchio distinguished between the manner of mathematicians (logical argument) and the persuasion of oratory (1438)[23] — but few switched back and forth between them in the same work, as does Manetti. Manetti's dual manner was understood by his biographer, Naldo Naldi, who commented that as philosophers we understand with our minds and spirits while as historians we perceive through both thought and the senses.[24]

The dialectical mode as taught in Italy from the thirteenth century was Aristotelian. Manetti says that, as a youth, the future Nicholas V was first in his class in dialectic, and, specifically, that he had eagerly devoted himself to the dialectic and physics of Aristotle.[25] In explaining Aristotle, Thomas's commentaries were known and read, but not exclusively used.[26] In the Quattrocentro, when Aristotelian texts were retranslated with greater accuracy and widely diffused, Thomas's position as the dominant interpreter of the Greek philosopher was strengthened rather than diminished. Certain audiences preferred to read and understand Aristotle in light of Thomas's commentaries, and not only his commentaries: he regularly includes, interprets, and evaluates Aristotle's opinions throughout the *Summa*. The rising importance of Aquinas in the fifteenth century is still inadequately studied, but by the second half of the century Thomas's work became newly authoritative.[27] Nicholas V, who owned forty-nine volumes of Aquinas's works, treated Thomas

---

[22] Discussed in M. Kempshall, *The Common Good in Late Medieval Political Thought* (New York, 1999), 131.

[23] Celenza, "Renaissance Humanism and the New Testament," 50.

[24] Naldi, "Vita Janotii de Manectis," 527.

[25] *Vita Nicolai V, RIS* 3:2.911. He reiterates the primacy of Aristotle in the treatise on the dignity of man at 2.10 and 4.32.

[26] P. Kristeller, "Thomism and the Italian Thought of the Renaissance," in idem, *Medieval Aspects of Renaissance Learning* (Durham, NC, 1974), 29–94, here 52.

[27] C. Stinger thought the revival of Thomism began in mid-century Rome: *The Renaissance in Rome* (Bloomington, 1985), 141–47. Only in the second half of the fifteenth century did the *Summa theologiae* replace Peter Lombard's *Sentences* as a basic text

as the first non-patristic Doctor of the Church, promoting his feast day with special ceremonial, attended by the Cardinalate, in the church of Sta. Maria sopra Minerva in Rome.[28] The leading theologian of the *Studium* of the Roman Curia, the Master of the Sacred Palace, was always a Dominican — under Nicholas, Torquemada and Jacobus Gil.[29] Thus while new translations of Aristotle's *Ethics*, *Politics*, and *Rhetoric* were available — including Manetti's own translations of the *Nicomachean Ethics* and *the Eudemian Ethics* — Thomas's commentaries were also more highly regarded and widely diffused.[30] Manetti himself owned three manuscripts of Thomas's *Summa* as well as his commentary on Aristotle's *De anima*.[31] Manetti would have appreciated Aquinas's Christian appropriation of the philosopher's teaching; for example, Aquinas had written an important commentary on the *Ethics*, tying it to theology and exalting the theological rather than the practical virtues.[32] Improved accessibility of the ancient sources meant that they could be used on their own, but the simultaneous growth in popularity of Thomas's Scholastic interpretation suggests that Aristotelian concepts in Manetti's or Nicholas's thought reflect also their Thomistic development. Nicholas's use of Ptolemy of

---

in theological teaching. The chair of Thomistic metaphysics was established at the university of Padua in 1442; that of Thomistic theology only in 1490. In the second half of the fifteenth century the professor of theology at the University of Pavia was required to teach from the texts of St. Thomas. In the same period the faculty of theology at the university of Ferrara was dominated by Thomism, and especially Dominican Thomists. A glance at the disciplines taught at the University of Rome (*Studium urbis*) from 1473 to 1484 shows that the largest number of courses were in canon and civil law, followed in order of size by grammar, medicine, rhetoric, philosophy, and theology; that is, in the traditional, or Scholastic, disciplines. See S. I. Camporeale, *Lorenzo Valla tra medieovo e rinascimento. Encomion S.Thomae, 1457* (Pistoia, 1977), 8; Kristeller, "Thomism," 46; D. Dal Nero, "L'insegnamento della teologia in Europa e a Ferrara," in *Rinascita del sapere. Libri e maestri dello studio ferrarese*, ed. P. Castelli (Venice, 1991), 246–63, here 256–57; E. Lee, "Humanists and the 'Studium urbis', 1473–1484," in *Umanesimo a Roma nel Quattrocento*, ed. P. Brezzi and M. de Panizza Lorch (Rome, 1984), 127–46, here 145.

[28] J. O'Malley's observation in "The Feast of Thomas Aquinas in Renaissance Rome: A Neglected Document and its Import," *Rivista di storia della Chiesa in Italia* 35 (1981): 1–27, here 14.

[29] Stinger, *Renaissance*, 141–47.

[30] On the new translations of Aristotle see C. Celenza, *Renaissance Humanism and the Papal Curia. Lapo da Castiglionchio the Younger's 'De curiae commodis'* (Ann Arbor, 1999), 8, 46–48.

[31] G. Cagni, "Agnolo Manetti and Vespasiano da Bisticci," *Italia medioevale e umanistica* 14 (1971): 293–312, here 305. Manetti's copy had the *Pars prima secundae* and *Pars secunda secundae*; he did not own the *Pars tertia*.

[32] Aquinas, *Commentary on the Nicomachean Ethics*, ed. A. Pirotta (Turin, 1934); trans. C. I. Litzinger (Notre Dame, 1993).

Lucca's *On the Government of Princes*, wrongly attributed to Aquinas and based on William of Moerbeke's translation of Aristotle's *Politics*, is an example of this practice (see Chapters 8 and 9).[33]

Manetti was drawn to Aquinas for a variety of reasons. The first was his own sense of order as paramount: belief that the world was ordered, that the mark of wisdom is the ability to produce order, and that order and clarity are virtues of a good literary style.[34] For Aquinas, order was a fundamental theological principle, and the logic, order, and comprehensiveness of his scholarly method reflects that. Second, Manetti may have viewed the precision of words and concepts in Scholastic discourse as a stage of evolution superior to patristic and biblical practice: it was, to him, modern and represented cultural progress. We often find Manetti's themes drawn from Augustine yet expressed in "modern" terms. Finally, and very importantly, were considerations of audience. The *Life of Nicholas*, for instance, was addressed to a cardinal theologian (Antonio de la Cerda) and to a banker Humanist (Giovanni de'Medici): Manetti required a language grounded in concepts familiar and persuasive to both. Comparison of his sources for the treatise on the dignity of man (for Alfonso, King of Naples) and for the *Life* shows that whereas Aquinas is hardly cited in the former (Cicero, Lactantius, and St. Augustine are the most frequently quoted), his work, and that of other medieval authors, is important for the latter. Of course, this may depend on the difference of subject and on Manetti's own greater exposure to Scholastic thinking in the intervening years in Rome. It seems right, nonetheless, to include the nature of his audience as a consideration.

Unlike many Humanists — and Voigt, in fact, excluded him from their ranks on this account — Manetti preferred philosophy and theology to poetry and literature.[35] Exceptionally, he was trained in logic and dialectic and learned Aristotle's *Physics* and *Ethics* from Augustinian canons who, we may be sure, consulted Aquinas for their interpretation. Manetti was almost unique as a layperson able to speak and write about theology at a level acceptable to professional theologians, most of whom were professed religious.[36] As a layperson and banker

---

[33] Howard concluded similarly about St. Antoninus that when the archbishop cites Plato, Aristotle, or Cicero, the source of the quotes is generally Thomas Aquinas: *Beyond the Written Word*, 46.

[34] O'Malley notes these aspects of order as appealing to Humanists in general, but they were particularly congenial to Manetti's personality: "Feast," 22–23.

[35] G. Voigt, *Il risorgimento dell'antichità classica ovvero il primo secolo dell'umanesimo* (1859), trans. D. Valbusa (Florence, 1968), 323.

[36] In Rome, for instance, most of the Scholastic theologians belonged to mendicant orders, taught at the *studia generalia* of their orders and the University of Rome, and supplied the Curia Romana and papal household with theological expertise: J. D'Amico, *Renaissance Humanism in Papal Rome* (Baltimore, 1983), 144.

Manetti understood that audience well and, indeed, addressed it very successfully from all reports, even though his later reputation has suffered by comparison with his more fluent contemporaries.

Manetti's approach to describing physical beauty illustrates how his oratorical manner, based in Humanist rhetoric, is founded on dialectical principles embedded in Thomistic Scholasticism and his study of philosophy. The classicizing speech marks "a conversion from the cerebral to the visual" and abounds in verbs of looking — *videre*, *aspicere*, *ante oculos ponere*, and so on.[37] The strongly visual language in both the *De pompis* and the *Life* aims to evoke emotions of wonder; in this, his work participates in the new style of oratory developed in mid-century Rome. Manetti's two most frequently used aesthetic terms, *speciosus* and *pulcher*, describe objects of beauty or wonder from the point of view of the perceiver. *Pulcher* seems to derive from an inherent quality within the object, while *speciosus* includes the affective response — an object becomes appealing, attractive: the eye is drawn to it and held there. This distinction corresponds to the essential difference between *forma*, the inherent pattern of order in a thing, and *figura*, its perceptible external boundary. Manetti's understanding of *figura* and *forma* follows Aquinas, whose usage assigned to these Latin terms a distinction ultimately found in Aristotle. "Form" refers not to the thing itself, but to its organizing pattern while "figure," instead, means its visible shape. In architecture, the design of the building as conceived in the architect's mind is its "form" — Aquinas says "the artist intends to make the house merge with the form he conceived in his mind" — but the resulting building is seen as *figura* or "shape."[38] Respecting the distinction between these technical terms makes sense, for example, of Manetti's observation on the shape of planned St. Peter's:

> If, therefore, the figure [*figura*] of this temple would have been like the human body, as seemed obvious above, surely it follows that it would have acquired the noblest appearance [*speciem*], since we are not unaware that the human form [*formam*] was by far privileged over all the other figures [*figuris*] of things animate and inanimate (51).

This complicated way of saying that the church was laid out in the shape of a human body is actually not verbose, but the expression of an old commonplace in precise philosophical language. Manetti is very clear: the noblest *forma* produces the most attractive *figura*.

---

[37] O'Malley, *Praise and Blame*, 62–63.

[38] So Aquinas, *ST* 1 q.15 a.1; so also *ST* 1 q. 15 a.2: "the form of the house in the mind of the architect is something understood by him, to the likeness of which he produces the form of the house in matter." On "figure," see U. Eco, *The Aesthetics of Thomas Aquinas* (Cambridge, MA, 1988), 169, 176.

For Aquinas, *figura* is form quantified in matter (*ST* 1 q.7 a.3 ad 2; 3 q.63 a.2 ad 1); its beauty is *species*, the outward appearance it presents (*ST* 1 q.51 1; 1–2 q.3 a.3).[39] *Pulchritudo* pertains to the beauty discerned in *forma* and is available to the senses of sight and hearing, but not the other senses (*ST* 1 q.5 a.4 ad 1; 1–2 q. 27 a.1 ad 3). But in Manetti's descriptions *pulcher* — beautiful by virtue of the intellectual *idea* of a thing — occurs far less frequently than *speciosus*, referring to the visible attractiveness of the object's *figura*. In this he is, in a general sense, following Aristotle (*De anima* 2). More precisely, he is taking technical terminology (and his understanding of perception) from medieval optics in which images that come to the eye are called *species*. We will be suggesting in another chapter that he culled this particular knowledge from Lorenzo Ghiberti's *Commentarii*, part two of which is a translation of excerpts from Alhazen (*De aspectibus*), Roger Bacon (*Perspectiva*), and John Pecham (*Perspectiva*).[40] Ghiberti uses the term "spetie" (3.11.1), meaning the similitudes of visible things received by the senses, and lists "figura" as one of the qualities of visible bodies (3.10.2). Thus Manetti prefers words that are especially close to the action of looking rather than to the bodies' abstract form or figure. In both descriptions, Manetti is more concerned with pleasingness than with perfection, and with the physical more than the ideal, for although his framework is Thomistic and Aristotelian, he draws on their physics rather than their metaphysics. Thus when Manetti describes the Vatican as a "speciosissime paradisi" (34), this should be understood as a paradise most pleasing to the sense of sight, "a paradise most attractive to see."[41]

Manetti's dual definition of the beautiful and its implications for epistemology need to be understood within the contexts of his own cultural background and that of curial Rome at mid-century. His earliest training was conventional in the sense that emphasis was placed on authority and memorization. This grounding in dialectic, in Manetti's case, was congenial to, not averse from, the new currents of Humanist learning and the decidedly non-dialectical ways in which it expressed itself. The paradox, then, is that the definitional, essentialist world of Aquinas is expressed anew in Manetti's affective, experiential rhetoric. The explanation may lie in Manetti's unique fusion of the two. He claimed to

---

[39] Eco, *Aesthetics*, 68. Passages in St. Augustine's *City of God* (which Manetti claimed to know by heart) are also relevant, especially 8.6 and 11.4.

[40] L. Ghiberti, *I commentarii*, ed. L. Bartoli (Florence, 1998).

[41] C. Westfall renders "speciosissime" as "most perfect" in the title of his excellent book on Nicholas V's building program, *In This Most Perfect Paradise: Alberti, Nicolas V, and the Invention of Conscious Urban Planning in Rome, 1447–55* (New Haven, 1974). This suggests a more Platonic and utopian significance than Manetti intended. For our understanding of the grammar of "speciosissime paradisi" see the Commentary at 34.

know three books by heart: Aristotle's *Ethics*, but also the Epistles of St. Paul and Augustine's *City of God* (Vespasiano, *Vite*, 1:485–86). These two Christian sources set out to describe the relationship between man and God not as a logical proposition, but as an irresistible response. Their rhetoric, like Manetti's, is concerned not only that we know something, but also that we do something. Manetti understood divine and human history within this Augustinian and Pauline, and therefore ethical and experiential, framework. He drew heavily on both, and particularly on Augustine, for both the language and the content of his architectural descriptions, so much so that they can be seen as extended expositions of themes found in Augustine. The argument of Book 2 of the *Life* is drawn from Book 18 of Augustine's *City of God* (which, in turn, comments on Paul's *Letter to the Romans*) and Book 19; and the rhetorical structure of the *De pompis* implements Augustine's view of liturgy.[42] In this, intellectual content and persuasive argument converge.

The Dialectical Manner

While Manetti rarely resorts to propositional logic or the "dialectical manner" in his argumentation, two qualities of his prose were consonant with traditional, and even Scholastic, training: his insistent emphasis on order; and a style more concerned with *brevitas* than with *copia*. This brevity serves to move his argument beyond the particular to universal human experience.

Manetti's reputation for clarity no doubt stems partly from the transparent organization of his work. He typically provides his reader with an outline of the order of presentation, and then explicitly notes as he moves from point to point. In the *De pompis*, his organizing principle is mainly chronological: the preparations (5), the procession to the church (19–24), and the ceremony itself (25–34), with a major digression to provide an ekphrasis of the basilica's interior (7–17). He provides an outline of what he calls "this order of speaking" (6); then justifies the digressive ekphrasis on the grounds it will contextualize his narrative better; and finally returns to his proposed order by cross-referencing where he left off ("as I said above," 19). His *Life of Nicholas*, though longer, is similarly marked by transparent organization, with markers to guide the reader from point to point and to signal the entry into and exit from digressions. Book 2 of the *Life* is organized not by chronology but by five narratives illustrative of Nicholas's achievements as pope: the Jubilee Year of 1450 (10–12), the founding of the papal library (13–16), the Vatican building project (28–62), the coronation of Frederick III (64–69), and the ratification of the Peace of Lodi (74–78). In the course of these

[42] See Chapters 2 and 9.

narratives, other accomplishments, given lesser attention, are connected to them: finances and the healing of the Schism with the Holy Year (4–5); Manetti's own scholarly projects with the library (17); the canonization of Bernardino of Siena, the plague (19–21), and other buildings in Rome and elsewhere (22–27) with the Borgo project; and papal diplomacy in Italy and the suppression of the Porcari conspiracy (70–73) with the ratification of the treaty. Within the major narratives Manetti may also announce his criteria for selecting details to be mentioned and how they will be ordered. For example, he tells us that his description of the papal building projects will touch upon only the ones that reveal Nicholas's magnificence, first outside Rome, then inside the city (22). Then the urban projects are further enumerated in an ascending order of importance: the walls, the station churches, the papal district, the Vatican Palace, and the Basilica of St. Peter, with more attention given to those that were unfinished and so cannot be viewed (25). He takes up each "in the announced order" (26). This metalanguage, that is, language calling attention to itself, is a feature of the oral style. Manetti is clearly conscious of doing this because he uses a different style for Nicholas's spoken testament in Book 3 in which the pontiff, a Doctor of Theology, addresses the cardinal theologians. Nicholas begins with an outline of the topics he intends to take up, noting: "we will explain one by one the three principal points into which we have subdivided the testament" (*RIS*, 947); having made a (duly noted) digression he informs them that he is returning to "the order of discourse that we proposed according to the established division" (*RIS*, 952). Nicholas speaks as a Scholastic theologian, while Manetti, in his own voice, does not.

Manetti's imposition of explicit order on his narratives reveals a mind that also searches for proper order in reality. So the "ordo" of paraders to the consecration is, in Manetti's view, natural and right, as is the "ordo" in which clergy and dignitaries are arranged in the physical space of the basilica. Manetti expressed this insight in his *De illustribus longaevis* (also from1436) with regard to the dedication of Solomon's temple: the procession entered the temple in "proper order" and "the wonderful order of the processions — as I imagine it again and again — always seems filled with great divinity."[43] The elements of the papal palace will be related to each other in proper order ("coordinabantur"); the "ordo" for the coronation of Frederick was meticulously followed. Thus Manetti tends to replicate in the orderliness of his works a hierarchical or historical order that he observes in the world, and this facilitates the listener's ability to absorb and remember its content. One of his most acclaimed performances was the speech given on the accession of Nicholas V to the papacy "in a new style of oratory which had been but a short time in use" (*Vite*, 1:59). The oration lasted an hour and a quarter, during which Nicholas appeared to sleep. At the conclusion, however, the

[43] *De illustribus longaevis*, fol. 73r.

pope repeated the speech almost word for word. Although the innovative qualities of the accession speech belonged to Manetti's "rhetorical manner," its appeal to the memory was due to the insistent clarity of organization characteristic of his "dialectical manner."

Manetti's prose is constrained by a self-imposed brevity. He does not amplify subjects about which we certainly would like to know more, for example, the exterior of Florence Cathedral, or the rebuilding of St. Peter's. His purpose in these texts is not to give a full account, however much we would wish it, but to develop a coherent theme, for which he only needs "enough." Thus he calls his *De pompis* a "sketch" (3, 35) and, in both our texts, generally omits the names of people. No prelates or secular dignitaries are named in the *De pompis*; Brunelleschi is never mentioned. We are in the dark about who Nicholas's architectural advisers and experts might have been, except for Bernardo Rossellino (54), and the translators he commissioned for his library are nameless. In our two texts, this leaves only Eugenius IV, Nicholas V, Frederick III, Stefano Porcari, and Manetti to move as identified individuals across the narrative. This anonymity permits Manetti to recount an historical event (a ceremony, a pope's life) without truly peopling it, and thus, undistracted by the particularity which detail would give, he can urge his theme more cogently. Manetti's brevity, then, does not serve as the vehicle for objectivity and fact, but is a reticence more closely linked to oratorical aims of persuasion. In this he seems to be very un-Ciceronian, but not unlike the Sophistic orators, who are more concerned with a vivid overall impression than with inclusiveness of detail.

Just as Manetti does not rely on abundance of factual detail to advance his themes, so his descriptive vocabulary is not copious. Physical objects are "large," "wondrous," "outstanding," or "attractive"; he sometimes will use these rather general descriptors twice in the same sentence. This verbal economy might seem strange in a narrative that seeks to persuade through the vividness of the impression it makes. And yet these adjectives have a precision in the definitional world of Scholastic philosophy. They all are attributes of works of magnificence: size, impact, unusualness, and appeal.[44] In the *De pompis*, Manetti uses the metaphor of the sketch to suggest that his true content eludes eloquence. Instead, the ordered structure of his narrative, though not filled with colorful language, leads climactically to a vivid experience that cannot be expressed by words. Since no words, not even the most expressive, can convey his experience, the words fixed in a dialectical tradition will serve as well. This terseness is associated with Manetti's conception of subjective experience. He believes that knowledge is completed in the self and that all individuals share common interior experience. Thus his subjectivity is not about individualism, but about universal human experiences realized in each individual.

---

[44] For discussion of magnificence, see Chapter 8.

Finally, Manetti includes in each of these two works lengthy passages filled with enumerated detail and sharpened by metaphors and historical comparisons. In each case, he marks them as digressions from the order of his discourse: the ekphrasis of Florence Cathedral in the *De pompis* and the descriptions of the papal library and of the papal building projects in the *Life*. These digressions, at the rhetorical level, function as *exempla*, the particular exemplifying the general. The most extended instance of this technique is the description of Nicholas's building projects in Book 2 of the *Life*, clearly marked as a digression by its concluding words: "Let us now, as if retracing our steps to the fatherland in a long journey home, return quickly to the order of our account" (63). As rhetoric, the account is meant to particularize the building program as an example of the larger theme of the historic significance of Nicholas's reign. As dialectic, it constitutes inductive evidence of the authority and dignity of the Roman Church.

The Rhetorical Manner

Manetti's rhetorical manner is the most pronounced feature of his writing, and yet it does not depend on the more dramatic oratorical strategies of ornamentation and copiousness. Though not propositional, it assumes a fund of ideas derived from dialectic. Perhaps formative in this regard were his intellectual experiences in the 1430s with Ambrogio Traversari, as part of a circle that included Niccolò Niccoli, Cosimo and Lorenzo de' Medici, Carlo Marsuppini, Paolo Toscanelli, and Antonio Pieruzzi.[45] Manetti, who began Greek with Traversari while Traversari was translating works attributed to Dionysius the Areopagite, benefitted from recent access to the study of Greek and to works in that language, as well as from the availability of Latin texts discovered in the first decades of the Quattrocento. He had access to the private libraries of Florence and accumulated an impressive personal library which included Greek and Latin patristic writers as well as classical authors.[46] His method of speaking experientially and historically draws on examples and observations to lead his reader in an orderly way to feel the same way about things as he does. One can see a similar strategy in Cicero, particularly in his philosophical works, and in the later orators of the Second Sophistic, whose handbooks Manetti knew.

Manetti's aesthetic terminology, we have seen, has both an intellectual and a sensual aspect. While intellectual probing can yield the truth, sensory experience persuades and therefore is the domain of the orator. Manetti's Nicholas in

---

[45] C. Stinger, *Humanism and the Church Fathers. Ambrogio Traversari and Christian Antiquity in the Italian Renaissance* (Albany, 1977), 30.

[46] He personally owned 140 Latin and 40 Greek codices: *Orationes*, ed. Wittschier, 29.

his deathbed testament puts it a bit differently: only the few understand intellectually the authority of the church and the Apostolic See from books, but the people become convinced when they see and are affected by great buildings (T2–3)[47]. Yet Manetti makes clear elsewhere that not only are the unlettered masses filled with wonder by visual display, but he himself, a man of letters, is overcome by visual pageantry, amazing buildings, and liturgical enactment. One thinks of Gregory the Great's famous saying that the unlettered "read by seeing on the walls what they are unable to read in books."[48] But Manetti does not mean, as Gregory does, that the viewer garners information from what he sees, but that the sense of sight, sometimes together with other senses, is so powerful that it is persuasive and transformative.

In Manetti's architectural ekphrasis, the visual quality that is most prized is that which makes an object *speciosus*; it possesses an allure so appealing that the eye is drawn to the object and held there. In the *Life of Nicholas*, the term recurs in its verbal form (*spectare*) and its nominal forms (*species*, *specimen*, *spectaculum*) as well. That sight is the highest and most informative of the senses had already been suggested by Plato (*Phaedrus*, 250d).[49] Aquinas reviews this idea in the *Summa* and agrees that vision is the superior cognitive sense because it and hearing are the only senses that experience *pulchritudo*, which flows from form; the others sense *suavitas* (*ST* 1–2 q.27 a.1 ad 3).[50] Plato and Aquinas both seem to prize sight as insight into the form of things, an intellectual activity. Pseudo-Dionysius argued similarly that material sight led to intellectual and spiritual

[47] Nicholas's testament comprises most of the third book of Manetti's *Life of Nicholas V*, discussed in Chapter 3. We have edited and translated the portion of the testament most relevant to Nicholas's building project (our T1–18); references to passages elsewhere in book 3 of the *Life* are to Muratori's edition in *RIS*.

[48] Gregory the Great, *Registrum epistolarum*, PL 78, 1128 (11.13). For fuller discussion of this theme, see Chapter 8.

[49] "Sight is the keenest mode of perception vouchsafed us through the body; wisdom, indeed, we cannot see thereby . . . nor yet any other of those beloved objects, save only beauty; for beauty alone this has been ordained to be most manifest to sense and most lovely of them all." Manetti surely knew the *Phaedrus* since he cites it in *De dignitate* 2.26.

[50] It is not clear, however, that Nicholas's buildings were intended to persuade through their beauty, as opposed to, instead, arousing wonder through their magnificence (a concept which we will explore in Chapter 8). Plato argues that beauty engenders love in the viewer; Aristotle, that the beautiful is that which gives pleasure. Augustine, in a median position, says: "If I were to ask first whether things are beautiful because they give pleasure [Aristotle's position], or give pleasure because they are beautiful [a watered-down version of Plato's position], I will have no doubt that I will be given the answer that they give pleasure because they are beautiful": *De vera religione*, 32.59 (PL 34.148).

insight.[51] Manetti's interest in sight might be characterized instead as volitional, an acceptance on the evidence of our eyes of the truths that are revealed. In this, Aristotle is closer to the link between sight and direct experience:

> Vision reveals to us the differences among things, since by means of vision we experience everything in the heavens and on earth (*Metaphysics*, 1.1.1).

In *De oratore*, Cicero applies this to persuasion, asserting the superiority of sight over hearing, of image over language:

> The keenest of all our senses is the sense of sight, and . . . consequently perceptions received by the ears or by reflection can be most easily retained in the mind if they are also conveyed there by the mediation of the eyes (2.357).[52]

The Greek rhetorical handbooks known to Manetti insisted that the purpose of ekphrasis was to present an object or an action "vividly to the sense of sight."[53] In this way, the language of rhetoric persuades by becoming a form of seeing, or, failing that, by leading the hearer to visualize for himself. This is an especially important device for Nicholas's building projects, so little of which were built, and Manetti alerts the reader that he will devote most of his efforts to their description precisely for that reason:

---

[51] For example, *The Celestial Hierarchy* 121C–D: "For it is quite impossible that we humans should, in any immaterial way, rise up to imitate and to contemplate the heavenly hierarchies without the aid of those material means capable of guiding us as our nature requires. Hence, any thinking person realizes that the appearances of beauty are signs of an invisible loveliness"; in *Pseudo-Dionysius: The Complete Works*, trans. C. Luibheid (Mahwah, NJ, 1987), 146.

[52] Cicero also praises sight as the keenest of the senses in *De natura deorum*, Book 2, in a passage quoted in Manetti's *De dignitate*, 1.3–12.

[53] Pope Nicholas had no fewer than seven copies of Hermogenes in Greek in his library. George of Trebizond's *Rhetoricorum libri V*, of 1433 or 1434, combined Hermogenes and the Greek tradition with examples from Cicero and Virgil. Since 1443 he had been in Rome at the papal court. Aristotle's *Rhetoric*, which was known in a medieval translation, was translated into Latin in 1430 by Filelfo and in the 1440s by George of Trebizond. Manetti owned a copy in Latin; copies in both Latin and Greek were in Nicholas's library. See E. Müntz and P. Fabre, *La bibliothèque du Vatican au XVe siècle* (Paris, 1887), 336–37, and 107 for Aristotle's *Rhetoric* in the old translation; G. Kennedy, *Classical Rhetoric and its Christian and Secular Tradition from Ancient to Modern Times* (Chapel Hill, 1980), 199; J. Monfasani, *George of Trebizond. A Biography and a Study of his Rhetoric and Logic* (Leiden, 1976), 55; R. Tobin, "Leon Battista Alberti. Ancient Sources and Structure in the Treatises on Art" (Ph.D. diss., Bryn Mawr College, 1979), 45; L. Onofri, "Sacralità, immaginazione e proposte politiche: La *vita* di Niccolò V di Giannozzo Manetti," *Humanistica Lovaniensia* 28 (1979): 27–77, here 36; Poggio, *Opera*, 297.

> I shall say little about the first two [projects] since we see that they are already carried through and completely finished. Then I shall treat the last three somewhat more fully because the buildings would have been unusual and quite wonderful if they had ever fully come into the light, completed and carried out as he had planned (25).

Since Manetti was not really interested in architecture for itself, in his writings the architectural ekphrases are first and foremost literary devices which enable him to exemplify non-architectural ideas. And conversely, his architectural judgment is more grounded in the ideas a building conveys than in technical questions of proportionality or engineering. In the accounts, Manetti views elaborately developed architectural settings as stages for significant human action, such as the consecration of Florence Cathedral and the coronation of Frederick III. In both cases, this action followed a prescribed liturgy, itself the subject of an abundant exegetical literature as well as associated with more general theological and ecclesiological ideas.

For Manetti, architectural ekphrasis is a vivifying rhetorical device enabling the reader to become, through imagination, a spectator. The reader sees, feels, and experiences the building in the context of the drama enacted within. Comparison of Manetti's description of St. Peter's with that of exactly the same date by Maffeo Vegio is especially illuminating in this regard.[54] Broadly speaking, all that is absent in Manetti's text is present in Vegio's and vice versa. For Vegio understood architecture to be a container within which significant objects were preserved: his edifice is empty of people, except as phantoms of memory, and the envelope itself is without observed qualities. More than Vegio, then, Manetti locates the built environment within a network of ideas and values, secular and sacred, and so enlarges their significance. His architectural texts testify to a particular, and in his own time persuasive, view of human nature and history.

Manetti the Orator

Cicero in his *De oratore* (1.34) asserted that the orator must in his training absorb all branches of liberal learning so that he could readily draw on them for his speeches. Manetti drew inspiration from both Scholastic and Humanist values and ideas from a large array of authoritative sources, classical, patristic, medieval, and modern. His practice was justified by both Cicero and Aristotle: perhaps, in this case, Aristotle through Cicero, since the latter translated the opening words

---

[54] Maffeo Vegio, "De rebus antiquis memorabilibus Basilicae Sancti Petri," in *Acta Sanctorum*, June 29 (Brussels, 1965–1970), 56–76.

of Aristotle's *Art of Rhetoric* — "Aristotle in the opening of the *Art of Rhetoric* says that art relates to dialectic as if its complement" — in the then recently discovered *Orator* (32.114).[55] In this, Manetti becomes a paradigm of the eclectic culture of the educated elite in the second quarter of the fifteenth century, above all in Florence and Rome. This is the audience to whom his works are addressed. This may make Manetti a more reliable spokesman for the values and culture he experienced than more striking, and therefore perhaps less typical, figures such as Alberti, whose brilliance and unstable temperament sometimes made him an outsider. But one ambition of his was unique among his peers: to produce the first new Latin translation of the Hebrew and Greek Scripture since Jerome.[56] This biblical project immersed him in philology and interpretation and left a distinctive imprint on his architectural language and thought. Though an eclectic and traditional mind may be more difficult to obtain access to than that of a brilliant and original thinker, Manetti's thought is unified by a world-view based on a Pauline and Augustinian understanding of human experience as essentially spiritual. Beyond the apparatus of Scholastic organization, technical terminology drawn from Aquinas, classicizing rhetorical tropes and *exempla*, and oratorical skills, we find a deeply religious person. Ancient and modern philosophers agree, he says in the *De dignitate* (3.46), that the obligation proper and peculiar to human nature is to act and to understand ("agere et intelligere"), the former depending on the latter.[57] Living according to one's nature in this sense, Manetti maintains, will bring beatitude in this life and the next (4.73). Both of the works studied here propose to readers who already knew what had been done the meaning of events as the basis for future action: Manetti the orator articulates the order and significance of contemporary life.

---

[55] "Aristoteles principio artis rhetoricae dicit illam artem quasi ex altera parte respondere dialecticae." As Panizza observed in "Pico della Mirandola," 72, *Orator* was known to the Humanists only after 1421.

[56] The justification for this project is spelled out in the first two books of his *Apologeticus*, ed. De Petris, 3–56. Augustine had added to the conviction that the Septuagint was inspired, obviating the need to consult Hebrew scripture, but Manetti sided with Jerome. As with Jerome, it was Manetti's version of the Psalms that was widely criticized, likely because the earlier Latin version was a familiar text used in liturgy.

[57] The passage in *De dignitate* is especially reliant on Cicero (*De finibus* 2.13.40) and, through him, on Aristotle (*Nicomachean Ethics* 1.6.1097b). But Manetti's understanding of human purpose and human history, as we will see, is entirely Christian.

Fig. 1. Eugene IV arriving at Florence Cathedral for the ceremony of consecration. Florence, Bib. Med. Laur., MS. Edili 151, fol. 7v.

Chapter Two

The Consecration of Florence Cathedral[1]

De pompis is, as Manetti says, an eyewitness account[2] of the events of 25 March 1436, from the gathering of the twin parades at Santa Maria Novella to their return there after the cathedral had been duly consecrated. The account is organized in four parts, with a brief conclusion: a prologue stating its intent (1–6); an ekphrasis of the cathedral and its ornamentation on the day of its consecration (7–15); a description of Brunelleschi's *ponte* or covered walkway, and the procession of secular and pontifical dignitaries who walked on it (16–24); the consecration proper, its Mass, and attendant ceremonials (25–34); and a conclusion (35).[3] At first glance, one might reasonably expect an accurate account of events anchored in historical reality, a type of chronicle. In fact, the *De pompis* was written at the request of Agnolo Acciaiuoli, himself a witness to and perhaps a participant in these very parades. His addressee, then, was asking him not for factual reportage, but for Manetti's explanation of what the event meant. Given Manetti's reputation for eloquence, Acciaiuoli would rightly have expected a rhetorically ordered and climactically revealing account of its significance. He would want Manetti to articulate what a participant should or could have made

[1] In 1997, while preparing a critical edition of and commentary on the text, the authors presented an earlier version of this chapter at a symposium celebrating the seven-hundredth anniversary of the foundation of the Cathedral of Florence, now published in the Acts of that conference, *Atti del VII Centenario del Duomo di Firenze*, vol. 2: *La cattedrale come spazio sacro: Saggi sul Duomo di Firenze*, ed. T. Verdon and A. Innocenti (Florence, 2001), 560–74. In the following year, a new transcription of the text and a literary analysis appeared: C. van Eck, "Giannozzo Manetti on Architecture: The *Oratio de secularibus et pontificalibus in consecratione basilicae Florentinae* of 1436," *Renaissance Studies* 12 (1998): 449–75. See our note to the text, p. 299.

[2] Early codices bind it with other contemporaneous Manettian works, the two *Laudes Januensium*, speeches given on diplomatic mission to Genoa, and his *De illustribus longaevis*, a compendium of famous people who lived long lives. MSS. Vat. lat. 2919 and Barber. lat. 120 contain the date 1436 in the explicit. Thus it is most likely it was written not too long after the events it describes.

[3] Our division differs from van Eck's principally in that hers is a more purely rhetorical analysis, dividing the text into *exordium*, *narratio*, and conclusion: van Eck, "Giannozzo Manetti," 451–52.

of this magnificent spectacle. Manetti obliged him, not just with a rhetorical retelling of the parades, as Acciaiuoli requested, but by situating this pageantry in the context of the consecration of the basilica which the Florentines had built. It is the relationship between the grand spectacle of the procession and its ultimate sacred purpose that gives the *De pompis* its meaning.

A comparison with other eyewitness accounts[4] and with the prescribed rites for the consecration of a church show that Manetti's purpose is not to give a full, literal description of either the parades or the consecration liturgy. Instead, he omitted significant details and rearranged others as it suited him. He elided most of the rite of consecration so that the procession to the church would be understood as the prelude to the events at the high altar. He conflated elements of the consecration with parts of the Mass and highlighted two ceremonials that belonged to neither. His account, then, cannot be used to document the events of the day accurately because that was not his intention.

"This sketch of that most glorious parade"

Manetti himself clearly states his purpose and his approach. He tells us that two themes guide his account: first, the ineffable glory of God, and second, the praise of the city (2). He warns us that this is not an objective and complete historical account, but an "adumbratio" or "sketch" with some parts "highlighted" and therefore visible, and others left in shadow (3). By this, Manetti not only means that he will be selective. He intends, he says, to imitate Timanthes who, in his painting of the Sacrifice of Iphigenia, did not depict the grief of Agamemnon, but instead covered his head. What could not be expressed through art the painter left to the judgment of the viewer. Manetti, too, will include only what can be expressed in words, while the most important part, surpassing words, will be left to the reader's imagination. By the conclusion of the *De pompis*, Manetti reaffirms that the wondrous nature of his subject has indeed eluded expression:

---

[4] Leonardo Bruni, *Rerum suo tempore gestarum commentarius*, in *RIS* 19.3, 423–58; also quoted in Vespasiano, *Vite,* 1.14 n.2. See also Feo Belcari in H. Saalman, *Filippo Brunelleschi. The Cupola of Sta. Maria del Fiore* (London, 1980), 275–76; St. Antoninus, *Chronicorum opus* (Lyon, 1586), 10.6 (527) (the chronicle is actually part 3 of his *Summa historiale*); Filippo di Cino Rinucci, *Ricordi storici dal 1282 al 1460, con la continuazione di Alamanno e Neri suoi figli al 1506*, ed. G. Aiazzi (Florence, 1840), 71; and Giovanni Cambi, *Istorie di Giovanni Cambi*, ed. I. di San Luigi, in *Delizie degli eruditi toscani* (Florence, 1785), vol. 20. Cambi's history is late fifteenth century but includes earlier chronicles. There are other published and unpublished accounts which we did not pursue since they would not shed further light on our text.

> These events were so wondrous that it seems I deserve to be forgiven if I did not have the power in words to explain worthily the unbelievable displays of things this great. Besides, these are clearly the ones least susceptible to eloquence (35).

The comparison with Timanthes goes beyond the rhetorical commonplace that the orator's words cannot do justice to the magnificence of events. It reveals his strategy for the development of his themes. Timanthes's painting is incomprehensible unless the viewer knows the story of Iphigenia's tragic betrayal by her father and the ethical burden of Agamemnon's choice. This need not be rehearsed; the artist's obligation is not to tell the story, but to lead the viewer to a moment where the emotional content must be discovered personally and experientially. So too Manetti. He does not need to catalogue each detail, describe each person and action, or explicate the civic and religious values which inform his narrative. Instead, by highlighting the elements he deems most rhetorically charged and sketching his own experience, Manetti can reconstruct events in such a way that his readers can feel within themselves what cannot be expressed directly in words.[5]

When Manetti says that his themes are the glory of God and the praise of the city, he means that the significance of the event is first theological and second political. But his narrative voice in the consecration account is that of a layman, and the theological content of his work is not explicit. The introduction and conclusion indicate a spiritual system of meaning, complementary to his rhetoric, which his eloquence can and will explore only indirectly and experientially, not in words. For example, instead of telling us that the bishop consecrating a church building represents Christ in his marriage to the Church, as do medieval commentaries on the consecration liturgy, Manetti writes that in the procession to the church the pope looked like God: he was "wondrously adorned with purple, gold, and interwoven gems of every sort; to those who looked upon him, the pope truly seemed more than a man, God himself" (23). Those, like Manetti, who were steeped in the symbolism of civic and religious ceremonial understood how this simple remark alluded to a developed system of theological thought and was enriched by it. Implicit in Manetti's narrative is the rich texture of images woven by medieval

[5] In his preference for emotion over reason and specific experience over logical abstraction as the basis for rhetoric, Manetti engages in a practice shared by other early Humanists. See Smith, *Architecture in the Culture of Early Humanism*, esp. 89; and P. O. Kristeller, *Renaissance Thought II. Papers on Humanism and the Arts* (New York, 1965), 30. Thus Pier Paolo Vergerio praised the power of history, saying that "I seem to live that age whose history I read," in *Epistolario*, ed. L. Smith (Rome, 1934), 172–73.

and Renaissance commentators on the consecration liturgy and which illuminate his apparently secular rhetoric.[6]

"A divine ranking of the Church Militant"

The double parade of secular and papal dignitaries that marched along Brunelleschi's covered walkway to the cathedral was a spectacle long remembered by contemporaries for its splendor. Manetti says it was "unparalleled in modern times" (1) and that both the Florentines and the papal entourage put such effort into their preparations that it seemed "a competition for the magnificence of parades was being waged between them" (5). An account of this memorable event would be worthwhile in its own right. Manetti must have seen Masaccio's fresco recording the consecration of Sta.Maria del Carmine (1422) showing the procession to the basilica and Bicci di Lorenzo's fresco of Martin V confirming the consecration of Sant'Egidio (ca. 1424) showing the crowd of lay and religious outside the church. Manetti, however, views the parades as continuous with the liturgical actions to be performed in the cathedral and endows them with a significance that arises from that liturgy. His purpose is to put before our eyes an idealized vision of the Church Militant which the rites inside the cathedral will perfect in its likeness to the Church Triumphant. As St. Antoninus put it: "Those things that are done in consecration signify those things which bring about the sanctification of the Church Militant." The church ceases to be the *tabernaculum* or tent of Christ's militant army and becomes the *Domus Dei*, the solidly founded, eternal dwelling of the King of Glory.[7]

The image of the Church Militant is perhaps most fully developed in St. Augustine's *City of God*, a work which Manetti claimed to know by heart (Vespasiano, *Vite*, 1:485–86). There the Church on earth is on pilgrimage, beset with danger and trials of all kinds, as it marches toward its goal which is the Heavenly Jerusalem. At the Last Judgment, the Church Militant will become the Church Triumphant. As expressed in Psalm 41 (42): "I shall make my way to the wonderful tabernacle, to the house of God."[8] Images of triumphal procession are

---

[6] In particular, Honorius of Autun, *Gemma animae*, PL 173.591; Sicardus of Cremona, *Mitrale*, PL 213. 30; Durandus of Mende, *Guillelmi Durantii Rationale divinorum officiorum*, ed. A. Davril and T. Thibodeau, CCCM 140–140A–140B (Turnhout, 1995); and St. Antoninus, *Summa Theologica* (Graz, 1959), esp. Book 12, chap. 6.

[7] St. Antoninus, *Summa*, col. 530.

[8] The psalms here reflect the Vulgate numbering, with that of the Authorized (King James) Version in parentheses. The translations provided are literal renderings of the Latin Vulgate text. The Vulgate psalms often differ greatly from the Hebrew text, as

frequent in the consecration liturgy: the bishop demands to be admitted to the church as "The Lord, valiant in battle" (Ps. 23[24]:8); at the anointing of the church the choir proclaims: "they have seen your procession, God . . . Princes go before him, joined with singers, in the midst of little girls playing drums" and "our feet were standing in your courts, Jerusalem" (Ps. 121[122]:2). And at the consecration of the altar, "the just shall feast and make merry in God's sight" and "the holy will make merry in glory" (Ps. 149:5).

Manetti's account exploits this military theme in various ways. First in his description of the decorations for the church, hung with shields and banners with insignia (14–15); then the canopied walkway built from S. Maria Novella to the cathedral, bearing the papal coat of arms (17). Since the pope's arrival in Florence almost two years earlier, he had hardly ventured out of the papal apartments at the Dominican convent (Vespasiano, *Vite*, 1:21–22). Thus his appearance before two hundred thousand spectators in the streets of the city in full regalia, and with all his court, in the person of the conquering Lord and of Christ, Bridegroom of the Church, was indeed a triumphal procession.[9] Brunelleschi's walkway, raised about four feet above the pavement and eight feet wide, must have been intended as a security measure. But it became the most striking spectacle of the day, carrying the highest dignitaries of church and state in their gorgeous robes above the heads of the people. For most, this was all they saw of the consecration: no account of the event fails to mention it and many describe nothing else.[10]

For Manetti, the procession was something more than a magnificent spectacle. In his account of the pontifical dignitaries (which includes, interestingly, the representatives of the Florentine Commune), he frequently uses the term *ordo*, "order."[11] He means by it not only the sequence of groups, but their relative status in the body of the Church Militant, its order made visible. In a Renaissance procession, the farther back in line, the greater the importance. Thus the civic dignitaries preceded the pontifical, and the pope came last of all. Manetti wants us to see the secular and papal *pompae* as a unified parade in two parts,

---

St. Jerome recognized. So too did Manetti, who published a poorly received translation from the Hebrew some twenty years after our text. But it is the Vulgate text which was sung in the liturgy and which endowed it with its spiritual meaning.

[9] The figure of 200,000 comes from Feo Belcari in Saalman, *Cupola*, 275.

[10] See our Commentary at 16.

[11] For example, "the huge line (*ordo*) of secular paraders" (19); "the line (*ordo*) of pontifical dignitaries seemed not human but divine" (21); "the divine ranking (*ordo*) of the Church Militant" (24). Manetti's account seems also to refer to Dionysius the Areopagite's concept of human and ecclesiastical hierarchies as reflections of the celestial hierachy: "Order and rank here below are a sign of the harmonious ordering toward the divine realm": *The Celestial Hierarchy* 124A, in *Pseudo-Dionysius*, trans. Luibheid, 146.

rather than two separate parades, even though the characters of the two are very different; he represents the event as the unification of Florentine polity and papal authority. This ideal, although it has some basis in contemporary politics, is an exemplification of the same metaphor underlying the ekphrasis of the cathedral: the Church — that is, all the faithful — as the body of Christ in the world. Unlike Paul's exegesis in 1 Corinthians 12, where the Church is made up of the different gifts of individuals, Manetti structures his exemplar according to classes within the ruling elite. He names none of the participants. For his account of the secular, or as he says, "human" part of the procession, Manetti uses classical Latin terms: the priors become *presides* and the city magistrates, *urbanis pretoribus*; they are said to wear togas (20). The courtly international culture of the fifteenth century is revealed, however, in the fact that ambassadors (*oratores*) of the Holy Roman Emperor and of kings, as well as princes, march with the Florentine leaders (20). Courtly also is Manetti's emphasis on the large numbers of youthful attendants and their lavish dress. Manetti takes this opportunity to state the equivalent value of the republican leaders in this gathering: "they seemed to the spectators to be kings — and justifiably so, because of their regal trappings" (20). This courtly theme is strong in the account: earlier, describing the cathedral, Manetti had praised the standards and banners bearing insignia which were hung all around the walls. The fifteen tribune chapels were said to be "so regally adorned that, without a doubt, they looked like royal rooms" (15). And the preparations of the Florentines were described as "royal, pontifical, and divine" (18). Manetti explicitly compares the procession of the Church Militant to the triumphal processions of the Romans (24), and indeed, what he describes is a socio-political, rather than a liturgical, procession. The head of the papal procession would have been the subdeacon with the processional cross, a figure who we know was there from other accounts (Vespasiano, *Vite,* 1:15), but about whom Manetti is silent. Also missing from his account are other figures known from papal ceremonial, such as the thurifer, the choir, and the subdeacon and deacon for reading the epistle and gospel.[12] There is, moreover, no mention of the abbots of major abbeys or the priors of convents in Florence, all of whom must certainly have been included. Finally, the liturgical character of the vestments of the pontifical paraders is de-emphasized by using Roman terms: copes become *subtalares togae* — ankle-length togas (23).

Manetti's papal procession begins with civil and canon lawyers and papal chamberlains (22). These three groups are not mentioned in any other contemporary source, but for Manetti's exemplar of the Church Militant, the placement

[12] For the typical participants in papal processions, see M. Dykmans, "D'Avignon à Rome. Martin V e le cortège apostolique," *Bulletin de l'Institut historique belge de Rome* 39 (1968): 203–308.

of papal interpreters of law and the executives of papal government behind, and therefore above, secular authorities is important. These are followed by bishops, archbishops, and patriarchs. Next to last come cardinals, "like Christ's true apostles" (22). Finally, the pope himself, who "seemed more than a man, God himself" (23). Manetti sums up the procession as a "divine ranking (*ordo*) of the Church Militant," a "great and divine spectacle" toward which "an unbelievable rush of people occurred" (24). Manetti takes the theme of triumphant entrance from the consecration liturgy and uses it to interpret the procession to the cathedral. Thus it becomes courtly and regal, like paintings of the Procession of the Magi done in Florence at this time, and it also becomes antique and Roman, acquiring the attributes of the classical ideal of the early Humanists, whose notion of civic virtue was formed by Livy and Cicero.[13]

"The most solemn rites of the whole consecration service"

The consecration service is elaborate, ancient, laden with symbolism, and time-consuming: it took about five hours to perform on that Annunciation Day, 25 March 1436.[14] The rite followed the ordo known from the Roman Curial Pontifical and elaborated in the thirteenth-century Roman Pontifical of Durandus of Mende, the pontifical widely diffused through the Christian West.[15] Durandus's

[13] One thinks, for instance of Gentile da Fabriano's Strozzi Altarpiece for the Sacristy of Sta. Trinità in which Palla Strozzi, represented as one of the Magi, wears the attributes of knighthood. H.Wohl observes that Leonardo Bruni, in his 1422 *De militia*, maintained that knighthood was Roman in origin (and therefore secular) and that the aristocracy of Florence were descendants of Roman and French knights: *The Aesthetics of Italian Renaissance Art. A Reconsideration of Style* (Cambridge, 1999), 27.

[14] Van Eck is mistaken in claiming that the liturgy which took place on 25 March 1436, was, in addition to the dedication of the high altar, the "pontifical confirmation of the previous dedication" because it had already been blessed in 1296 ("Giannozzo Manetti," 453). The blessing in 1296 would have been the liturgy for the blessing of the cornerstone of the new structure. That the 1436 liturgy was a consecration of the entire structure is confirmed by the anointing of the walls. As St. Antoninus reminds us in his *Summa*, a consecrated church must be reconsecrated if its walls have been destroyed in all or major part, or if the entire roof has been destroyed (535E). Since this is what had occurred when Sta. Maria del Fiore replaced Sta. Reparata, the church required a new consecration.

[15] For these two Pontificals, see M. Andrieu, *Le pontifical romain au moyen-age II: Le Pontifical de la curie romaine au XIIIe siècle*, Studi e Testi 87 (Vatican City, 1940), 421–40, and *Le pontifical romain au moyen-age III: Le pontifical de Guillaume Durand*, Studi e Testi 88 (Vatican City, 1940), 455–98. Both were well known and in use, though in the

commentary on liturgy, the *Rationale divinorum officiorum*, commanded great authority in the Quattrocento; it was the first work by a non-biblical writer ever printed (1459) and it went through forty-three printings in that century alone.[16] The liturgy performed in Florence and its interpretation are both clarified in the work of this thirteenth-century Scholastic. It has two distinct parts: the consecration of the building and altar (Durandus, *Rationale*, 2:1–99; 3:2–80) and then the Mass on the newly consecrated altar (2:100–110). The first and much lengthier part consists of actions accompanied by prayers and the singing of antiphons, responsories, hymns, and psalms, each of which endows the stages of the rite with mystical significance. The Mass contains service music (the "Ordinary"), the words of which were known to all (Kyrie, Gloria, Sanctus, etc.), the musical settings proper to the consecration (Introit, Gradual, etc.), and readings from Scripture. While the Mass is shorter than the rite of consecration, its impact is more concentrated: the scriptural readings firmly fix its themes; the musical settings are grander; and the eucharistic action is both sacred and familiar.

During the course of the consecration rite, the complexity with which meanings are interwoven can be seen from the chanting of all or part of eighteen different psalms, most prefaced by antiphons which aid in their interpretation. While the ritual is a dramatization, a sacred action and spectacle, the psalms and antiphons add words to comment on and contextualize the actions performed by the bishop. Taken together, these texts reveal several levels on which every consecration liturgy can be understood: historical (consecrating the church building); allegorical (the descent of the Heavenly Jerusalem); and anagogical (the passage from earthly life to the beatific vision). While Manetti's account is informed by all three senses, the anagogical — that is, the spiritual — corresponds to the ineffable experience at the heart of his sketch. Not only are these multiple

---

later part of the fifteenth century Durandus's clearer, fuller, and better organized work would supersede its predecessor. In any case, there is no disparity between the two on the actions, hymns, and prayers which constitute the liturgy of consecration. Durandus's pontifical is also consonant with his liturgical explications in the *Rationale*. See Andrieu, *Pontifical III*, 17–19. The numbers cited in parentheses refer to the book and section of Durandus's pontifical in Andrieu's edition. It may be that a still-extant manuscript owned by a participant in the ceremony, Antonio Casini, was used at the consecration. This is now MS. Edili 120 in the Biblioteca Laurentiana, an early fifteenth-century manuscript which was given to the cathedral in 1439. There is an illumination of the consecration of a church on fol. 42r: L. Fabbri and M. Tacconi, *I libri del duomo di Firenze: Codici liturgici e biblioteca di Santa Maria del Fiore* (Florence, 1997), 67, 210. For Casini's role in the consecration liturgy, see the Commentary at 22.

[16] On its popularity and the editions, see Durandus of Mende, *The Symbolism of Churches and their Ornaments. A Translation of the First Book of the 'Rationale divinorum officiorum'*, trans. J. M. Neale and B. Webb (London, 1843), xi.

senses all available within the liturgy, but they are also progressively developed through the interplay of actions and song, towards a culmination which completes and reveals its plenitude of significance. And even though Manetti's account does not describe most of the individual stages in the liturgical drama, its general effect is ordered by this same principle.

The psalms sung at various stages of the consecration show how the actions become part of the development of core ideas and themes. As the bishop circles the exterior of the church three times, sprinkling its walls, the choir sings from Psalm 50 (51):9: "you shall sprinkle me with hyssop and I shall be cleansed; you will wash me and I shall become whiter than snow." After each circuit, the bishop knocks on the door of the church and has the following exchange, from Psalm 23 (24):7–8, with a deacon inside. The bishop: "Lift up your gates, o princes; and be raised, eternal gates, and there will enter the king of glory." The deacon: "Who is this king of glory?" The bishop: "The Lord the mighty, the valiant, the Lord valiant in battle." Thus the liturgy begins with purification, followed by the announcement of the triumphant entry of God, in the person of the consecrating bishop (Durandus, *Rationale*, 2:24–36). During the rites leading up to the anointing of the altar the musical texts stress the identification of the church being consecrated with the Temple in Jerusalem. Thus, Psalm 67 (68):25: "They have seen your processions, God, the processions of God, my king, who is in the sanctuary"; from Psalm 121 (122):2: "our feet were standing in your courts, Jerusalem"; and from Psalm 25 (26):6: "I will wash my hands among the innocent and encircle your altar" and "I have loved the beauty of your house and the place where your glory dwells."

When the activity then moves to the area around the altar, the chants underscore the connection of the sanctuary to the dwelling place of God and the saints, the triumphant Church in heaven. Psalm 86 (87):1–2: "Its foundations are on the holy mountains; the Lord loves the gates of Sion over all the tabernacles of Jacob"; Psalm 67 (68):4: "The just shall feast and make merry in God's sight and they shall delight in gladness"; Psalm 149:5–6: "the holy will make merry in glory, they will be glad on their couches, God's joyous praise in their throats"; and Psalm 62 (63):3: "I have served you in your sanctuary, to see your power and glory."

The house now consecrated, a new phase in the action begins. The church is finally flooded with light; the ministers reemerge from the sacristy, having changed into Mass vestments; and the Introit for the Mass in sung. The text is taken from Genesis 28:17, where Jacob, having seen angels ascending and descending from heaven exclaims: "How awesome is this place! This is none other than the House of God and the gate of heaven." The epistle reading, from Revelation 21:1–3, summarizes how the rite of consecration has endowed this space with new meaning:

> And I saw a new heaven and a new earth, the first heaven and the first earth had gone away, and the sea was no longer. And I, John, saw the holy city, the new Jerusalem, coming down from God out of heaven, readied as a bride adorned for her husband. And I heard a great voice from the throne, saying 'Behold the tabernacle of God among men, and he will dwell among them.'

The drama of the liturgy began with penitence and purification, the sanctification of an earthly place to await the coming of God. God is then seen approaching victorious, the faithful rejoice, and, finally, God enters, fills and transforms the new church, as a new reality of heaven on earth is revealed.

"This Temple, so magnificent, so wonderful, and ultimately so unbelievable"

The conceptual basis of the liturgy of consecration draws on three Old Testament biblical narratives, the common theme of which is that there are indeed places where heaven is revealed on earth. These can be seen as affirmative replies to the question posed by King Solomon at the dedication of the Jerusalem Temple: "Is it believable that God lives among men on the earth? If heaven and the heavens' heaven cannot contain you, how much less this house that I have built!" (2 Chronicles 6:18). That God is present in a special way in certain places is shown in the story of Jacob's dream: as we saw, parts of this text are quoted during the consecration liturgy, specifically at the consecration of the altar and at the introit of the Mass: "This is none other than the House of God and the gate of heaven." That God really will inhabit a temple made by human hands is clear from the dedication of Solomon's Temple (2 Chronicles 7:1–3) at which "the majesty of the Lord filled the Temple . . . and all the sons of Israel saw the fire descending and the glory of the Lord upon the house"; and Ezekiel's vision of the restoration of the Temple (43:1–5), "I saw the glory of the God of Israel approaching from the east . . . the earth shone with his majesty . . . [and] I saw the majesty of the Lord fill the Temple."

The Temple means something additional to Christians, who understand it allegorically and anagogically as well as historically. As allegory, we find it most fully expressed in 1 Corinthians 3:16, when Paul says: "Do you not know that you are God's temple and that the spirit of God lives among you?" For Christians, the *ecclesia* is not only a structure in which the mysteries of salvation are enacted, but also the *Ecclesia*, the collectivity of believers, the visible church which embodies Christ's kingdom on earth (the Church Militant) and the church in glory, the angels and saints around the throne of God (the Church Triumphant). The progress from one to the other is evoked in the consecration liturgy as also in Manetti's account. The allegorical sense emphasizes the corporate and sociopolitical significance of the event.

Augustine wrote that whatever is done in a church at its dedication signifies an analogous operation in the soul:

> Then our conversation will cohere if it includes something about building which augments your souls' advantage while God builds us inwardly. What we see here made bodily in the walls, let it be made spiritually in our minds. And what we here observe completed in stone and wood, let this, as God's grace builds it, be completed in your bodies.[17]

Augustine expressed the progression of the soul to God as types of vision: corporeal (seen by the body); imaginative (seen in the mind's eye); and intellectual (divine illumination beyond intellection) (*De Genesi ad litteram libri XII* 12.6). So Manetti, wanting to alert the reader to the double significance of the consecration as a human as well as an architectural event, tells us that to him, "looking carefully and often at the admirable building of this sacred basilica, it seems to be almost the same as the human body" (7). There is nothing original in this image. The analogy between the human body and architectural form, already in Vitruvius, was repeated throughout the Middle Ages, not least by Durandus who tells us that churches are shaped like the human body.[18] But there is a great difference between Durandus's interpretation — that this is to remind us of the body of Christ on the cross — and Manetti's reference in the context of consecration liturgy which enacts the drama of human salvation, specifically, of the Last Judgment, Second Coming, and descent of the Heavenly Jerusalem: a drama experienced both as spectacle and as insight.

For Christians, moreover, the Temple is indistinguishable from the Heavenly Jerusalem for, as we hear in Revelation, the epistle reading for the dedication of a church: "I saw that there was no temple in the city since the Lord God Almighty and the Lamb were themselves its temple . . . for the brilliance of God illumined it"; and "It had all the radiant glory of God" (21:9, 22).

"The ineffable glory of God"

The glory referred to here is not "reputation" or "honor" but the distinctive attribute of God's presence, often imagined as a particular kind of light, and therefore visible on earth.[19] Just as it filled the Temple in Jerusalem, so it descends on the

---

[17] St. Augustine, "Sermones de tempore," 336, PL 38.1475. See discussion in L. Bowen, "The Tropology of Mediaeval Dedication Rites," *Speculum* 16 (1941): 469–79, here 476–77.

[18] Manetti's image is discussed in Chapter 9.

[19] The representation of glory in art was studied by W. Loerke in "'Real Presence' in Early Christian Art," in *Monasticism and the Arts*, ed. T. Verdon (Syracuse, 1984), 29–52.

newly consecrated church. When Manetti says that his subject is "the ineffable glory of immortal God" (2), he does not mean that his purpose is to give glory to God, but to describe and testify to God's "glory" in this technical, biblical sense, as manifested in the great events surrounding the consecration of 1436. "Glory," as St. Antoninus defined it, is a technical term meaning "bringing into the light and celebrating."[20] The term occurs twice more in Manetti's narrative. We are told that the pope prepared for the consecration "so that he might exhibit to our people an exemplar of divine glory" (5). The round windows of the clerestory and drum of the cathedral "illumine with their light not only the individual places of the east end, but seem also to provide viewers with a specimen of divine glory" (11). The glory of God is God manifesting himself to the human senses, especially sight. Manetti tells us that the glory of God is seen by the eyes of the body as specimen and exemplar. But it is also ineffable, and what goes beyond the power of words, though mediated through physical sight, must be left to the imagination of the reader. And so Manetti will allude to, but not describe, the glory of God that filled Florence Cathedral.

While a specimen of God's glory may be seen in the light of a church building, it is fully revealed in the individual soul. Paul writes: "It is the same God that said, 'Let there be light shining out of darkness', who has shone in our minds to radiate the light of the knowledge of God's glory"; and: "We, with our unveiled faces reflecting like mirrors the brightness of the Lord, all grow brighter and brighter as we are turned into the image that we reflect" (1 Corinthians 4:6, 3:18). Manetti tells us of his beatific vision, at the elevation of the Host, the focal point of the Mass for a fifteenth-century congregation.[21] He says, "I indeed obtained so many pleasures that I seemed to be enjoying the blessed life here on earth" (33). This inner vision of the glory of God, the goal of the liturgy and the subject of his account, because of its inexpressibility, must be experienced individually, even as the viewers of Timanthes's Agamemnon had to choose how to respond: "Whether others standing there experienced the same thing, I clearly do not know; about myself, however, I am a competent witness" (33).

---

[20] St. Antoninus, *Summa*, 2.4.1, cols. 544–547: discussed in Howard, *Beyond the Written Word*, 101.

[21] For the congregation's perception of the Mass in the fifteenth century, see T. Klauser, *A Short History of the Western Liturgy* (London, 1969); G. Dix, *The Shape of the Liturgy* (London, 1945); and J. Jungmann, *The Mass of the Roman Rite. Its Origins and Development* (New York, 1951). For the elevation of the host, see M. Rubin, *Corpus Christi* (Cambridge, 1991), 55–70.

"What the pope did in the consecration of the basilica"

When Manetti describes events within the cathedral, he takes liberties not only in omitting most of the specific rites performed in the sanctification of the building and the conduct of the Mass, but also in rearranging the elements he does describe to produce a succession of events that lead climactically to his experience of overwhelming joy. In Manetti's account, Eugenius enters the church and immediately proceeds to the altar where he prays briefly before ascending the papal throne where he sits, ringed by his entourage assembled by rank (25), the Gonfaloniere della Giustizia seated at his feet (26). Immediately, a cardinal vested for Mass begins the service. Manetti is at once transported by the music, presumably of the Dufay setting for the Introit "Terribilis est locus iste" (26). His senses piqued by the sounds and smells and sights (27), Manetti next recounts a gang of captives liberated by the pope, followed by the investiture of the Gonfaloniere as a knight (29–30). While this was happening, a cardinal begins anointing the images of the twelve apostles around the church's perimeter (31). After a pause, the pope rises from his throne to anoint the table of the altar, and then to deposit within it the relics of the martyrs, and finally washes his hands with the assistance of the prince of Rimini (32). In Manetti's account, the consecration and elevation of the host occur amid music of such sweetness Manetti imagines he hears sounds from paradise (33). Then he recounts that the pope endowed the basilica with indulgences and returned with the paraders to his apostolic residence by the same route from which he had arrived (34).

Manetti recognizes that any participant in the service would understand how much he had omitted. For the Mass alone, the liturgy of the Word during which the epistle and gospel were read is missing; the Canon is shortened to the elevation of the host; the actual reception of communion is not remarked; and the blessing and dismissal is reduced to the announcement of spiritual privileges. While he is at pains to convey the beauty of the music, he divulges none of its content. Despite this foreshortened description, he acknowledges that "all the most solemn rites of the whole consecration service had . . . been performed and the whole divine service (the Mass) reverently celebrated" (34). His selectivity is obviously in service to the interpretation he wishes to convey. But equally important is the rearrangement of the elements he does report. Neither the anointing of the walls nor of the altar would have occurred during the Mass, but rather as the climax to the consecration rites where the altar would have been anointed first and then the walls. The liberation of captives and the investiture of the gonfaloniere are not part of either the consecration or its Mass, and yet they receive prominent attention. And Manetti's own reaction to sensory stimuli, particularly the music, occupies almost as much space in the account as the events that are described.

The following table schematizes the ritual as required by the Roman Pontifical and includes the two ceremonials, the freeing of captives and the knighting of the gonfaloniere, known to have been inserted into the Florentine liturgy.

Actual Liturgy	Manetti's Account
A. 3 circuits	
B. knocking on door	
C. entrance	C. entrance
D. litany	
E. alphabets	K. Mass begins
F. lustrations	L. music (Introit)
G. relics	O. captives freed
H. altar	J. knighting
I. walls	I. walls
J. knighting	H. altar
K. Mass begins	G. relics
L. Introit	
M. readings	
N. Creed	
O. captives freed	
P. offertory	
Q. elevation of host	Q. elevation of host
R. Benedictus	R. music (Benedictus)
S. communion	
T. blessing	
U. indulgences	U. indulgences

Manetti's economical description underscores the theme of triumphant entrance, but in a different way from the "King of Glory" reenactment that actually comprised the liturgical entrance. In Manetti's account, the pope magnificently enters the basilica and takes his place on "the most regally adorned pontifical throne" beneath the dome (25). The Mass begins, but its first noted actions are the freeing of captives and the knighting of the Florentine Gonfaloniere della Giustizia "to greatly honor the Florentine name" (29). From other testimony, we know that the knighting took place while the ministers were vesting for the Mass, that is, after the altar had been consecrated, but before that Mass had begun. The freeing of prisoners was done after the Creed and before the Offertory of the Mass.[22] Manetti's order is invented to further his theme of a royal papacy presiding over a militant church celebrating a victory in the manner of an imperial *adventus*: captives are freed and loyal supporters rewarded on the arrival of

[22] Belcari in Saalman, *Cupola*, 276; and Cambi, *Istoria*, 208.

the *triumphator.* In this way, Manetti invites us to share the transformation of the Church Militant as it becomes the Church Triumphant.

This transformation has also determined Manetti's narrative realignment of the anointing of the altar with the eucharist. In reality, they occurred hours apart, but theologically and experientially, they are a single unified action. The anointing of the altar enables the "consecrating of the Lord's body" (33). The creation of the cathedral's sacred space makes it a place where God can be present on earth, and an actualization of the Heavenly Jerusalem and the Church Triumphant in God's glory. This temporalization of the eternal makes available to the participant an experience of the joyous paradise and its pleasures. In Manetti's version, the anointing of the walls of the cathedral precede the anointing of the altar, so that the sacred action narrows on the holy spaces of the *tabulatum* where are located the altar, the papal throne, the relics of the martyrs, the seats of ranked dignitaries, and the choir. These comprise a vision of a transcendent order where, the victory won, the Church on earth finds its proper place within the eternal order of angels (music) and saints (relics) in the reign of the King of Glory (the papal throne, Christ in the Eucharist).

"The great praise of our city"

The praise of Florence, Manetti's secular theme, is inextricably bound up with the sacred. The two parades form a unified panorama of the structure of the Church Militant, its lay and clerical leaders processing by rank on the elevated *ponte* and seated within the choir as an ordered assembly, with "children of both sexes and men and women of all ages" (24) crowding the streets. The knighting of the Gonfaloniere della Giustizia "to honor greatly the Florentine name" (29) incorporates a Florentine dignitary, and by extension the city, into the spiritual service of the militant church. But most of all, the city is praised for the completion of its cathedral, magnificent enough to merit an apostolic consecration. The fabric of the cathedral, recounted in great detail in the ekphrasis of 6–15, Manetti insists, places it among the Seven Wonders of the World and equals the Athenian achievement in the building of Philo's magnificent armory: "ought not the Florentines also take the highest pride because they have built a wondrous work?" (12) The cathedral on the day of its consecration is vividly described so that it can be visualized as the setting for the grand spectacle that will occur within. But more than this, the cathedral is not simply the place within which sacred actions are performed. It is the very object of those actions. What the Florentines have built, the pope has sanctified as a new Jerusalem, an exemplar of the triumphant church, and a place where the pleasures of paradise are available to men. Thus civic praise is inseparable in Manetti's account from his witness to God's glory.

Manetti's account of the consecration begins with a physical description of the cathedral which anyone in Florence could check against the building; continues with the procession and liturgy, which can be imagined on the basis of his description; and closes with the author's beatific vision at the elevation of the host: "At that very moment, I managed to take so many pleasures that I truly seemed to be enjoying the blessed life here on earth" (33). This progression is embedded in the consecration liturgy itself, but Manetti's response to it reveals his broader cultural experience. Certainly this Florentine's account is informed by Dante's *Divine Comedy* where in the "Paradiso" we find that:

> The passing beyond humanity [to gaze on the glory of God] may not be set forth in words: therefore let the example suffice any for whom grace reserves that experience (Canto 1.70–72).

"This most solemn day when the first event of human salvation appeared"

A final word about the consecration. We know that the first stone of the cathedral was laid on 8 September 1296 or 1298, on the Feast of the Birth of the Virgin.[23] The consecration occurred on 25 March, the Feast of the Annunciation. Luke's Gospel tells us that at the incarnation, "the power of the Most High" covered Mary with its shadow (1:35). Like the glory of God, usually thought of as light, the shadow or cloud of the power of God is visible evidence of his divine presence. In early Christian art, these images are usually conflated, divine presence being depicted by light-filled clouds.[24] We saw that the body of Christ, of which the faithful are all mystically members and which is signified in the shape of Florence Cathedral, will be filled with God's glory at the consecration. But the body of Christ took historical shape within the Temple of the body of the Virgin. The body of the cathedral, then, like the Virgin to whom it is consecrated on the day commemorating the Incarnation in her body, is the means by which Christ becomes part of the material world and the material world in turn is transformed to the divine. The importance of Mary and the Annunciation to the consecration ceremony was expressed in the music commissioned for the occasion from Guillaume Dufay, especially the motet "Nuper rosarum flores" which sets a text

[23] The text of the foundation stone is in T. Verdon, "L'opera di Santa Maria del Fiore: Sette secoli di laboriosa fedeltà," in *Alla riscoperta di Piazza del Duomo in Firenze. 6. I tesori di Piazza del Duomo*, ed. idem (Florence, 1997), here 109.

[24] See Loerke, 'Real Presence,' 16–17.

praising the Virgin in counterpoint to the Introit "Terribilis est."[25] Manetti celebrates the angelic annunciation, telling us that "the songs appeared angelic and divine" (33) and were like those sung in heaven "by the angels every year on this most solemn day on which the first event of human salvation appeared" (26).

Sicardus of Cremona compares an unconsecrated church to an unmarried maiden, who at the consecration becomes the bride of Christ, for the liturgy signifies "a copulation of the soul" (*animae copulatio*).[26] And Honorius of Autun adds that "the dedication of a church is the consummation of the marriage (*nuptialis copulatio*) between the Church and Christ. The bishop who consecrated it is Christ who has betrothed the Church."[27] The metaphor is thus one of the sexual union between husband and wife necessary for marriage to become sacramental and sacred. This metaphor is rooted in the consecration liturgy, where the procession to the sanctuary is also a marriage procession, as in Psalm 44 ([45]:14–16), the royal wedding song: "All the glory of the daughter of the king comes from within, amid golden fringes, dressed in brightly colored robes; behind her, the bridesmaids shall be led to the king." And in Revelation 21:9, where an angel shows John the Heavenly Jerusalem, saying: "I will show you the bride, married to the Lamb"; the bride is said to be radiant with the glory of God and to glitter like a diamond (Revelation 21:11). As in historical time the power of God filled Mary with the incarnate Christ by a "copulation of the soul" at the Annunciation, so in the liturgy of consecration Christ marries the Church by filling it with the glory of God.

Of the seven stained glass windows filling the oculi of Brunelleschi's dome — which Manetti told us were a specimen of God's glory (11) — only one was commissioned before the consecration and the others almost a decade later.[28] The window ordered from Donatello in 1417, but not installed until 1437, shows the Coronation of the Virgin, Mary as the Church taken as bride by Christ (fig. 2). Her garments — unheard of in stained glass — are white and faceted, glittering "like a diamond."

Manetti's account of the consecration interweaves the ceremony of consecration with the Feast of the Annunciation to Mary, patroness of the city of

---

[25] C. Wright, "Dufay's *Nuper rosarum flores*, King Solomon's Temple, and the Veneration of the Virgin," *Journal of the American Musicological Society* 47 (1994): 395–441, with further bibliography, and our Commentary at 26.

[26] Sicardus, *Mitrale*, 1.6, PL 213.28B.

[27] Honorius of Autun, *Gemma animae*, PL 173.590.

[28] On the glass windows, see C. Acidini Luchinat, "The Stained-Glass Windows," in *The Cathedral of Santa Maria del Fiore in Florence*, ed. idem (Florence, 1995), 273–302, here 279; and idem, "Quarantaquattro vetrate d'artista, un tesoro del Rinascimento in Duomo," in Verdon, *L'opera*, 40–66.

Florence and of the cathedral named for her. The Church Militant, or the body of Christ on earth, begins at the Incarnation; the Church Triumphant, or the Heavenly Jerusalem, begins with the marriage of Christ and the Church, who is S. Maria del Fiore.

Fig. 2. Donatello's "Coronation of the Virgin" window in the tambour of Florence Cathedral's dome. Scala/Art Resource, NY.

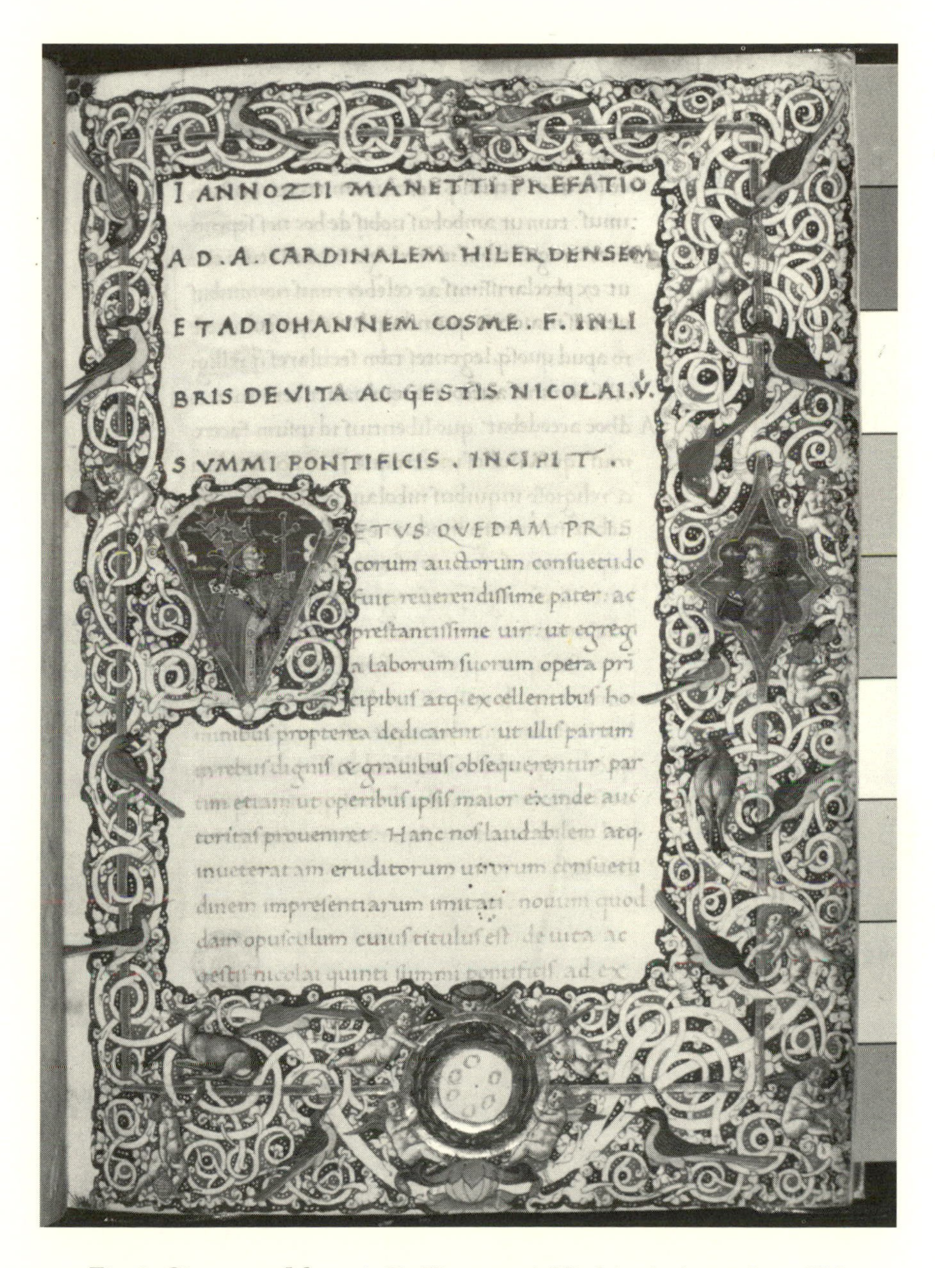

IANNOZII MANETTI PREFATIO
AD D. A. CARDINALEM HILERDENSEM
ET AD IOHANNEM COSME. F. IN LI
BRIS DE VITA AC GESTIS NICOLAI. V.
SVMMI PONTIFICIS. INCIPIT.

VETVS QVEDAM PRIS
corum auctorum consuetudo
fuit reuerendissime pater ac
prestantissime uir ut egregi
a laborum suorum opera pri
ncipibus atq excellentibus ho
minibus propterea dedicarent ut illis partim
in rebus dignis et grauibus obsequerentur par
tim etiam ut operibus ipsis maior exinde auc
toritas proueniret. Hanc nos laudabilem atq
inueteratam eruditorum uirorum consuetu
dinem impresentiarum imitati nouum quod
dam opusculum cuius titulus est de uita ac
gestis nicolai quinti summi pontificis ad ex

Fig. 3. Giannozzo Manetti, *De Vita ac gestis Nicolai quinti summi pontificis*, depicting the pontiff in the initial and the author at right. Florence, Bib. Med. Laur., MS. Plut. 66.22, fol. 1r.

Chapter Three

Manetti's *Life of Nicholas V*

Early in Book 1 of the *Life of Nicholas V* (fig. 3), Manetti relates a dream which came to Tommaso Parentucelli's mother, Andreola. Her ten-year-old son had become so seriously ill that, despairing of medical cure, she resorted to prayers and devotions. One night, she dreamed that she was visited by a priest in white vestments who admonished her to lay aside her anxieties and to encourage her son to enter the clerical life, because it was there that he was destined for greatness. After the vision, the boy, the future Nicholas V, was restored to health and accepted first tonsure (*RIS* 910). Manetti affirms this event with a digression on dreams in classical antiquity[1] and in the Old Testament, a digression Muratori refused to publish.[2] One dream, that of Eudemus of Cyprus, holds special interest for Manetti's purpose in the *Life*. According to Cicero (*De divinatione* 1.25.53), Eudemus's dream, recounted by Aristotle in his lost dialogue *Eudemus*, occurred when he became deathly ill during his exile from Cyprus. A young man appeared to him to say that he would soon be cured, that the Cyprian tyrant would die, and that Eudemus would return home after five years. Indeed within a few days Eudemus was healed and news arrived that the Cyprian tyrant had been assassinated. When the predicted five years had elapsed, Eudemus made his way to the port to sail home, but was killed there. Aristotle resolved the oracular conundrum by arguing that Eudemus had indeed "returned home" from exile since human life was itself an exile. Death released his soul to return, not to Cyprus, but to its true home. This particular example shows the retrospective and interpretative way in which dreams must be verified. As they occur in time, they may seem to portend one thing, but their true value can clearly be discerned only in hindsight.

The same may be said for Manetti's biography of Nicholas V. Andreola's dream and the three other dreams that Nicholas experienced — Eugenius IV revealing he will be elected his successor, the same Eugenius predicting he will

---

[1] Manetti draws his illustrations from Cicero, *On divination*. *Vita*, trans. Modigliani, 79–86 gives a translation of the passages Muratori excised (see following note).

[2] *RIS* 3.2: 911. Muratori explains: "Manetti inserted here and dragged on for some pages some mishmash about the dreams of the ancients, if not tasteless, at least idle and unsuited to the context. Let me be permitted to cut them out and leave them to their darkness. The reader demands a life of Nicholas V, not a pile of dreams, some of which must be regarded as fables."

be cured of his disease but the eighth year of his rule would hold danger, and Stephano Porcari entering his bedroom with a cudgel — are sent as "oracles of almighty God" (*RIS* 911). Read chronologically in the biography, they mark turning points in his life story: he becomes a priest; he is elected pope; he survives a life-threatening disease but succumbs to illness in the eighth year of his pontificate; and he exposes the Porcari conspiracy. Read retrospectively, in the light of his pontificate, they confirm a divinely willed and communicated destiny, or as Miglio puts it,[3] a predestined papacy, affirmed by visions. Even if Manetti cannot discern God's will in Nicholas's premature death, he does not doubt the operation of a divine plan, only his own ability to comprehend it (*RIS* 958). Similarly, when Manetti considers what Nicholas achieved in his life before the papacy, during his reign, and in the legacy he intends to leave on his deathbed, he argues in retrospect a coherent meaning and unified purpose that was not obvious to everyone while the pope lived.

Although Manetti is prepared to treat dreams as credible, portending and confirming a life of extraordinary importance to a divine plan, his biography of Nicholas is not hagiography. Dreams are not miracles. They do not suspend the laws of nature or contradict science; indeed, their occurrence in pagan antiquity and in the Old Testament confirms them as occasional indicators of a deeper meaning under the surface of events. Moreover, Manetti says nothing of any ascetic practices Nicholas may have engaged in[4] or spiritual heights he may have experienced. Nor is the *Life of Nicholas V* a papal chronicle, such as might be found in the *Liber Pontificalis*, which enumerates in a detached manner the material and administrative achievements of a successor to Peter's throne. In the *Life*, Nicholas's material legacy, especially in the city of Rome, and his papal policy within Italy and beyond, are inextricably linked to his human character and to the historical moment to which he responded.

In this respect, the *Life of Nicholas V* resembles Manetti's biographies of the Florentine poets, composed in the 1430s, and his later biographies of the pagan philosophers Socrates and Seneca. As compositions, they all share similarities of literary structure and character analysis. In two important respects, however, they are radically different. First, the subjects of Manetti's other biographies, the Florentine poets and the ancient philosophers, were figures of the past, already fixed in memory, about whom much had been written. But Nicholas V was Manetti's contemporary. Manetti had known the man in his youth, had seen him rise to the papal dignity, had officially greeted him on his accession,

[3] In *Vita*, trans. Modigliani, 19–23.

[4] In contrast, for example, to Vespasiano's account of Eugenius IV, where the opulence of the papal display he accepted is contrasted to the pontiff's personal simplicity of life and his penitential practices (*Vite*, 1:22).

and had come to Rome at his bidding to engage in scholarly pursuits at the papal court. And the *Life* was composed soon after Nicholas's death in 1455, when assessments of the man and of his achievements were mixed and his historical reputation fluid. Second, among the subjects of Manetti's biographies Nicholas was unique in status. Poets and philosophers mattered greatly to men of culture and learning. Even if they entered into politics and affairs of state, as did Dante and Seneca, their importance derived from their contributions to the life of the mind, not to their public deeds. In fact, in the case of Dante, Manetti argues that he is to be admired all the more because he achieved greatness as a poet despite his active and honorable engagement in public life.[5] A pope, however, is a prince among princes and bears an institutional identity with his church and its mission. This public and historic role demands that his life be measured by his deeds, by the quality of his pursuit of the active, not the contemplative life.

Manetti as Biographer

Manetti's biographies of the Florentine poets were written at a time when the history and biography of the ancients were becoming increasingly well known through the production of Latin translations of Herodotus, Thucydides, and especially Plutarch.[6] Manetti owned these works, and it is not surprising that Plutarch influenced both the literary structure and the purpose of his biographies. As he explains in his preface to his *Lives of Three Illustrious Florentine Poets*, this work grew out of his earlier *On Famous Men of Great Age* (*De illustribus longaevis*), a compilation of brief biographical sketches of prominent men of the distant and recent past who were both memorable and long-lived, a task enabled by the recent recovery of lost and neglected source material. His task in these biographies was to render fitting praise, in Latin, to an audience of erudite men who might otherwise disdain the vernacular literature these poets produced.[7] To do so, he adopted a literary structure modeled on Plutarch for each life, with a concluding comparative assessment in imitation of Plutarchan parallelism. This is the same structure he would later adopt for an even lengthier parallel set of lives of the philosophers Socrates and Seneca for King Alfonso of Aragon.[8] The first part

---

[5] *Biographical Writings*, ed. and trans. Baldassarri and Bagemihl, "Life of Boccaccio," 103.

[6] On the recovery and use of Plutarch's *Lives* in early Quattrocentro Florence, see Gary Ianziti, "The Plutarchan Option: Leonardo Bruni's Early Career in History, 1405–1414," *I Tatti Studies* 8 (1999): 11–36.

[7] *Biographical Writings*, 2–7.

[8] *Biographical Writings*, 164–287.

of each life contains a family history, a discussion of the youth and education of its subject, and then a description of the most important events and accomplishments in chronological order. This is followed by a *prosopopoeia*, that is, a sketch of physical attributes and a character assessment. Afterward, each life continues with an analysis of the subject's major achievements in the area on which his fame rests.

The structure accommodates anecdotes for vivid narrative and digressions for fuller treatment of topics the writer chooses to endow with greater importance. Among these topics is often Manetti's own explanation of items that remained controversial or his defense of his subject from charges he considers ill considered. In Dante's case, for example, he justifies the poet's refusal to return to his native land by showing how the conditions of that return would have brought dishonor; in the same vein, he argues that the behavior some have interpreted as arrogance should be seen as patriotism or idealism.[9] Manetti's life of Seneca is distinctive for its efforts to correct a variety of misinterpretations: attacks on the philosopher's lack of rigor, rhetorical style, and erudition;[10] the alleged hypocrisy of his wealth and connections to Nero;[11] and the hotly debated philological question of the authenticity of works attributed to Seneca.[12]

All the biographies take note of the circumstances of the subject's death, including any telling details such as subsequent memorial dedications. The death of Socrates is related at great length because of the abundance of information supplied by Plato, including the content of his last philosophical discourses, and because the manner of his death is connected thematically to the source of his fame.[13]

Manetti's use of the form of Plutarchan biography suits the purposes for which he undertakes these various lives. His stated intention is to accord praise due to great men for the edification of a specialized audience: for the poets, the erudite; for the philosophers, a prince. Each biography constitutes a rhetorical argument favoring its subject by presenting his character as virtuous and his deeds as praiseworthy, appealing to the values his audience would find convincing. In this way, he portrays his subject's actions in a positive light and sometimes explicitly deflects or rebuts past or potential criticism. Where previous accounts exist, his new version invites the reader to prefer his alternative understanding. Manetti's purpose, then, is not simply to recount, but to explain these famous lives in ways that make sense to his audience and affect how his subjects are remembered.

---

[9] *Biographical Writings*, "Life of Dante," 52–55.
[10] *Biographical Writings*, "Life of Seneca," 252–67.
[11] *Biographical Writings*, "Life of Seneca," 268–81.
[12] *Biographical Writings*, "Life of Seneca," 280–87.
[13] *Biographical Writings*, "Life of Socrates," 226–33.

The power of the writer to shape this historical memory was well understood in Manetti's culture. Poggio Bracciolini in his *De varietate fortunae*, presented to Nicholas in 1447, takes up this very issue. Poggio represents himself in conversation with Antonio Loschi discussing the vagaries of Fortune, particularly among the ancients. Our times, Loschi ventures, lack gifted writers to memorialize great deeds, while antiquity enjoyed abundance:

> There was a great supply of writers who did not allow the deeds of their own time to be interred; each extolled them and embellished them in words so that they might be read with pleasure. So it happened that what the earlier times endured is better known to us than what has been done in our own age. We are lacking people to bring to light deeds which, left in darkness, grow obscure.[14]

Poggio concurs and attributes the contemporary lack to rulers who surround themselves with flatterers and offer no incentive, reward, or favor that might attract the learned and eloquent. Loschi continues:

> I encourage whoever can to take up the task of at least representing this age in writing . . . [The accounts of antiquity] are as credible as their writer's authority and eloquence. But we have lacked writers for some time and, because of this lack, the deeds of our day, some quite magnificent and extraordinary, slide into never-ending oblivion.

Poggio and Loschi seem to share Manetti's conviction that the "learned desire and hope for praise that comes from erudite men," who will write "effusively and at length about the wealth of their accomplishments."[15] Poggio and Loschi imagined that the practice of biography was the eloquent rendering of a life memorable for magnificence or extraordinary deeds, and urged writers to memorialize the great deeds of their own time, as had the writers of antiquity. Such writers, by their authority and eloquence, would make such deeds credible, that is, they would convince future readers of their truthfulness. Manetti, eight years later, had just such an urgent and far-reaching purpose in his construction of the *Life of Nicholas V.*

Nicholas V (fig. 4) died in Rome on 24 March 1455. Between then and the end of the year, as Modigliani has pointed out,[16] Manetti wrote his biography amid tension and personal distress that the papal projects with which he himself identified and which he would eloquently articulate might not come to fruition.

[14] *De varietate fortunae*, ed. Merisalo, 106–7.

[15] *Biographical Writings*, 7.

[16] *Vita*, trans. Modigliani, 49–52.

Fig. 4. Coin portrait of Nicholas V, obverse. Bib. Vat., inv. 766.

Nicholas had his detractors, and the newly elected pontiff, Callixtus III, had shown little enthusiasm for continuing his predecessor's ambitions in augmenting the papal library or completing the architectural program for the Vatican. Manetti's alarm breaks through in his account of Nicholas's commissions for translations and new works for his library; the pope's untimely and hurtful death has damaged and perhaps wrecked his own plans to compose a new translation of Hebrew and Greek Scripture and a long critique of pagan and Jewish thought (2.17). The threnody and prayer which close Book 3 of the *Life* constitute an impassioned questioning of God's incomprehensible judgments, while still expressing hope that God had not endowed Nicholas with such abundant gifts in vain (*RIS* 958). Manetti's biography, in contrast with Canensi's account written during the pope's life, or Vespasiano's or Platina's chronicles written several decades later,[17] seems particularly informed by an unstated intimacy between the pope and his biographer and a sense of urgency to preserve an historic legacy. As the first, most complete, and most eloquent of the biographies, Manetti's would seem not only to have achieved the purposes that characterized his earlier accounts of the Florentine poets — to praise his subject convincingly to a learned audience — but also to command historical memory because of its eloquence and special authority. In this case, as earlier in his depiction of the consecration of Florence Cathedral, he intends to represent, not the past, but his own age in writing. The form here, however, is biography, and its subject, the successor of Peter, prince of the Apostles, and himself a prince, commands far broader scope — not the crowning achievement of a flourishing republic, but a magnificent papal reign in the developing story of the Roman church.

The two principal achievements of Nicholas's reign, his library and his building program, are the centerpieces of Manetti's argument in the *Life* (2.13-63). Other admirers of Nicholas, including the two eulogists at the papal funeral whose speeches survive,[18] also emphasize books and buildings as the major material legacy of his reign and worthy of praise. This suggests that Manetti's extensive treatment of these two themes arises from a shared view within the Roman Curia that they best characterize the nature of this pope's tenure in office. Manetti's discussion of them so dominates his assessment of Nicholas that it is difficult to remember that he formally treats them as if they were digressions, lengthy interruptions in the narrative of a life. Yet they provide the most tangible evidence of Nicholas's greatness as the most extraordinary and enduring achievements of his pontificate. In fact the rest of the *Life* seems to frame these two pontifical deeds; their prodigious cost and comprehensiveness made them marvelous. What sort of man conceived these projects and to what purpose? What have they to do with Rome, with the church, with human destinies or the divine plan? We shall see that Manetti's conception of the nature and purpose of both these projects is key to understanding his interpretation of this pope. As with his lives of the Florentine poets, his representation of Nicholas strives persuasively to demonstrate a coherence between the man and his works and to argue that his subject is deserving of praise and glory. And he will anticipate and attempt to correct or counterbalance any criticisms of Nicholas or his achievements that might tarnish this assessment.

---

[17] M. Canensi, "Ad beatissimum D. N. Nicolaum Pontificem . . . de ipsius laudibus et divina electione," in Miglio, *Storiografia pontificia del Quattrocento*, 205–43; Vespasiano, *Vite*, 1:35–81; Platina, *Liber de vita Christi ac omnium pontificum*, *RIS*, 3:1, 328–39. Vespasiano's account is drawn from Manetti's, though it contains some additional details.

[18] Niccolò Palmieri and Jean Jouffroy.

To underscore this interpretative aim, Manetti uses the same device to introduce the *Life* as he had in the *De pompis*: ideal sympathetic addressees who have requested this work from him. In this case, Manetti says, the requesters, Cardinal Antonio de la Cerda[19] and Giovanni de'Medici, son of Cosimo,[20] representatives of the clerical and lay elite, will lend authority to his work among secular and religious readers, since no one, lay or cleric, knew the pope's qualities better than they. But if they knew Nicholas so well, why did they need this biography? Precisely because they expected Manetti to accomplish what Antonio Loschi argued was needed for his time: Nicholas's great and memorable deeds would be transmitted to history and made credible by eloquence and authority.

The Structure of the Life

Though the *Life of Nicholas V* is in three books, its kinship with other Manettian biographies is apparent. Its format is recognizably, but not strictly, chronological. Book 1 traces the future pope's career from his origins to his election as pontiff. It treats his background, early education, youthful connections with Florence's noble families, theological training, ordination, apprenticeship, mature duties before and after the death of his patron, diplomatic successes, and induction into the cardinalate. It concludes with a formal *prosopopoeia*, containing a physical description and character analysis. The latter summarizes the intellectual and moral qualities as well as personality quirks manifest during his reign as pope, and we therefore have a fairly complete assessment of Nicholas the man before his papal accomplishments are introduced. Book 2 contains the *gesta pontificalia*, his principal deeds as pope which make him deserving of praise and fame. Three major events are treated in detail: the Holy Year of 1450, the imperial coronation of Frederick III, and the pacification of Italy. His patronage of the growth of the papal library and his plans for the reconstruction of the papal enclave in the city are fully developed as the permanent legacies which define his particular greatness. Of these, the architectural description is by far the more elaborated and includes an extended ekphrasis of the Curial District, the papal palace, and a new basilica over Peter's tomb. Book 3 records the pontiff's death and features a long "Testament" purportedly in Nicholas's own words, which, for the first time in the *Life*, acknowledges that some of his policies and projects had been criticized and offers a defense.

---

[19] A theologian and philosopher of some prominence, and bishop of Messina from February of 1448, he had been made a cardinal and bishop of Ilerda by Nicholas on 28 March 28 1449 (Vespasiano, *Vite*, 1:61, n. 4).

[20] Himself an avid collector of books and a devotee of music and poetry; he was 34 in the year of Nicholas's death.

The division into three books, each with its own distinctive focus, has another advantage: Manetti can refer to the same topic several times, varying its context and so its significance. The most striking example of this, which Modigliani also noticed,[21] is the starkly different treatment of Stefano Porcari in each of the three books. In Book 1, Nicholas has a dream of his would-be assassin entering his room carrying a cudgel which he swings to no effect. In Book 2, Manetti explains that Nicholas recognized the latent talent of the young firebrand and hoped to win him over with favored treatment within the papal service, but Porcari instead put his twisted views into action. In Book 3, Nicholas himself says nothing of either the dream or his disappointment at a protegé's betrayal, but adds Porcari to the long list of villains who assailed or threatened the person of the pope. Each serves a different purpose within its context. The first elevates the conspiracy beyond the personal to an attack on a divinely sanctioned, predestined papacy, affirmed by visions. In the second, a conciliatory and compassionate pope is betrayed. To restore security and tranquillity to the city, Nicholas was forced to lay aside his accustomed clemency and pursue justice. The fault lay in Porcari's defects of nature, including ingratitude to his benefactor. In the third allusion to the conspiracy, Nicholas is severe. Porcari is a traitor to the Holy See, not unprecedented in papal history. He joins the company of other assailants on papal security, like Arnold of Brescia, and makes the case for Nicholas's building program as a security measure. In fact, Porcari was not without his sympathizers both inside and outside church circles; he was well educated and had influential family connections. Manetti's Porcari, however, is credited with no ideas; his execution is justified in multiple ways, all of which exonerate Nicholas from blame, either by suggesting he had no choice or by invoking the divine institution of the papacy or the divinely ratified calling of its current occupant. This version of the conspiracy seems to have become historically authoritative, at least in Curial circles.[22]

Similarly, Nicholas's magnificent legacy of the library is given three alternative explanations in the three books. Manetti does not tell us of Nicholas's early book-collecting habits, even though we know from Vespasiano that he was so well regarded as a collector in his years in Florence that he advised Cosimo de'Medici on the planning of his library at San Marco (*Vite,* 1:46–47). Instead, he gives some insight into his reading, providing a lengthy list of church fathers

---

[21] *Vita*, trans. Modigliani, 51–52.

[22] Alberti's account of the conspiracy also argues the perfidy of the conspirators. In contrast to Manetti's approach in which no details of the plot are given, Alberti's *De coniuratione Porcariana* (*RIS* 25) contains a vivid account of the plot, its discovery, the pursuit of the conspirators, and their execution. It is obvious that Manetti's purpose is not to chronicle the event, but to justify the outcome.

and "modern" theologians that occupied his study between his return to Bologna and his ordination (1420–1423). We are told that he had such a thirst for learning that he "took it in like honeyed wine, or drank and drained it like nectar" (*RIS* 911). From Book 2, we learn the organization of his library and a list of works recovered, compiled, and translated during his reign. Manetti tells us that books sustain the church's authority among the learned and that the library building he planned would be open to all the Curia (15). Nicholas's own reference to the library in his Testament is brief: it was part of his intent to increase the church's material and intellectual wealth, by acquiring treasure such as gems, vessels, and vestments, fortifying and building the urban fabric, and by attracting to the papacy men of great learning by offering them generous stipends and the means for study (*RIS* 956). His early education suggests that the papal library project, extolled as magnificence in Book 2, should be understood in the context of the pope's own vast reading and his commitment to the life of the mind. The Testament, by contrast, sees it as a strategy to increase the prestige of the Roman church by adorning it with wealth and opulence.

Book 1: The Making of a Pope

In the comparison which concludes his biographies of the three Florentine poets, Manetti remarks: "We find it first necessary to say what everyone agrees on: the human race is subject to a two-fold life, namely active and contemplative."[23] Dante, he decides, is to be preferred to Petrarch and Boccaccio because, in addition to his literary studies, he both courageously fought for his country and participated honorably in civic government. In fact, the absence of tranquillity in Dante's life proved no impediment to his acquiring "a vast knowledge of things human and divine, thanks to the almost divine excellence of his intellect." Throughout the *Life of Nicholas V*, Manetti portrays a pope whose exercise of governance, in times both of stress (schism, war, the plague) and of peace, is complemented by the intellectual virtues. He unites, as did Dante, the active and contemplative lives; in contrast with Dante, his fame is achieved primarily through action. Book 1 narrates how this was possible. As a youth, endowed with prodigious natural talents, he mastered all the liberal arts. Later, he combined this learning with the practical and efficient management of church affairs. He united what was best in the contemplative sphere with solid experience in the active life. This accounts for his rise to the papal dignity and his success in achieving his ambitious goals.

[23] *Biographical Writings*, 103.

Manetti's usual biographical practice is to anticipate the subject's later prominence by finding something of note in his family of origin. Nicholas, however, came from social obscurity and penury to rise to the pinnacle of ecclesiastical power. Although Nicholas as pope will be amused at the general astonishment that a "priest who once rang the bells" had ascended Peter's throne (Vespasiano, *Vite*, 2:56), Manetti, himself a scion of an important and wealthy Florentine family, seems to have been sensitive to Tommaso Parentucelli's lesser pedigree. He compensates by claiming that Nicholas's family was not as obscure as has been reported. Manetti is among the few biographers to challenge that Tommaso da Sarzana, as Parentucelli was commonly known, was actually born in Sarzana.[24] In this account, his birthplace was Pisa, a city ennobled by a mention in Vergil, and his father was a prominent professor of arts and medicine, of good family. Political intrigue and then his father's untimely death accounted for both the obscurity of his origins and his early financial problems; both are unlucky reversals, *variante fortuna vices*, that carry no stigma (*RIS* 907–909). Divine favor, as we have seen, is indicated by the series of dreams which associate him with great classical and Old Testament figures whose destiny was revealed through dreams and omens.

What he lacked in material support, the young Tommaso supplied with innate talent and studiousness. According to Manetti, he was gifted with a natural facility at language and an extraordinary memory. His natural expressiveness manifested itself even in his infancy, before he learned to speak, and again in early childhood before his formal schooling began, when the maturity of what he said and the eloquence of how he said it astounded his hearers (*RIS* 909). Though his training in grammar began late because of his mother's financial difficulties, he was able to complete his early studies by age twelve, when he began the study of dialectic at Bologna. His acquisition of dialectic occupied four years, during which time, Manetti tells us, he was absorbed in his study and thirsted for learning, and emerged first in his class (*RIS* 911). In the ensuing two years, he devoted himself to natural philosophy, virtually memorizing the works of Aristotle.[25] In the Testament, Nicholas himself refers to this training in a prayer of thanks:

> I give you thanks, almighty and everlasting God, because you have adorned our person from its beginning with health of body and unique talent and

---

[24] Vespasiano, whose account is closely based on Manetti, agrees with the Pisan birthplace, but says his parents were "humili" (*Vite*, 1:35); Platina outright rejects the opinion of "some" that Pisa, not Sarzana, was the place: *RIS* 3.1: 328; while von Pastor was convinced on the basis of archival work that the Parentucelli were from Sarzana: *A History of the Popes*, trans. and ed. F. Antrobus (London, 1891), 2:14, note.

[25] Manetti would know something about this, having memorized and translated the ethical works of Aristotle (Vespasiano, *Vite*, 1:486).

> extraordinary memory, and granted us the grace even in our childhood so that we, aided by those extraordinary and uncommon props of nature, turned ourselves towards the study of letters, in which, in a short time, due to the particular excellence of these natural gifts, we so progressed that we acquired in a wonderful way all the arts worthy of a free man (*RIS* 954).

At the age of eighteen, his family was no longer able to support his education; two other children had been born, and Tommaso had to fend for himself. He did so by tutoring for four years[26] in the Albizzi and Strozzi households (*RIS* 912). Manetti and Nicholas are both silent about the influences on the youth during his years in Florence. We learn nothing of his exposure to the intellectual currents in the Republic during the years 1416–1420, but the stay enabled him to resume his studies in Bologna and serve as majordomo in the house of the archbishop, Niccolò Albergati. Vespasiano represents him later, when Eugenius's Curia resided in Florence and Tommaso tended to the affairs of Albergati, as an intimate and avid participant in the inner circle of Florentine intellectuals, among whom Manetti was prominent (*Vite*, 1:42–43). But the story which Manetti relates and which Nicholas in his Testament confirms portrays him rather as a loner during his long years of study, as though his learning was acquired in isolation. His teachers are not mentioned by name; we are only told that they were astonished at the young cleric's extraordinary intellect. The anecdote Manetti uses to crystallize this portrait is Tommaso's scrutiny before his ordination. Asked the usual questions about canon law, the ordinand displayed the range of his learning by working into his answers all the liberal and sacred arts, including poetry, oratory, cosmography, history, and a grasp of international relations. So astonishing was the performance, Manetti tells us, that the examiners marveled as though he were divine, not human, and spread the word through Italy and beyond (*RIS* 912–913).

His early intellectual formation was advanced by what Nicholas himself called "our extraordinary memory." In Book 1, Manetti tells us that whatever he read in youth, whether secular or sacred learning, he stored in the "treasure house of his ageless memory" (*RIS* 912). Vespasiano, in an anecdote about the papal coronation, tell us that while the pope seemed to doze as Manetti delivered Florentine congratulations, at the end Nicholas was able to recite back to the orator the entire speech (*Vite*, 1:59). What might seem to us a parlor trick was in large measure at the center of early humanist understanding of the intellectual life, and Cicero himself had emphasized the difficulty and necessity of retentive memory for the practice of oratory.[27] Many of Manetti's own works are phenomena of

---

[26] So Manetti. Vespasiano says two years (*Vite*, 1:38).

[27] Cicero, *De oratore* 2.359.

memory, in particular the encyclopedic recall to be found in *On Famous Men of Great Age* or *Against the Jews and the Pagans*. Among a learned class that prized memory, Nicholas's memory was prodigious, fortifying the pope with the means throughout his life to engage in intellectual exchange. His mastery of Aristotle's dialectical and physical works during his years in Bologna were a prelude to a lifelong ability, which Manetti "shudders to recall," not only to retain the gist of everything he had ever read, but to summon it up verbatim. His memory enabled him to pursue "all branches of every single discipline" (*RIS* 919). It also made him a formidable conversationalist and interlocutor in public and private debates, domestic get-togethers, and diplomatic missions because he could draw on such an extensive fund of ideas and quotations. This representation of the engaged Nicholas makes more credible Manetti's depiction of him directing his various projects by recalling what "he had read in the pertinent authors" (15) and "the ancient learning of the proven architects" (31).

Tommaso's devotion to the intellectual life is balanced by the practical competences Manetti claims he possessed. In Book 1, the Archbishop of Bologna, Niccolò Albergati, is credited with preparing his apprentice for a career of high responsibility in the church. Albergati fostered in his protegé two practical virtues, one domestic, the other political. The domestic management of the bishop's, then cardinal's, household continued from the time Tommaso entered Albergati's service until his mentor's death in May of 1443, over twenty years. Manetti insists that Tommaso was completely in charge of every aspect of his affairs, especially after Albergati received the red hat in 1426: "He was confirmed in the same office of governing the household, and he did govern everything at his own nod and at his own personal discretion" (*RIS* 913). This proved true as well during Albergati's lengthy diplomatic assignments abroad: "During the mission, as before, our Tommaso continued as governor of the whole household and of the person of his master" (*RIS* 914). The personal tendance of his master was no less taxing as Albergati aged and became chronically ill: "Because of this, in the long travels, he would perform the duties of guide and minister, and manager, and doctor with the utmost loyalty and precision" (*RIS* 914–915).

Albergati also initiated Tommaso into the arts of diplomacy, teaching the practical knowledge of "how to get things done, including great things" (*RIS* 914). These missions were of the greatest moment to peace both in Europe and in the church. The cardinal served Eugenius on diplomatic assignments in Italy, France, and Germany, and as papal representative to the Council of Basle in 1434 and at Florence during the Council of Union in 1439. And while Manetti does not state it, Vespasiano notes that when Eugenius and his Curia were in residence in Florence, Tommaso was there as well, not just managing the cardinal's staff, but also involved in the negotiations with the Eastern churches (*Vite*, 1:44–45). His future role, developed in Book 2, as a pope of peace and healer of schism owes something to Albergati's direction, but also to the skills he acquired in diplomatic service and to his reputation in the international community. Not long after Albergati's death, Eugenius, now back in Rome, appointed Parentucelli to responsibilities within the papal household and entrusted him with embassies within Italy and to France, Britain, and Germany where he became known for his effective diplomatic oratory. For the latter mission he was awarded the cardinal's red hat, entered Rome in triumph, and received a special benediction from the pope (*RIS* 916). Shortly thereafter, Eugenius died, and the conclave convened to elect the new pontiff.

It is at this point that Manetti relates the dream in which the dead Eugenius predicts to Parentucelli that he will be his successor. He then adds two other dreams (the cure from the plague and the attack by Stefano Porcari) which he acknowledges properly belong to the papal years, but saves all other discussion of his papacy for Book 2. The first book then concludes with the *prosopopoeia* of Nicholas. Elsewhere in Manetti's biographies, this character sketch is placed at the end of the chronological narrative before the assessment of his subject's achievements. We shall return to this *prosopopoeia* presently, since it summarizes particular virtues and alludes to criticisms related to Nicholas's conduct of his office.

Book 2: Pontifical Achievements

Biographies are written of the famous, and fame depends on achievements which are generally recognized as extraordinary and which the biographer seeks somehow to explain. Manetti's practice is to attempt to explain the deeds eloquently to a learned and interested audience; in Nicholas's case, this audience includes both prominent churchmen and influential laity. His orderly progression in the *Life of Nicholas V* is to reserve all discussion of Nicholas's achievements as pope to Book 2, where he will both relate the deeds that are most worthy of praise and fame and assess their meaning. The double purpose of the book — to recount and to evaluate — partly explains its dual structure, a chronological account of the conduct of Nicholas's papacy from his accession to his final illness, and two inserts, marked as digressions, which treat at length his ambitious plans for a papal library and an extensive building program, neither complete at his death. The architectural ekphrasis, which has often been discussed by scholars independent of the events that surround it, occupies fully half of the book.

The Narrative of Book 2

Book 2 of the *Life*, "The Pontifical Deeds of Pope Nicholas V," is not merely a chronological account of Nicholas's deeds as pope, nor of his building program. Rather, it is a rhetorically structured argument about the pontiff's place in secular and sacred history, casting in narrative form *exempla* of how Nicholas achieved certain aims.[28] Since Manetti's approach is rhetorical rather than theological or doctrinal, he argues by means of historical example, placing the matter before the reader's eyes. Most of his *exempla* are historical events such as the Jubilee, the imperial coronation, and the conclusion of peace; two *exempla*, the Library and the buildings, treat patronage. The overall structure of Book 2 is chronological, from Nicholas's accession to the papacy to his death. Within this chronological framework the narrative is hierarchical, ending with the pacification of western Christendom which Manetti attributes to Nicholas's diplomatic skill. It is, in a certain sense, also periodic since two long excursuses in the center of the book (on the Library and building projects) rather than a summation at the end convey Manetti's conclusions regarding the significance of Nicholas's pontificate. The most prominent theme is Nicholas's achievement of peace through the progressive recognition of his authority, moving from the pacification of the church to the pacification of all of Italy. His goal, unity, is to be understood in an ecclesiological rather than a secular and political framework.

Manetti characterizes Nicholas's achievements in his first year of rule as "the remarkable foundations of his future building most soundly and handsomely laid" (5). These were the resolution of schism, the end of war and recovery of the papal cities, and the repayment of debt. In his second year, which Manetti characterizes as the imposition of order (7), Nicholas preserved the peace, organized the lands outside the city, fixed taxation in Rome, and appointed eight cardinals. This done, he turned his mind to projects that would "somehow be related to enlarging the prestige of the Roman Church and enhancing the dignity of the Apostolic See" (7). Then comes the account of the Jubilee (10–12). The Jubilee signals the first universal recognition of Nicholas's greatness, for "because of the wonderful attributes of the pontifical person, his fame, which had already traveled through virtually all the world, thundering everywhere" (10) attracted greater crowds to this Jubilee than to any since the time of "the divine Lawgiver Moses."[29] Manetti situates the accounts of Nicholas's Library and architectural projects between the Jubilee (25 December 1449 to 25 December 1450) and the coronation of the Holy Roman Emperor, Frederick III (19 March 1452). These accounts are so long, occupying sections 13 to 62, that scholars have treated them as self-contained ekphrases, independent from the narrative structure. But Manetti alerts the reader that they are digressions from the thread of his account. At

[28] Miglio also suggested that the whole of Book 2 is strongly ideological in organization, focused on the qualities of the pope and on the exemplification of these qualities in deeds: Miglio, "L'immagine del principe e l'immagine della città," in *Principe e città*, ed. S. Gensini, 321.

[29] The Jubilee also illustrates Nicholas's generosity (another theme of Manetti's biography), since the biblical passages on the Jubilee established by Moses say it included the forgiveness of debt and the liberation of slaves (Leviticus 25:8–17, Deuteronomy 15:1–11).

the end of section 17, concluding his discussion of the Library with a lament over its interruption by Nicholas's death in 1455, Manetti resumes his account of the Jubilee Year (1450) saying: "Now let us return to the agreed order of discussion." We then hear briefly about the canonization of Bernardino of Siena and, in order "not to distort the narrative order" (19), about Nicholas's retreat to Fabriano in the summer of 1450 to avoid the plague (19–21). Then Manetti turns to the buildings, the longest single topic in Book 2 (22–63), but again characterized as a digression, concluding with these words: "Let us now, as if retracing our steps to the fatherland in a long journey home, return quickly to the order of our account" (63).

The narrative resumes in 1451–1452 with Frederick's request to come to Rome to be crowned emperor. Manetti tells us that he was eyewitness to the imperial coronation as an ambassador of Florence, and what follows is not unlike the account of the consecration ceremony in Florence, which Manetti observed from the same vantage point.[30] In both, he recounts only those aspects of the liturgy which further the purpose of his narrative. The account begins with Frederick's petition to be crowned in Rome which (Manetti says) Nicholas granted because the pope had decided to observe the previously neglected practice of confirming the rule of the Roman Empire (64).[31] The rebuilt St. Peter's, Vatican Palace, and Borgo which Manetti had just described are the settings for the coronation. Manetti employed this same rhetorical strategy in describing the consecration of Florence Cathedral (6), first giving the visual setting and then the events which took place in it. The narrative of Book 2 concludes with the delineation, as a kind of coda, of Nicholas's guidance of the diplomatic initiative which pacified all of Italy, himself remaining a neutral party.

The Architectural Ekphrasis as Digression

When Manetti's digression on buildings is taken out of its literary context and scrutinized for its factual content, distortion is bound to occur. Few scholars have cared to read Manetti's text as he instructs, that is, as a distinctive element in

---

[30] There are at least fifteen mostly eyewitness accounts of Frederick's coronation as well as the account of Nicholas's Master of Ceremonies, Pietro de Burgos, cited in M. Dykmans, "Le 'Cérémonial' de Nicolas V," *Revue d'histoire ecclésiastique* 63 (1968): 780–825, here 785.

[31] Nicholas's reasons for granting Frederick's request for a pontifical coronation in Rome are stated in a document dated 19 March 1452: in *Bullarium diplomatum et privilegiorum sanctorum Romanorum pontificum Taurinensis*, ed. S. Franco and H. Dalmazzo (Turin, 1857–1872), 5:109–10.

a larger agenda.[32] Manetti had no particular interest in architecture for its own sake, as we have seen, and he was an orator, not a chronicler. Therefore, since Book 2 is not merely a chronological account, but a rhetorical exposition of the papacy, Manetti's *Life* in general, and the architectural description in particular, must be approached with caution as evidence for what literally happened or what was built. The extended digressions on the Library and building projects, standing outside of the narrative order and interrupting the narrative almost exactly in the middle, enable Manetti to articulate the significance of the already recounted historical events (the end of the schism, the Jubilee) and prepare the framework within which the events that follow (the coronation of Frederick, the peace of Lodi) should be understood.

As with the Library, Manetti gives the whole building narrative at the place where it best falls in the structure of his argument. But unlike the Library, Manetti needs to put before the reader's eyes the full extent of the building project as if complete before he describes the coronation. Since his readers could see for themselves that even by 1455 the buildings which Manetti describes did not exist, they presumably understood the rhetorical nature of the narrative. If Manetti had described St. Peter's as it actually had been in 1452, the real building would have presented an inadequate, not to say miserable, frame for an imperial coronation. Certainly, he could have moved the architectural digression to the end of the *Life* and described the state of Nicholas's projects in 1455 as uncompleted initiatives. But he needed his account to contain completed buildings for at least three reasons: as imagined settings for the coronation liturgy; as metaphorical images for themes of the papacy; and to defend Nicholas against criticisms.[33]

The placement of the two "digressions" is not primarily determined by chronological accuracy any more than their purpose is primarily informative. Nor should they be related in a causal way to the Jubilee, the revenues from which made it possible for Nicholas to embark on such projects. Manetti is careful to say that the plan for the Library and for the buildings pre-dated the Jubilee (9 and 13). This claim portrays the papal plan as unified and conceived from the beginning of the papacy, a claim which likely does not correspond to how these projects actually developed. Therefore, the placement of the building account as though it fits the context of 1450 is not a reliable *terminus a quo* for the start of a unified construction program. Manetti himself tells us that some building had been begun before the Jubilee and that some was incomplete at Nicholas's death

[32] Miglio has repeatedly called for a re-evaluation of the whole Manettian composition instead of privileging isolated sections: "Immagine," 317; idem in *Vita*, trans. Modigliani, 14.

[33] Manetti's defense of Nicholas's building project is taken up in Chapter 7; the images of the papacy in Chapter 9.

(13, 37, 57). But his description makes a project that grew and changed over time seem as if unitary from the beginning. He, in fact, is largely responsible for the notion that, by the time of the Jubilee, Nicholas had arrived at a full agenda for his papacy which was only partly realized because of his untimely death.[34] Documentary evidence for the building projects suggests otherwise, that the projects were not conceived as a coherent program but evolved gradually.

With these *caveat*s, something can be gleaned about the building projects from Manetti's narrative. For instance, it is not improbable that experiences of the Jubilee, including the disastrous loss of life on an overcrowded bridge (11), and of the canonization of San Bernardino, revealed all the inadequacies of St. Peter's and the Borgo as settings for large-scale ceremonies. Nicholas addressed these shortcomings afterward even though they may not have been completed in time for the coronation, or even by his death. And it probably is true that the projects entered a new and more ambitious phase following the trip to Fabriano, with the help of the Jubilee revenues and with Frederick's imminent arrival in view. Work on the walls of Rome, for instance, seems to have been undertaken with Frederick's visit in mind.[35] The enlargement of the piazza in front of St. Peter's, where the pope first received Frederick, is also dated to 1451 by a contemporary diary.[36]

The Coronation of a Roman Emperor

The architectural ekphrasis preceding the coronation in the *Life* provides details which flesh out that narrative in two ways: (1) the order of places in the architectural ekphrasis and that in the coronation narrative are not only parallel, but

[34] Most scholars have assumed that the whole building program was conceived around 1450 and revised in 1452–1453 in response either to the Porcari conspiracy or to Alberti's criticism. See, for instance, Magnuson, *Studies in Roman Quattrocento Architecture*, 91; M. Tafuri, "'Cives esse non licere'. Nicolò V e Leon Battista Alberti," in idem, *Ricerca del Rinascimento. Principi, città, architetti* (Turin, 1992), 33–84, here 47; C. Burroughs, "Alberti e Roma," in *Leon Battista Alberti*, ed. J. Rykwert and A. Engel (Milan, 1994), 134–57, here 154.

[35] Stefano Infessura's *Diario* dates this work to 1451, and Platina's *Liber de vita Christi ac omnium pontificum* connects their repair with preparations for the coronation. See S. Infessura, *Diario della città di Roma*, ed. O. Tommasini (Rome, 1890), 49; Platina in *RIS*, 3.1: 334. Maffeo Vegio makes the more guarded comment that repair of the walls resulted in greater security for St. Peter's and the city of Rome by deterring barbarian nations from attack: *De rebus antiquis*, 3.63.

[36] Infessura, *Diario*, 50.

complementary; and (2) the description of St. Peter's serves as an ideal, and ideated, setting for the coronation liturgy.

Manetti's account of the architecture is organized in an experiential order, beginning with papal towns, proceeding through the gates of Rome, then through the Borgo and Vatican Palace, and culminating in St. Peter's, as scholars have noted.[37] And Manetti's order is also hierarchical, beginning with lesser projects and culminating in the most sacred — again well-known. But what has not been noticed is that since the order and subjects of the architectural description correspond to Frederick's processional route through the papal lands, into the City, the Borgo, the Vatican Palace, and finally to St. Peter's, the ekphrasis and the narrative event are complementary. For instance, Manetti collapses Frederick's journey from Germany to the Vatican Palace into a short paragraph (65) because that aspect of the ceremonial procession to Rome which was relevant for Nicholas — the progress through the papal lands — had already been covered in the architectural ekphrasis (23). We know from Nicholas's Master of Ceremonies, Pietro de Burgos, that the imperial cortège arrived in papal territory at Viterbo.[38] This may explain why Manetti gives a disproportionately detailed account of Nicholas's renovation of the baths there, describing the new lodgings as "palaces fit for kings" (24).[39] The cortège spent the night of 7 March outside the walls of Rome and was joined there by the Florentine embassy, which included Manetti.[40] The Roman walls were Manetti's next topic in his architectural digression (26). On 9 March the cortège entered Rome at Castel Sant'Angelo and visited relics in various parts of the city: Nicholas's repairs to the major Roman basilicas were Manetti's next architectural subject (27). The cortège then proceeded from Castel Sant'Angelo to the piazza before St. Peter's (fig. 13, see page 152). Once again Manetti's order of architectural description followed the imperial route, with sections 28 to 30 describing the Borgo. The liturgy for Frederick's reception, which Manetti describes (66), required that the king, accompanied by his own archbishops and bishops, princes, dignitaries, and nobility, approach the pope enthroned in front of the closed doors of the basilica, genuflect, and kiss

[37] Westfall, *In This Most Perfect Paradise*, 106.

[38] Petrus Burgensis, from Burgos in Spain, was a canon of St. Peter's; he was made Master of Ceremonies by Eugene IV and remained in that position under Nicholas V. Dykmans published a part of his diary which had been copied in the early sixteenth century in MS. Vat. lat. 14585, fols. 207–219: Dykmans, "Le 'Cérémonial'," 780–825.

[39] For the baths, see our Commentary at 23.

[40] Dykmans, "Le 'Cérémonial'," 801–2; and von Pastor, *The History of the Popes*, 2:149.

his foot.[41] The reader knows the site of this liturgy from the ekphrasis where Manetti noted that there was "a great platform with a spacious surface which would seem to provide plenty of room in its length and breadth for the largest crowd of people" (41). After the reception, the emperor and empress lodged in the Vatican Palace where on 12 and 13 March they attended Mass in the "capella magna palatii": Manetti had furnished an account of the Vatican walls (31 and 32) and a detailed description of the Vatican Palace (33–38) beginning with its entrance from St. Peter's Square. On March 16, Frederick's marriage to the Empress Leonora was celebrated in the main apse of St. Peter's; the coronation followed on March 19. Like the coronation narrative, the architectural description culminated in the apse of St. Peter's (39–63).[42]

Although Manetti omits almost all of the coronation liturgy (67–68), it is known from other sources, especially the Pontifical of Durandus, a nearly contemporary Book of Ceremonies, and other eyewitness accounts.[43] Since the liturgy stipulates where the actions are to be performed, we can reconstruct how

---

[41] This ceremony, like that of the coronation proper, would have been directed by the masters of ceremony, ministers assisting the Cappelle and chaplains of the papal cantors, supervised by the *prelato maggiordomo*, prefect of the apostolic palaces: G. Moroni, *Le cappelle pontificie cardinalizie e prelatizie* (Venice, 1841), 1. At the death of Eugene IV, there were five masters of ceremony, but only under Nicholas are they called "masters" rather than "clerks" of ceremonies. See Dykmans, "D'Avignon à Rome. Martin V e le cortège apostolique," 288; G. Bourgin, "La 'familia' pontificia sotto Eugenio IV," *Archivio della Società romana di Storia Patria* 27 (1904): 205–24, here 223; Dykmans, "Le 'Cérémonial'," 803–4.

[42] Dykmans, "Le 'Cérémonial'," 806–12. Scenes from the coronation on a Florentine cassone panel in the Worcester Art Museum showing Frederick receiving his crown on the steps of St. Peter's, instead of in its apse, represent the view of someone to whom liturgical precision was not of great importance. The cassone is reproduced in C. Burroughs, *From Signs to Design. Environmental Process and Reform in Early Renaissance Rome* (Cambridge, MA, 1990), fig. 12.

[43] We follow the account in the Pontifical of Durandus supplemented by the notes of Pietro de Burgos and Patrizio Piccolomini: M. Dykmans, *L'Oeuvre de Patrizi Piccolomini: ou le cérémonial papal de la première Renaissance* (Vatican City, 1980–1982); idem, "Le 'Cérémonial'"; idem, *Le pontifical romain au moyen-age, III: Le pontifical de Guillaume Durand*. We can be confident that the service for the coronation of an emperor was that in the Pontifical of Durandus. Confirmation that this was the text in use in mid-century Rome is that Giovanni Barozzi, bishop of Bergamo from 1449 to 1464 and Nicholas's subdeacon from 1448, used Durandus's text for a Pontifical he commissioned in 1451: Dykmans, "D'Avignon à Rome," 288. We also consulted other eyewitness accounts. Gaspar Enenkel's account is in von Pastor, *History*, 2:153. Aeneas Silvius Piccolomini, later Pius II, is an especially well-versed observer of liturgical ceremony who commemorated the event in a book: *Historia Friderici III imperatoris*, ed. B. Ziliotti (Trieste, 1958), 61–86.

the old basilica must have been used at Frederick's coronation.[44] From this we can conclude that it was woefully inadequate for the ceremony. By describing the church as Nicholas would have rebuilt it instead of as it was, Manetti impressed on the reader's imagination a setting both dignified and splendid.

Let us begin with the coronation liturgy, matching its actions to the places described in the ekphrasis and commenting on what was actually there in 1452 (fig. 23, see page 249). Giulio Romano's depiction of the Donation of Constantine (fig. 5) will aid our visualization since it shows us the nave and apse of old St. Peter's. Of course, the apse had been enclosed in Bramante's temporary housing and some of the old church demolished when Giulio painted this fresco around 1520 and his view is not only reconstructive, but ideal. Additionally, he omitted much of the liturgical furniture — crucial to our account — which is shown on our plan of the basilica (fig. 23), and he places the interaction of pope and emperor in the nave rather than the apse for greater visibility. Nonetheless, the fresco helps the reader to imagine the grandeur of a papal ceremony within the setting of the old church.

On the day of the coronation, the pope and his entourage, having vested for Mass, process from the palace into the church and take their seats in the apse.[45] Manetti describes the passage to the basilica from the palace, reworked by Nicholas so that "the supreme pontiff, accompanied by a large retinue of prelates, could make his entrance into this temple from the palace through many very lovely entrances. The procession would move from an entrance more splendid than the rest along "a very beautiful spiral staircase" (50).[46] Since this staircase gave onto the narthex (see Chapter 6), the pope would have had to process down the central nave, which, says Manetti, "would afford a more open view than the

[44] S. De Blaauw also analyzed the liturgy of coronation in relation to the architecture of St. Peter's: *Cultus et decor: Liturgia e architettura nella Roma tardoantica e medievale: Basilica Salvatoris, Sanctae Mariae, Sancti Petri* (Vatican City, 1994), 732–43.

[45] The pope would vest in the Sala dei Paramenti, as would the cardinals, including the eight new cardinals created by Nicholas: Dykmans, "Le 'Cérémoniale'," 808, n. 2. The procession began as this room was exited: or so it would appear from the notes of Petrus de Burgos who, describing the entry for Easter of 1452, says the King of Hungary carried the pope's train from the time he exited the "camera paramenti" until he came to the altar of St. Peter: "Le 'Cérémoniale'," 376. The sacrament would be taken from the tabernacle, probably that made by Donatello, in the Chapel of the Sacrament, perhaps identical with the Cappella di S. Nicola or "cappella parva." Vasari says the chapel had been frescoed by Fra Angelico with scenes from the life of Christ, including portraits of Nicholas and Frederick, frescoes therefore presumably painted after the coronation. In this chapel Nicholas had received Frederick in audience: D. Redig de Campos, *I Palazzi Vaticani* (Bologna, 1967), 37.

[46] We identify this staircase with the old Scala Regia in Chapter 6.

Fig. 5. The Donation of Constantine imagined in St. Peter's. Giulio, Romano, Saladi Costantino, Vatican Palace.

others on the sides both because its walkway was to be more spacious and because from there the marvelous panorama of the whole temple would be more freely visible" (44).[47] Having reached the transept, a rebuilt version of which Manetti describes (45), the processors must have moved through the chancel barrier with its twelve spiral columns, ascended the presbytery steps, and taken places on the *subsellia* which ringed the apse ("G" and "I" on our fig. 23).[48] Manetti, rather than describing the east end of St. Peter's as it existed, describes Nicholas's new choir in an imagined state of completion. He omits the liturgical furniture, except for the papal throne and papal altar. The visibility of the pontiff was important to Manetti, who describes Nicholas's new apse as having "a taller pontifical throne . . . so that he could be viewed by all the bystanders and likewise that he might view everyone, whether they were standing or seated" (46).[49]

At Frederick's coronation, an enormous number of people had to be accommodated according to rank on the *subsellia* in the apse. The Master of Ceremonies would have been in charge of determining how cardinals of various ranks down to senators, counts, protonotaries, bishops, and abbots were to be placed. There was room for about thirty-four people on the *subsellia* of St. Peter's as they existed in 1452, not nearly enough for the number of people who had to be accommodated from the papal Curia and far too few for all the additional participants in

---

[47] The panorama was not always visible: Paschal I gave St. Peter's two forty-six-piece sets of tapestries. Since there are twenty-three intercolumniations in each of the four nave colonnades, these tapestries could be hung in the basilica in such a way as to block each of the aisles as a separate corridor: J. Shearman, *Raphael's Cartoons in the Collection of Her Majesty the Queen and the Tapestries for the Sistine Chapel* (London, 1972), 7.

[48] The chancel barrier was almost thirty feet before the apse entrance; the presbytery steps some 18 feet (5.8 m) before the apse; the apse was 55 feet (17.87 m) in diameter. The area behind the barrier (which was raised 18 cm above the nave), the front face of the podium, and the steps leading up to it were all covered in porphyry: De Blaauw, *Cultus et decor*, 552. Above, on the wall of the apse, were painted five scenes from the Life of Christ; these were either replaced or complemented by a series of scenes of the life of Peter completed under Nicholas and painted by Fra Angelico between 1447 and 1449: Redig de Campos, *Palazzi*, 50.

[49] The actual papal throne, commissioned by Innocent III (1198–1216), was of Cosmatesque work with lion-head arms; its porphyry panels had been stolen in 1436. It was elevated six steps so that its base was about three feet (1 m) above the presbytery, itself about five feet above the pavement of the basilica. Paris de Grassis, Master of Ceremonies under Julius II, said that this enabled the pope to be seen by the people above the altar of St. Peter, which stood in front, at the edge of the presbytery: De Blaauw, *Cultus et decor*, 652. Shearman pointed out this must have meant that he was visible through the ciborium (as the *Cattedra Petri* was later arranged also by Bernini): Shearman, *Raphael's Cartoons*, 28.

the coronation ceremony as described in the Pontifical.[50] We know from Aeneas Silvius Piccolomini's eyewitness account that the cardinals sat to Nicholas's right while bishops and prelates were at his left.[51] The apse of St. Peter's as it actually was at the coronation was not an adequate setting for a courtly ceremony requiring seating for many different ranks of secular and religious persons to be distinguished. In the new apse which Manetti describes, seventy-five cubits deep and forty wide, many more people would have been accommodated behind the altar, which Manetti tells us was to be kept in the same place "at the farthest reach of the great crossing" (45). The increased, and better differentiated, seating capacity between the papal throne and the altar is an obvious advantage of the new apse begun by Nicholas, as Manetti acknowledges: "Both sides of this tribune were being expanded in various places for seats to enlarge its capacity for people" (46). Although scholars have recognized this functional reason for the rebuilding of St. Peter's, the literary purpose of Manetti's evocation of the improved apse has been overlooked.[52]

Returning to the liturgy, when the pope had reached his throne, word was sent and the king was escorted from the Vatican Palace into the square from which he mounted the steps of St. Peter's and entered the atrium's vestibule where the chapel of Sta. Maria in Turribus was. Manetti began his description of St. Peter's with the square, the stairs, platform, and vestibule (41–42). He omits from the coronation narrative a series of the king's actions with the canons, cardinals, and Roman dignitaries taking place between the entrance of the basilica

---

[50] Paris de Grassis said that when 34 cardinals were present they could hardly fit on the *subsellia*: De Blaauw, *Cultus et decor*, 684. Where, then, would the canons, beneficiati, and clerics of St. Peter's sit? In the canons' choir at the end of the nave before the crossing? Where the urban clergy and magistrates? Perhaps in the right transept?

[51] Piccolomini, *Historia Friderici*, 79. Aeneas Silvius, who was subdeacon under Nicholas, also gives us the order of seating for the Capelle Pontificie: the pope would be on his throne with cardinals at his right, and at his left bishops, abbots with mitres, protonotaries, and ambassadors. To one side were the *uditori* and on the other *chierici di camera*, then the *procuratori* of the Orders: subdeacons, acolytes, and *cubiculari* of the pope would be seated on the second step: *Aeneae Sylvii Piccolominei Senensis . . . Opera quae extant omnia* (Basle, 1571; repr. Frankfurt, 1967), 739. Probably the two cardinal deacons sat on faldstools flanking the pope; they had to remain near since they assisted him during Mass and also walked just in front of him in procession: Dykmans, "Le 'Cérémonial'," 808.

[52] G. Urban realized the connection between the new apse and liturgy without, however, working out the specific inadequacies of the old basilica in relation to specific liturgies which Nicholas performed in it: "Zum Neubau-Projekt von St. Peter unter Papst Nikolaus V," in *Festschrift für Harald Keller* (Darmstadt, 1963), 131–73, here 133.

and the apse.[53] Arriving before the *confessio* of Peter,[54] the king prostrated himself while the archdeacon led the litany of saints. Going then to the altar of St. Maurice which was at the entrance to the transept from the southern side aisles ("J" on our fig. 23), the king was anointed on his right arm and between his shoulders by the Bishop of Ostia.[55] In order to get from the *confessio* to the altar of St. Maurice in 1452, Frederick and his attendants would have had to squeeze through the narrow passage between the Gospel pulpit and the canons's choir if temporary walkways had not been constructed for the occasion ("F," "G," and "H" on our fig. 23). The king would have had then to repeat this maneuver in order to retrace his steps to the *confessio* before ascending the presbytery platform to receive the kiss of peace from the pope.

Returning to the liturgy, the king then goes to his pavilion, which was just outside the southern perimeter of the chancel barrier in the old church, where he is met by his own archbishops and other members of his entourage. The empress's pavilion was in the same position but north of the chancel barrier. Piccolomini tells us that these pavilions were very tall and were connected by raised walkways to the altar area.[56] Although the walkways temporarily solved the problems caused by the basilica's actual liturgical furnishings, the difficulty of processing between the transept and apse in old St. Peter's helps explain why Nicholas wished to create the "larger and more spacious crossing" which Manetti describes (45).

---

[53] For instance, Frederick was made a canon of St. Peter's, dressed in imperial insignia, and given a pallium as *camerarius* of the pope. Led by the canons and choir and escorted by the *comes* of the Lateran Palace and the *primicerius* of the Roman judges, the king processed into the basilica by the central door (Porta Argentea). He stopped at the porphyry disc in the pavement about halfway down the nave, where the cardinal bishop of Porto (Francesco Condulmer) said a prayer, and then proceeded through the chancel barrier before the presbytery; Dykmans: *Oeuvre*, 110.

[54] The *confessio* was a shrine in the front side of the raised presbytery, directly under the altar. It had a grill (installed by Innocent III), which was kissed by pilgrims, and a closure of Limoges enamels. For the layout, see B. Kempers and S. De Blaauw, "Jacopo Stefaneschi, Patron and Liturgist. A New Hypothesis Regarding the Date, Iconography, Authorship, and Function of His Altarpiece for Old St. Peter's," *Mededelingen van het Nederlands Institut te Rome* 47 (1987): 83–113, here 97; for the closure, see M. Gauthier, "La cloture émaillée de la confession de Saint Pierre au Vatican, lors du concile de Latran IV, 1215," in *Synthronon. Art et archéologie de la fin d'antiquité et du moyen age. Recueil d'études par André Grabar et un groupe de ses disciples* (Paris, 1968), 237–46: the reconstruction is fig. 9, 246.

[55] The Bishop of Porto replaced the Bishop of Ostia at Frederick's coronation: Dykmans, *Oeuvre*, 110.

[56] Piccolomini, *Historia Friderici*, 79. De Blaauw is in error in interpreting the king's *thalamus* as a wooden throne in the choir: *Cultus et decor*, 738.

The coronation continues with the Introit being sung by the choir in front of the altar of St. Peter: the ten or fifteen singers were probably in the *schola cantorum* in the center of the transept which was dismantled in 1462. Perhaps they would have been moved up into the new apse in Nicholas's rebuilt scheme.[57] Mass begins. The coronation would have been one of the rare occasions on which the pope would actually officiate at the Mass.[58] After the Gradual is sung but before the Gospel is read (from the ambo in the crossing), the king again ascends to the presbytery where, in the space between the altar and the papal throne, the pope invests him with a sword, a sceptre, and the orb and diadem[59] taken from the altar of Peter. Manetti selects these symbolic acts of investiture for his account, even noting with which hands Frederick received the imperial regalia (67).[60] Yet since Frederick knelt behind the main altar during this portion of the liturgy, he would have been invisible to all except those in the apse proper. In the new apse, with its long extension between the papal throne and the altar, these climactic actions of the coronation could have been witnessed by many more people. Manetti records prayers of the pope and emperor immediately after the investiture, adding that the pope prayed "in a rather high voice" (68). Nicholas's prayer (according to Manetti), asserting that God "provided the Roman Empire for the preaching of the Gospel," exhorted Frederick to defeat "the enemies of peace and the Catholic faith" (68). And Frederick, says Manetti, responded that his intent was to wipe

[57] Nicholas's reign marked a turning point for music in regard to the papal choir, and presumably on this occasion it would be the Capella Pontificia rather than the quite distinct St. Peter's choir that sang. Under Nicholas the papal choir grew from ten to fifteen singers, some from northern Europe; their wages were increased by almost fifty percent, and they could be granted benefices: C. Reynolds, *Papal Patronage and the Music of St. Peter's, 1380–1513* (Berkeley, 1995), 34.

[58] As Prodi and others have shown, until Nicholas's reign, the papal liturgy was pastoral, with the pope himself saying Mass and preaching. But after the return from Avignon the liturgy had become increasingly a palace liturgy, separating the pope from the people. The liturgy became more solemn and rigidly structured, and at the same time more sensitive to secular diplomacy, for instance in the hierarchy of seating. Hence the rise in status of the masters of ceremony. Although only the pope may say Mass at the main altar of St. Peter's, this function was normally delegated to cardinals: see P. Prodi, *The Papal Prince. One Body and Two Souls: The Papal Monarchy in Early Modern Europe* (Cambridge, 1982, repr. 1987), 45; M. Borgolte, *Petrus Nachfolge und Kaiserimitation: Die Grablegen der Päpste, ihre Genese und Traditionsbildung* (Göttingen, 1989), 254; Kempers and De Blaauw, "Jacopo Stefaneschi," 95.

[59] This crown was that of Charlemagne, which Frederick had brought with him from the treasury at Nürnberg: Piccolomini, *Historia Friderici*, 81.

[60] Enenkel confirms that Frederick's investiture exactly followed the Pontifical: von Pastor, *History*, 2:153.

out and eliminate such enemies, bringing about a "sure and secure family of all our faithful nations" (68). The Gospel was then read, Mass said (with the emperor serving the pope as subdeacon), and the kiss of peace exchanged.

Manetti selected three moments of the long liturgy for his account of the coronation: the initial reception on the steps of St. Peter's, in which the king enacts submission to papal authority; the pope's investiture of the king with the authority of empire in the apse (66–67); and the prayers. Manetti's version of the prayers, articulating the proper relation of church and empire in the Church Militant, owes much to Juan de Torquemada's 1450 *Summa against the Enemies of the Church*. In the *Summa*, Torquemada urged that soldiers of Christ were needed to protect the Church in these troubled times lest many, led astray, forsake her fold; and to combat those who wished to crush the primacy of the Apostolic See and maim the supreme authority conferred on it by God.[61] An eyewitness, Gaspar Enenkel, however, only heard Nicholas recite appropriate collects in Latin and does not report that Frederick spoke; Piccolomini mentions neither Nicholas's prayers nor Frederick's response.[62] In fact, Manetti puts into the mouths of Nicholas and Frederick, word for word, the very prayer with which he himself had closed his own oration, delivered earlier in the day as Florentine ambassador to the coronation.[63] These are Manetti's words, spoken by him, and not by the pope or the emperor.

Manetti omits from the coronation account all actions performed by anyone except Nicholas. In his version, the event was a stunning affirmation of a political theory concerning the right order of powers which the church had urged since the eighth century, and it embodied that vision of the Church Militant favored by Nicholas and his apologists (see Chapter 8). Had the coronation taken place in the transept and apse which Manetti describes, the setting would have enhanced its significance. In the old St. Peter's, it must have been crowded and difficult to see.

Understanding the architectural digression as a foil for the coronation narrative explains certain of Manetti's omissions, especially of work on the Campidoglio and other sites connected with the power and prestige of the Roman Commune. These correspond to his omission of the important roles played by governmental officials of Rome, such as the urban prefect and senators, in the coronation ceremony. Further, just as Manetti's account of the Vatican complex largely excludes buildings used by the canons of St. Peter's (a lacuna filled by Vegio, a canon himself), so his coronation narrative omits their actions. For example, we do not learn

---

[61] Quoted in von Pastor, *History*, 2:51.

[62] Von Pastor, *History*, 2:155; Piccolomini, *Historia Friderici*, 81.

[63] G. Manetti, "Florentinorum legatorum oratio in fausta ac felici Federici III Imperatoris coronatione," in *Germanicarum rerum scriptores*, ed. Freher, 3:14.

that the king is made a canon of St. Peter's or escorted into the basilica by them, as the liturgy requires and as in fact occurred. We do not even hear of actions performed by the cardinals, the litany of saints, or the anointing. In Manetti's account, Frederick is received by a monarch who also, as Vicar of Christ, crowns him: there is only one figure of power in Rome in Manetti's version, namely Nicholas.

The building and coronation accounts are complementary. The deficiencies of St. Peter's as a setting for the actual event explains why Manetti places the architectural digression between the Jubilee and the coronation. It enables him to show us an exemplar of the supreme authority of the Roman church revealed in the person of Nicholas and publicly confirmed by Frederick at the coronation. Nicholas's plan, Manetti suggests, had it been carried out, would have provided the setting he describes for the ceremony of coronation. By his rearranging of the chronology of Nicholas's achievements they mutually reinforce one another: the greatest liturgical celebration of the papacy can be seen to take place in the completed architectural setting. Manetti's choice of the coronation liturgy rather than a pontifical Mass, the canonization of a saint, or the celebration of Peter's feast day as exemplar is itself significant for the meaning of Book 2. The coronation marked a diplomatic and indeed political triumph for the Roman church in the person of Nicholas.

Book 3: Legacy and Lament

Manetti titles the concluding book of the *Life* from its most prominent feature, Nicholas's Testament spoken on his deathbed to the cardinals and other prelates of his Curia. It is impossible to determine with any certitude the extent to which the words recorded were actually spoken by Nicholas. In his *Life of Socrates*, Manetti refers to the philosopher's similar discourse to his pupils recorded in Plato's *Phaedo*. Manetti would also likely recall the historian Thucydides's explanation of the speeches which he reported, that he had faithfully represented what the speakers must have said (1.22). Piccolomini, as papal secretary and eyewitness, had reported in the pope's own words the instructions of the dying Eugenius as he entrusted the care of the church to his cardinals.[64] Manetti, a long-time collocutor of Nicholas's and member of the papal court in the latter years of his reign, was perhaps in as good a position as any layman to know something of the pope's mind. It is likely that Manetti learned what was said from eyewitnesses, perhaps Jean Jouffroy who is named, or Antonio de la Cerda who requested the account. In any case, the curial eyewitnesses who would read his account would

---

[64] "De morte Eugenii IV creationque et coronatione Nicolai V," *RIS* 3.2:878–98.

detect any false notes. Granted that Manetti elsewhere chooses the precise wording and may have done so here, it is safe, we believe, to assume that the Testament is a true record of the substance of Nicholas's last discourse.

The credibility of the Testament as the pope's own version of his story, independent of the way Manetti has told it, is suggested by divergences in interpretation between the two accounts. This is especially true in the autobiographical synopsis that Nicholas provides. For example, when Manetti describes him managing Cardinal Albergati's household, his focus is on two things: the magnitude of responsibilities with which he was entrusted, and his indefatigability. Nicholas, by contrast, emphasizes primarily fiscal management in papal domestic affairs, in particular the quick elimination of foreign debt. In Book 2, Manetti attributes papal prosperity to the unprecedented success of the Jubilee, with revenues coming from taxes, the sale of goods, and voluntary contributions (12). Nicholas, however, connects it to his diplomatic agenda of pacification. His resolution of the schism and the abdication of the antipope Felix, together with his secular diplomacy resolving disputes among the principates and republics of Italy, allowed him to recover and rebuild the cities of the Patrimony that had passed from papal control. The tranquillity which ensued not only retired the debt incurred under Eugenius, but also provided him with the surpluses needed to leave as a legacy a church not just financially sound, but visibly opulent (*RIS* 955–956).

In Nicholas's view, then, the good management of his household is tied to his successes in achieving ecclesiastical and secular concord. He gives very little explanation of how he managed to acquire the diplomatic skills needed for the task. His own brief autobiography embedded in the Testament leaps from his academic background — doctor of arts, then priest, then professor of Scripture — to his service under his predecessor Eugenius. There is no mention of the years of tutelage under Albergati, though Manetti assures us in Book 2 that he took the name "Nicholas" on his accession to the papal throne out of devotion to his beloved mentor.[65] Instead, Nicholas very briefly summarizes his meteoric rise under Eugenius as explaining his election to the Apostolic See. Manetti emphasizes the training under Albergati to show certain qualities of stamina and organizational skills which will be echoed in his account of pontifical deeds. Nicholas underscores the connection with Eugenius, first suggested by the two visions he experienced of his predecessor, to claim a continuity of mission between the two vicars of Christ. But in both accounts, that of Manetti and that of Nicholas, the competence of this pope rested on his prodigious mental powers

[65] This is also confirmed by Aeneas Silvius Piccolomini, "De morte," 894.

and his vast experience in managing a cardinal's and then a pope's household and in conducting international affairs of state. This pointed insistence on intellect and competence, the contemplative pope in action, takes on special significance if Nicholas's deeds had been criticized as ill-conceived or poorly executed.

Nicholas orders his speech around three points. He wishes, first, to give thanks to almighty God for the gifts he has personally received since his birth; second, to give an account of the state of the church; and third, to exhort his hearers to love and care for the church he leaves behind. Before he takes up these issues in order, however, he wants to remark on the sacraments and to refute some accusations that have been brought against his building program. This is the first time in the *Life* that criticisms are explicitly mentioned, and this fact sheds light on certain elements in the first two books. It is not unusual for Manetti to take up criticisms both of actions and of character as part of his assessment of his subjects' lives. It is a different strategy to hear the rebuttal in the subject's own words.

Praise and Blame of the Building Project

Of his two principal achievements, criticism focused more on his building project than on his book collecting. Indeed, Nicholas does not defend the library in his deathbed speech, an indication that book collecting was less controversial. Buildings cost more than books, even the expensive books made for Nicholas; and buildings are much more in the public eye. More importantly, however, building patronage reflects on the moral qualities of the builder as book collecting does not: "Great buildings are perpetual reminders of a generous and magnificent constructor," as it was put as early as the fourteenth century.[66] For this very reason, buildings can be interpreted as works of vanity, arrogance, immoderate passion, or attempts at subjugation, all of which Nicholas was accused of. The most serious charge, because it attacked the monarchical concept of the papacy, was the suspicion of tyranny: that is what Manetti most elaborately refutes (see Chapter 8). Especially in the case of priests, large-scale building activity which diverted funds from charitable works was viewed with reservation.[67] And for a head of state, large building programs might be viewed negatively (as

[66] Baldo degli Ubaldi, *In decretalium volumen commentaria*, fol. 6a: in P. Spilner, "Giovanni di Lapo Ghini and a Magnificent New Addition to the Palazzo Vecchio," *Journal of the Society of Architectural Historians* 52 (1993): 453–65, here 460.

[67] As Matteo Villani expressed it: "Io non so s'egli e da lodare o da biasimare il prelato che spende negli edifici magnifichi il danaio che trae del beneficio a lui conceduto": quoted in Spilner, "Giovanni di Lapo Ghini," 460, with further examples of opposition to spending on big buildings.

Nicholas's were) for distracting attention from foreign and domestic politics. Indeed, the buildings were first viewed negatively in 1453 when they were seen as diverting funds from the rescue of Constantinople.

The first extended written reaction to Nicholas's earliest program of repair and improvement is Michele Canensi's eulogy of the pope early in 1451.[68] Canensi praised Nicholas for his skill in the "art of building" and his "most exact knowledge of building" as well as for his restoration of old buildings.[69] In particular, he praised the care and concern Nicholas showed in his "perspicacious invention" in "building the houses of the canons of the churches and refashioning their other holdings."[70] In fact, having rebuilt the canonicate, Nicholas continued work on the canons' sacristy and began renovating their property in the Borgo. While Canensi's evaluation of the building activity was positive, he suggests that others had been critical and had prejudged these activities:

> What man is there of such depraved mind or hardened heart that he is unmoved and ill disposed towards the liberal arts, towards decency, and towards religion itself when he has decided to bend his heart towards you and furthermore gaze upon your holiness with devotion?[71]

Canensi wrote after the Jubilee and the canonization of San Bernardino, but before the imperial coronation, exactly the chronological period in which Manetti situates his digression on the building projects. Yet no unified overall plan such as Manetti describes in the architectural ekphrasis could be deduced from the works actually begun by 1451. And there is certainly no evidence, by 1451, of an intention to replace St. Peter's from the foundations up, although Manetti twice says that this was Nicholas's plan (25, 27). Aeneas Silvius Piccolomini's eyewitness account of the coronation evaluates the architectural program as it was in 1452. The Emperor Frederick, he says, praised Nicholas's buildings as the best of all modern work and, since Frederick was also an ambitious patron, the king and pontiff conversed about architectural matters during the visit.[72]

---

[68] M. Miglio, *Storiografia pontificia del Quattrocento* (Bologna, 1975), 83. Canensi's list of projects differs significantly from Manetti's. He mentions work in Rome on SS. Apostoli, San Paolo fuori le mura, St. John Lateran, Sta. Maria Maggiore, the Pantheon, Sto. Stefano Rotondo, Sta. Susanna, and Sta. Prassede; outside Rome, on S. Petronio in Bologna, and in Fabriano and Assisi. There is also a paragraph on work at the Vatican Palace, Castel Sant'Angelo, and St. Peter's.

[69] M. Miglio, "Una vocazione in progresso: Michele Canensi, biografo papale," *Studi medievali* 12 (1971): 463–524, here 516.

[70] Miglio, "Vocazione," 516.

[71] Miglio, "Vocazione," 516–17.

[72] Piccolomini, *Historia Friderici*, 69.

The year 1453 was the political nadir of Nicholas's pontificate. Nicholas's building projects were evaluated no longer as the settings for the Jubilee and the coronation, but in the light of the conspiracy of Stefano Porcari (Epiphany 1453) and the fall of Constantinople (29 May of the same year). Because of the conspiracy, some saw Nicholas's building activity as prudent because it provided new fortifications. In his dialogue on the Porcari conspiracy of 1453, for instance, Pietro de Godi of Vicenza enumerated projects underway like the palace at Sta. Maria Maggiore, the Palazzo dei Conservatori on the Campidoglio, the fortification of Castel Sant'Angelo, roofing of the Pantheon, work on Sto. Stefano Rotondo, and repair of the city walls.[73] Coming to the Vatican area he observed:

> New walls are being made and the palace at St. Peter's basilica is being rebuilt extensively with magnificent beauty; those towers and the very thick walls enclosing the palace are being constructed from the very foundations . . . and the magnificent and sumptuous tribunal of St. Peter's basilica is likewise being built whose deep foundation stands at the center of the earth and is 25 cubits in width.[74]

Amid these admiring descriptions, one sour note is struck. San Teodoro, a small church on the Forum which Nicholas had rebuilt on the old foundations, had collapsed and was rebuilt on new ones.

By contrast, the building activity was denounced as wasteful and fiscally irresponsible by those who saw it in relation to the fall of Constantinople: indeed, George of Trebizond said he had lost the pope's favor because of his insistence that the money should be used for holy war.[75] Even here, Nicholas had defenders. Lampugnino Birago wrote, in his *Strategicon adversus Turcos*:

> Some people say he is too eager to build; nothing should be overlooked or ignored that might constitute an objection. I admit he has been most sumptuous in building; I shall not run away from that charge. But what was he building, a private home or some other insignificant work? He adorned Rome, the head of the world, he adorned its temples, he constructed a seat worthy of pontifical majesty, and equally outfitted it with its furnishings but at a time when there was an abundance of money clearly at his disposal and which he was able to set aside and retain for his use.[76]

---

[73] Pietro de Godi, *Dyalogon de conjuratione porcaria*, ed. M. Perlbach (Greifswald, 1879), 20–21.

[74] *De conjuratione*, ed. Perlbach, 21.

[75] L. Onofri, "Sacralità, immaginazione e proposte politiche: La *Vita* di Niccolò V di Giannozzo Manetti," *Humanistica Lovaniensia* 28 (1979): 27–77, here 70.

[76] Quoted in Tafuri, "'Cives esse non licere'," 73 note.

One wishes that the first biography of Nicholas, Francesco Filelfo's *Liber de vita et moribus*, had survived, but upon receiving it in the spring of 1453, Nicholas burned the manuscript in his fireplace.[77]

This same year saw the departure of Poggio Bracciolini, Nicholas's long-time supporter, from court and the return of Flavio Biondo. Poggio had known Nicholas since 1427; dedicated a dialogue on the unhappiness of princes to him in 1446; referred to himself as an "old friend" in his congratulatory speech on Nicholas's election as pope in 1447; and dedicated *De varietate fortunae* to him in that same year.[78] But in the first half of 1453, Poggio left Rome to become Chancellor of the Florentine Republic. In July of that year, he begged Piero da Noceto to admonish the pope "to stop spending on building which, to tell the truth, everyone at the moment does not simply blame but detests."[79] In his very next letter to Piero, Poggio announced Manetti's immanent arrival in Rome: Voigt suggested that the two letters were connected and that Poggio may have thought Manetti would influence Nicholas to stop building.[80]

Although he denounced the building project in the 1453 letter, in his *De officio principis* (usually dated 1453–1459), in a long section on the virtue of magnificence, Poggio included Solomon, Constantine, and Nicholas as examples of princes who displayed this virtue through building.[81] Most likely Poggio's treatment of magnificence in *De officio* draws on Manetti's *Life*, which seems first to have associated Nicholas with this virtue. If *De officio* was written shortly after the pope's death, it suggests that Poggio's attitude toward Nicholas's building activity had changed between 1453 and 1455–1459, aligning itself with Manetti's assessment of its historic importance.

It could hardly be expected that the cardinals' funeral orations would criticize the dead pontiff. Jean Jouffroy's oration, on the sixth day, cited as testimonies of Nicholas's virtue and liberality St. Peter's, "which he raised with such grandeur," San Paolo fuori le mura, Sto. Stefano Rotondo, Sta. Maria Maggiore, the Pantheon, and Sta. Maria in Trastevere.[82] But his fuller praise had as its subject fortifications: like Romulus, Nicholas rebuilt the walls of Rome.

---

[77] S. Borsi, *Momus o del principe. Leon Battista Alberti, i papi, il giubileo* (Florence, 1999), 59.

[78] Voigt, *Il Risorgimento dell'antichità classica*, 2:73–74.

[79] *Poggii epistulae*, ed. Tommaso de Tonellis (Florence, 1832), 11.6. The letter dates to 25 July 1453. See also V. Fontana, *Artisti e committenti nella Roma del Quattrocento. Leon Battista Alberti e la sua opera mediatrice* (Rome, 1973), 26.

[80] Voigt, *Risorgimento*, 80, n. 3. Poggio had been the personal secretary of Eugenius IV; Piero occupied that position of trust with Nicholas, an intimacy which Poggio seems to have counted on in criticizing the pope.

[81] Poggio Bracciolini, *De officio principis* (Rome, 1504), unpaginated.

[82] Jean de Jouffroy, "Oratio Episcopi Atrebatensis habita Rome in funeralibus Nicolai Pape Quinti incipit feliciter," in MS. Vat. lat. 3675, fols. 30r–37r, here 33r–v.

After Nicholas's funeral, however, controversy over the projects resurfaced at the Curia for the same reasons voiced in 1453. Giovanni da Capistrano wrote to Callixtus III in 1455 urging him to spend the Church's money on crusade rather than building:

> I truly think it would be more pleasing to Peter and to God that in this obvious time of need and peril to the faith the ornaments of the basilica of the Savior and of the apostles Peter and Paul would be melted down and diverted to protect Christian religion than if all the churches of the city and the world and the towers and palaces were fashioned of pure gold and inlaid with precious stones.[83]

Evidently he did not believe that the safety of the Church could be assured through the persuasive effects of Nicholas's buildings. But Giuseppe Brippi addressed to Callixtus a work titled *Exhortatio ad complendam mirabilem capellam ecclesiae S. Petri*.[84]

Like almost all the sources written immediately after Nicholas's death, Vegio is discreet in his *De rebus antiquis memorabilibus basilicae S. Petri Romae*, probably composed in 1455.[85] He seems genuinely to have admired Nicholas, whom he refers to as "another great master of mine, never to be erased from my memory" (4.132). However, the examples of arrogance in his vehement denunciation of this sin — "so enormous a sin, and above all others so contrary to Him, and so detestable" (1.5.40) — fairly catalogues all that Nicholas paid for during his pontificate except the library:

> For it was not with a longer and more noble retinue, nor with more refined and flowing clothing, nor with more magnificent cavalry, nor with more splendid armaments, nor with more elegant companions, nor with loftier buildings, nor with fuller titles and scepters, that our savior Jesus Christ came to us. (1.5.40)

Since Nicholas's projects changed over time, criticisms of them made in the earlier years of the pontificate are not criticisms of the final project Manetti describes, nor can they be used to reconstruct it. Further, the continually evolving political, administrative, and religious contexts of Nicholas's pontificate within which the pontiff responded successfully or unsuccessfully to a sequence of challenges provided a changing background against which the building program was

---

[83] Quoted in C. D'Onofrio, *Visitiamo Roma nel Quattrocento. La città degli umanisti* (Rome, 1989), 54–55.

[84] Von Pastor, *History*, 2:357.

[85] In *Acta Sanctorum*, June 29, 27:56–76.

evaluated by those around him. The above texts reveal the contexts within which opposition to building could be framed at the Curia. That criticisms of Nicholas's character almost all date after his death is not surprising: candid evaluations can hardly be expected from authors whose livelihood depended on Nicholas's favor, nor debates about architectural form from diplomatic advisors. Criticisms directed at Nicholas's procedures as building patron while he was still alive can only be reconstructed indirectly (as subjects of Manetti's defense) and through circumstantial argument. Among these, charges of ineptitude and over-ambition are of special interest for art historians since they furnish new insight into the building program and its procedures. These are treated at greater length in Chapter 7.

In Book 3, Nicholas responds also to attacks on his building projects, especially at the Vatican. In Manetti's narrative in Book 2, they are evidence of papal magnificence, a virtue exercised only by the wealthy and powerful. In the Testament, Nicholas's justifications are twofold and pragmatic. The first (T2–3) is ecclesiological and pastoral, amplifying Manetti's earlier assertion that Nicholas believed impressive buildings safeguarded the faith of Christian peoples (13). The pope argues that although the majority of Christians, being unlettered, hear solid doctrine about the Church's authority from the experts, unless they are emotionally moved, particularly by what they see, they can slip away. Grand buildings and monuments, built to last through the ages and seemingly fashioned by God, strengthen, confirm, preserve and increase their loyalty to God's church. They exist not just for the present time, but continuously as future generations witness their wonders. The tens of thousands who streamed into Rome from the ends of the earth to celebrate the Jubilee exemplify the potential of material, visible monuments to draw the faithful in.

The second justification (T4–18) is new, one which Manetti never mentions in his ekphrasis in Book 2. Nicholas argues that his building program promotes security, particularly the safety of the pope's own person. Even the extra-urban renovations in the papal towns were calculated not just for the loyalty they would inspire but also for the defensive fortifications they would provide. Nicholas intended that his city would remain the permanent home of all future popes, and to this purpose he undertook not only to repair and adorn churches and public places, but also to ensure the defensive perimeter of the walls and fortify them with battlements. This was true of the Borgo as well, which he desired to be a safe and comfortable dwelling place for the pontiff and for the curial staff, whose numbers he had so augmented. He was prompted to move with urgency and at great expense for an obvious reason. The history of the last eight hundred years of the papacy, he says, is littered with instances of assaults on the person of the pope by both external and internal enemies, and he lists twenty-one popes who had been killed, assaulted, maimed, imprisoned, and driven into exile. These beleaguered pontiffs include his predecessor Eugenius who had narrowly fled with his life from the besieged Castel Sant'Angelo in 1434, and Nicholas himself, endangered by the Porcari conspiracy of 1453. This history of violence places the building program and the Christian loyalty it inspires in a very different context: such loyalty to Rome is not only a means towards salvation, but also a guarantor of security against anti-authoritarian movements such as that led by Stefano Porcari.

Manetti is defending not the living pope, who might be influenced to change, at any specific moment in his papacy — the Jubilee, the imperial coronation, the fall of Constantinople, or the Porcari conspiracy; but the deceased pontiff, the significance of whose tenure can now be evaluated as a whole. The parameter of discussion, both for praise and blame is, consistently, the furthering of the political and religious goals of the church as reflected in expenditure of resources. It is Nicholas's legacy which Manetti intends to articulate and affirm, and the pontiff's image for posterity which he intends to construct.

"Accusations made against us"

Besides answering the critics of his building program in the Testament, Nicholas also defends his actions at the time of the fall of Constantinople. The two are interrelated. Critics bristled at Nicholas's profuse expenditure of funds on Roman projects while Constantinople was imperiled by the Turkish advance. Instead of presenting the issue as one of resources, Nicholas sees this accusation as an attack on his command of diplomacy. His response is a succinct narrative of the negotiations between himself and the ambassadors of the Byzantine Emperor. He is careful, in case there should be some doubt, to couch his remarks in language that shows he is upset and saddened by the fall of the Christian city: "the doleful capture of Constantinople"; "O crime undeserved which all Christians in every age must mourn and detest." When he learned that Mehmet, "the most bitter enemy of the orthodox faith and the name of Christ," had besieged Constantinople, he decided to provide whatever aid he could to the Greeks, but, realizing that his resources alone were insufficient against the superior numbers of the Turks, he tried unsuccessfully to gather additional troops and munitions from Christian princes and republics. Despite his disappointment, he decided no longer to defer his reinforcements, but before the relief forces embarked for besieged Constantinople, the city fell to the Turks. Perhaps it was God's will or perhaps the enemy began to fight more strenuously knowing reinforcements were on the way (*RIS* 953). By offering the latter alternative, Nicholas leaves open the possibility that the Byzantine plea for Western troops had been bad strategy on their part and that it, rather than papal inaction, had hastened the fall.[86]

---

[86] See A. Kazhdan, "Nicholas V," in *Oxford Dictionary of Byzantium*, 3 vols. (New York, 1991), 2:1468.

The failure of negotiations to speed relief to Constantinople opened the question of papal diplomacy, and in particular the ability of this pope to deal with international crisis on this scale. For this reason, Manetti had developed in Book 1 the case for Nicholas as an exquisitely skilled and experienced diplomat. There we also learn that no matter how skilled the negotiator, diplomacy is not always under the control even of the most gifted emissary. Thus in his mission to resolve the outbreak of hostilities between Britain and France:

> He stayed on for months trying to work out a peace. I cannot tell you how much work he undertook day and night in hopes of fulfilling the precise charge of his mission. When he finally understood that his various effective and elegant attempts at persuasion were having little or no effect on the peace process, he returned to Rome with the matter unresolved. (*RIS* 916)

Thus Nicholas's failure in the matter of Constantinople need not be viewed as bad policy or botched diplomacy; failure was part of the reality of international relations, which no one person, not even a pope, could hope always to control. Yet his papacy is a long record of peace-making and diplomatic detente, of which the coronation of Frederick III marks a special highlight. Indeed, the main theme of Book 2 is Nicholas's successful pacification of western Christendom through skilled negotiation.

Two explicit objections — his absorption with building and his failure to prevent the fall of Constantinople — Nicholas rebuts directly in Book 3, and the *Life* elsewhere confirms indirectly. The *Life* addresses two other implicit criticisms. First, were the sources of papal wealth legitimate? And second, was the character of this pope admirable?

We have mentioned that Nicholas glossed over the fact that the papal treasury had been so enriched by the Jubilee Year that debt was retired and expensive projects could be lavishly funded.[87] Manetti tells us that so many pilgrims came to Rome because "sure remission of all old sins and explicit forgiveness of every fault could be acquired by all who arrived with penance and confession" (10). Since sacramental penance is a precondition of this remission and forgiveness granted in Rome, Manetti is not really talking about pilgrimage as efficacious in reconciling the sinner to God, but rather about indulgences, such as those with which Eugenius had endowed Florence Cathedral at the conclusion of the papal consecration (*De pompis* 34). This was a papal privilege, symbolized in the Keys of Peter, whereby the treasury of grace could be opened so that sins, already

[87] Manetti tells us that the revenues were so great that he was able to issue a new denomination of gold coin called the "jubilee" at three times the weight of the standard coinage (12).

forgiven, might have any lingering consequences reduced or canceled and full atonement made.[88] While the financial metaphor of the church's spiritual treasury is ingrained in the discussion of indulgences, an actual monetary transaction in exchange for spiritual benefits constituted the grave sin of simony.[89] The Jubilee indeed dispensed spiritual treasure, while at the same time taking in a great deal of material wealth. Manetti claims that by the second year of his reign Nicholas had reformed urban taxation and thus eliminated papal debt "without resorting to the illegal, though previously common, sale of sacred benefices" (7), and he specifies that the income from the Jubilee of 1450 consisted of tax revenues, the sale of provisions, and free offerings (12). He had surrounded himself with a "trustworthy and competent staff, without a hint of corruption and simony" (3). When Nicholas himself testifies to God about the wealth he amassed to glorify the Church, he denies that simony or other vices played a role: "Not out of greed, not out of simony, not out of bribery, not out of stinginess" (*RIS* 956). Yet the fine line between the pilgrim's voluntary and pious contribution and a quid-pro-quo exchange of money for grace can be obscure. The liturgical reforms Nicholas initiated, the ceremonial he performed, the ornamentation, repair, and enlargement of churches, and the frequency and splendor of papal audiences encouraged a great influx of pilgrims and tourists and enriched the papal treasury. Criticisms, if they arose, would likely attach to what Manetti calls "general offerings made by individuals" (12).

If Nicholas's critics were suspicious of the nature of papal income, his deathbed discourse on the sacrament of penance serves as a defense against any charge of simony because it affirms that penance is the true means for the remission of sins. He takes the Augustinian point of view that Adam's original sin left humans in a weakened condition, more prone to sin. While baptism washes away the original sin, there remains a taint and a tendency to sin which is compensated for in the sacramental life of the church, particularly in the necessary and repeatable sacraments of penance, holy eucharist, and extreme unction. In Nicholas's view, sacramental penance is the most important because it is the most connected to the Church's authority to bind and loose sins. Eucharist, after confession, fortifies the soul, and unction helps the sick and dying persevere, but only penance remedies the defect in our nature inherited from Adam's sin (*RIS* 948). While there is nothing

---

[88] See Thomas Aquinas, *ST*, suppl. q. 25, 1–3. In the Thomistic view, indulgences remit punishment in purgatory for sins already confessed and forgiven; only the pope may grant a "plenary" indulgence, cancelling all future punishment.

[89] Aquinas, *ST* 2/2 q.100 a.1, defines simony as the "deliberate willingness to buy or sell anything spiritual," and he counters Albertus Magnus's contention (*In sent.* 1.4 d.25 a.4) that a pope is permitted to buy and sell spiritual goods by stating that popes who do so are in fact engaging in simony and commit a greater sin because of their greater status.

theologically innovative in Nicholas's discourse, his age saw a revival of preaching on penance which he encouraged. The discourse on sacraments shows, then, that the pope acknowledged the difference between pious activities such as pilgrimage and the spiritual benefits they might confer, and the theology of sacramental penance. The content of the discourse is theological, but its intent is political.

The *Life* also suggests that the pope's personal character had come under attack. Some of the criticism of the building program suggested it was driven by vainglory. Beyond this, the very qualities which Manetti holds in such high esteem, eloquence and formidable learning, left the pope vulnerable to derision. What Manetti and Nicholas regard as the fruits of the liberal arts others could construe as a dilettantish lack of seriousness. Manetti acknowledges the potential for satire in the *prosopopoeia* at the end of Book 1. Manetti wishes to leave the reader with a distillation of Nicholas's character, one that portrays him as a paragon of the moral and intellectual virtues. He does so by enumerating the qualities that comprise his complex personality: "humane, agreeable, witty, sophisticated, generous, magnificent, brave, just, and moderate, except when he was angry and became hot at the bad behavior of his staff" (*RIS* 919). Then, as he had earlier, Manetti surveys the branches of knowledge of which he was master: "grammarian, dialectician, poet, historian, cosmographer, orator, philosopher, physical scientist, and theologian." Might not someone who did not know him well mistake him for a dilettante? To counter this charge, Manetti insists that Nicholas was not absorbed with "Greekish showmanship" like the hungry Greek that Juvenal flailed, who could assume any number of personalities to service his opportunistic ambitions: "grammarian, rhetor, geometer, painter, wrestling coach, augur, acrobat, doctor, magician — he knows it all" (*Satire* 3.76–78). Nor was Nicholas like Gorgias of Leontini, the Sophist whom Cicero denounced as being prepared to tell people whatever they wanted to hear (*De oratore* 1.22). These two allusions suggest two very serious charges: the first, intellectual fraud; the second, pandering. Nicholas's polymathy, which Manetti insists on, might indeed remind critics of Juvenal's low-born, jack-of-all-trades, opportunistic Greek pretender. Nicholas was in fact the butt of satire (see Chapter 7). His rise from obscurity, his need to fend for himself in acquiring an education, his intellectual ambitions, and his tendency towards self-promotion likely irritated those who opposed his policies. His vaunted tact in pleasing all who approached was a quality Manetti found admirable: "He would make himself accessible and courteous to all who approached him. He would answer all petitioners and supplicants in a way that made them leave delighted and cheered because they had been welcomed courteously and graciously" (3). His purpose in this, according to Manetti, was to gain a reputation as a "cultured, good, and generous pontiff." But to others it was a sign of inconstancy or, on the example of the Greek orator Gorgias, insincerity and sycophancy. Poggio saw this as Nicholas's one glaring character flaw:

> In one respect fault can be found in him. He was more frivolous in character than the seriousness of his position demanded and he revoked, on the prompting of certain cardinals, many favors he had conveyed. This is the greatest vice in a prince of his station, where no urgent cause is brought to bear.[90]

In the end, Manetti, not Nicholas's critics, provided the template by which to assess Nicholas's accomplishments, the greatness of character and learning which he brought to his eight-year reign, and his vision of the spiritual, cultural, and political authority of the Roman See. Manetti's version was and still is the authoritative account of the pope and his reign, which subsequent writers from Vespasiano on have adopted. Written in the months after the pope's untimely death, Manetti's *Life of Nicholas* is at once an encomium and a defense. As such, the *Life* not only represents but also interprets his magnificent achievements, his acquisition of books and his building projects in particular, within the framework of an understanding of the man and of the papacy which Manetti so brilliantly articulates. In doing so, he not only fulfills Antonio Loschi's desire that a man of authority and eloquence preserve the memory of magnificent and extraordinary contemporary deeds, but he provides an exposition and vindication of Nicholas's character and deeds meant to persuade the uncommitted that the work must go forward.

---

[90] *Le Liber Pontificalis*, ed. L. Duchesne (Paris, 1886–1892), 2:558.

Chapter Four

What do Athens and Jerusalem Have to Do With Rome?: The Library of Nicholas V

Manetti singles out the two achievements of Nicholas's reign that will establish the pontiff's historical significance: a massive program of renovation and building in Rome and in the Borgo, largely unfinished, and the assembly of the largest collection of Greek and Latin codices in Europe, the foundation of the Vatican Library. This two-part plan had a single purpose differentiated in its means by audience: the book project was aimed at the reading public, that is, the educated elite, while the building campaign was intended for the masses. Manetti records Nicholas's explanation of the plan on his deathbed:

> That the authority of the Roman Church is greatest and supreme is understood only by those who have learned its origins and growth from their knowledge of reading . . . the conviction of common people grows strong through buildings. (T2)

What was most original about the library and essentially different from any previous library project, was its stated ideological — ultimately ecclesiological — goal. For Nicholas did not intend to provide scholars with a resource with which to explore learning only for its own sake, for their enjoyment, their improvement, or even for the betterment of human society: study was to result in an understanding of the supreme authority of the Roman church.

How does this perspective affect our understanding of the library's well-known activities and acquisitions? Why would Nicholas want to acquire the classics of Greek literature, making them available in translation? And what of the project to translate the Old Testament from the Hebrew? How would these projects further Nicholas's ideological purpose for the library? We remember the controversy over the role of pagan learning in the early Church, expressed by Tertullian as: "What does Athens have to do with Jerusalem? The Academy with the Church?" (*On the Pretenses of the Heretics* 7.9–10 [PL 2.20B]). Indeed, Nicholas's project revivified a problem much discussed by the early Fathers: the relevance of pagan and Jewish tradition for Christianity. Since the literary contexts for both the problem and its solution as presented by Manetti are to be found in patristic writers, a variant of Tertullian's question is an appropriate title for this chapter.

The fullest contemporary account of the library's program is in Book 2 of Manetti's biography of Nicholas V where he claims that the pope "imitated Ptolemy Philadelphus, that renowned king of Egypt, who, he had read in the pertinent authors, had held to this method of collecting books while building that much-celebrated library of his, where it is reported he had collected about sixty thousand just of Greek books (unbelievable to tell!)" (15). Recent analyses have shown that the comparison is not merely a flattering classical allusion but an expression of Nicholas's intentions which his actions substantiate.[1] For example, both pope and king collected voraciously, sending emissaries to distant lands to recover rare or previously unknown works for their collections: in Nicholas's case these included Greek codices acquired both before and after the fall of Constantinople in 1453. Niccolò Perotti was able to obtain in Trebizond a codex containing Aristotle's *Problems* and another of Demosthenes's private speeches; Enoch of Ascoli searched on the pope's behalf in Denmark, Germany, and the cities of the lower Rhine.[2] Nicholas, like Ptolemy, intended to house the collection splendidly in a special part of the palace and to grant access to scholars.[3] Nicholas, like Ptolemy, accelerated the diffusion of knowledge by promoting translations of texts. Here Nicholas's scope begins to exceed that of the king of Egypt: Ptolemaic translations were made because his library, by rule, contained only books in Greek. Nicholas's library was both Greek and Latin, and therefore more diverse. In fact, the translation projects under Nicholas, more than the new works he specially commissioned, were the objects of amazement to his contemporaries. On these the most distinguished Humanists of the day labored: Lorenzo Valla's prose translations of Homer; those of Carlo Marsuppini and Guarino Veronese in verse; Guarino's Strabo; Valla's Thucydides; Poggio Bracciolini's Xenophon and Diodorus; Perotti's Polybius; Manetti's Philo and his version of Aristotle's ethical works; Traversari's Dionysius the Areopagite, Eusebius, Gregory Nazianzus, Basil, and

[1] S. Rizzo, "Per una tipologia delle tradizioni manoscritte di classici latini in età umanistica," in *Formative Stages of Classical Tradition: Latin Texts from Antiquity to the Renaissance*, ed. M. D. Reeve and O. Pecere (Spoleto, 1995), 371–407; L. Canfora, *Il viaggio di Aristea* (Bari, 1996), 61–70.

[2] For Nicholas's acquisitions, see esp.Vespasiano, *Vite*, 1:35–81. The acquisitions and translations also occupy an important part in Voigt, *Il risorgimento dell'antichità classica*, *passim*.

[3] The location of Nicholas's library is the subject of debate. See our Commentary at 35. Nicholas told Enoch of Ascoli that he intended to ensure that "for the common convenience of the learned we may have a library of all books both in Latin and Greek that is worthy of the pope and the Apostolic See": Letter of 1451 quoted in *Rome Reborn: The Vatican Library and Renaissance Culture*, ed. A. Grafton (Washington, DC, 1993), xii. Manetti also mentions the benefit to present and future scholars at 11, yet at 15 he qualifies this as "for the common use of all the prelates of the Roman Church."

Chrysostom; Theodore of Gaza's Theophrastus; and the dozen or so Aristotelian, Platonic, and patristic works translated by George of Trebizond (Vespasiano, *Vite*, 1:65–67). As at Alexandria, all branches of learning were to be represented. Jean Jouffroy sums up:

> Collecting throughout the world, he brought over six hundred rare books to light; he made the philosophy of Aristotle, Plato, Theophrastus, and Ptolemy, and the wonderful but previously unknown histories of Thucydides, Herodotus, Appian, Diodorus Siculus, and Polybius accessible to us [in our own language]. He brought us the heavenly manna of Chrysostom, Basil, Gregory of Nazianzus, and Eusebius. . . .[4]

In the end, only the pope's untimely death stemmed the growth of his amazing collection.

In the mid-Quattrocento, there were those who believed that clerics should read only sacred and not profane works; those who doubted the value of studying classical authors; and those, especially connected to the Observant movement's ideal of *sancta rusticitas*, who advocated the renunciation of all cultural pretension.[5] This line of thought goes back at least to St. Jerome's dream of God condemning him as a Ciceronian rather than a Christian (*Letters* 22.30 [PL 22.416]). It was reactivated by the new interest in pagan authors in the early Quattrocento and was the subject of an exchange between Coluccio Salutati and Giovanni da San Miniato in 1400: Salutati employed St. Basil's *Letter to Young Men on Reading Pagan Literature* to support his position that Christians could select what was good in pagan letters and ignore mistaken theological notions.[6] While Manetti also adopts patristic authority as justification, his argument is different, as we will see.

---

[4] "Oratio Episcopi Atrebatensis habita Rome in funeralibus Nicolai Pape Quinti," MS. Vat. lat. 3675, fol. 34r–v; the Latin text has been published by L. Onofri, with J. IJsewijn, "*Sicut Fremitus Leonis ita et Regis Ira*: Temi Neoplatonici e culto solare nell'orazione funebre per Niccolò V di Jean Jouffroy," *Humanistica Lovaniensia* 31 (1982): 21–28.

[5] The most recent discussion, with further bibliography, is in C. Bianca, "Il pontificato di Niccolò V e i padri della chiesa," in *Umanesimo e padri della chiesa*, ed. S. Gentile (Milan, 1997), 85–92, esp. 89; and Rummel, *The Humanist-Scholastic Debate*, 35, where she quotes Jean Gerson (1363–1429), Chancellor of the University of Paris: "Theologians are open to criticism when they put the study of grammarians, secular historians, poets, ancient orators, and mathematicians first and persist in those studies rather than in theological subjects." Such reading is acceptable, according to Gerson, only for pleasure and recreation.

[6] Bruni translated this letter for Salutati and dedicated it to him. The dedication letter is in H. Baron, *Leonardo Bruni Aretino: Humanistisch-Philosophische Schriften* (Leipzig, 1928), 98–100; idem, *Humanistic and Political Literature in Florence and Venice* (Cambridge, MA, 1955), 117–19, and 160 n. 4.

Especially after the fall of Constantinople and the conspiracy of Stefano Porcari, both events of 1453, some in Nicholas's circle felt that funds should be spent on military security instead of the library and construction.[7] Many, however, seem to have understood Nicholas's two projects as a direct response to the Humanist complaint, on the theme of *ubi sunt*, that the two things which best revealed and preserved the memory of a culture were books and buildings: these had distinguished ancient Rome, but their ruin evidenced the destruction of that culture.[8] That Nicholas joined in this Humanist view is certain, for Manetti records that Nicholas always considered "no memory of human affairs lasts longer than that which is committed to enormous permanent buildings and imperishable literary records" (13).

In the early Quattrocento, with the return of the papacy from Avignon to a destitute and deserted city, Rome's reputation for book learning was low indeed. It was widely believed that Gregory the Great had destroyed the monuments and libraries of pagan antiquity that had once rivaled the Wonders of the World.[9] Cencio Romano, in 1415, implicated the Church in this devastation, driven "partly by ignorance and partly so that the divine face of Veronica might be painted," referring to the tourist souvenirs made by detaching pages from old codices, scraping them clean, and overpainting them with images of the *sudarium*, Veronica's veil with the imprint of Christ's face that was among the principal relics of St. Peter's.[10] Nicholas's rescue of forgotten and neglected books was to reverse this public image of papal philistinism.

Nicholas's library was also an assertion of hegemony over the city of Rome, from which the papacy had been exiled for most of the preceding century. Moreover, it was necessitated by that same exile, since when Martin V returned to Rome the Avignon library was dispersed, part staying in Avignon, part going to Toulouse, with only some volumes ending up in Rome.[11] How many, if any, books had remained in the papal collection at the Vatican or Lateran Palaces is impossible to determine; although we know that Nicholas's predecessor Eugene IV left at least three hundred and forty codices, Ambrogio Traversari considered

---

[7] For criticisms, see Miglio, *Storiografia pontificia del Quattrocento*, 105, n. 55. We explore these criticisms in the context of the building projects in Chapters 3 and 7.

[8] See, for instance, a letter by Pier Paolo Vergerio in R. Valentini and G. Zucchetti, *Codice topografico della città di Roma*, 4 vols. (Rome, 1953), 4: 97: "There would be two things by which the memory of events endures, namely, books and buildings."

[9] T. Buddensieg, "Gregory the Great, the Destroyer of Pagan Idols," *Journal of the Warburg and Courtauld Institutes* 28 (1965): 44–65.

[10] L. Bertalot, "Cincius Romanus und seine Briefe," *Quellen und Forschungen aus italienischen Archiven und Bibliotheken* 21 (1929–30): 209–51, here 224.

[11] Dykmans, "D'Avignon à Rome," 254.

nothing in either the papal library or that of St. Peter's to be of real value.[12] Thus a papal, palatine library of unprecedented amplitude "per comune uso di tutta la corte di Roma" (Vespasiano, *Vite*, 1:65) did not rival, but far surpassed, any other secular or ecclesiastical library in the city. This appropriation of cultural primacy was warmed by the currents of Florentine humanism and energized by the steady recovery of Greek and Latin texts from classical antiquity; but at heart its vision was larger.

The library at Alexandria (Alexander's city in Egypt, on the Nile delta), the first to unite all secular and sacred wisdom and the most comprehensive collection ever created, became the possession of Rome after 31 B.C., and the Greek-language culture of its founder gave way to the successor Latin-language culture of the Romans, whose own libraries rivaled the Seven Wonders (as Cencio Romano had claimed). After the destruction of the library at Alexandria, the Roman libraries in their turn were destroyed. Nicholas's purpose was to transfer the center of the civilized world to the revitalized papacy and to Old Rome, superseding both Constantinople and Florence, bringing there all the treasures of past learning, and endowing a cultural legacy for posterity. By reinstating Rome as a great center of learning, Nicholas demonstrated the papacy to be the successor of ancient Roman cultural achievement. This new culture, similar to the last because Roman but new because Christian, had assumed the rights of inheritance and claimed legitimate succession, a claim challenged by attacks on the authenticity of the Donation of Constantine brought by Nicholas of Cusa and Lorenzo Valla, among others.[13] If it were not true that Constantine gave the bishop of Rome *imperium* over the western portion of the Roman Empire, then the church's authority would have to be grounded on other evidence. Nicholas's many commissions for the translation of texts into Latin suggests a partial response

[12] P. L. Rose and S. Drake, "Humanist Culture and Renaissance Mathematics: The Italian Libraries of the Quattrocento," *Studies in the Renaissance* 20 (1973): 46–105, here 76; Voigt, *Risorgimento*, 197. The main part of this latter collection, in the care of the canons, was built up with Cardinal Giordano Orsini's books, some 250 volumes, housed in the sacristy of the basilica during Nicholas's pontificate. Estimates of the number of volumes varies. See G. Lombardi and F. Onofri, "La biblioteca di Giordano Orsini (c.1360–1438)," in *Scrittura, biblioteche e stampa a Roma nel Quattrocento: Aspetti e Problemi*, ed. C. Bianca, P. Farenga, and G. Lombard (Vatican City, 1980), 371–82, here 372, 374; Müntz and Fabre, *La bibliothèque du Vatican au XVe siècle*, 42.

[13] Valla wrote *On the False and Lying Donation of Constantine* around 1440. See R. Black, "The Donation of Constantine: A New Source for the Concept of the Renaissance?" in *Language and Images of Renaissance Italy*, ed. A. Brown (Oxford, 1995), 51–85; and S. I. Camporeale, "Lorenzo Valla e il 'De falsa credita donatione': Retorica, libertà ed ecclesiologia nel' 400," *Memorie Domenicane* 19 (1988): 191–293.

to this challenge, for, as Valla explained, the real dominion of the Roman Empire had been based not on military conquest but on the diffusion of the Latin language: "There is the Roman Empire, wherever the Roman language rules."[14] But how would it teach that "the authority of the Roman church is greatest," in regard to its religious rather than secular hegemony? In part, because while vernacular languages were increasingly used by states, Latin remained (and remains) the official language of the Roman Curia. Thus the Roman Empire lived on in the Curia and it could even be claimed that Christianity and Latin were co-extensive and eternal.[15]

The point of the comparison between the planned papal library and its ancient Ptolemaic exemplar is at first glance entirely secular, and it has invariably been analyzed as such. But it is also clear that Manetti and Nicholas saw the connection with Ptolemy in yet another historic way, one that was programmatic for redefining the nature of Christian humanist learning. Ptolemy's library had received abundant attention in Jewish and Christian sources because it had been the site of the translation of Hebrew Scriptures into the Greek of the Septuagint version. Manetti would have known of the Alexandrian library not only from classical references and from Tertullian and Isidore, but primarily from Jerome, Augustine's *City of God*, Josephus's *Jewish Antiquities*, Aulus Gellius's *Attic Nights*, and, most particularly, Eusebius's *Preparation for the Gospel*.[16] These are the authorities Manetti quotes in his discussion of the Septuagint translation at Ptolemy Philadelphus's Alexandrian Library, the subject of the second book of his *Apologeticus*.[17] Nicholas surely knew of the Library from the same sources, and from Eusebius, whom he had commissioned George of Trebizond to translate

---

[14] Lorenzo Valla, *Elegantiae latinae linguae*, in idem, *Opera omnia*, ed. E. Garin (Turin, 1962), 3–5. For the translations, see Vespasiano, *Vite*, 1:66–69. Arguments for the authority of the Roman church are examined in Chapters 7 and 9.

[15] Suggested by D'Amico, *Renaissance Humanism in Papal Rome*, 119.

[16] On the Library at Alexandria and its literary heritage, see Canfora, *Viaggio*; also idem, *The Vanished Library: A Wonder of the Ancient World* (Berkeley, 1990); and E. A. Parsons, *The Alexandrian Library* (New York, 1952).

Manetti may have known the copies of Josephus and Gellius owned by Niccolò Niccoli. He surely knew the *Jewish Antiquities* by 1452, as it is a frequently cited source in his treatise on the dignity of man (see the "Index auctorum" in the edition of Leonard). Nicholas had three copies of Josephus, of which one was surely the *Jewish Antiquities*. See R. Sabbadini, *Le scoperte dei codici latini e greci ne'secoli xiv e xv* (Florence, 1967), 1:55, 92, and Müntz and Fabre, *Bibliothèque*, 78, 79, 86. On the availability of Aulus Gellius see H. Baron, "Aulus Gellius in the Renaissance: His Influence and a Manuscript from the School of Guarino," in idem, *From Petrarch to Leonardo Bruni. Studies in Humanistic and Political Literature* (Chicago, 1968), 196–216.

[17] Manetti, *Apologeticus*, ed. De Petris.

into Latin. A copy of Eusebius was in his private rooms after his death, together with some of the new translations.[18]

In the *Apologeticus*, written in 1455–1456 and thus virtually contemporary with the *Life*, Manetti needed to contend in detail with the Eusebius account, since his purpose was to defend his own new Latin translation of the Psalms. Eusebius, in turn, had quoted at length from another source, the so-called *Letter of Aristeas*, considered the first-hand account of the intermediary between Ptolemy and the High Priest Eliezar who facilitated the arrival of the Scriptures and their bilingual translators from Jerusalem to Alexandria. Aristeas's account and Eusebius's explication were considered from the time of Augustine (*City of God* 18.43) definitive in suggesting not only that the Septuagint was accurate, but also that it was inspired by the Holy Spirit. This claim is one which Manetti, fortified by Jerome and secular parallels, was obliged to challenge if he was to defend his return to Hebrew Scriptures as the criterion of Old Testament authority. Thus Manetti provides us with extended quotations, in the Latin translation by George of Trebizond, from the Aristeas account as embedded in Eusebius.[19] Oddly, in the passage from the *Life* quoted above, Manetti credited Aristeas with the project, though it is clear from the *Apologeticus* that Manetti was quite aware that Aristeas himself had attributed the initiation, organization, and direction of the translation to Demetrius of Phalerum, thought to be Ptolemy's librarian.[20] Manetti does not hesitate to question certain details of the account where he has

---

[18] A. Manfredi, *I codici latini di Niccolò V: Edizione degli inventari e identificazione dei manoscritti* (Vatican City, 1994), Inventory of the *cubiculum*, numbers 2, 3, and 4. The Eusebius manuscripts are now Vat. Lat. 228 and 234; cf. G. Sforza, *La patria, la famiglia e la giovinezza di Papa Niccolò Quinto* (Lucca, 1884), 385. Manetti and Vespasiano after him consider the Eusebius translation among the premier works commissioned by Nicholas: Manetti, "preclarum illud de preparatione evangelica Eusebii cesariensis," *Life* 16; Vespasiano, "il mirabile libro de Praeparatione evangelica, d'Eusebio Panfilo, libro di grandissima cognitione," *Vite*, 1:68–9.

[19] Manetti knew Aristeas as "Aristeus," a common variant. In general, Manetti accepted Aristeas's historical account (with the exception of the number of Ptolemy's books). He chose instead to undermine Eusebius's and Augustine's inspiration theory by noting a parallel concord among a group of secular editors establishing the text of Homer under the Athenian tyrant Pisistratus and citing the authority of the great Jerome, who vehemently rejected the story of identical simultaneous translations. In addition, inaccuracies in translation from the Hebrew had led to at least six other Greek translations/emendations: *Apologeticus* 2.28–57.

[20] Modern scholars conclude that this cannot be so, that Demetrius of Phalerum is to be connected with Ptolemy I Soter, and suffered the enmity of Philadelphus, dying in exile in 383 B.C., at the king's instigation. See the summary in *Apologeticus*, ed. De Petris, 29, note to lines 7–10.

other evidence; for example, he uses a remark in Aulus Gellius to deflate the number of Ptolemy's books from 200,000 to 60,000 (*Apologeticus* 2.16–17). His substitution of Aristeas for Demetrius in the papal life, then, is no slip but an intentional highlighting of the Septuagint project.[21] In the *Apologeticus* Manetti was concerned with the particulars of a historical biblical translation in order to demystify it. In the *Life*, he was interested in how the Hebrew Scriptures became assimilated into Hellenic culture, and to this purpose the bilingual Aristeas, a classically educated Jew who recorded the event, suited Manetti's purpose more than the monolingual royal librarian who sought to please Ptolemy.[22]

By the mid-Quattrocentro, the so-called *Letter of Aristeas to Philocrates* was circulating in Italy and accepted as genuine.[23] Mattia Palmieri of Pisa translated it into Latin in the 1460s; its *editio princeps* was early, in 1471. Whether, in the 1450s, Manetti knew of this document — a detailed narrative of the Septuagint's production — is not clear; the fact that the quotes in the *Apologeticus* are from George of Trebizond's Latin translation of Eusebius suggests he does not. But Eusebius's extended quotations in Book 8 of the *Preparation for the Gospel* were sufficient and suited the project for which Manetti had been called to Rome in 1453: a new Latin translation, from the original Greek and Hebrew, of the Scriptures — a Renaissance version of the Septuagint produced in a papal library that rivaled that of Ptolemy Philadelphus, in the successor language of high culture, Latin. Manetti writes:

> And then a new translation into Latin of both the Old and New Testaments, from the Hebrew and Greek, since clearly they had been originally entrusted by their writer to their own forms of writing, had not unjustifiably crept into his mind. (*Life* 17).[24]

Only Nicholas's death, he says, prevented its completion. In addition to these translations, Manetti was preparing a new apologetical work, his *Against the Jews*

---

[21] Even though he does not mention Demetrius of Phalerum in the *Life*, Manetti is well aware in the *Apologeticus* that Ptolemy's librarian was involved in every stage of the Septuagint project from first suggesting it to the king to the oath at the end against changes in the text (2.4–26). Compared to Demetrius, Aristeas's role was relatively minor.

[22] Near the end of his discussion of the Septuagint, Manetti attributed later Jewish opposition to translations, including his own, to their ignorance of classical literature and their loss of command of Hebrew; this cultural fusion of Greek and Hebrew had disappeared with Philo and Josephus (*Apologeticus* 2.67–68).

[23] For a text, translation, and commentary on the Letter of Aristeas, see M. Hadas, *Aristeas to Philocrates (Letter of Aristeas)* (New York, 1951); *The Old Testament Pseudepigrapha*, ed. J. Charlesworth (Garden City, 1985), 2:7–34.

[24] In fact at the pope's death, Manetti, unable to return to Florence, moved to Naples at the sponsorship of King Alfonso and was able to produce only a Latin translation of the New Testament, and, from the Hebrew, a new Latin Psalter before his death in 1459.

and the Pagans, in which he would try through his vast learning to articulate a new synthesis of Latin Christian culture which was more sympathetic and assimilative towards Hebrew and pagan learning. Manetti was uniquely qualified to approach this subject. By 1430, he had already embarked on his studies of Hebrew at his home in Florence with a tutor.[25] Having learned the language, in 1442 Manetti began to read through the Old Testament (twice) with Immanuel ben Abraham da San Miniato and studied medieval Hebrew biblical commentaries. His spoken Hebrew was polished by Giovanfrancesco Manetti — not his son, but a Jew he had converted and who took his name in baptism — who lived with him until 1449. Manetti collected some of the Hebrew works now in the Vatican collection: a Bible and a Psalter, both with commentaries by David Kimchi; a copy of Josippon bought in 1443; and Moses Maimonides's *Guide for the Perplexed*, acquired in 1457.[26] Stinger rightly observed that people like Manetti distinguished between Old Testament Jews, whose history and culture had been incorporated into Christian tradition and belief; and those born after the birth of Christ, whose religion he rejected and whom he tried to convert.[27] While in Rimini in 1447, he debated for six hours with learned Jews whom Sigismondo Malatesta had invited to a conference; his facility in Hebrew enabled him to do this successfully (Vespasiano, *Vite*, 1:504). Manetti did not share the anti-Semitism preached especially by fifteenth-century Franciscans and practiced by many Italian cities, including Florence.[28] His anti-Judaism, that is, his opposition to Jewish tenets and doctrines, was very different from the anti-Semitism common in his time.[29] It occupies a

[25] On Manetti's Hebrew studies see Cagni, "Agnolo Manetti and Vespasiano da Bisticci," 294; C. Dröge, *Giannozzo Manetti als Denker und Hebraist* (Frankfurt, 1987); and Trinkaus, *'In Our Image and Likeness'*, 581, and, on his relations with contemporary Jews, 591–92.

[26] U. Cassuto, *Gli ebrei a Firenze nell'età del Rinascimento* (Florence, 1948), 275–76; and Dröge, *Giannozzo Manetti*, 24–36.

[27] Stinger, *Humanism and the Church Fathers*, 132.

[28] R. Bonfil, *Jewish Life in Renaissance Italy* (Berkeley, 1994), 25–26; Cassuto, *Gli ebrei*, 370; G. Brucker, *The Society of Renaissance Florence. A Documentary Study* (New York, 1971), 240; F. Mormando, *The Preacher's Demons. Bernardino of Siena and the Social Underworld of Early Renaissance Italy* (Chicago, 1999), esp. 164–218; and K. Stow, *An Alienated Minority: The Jews of Medieval Latin Europe* (Cambridge, 1992).

[29] The distinction is Andrew Gow's, not, however, in reference to Manetti: A. Gow, *The Red Jews: Antisemitism in an Apocalyptic Age 1200–1600* (Leiden, 1995), 1. Manetti's criticism that the Jews had lost the tradition of learning they once enjoyed in antiquity is developed in his *Apologeticus* 2.66–71. Manetti's work has been studied by G. Fioravanti, "L'apologetica anti-judaica di Giannozzo Manetti," *Rinascimento* 23 (1983): 3–34, in relation to its literary tradition. See also A. L. Williams, *Adversus Judaeos: A Bird's Eye View of Christian Apologiae until the Renaissance* (Cambridge, 1936) and H. Schreckenberg, *Die Christlichen Adversus-Judaeos-Texte und ihr literarisches und historisches Umfeld (13.–20. Jh.)* (Frankfurt, 1994).

relatively unexplored corner of early Renaissance ecclesiology which would require a separate study. For our purposes it suffices to demonstrate that Manetti would have known, and later in his *Apologeticus* shows that he did indeed know, the history of biblical texts. While the date of the *Against the Jews and the Pagans* is uncertain, a letter of 1448 from Manetti to Nicholas shows it had already been begun and was of interest to the pontiff.[30] These tasks, patronized by Nicholas, rise beyond the antiquarianism or curiosity of a collector, and point towards an aspect of the library's program that sets it apart from Ptolemy, even in his patronage of the Septuagint.

Nicholas V and Giannozzo Manetti shared a background in the Humanist Florence of the early Quattrocento in which the collection, composition, and translation of books proceeded at an exhilarating pace, and this provides the first context in which we can explore Nicholas's Vatican library project. Manetti had been a longtime friend of the pope and a fellow bibliophile. Their acquaintance may have reached back as early as 1417, when the future pontiff, Tommaso Parentucelli, was tutor in the households of the Albizzi and Strozzi families in Florence. This earliest contact might have coincided in time with Palla Strozzi's project, recounted by Vespasiano da Bisticci, to found a public library at Sta. Trinità which, because it was in the center of Florence, would give convenient access to everyone (*Vite*, 1:146–47).[31] Although this intention is not otherwise documented and most of Palla's books were, in the end, given to Sta. Giustina in Padua, where he had been exiled in 1434, the idea of a public library was not new to Florence by 1420.[32] Some of its essential elements may be traced back to Petrarch. For instance, in Petrarch we find the notion of cultural succession: because Alexandria and Athens lost to Rome, and Egypt and Greece to Italy, we also have princes who love letters (*Letters to Friends* 3.18). Petrarch gathered the relevant classical exemplars: the Library of Ptolemy in Alexandria; the private library of Gordianus; and the public libraries of Julius Caesar and Augustus in Rome (*On the Remedies for Both Kinds of Fortune* 1.43 and *Letters to Friends* 7.4.2).

[30] A. De Petris, "*L'Adversus Judeos et gentes* di Giannozzo Manetti," *Rinascimento* 16 (1976): 193–205, here 193. De Petris suggests that Books 1–8 were written in Rome and Florence and 9–10 in Naples. Vespasiano says that in Naples Manetti corrected and emended what he had written earlier and added a few more books (*Vite*, 1:534), but the work never attained the 20 books Manetti originally planned (*Life*, 17).

[31] According to Vespasiano, this library was to contain books "d'ogni facultà," both sacred and secular, and in both Greek and Latin. See H. Gregory, "Palla Strozzi's Patronage and Pre-Medicean Florence," in *Patronage, Art and Society in Renaissance Italy*, ed. F. W. Kent and P. Simons (Oxford, 1987), 201–20; see 216 for reasons to doubt Vespasiano's story.

[32] Gregory, "Palla Strozzi's Patronage," 207 for the library. The notion of a public library in Florence is surveyed by E. Garin, *La biblioteca di San Marco* (Florence, 1999).

And he compared a modern figure to a classical prototype: thus Giovanni Coci, librarian to Clement VI, was said to be a Varro (in charge of Caesar's library); a Macro (for Augustus); and a Demetrius of Phalerum (Ptolemy's librarian) (*Letters to Friends* 7.4.2).[33] Roman exemplars of public libraries like those of Julius Caesar, Augustus, and Trajan may have been especially relevant for Florence where the goal was to create an educated citizenry.[34] Coluccio Salutati urged the creation of a public library in Florence, and Niccolò Niccoli stipulated that his books be preserved for the use of "all studious citizens."[35] It was Niccoli who arranged in cupboards the books which Giovanni Boccaccio had left to Sto. Spirito (Vespasiano, *Vite*, 1:46).[36] Like these, Palla Strozzi's project would have offered public access to a collection housed in a religious institution. And, in a similar project, the prior of S. Bartolomeo in Florence thanked Cosimo de'Medici for endowing his library with books, "a place to which men of study and letters could withdraw as into the most pleasant haunt of the Muses."[37] Cosimo, who had had Michelozzo build a library at San Giorgio Maggiore during his own exile in Venice in 1433, was responsible for the creation of the first public library in Florence at San Marco, after 1444.[38]

---

[33] In Canfora, *Viaggio*, 48, 53.

[34] Caesar's plans for the first public library in Rome were carried out by Asinius Pollio in 39 B.C. and extended by Augustus's addition of Greek and Roman libraries to the portico of the new Temple of Apollo on the Palatine. See D. Favro, *The Urban Image of Augustan Rome* (New York, 1996), 96, 165.

[35] For Salutati, see Rizzo, "Per una tipologia," 391; B. L. Ullmann and P. A. Stadter, *The Public Library of Renaissance Florence. Niccolò Niccoli, Cosimo de'Medici and the Library of San Marco* (Padua, 1977), 6; and C. Celenza, "The Will of Cardinal Giordano Orsini (ob. 1438)," *Traditio* 51 (1996): 257–86, here 271, n. 53, where he gives the quotation from Salutati's *De fato* 2.6. Although Rizzo believed Salutati's model to be Ptolemy because of its philological activity, its political role is modeled on Roman exemplars. Poggio Bracciolini, in his funeral oration for Niccoli, said he lent his books freely, even to people he didn't know, so that his home seemed a public library: also quoted in Rizzo, "Per una tipologia," 379. Manetti, too, echoing Poggio, says in his *De illustribus longaevis hominibus* that Niccoli's collection of Latin and Greek books became "publica quaedam bibliotheca": Vespasiano, *Vite*, 2:238, n. 1.

[36] A. Mazza, "L' Inventario della 'parva libraria' di Santo Spirito e la biblioteca del Boccaccio," *Italia medioevale et humanistica* 9 (1966): 1–74, esp. 6–7.

[37] Latin quoted in A. D. Fraser Jenkins, "Cosimo de Medici's Patronage of Architecture and the Theory of Magnificence," *Journal of the Warburg and Courtauld Institutes* 33 (1970): 162–70, here 170.

[38] Ullmann and Stadter, *Public Library*, 5. Most recently on the library at San Marco, see *La biblioteca di Michelozzo a San Marco tra recupero e scoperta*, ed. M. Scudieri and G.Rosario (Prato, 2000).

Interestingly, both Manetti and Parentucelli were involved in the San Marco project. In order to guide his acquisitions in completing the holdings of this library, founded with four hundred volumes mostly from Niccoli's collection, Cosimo asked Parentucelli to draw up a canon.[39] Manetti, not named as a trustee of Niccoli's collection in his first will of 1430 (in which the books were to go to Sta. Maria degli Angeli), is named as such in the 1437 will, which was subsequently executed.[40] Thus we find Manetti as trustee of a collection the growth of which was shaped by the future pontiff. Parentucelli's "wish list" for a monastic library open to the public included rather more sacred than secular texts and foresaw Greek and Hebrew works in Latin translation only.[41] While scholarly interest in Renaissance libraries has focused on *recovery* and therefore on secular classical literature and, secondarily, on patristic texts, the core of this collection — one-third — was texts of medieval theology and philosophy.[42] The example of San Marco suggests that new acquisitions need not imply a shift of value from what was already in the collection (mostly sacred) to what ought to be added (mostly secular). Excitement might have been expressed about new books which were secular, Greek, or patristic (as we saw in the accounts of Nicholas's library above) precisely because the collection was more complete in the standard works of Scripture, canon law, and theology. In these areas too, however, new acquisitions were made for San Marco.[43] The hierarchical ordering of subject matter in Parentucelli's canon — according to which church history and theology were most highly regarded (and also most numerous) and poetry and geography were among the least important — also governed how books were distributed in armoires in the papal collection at the Vatican, as we know from the inventory of 1455 as well as from Manetti's list of the subjects. If we go by the inventory compiled by the papal chamberlain Cosimo de Montserrat after Nicholas's death but before the accession of Callixtus, in the papal apartments Nicholas's Latin books were arrayed in eight armoires, each holding about a hundred codices: 824 Latin volumes in all.[44] The sequence follows a hierarchical order beginning with the

---

[39] See most recently M. G. Blasio, C. Lelj, and G. Roselli, "Un contributo al canone bibliografico di Tommaso Parentucelli," in *Le chiavi della memoria. Miscellanea in occasione del I centenario della Scuola Vaticana di Paleografia, Diplomatica e Archivistica* (Vatican City, 1984), 125–65.

[40] Ullmann and Stadter, *Public Library*, 7.

[41] Ullmann and Stadter, *Public Library*, 16; and Sforza, *La patria*, 379–89, for the canon.

[42] Blasio et al., "Un contributo," 130.

[43] Garin, *La biblioteca*, 35–36. For instance, a group of works on canon law and 34 works of Scholastic theology and philosophy, mostly by Thomas Aquinas, in 1445 and, in 1464, a group of Scholastic texts on logic.

[44] The most complete treatment of the inventory is Manfredi, *I codici latini.*

Bible and commentaries, ranging through patristics, theology, canon law, and decretals, filling the first six armoires to the right of the window; on the left side, the two remaining cupboards contain the volumes of classical writers — philosophers, historians, and poets. The author most fully represented is Augustine with fifty codices; the second is Aquinas with forty-nine. Thus three out of four books in the Latin inventory are theological or ecclesiastical in nature and only one in four is secular; one volume out of eight is either Augustine or Aquinas. An additional inventory of Greek books, not so detailed, yields another 429, about half of which are biblical or theological.[45] The entire documented library thus slightly exceeds 1,250 codices. Nonetheless, the assertion that their scope covers all learning (Manetti's "in omni doctrinarum genere"; Vespasiano's "d'ogni facultà") is borne out by Manetti's classification of the categories comprised in the library: works on grammar, poetry, history, rhetoric, oratory, dialectic, cosmography, architecture, geometry, music, arithmetic, astrology, painting, sculpture, military science, agriculture, ethics, physics, medicine, civil and canon law, and theology; plus commentaries on all the above (14). The aim, then, was not to substitute one kind of literature for another, nor even to achieve equal representation among the categories, but to make it universal in scope. Both of Manetti's charges from the pope in connection with the Roman project pertained to the highest class of subject: a treatise against Jews and pagans (theology), and new translations of the New and Old Testaments, including the Psalms (Scripture). Thus, when in his account of Nicholas's library he lists the subjects of the collection in ascending order culminating in his own contributions, this is not mere vanity on his part, but the reflection of an acknowledged hierarchy (17).

Parentucelli was also instrumental in the formation of the next major library in Florence, that of the cathedral. Responding to requests from the Florentine Signoria in 1447, the first year of his pontificate, Nicholas V gave permission for the transformation of S. Pietro in Celoro into a library. This library, which had been urged by the Consuls of the Arte della Lana and the Signoria, as well as by Archbishop Antoninus, was to be open to the public.[46] But in reality, since the library stood within the canons' cloister, access was limited and the collection never played a major role in Florentine civic culture. Whereas Salutati and Niccoli had emphasized the benefit of a library for the public, the founding statute of the cathedral library presents the books as a precious collection augmenting the prestige of the principal church of Florence, a treasure to be cared for, and an

[45] R. Devreesse, *Le fonds grec de la Bibliothèque Vaticane des origines à Paul V* (Vatican City, 1965), 9–43.

[46] The cathedral library was the subject of a recent exhibition and catalogue: *I libri del Duomo di Firenze: Codici liturgici e biblioteca di Santa Maria del Fiore (sec. XI–XVI)*, ed. L. Fabbri and M. Tacconi (Florence, 1997).

aid to divine worship, but not as a source of knowledge for the general citizen.[47] Thus, although the cathedral library could be described as public, enhancing the prestige of the Republic, and secular, including secular as well as sacred works, its primary purpose does not seem to have been to promote learning and foster intellectual discussion among educated Florentines.

The Florence Cathedral statute was composed by a committee, but the final version of November and early December 1451 was written by one of the Consuls of the Arte della Lana, Francesco di Tommaso Giovanni, and by Giannozzo Manetti.[48] Since Manetti had been appointed papal secretary in July of 1451, it is not surprising that the statute refers to the library being assembled by Nicholas as a model; nor, since Manetti was a trustee of Niccoli's collection by now at San Marco, that Cosimo is praised as a great patron of libraries.[49] But what is critical for this study is that the passage on Ptolemy Philadelphus in Manettis *Life* is clearly a reworking of the Florentine statute:

> Statute
>
> For it is clear that Ptolemy, surnamed Philadelphus, the second king of the Egyptians, so built that celebrated and marvelous library (*celebratam illam et admirabilem bibliothecam . . . construxisse*) that he gathered in one place about 60,000 different volumes (*millia circiter sexaginta diversorum librorum*), unbelievable to tell (*incredibile dictu*) if it had not been recorded by the pertinent authors (*ab idoneis auctoribus scriptum*) . . . and there the Hebrew laws were translated into Greek. . . .[50]

> Life of Nicholas V
>
> In this [Nicholas] quite remarkably imitated Ptolemy Philadelphus, that renowned king of Egypt, who he had read in the pertinent authors (*apud idoneos auctores*) had held to this method of collecting books in the building of that much celebrated and wondrous library of his (*in construenda illa sua tam celebrata ac tam admirabili bibliotheca*), where it is reported he had collected about 60,000 just of Greek books (*sexaginta circiter librorum duntaxat grecorum milia*), unbelievable to tell (*incredibile dictu*). (15)

Only Manetti among the writers of the Quattrocento put the number of Ptolemy's books at 60,000. The received tradition, used by Leon Battista Alberti

---

[47] The Statute is published in *I libri*, ed. Fabbri and Tacconi, 51–52.

[48] *I libri*, ed. Fabbri and Tacconi, 40.

[49] For the date of Manetti's appointment see F. Pagnotti, "La vita di Nicolò V scritta da Giannozzo Manetti: Studio preparatorio alla nuova edizione critica," *Archivio della Società Romana di Storia Patria* 14 (1891): 411–36, here 413.

[50] In *I libri*, ed. Fabbri and Tacconi, 51.

and others, accepted the high estimate of classical antiquity, 700,000 volumes. But Manetti objected to this on scholarly grounds — his only revision of the historical information he found about the Library in his principal source, Eusebius's *Preparation for the Gospel.* He drastically revised downward, based on his reading of Aulus Gellius (*Attic Nights* 7.17.1–3), where the holdings at Alexandria under the Ptolemies were stated to be about 70,000.[51] The fact that Manetti's idiosyncratic assessment of the library's size appears in both instances, together with the other striking verbal parallels, assures us that he is indeed the author of both passages.

This means that Manetti's comparison with Ptolemy was invented not within the context of papal Rome, but in bibliophile Florence. Petrarch had first cited the exemplar, and Rizzo thought it was what Salutati had in mind when he suggested that variant textual readings should be resolved through the collation of manuscripts.[52] Undoubtedly, Salutati knew of the Alexandrian library since in a manuscript of St. Jerome's works which he owned ultraviolet rays have revealed his marginal notation "Ptholomaeus" in the *Hebrew Questions.*[53] This manuscript then passed to Niccoli before entering the collection at San Marco. Canfora believes that a letter about Enoch of Ascoli's mission which Poggio wrote as Nicholas's secretary in 1450 already has all the salient elements of the Ptolemaic story as told by Epiphanius of Salamis (A.D. 315–403).[54] Whether the source was Epiphanius is uncertain since Nicholas possessed no works by him, but if Nicholas's project was already modeled on Ptolemy by 1450, then the image might have been suggested to Manetti first by the pontiff himself before he used it either for the statute or the *Life.*[55] What is certain is that the comparison was current in Florentine circles in the 1450s.

The image of Ptolemy's library could be used as an exemplar either of personal power and wealth — the books as possessions — or as a public work bringing glory to the city. Petrarch had used the image in this first sense: libraries are created by princes who love letters. The Florence Cathedral library statute also presented book collections as achievements of great individuals (extended in this case to reflect the greatness of the Florentine Republic through its representative individuals) and as precious possessions, not unlike collections of other rare and refined objects. In it, Ptolemy appears in a list of other famous private collectors

[51] Manetti's argument is explained in the *Apologeticus* 2.17.

[52] Rizzo, "Per una tipologia," 391.

[53] *Umanesimo*, ed. Gentile, 149. The manuscript is now MS. Laur. San Marco 600, c. 1r; the notation is on fol. 1v.

[54] Canfora, *Viaggio*, 61; Epiphanius, "On Weights and Measures," PL 43.252.

[55] In the *Life of Nicholas V*, Manetti represents the pope as collecting codices even before the phenomenal revenues of the Holy Year 1450 allowed him to expand his bibliophile ambition (13).

like Lucullus and Cosimo as models for the action of the Signoria of Florence in founding the library.[56] Manetti also cites Nicholas in that list. But Alberti's discussion of libraries in *De re aedificatoria* includes that of Ptolemy Philadelphus as a classical example of a secular public work bringing dignity to a city; he differentiates it from a classical instance of a private library, that of Gordianus (8.9). Since Nicholas's library was not a secular public work in the sense that Alberti intended by his Ptolemy citation, perhaps the reference was a veiled criticism of the project.[57] Unlike Salutati's and Niccoli's ideal of a civic library, Nicholas's library did not purport to create an educated citizenry but, closer to the aims of the cathedral library, it was intended to enhance the dignity and influence of the Roman See. Seen in the context of other Ptolemy citations, it would seem that in the *Life*, which postdates the statute and some parts of Alberti's treatise, Manetti exploited the ambiguity inherent in the image, presenting the Vatican library as the possession of a great prince, "a permanent and everlasting ornament to the sacred palace"; limited in access like the cathedral library in Florence, "for the common use of all the prelates of the Roman church"; but open to the public, so "much benefit might be supplied to present and future scholars" (13).

Our analysis suggests that the Florence Cathedral library project differed from other Florentine libraries in ways that make it closer to the Vatican project than had been realized. But the cathedral library did not exploit the possibility of using books for ideological argument. There is an important difference, therefore, in Manetti's use of the same literary topos for Florence on the one hand and for Nicholas's Rome on the other. Whereas in the Florentine document Ptolemy's library serves only as a classical allusion, and an exemplar of great patronage, in Rome the model is richly meaningful.

The Library at Alexandria was the first to collect all secular and sacred wisdom. It was renowned in particular for a series of brilliant librarians who refined and purified the text of Homer.[58] In this, they harked back to the sixth-century B.C. Athenian tyrant Pisistratus who was thought to have used seventy-two learned Greeks to establish the first recension of the Homeric corpus. It was logical that this Pisistratid recension would become a paradigm for the creation of the Septuagint, translated by seventy (in some versions, seventy-two) Greek-speaking

---

[56] *I libri*, ed. Fabbri and Tacconi, 51.

[57] For other criticisms of Nicholas in Alberti's writings, see Chapters 7 and 8.

[58] For the Alexandrian scholarship on Homer, see Parsons, *The Alexandrian Library*, 230–69; L. Casson, *Libraries in the Ancient World* (New Haven, 2001), 41–45; and the "Homer and the Papyri" database at http://www.chs.harvard.edu/homer_papyri/index.html. The system of obeli and asterisks which St. Augustine knew from critical editions of the Scriptures, in the passage Manetti quotes from the *City of God* 18.43 (*Apologeticus* 2.40), derived from notations first used in Alexandrian editions of Homer.

Jews. Manetti, in fact, connects the two stories in his *Apologeticus*. Having told at length the story of the Septuagint following Eusebius, he immediately recounts that of the Homeric corpus following Cicero. Manetti's purpose in calling attention to the parallel ("simile quiddam esse videbitur" [2.33]) is to question the divine inspiration of the Septuagint, while at the same time asserting that both the secular and the sacred enterprises were remarkable feats of learning with tremendous cultural consequences. The two projects are, as De Petris observed, thus put on the same level and seen as complementary.[59] And not surprisingly the verse translation of Homer, commissioned by Nicholas, was a project singled out by Manetti as specially difficult (16).[60] Canfora believed that this linkage was first suggested to Nicholas through the Scholium Plautinum, which excerpts the information on Ptolemy and Pisistratus from Tzetzes's *Prolegomenon to Aristophanes*. Evidently this scholium was done by Giovanni Andrea Bussi, who served Nicholas since 1450 and was later librarian of Sixtus IV's Vatican collection.[61] But the Scholium Plautinum was not in Nicholas's library — it came to the Vatican only in the nineteenth century — nor was Tzetzes.[62] That the scholium includes a reference to Lorenzo de'Medici suggests a date for it after Nicholas's death, unless Cosimo's brother Lorenzo who died in 1440 is meant. The connection, though, was a natural and likely one for Manetti to make; it suited his argument, as he acknowledges, to pair Eusebius with Cicero.

The *Apologeticus* was written in the year following Nicholas's death, so it is not certain that the Pisistratus-Ptolemy parallel was part of the original conception of the papal library. Indeed, it might have been developed as a defense against criticism leveled at the pontiff's famously expensive project of collecting and translating; at least this is how it appears in Manetti's *Life*. This criticism would have been of two kinds: attacks on the propriety of reading pagan authors and disapproval of revising Jerome's Vulgate. The Ptolemy comparison is Manetti's exemplar for the position that the supreme authority of the Roman church

---

[59] Manetti quotes Eusebius, *Preparation for the Gospel* 8.1–2 and Cicero, *On the Orator* 3.34.137 (*Apologeticus* 2.13–15, 18–24, 28–32). See De Petris's remarks, xxxi.

[60] "It is a truly difficult and arduous task . . . it is far easier to make a translation in prose than in poetry." Manetti does not name the verse translators, but Greco identifies them as Carlo Marsuppini and Guarino Veronese, and not Valla, who at the pope's bidding had produced a prose translation of 16 books of the *Iliad*: Vespasiano, *Vite*, 1:66, n. 1. Manetti contrasts the translations in verse with a prose *Iliad* by Leontino of Thessalonica done at the time of Boccaccio. See also C. Santini, "La versione latina dell' *Iliade* di G. P. Marinelli," in *Acta Conventus Neo-Latini Cantabrigiensis*, ed. R. Schnur et al., MRTS 259 (Tempe, 2003), 493–501.

[61] Rizzo, "Per una tipologia," 389, n. 67; Canfora, *Viaggio*, 64.

[62] The Scholium Plautinum is in MS. Vat. lat. 11469, fol. 184v. It forms the frontispiece for Parsons's *Alexandrian Library*; see also Parsons's discussion, 106–21.

rests on the acceptance of the former and the revision of the latter. Once again, the papal library of Nicholas could only be understood by its single historical rival: the Great Library of Alexandria. Site of the translation of the Hebrew scriptures into Greek and a repository of secular learning, it marked the beginning of the transference of Judaism and ultimately Christianity to the Hellenized West.

The significance of this transfer, debated by the early Fathers, was re-examined in the early Renaissance. One of the peculiarities of this discourse is that Renaissance authors, instead of raising the question directly, spoke through the writings of the early Fathers of the Church rather than in their own voices. There seems, therefore, to be a curious anachronism in Nicholas's thought, at least as we know it from Manetti, for the terms of debate and arguments for the papal view are situated not in the fifteenth but the fourth and fifth centuries. The authenticity of a supposedly fourth-century document — the Donation of Constantine — is hotly debated; Augustine's view of Christian culture in the fifth century as evolving from gentile and Jewish history is affirmed; Nicholas claims succession from a culture which modern historians would see as having lapsed almost a thousand years earlier. In this historical perspective — or lack thereof — the Middle Ages is like the blink of an eye interrupting a continuous conversation between fifth- and fifteenth-century authors. In this discourse, difference was primarily a matter of degree of authority. In it, patristic and Renaissance argument was intertwined.

One argument for the relevance of gentile and Jewish culture for Christians is that all truth is one. The Letter of Aristeas, even as known through Eusebius, showed the compatibility of Hebrew and Greek thought, since much of it recounts the questions Ptolemy asked the seventy-two Jews and their wise replies. Philo of Alexandria had tried to show the compatibility of the content of the Old Testament and Greek philosophy; Manetti was translating his work for Nicholas.[63] Clement of Alexandria argued that each philosophy contains a fragment of truth, which is one.[64] Tertullian's position was that Homer and Plato had drawn whatever insight they had on God and man from their knowledge of the Old Testament authors who lived before them.[65] And Augustine showed the essential harmony between Jewish prophecies and those of the Sibylline Books, Rome's own pre-Christian source of divine revelation. Manetti's parallel with Ptolemy's

[63] Vespasiano, *Vite,* 1:67; see Greco's note, quoting a letter from Manetti to Panormita regarding a corrupt manuscript of Philo which Manetti had in his possession, and their mutual interest in seeing a new translation produced.

[64] Clement of Alexandria, *Stromata* 1.16.80; M. Simonetti, "Alle origini di una dialettica culturale: I padri della Chiesa e i classici," in *Umanesimo*, ed. Gentile, 7–20, here 11–12.

[65] Simonetti, "Alle origini," 9.

library fits the Augustinian scheme in which truth is progressively acquired in the process of historical succession: the Greeks, having conquered the Jews, absorbed their truth by translating it into Greek in Alexandria; the Romans then conquered the Greeks and Augustus, the conqueror of Egypt, founded the Palatine library; now Nicholas, Vicar of Christ, gathered all the truths of all the ancients — Jewish, Greek, and Latin — at the Vatican Library.

An implication of this theme, developed by Manetti for and with Nicholas, is that Christianity was forged from the confluence of pagan and Jewish traditions.[66] In Paul's Letter to the Romans (which Manetti translated for Nicholas) the Apostle to the Gentiles writes: "Whether we were Jews or pagans we are the ones he has called" (9:24). It was Augustine who extended this theological understanding to the process of history. Almost all of Book 18 of the *City of God* — a work which Manetti claimed to have known by heart (Vespasiano, *Vite*, 1:521)—recounts the parallel histories of Jews and gentiles up to the birth of Christ. In one of the panels of Ghiberti's Gates of Paradise, for which Traversari seems to have given the program, Solomon and Sheba are depicted holding hands (fig. 6). Krautheimer's suggestion — that the scene anticipates the union of the Eastern and Western Churches — has been widely accepted, but an alternative, more literal, interpretation may be considered, in which the pair represent the union between Gentile and Jew.[67] They stand before the Temple of Jerusalem depicted, however, as a gothic church. If we are to understand that the fruit of their union is the Church, then another important element of Manetti's argument can be traced to Florence, since Traversari was his teacher and influenced his interest in Hebrew.[68] In any event, Manetti would have seen Ghiberti's doors, installed the year before he left Florence for Rome to assume his papal commission.

Considered as cultural history, the union of Greek and Jewish wisdom in Christianity can be described as confluence, but within the history of salvation it is supersession: Christianity must be shown not only as superior because more advanced, but also as possessing a truth which reveals earlier beliefs as imperfect and partial. A fresco representing the "Triumph of the Church over the Synagogue" painted in 1420 by Giovanni da Modena in San Petronio in Bologna

---

[66] This theme is discussed in De Petris, *Apologeticus*, ix, and especially by Trinkaus, *'In Our Image and Likeness'*, 726–34, on Manetti's *Adversus Judeos et gentes* ("Against the Jews and the Pagans").

[67] R. Krautheimer, *Lorenzo Ghiberti* (Princeton, 1982), 181. F. Hartt believed that, except for the Solomon and Sheba panel, the program for the doors was related to St. Antoninus's *Opus chronicorum*. That Antoninus doesn't discuss this subject seemed to confirm Krautheimer's suggestion that this scene related, uniquely, to a contemporary event: F. Hartt, "*Lucerna ardens et lucens*. Il significato della Porta del Paradiso," in *Lorenzo Ghiberti nel suo tempo* (Florence, 1980), 1:27–57.

[68] Trinkaus, *'In Our Image and Likeness'*, 581.

Fig. 6. Solomon and the Queen of Sheba, Lorenzo Ghiberti, Gates of Paradise, Baptistery of Florence. Scala/Art Resource, NY..

and commissioned by the Dieci di Balìa expresses this idea in relation to Jewish truth. Historical evolution from the perspective of the working out of God's plan for salvation is inherently teleological, looking back in time from revelation concerning the Last Things. Nourished by Paul's Letter to the Romans — "Now the Law has come to an end with Christ, and everyone who has faith may be justified" (10:4)–and by Augustine's *City of God*, a teleological interpretation of cultural evolution was deeply embedded in medieval liturgy. At the consecration of a church, the Greek and Latin alphabets, the languages signifying the two

Testaments, are written in ashes in a cross traced on the floor.[69] Although the Hebrew alphabet is not written because, as Sicardus of Cremona tells us, "it is not uttered in church," the pattern itself expresses the parallelism of gentile and Jewish sources of Christianity. The eastern, left corner of the church is identified as Judea because there Christ took on flesh, but reckoned "sinister" because of the "perfidy" of the Jews. The line begun there terminates in the right, western corner, representing *gentilitas* ("pagan-ness") in which perfidy fell and where Christ, the Sun of Justice (Malachi 4:2), sets. This line from east to west is written in memory of the transferral of God's favor from the Jews recorded in Matthew 21:43: "I tell you, then, that the kingdom of God will be taken from you and given to a people who will produce its fruit." The right, eastern corner signifies the early church; it runs to the left, western corner, again occupied by the Jews. These are the remnant of unconverted Jews who, after all the gentiles are converted, will also be converted at the end of time, as Paul writes: "One section of Israel has become blind, but this will last only until the whole pagan world has entered, and then after this the rest of Israel will be saved as well" (Romans 11:25–26). Augustine follows Paul in his discussion of the role of the Jews in the economy of salvation in the *City of God* (18.48) which, we should remember, is properly titled *About the City of God Against the Pagans*. Thus, while Paul shows the transferral of divine favor from the Jews to the gentiles, Augustine demonstrates the subsequent transferal from the gentiles (now pagans) to the Christians.

Manetti makes the argument for supersession elsewhere in the *Life*. Describing Nicholas's proposed papal palace and new basilica over Peter's tomb, for which Constantine's great edifice would have been razed, Manetti suggests the scarcity of ancient antecedents to which Nicholas's building might justly be compared. He rejects the conventional comparison with the Seven Wonders of the Ancient World: only the walls of Egyptian Thebes and of Semiramis's Babylon could rival the scale of Nicholas's project (55–56). Instead, he finds his model in Scripture: the temple and palace of Solomon. But even here, in both size and quantity Nicholas's structures would have been superior, had they actually been built (57–62). In this we see Manetti engaging in persuasive association; the basilica and palace of Nicholas would have been on a par with, or rather would have superseded, the greatest known analogies from both classical and Jewish antiquity.

Interestingly, Manetti finds it easier to dismiss the former than the latter. And other evidence shows that contemporaries shared his concern. Eusebius's *Preparation for the Gospel*— Manetti's source for the Ptolemy story and translated at Nicholas's request in 1448—was written to defend Christians against the accusation of being Jews. Since at least forty-six manuscripts of it were made in

[69] Honorius of Autun, PL 172.591–592; Sicardus of Cremona, PL 213.30–31, on the significance of the two languages.

the fifteenth century, it must have been popular.[70] Tertullian's *Against the Jews* and *Against All Heretics* were acquired by Giordano Orsini in 1426, were read by Traversari, and passed into the San Marco library.[71] This might shed light on Traversari's translation of Chrysostom's *Homilies Against the Jews*, the motivation for which so puzzled Stinger that he concluded it must have been done for the rhetoric rather than the content.[72] But Manetti's *Against the Jews and the Pagans*, also written for Nicholas, suggests a new interest in demonstrating that everything of value in ancient Jewish and pagan culture culminates and is unified in Christianity.

The Renaissance interest in supersession might have been nourished by Early Christian pictorial decoration in Rome where, for instance at Sta. Maria Maggiore and St. Peter's, stories from the Old and New Testaments were juxtaposed and the iconographic schemes culminated in the apse in a vision of the end of time. The theme of Christianity as the supersession of Jewish and gentile tradition also sheds new light on the frescoes painted by Fra Angelico in Nicholas's study in the Vatican Palace in 1449 (fig. 7).[73] These depict scenes from the lives and martyrdoms of Stephen and Lawrence, whose bodies had been discovered together at San Lorenzo fuori le mura in Rome in 1447.[74] Burroughs has already pointed out that the choice of these saints, Stephen the patron saint of builders and Lawrence the patron of librarians, parallels the two parts of Nicholas's achievement: books and building.[75] Relevant here, apart from Nicholas's evident devotion to these saints, is that Stephen, a Jew, was martyred for his faith by the Jews and Lawrence, a gentile, was martyred by a pagan emperor. Both saints, according to their legends, opposed the religious architecture of their heritage. Stephen spoke against the Temple of Jerusalem (Acts 6:8–7:50) and Lawrence

[70] *Umanesimo*, ed. Gentile, 275.

[71] *Umanesimo*, ed. Gentile, 223. For the disposition of Orsini's other books see Celenza, "The Will."

[72] Stinger, *Humanism*, 132.

[73] On the question of their date and the original purpose of the room, see C. Gilbert, "Fra Angelico's Fresco Cycles in Rome: Their Number and Dates," *Zeitschrift für Kunstgeschichte* 38 (1975): 245–65, here 261; J. Pope-Hennessy, *Fra Angelico* (London, 1974), 30; Burroughs, *From Signs to Design*, 50–51. The most recent study of the iconography is by Renate Colella in I. Venchi et al., *Fra Angelico and the Chapel of Nicholas V* (Vatican City, 1999).

[74] Burroughs, *From Signs to Design*, 53. Nicholas appointed a commission to investigate the finding; his arms are on the church (whose restoration was carried out by Guillaume d'Estouteville) and he restored Sto. Stefano Rotondo.

[75] Burroughs, *From Signs to Design*, 55.

Fig. 7. St. Peter Ordaining Stephen. Fra Angelico, Chapel of Nicholas V, Vatican Palace.

is supposed to have destroyed the Temple of Mars in Rome.[76] Both men delivered long speeches against the faith of their executioners: Stephen's is recorded in Acts; Lawrence's in his *Passio*. On Stephen's feast day the appointed reading (Matthew 23:34–39) is taken from Jesus's sevenfold indictment of the scribes and pharisees and concludes: "Jerusalem, Jerusalem, you that kill the prophets and stone those who are sent to you! How often have I longed to gather your children, as a hen gathers her chicks under her wings, and you refused! So be it! Your house will be left to you desolate, for, I promise, you shall not see me any more until you say 'Blessings on him who comes in the name of the Lord'."

Manetti, in fact, includes these saints as exemplary of Jewish and gentile Christian martyrs in his *Against the Jews and the Pagans*.[77] Whereas the Church of the Jews and the Church of the Gentiles had been depicted as personifications in early Christian mosaics in Rome, at Sta. Sabina and Sta. Pudenziana for instance, Manetti and Nicholas share the Humanist belief in argument made through historical exemplars of human action.

But what, then, do Athens and Jerusalem have to do with Rome? Two weaknesses in the notion of supersession became apparent and had to be dealt with. In regard to pagan learning, discoveries of unknown works revealed that the legacy was incomplete: not all of the pagan heritage had been included in, and therefore forged into union with, Christianity. This was especially evident for Greek literature. Until this was absorbed, through acquisition, translation, and interpretation, it might be claimed that some fragments of truth were independent from — even in conflict with — Christian revelation. Second, the transferred heritage was flawed: manuscripts of both pagan and Jewish truth were corrupt and their original significance, therefore, uncertain. The authority of the Roman church could be proven only if it possessed *all* of truth, its own truth therefore being both complete and perfect.

From the perspective of cultural history, Jerusalem could be seen as irrelevant. Bruni, for instance, admitted the importance of Greek, a language which lends itself to philosophy, but not of Hebrew, the literature of which in his opinion had no philosophy, no poets, and no orators.[78] Besides, everything worthwhile had already been translated, he said, "unless perhaps you distrust Jerome,

---

[76] Burroughs, *From Signs to Design*, 63. Stephen's objection to Solomon's Temple and the Temple cult is especially relevant given Manetti's comparison of Nicholas to Solomon. On Stephen's objections see A. Klijn, "Stephen's Speech–Acts 7, 2–55," *New Testament Studies* 4 (1957–1958): 25–31; and M. Simon,"St. Stephen and the Jerusalem Temple," *Journal of Ecclesiastical History* 2 (1951): 127–42.

[77] MS. Urb. lat. 154, fol. 155r (Stephen) and fol. 168r (Lawrence).

[78] Trinkaus, *'In Our Image and Likeness'*, 578. See also De Petris, ed., *Apologeticus*, xxxix, quoting a letter to Giovanni Cirignani.

a most learned man, and are confident that you yourself can know better than he knew."[79] The cultural question, then, turned on the accuracy of the Vulgate.[80] So does the issue of superiority. As Manetti wrote in the *Apologeticus*, "the Holy Scriptures, because of their divine authority in all matters . . . seem to exact and demand especially and chiefly a certain solemn and accurate . . . translation" (5.81).[81] Since, without question, the Divine Word had been entrusted to Scripture as its original source, it was essential that nothing of the original meaning be lost or altered in translation. This explains why chapters 3 and 4 of the *Apologeticus* are devoted to the enumeration of erroneous deletions from and additions to the Psalms. And, argued Manetti, it would be intolerable to believe, because variant versions of the Septuagint do not agree, that there are contradictions in what Scripture says (2.61–62). Bessarion and Valla had already realized that the texts were corrupt.[82] But since Jerome had long ago noticed this, Manetti cites the great translator's authority not only to confirm that the various translations are filled with discrepancies and contradictions (2.62), but also to make a sharp distinction between inspiration and translation. He quotes Jerome's acid remarks in the *Preface to the Pentateuch* debunking the myth of an inspired Septuagint: "It is one thing to be a prophet, quite another to be a translator. In the first instance, the Spirit foretells what is to come; in the second, a man's learning and verbal proficiency transfers what he understands" (2.48). Though Old Testament scholars are fallible mortals and not instruments of the Spirit, Manetti, like Jerome, is well aware not only that an accurate translation into Latin, for use within Latin culture, is useful and needed, but also that it advances the plan of human salvation (*Apologeticus* 2.64). Augustine took a different position, arguing that since the Septuagint translation was itself divinely inspired, it had greater authority than Jerome's translation (*City of God* 18.42). And if certain parts of the Hebrew were not translated in that version, this was because the Holy Spirit judged the time not ripe for certain things to be revealed in Greek (18.43). But if that were true in Ptolemy's time, before the birth of Christ, it could not be true in Nicholas's Rome. Surely, now, the Holy Spirit would reveal all truth (cf. John 16:13) in Latin.

Manetti, citing inaccuracies in the Septuagint translation and in Jerome's translation as the reasons for which he undertook to produce new versions of all

[79] Translated by Trinkaus, *'In Our Image and Likeness'*, 580.

[80] Recent discussion, mostly for a slightly later period, is in Rummel, *The Humanist-Scholastic Debate*, chap. 5.

[81] Translation in Trinkaus, *'In Our Image and Likeness'*, 599.

[82] De Petris, *Apologeticus*, xxv. On Valla see Celenza, "Renaissance Humanism and the New Testament," 33–52; and more generally, S. Garofalo, "Gli umanisti italiani del secolo XV e la Bibbia," *Biblica 27* (1946): 338–75; and Bentley, *Humanists and Holy Writ.*

Scripture, said that the Jews claim that the theological errors of the Christians were due to wrong interpretations of the truth in the Hebrew originals (*Apologeticus* 2.62). His attempt has been seen in the context of a new Humanist study of the Bible in his desire to return to original sources, his understanding of philology as a necessary tool, and his interest in the problem of translation (*Apologeticus* 2.64).[83] These may be related to the revived interest in patristic authors: Origen, for instance, believed spiritual progress to be founded on a philological approach to Scripture, through comparison of various Greek versions with the Hebrew in order to establish the text (*Letter to Gregory* 1–2). Such progress was also, he believed, fostered by the study of pagan philosophy, as well as of seemingly unrelated branches of knowledge like geometry and astronomy. But Manetti's approach also finds precedent in medieval biblical scholarship. Smalley's pages on thirteenth-century Hebrew studies show a number of Scholastics attempting new translations from the original Hebrew, culminating in the work of Nicholas of Lyra, an author especially well represented in Nicholas's library.[84] Similar arguments for studying Scripture in the original languages had been made by Roger Bacon in the thirteenth century. Without Hebrew and Greek, he said, it was impossible to understand the idiom, the rhythm, and hence the meaning of the texts.[85] And he asked the pope to set up a commission to revise the Vulgate since the text had been corrupted by insertions and additions. This is also exemplified in the Ptolemy image. Rizzo observed — although only in regard to secular literature — that Nicholas, like Ptolemy, wanted to create normative exemplars for his library.[86] Manetti's image suggests that, just as the Septuagint was intended to be a normative exemplar (which is why seventy translators were employed), so were his own translations. So there was nothing new in Manetti's translation projects for Nicholas; nothing that is, except its purpose. And this we find in the *Apologeticus*. Again, he follows Jerome's lead; the project to retranslate the Bible from the original languages was founded on the realization that discrepancies

[83] On Manetti's own translations of the Psalms and on debates about biblical translation in the early Quattrocento, see Dröge, *Giannozzo Manetti*, 42–64; idem, "The Pope's Favorite Humanist in the Land of Reformation: On the Reception of the Works of Giannozzo Manetti in Sixteenth-Century Germany and France," in *Acta Conventus Neo-Latini Bariensis*, ed. R. Schnur et al., MRTS 184 (Tempe, 1998), 217–24; and Botley, *Latin Translation*, chap. 2 and appendix.

[84] B. Smalley, *The Study of the Bible in the Middle Ages* (Notre Dame, 1978), 338–55; and M. A. Signer, "Polemic and Exegesis: The Varieties of Twelfth-Century Hebraism," in *Hebraica Veritas?*, ed. Coudert and Shoulson, 21-32.

[85] Smalley, *Bible in the Middle Ages*, 331.

[86] Rizzo, "Per una tipologia," 390, 393.

among translators undermined the authority of sacred Scripture in the minds of Christians, and that the Old Testament, in Greek as well as in Latin, was regarded, particularly by Jewish scholars, as lacking fidelity to the Hebrew original (*Apologeticus* 2.75). This sentiment expresses, in reverse, the same idea about authority which Nicholas's aim for the library states in the positive.

The religious implications of the comparison Manetti invites with Ptolemy Philadelphus's great library at Alexandria disclose aspects of the project insufficiently appreciated by scholars. First, while many have observed that Nicholas's library project imported to Rome the bibliophile culture of early Renaissance Florence, characterized by the collection of both sacred and secular, Greek and Latin, works and by being open to the public, it has escaped remark that the Vatican collection, papal and Roman, differed from them in its didactic and religious purposes. Reconsideration of the relation between the Florentine and Roman library projects reveals closer collaboration on these by Manetti and Nicholas and more common features between the Vatican and Florence Cathedral libraries. Next, while the content of the Vatican library has been discussed exclusively with regard to classical literature and its translation, Manetti's image reveals that, for him at least, its conceptual principle was that it gathered in one place all secular and sacred wisdom. From his point of view, the library was not about language but about types of content. It is in this expanded context that Rizzo's intuition — that Nicholas intended to produce normative exemplars (the Quattrocento equivalent of critical editions)—acquires fuller resonance, clarifying by what means books could implement the stated ecclesiological goal. Manetti's new, exemplary, and normative translation of the Bible was the cornerstone of this desired ecclesiological authority. In particular, since the new version would be nearer the truth of divine revelation, the project suggests that Nicholas's Humanism is manifest not only in the acquisition of classical texts, as scholars have long realized, but also in his philological, and therefore historical, approach to Sacred Scripture. Finally, while the comparison with Ptolemy has a long tradition in Florentine bibliophile culture, its meaning in Manetti's biography is infused with cultural and theological ideas drawn from St. Paul's Letter to the Romans and Book 18 of St. Augustine's *City of God* (itself in part a response to the themes of the Pauline letter). The historical exemplar of Ptolemy's library encapsulates Manetti's answer to the problem, newly current in the Quattrocento, about the value of pagan and Jewish tradition for contemporary Christians.

Chapter Five

Manetti's World Through His Words

Most of Manetti's words seem not to pose translation problems. Yet an *ad verbum* rendering often produces a reading which cannot be related to the known physical reality. To interpret his meaning while respecting his language we sought the sources and context of his words. As an example, describing Nicholas's repairs to the walls of Rome Manetti identifies the circuit using names of gates in the Servian, not Aurelian, walls (*Vita*, 26). Since these gates no longer exist, the text seemed to make no sense. Our clue was that Manetti lists them in an order, beginning "at the bottom" and continuing "at the top." If we could establish what he meant by "up" and "down" we might identify the gates and understand why he misnames them. Unexpectedly, investigation of "upper" and "lower" sheds light on whether Nicholas's building program existed in plans or drawings or was a purely conceptual, utopian, or *ad hoc* scheme. In his architectural descriptions, some of Manetti's most distinctive terms are not transparent. Sometimes a term that would seem to mean one thing evidently had different significance for our author. *Intercolumnium* — "between columns" — is one such; "fenestras obliquas," "oblique windows," is another. *Intercolumnium* reveals how Manetti conceptualizes architectural structure and, by extension to *porticus*, enabled us to clarify a much-debated passage about the form envisioned for St. Peter's square. With *area*, instead, we were unsure what physical form it signified. It brought us to how Manetti understood interior and exterior space, and to the conceptually related terms *locus*, *spatium*, and *platea*. In these and other examples, many found in our Commentaries, we were able to identify the kind of literary source from which Manetti took his words: since we suppose he considered these authoritative on architectural matters, we also learned something about his values. In most instances we can distinguish Manetti's way of thinking and writing about architecture from that of Alberti, evidence that Manetti is not Alberti's spokesperson, as has been thought. Clarifying the manner by which Manetti selected vocabulary aids in the interpretation of his content not only in problematic architectural passages but more generally. Understanding his categories of thought, his assumptions about physical reality, and his authorities, we begin to see his world through his eyes.

Upper and Lower

Manetti's words of directions, "upper" (*superius*) and "lower" (*inferius*), are a key to how he envisions buildings and building elements in relation to one another. His description of Nicholas's repair of the walls of Rome is an especially telling example. The account of the walls, identified by gates, begins at the north of the city, describes a half circle clockwise to the south, then in another clockwise movement returns northward and concludes with the fortifications of the Leonine City. His use of "upper" and "lower" in this passage points to some sources used for the *Life* and a criterion for evaluating the actuality of Nicholas's building projects at the Vatican:

> To proceed in our announced order, he quite nobly and usefully repaired the city walls from the Porta Flumentana at the bottom (*ex parte inferiori*) moving towards the east through the Portae Collatina, Viminalis, Naevia, Latina, Capena, all the way to the Trigemina, joining many places with battlements wherever they threatened ruin, across the stone pyramid that stands up against the walls, some miles altogether. At the top (*a parte superiori*) towards the west moving as far as the Hadrianic Mass he had them remodeled very handsomely. . . . He added nothing new from the bridge to the gate of the palace, not just because the walls there looked stout and solid but also because in the construction of the District, about which I shall talk in a moment, he had decided to completely raze and demolish them to enlarge it. Going across the hill almost at its peak towards the south he brought, at great expense, that entire region to wonderful completion with new walls, close towers, and frequent battlements beyond the gate commonly called the Porta Pertusa, and finished it all the way to the region that faces the hospital of Sto. Spirito. (26)

Manetti's identifications of the city gates tell us something about what kind of a source he used, for most of these are not the fifteenth-century names, or the modern names, or even the common classical names, but antiquarian names for the gates explained by Flavio Biondo in *Roma instaurata* (1444–1446).[1] Thus (following Biondo) the Flumentana, actually near S. Maria in Cosmedin, is identified with the Flaminia, now Porta del Popolo; the Collatina is the Pinciana (another misidentification); Viminalis is the ancient name for the Nomentana or

---

[1] Biondo's sources were Livy and Festus Pompeius. For a discussion of Biondo's identifications see C. D'Onofrio, *Visitiamo Roma mille anni fa. La città dei Mirabilia* (Rome, 1988), 102–11; and P. Jacks, *The Antiquarian and the Myth of Antiquity. The Origins of Rome in Renaissance Thought* (New York, 1993), 114. G. Scaglia recognized that some of the ancient identifications proposed by Biondo were adopted by Manetti: "The Origin of an Archeological Plan by Alessandro Strozzi," *Journal of the Warburg and Courtauld Institutes* 27 (1964): 137–59, here 143, n. 26. On the ancient walls and gates see L. De Carlo and P. Quattrini, *Le mura di Roma tra realtà e immagine* (Rome 1995).

S. Agnese; Naevia is the Porta Maggiore (again wrong — the Naevia was near the Aventine); the Porta Latina is the Porta Latina; the Porta Capena is the Porta Appia or Porta San Sebastiano; and the Trigemina is the Porta Ostiensis or Porta San Paolo. Manetti's names also appear in Giovanni Tortelli's entry on Rome in *De orthographia* (1449), another work written for Nicholas (he gives Flumentana, Collatina, Collina, Exquilina, Viminalis, Naevia, Querquetula, Gabusia, Lavernalis, Rudusculana, Rutumena, Latina, Appia or Capena, Trigemina, Aurelia, Fontinalis, Carmentalis or Scelerata, Pandana or Libera, Mugonia or Trigonia, Catularia, and Triumphalis).

Why does Manetti use these names? First, Manetti's source, if not Manetti himself, had fallen into one of the difficulties of imagining ancient Rome. The information on the ancient city given by literary sources like Varro, Livy, Dionysius of Halicarnassus, Festus Pompeius, and Pliny included little in the way of urban description.[2] All these literary sources referred to the fourth-century B.C. Servian walls instead of the late third-century A.D. Aurelian walls, which still stand, and which replaced them.[3] Nicholas, of course, repaired gates in the Aurelian and Leonine, not the Servian, walls. The false assumption that the names of gates recorded for the latter must somehow correspond to portals in the former led to the kind of mistaken identification we find in Manetti and Biondo. Early Renaissance antiquarians did not realize that the gates listed by Livy and others no longer existed. While most of the gates Manetti lists actually belonged to the Servian walls, the great exception is the Porta Pertusa, added by John XXIII in 1411 to the Leonine walls. This exception suggests that Manetti was not copying from an ancient source, in which this gate would not have appeared, but rather from a nearly contemporary text or texts, or a drawing or drawings. Other evidence strengthens this hypothesis.

Manetti is relying on a specific source, and not simply reflecting an understanding common in mid-fifteenth-century Rome, because his contemporaries discuss the walls very differently. In *De varietate fortunae*, begun in the early 1430s, but presented to Nicholas in 1447, Poggio Bracciolini was one of the first to realize that the walls he saw were late antique, and that the ancient walls had been burnt by the Gauls. Using Livy, Dionysius of Halicarnassus, Pliny, and the

[2] Pagliara suggested that antiquarians proceeded on the notion that *Roma quadrata* was succeeded by the administrative and topographical divisions of Severus and Augustus: P. N. Pagliara, "La Roma antica di Fabio Calvi. Note sulla cultura antiquaria e architettonica," *Psicon* 8–9 (1976): 65–88, here 73.

[3] Biondo also knew a fourth-century source, the so-called Flavius Vopiscus, as well as the Regionary Catalogues, but these did not clarify the nomenclature of the gates. That his source was Festus Pompeius (perhaps the manuscript discovered at Speyer in 1436) is suggested by his repetition of an error: the Porta Collina was the gate in the Servian walls, but Festus gives it as Porta Collatina (33L), as does Biondo.

Liber Pontificalis, Poggio attempts to reconcile eyewitness observation of extant remains with information from these literary sources.[4] Of the thirty-seven gates mentioned by Pliny, only thirteen were in use in the fifteenth century, he says: three — the Portuense, Aurelian, and Cassian — enclosed Trastevere. Of the remaining ten, three were walled up: one between the Ostian and Appian, which Poggio thinks was the Capenan; another between the Latin and Asinarian gates; and a third between the Tiburtine and Nomentanan. A fourth gate, opposite the Nomentanan, is in a kind of second wall which runs for fifty feet at that point. This leaves only three antique gates in use on the south bank of the Tiber: the Praenestine, "popularly called the Maggiore"; the Tiburtine, known as S. Lorenzo; and the Nomentanan. All the rest are more recent. Among these are the Flaminian and the Pincian, inserted in walls which consist of public and private buildings.

Poggio's discussion of the walls cannot be reconciled with Biondo's, although both works were written in Rome in the 1440s. Their identifications are entirely different, and Poggio's sense of the walls as the product of historical evolution is less pronounced in Biondo. It is hard to believe that Manetti did not know Poggio's work as well as Biondo's. If he ignores Poggio's clarifications about the relationship of the then existing walls to the walls as discussed in ancient sources, it could be because he wishes to represent Nicholas as restoring the ancient gates of Rome, or because at the moment of describing the gates of the city Manetti referred to a map and not a literary text.

The distance between Manetti's account of the gates and that of Alberti is even greater. In his *Descriptio urbis Romae* prepared sometime before 1452,[5] Alberti refers to the Roman gates by the names used at the time he was writing and not by their ancient names. Sharing Poggio's grasp of their evolution, he says: "no remnants of the ancient walls are anywhere evident."[6] Thus Manetti could not have used the *Descriptio urbis Romae* as his source for the account of Nicholas's repair to the walls of the city.

While the order in which Manetti gives the gates agrees with Biondo and Tortelli, this does not explain his indications of bottom and top, north and

---

[4] *De varietate fortunae*, ed. Merisalo, 99–100.

[5] J. Spencer, *Leon Battista Alberti. On Painting* (New Haven, 1966), 113, dated the *Descriptio* 1431–1434; L. Vagnetti, "Lo Studio di Roma negli scritti albertiani," in *Convegno internazionale indetto nel V centenario di Leon Battista Alberti* (Rome, 1974), 73–110, here 77, dated it to 1443–1445; Jacks, *Antiquarian*, 102, suggested 1452–1453, just after *Ludi rerum mathematicarum*, although in this latter text Alberti comments "come feci quando ritrassi Roma" — probably a reference to the *Descriptio*. The most recent edition dates it to 1443–1450: M. Furno and M. Carpo, *Descriptio urbis Romae. Edition critique, traduction et commentaire* (Geneva, 2000), 98; while a recent monograph on Alberti dates it to ca. 1444: R. Tavernor, *On Alberti and the Art of Building* (New Haven, 1998), 14.

[6] The translation is Philip Jacks's, as also the idea that Poggio's and Alberti's accounts show a similar understanding of the walls: *Antiquarian*, 100.

south. "Upper" and "lower" cannot have topographical significance in describing Rome's gates, and must refer to relative positioning. Julius Caesar had used *superior* for things nearer the origin of an itinerary and *inferior* (really meaning *ulterior*) for things farther away; Strabo uses analogous forms in Greek.[7] But if the choice of vocabulary might be self-consciously classicizing, Manetti is describing not a journey, but a single physical form, most probably as it appears on a map. In what sense could north be the bottom and south be the top, as he describes them, except in reference to the well-established conventions of maps of Rome which have this orientation? This cartographic convention is ancient and not unique to depictions of Rome: the Barberini mosaic at Palestrina, of 120–110 B.C., already places north (the Nile delta) at the bottom and south (Ethiopia) at the top.[8] By contrast, medieval maps, including maps of Rome such as Fra Paolino da Venezia's fourteenth-century example, are oriented with east at the top. But in the fifteenth century, beginning with Taddeo di Bartolo's map of Rome in the Palazzo Pubblico in Siena (1414), south is again at the top and north at the bottom.[9]

Three graphic representations of Rome, all with north at the bottom, were produced in the 1440s or early 1450s: Alberti's *Descriptio urbis Romae*; an illustration to Biondo's *Roma instaurata* known from a copy by Alessandro Sforza of 1474 (fig. 8); and the illustrations in Ptolemy's *Geography*, also based on a lost prototype probably of the 1440s and perhaps identical with the model for the Sforza drawing.[10] Maddalo has argued that the Ptolemy and Sforza draw-

---

[7] R. Dion, "Sur l'emploi des mots *ulterior, superior, inferior, infra* dans les passages du *De Bello Gallico* relatifs à la Bretagne et aux expéditions de César en cette île," *Latomus* 22 (1963): 191–208, here 198.

[8] On the mosaic and the conventions of ancient maps, see P. Meyboom, *The Nile Mosaic of Palestrina: Early Evidence of Egyptian Religion in Italy* (Leiden, 1995); and P. Holliday, "Roman Triumphal Painting: Its Function, Development, and Reception," *Art Bulletin* 79 (1997): 130–47, here 139.

[9] For representations of Rome see S. Maddalo, *Appunti per una ricerca iconografica: L'immagine di Roma nei manoscritti tardomedievali* (Udine, 1987).

[10] For these works, see Scaglia, "The Origin," esp. 139 where the Ptolemy illustrations and the Strozzi plan are said to depend on the same lost prototype; J. Schulz, "Jacopo de'Barbari's View of Venice: Map Making, City Views, and Moralized Geography before the Year 1500," *Art Bulletin* 60 (1978): 425–74, esp. 456, 458 n. 114, where he agrees with Scaglia. Further discussion of maps and views is in Westfall, *In This Most Perfect Paradise*. We are not considering the view in the manuscript of the *Dittamondo* in a manuscript written by Andrea Morena in 1447 because this depends on a 14th-century prototype: H. Stevenson, "Di una pianta di Roma dipinta da Taddeo di Bartolo nella cappella interno del Palazzo del Comune di Siena (1413–1414)," *Bollettino della Commissione archeologica comunale di Roma* 9 (1881): 74–105, here 85. Jacks, *Antiquarian*, 457, thinks the earliest Ptolemy manuscript (Paris, BN MS. lat. 4802) is before 1456 (but based on an earlier, lost, view). The manuscript of the *Descriptio urbis Romae* in Venice (Bib. Marciana, Cod. Ital. CL XI,67, fol. 123v) shows north at the bottom.

Fig. 8. Map of Rome, Alessandro Sforza. Florence, Bib. Med. Laur., Inv. Redi 77, cc VII–VIII.

ings share similarities (including errors) and that they show no influence from Alberti.[11] Nicholas had two works by Ptolemy in Latin and one in Greek; one can be identified as the unillustrated translation of the *Geography* made in 1409 by Jacopo da Scarperia.[12] However, except for the Porta Pertusa (where Manetti also departs from Biondo), all of Manetti's identifications appear on the Strozzi drawing.

[11] S. Maddalo, *In figura Romae. Immagini di Roma nel libro medioevale* (Rome, 1990), 123–34 and 126.

[12] Müntz and Fabre, *Bibliothèque*, 98, 102, 341. Manfredi identified MS. Vat. lat. 2974 as the translated *Geography*: *I codici latini*, no. 661. Ptolemy also wrote other works, such as the *Almagest*, which were fairly common in Renaissance libraries.

Manetti's descriptive terminology for the walls and gates of Rome was most likely determined by the graphic image he looked at as he wrote. Either this was the prototype of the Strozzi drawing, which would show us Manetti consulting Flavio Biondo (who returned to the court in 1453), rather than Alberti (still in Rome), or else it was a related drawing showing, in addition, the gates of the Leonine city.

Now if "upper" and "lower" in his description of walls and gates suggests that Manetti's account was guided by a graphic representation, is it also the case in his description of the Vatican buildings? Describing the Apostolic Palace, Manetti speaks of "the lower part of the palace" (34), and a theater "in the lower part." "A bit higher" than the court beyond the garden wall was the library (35). Then, beyond the library, "towards the north," a court, next to which "on the upper part" were kitchens (35). Again (at 36) "in the upper part towards the west" another garden could be seen.

Magnuson argued that in these instances Manetti's terminology referred to the slope of the Vatican hill, which slopes from west to east and north to south.[13] It is quite true that "upper" and "lower" as applied to parts of the Vatican Palace in the fifteenth century sometimes refer to relative grade level. For instance, the *palatium inferius* north of the atrium of St. Peter's was topographically below the *palatium superius* on Mons Saccorum. In order to determine whether the other sites described as "upper" and "lower" in Manetti's text were actually higher or lower in a topographical sense, or whether this terminology refers to their position on a map or plan, we would have to know their exact locations. Where these sites can be identified,[14] it does seem that in describing the palace "upper" and "lower" are determined by topography. Because the palace had several stories in different wings and wings at different grade levels, Manetti would have had to refer to plans of the different levels. Whether or not these existed — and there is no evidence in this case that they did — plans were not Manetti's primary locators for his description of the palace.

Manetti also applies this terminology to St. Peter's basilica, the site of which is perfectly well known: next to the crossing, he says, "from the upper part" was the tribune "at the highest point" of which was the papal throne (46). To the left of the basilica "a parte superiori" a sacristy was to be constructed (44). In this case, then, the terminology is like that of the city walls: "upper" and "highest" must mean as seen looking at a plan of the building oriented so that the atrium is at the bottom of the sheet (that is, the east).

Was this plan the prototype for Uffizi 20A (fig. 9)? Many scholars now accept that the apse and transept walls shown on Uffizi 20A record a fifteenth-century

---

[13] Magnuson, *Studies in Roman Quattrocento Architecture*, 132.

[14] See Chapter 6.

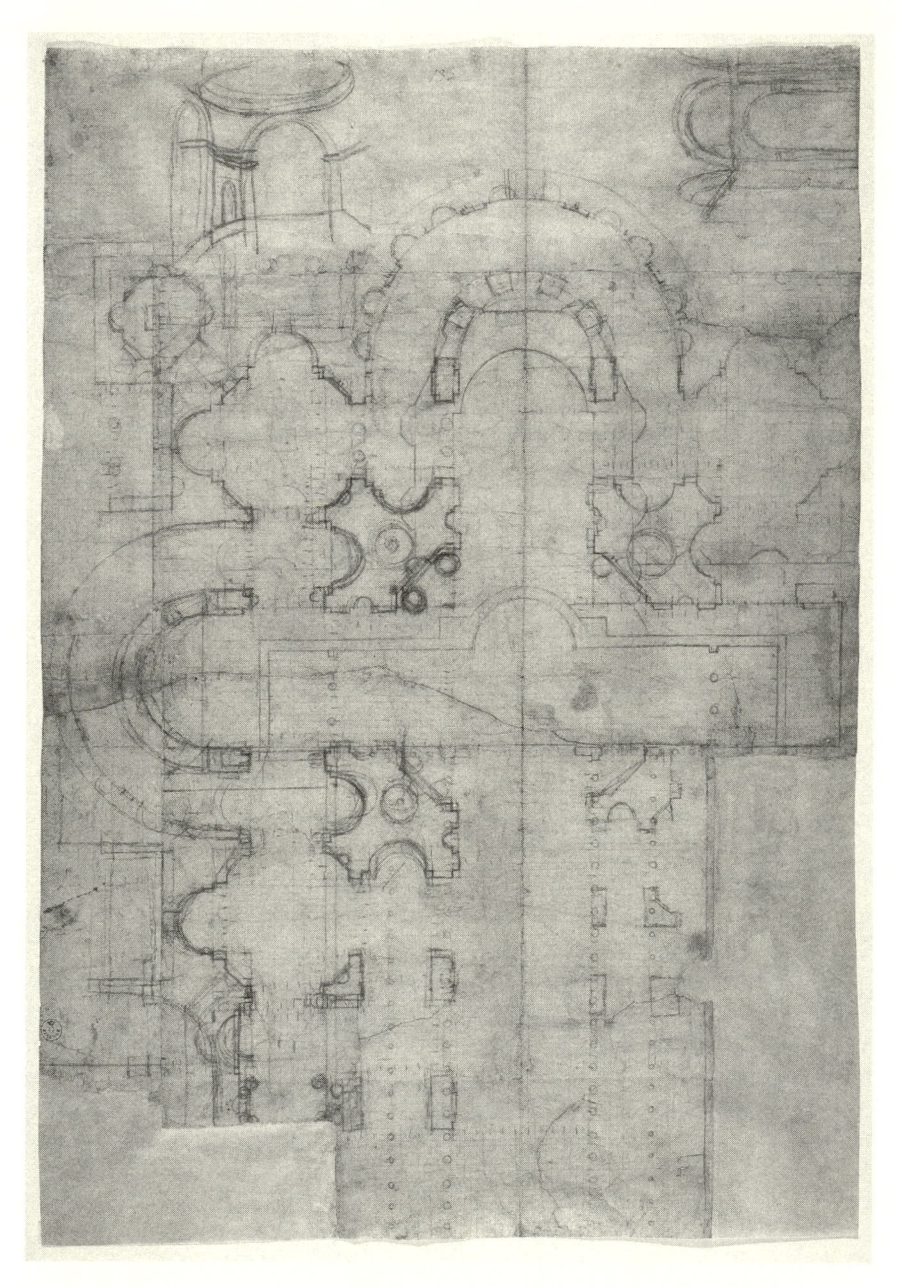

Fig. 9. Plan for New St. Peter's superimposed on the old basilica and perhaps incorporating Nicholas's apse and transepts. Bramante, Uffizi 20 A. Scala/Art Resource, NY

project for St. Peter's, presumably a lost drawing, rather than the remains of Nicholas's project in Bramante's time.[15] Although from the time when Geymuller first proposed it in 1875 until quite recently Uffizi 20A has been the basis for all reconstructions of Nicholas's project, we now know that this (or its prototype) was not the graphic Manetti describes.[16] Whereas the apse wall (the so-called "Rossellino choir") in the drawing is 13 braccia wide, as Matteo Palmieri also described it in the 1470s, its measurement does not correspond to Manetti's account, and the drawing shows more built than actually was, for example in the south transept. While Manetti provides a very detailed account of Nicholas's new choir and transepts in the *Life*, the parts depicted also in Uffizi 20A, his information about the new nave is sparse (44–49). Nonetheless, since he gives the overall measurements of the building, and refers to elements in the transept in the comparative — "above" or "higher" — he must have seen a drawing that, unlike Uffizi 20A, showed the whole edifice.

In the *De pompis*, Manetti uses "superius" to distinguish Florence Cathedral's east end from the nave in a passage where he gives measurements (8), but to indicate height he uses "altitudo" (9).[17] Since Manetti claimed the cathedral was 260 *paces* long (1 pace = 3 *braccia*); Bartolommeo Scala that it was 260 *cubits* long (1 cubit = 1 *braccia*); and Giorgio Vasari that it was 260 *braccia* long (see Commentary 8), it is not unlikely that all three referred to a plan which gave numbers, but not the unit of measurement. Could this also be the case at the St. Peter's project? Scholars have been troubled by Manetti's inconsistent use of measurement. For instance, the platform before the basilica is said by Manetti to be seventy-five *cubits* wide and one hundred and twenty *paces* long (41); the open area before the steps is five hundred of an unspecified unit in length and one hundred *cubits* in width; he then adds that the area would be five hundred *paces* in length (39) but at 49 he tells us it was five hundred *cubits* in length. Is Manetti

[15] Suggested by H. Millon, "Da Nicolò V a Giulio II, da Bernardo Rossellino a Donato Bramante: Timori per l'antica basilica e progetti per la nuova," in *San Pietro. Antonio da Sangallo. Antonio Labacco*, ed. P. L. Silvan (Milan, 1994), 11–13, here 11; C. Frommel, "Il San Pietro di Nicolò V," in *L'Architettura della Basilica di San Pietro: Storia e costruzione*, ed. G. Spagnesi (Rome, 1997), 103–10, here 103. M. Curti, however, suggested that Uffizi 20A is a reconstruction of a hypothetical project, perhaps of that described by Manetti: "L''Admirabile Templum' di Giannozzo Manetti alla luce di una ricognizione delle fonti documentarie," in *L'Architettura della Basilica*, ed. Spagnesi, 111–18, here 115.

[16] H. Geymuller, *Die Ursprünglichen Entwürfe für Sankt Peter in Rom* (Vienna, 1875), 130.

[17] An ambiguous case is his reference to the "superiora loca" where myrtle and laurel were placed (13): whether he means strewn on the pavement of the east end or attached to the upper part of the walls is problematic.

more interested in the numbers written on a plan than he is in the spatial extension which they designate?

The most recent publications on this problem do not think so, taking very seriously the values of Manetti's units of measurement. Reconstruction of Nicholas's project for St. Peter's depends on comparing the measurements of the old basilica with those which Manetti gives for the new. This can be done only if we know the value of his unit of measurement. Manetti's *cubitum*, the distance from the elbow to the end of the middle finger, may be the Latin equivalent of the *braccio*, which means "arm" and is similarly a measurement of the forearm. The metric equivalents of the pace (*passus*) and the cubit are not certain. Whereas for Magnuson, Manetti's cubit equaled the Roman *braccio* (55.8 cm); for Frommel, Manetti's cubit is close to the Florentine *braccio* (ca. 58 cm); while Curti is convinced that the cubit's value is 47.5 cm.[18] Comparison of Frommel's and Curti's reconstruction of Nicholas's scheme for St. Peter's shows the radically different results a 10 cm difference in the cubit's value produces (figs. 10 and 11). In particular, while the larger unit produces an apse similar to that of Uffizi 20A, the smaller results in an east end more reasonably proportioned in relation to the old basilica's nave. Without Uffizi 20A as a model and with the value of Manetti's cubit in question, long-held assumptions about the form of the new St. Peter's are being re-evaluated. Rocchi Coopmans de Yoldi, for instance, noted similarities with the Cathedral of Milan, undoubtedly the largest building enterprise in Italy at the time as well as the most fully gothic.[19] Curti proposed a reconstruction of Nicholas's project which has similarities with Martino Ferrabosco's attempt to visualize it in 1619 (fig. 12).[20] Boccardi Storoni assumed that Nicholas's plan was what is shown on the Ferrabosco drawing.[21] Since we know that Manetti gives measurements of diverse kinds and diverse measurements for the same architectural feature, and since the values of his units of measurement are uncertain, his numbers will always be unreliable evidence for reconstructing Nicholas's scheme. Stylistic analysis and comparison with Nicholas's built work in Rome and elsewhere must therefore be given greater weight and any reconstruction of the rebuilt St. Peter's should be plausible in terms of such criteria.

[18] See the recent discussion in Frommel, "San Pietro," 104; Curti, "L''Admirabile Templum'," 112; J. Rykwert, N. Leach, and R. Tavernor, *Leon Battista Alberti. On the Art of Building in Ten Books* (Cambridge, MA, 1988), glossary, 423. As for the *passus*, Frommel thought it equaled 3 florentine *braccia*, hence 1.74 m ("San Pietro," 104) but Rykwert 1.77 m (*Art of Building*, 423).

[19] G. Rocchi Coopmans de Yoldi, "La fabbrica di San Pietro da Niccolò V a Urbano VIII," in *San Pietro. Arte e storia nella basilica vaticana*, ed. idem (Bergamo, 1996), 71–167, here 76–77.

[20] Curti, "L''Admirabile Templum'," figs. 9, 12.

[21] P. Boccardi Storoni, *Storia della Basilica di San Pietro* (Pavia, 1988), 82.

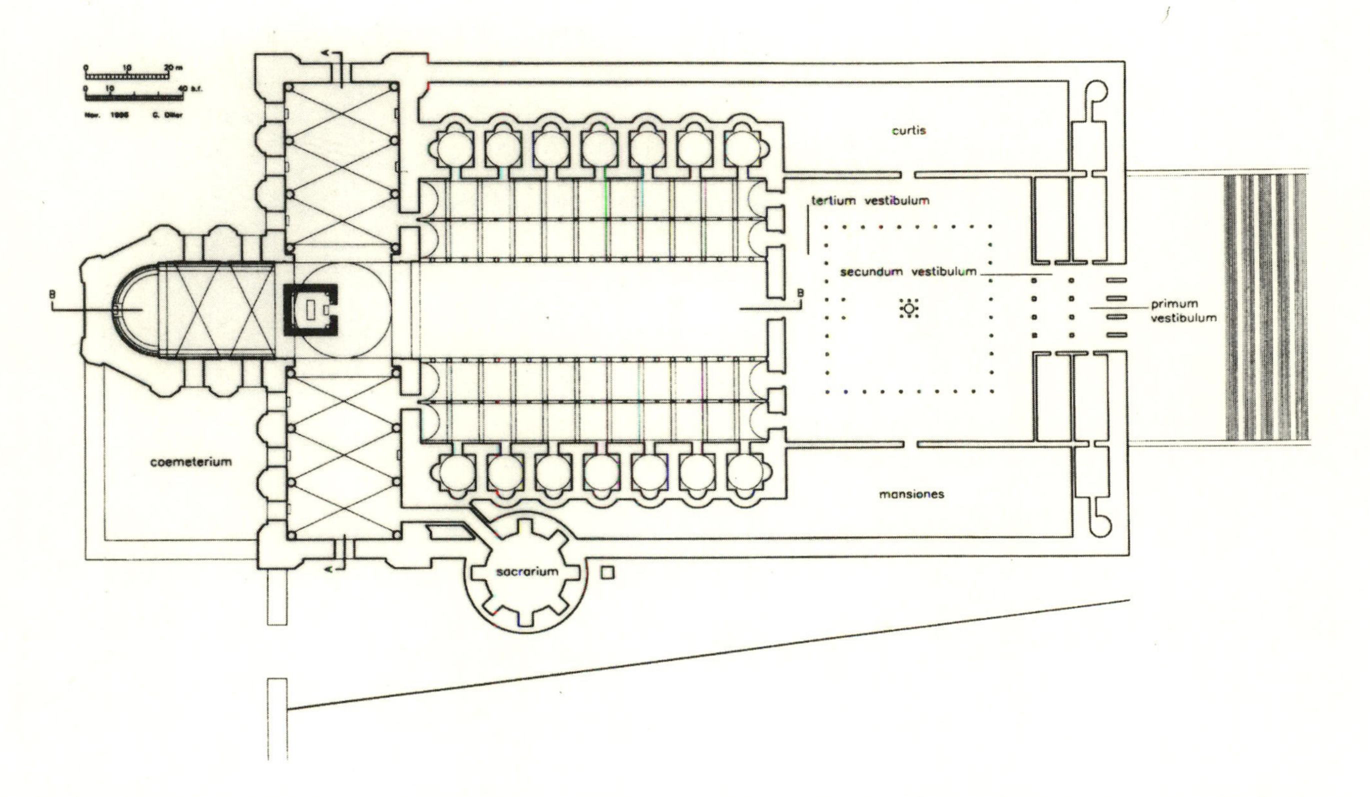

Fig. 10. Reconstruction of Nicholas's plan for St. Peter's by C. L. Frommel, using a 5.58 cm. cubit. From "Il San Pietro di Nicolò V," in *L' Architettura della Basilica di San Pietro: Storia e costruzione*, ed. G. Spagnesi (Rome, 1997), fig. 7.

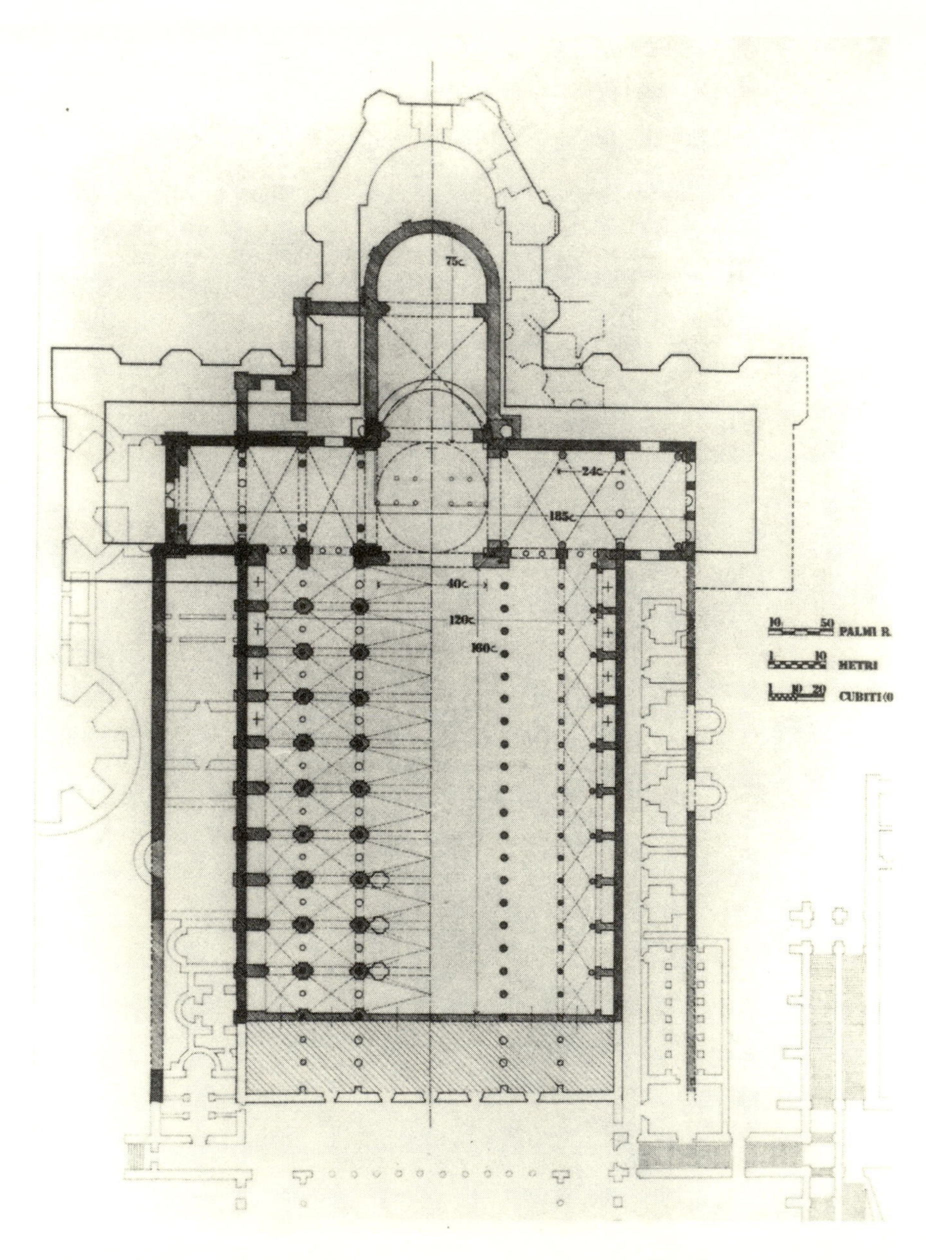

Fig. 11. Reconstruction of Nicholas's plan for St. Peter's by M. Curti, using a 4.75 cm. cubit and shown in relation to Old St. Peter's and U 20 A. From "L' Admirabile Templum' di Giannozzo Manetti alla luce di una ricognizione delle fonti documentarie," in *L' Architettura della Basilica*, ed. Spagnesi, fig. 9.

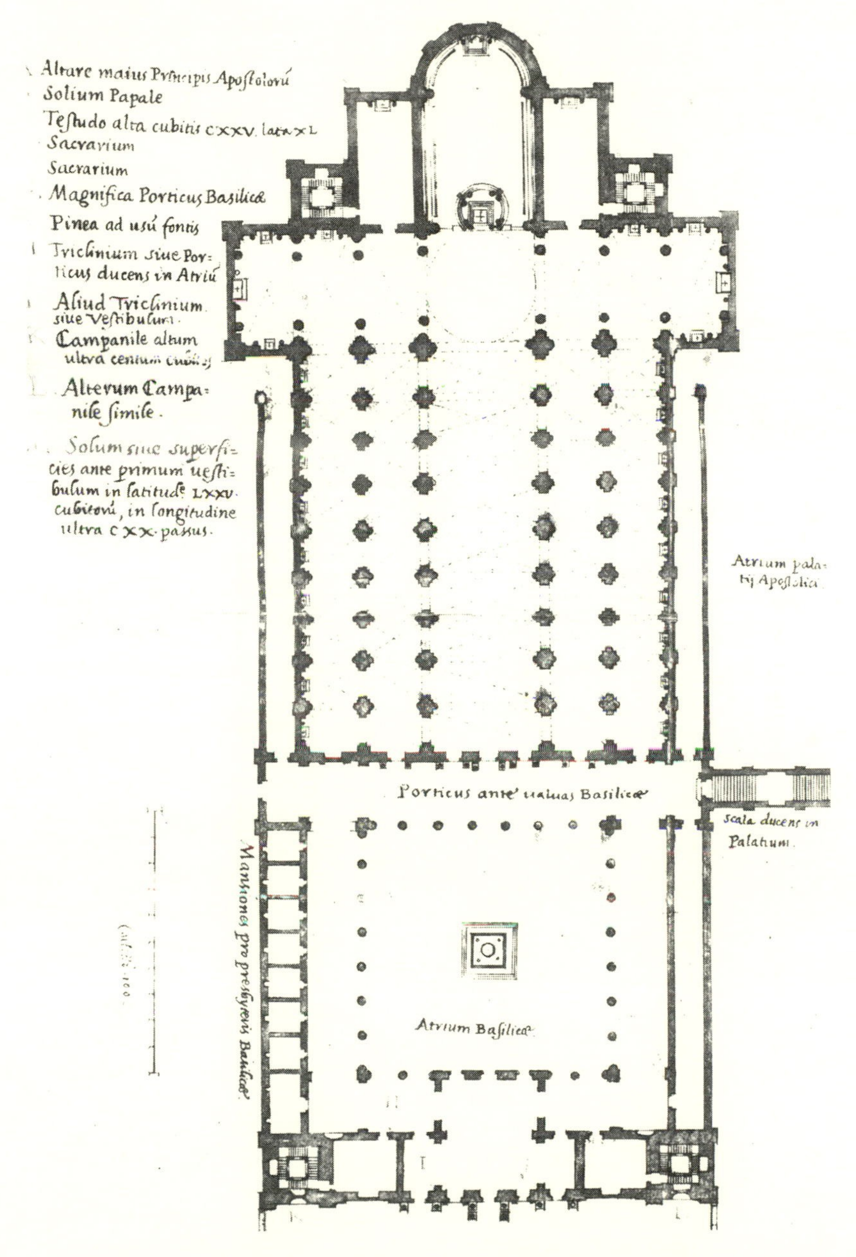

Fig. 12. Reconstruction of Nicholas's plan for St. Peter's by Martino Ferrabosco, published by Giacomo Grimaldi in 1619 in *Descrizione della basilica antica di S.Pietro in Vaticano*, ed. R. Niggl (Vatican City, 1972).

Manetti gives measurements in several different kinds of units, sometimes using units presumably different in value (paces and cubits) for the same thing. The question relevant for reconstructing Nicholas's projects is not what unit of value Manetti uses, since he is cavalier in this regard, but what unit governed the drawings he saw. Unfortunately, an analysis of Manetti's language and culture is not useful in answering this and cannot lead beyond the present state of scholarship in resolving the problem of Nicholas's plan for St. Peter's. If Manetti preferred to express the numbers on a plan in terms of the cubit, perhaps because this is the Scriptural unit of measurement, it would warn us that his description negotiates conflicting aims of factual precision and literary content. Inconsistencies in Manetti's measurements, for instance giving 180, 185, and 184 for the length of the new transept of St. Peter's (45, 49), also might refer to a drawing which provided measurements at different points (such as clear distance and distance including wall thickness) which Manetti consulted somewhat carelessly.[22]

We cannot be certain that Manetti was reading from a plan of Florence Cathedral in the passage giving measurements where "superius" occurs. But we can say that "superius" and "inferius" are almost entirely absent from his eyewitness description of that building, whereas they are frequent words in the *Life* for unbuilt and incomplete structures (the tribune and sacristy of St. Peter's), or structures too large to be taken in all at once by the human eye (like the walls of Rome). The implication is that for these, Manetti wrote his description looking at some kind of graphic representation, quite possibly a plan showing Nicholas's proposed additions and changes. Yet this has always been denied. Westfall was quite definite on this point:

> The project as a whole doubtless never existed in the form of models, drawings, diagrams, explanations, statistics, and analyses, which precede modern undertakings . . . Instead, it existed in the form of a concept that . . . was worked out in detail as time and circumstances demanded.[23]

Mack thought that apart from the new apse of St. Peter's, the whole building program was "just sort of an utopian dream."[24] Magnuson was less certain, but concluded that no models or designs were ever made, "as no contemporary reference to them exists."[25] Only Massimo Miglio, an historian not an architectural

---

[22] Curti analyzes this inconsistency: "L''Admirabile Templum'," 118, n. 19.

[23] Westfall, *In This Most Perfect Paradise*, 183–84.

[24] C. Mack, "Bernardo Rossellino, L.B. Alberti, and the Rome of Nicholas V," *SECAC Review* 10 (1982): 60–69, here 64.

[25] Magnuson, *Studies in Roman Quattrocento Architecture*, 59. E. MacDougall pointed out in her review of Magnuson's book (72) that he had settled the problem of whether Manetti's description was real or an invention by showing its relation to existing conditions, which it would have corrected, and at least some links to payments.

historian, thought that Manetti consulted sources relevant to the projects for his description.[26] Our analysis of Manetti's language supports his view.

In fact, drawings and models were more commonly used in the fifteenth century than was supposed when Magnuson and Westfall wrote. Brunelleschi prepared a model for the dome of Florence Cathedral in 1419; Giovannino de Grassi's lost wooden model for Milan Cathedral was used as a guide by the builders until the mid-fifteenth century.[27] Nicholas, who had spent time in both Bologna and Florence, certainly knew that it was common practice to prepare models. Less is known about the frequency of architectural drawings, very few of which survive from our period.[28] In 1391 Antonio di Vincenzo made drawings based on the drawings or models for Milan Cathedral which then served him for his own project for San Petronio in Bologna.[29] Nicholas might have seen these in Bologna in 1437, when he was involved in building for Cardinal Nicholas Albergati, or in 1444 when he himself became Bishop of Bologna. Alberti wrote vehemently about the need for both drawings and models: in a later chapter, we will consider his views in relation to Nicholas's projects. If Alberti's drawing for a bath, his only autograph plan drawing, were associated with Nicholas's project to renovate the baths at Viterbo or if his reconstruction of Hadrian's Bridge (*De re aed.* 8.6) were part of the renovation of the Borgo, then this practice would be documented within Nicholas's circle of patronage.[30] Filarete, writing just after 1460, tells how

---

[26] Miglio, "L'immagine del principe e l'immagine della città," 322.

[27] A. Cadei, "Cultura artistica delle cattedrali: due esempi a Milano," *Arte medievale* 5 (1991): 83–104, here 104; A. Lepik, *Das Architekturmodell in Italien 1335–1550* (Worms, 1994).

[28] A recent overview of architectural drawing is J. Ackerman, *The Reinvention of Architectural Drawing 1250–1550* (Otley, 1998).

[29] V. Ascani, "I Disegni architettonici attribuiti ad Antonio di Vincenzo. Caratteristiche tecniche e ruolo degli 'appunti grafici' nella prassi progetturale tardogotica," *Arte medievale* 5 (1991): 105–16, here 112; the drawings are in the Archivio della Fabbriceria di San Petronio, disegno M1. Antonio di Vincenzo's drawings were recorded by Cesare Cesariano who reproduced the plan, elevation, and triangulation of Milan Cathedral in his illustrated Vitruvius with the remark: "et questa e quasi como la regula che usato hano li Germanici architecti in la sacra aede baricephala de Milano." See H. W. Kruft, *A History of Architectural Theory from Vitruvius to the Present* (Princeton, 1985, repr. 1994), 68; Cesare Cesariano, *De Lucio Vitruvio Pollione de architectura libri decem traducti de latino in volgare* (Como, 1521), fol. xiiiv.

[30] C. Mack, "The Bath Palace of Pope Nicholas V of Viterbo," in *An Architectural Progress in the Renaissance and Baroque, Sojourns in and out of Italy*, ed. H. Millon and S. Scott Munshower (University Park, 1992), 45–63. But there is no agreement on this. Tavernor argues that the drawing of a bath was for Federico da Montefeltro's palace at Urbino, which would place it a decade or so later; the drawing of the bridge is known only from Vasari, who claimed to have owned it: R. Tavernor, *On Alberti and the Art of Building* (New Haven, 1998), 19, 194–200.

after the architect describes a project verbally to his patron the patron says that in order to understand it he needs to see a "disegno", which the architect then produces.[31] By the 1470s, architectural drawings begin to be common, as do architect's sketchbooks. If Nicholas's project for the Vatican and St. Peter's were real, there were surely drawings and probably models: at issue is not whether drawings were made for the project, but the reality and extent of the project itself. Yet some project did exist, as Magnuson demonstrated by correlating the existing conditions in Rome and the Vatican with payments for work and Manetti's description; and some parts of the project were executed since the Great Tower was built, the Vatican palace enlarged, and a new apse for St. Peter's begun.[32] We may propose that some drawings existed for Nicholas's projects, and that Manetti used these for his description. Indeed, the abundance of measurements he gives for St. Peter's and the Great Tower and the absence of precise figures for the Vatican Palace and Borgo may be indicative of the relative availability of measured drawings. The terms "upper" and "lower", then, probably describe position on a plan or map when they occur in conjunction with measurements or where they are meaningless topographically. But where they occur without accompanying measurements and on a hilly site, as in the account of the Vatican Palace, they record empirical impressions and suggest that graphics were not referred to.

Excursus: Relative Position

The problem of "upper" and "lower" opens up a much broader subject of enquiry, which we can sketch only briefly here. As relative terms, they raise a question very important in the fifteenth century: relative to what or whom? A good example are the terms "left" and "right". In placing statues on the new stairs before St. Peter's, Francesco dal Borgo had put Peter on the left of who goes up and Paul on the right, an arrangement opposite to the arrangement of the two heads on the lead seals of papal Bulls and of the two statues of the apostles on an altar in the basilica. Biondo wrote to Gregorio Lolli Piccolomini (18 and 30 September 1461) showing, on the authority of ancient linguistic example as well as in the composition of the apse mosaic of St. Peter's, that "left" and "right" are established in relation to the person who observes, speaks, or writes.[33] This

[31] *Antonio Averlino detto Il Filarete: Trattato di architettura*, ed. A. M. Finoli and L. Grassi (Milan, 1972), 15:448. The treatise dates ca. 1462.

[32] Magnuson, *Studies in Roman Quattrocento Architecture*, 58–59; payments are in E. Müntz, *Les arts à la cour des papes* (Paris, 1882), now with additions by Burroughs, *From Signs to Design*.

[33] In *Scritti inediti e rari di Biondo Flavio*, ed. Nogara, 202–7, esp. 206. Relative position has recently been discussed in A. Grafton, *Leon Battista Alberti: Master Builder of the Italian Renaissance* (New York, 2000), 262.

understanding is consonant with the assumptions of one-point perspective in painting, and with the more general significance Erwin Panofsky attributed to perspective: the individual subject determines order.[34] Biondo went so far as to suggest that it was determined by the human body: "A person who approached the altar of the Prince of the Apostles in the basilica makes the parts right and left that correspond to his right and left hand."[35] But the question of right and left was resolved in a different fashion by Innocent VIII (1484–1492), as Shearman has shown, defining it with respect to the object or image in question rather than the view of the spectator.[36] This is what Francesco dal Borgo had done with the statues on the stairs of St. Peter's, since Peter was on the right in respect to the basilica, but not to the spectator.[37] The grammar of relative position focuses, in microcosm, value assumptions of two cultures in Quattrocento Rome. One, usually identified with Humanism, privileged the individual spectator, his body, and his subjective experience; while the other, for want of a better term characterized as Scholastic, asserted the superiority of objective criteria. As we have maintained, and as is confirmed by his use of "upper", "lower", "left", and "right", Manetti adopted the Humanist position in the rhetorical apparatus of his writing: this remains true whether he is referring to a map, plan, or landscape.

Once again we find Manetti's usage consonant with Flavio Biondo's. Just as "upper" and "lower" are determined in Manetti's account by the orientation of the object to the viewer's eye, so he guides the reader with the descriptive device of the spectator's point of view. In general, the order of the ekphrasis follows the footsteps of some ideal viewer in that things are described in the order in which they would be encountered. There are also specific kinesthetic indications which permit Manetti to include the impression made on the spectator: "First one would gradually ascend along accommodating stairs into a huge court" (33); "the main atrium of this palace opens here and there widely and spaciously" (36); "from this first vestibule (of St. Peter's), one passes into another similar one," "but before one reaches the doors of the temple" there was the atrium (43).

Maffeo Vegio's description of St. Peter's of about the same date also relied on this device: however, he used it to the exclusion of all others, whereas some of Manetti's descriptive strategies refer to plans and some to spectator experience.[38] This is especially the case in Manetti's description of the Vatican Palace,

---

[34] E. Panofsky, *Renaissance and Renascences in Western Art* (New York, 1972), 42–113.

[35] *Scritti*, ed. Nogara, 204.

[36] Shearman, *Raphael's Cartoons*, 39. The information is drawn from Burchard's Book of Ceremonies of 1488, fols. 124r, 137v.

[37] Biondo explicitly blames Francesco dal Borgo for the arrangement: *Scritti*, ed. Nogara, 202.

[38] *De rebus antiquis*.

where his subject consisted of many tangentially related structures disposed on four different levels (see Chapter 6). In general, those passages in which Manetti uses the kinesthetic device describe buildings which actually exist. Further, while Vegio exploits the periegetic voice as a way of creating a relationship with the reader ("but let us depart this place and come to the left hand section of the basilica's entrance" [4.118]; and "now let us enter the basilica proper" [4.129]), Manetti, instead, invites the reader to accompany the train of his argument, but does not use this language of comradeship in the ekphrasis: "Now at last let us proceed to that admirable and truly magnanimous and most reverent plan for the apostolic temple" (39); and "while I may seem already to have said much about this temple's marvelous structure, it still remains for me to add a few brief remarks on its dimensions" (49).

Area

Manetti uses "area" to designate a feature of urban planning of special interest to architectural historians, a planned open space. One of the *areae* is at Castel Sant'Angelo: "He [Nicholas] was creating a large open area (*area*) in front of Hadrian's Mass by completely razing all the houses that stood between the city walls . . . and the Tiber" (28). From this *area* a route "is arranged on a straight line from that first open area (*area*) to the middle of the basilica's five doors" (28). Later Manetti describes the space before St. Peter's again: "a very great open area (*area*), five hundred in length and a hundred cubits in width, comes into view" (39); and also at 49, "the open space (*area*) covers five hundred in length and one hundred cubits in width."

When Manetti uses the term "area," he does not quite mean "piazza" in the Italian word's connotation of a planned open space with positive qualities such as shape and intentional relation to the structures which bound it. Whereas Manetti locates an *area* by proximate relationship to one or more structures at its limits and often defines its extension in numerical length and width, the *area* itself is not perceived as shaped space. For Manetti, an *area* is the measured or unmeasured extension between significant solids.[39] Classical and late antique usage, for instance in the *Digest*, gives a negative definition of *area* as "a place without buildings in a city," which seems to fit Manetti's text better.[40] That is,

[39] On "area" as geometric extension, often connected to measurement, see *TLL* 2:497, s.v.; also, DuCange, *Glossarium*, 1:375–76.

[40] *Digesta Iustiniani Augusti*, ed. T. Mommsen and P. Krüger (Berlin, 1870), 50.16.211, 2:952: "locus sine aedificio in urbe."

area is defined not by the presence of space but by the absence of buildings, and not as focusing built form around a core of space but as interruption or discontinuity in the urban fabric. The word also appears in Scripture, for instance in 1 Kings 22:10, 2 Chronicles 3:1, and Matthew 3:12: all three instances translated as "threshing-floor" in the Jerusalem Bible but implying (at least in the Old Testament instances) a place of public assembly.[41] There is no clear case in the *Life* where Manetti associates the term with this function. Manetti tells us that "area" is called by the Greeks "platea" (40). Yet he seems to distinguish between the two when he says that Nicholas built an "aream magnam . . . quo catervae hominum in plateae latitudinem egrederentur" (11). It seems from his use at 40 that a *platea* is an *area* which has certain positive qualities, such as amplitude and ornateness, and is thus something more positive than an unbuilt urban space, something in fact approaching a piazza. Both are described as places *through* which people pass and not as places *in* which they gather. In 2 Chronicles, the *area* is the place on Mount Moriah where Solomon built his palace, on the site designated by David. Since Manetti quotes from this passage in the *Life*, comparing the palace and Temple of Solomon to those of Nicholas, we know that he was particularly aware of its vocabulary. His choice of the word "atrium", for instance, seems to be influenced by it (see below). That Manetti prefers biblical words, and especially the vocabulary of Solomon's buildings, strengthens his parallel between Nicholas and Solomon. But it is also a literary device enhancing the dignity of his subject matter, since architecture was, after all, a mechanical art and not yet an appropriate subject for Latin prose composition.

Manetti's architectural vocabulary is different from Alberti's, in whose work we consistently find "forum" rather than "area" for this kind of urban feature.[42] Alberti does use the word *area* to mean: (1) all that is covered by the building; (2) aspects of a locality; (3) the arrangement of the plan; (4) foundations; or (5) parts of the walls above ground.[43] Surprisingly, then, Manetti's vocabulary is more consistent than Alberti's in the use of *area*; moreover, what Alberti at least sometimes means by "area" Manetti calls "solum" (see our Commentary at 31).[44] Despite their divergence in spatial terminology, we will see that Manetti's understanding of topographical extension has affinities with Alberti's cartography and with his understanding of planes.

---

[41] "Rex autem Israhel et Iosaphat rex Iuda sedebat unusquisque in solio suo vestiti cultu regio in area iuxta ostium portae Samariae." 1 Kings 22:10.

[42] See, for instance, the discussion in 7.6 of *De re aedificatoria*.

[43] This is the analysis given in Rykwert's glossary to his English translation of *De re aed.*, *Art of Building*, 420, where he cites the relevant passages.

[44] In the case of the Etruscan Temple Alberti calls the building platform the *area*: *De re aed.*, 7.4.

Excursus: Space

The description of interval, what we call "space," seems to have posed Manetti considerable difficulty, and since his linguistic dilemma reflects issues central in the interpretation of Renaissance urban and architectural design, we will sketch the principles of Manetti's usage in broad outline. One of the novelties of the fifteenth-century understanding of space is the importance laid on interval (i.e. space) as that which reveals the relationship of solids to each other. The development of one-point perspective, in particular, made spectators aware of relationships between objects as perceptible as well as measurable.[45] Thus the new perception of space as significant interval, incipient in the Strozzi drawing (fig. 8), must also have represented a novelty in the lost prototype for that drawing which, we have suggested, was known to Manetti.[46] Although his language does not embody this new way of thinking, he does show some concern with defining spatial relationships between things, by using "upper", "lower", "left", "right" and so forth. He also reflects the new interest in relations between solids across distance in other ways.

By *area*, Manetti conceives of something not yet a piazza, an empty space in a city and/or a broadening-out of a thoroughfare.[47] He envisions neither an ideal Renaissance piazza where "the space itself is a primary object of vision" nor a Trecento piazza where "space is essentially a transparent medium that one looks through to the monument which it envelops," but a third kind of space not included in Trachtenberg's recent analysis of Italian Trecento urban form.[48] Trachtenberg deduced the principles and methods of urban development in Trecento and early Quattrocento Florence from physical and visual evidence, believing them not to be found in written sources if, indeed, ever systematically defined.[49] Our approach is different, concerned not with the urban planning principles of Nicholas's scheme as it can be reconstructed, but with Manetti's understanding of space in so far as it can be deduced from his language.

---

[45] S. Edgerton, *The Renaissance Rediscovery of Linear Perspective* (New York, 1975).

[46] Westfall observed, for instance, that the Strozzi drawing emphasizes the spatial relationships between buildings, especially topographic relationships: *In This Most Perfect Paradise*, 89–90.

[47] Westfall, *In This Most Perfect Paradise*, 113, already noted that Manetti has almost no awareness of urban space or of a "piazza" in the later Renaissance sense.

[48] M. Trachtenberg, *Dominion of the Eye. Urbanism, Art, and Power in Early Modern Florence* (New York, 1997), 150.

[49] Trachtenberg, *Dominion of the Eye*, 157.

How space, especially empty space, was understood in the mid-fifteenth century is fundamental for historians of art and architecture, since any understanding of pictorial, architectural, or urban design depends on it. In a recent work on Renaissance aesthetics Wohl has argued against the traditional opinion that a mathematically correct and coherent image of three-dimensional space was achieved in the fifteenth century.[50] The theory of a homogeneous spatial continuum, and the notion that space and bodies are the same in that both have extension in length, breadth, and depth, are discoveries of the seventeenth century. Thus the aim of Renaissance painters in using perspective, he argues, was the representation not of space, but of relief. Elkins's recent study of perspective makes a similar case, also asserting that the Renaissance view is object-oriented, not space-oriented.[51] The word "space", he notes, first appeared in an architectural treatise in the eighteenth century. Like Wohl and Elkins, Trachtenberg also rehearsed the traditional view, established mainly by Panofsky and Edgerton, and found it not to correspond to observed practice.[52] So in the last decade one of the most fundamental assumptions about Early Renaissance spatial thinking has been challenged in three important books. Yet the implications of these reversals of the traditional view for architectural history have not begun to be explored, although they are even more revolutionary for building than for painting, and it is still assumed that Renaissance architecture and urbanism were concerned with the shaping of space. Whether one reads the solids or the voids on a plan as primary makes all the difference in the world, and we have learned to do the latter, assuming that this revealed the architect's idea. But if fifteenth-century architecture is about planes and solids rather than intervals and voids, we have misunderstood it. While Trachtenberg's study of the perception of architectural solids is an important breakthrough, his subject did not require an answer to the basic question: "Did anyone perceive space as such?" We can answer that question for one Renaissance person, Manetti, through analysis of his spatial vocabulary since the example of *area* asks us whether Manetti conceived of the Borgo as organized by empty spaces — two piazzas and three streets — or not.

Manetti does not describe that positive void, or incorporeal body, which we call space.[53] His understanding of "space" owes something to Aristotle, who in

---

[50] Wohl, *The Aesthetics of Italian Renaissance Art,* 3–4, 88–90.

[51] J. Elkins, *The Poetics of Perspective* (Ithaca, 1994), 23.

[52] Trachtenberg, *Dominion of the Eye*, 151. The older view is in E. Panofsky, *Perspective as Symbolic Form* (New York, 1991), 29ff.; and. Edgerton, *Discovery of Linear Perspective*, 23 ff.

[53] The formulation is E. Cassirer's in *The Individual and the Cosmos in Renaissance Philosophy* (Philadelphia, 1927), 184.

the *Physics* and *Categories* defined "space" as the sum total of all places occupied by bodies (*Physics*, 4.211; *Categories*, 5a.8–14). Aristotle used the term "place" (*topos*) but not a term for space. Manetti understands "place" as "locus", the Latin equivalent of *topos* (see below). Aristotle's theory of positions in space was really a theory of places which did not consider space itself as the homogeneous and infinitely extending if incorporeal body that it came to be understood as in the modern period.[54] Rather, Aristotle defined space as the sum total of all places (*Physics*, 4.211). For the most part Manetti follows Aristotle, conceiving of general space as the aggregate of all the separate places. This results in what seems today a very odd way of describing space. In the *De pompis*, round windows in the upper part of Florence Cathedral light "the individual places [*singula loca*] of the east end" (11); and during the consecration ceremony a cardinal "was carried here and there throughout all the sacred places [*sacra loca*] of the basilica" (31). In the *Life*, the windows "illuminate with their splendor every single place of the long and ample space [*singula queque ampli et longi spatii loca*] lying below that great crossing" (47). And the windows of the basilica illuminated "the individual places of the dome [*singula testudinis loca*] with their light" (47). Interior space, in these Manettian examples, is the sum of individual places. However, space is not, as in Aristotle, just object dependent — that is, generated by and enveloping solids — but it is itself an entity composed of sub-units (places), rather like a bunch of grapes in the discrete nature of each unit, but more like a sheet of bubble-wrap in their horizontal arrangement. Thus his notion of space diverges slightly from Aristotle's definition of place as determined by bodies ("the boundary of the enclosing body around the enclosed body"), and as a quality of bodies (position or location).

Manetti's choice of *locus* for spatial description is unusual and indicates that he is using a technical term from Aristotle. Since we know that he read the *Physics* with Luigi Marsigli in his early study in Florence, we can suggest this formed his understanding of the natural world.[55] But he is not deeply concerned with theoretical physics, as a comparison of the relevant passages in Aristotle's *Physics* and Aquinas's commentary on them (*ST* 1a, q.46. art.1 ad 4) with Manetti's usage makes clear. Manetti, for instance, has no interest in the problem of whether a void can exist; he knows that these authorities concluded that it cannot and he does not admit voids into his view of space. Instead, he is interested in perception, studied in his time as optics or *perspectiva*. He seems to have read Alberti's *Della pittura* in 1436, in which one-point perspective was explained for painters, and he had a second opportunity to encounter Alberti's explanation of the difference between points and lines as understood by mathematicians and by

[54] On this see M. Jammer, *Concepts of Space* (Cambridge, MA, 1954), 15–16.
[55] Voigt, *Il risorgimento dell'antichità classica*, 323.

painters at Nicholas's court since Alberti re-examined the issue in *On Points and Lines for Painters*, written between 1450 and 1455.[56] Another source for Manetti's knowledge of vision, however, seems to have been more influential. Around 1448 Lorenzo Ghiberti assembled the material known as *I commentarii*, almost two-thirds of which is his translation into the vernacular of passages from three medieval texts on vision: the *De aspectibus* of Alhazen, the *Tractatus de perspectiva* of Roger Bacon, and the *Perspectiva communis* of John Pecham.[57] Ghiberti's work was produced in the same intellectual ambient in which Manetti participated during the 1440s in Florence, and it was most probably through the *Commentarii* that he became aware of optical theory. Nicholas owned a copy of Witelo's *Perspectiva*, which Manetti does not seem to have consulted.[58] He does show awareness of another book owned by Nicholas, Roger Bacon's *Tractatus de perspectiva*.[59] Whether he read the original in Rome or only knew Ghiberti's translated excerpts is less important than that his spatial understanding comes from thirteenth-century treatises, themselves derived from Aristotle, which were current in his ambient culture.

Bacon's treatise used Aristotle to develop a science of vision using *On Animals* and *On the Soul* rather than the *Physics*. His translation into Latin of Aristotle's definition of sight ("sense receives the species of sensible things" [*On the Soul* 2.12.424a–424b]) prefers the word *species* for what appears in other Latin Aristotle renderings as *forma*, and Ghiberti retains this in his vernacular translation as "spetie".[60] As we saw, Manetti's vocabulary is especially rich in "spec-" words: he uses *forma* very rarely, and then in contexts in which the Aristotelian source is mediated by Aquinas. This is not the case in describing what he sees. Seeing, we

[56] L. B. Alberti, "De punctis et lineis apud pictores," in *Opera inedita et pauca separatim impressa*, ed. G. Mancini (Florence, 1890), 66.

[57] Lorenzo Ghiberti, *I commentarii*, ed. L. Bartoli (Florence, 1998).

[58] Nicholas's copy is in Müntz and Fabre, *Bibliothèque*, 98; Manfredi (*I Codici*, number 620) has identified it as MS. Vat. lat. 3102. See also L. Benevolo, *Storia dell'architettura del Rinascimento* (Bari, 1977), 1:17.

[59] David Lindberg cites MSS. Vat. lat. 3102, fols. 1r–28r (14th c.); Barb. lat. 350 (14th c.); and Pal. lat. 828 (of 1349) in *Roger Bacon and the Origins of "Perspectiva" in the Middle Ages* (New York, 1996), civ.

The papal court had been a center for the study of optics in the late thirteenth century. Witelo finished his *Perspectiva* at the Curia, as did John Peckham his *Perspectiva communis*. Roger Bacon had sent Clement VII his *De radiis* in the 1260s. See A. Paravicini Bagliani, *The Pope's Body* (Chicago and London, 2000), 197.

Manetti may have seen a copy of John Peckham's *Perspectiva* circulating in Florence while he was there: E. Garin, *Science and Civic Life in the Italian Renaissance* (Garden City, 1969), xviii.

[60] Noted in Lindberg, *Bacon*, 61.

learn in Roger Bacon, is the visual power extending to the visible object (the theory of extramission). Since visible objects must have a density exceeding that of air (1.9.1–4), it follows that Bacon's theory does not recognize the perception of space. Ghiberti's excerpt from Pecham elaborates this point. We see only things that are luminous and colored, and only dense objects have these qualities: since air cannot fix light in itself, it cannot send rays to the eye and thus is not visible (*Commentarii* 3.21.2). Indeed, since all theories of vision up to 1500 whether classical, Arabic, or medieval assume that vision is a relationship between the eye and a plane, the perception of void or space is excluded.[61] Among the twenty-nine sensibles which vision does perceive, according to Bacon (1.1.3), four are especially relevant for Manetti's understanding of space: light, continuity, distinction, and separation. In all but one of the examples of *locus* given above, Manetti says that light illuminates the *loca* in an interior, presumably thereby rendering them visible. Indeed, Bacon explains that we are able to see rays of light because "the air in the window increases in sensibility since it is confined within a clearly bounded figure by the sides of the window and the ground on which it falls" (1.9.1–4). Thus Manetti says:

> Both sides of this temple [St. Peter's], adorned with huge windows facing one another, illuminate with their splendor every single place [*singula queque loca*] of the long and ample space [*spatium*] lying below that great crossing. Round windows, exquisitely fashioned in the form of great eyes, as we have said, ring the whole circuit most attractively, like a shapely crown of windows, through which the sun's rays enter and not only illuminate the individual places [*loci*] of the dome with their light, but also display to all devout spectators a model of divine glory. (47)

Bacon wrote that sight occurs along a straight line (1.7.4) and that its object must be located opposite the eye (1.8.1–3): "Whatever terminates vision is truly visible" (1.9.1–4). This is Manetti's understanding too. But we need to keep in mind that Manetti's is not entirely an account of things actually seen. Rather, for some projects he recounted as if seen buildings which he knew only from verbal or graphic representations. In many cases, his expression of extension is colored by non-visual information. Describing the Borgo, Manetti presents the urban design as two points — the two open areas — joined by three lines, the streets:

> From this great open area three broad and spacious avenues derive, set off from one another, one on either side and the third in the middle, and reach the other enormous open area visible [*apparentem*] in front of the apostolic church. (28)

[61] See D. Lindberg, *Theories of Vision from al-Kindi to Kepler* (Chicago, 1976), passim.

This would seem to be the unique case in Manetti's writing where an open space is said to be visible, and, given what we know of the urban fabric of the Borgo, we can be fairly sure that St. Peter's Square was not visible from Castel Sant'Angelo. Manetti is imagining in elevation what he is actually seeing in plan only. Moreover, each of these streets is described as terminating not in the open *area* but at a specific point, or sensible object, beyond the *area*: at the middle door of the basilica, at the door of the apostolic palace, and at the obelisk, where the living quarters for the canons would go. These points are, as Bacon required for vision to occur, opposite the eye (not at ground level or high up); they have sensible magnitude; and above all, they terminate vision (1.9.1–4). Interestingly, none of the streets is said to terminate at the fountain which we know was in St. Peter's square.[62] Nor does Manetti mention as a visual terminus the obelisk which, he tells us (40), was to be moved "in the very center of the area, aligned with the middle door of the vestibule." Thus the description is not so much an evocation of vista, as Frommel recently suggested, as a definition of point-to-point extension.[63] And in fact, once again Manetti must be describing the elevation of what he sees in plan.

Although Manetti almost never understood space as *figura*, that is, as a shape, his expression of extension may reveal a basic knowledge of arithmetic and plane geometry. In Pythagorean number theory, two points have no extension, but by permitting a line to be drawn between them, extension is created. Space, understood as the extension between two bodies (points), is that which puts them in relation to one another or, in Euclid's *Elements*, as the description of two-dimensional and three-dimensional figures. And this understanding is the graphic analogue to the notion that vision occurs between the eye and the sensible object (two points) across distance (extension). As Ghiberti quoted Alhazen, spatial quantities are understood only as the interval between the extremities of visible bodies (*Commentarii* 3.22.4). This is the understanding of space that organizes the Portolan Charts, maps for sailors which show the direction and distance between two ports.[64] Alberti's *Descriptio urbis Romae*, too, owes much to point-to-point sighting but goes beyond it in subjecting all such points to an

---

[62] On the fountain, which stood in the piazza until its enlargement in 1564, see T. Marder, *Bernini's Scala Regia at the Vatican Palace. Architecture, Sculpture and Ritual* (Cambridge, 1997), 37; C. Thoenes, "Studien zur Geschichte des Petersplatzes," *Zeitschrift für Kunstgeschichte* 26 (1963): 97–145; and H. Grisar, *Roma alla fine del mondo antico* (Rome, 1943), 240, where he suggests it was originally in the center of the space; it was replaced by Innocent VIII in 1490 by one off-axis to the north. However, the exact location of the fountain before 1490 remains uncertain.

[63] Frommel, "San Pietro," 109.

[64] On the Portolan maps, see A. Crosby, *The Measure of Reality. Quantification and Western Society, 1250–1600* (New York, 1997), 97.

overall system of relationships. The linear approach was congenial to Manetti, not only because if a line comprises an infinite number of points extension can be expressed as a segment of it, but also because a line drawn between two points, as on a plan, can be understood as a graphic representation of the act of vision. This understanding recalls Alberti's mathematical exposition of planes in *Della pittura*, where he explains that a line is made up of points joined together in a row; lines woven together make a plane which is "that certain external part of a body which is known not by its depth but only by its length and breadth and by its quality" (1). How, then, does Manetti apply this knowledge?

Although modern discussion of the Borgo project has tended to focus on the diverse nature of the shops which would line the three streets (29), in Manetti's two-dimensional spatial thinking this is secondary to the relation between the paired points: from the entrance to the District at the first *area*, one street is for the pope, his household and his visitors, since it leads to the door of the palace; one is for pilgrims and other faithful, leading to the door of St. Peter's; and one is for the canons, leading to their compound. The defining points, then, are not really the two *areae* but, in each case, the spectator and his destination. The social planning inherent in this urban scheme, expressed according to the Manettian understanding of space, is a by-product of functions generated by St. Peter's: presided over by the pope, visited by the pilgrims, and served by the canons. In the next paragraph, Manetti returns to the streets as three-dimensional volumes and explicates their forms and functions. To use Trachtenberg's terms, Manetti's streets are first of all "paths" and second "places".[65]

Manetti uses the word "spatium" to describe a mathematically measurable plane: the interior of St. Peter's is an "amplo templi spatio" which was to extend one hundred and sixty [cubits] in length to the crossing (44); its width was one hundred and twenty cubits "for almost the entire space" (*per totum pene spatium*) (49); the transept was "made of vaults and arches within a long space [*spatium*] of one hundred and eighty-five cubits" (45). These spaces are always described as having been extended — *extendebantur* — or stretched out — *portendebantur*[66] — word choices which emphasize their planarity. Space is connected to the *solum*, or building platform; perhaps it *is* the plane of the platform: in the Vatican palace area, "in this ample space for building the whole platform [*totius soli aedificandi spatio*]" (34) were gardens and other buildings. We learn from this that the "building platform" is an area prepared or designated for building, but not always a physical object. Above the building platform are bodies which are the object of vision. Again, about the interior of St. Peter's, "in the platform's remaining space

[65] Trachtenberg, *Dominion of the Eye*, 151.

[66] For Manetti's consistent use of *portendere* for *protendere*, see our introduction to the Latin text.

[*soli spatio*] six beautiful and attractive colonnades dominate the view" (44). But solid objects seem to be on, rather than in, the *spatium*: in St. Peter's, "all the pavement of the entire space [*totius spatii*] is ornamented" (47). That is, the pavement is on the *spatium*, suggesting that *spatium* is the boundary or plane of the building platform. Views are afforded by elements seen in elevation and the intervals between them: such intervals are not "spacious" but "ample": the main nave (*intercolumnium*) of St. Peter's "affords a more open view than the ones on the sides both because its walkway is more ample [*amplius*] and because from there the marvelous panorama [*spectaculum*] of the whole temple is more freely visible" (44). It may be that "ample" suggests "capaciousness", that is, the ability to hold many people or objects, and is therefore indirectly related to function.

Spatium may itself be perceived by the senses, although this is more often the case in the earlier *De pompis* than in the *Life*, and in neither is it certain that *spatium* is an incorporeal entity in three dimensions rather than the plane of the *solum*. For instance, the central nave of Florence Cathedral is defined as "the rest of the space [*spatii*] lying in the middle of these same side columns" (9); this "wonderful space [*spatium*] of the east end" is defined by the three tribunes (10); and "in the middle of the space [*spatii*] below" is an altar (10). In the *De pompis*, Manetti invites us to admire the shape of space. We are told that the piers create three naves each "in the form of a ship [*formam navis*]" (9); the form (*forma*) of the human body from the chest to the feet looks "very much like the elongated space [*oblongo spatio*] of our cathedral" (7); "the remaining space [*spatium*], enclosed further down by the perimeter of the east end" (7) resembled the upper part of a man's body. In the *Life*, the human analogy is similarly made with spatial units: the nave is an "elongated space [*oblongo . . . spatio*]" (51); and the transept, the "crucis spatium" (51); while the apse is "the remaining space [*spatium*], enclosed by the circuit of the great tribune" (51). In these cases, space would seem to be defined by its perimeter. However, we should remember that in both usages of the human analogy the figure is "stretched out," "extended" (*porrigitur* [7]; *porrigebatur* [51]) on what Manetti refers to as "in superiori huius templi parte," and is therefore understood as extension. Space, in the *De pompis*, also has a defined perimeter: "the figure of the space [*spatii figura*] below [the vaults of the east end] seems to come close to being a rotunda" (10). And this shape depends not only on outline, but also on proportion: even though the nave is wider than the side aisles, it "still renders perfectly the form [*formam*] of a ship" (9). *Spatium* is a vessel holding light: the crossing dome of St.Peter's had a lantern "so that light is diffused more brightly and openly in every direction throughout the whole space [*per totum spatium*]" (45). In one case only does it seem to contain buildings: the Vatican palace garden is a "space [*spatio*] of a most lovely paradise" in which ("in hoc") there were three buildings (34). But this is a misreading of the grammar and it is, once again, the building platform that is meant (see Chapter 6).

Manetti did not extend this understanding of shaped interior space to the exterior spaces of the urban fabric, which are conceived of as numerical extension between solids. Nor does he use *spatio* to define the open area which we would call "piazza". The *area* in front of St. Peter's, he says, began at the steps of the church and extended (*extendebatur*) five hundred paces to the colonnaded streets. Although the *area* is said to have qualities — it is ample (*amplissima*) and ornate (*ornatissima*) (40) — not the extension, but the view of three-dimensional objects is what elicits aesthetic experience. The porticoed streets are "speciosorum omnium spectaculorum visu pulcherrimum specimen" ("an exemplar most beautiful to see of all lovely visual delights" [39]). Once again Manetti's linguistic practice is consonant with thirteenth-century optical theory. Visible distance, continues Pecham in Ghiberti's translation, is understood not by sight, but by reason, and is deduced either from the size of bodies distributed in spatial extension or by measurement (3.21.13).

In conclusion, Manetti understands *spatium* as a magnitude but not a body, consonant with Aristotle's distinction between the two: if a magnitude is divisible one way it is a line, if two ways a surface, and if three a body (*On the Heavens* 1.1.268a). For him, space is a question of lines and surfaces which have extension and are sometimes figures; but perceptible bodies are three-dimensional solids. This understanding is fundamental for our next topic, for, as Manetti does not perceive voids, he does not recognize the spaces between columns.

Intercolumnium

Manetti's primary meaning for *intercolumnium* is a series of vertical supports together with the space between them, whether as a free-standing row of columns, as piers dividing the aisles in a church, or as the front facade of a portico. Thus he describes the nave of St. Peter's as having "six beautiful and attractive colonnades [*intercolumnia*] . . . facing each other in alignment, three on each side" (44). Manetti also uses *intercolumnium* in a second sense, to mean the aisles of a church — that is, the space between two colonnades — although he also calls this the *ambulatio*.

The term *intercolumnium* is rare, and therefore Manetti's source should be traceable. In the *Ad Herennium*, the work on rhetoric most familiar in Manetti's time,[67] the author gives as examples of backgrounds which can be used for artificial memory "aedes, intercolumnium, angulum, fornicem et alia" (3.16.29). Given Manetti's understanding of space, he would have assumed that these were

[67] The *Ad Herennium* was wrongly attributed to Cicero in the Renaissance.

all solids: a house, a colonnade, a corner, and an arch (or vault). The void between two columns, which is what an *intercolumnium* is (*intercolumnium* appears in Cicero at least twice in this sense),[68] would not be an entity for Manetti. However, this did not exclude the possibility that a space between two colonnades could be an *intercolumnium*. A likely source for this alternative meaning is John of Genoa's *Catholicon*, of which Nicholas had three copies and which must have been popular since its *editio princeps* is very early, dating to 1460.[69] In his commentary on the base of the bronze Ocean in 3 Kings 7:31 ("et media intercolumnia quadrata non rotonda"), John defines *intercolumnia* as "that which is placed between columns, the space which divides them."[70] Thus in Manetti's usage, while the nave of St. Peter's consists of six *intercolumnia*, the central aisle is the "medium intercolumnium" (44). These spaces are extensions from the sides of the colonnades: at Florence Cathedral, "huge stone columns . . . seem to create three naves [or 'ships'] for each intercolumniation splendidly presents from each side the form of a ship" (9); in St. Peter's, the six *intercolumnia* rendered "these five lateral spaces into the form of a ship" (44). The *intercolumnium* is counted by the solids and not by the voids: thus each arm of the transept of St. Peter's had a colonnade (*intercolumnium*) with eight columns (45). Since we presume each transept to have had two colonnades of four columns each, the term, again, also means aisle. In so far as Manetti understood an *intercolumnium* to be a series of points joined together, or two such series defining the interval between them, this term reveals the same understanding of space that we examined above.

Vitruvius also uses "intercolumnium" to mean spaces between columns in a colonnade, but elaborates it as "intercolumniation" to be part of the system of proportions of the Orders (*Ten Books on Architecture*, 3.3; 4.4; 4.8; 5.1; 5.9). Alberti's usage follows Vitruvius. In his architecture treatise he tells us that "in porticoes along the sides of temples the columns should be as far from the wall as they are from each other" ("columnae a parietibus cellae spatio distabunt intercolumnii").[71] Later in the same text we learn that the intercolumniations should

---

[68] Cicero, *Against Verres II*, 1.19.51: statues were "nuper ad omnes columnas, omnibus etiam intercolumniis"; *Ad Quintum Fratrem III*, 1.5: ivy was planted "qua intercolumnia ambulationis."

[69] Johannes Januensis, or Johannes Balbi, was a Dominican who died in 1298. The *Catholicon*, written in 1286, was published in Paris and Mainz in 1460, Venice in 1487, and Lyons in 1514. For Nicholas's copy, see Müntz and Fabre, *Bibliothèque*, 100; and Manfredi, *Codici latini*, numbers 635, 636, and 637, now MSS. Vat. lat. 1474, 1472, and 1473.

[70] "illud quod ponitur inter columnas, spatium quod dividit eas": C. Du Cange, *Glossarium mediae et infimae latinitatis* (repr. Graz, 1954) s.v. "intercolumnium."

[71] L. B. Alberti, *De re aedificatoria*, ed. G. Orlandi (Milan, 1966), 7.5, 557.

be uneven in number and that they must be in proportion to the thickness of the column (*De re aed.*, 7.5). In all these cases, *intercolumnium* means the intervals between columns, not the columns and intervals together or the intervals between colonnades, as in Manetti. Although Manetti owned a copy of Vitruvius and knew Alberti, they are not the sources for *intercolumnium* in his work.[72] Moreover, he displays virtually no interest in the Orders or their proportions. For him, an *intercolumniation* always includes both solids and voids, and, except for the two cases where he means "aisle", the emphasis is on the solids.

Magnuson suggested that while Manetti usually (in his view, erroneously) means "colonnade", he also uses *intercolumnia* and *porticus* as interchangeable terms and that this was "characteristic of Manetti's rather arbitrary use of architectural vocabulary."[73] But in fact these are two different things for our author. His idea of the relationship between a *porticus* and an *intercolumnium* might come from Jerome's commentary on Ezekiel 12:17–19 where Jerome confronts the Vulgate version, translated from the Hebrew, with a Latin translation of the Septuagint, that is, Greek, version. Where the Septuagint had: "And he brought me into the inner court, and, behold, there were chambers, and peristyles (*peristula*) round about the court, thirty chambers in the peristyles (*en tois peristulois*)," Jerome translated "Et introduxit me in atrium interius, et ecce thalami et intercolumnia atrii per circuitum, triginta thalami inter columnas."[74] Although the Greek "peristyle" could mean "porticoes", Jerome seemed to think that the *intercolumnia* were colonnades, between the columns of which (*inter columnas*) there were chambers. This closely parallels Manetti's statement that in the Borgo there were shops in the porticoes behind the colonnades:

> These three streets are furnished with six colonnades [*intercolumniis*] in such a way that they form six continuous porticoes [*porticus*], two facing each other on each street, with great beauty and utility since the miscellaneous shops of the various tradesmen are built near the living quarters of the homes above them. (29)

It is not clear that Manetti meant to associate the Borgo with the court outside the temple in Ezekiel's vision — although once again we note a preference for vocabulary associated with the Temple; he may simply have remembered Jerome's term because the passage poses a problem of translation. What the problem was

[72] Cagni, "I codici," 42. Manetti's copies were MSS. Vat. Pal. lat. 867, which contains Vitruvius 2, 8, 10 and 11 and Pal. lat. 1562 with 130 folios. See S. Schuler, *Vitruv im Mittelalter* (Cologne, 1999), 360, 380.

[73] Magnuson, *Studies in Roman Quattrocento Architecture*, 72, 184.

[74] Jerome, *Commentariorum in Hiezechielem libri XIV*, ed. F. Glorie, CCSL 75 (Turnhout, 1964), 568.

becomes evident by confronting Jerome's translation in the *Commentary* with his translation in the Vulgate, where he gives: "Et eduxit me ad atrium exterius, et ecce gazophylacia, et pavimentum lapide stratum in atrio per circuitum, triginta gazophylacia in circuitu pavimenti." Thus the Hebrew word rendered as "peristyle" by the Septuagint was translated as "pavement" by Jerome. As a Hebrew scholar himself charged with the translation of the Bible, Manetti would have been interested in this passage. And it is interesting that he rejects the authority of the Vulgate in this case, preferring other sources. Manetti undoubtedly consulted exegetical aids for the meaning of *intercolumnia*. One of these may have been Josephus, who says that in the court outside the temple "the figure of which was that of a quadrangle," Solomon "erected for it great and broad porticoes (στοάς)" (*Jewish Antiquities*, 8.9).

We saw that Manetti described the structures lining the streets of the Borgo as having six colonnades forming six continuous porticoes: people would be able to walk "sub porticibus" (29). Here *intercolumnia* are clearly different from porticoes. The same distinction is made in describing the first courtyard of the palace, which was built "with colonnades and porticoes" (*cum intercolumniis et porticibus*) (33). For Manetti, an *intercolumnium* is essentially a facade with apertures; a portico, instead, is a covering which creates a roofed space — something you can walk beneath and in which there may be rooms. A similar usage occurs in the description of the atrium of St. Peter's: "at the sides of each portico [*porticus*] two colonnades [*intercolumnia*] facing one another were inserted" (43); "from the left portico [*porticu*] . . . rooms are built. . . . Intersecting these two colonnades [*intercolumniorum*], a third colonnade [*intercolumnium*] extends between the two porticoes just mentioned. On top of this huge arches are sprung for the third vestibule of the temple" (43). Again, the *intercolumnium* is a facade, a wall with apertures or a screen, and the roofed space behind them is the portico or, at the entrance to the church, a vestibule.

Alberti does not share Manetti's architectural conception of the portico, considering the columnar facade to be a perforated side of a four-sided structure: "The portico, by definition, consists of one continuous, complete wall only, the other sides being perforated with openings" (*De re aed.*, 7.5 [199]). The very same porticoed road running from Castel Sant'Angelo to St. Peter's which formed the basis for Manetti's description of the paired colonnades fronting roofed porticoes, Alberti described as "protected by a portico of marble columns and lead roofing" (*De re aed.*, 8.6 [261]). It may be that what Manetti calls an *intercolumnium*, Alberti calls a *columnatio* (*De re aed.*, 7.6), comprising a pedestal, base, column, capital, beam, frieze and cornice, that is, both the load and the load-bearing elements of the Orders in elevation.

Manetti's most troubling use of *intercolumnia* occurs in defining the juncture between the *area* in front of St. Peter's and the Borgo, in a passage we examined above for other reasons: the *area* "extends, as I said, a full five hundred paces in length all the way to the exceptional and ennobled colonnades [*intercolumnia*], upon which [*super*] the three porticoes [*porticus*] of the district just discussed were supported" (39). Manetti's meaning here has long vexed scholars. In order to make sense of this sentence, Magnuson suggested that "porticus" be translated as "arches": only thus would it make sense for the porticoes to be supported on the colonnades, as the sentence grammar unequivocably requires. He rendered the meaning as: "each of the three streets was to have entered the piazza through an archway."[75] MacDougall, instead, translating "super" as "beyond", proposed that the *area* was bordered along its east side by a colonnade, beyond which were the porticoes of the three streets.[76] This solution was adopted by Westfall, who described "a facade of the piazza with colonnades that recall those of the three streets leading through the Borgo."[77]

But in fact Manetti's sentence is perfectly consistent with his usual descriptive vocabulary as we have analyzed it, and exactly parallels his terminology in the account of the atrium of St. Peter's where he said that on top of the third *intercolumnium* arches were to be sprung for the vestibule (43). Manetti always gives the element at ground level first: here, colonnades. Since colonnades support diverse architectural elements, he then distinguishes them by what they support (a portico or a vault) or how they relate to other colonnades to divide or define space. In this case, then, the open space in front of St. Peter's ended at the colonnades, the ones which support porticoes along the streets of the Borgo. The problem is not terminological, but comes from a confusion between plan and elevation. Manetti had first told us that there were to be six porticoes, two facing each other on each street (29). This means that they would have covered sidewalks flanking the street and been attached to the house and shop facades. But at 39 he says that there were only three porticoes, meaning that the roads rather than the sidewalks were covered. In each case the number and even the placement of colonnades is the same, and that must be what Manetti saw on the plan: a row of dots, representing columns at ground level. Once again an error in the text reveals the existence of graphic images made for the building projects, and suggests that what is fictional is not the reality of the building program but Manetti's attempt to describe the visual impression in elevation of elements which he knew only from two-dimensional depictions. And this itself is extraordinary, for we have little or no other evidence that someone other than an architect was able to do this in the mid-fifteenth century. Yet if Manetti could infer elevations from such plans, at least Nicholas, for whom they were made, must also have done so.

---

[75] Magnuson, *Studies in Roman Quattrocento Architecture*, 72.

[76] MacDougall, review, 73.

[77] Westfall, *In This Most Perfect Paradise*, 113.

Chapter Six

The Vatican Palace

Manetti refers to the Vatican Palace — that complicated aggregation of structures — as a labyrinth, albeit a "lovely and well-marked" rather than an "entangled and involved" one (37) (fig. 13).[1] In his day, nomenclature defined it as having two main parts. The *palatium inferiore* had grown out from the north arm of St. Peter's' atrium probably in the ninth century although it appears in documents first in 1367–1370. The *palatium superiore*, where the episcopal reception halls and residence were, had been established by Innocent III (1198–1216) on the Mons Saccorum some 16 m higher up, and expanded by Nicholas III (1277–1280) who built a new wing with a suite of rooms and loggia east of, and almost perpendicular to, the earlier core and a west block (or its upper story) with the main reception hall — the *aula prima* — perpendicular to St. Peter's.[2] The sloping site of the Mons Saccorum, an eastern spur of the Vatican Hill, favored a north/south orientation of the east and west wings of the upper palace, straddling the crest of the spur. The upper palace on the spur and St. Peter's on its artificial platform were separated by the lower palace in the declivity between the two. The platform of Old St. Peter's was some 30 meters above sea level; the piazza before the basilica was about 20 meters asl; the site of the present Cortile di San Damaso on the crest of Mons Saccorum at 38.8 meters asl; and the present Cortile di Belvedere, in a valley north

[1] On the labyrinth as a metaphor, see the Commentary at 37.

[2] On the development of the Vatican Palace, see F. Ehrle and H. Egger, *Der Vatikanische Palast in seiner Entwicklung bis zur Mitte des XV. Jahrhunderts* (Vatican City, 1935); *Il Palazzo Apostolico Vaticano*, ed. C. Pietrangeli (Florence, 1992); K. Steinke, *Der mittelalterlichen Vaticanpaläste und ihre Kapellen: Baugeschichtliche Untersuchung anhand der schriftlichen Quellen* (Vatican City, 1984); A. M. Voci, *Nord o sud? Note per la storia del medioevale Palatium Apostolicum apud Sanctum Petrum e delle sue cappelle* (Vatican City, 1992); D. Redig de Campos, *I Palazzi Vaticani* (Bologna, 1967); idem, "Di alcune tracce del palazzo di Niccolò III," *Rendiconti della Pontificia Accademia di Archeologia* 18 (1941–1942): 71–84; idem, "Testimonianze del primo nucleo edilizio de'palazzi Vaticani e restauro delle pitture delle stanze della 'Bibliotheca Latina' e della 'Bibliotheca Graeca'," in *Il restauro delle aule Niccolò V e di Sisto IV nel Palazzo Apostolico Vaticano* (Vatican City, 1967), unpaginated; idem, "Les constructions d'Innocent III et de Nicholas III sur la colline Vaticane," *École Française de Rome, Mélanges d'archéologie et d'histoire* 71 (1959): 359–76; and idem, "Bramante e il Palazzo Apostolico Vaticano," *Pontificia Accademia Romana di Archeologia. Rendiconti* 43 (1970–1971): 283–99.

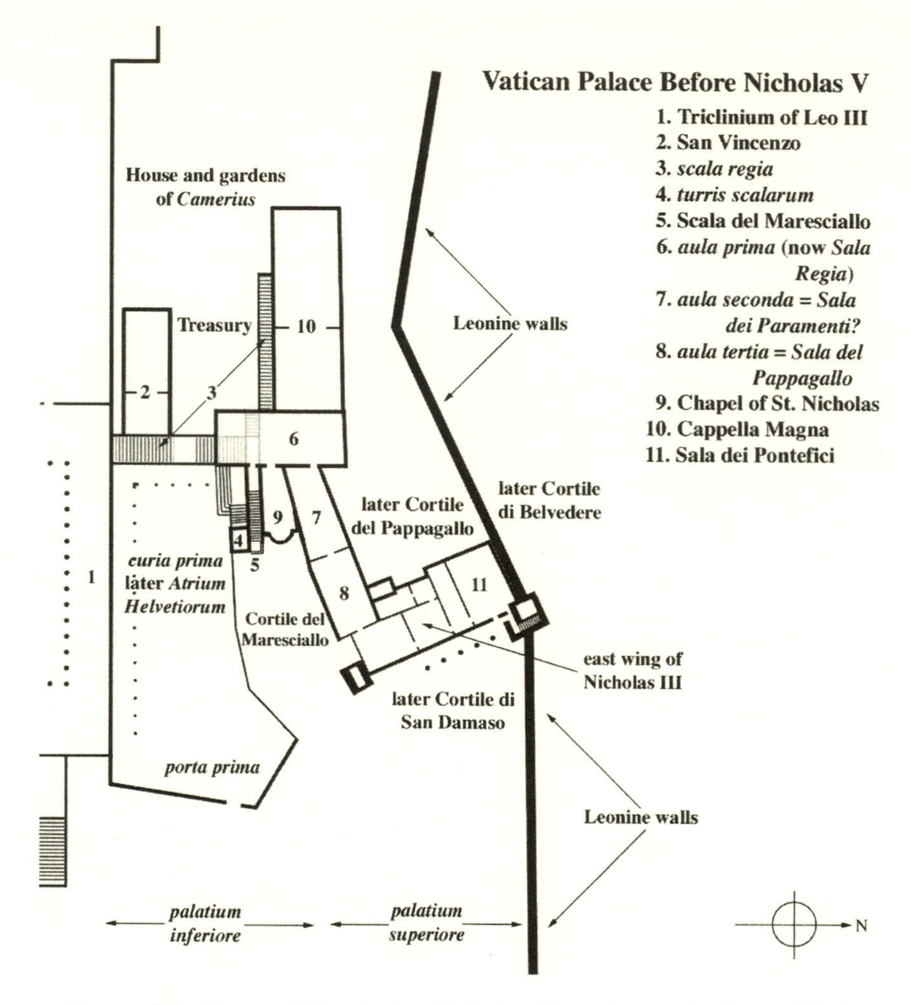

Fig. 13. The Vatican Palace before Nicholas. Digital image by Steven Wolf.

of the Mons Saccorum, at 27 meters asl.[3] Disjunctions in level between the upper and lower palaces, and between the different wings of the upper palace, resulted in disparities in the number of stories throughout the complex and difficulties in

[3] E. Josi, in *Enciclopedia cattolica* (1954), s.v. "Vaticano," 12:1054; Voci, *Nord o sud*, 28. Later construction makes it impossible to know the exact grade quotients for the Vatican Palace in the fifteenth century, and the figures cited are intended as rough indications.

communication between them. The regularization of grade level and provision of better access by stairways would be essential to Nicholas's renovation.

Without exception, scholars have assumed that most of the buildings Manetti describes in his section on the Vatican Palace complex (33–38) were new structures, of which only a westward extension of the east wing from its north end and some fortifications were actually built.[4] Work involving renovation or modernization of existing structures in the palace under Nicholas has been related to Manetti's account, but seen as secondary to the new structures planned.[5] Magnuson, for instance, having matched Manetti's account of the palace with what was there, concluded that Nicholas's plan much enlarged the old palace, especially with the addition of new buildings.[6] Of course, some of the physical evidence of the palace in Nicholas's time is irretrievably lost, especially in the area immediately north of the basilica (the *palatium inferiore*), but also in the *palatium superiore* where major rebuilding in the sixteenth and seventeenth centuries has altered or erased it. Supplementary information gleaned from contemporary pictorial sources and sporadic documentation leaves many elements conjectural. Even so, recent research on the medieval palace and its transformation in the following century enables us to compare Manetti's account to the site as it was during Nicholas's pontificate with a greater precision than was previously possible.[7] Matching structures known from the now available documentary and archeological evidence with Manetti's account illuminates the locations and nature of Nicholas's planned interventions in unexpected ways. Especially useful for this analysis is the most accurate and detailed plan of the palace before major renovation, a drawing from Bramante's workshop, dating to 1505–1507 and probably by Antonio del Pellegrino, Uffizi 287A (fig. 14). Although the extent to which the large drawing represents the actual state of the palace complex as opposed to Bramante's plan for its renovation is debated, it contains precious information about the palace before the major rebuilding projects of Julius II and his successors and supplies a visual complement to Manetti's verbal account.[8] Areas not on

---

[4] Recently, C. L. Frommel, "Il San Pietro di Niccolò V," in *L'Architettura della basilica*, ed. Spagnesi, 103–10, 120.

[5] On this, see especially Redig de Campos, "Testimonianze."

[6] Magnuson, *Studies in Roman Quattrocento Architecture*, 126–41.

[7] For instance, the bibliography cited in notes 2, 4, and 11, some of which was not available to either Magnuson or Westfall.

[8] Magnuson also realized its usefulness and referred to it in his discussion of the project: *Studies*, 124–41. More recently, Frommel suggested that in instructing Bramante to enlarge and reorganize the Palace, Julius II based his ideas on Nicholas V's project: C. L. Frommel, "Il Palazzo Vaticano sotto Giulio II e Leone X: Strutture e funzioni," in *Raffaello in Vaticano*, ed. C. Pietrangeli (Milan, 1984), 118–35, here 122.

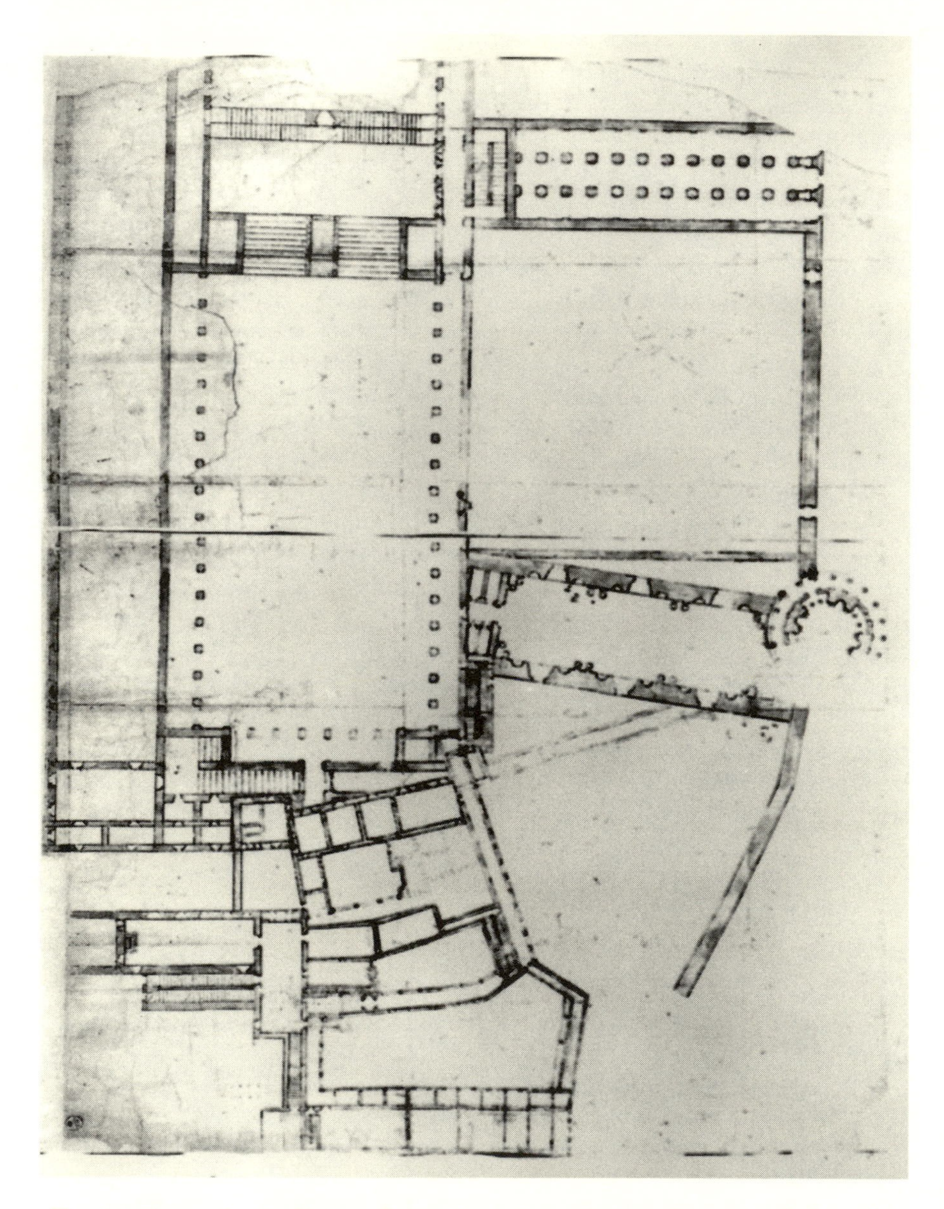

Fig. 14. Project for the Vatican Palace from the workshop of Antonio da Sangallo (Antonio del Pellegrino?), Uffizi 287 A.

the plan or known from other sources, especially ancillary structures north and west of the palace, remain hypothetical. But the evidence which does exist suggests that Nicholas's ceremonial rooms were, except for the north wing, not new constructions but renovations of existing rooms in the extant palace.

Nicholas's project for the palace has not been recognized as consolidation and improvement rather than expansion because of Manetti's architectural terminology — "theatrum" and "atrium" have not seemed applicable to any then existing Vatican buildings — and because a crucial sentence in his description seems to locate a "theater," "atrium," and "chapel" in the garden (34). Scholars' understanding of the building types Manetti mentions has been largely determined by Vitruvius's and Alberti's terminology:[9] since there was no "theater" in the palace as these authors use that term, it seemed that new structures were meant. Nor are Manetti's the usual terms in contemporary or earlier sources referring the medieval palace. Compounding the problem of Manetti's terminology is the unity and ideality of his account: it seemed impossible that he would describe the status quo. Thus the most recent visualization of Nicholas's project for the palace (fig. 15) continues to posit entirely new structures in previously unbuilt areas, reaffirming an established assumption that this is the right approach.[10] Manetti's terminology does not follow Vitruvian or Albertian usage, as has been shown in other instances, but derives instead from other contexts peculiar to his culture and interests. Identifying the sources, and therefore the meaning, of Manetti's terms and comparing his account of the palace project to what we know was there shows that a high percentage of what he describes already existed in much the form that he says.

Fortifications

The key to Nicholas's palace project was defense and security, as he himself made clear in his deathbed speech (T17–18) and as did Manetti by beginning his account of the palace with the Great Tower (31). That is where we also will begin.

The ninth-century Leonine fortification had enclosed the Vatican area with a wall some three kilometers long, between 1.5 and 2.5 m thick and 7–8 m high

[9] In Linda Pellecchia's excellent article on the interpretation of "atrium" in the Renaissance, for instance, she never encountered the usage we will show to be Manetti's, probably because she did not consider the kinds of sources he relied upon: "Architects Read Vitruvius: Renaissance Interpretations of the Atrium of the Ancient House," *Journal of the Society of Architectural Historians* 51 (1992): 377–416. Westfall, however, recognized that Manetti did not intend a "theater" as a place for the performance of drama: *In This Most Perfect Paradise*, 153.

[10] Frommel, "San Pietro."

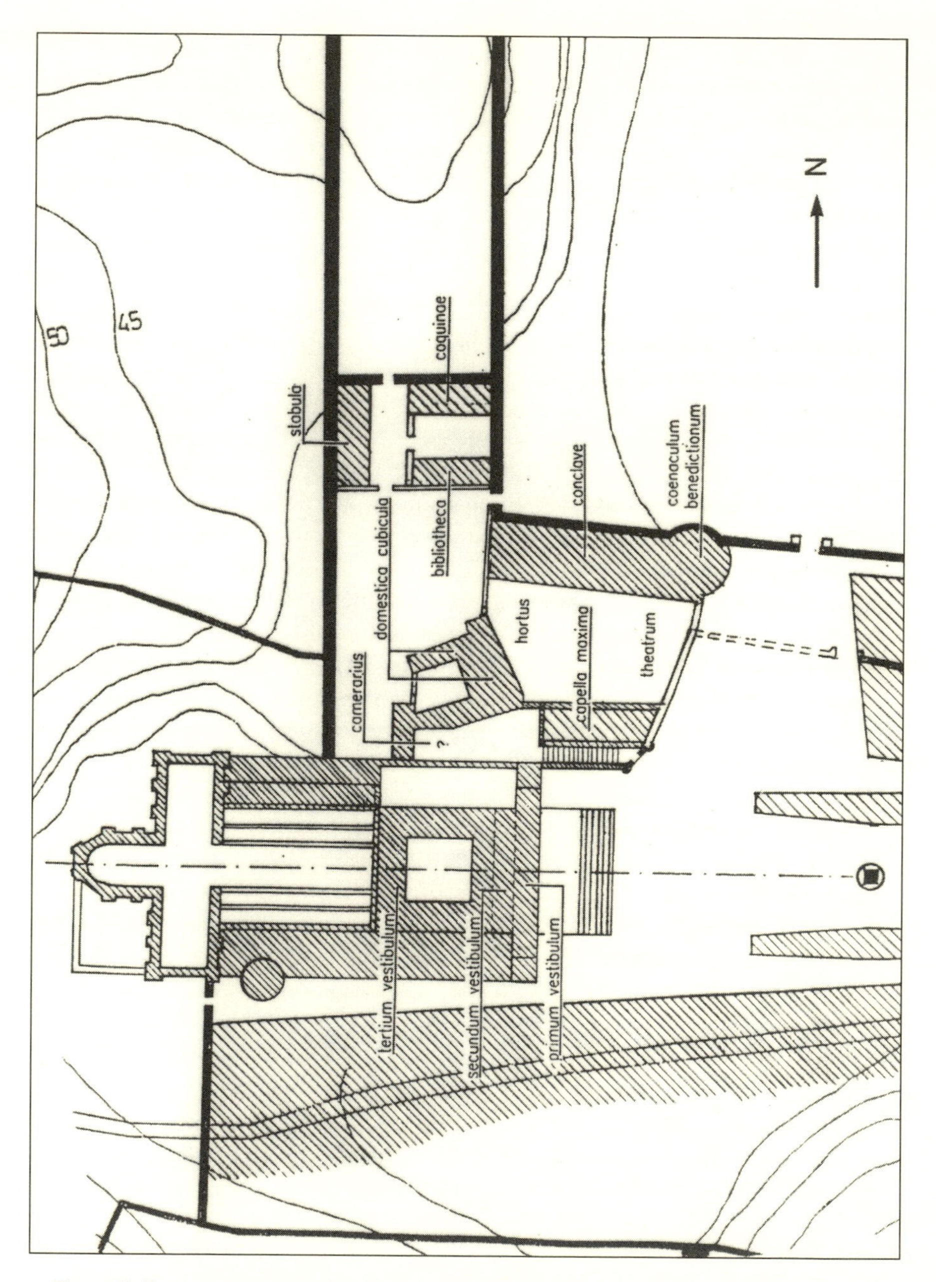

Fig. 15. Reconstruction of Nicholas's plan for the Borgo, palace and basilica by Frommel from "Il San Pietro," fig. 1.

(fig. 16).[11] It ran, wherever possible, over the crests of the hills, crossing the spur of the Janiculum at south/east, then up to the crest of the Vatican hill at the west and down along the Mons Saccorum at the north. The Leonine Walls had only one main gate, variously called the Porta Sancti Peregrini (or Pellegrini), Porta Palatii, Porta Viridaria, or, later, Porta San Pietro, near the present Porta Angelica.[12] But there were smaller openings in the walls near Sto. Spirito on the south and Castel Sant'Angelo on the north. John XXIII (1410–1415) opened a second main gate, the Porta Pertusa, behind the basilica on the crest of the Vatican hill, and two smaller gates, the Porta Vaticana near it and another on the south near the Schola Langobardorum: Nicholas enlarged this last and opened yet another gate in that tract of the wall (the present Porta Cavalleggeri). To the original circuit, Nicholas III had added walls enclosing the lower part of the Vatican hill on its western slope, encircling its northern spur, the Mons S. Egidi, and — in a portion now lost but which surely closed off entrance to the valley between the Mons Saccorum and Mons S. Egidi — returning to the Leonine Walls just east of the Vatican Palace. After this extension, the western portion of the original northern tract of the Leonine Walls was superfluous and seems not to have been maintained. In Nicholas's time the eastern slope of the Mons Saccorum was surely traversed by the Leonine Walls, even though their exact course between the juncture with Nicholas's new wall at the east and the tract west of the present Cortile di Belvedere is partly conjectural. The problem that Nicholas faced was whether to rebuild the northern stretch of the Leonine Walls or maintain the larger area enclosed by the walls of Nicholas III in which by this time vineyards and gardens had been established.

Two documents from a later period help conceptualize what was at issue in regard to defensive strategy: a report on the fortification of the Borgo written by Francesco Montemellino in 1547, and a plan of the fortifications of 1548. The report evaluates the relative advantages of (1) building walls along the heights and shrinking the enclosed area in order to stay clear of the nearby hills and (2) building on the low-lying ground and including more of the site, in order to flank the nearby hills.[13] The first alternative is said to be safer, cheaper, quick-

[11] S. Gibson and B. Ward Perkins, "The Surviving Remains of the Leonine Wall," *Papers of the British School at Rome* 47 (1979): 30–57, and eidem, "The Surviving Remains of the Leonine Wall: Part II. The Passetto," *Papers of the British School at Rome* 51 (1983): 222–39, here 236.

[12] L. De Carlo and P. Quattrini, *Le mura di Roma tra realtà e immagine. La riscoperta del monumento 'mura' nel suo rapporto con la città dal Medioevo all'età moderna* (Rome, 1995), 177.

[13] L. Bianchi, *Roma. Il monte di Santo Spirito tra Gianicolo e Vaticano* (Rome, 1999), 215–21.

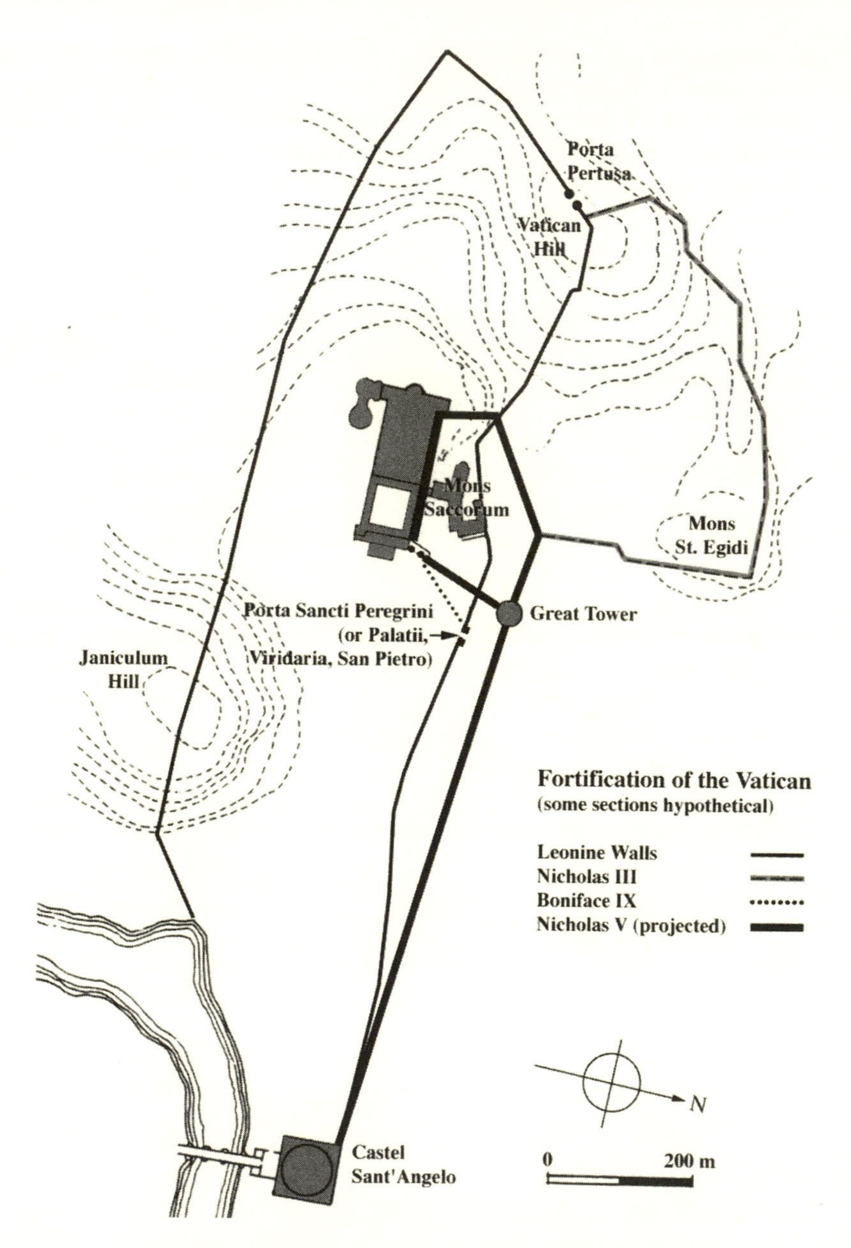

Fig. 16. Fortification of the Vatican area. Digital image by Steven Wolf, redrawn from S. Gibson and B. Ward Perkins, "The Surviving Remains of the Leonine Wall," *Papers of the British School at Rome* 47 (1979): 30-57.

er, sanctioned by the authority of the ancients, and having the advantage of a natural embankment. Clearly the Leonine Walls were of this type, built along the heights. But they obstructed the further expansion of the palace by bisecting the spur along its crest, and produced walls which, since they followed the terrain, were not uniform in elevation. Because it shows the topography of the Vatican area without buildings, the 1548 plan (fig. 17) reveals that Nicholas's Great Tower buttresses the foot of the Mons Saccorum, and its short westward extension encloses the base of the hill as does the short extension to the south.[14] In other words, Nicholas's defensive perimeter was of the second type. Although the course of his northern wall remains open to debate, if it followed the principle evident in the drawing it would have fortified the Mons Saccorum at its base, running through the present Cortile di Belvedere more or less where Domenico Fontana's fountain is, and where remains of walls have been found.[15] The alley marked "Silva" on Bufalini's plan (1551) (fig. 18) may mark its course up to the Porta Vaticana where it joined another tower built by Nicholas.[16] Nicholas's extension from the Great Tower to the south also embraces the foot of the spur and, Manetti says, would have joined a wall running east/west in the declivity next to St. Peter's. A fourth wall at the west, joining this to the northern tract — perhaps where the topography dips behind the present Sistine Chapel (the Piazza del Forno) — would have completed the circuit. It would seem that Nicholas planned not to rebuild the wall circling the Mons S. Egidi but only to add some short stretches enclosing the Mons Saccorum.[17] Magnuson and Westfall were probably correct that at the north, the new wall loosely paralleled the earlier Leonine Walls.[18]

Manetti tells us that the palace was enclosed by two sets of walls (38). But on the north side it was really protected by three since it seems that the Leonine

---

[14] The wall which runs from the Great Tower to Bramante's wing of the Cortile di Belvedere is assumed to have been built by Nicholas because its moldings and windows are the same as on the tower and the wall running south. But if Magnuson is correct that all these elements were refaced by Bramante, who also added their moldings, this identification falls: Magnuson, *Studies*, 117–18.

[15] Pietrangeli, *Palazzo*, 35; E. Ercadi, "La fontana del Cortile del Belvedere in Vaticano," *Monumenti, musei e gallerie pontifiche. Bollettino* 15 (1995): 239–55.

[16] Ackerman thought the alley might indicate the course of the Leonine Wall, but recent research has shown that it ran south of this: J. Ackerman, *Il cortile di Belvedere* (Vatican City, 1954).

[17] We disagree with Frommel on this point. Manetti says that the wall from the Great Tower ran toward the crest of the hill and that at the point where it passed by the upper palace it met another wall running south (33). If it passed the palace as it extended toward the crest, it must have been running almost directly west. See Frommel's alternative reconstruction from his "San Pietro," 103, our fig. 13.

[18] Westfall, *In This Most Perfect Paradise*, 102.

Fig. 17. Plan for the fortification of the Vatican and Borgo, attributed to Jacopo Castriotto or Nanni di Baccio Bigio, 1548, Bib. Vat., MS. Barb. lat. 4391b Stragr., c. 2.

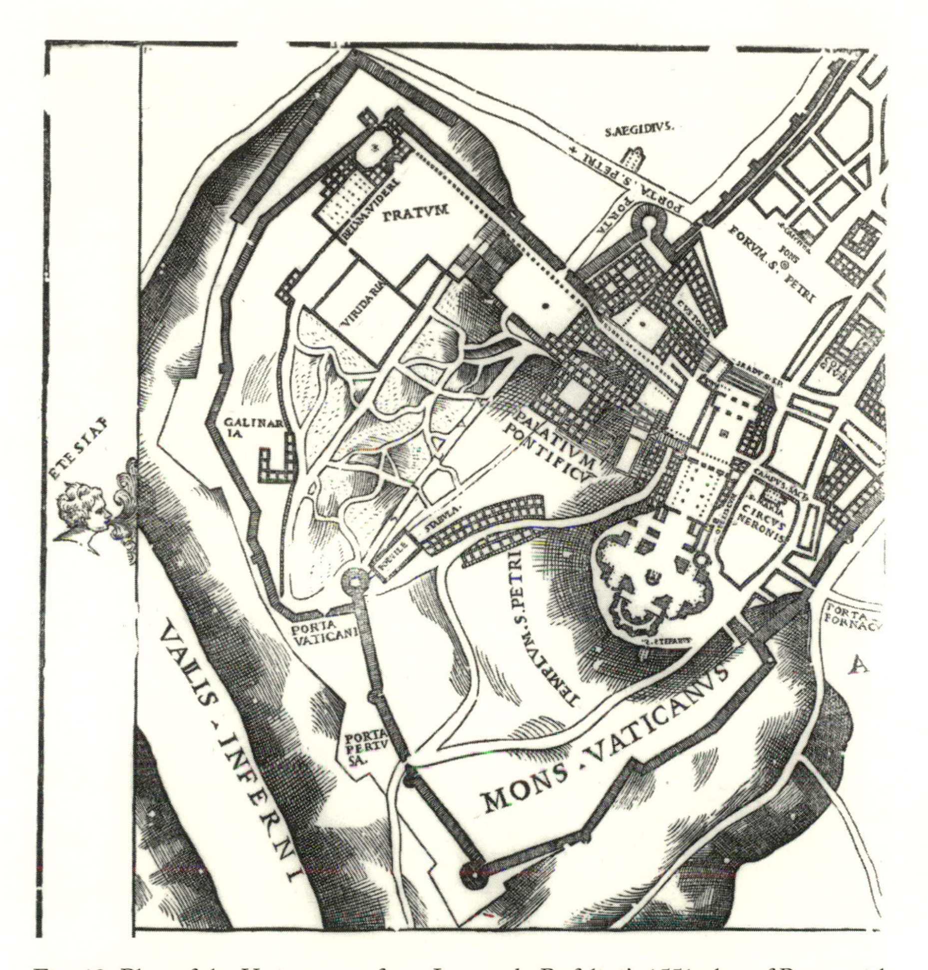

Fig. 18. Plan of the Vatican area from Leonardo Bufalini's 1551 plan of Rome with orientation reversed.

Walls ran along the line of Nicholas's new wing, and that his fortified palace wing substituted for them, indeed was built on them, at this point.[19] This new northern facade of the palace presented a sheer vertical surface of great height — Manetti says one hundred cubits (38) — a figure which has seemed excessive for

[19] As F. Erhle and H. Stevenson first suggested in *Gli affreschi del Pinturicchio nell'Appartamento Borgia* (Rome, 1897), 30 and now confirmed by Gibson and Ward Perkins, "Surviving Remains."

the palace alone but which can be understood as the height of fortified wall (or basement zone) and palace together. A similar condition existed in the walls facing St. Peter's Square, where Nicholas's new facade wall was set behind an existing stretch of wall built by Boniface IX. The new walls at the north and east created enclosed courtyards between them and the palace proper not unlike the already existing courtyard of the *palatium inferiore* to the south. These intermediate spaces between the new and old walls served functional purposes. For instance, entrance to the palace from the north would be more strictly controlled: one passed through a gate in the new wall and dismounted in the newly created intermediate space; stairs leading to the palace proper were in the defensive tower on the north corner of the east wing, the foundations of which were on the level of this courtyard.[20]

While the rebuilding of defense walls at the base of the hill was motivated by a desire for heightened security and the need to replace that stretch of the Leonine Walls on the eastern slope of the Mons Saccorum, the project presented an advantage which Nicholas exploited: building on top of them. Nicholas III had created the precedent for this by sinking the foundations of the end rooms of the east wing (the present Sala dei Pontefici and Sala di Costantino on the second and third floors respectively) down to the valley floor, creating a basement level or, put differently, adding more than ten meters of fortification below the Leonine Walls, a solution which Nicholas V continued in his own new wing.

Manetti's description begins with the Great Tower and with the notion that its height, thirty cubits, reached the platform of the palace (31). This new tower at the north/east foot of the Mons Saccorum (ca. 22 m asl) did indeed rise to the maximum height of the existing palace ground floor level (38 m asl). From this it seems that Nicholas had decided not to accept the sloping topography of the site but, establishing the crest of the Mons Saccorum as the "main floor" level of the palace, to extend an artificial platform from the east wing to the tower some 100 meters further east. This thirty-cubit mark also determined the height of the fortified basement zone of his new wing, extending some 50 meters west of the old east wing: its main floor rooms were at the height of this conceptual platform. Nicholas raised the original ground floor pavement level of the eastern wing itself approximately eight meters, presumably to regularize the level of the *palatium superiore*.[21] The new walls built out from the Great Tower at east and north were retaining walls for this artificial platform.

Thus the first concerns of the project were engineering and fortification, proposing the creation of a level building platform buttressed and protected by

---

[20] This interpretation supports Frommel's hypothesis that the tower on the north corner of the east wing was built by Nicholas: Frommel, "Palazzo Vaticano," 120.

[21] Redig de Campos, *Palazzi Vaticani*, 32.

the new walls. The level platform would have extended over the mostly unbuilt area between the east wing of the palace and the Great Tower. In fact, this area is now entirely built over on a level platform and is the location of the palace wings of Sixtus V and Gregory XIII. Nicholas's engineering project has analogies with the work subsequently overseen by Bernardo Rossellino for the garden of the Piccolomini Palace at Pienza, the level platform for which was artificially created with the help of walls at the foot of the hill. That Aeneas Silvius Piccolomini, the patron at Pienza, was a member of Nicholas's curia and Manetti attributes the Vatican projects to Rossellino strengthens this connection, suggesting that since Nicholas's concept was used elsewhere shortly after his death it was known and understood during his pontificate. However, Manetti's continued use of "lower" and "upper" when referring to the topography of the eastern slope of the Mons Saccorum suggests that the artificial platform was not realized under Nicholas.

What became of the stretch of Leonine Walls that ran from the foot of the Mons Saccorum up to the palace? Platina commented that Nicholas began to build the walls and palace "after the unsound foundations for the towers had been razed."[22] This could mean, as Magnuson thought, that after the Great Tower fell in 1454, its foundations were razed and building began again.[23] But another explanation seems more likely. In 1411, John XXIII began to replace the wall between the Porta Viridaria and the palace; he also restored the *passetto* (access passage) atop it from Castel Sant'Angelo to the palace and opened a new gate, the Porta Pertusa, on the crest of the Vatican Hill (which made it necessary for Nicholas to close off the palace precinct with walls to the west).[24] It may be suggested that the tract running up the slope of the Mons Saccorum (that is, between the wall of Boniface IX and the palace) was unsound and had to be replaced. Nicholas, concluding (not wrongly) that walls on an inclined plane, subject moreover to constant erosion, were unstable, replaced them with a buttressing/fortification wall and tower the foundations of which stood at the foot of the hill. The substantial earthworks to fill in the resultant depression and create a level platform would have buried parts of the old walls and towers; the rest would have been razed. Platina probably refers to Nicholas's continuation of John XXIII's work on those portions of the Leonine Wall on the eastern slope of the Mons Saccorum, and specifically to the razing of its towers in that stretch, remains of which have been found in the present Cortile di San Damaso. But how would the *passetto* now reach the palace?

---

[22] Platina, "Vita Nicolai Quinti," *RIS*, 3.1:338.

[23] Magnuson, *Studies in Roman Quattrocento Architecture*, 63–64, 127.

[24] Reported by Pietro dello Schiavo's contemporary chronicle in Ehrle and Egger, *Vatikanische Palast*, 89: "fuit inceptum fundamentum inter palatium apostolicum et portam Viridariam." For recent discussion, see De Carlo and Quattrini, *Mura*, 177.

Manetti says that the palace "was being raised from the platform to such a degree that it would extend to a height of one hundred cubits all the way to where the Great Tower rose" (38). The wing of Nicholas V facing the present Cortile di Belvedere is clearly one portion of this project, but a second wing, connecting the eastern wing of Nicholas III to the Great Tower, was apparently never built. A wall, faintly drawn on Uffizi 287A (fig. 14), connecting the Great Tower to the tower at the north/east angle of the palace's east wing and essentially continuing the facade of Nicholas's new wing may mark its intended site. Of course, it could not be begun until the artificial platform was completed, and thus was not built. The width of the wall shown on the drawing (about five meters) is even greater than that of the facade wall surely built by Nicholas running south from the tower towards St. Peter's on the same drawing. This second wing also had a defensive purpose. The access corridor between the fortress and the palace would connect to the Great Tower and then through the new wing to the corner tower of the east wing and into the upper floor of an inaccessible portion of the residence. Manetti says of Nicholas's renovation of Castel Sant'Angelo that "on the inside he so divided its spaces between halls and triclinia that it seemed quite nicely to serve the dual function of citadel and palace" (26). In other words, it stood as a fortress guarding access to the Borgo from the Tiber and the plain, but could also be used as a residence should the Vatican Palace be taken. However, should the fortress fall into enemy hands, as it had in 1379, the *passetto* would provide dangerous access to the palace. The *passetto* was both an advantage and a liability, and the pope needed to be able to block it if necessary. Thus the need for fortified checkpoints — the Great Tower and the corner tower — between the fortress and the residence. Nicholas also intended to rebuild the wall between Castel Sant'Angelo and the Great Tower (28, 30, 32), as Pius V (1559–1565) later did.

The decision to retrench, rendering the Mons Saccorum a fortified citadel, was made for defensive purposes: it produced a fortification at the foot of the hill which was simultaneously a retaining wall, the substructure of the palace, and a defensive circuit. Yet the Great Tower was something more than a defense tower. It was a bastion — a solid platform thrust forward to get a wide field of fire for cannon while still providing flank cover to adjacent parts of the fortification — and therefore an aggressive, rather than purely defensive, form.[25] This explains why its height was dropped to the level of the walls and of the building platform, a novelty which attracted criticism which Manetti rebuts (see Chapter 7): this made it accessible to run guns out onto it. And it was also a ravelin, an embankment in front of the main gate to the Leonine City placed so as to be able

[25] J. Hale, "The Early Development of the Bastion: An Italian Chronology c. 1450–c.1534," in *Europe in the Late Middle Ages,* ed. idem, J. Highfield, and B. Smalley, (Evanston, 1965), 466–94, here 483.

to break up an attack heading to the gate both at a distance and with flanking fire at the gate itself.[26]

Instead of enlarging the enclosed area of the palace the new walls reduced it, isolating the Mons Saccorum as a fortified acropolis cut off from the rest of the Vatican Hill and its valley. This area Manetti designates as "the ample space for building the whole platform" (34) and "this space of a most beautiful paradise" (34). Yet the principal advantage of the project was not amenity, providing more extensive palace grounds, but security. The Vatican Palace was not, in other words, a miniature city but the fortress of a tyrant.

The Entrance

The palace would be entered through a triumphal arch flanked by two towers (33) in the wall running south from the Great Tower (fig. 19).[27] This gate would have been about 30 m east of the old *porta prima*, and behind it would have been a ramp for horses and carriages (33) because the *curia prima* was about two meters higher than the public square. Since this ramp was actually built or rebuilt under Pius II (who also rebuilt the *porta prima* rather than bringing it forward to Nicholas's new boundary), we know where the topography changed level.[28] The ascent in level from St. Peter's square to the *curia prima* (later the *Atrium Helvetiorum*) was located outside the old *porta prima* (as one still sees in Marten van Heemskerck's drawing). Therefore, since Manetti says that the ascent took place just behind the entrance, the gate must have been in front of the ramp. Since the old *porta prima* was not dismantled, another intermediate courtyard would have been created between the two gates, an additional security measure.

The Curtis

Nicholas's project envisioned the fortification of the *curia prima*, a courtyard which Manetti designates as "curtis" (33).[29] This is where Nicholas demolished the old church of St. Benedict, presumably to clear the area.[30] One entered, Manetti says, a huge court, with colonnades and porticoes. Manetti may be describing

[26] Hale, "Early Development," 479.

[27] Frommel also realized that this was the location of the entrance: "San Pietro," 103.

[28] T. Marder, *Bernini's Scala Regia at the Vatican Palace. Architecture, Sculpture and Ritual* (New York, 1997), 37.

[29] For "curtis" see the Commentary at 33.

[30] See Chapter 7.

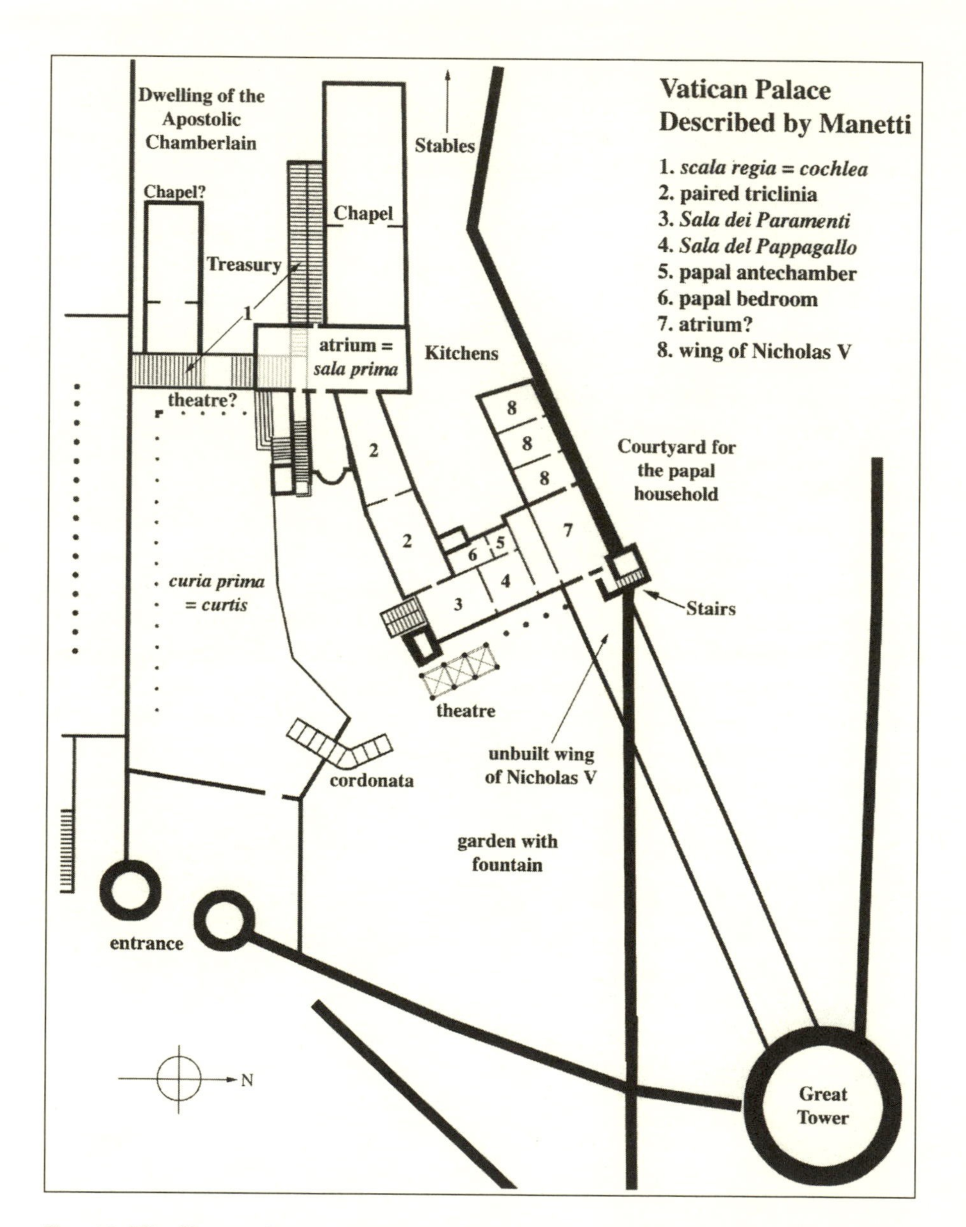

Fig. 19. The Vatican Palace as described by Manetti. Digital image by Steven Wolf.

colonnades already in this courtyard since the fourteenth century.[31] Some idea of their arrangement might be gleaned from the three-storied porticoes later built on the south and west sides of the *curia prima*: Vasari says they were of travertine and had columns on the ground floor.[32] The court, says Manetti, was enclosed to the south by a wall dividing the basilica from the palace (the third side of the fortification walls ringing the Mons Saccorum).

In Manetti's time, the Triclinium of Leo III with the main hall of the *auditorium rotae* was on the south side of the courtyard.[33] The Rota, part of the judicial branch of the Curia, dealt with spiritual or temporal issues which did not require the intercession of the pope.[34]A few decades later Innocent VIII replaced the Triclinium with a new edifice (demolished in 1610) for the *auditorium rotae*, the *dataria* (where dates were put on bulls, the final administrative step in their promulgation, but also the office that fixed fees for services), and with a room used for princes.[35] This last, perhaps identical in function with the *camera imperatoris*, was also in the lower palace in Manetti's time: Stefano Infessura tells us that Frederick III stayed "in quello palazzo che sta sopra le scale di Santo Pietro" ("in that palace which is above St. Peter's' stairs") when he came for the coronation in 1452.[36] Although Magnuson thought this meant in the south or east wing of the *palatium inferiore*, those nearest the stairs in front of the basilica,[37] we will show that "above St. Peter's' stairs" suggests that it was in the west wing of the courtyard, which housed the stairs connecting the palace to the basilica. The offices of the Apostolic Camera (the financial branch of the Curia which collected monies, governed the papal states, and directed the pope's finances), the Treasury, and Offices of the Curia were in the *palatium inferiore*.[38] The *Camerarius*

---

[31] For the earlier colonnades, see J. P. Kirsch, *Die Rückkehr der Päpste Urban V und Gregor XI von Avignon nach Rom* (Paderborn, 1898), xxxii.

[32] They were probably begun by Sixtus IV and completed by Innocent VIII, although Vasari attributes them to Paul II in his Life of Giuliano da Maiano. See Marder, *Scala Regia*, 40; G. Zippel, "Paolo II e l'arte, note e documenti: IV: Gli edifici di San Pietro," *L'Arte* 14 (1911): 181–97, here 193.

[33] H. Egger, "Quadriporticus S. Petri," *Papers of the British School at Rome* 18 (1950): 101–3, here 101; idem, "Das päpstliche Kanzleigebäude im 15. Jahrhundert," *Festschrift zur Feier des Zweihundertjahrigen Bestandes des Haus- Hof- und Staatsarchives* (Vienna, 1951), 487–500.

[34] For the structure and function of the Curia we follow D'Amico, *Renaissance Humanism*, esp. 21–27.

[35] G. Grimaldi, *Descrizione della basilica antica di S.Pietro in Vaticano*, ed. R. Niggl (Vatican City, 1972), 277.

[36] Infessura, *Diario*, ed. Tommasini, 52.

[37] Magnuson, *Studies*, 104.

[38] Voci, *Nord o sud*, 50.

(superintendent of the administration and finances of the papal court) had twelve or thirteen rooms in and behind the west wing, perhaps in a now-destroyed block flanking the Sistine Chapel; his garden was along the north flank of St. Peter's.[39] The medieval retaining wall which was the northern boundary of the old *curia prima* must be Manetti's "second wall" (33), extended eastward to the north tower of the new entrance. Those offices, then, which received most visitors and which dealt directly with secular matters were located in the *palatium inferiore.*

Manetti tells us that in this courtyard people would dismount. Some did dismount in the *curia prima* and, at least in the sixteenth century, their horses were taken through a passage in the west wall of the atrium up to the stables near the Porta Vaticana, as shown on Bufalini's woodcut (fig. 18). We will see that Bufalini's stables are in the approximate location Manetti gives for those of Nicholas (35), so a passage in the west wall either already existed or was planned.[40] Dismounting in the securely enclosed *curtis* cleared of other buildings would have tightened security at the palace. Other stables seem to have been outside the palace entrance, in the north/east corner of the Square: these might have been between Nicholas's new wall and that of Boniface IX.[41]

During Nicholas's time some visitors on horseback, however, passed through the guarded *turris scalarum* in the north/west corner of the courtyard and ascended to the Cortile del Maresciallo. There they dismounted, and their horses were stabled near the quarters of the *marescalcia*, the stable-master, from whose title the room directly beneath the *aula prima*, or main reception room of the palace, takes its name. In 1538 it was still traditional for cardinals to dismount in the Cortile del Maresciallo although most people dismounted in the *curtis*.[42] We will see that Nicholas planned a new access route leading up from the *palatium inferiore* to the *palatium superiore*, the level of the Cortile del Maresciallo.

The First Garden and Fountain

Manetti begins his description of the palace proper "ab inferiori palatii parte" (34) referring to (1) the *palatium inferiore*; (2) the part at the bottom of a plan; or (3) the terrain. This part was lower than the "supernam palatii partem" he had

---

[39] Voci, *Nord o sud*, 52; Magnuson, *Studies*, 104. The block is shown on a plan by Ottaviano Mascherino (Accademia di San Luca, 2489) and is discussed in M. Kuntz, "Designed for Ceremony. The Cappella Paolina at the Vatican Palace," *Journal of the Society of Architectural Historians* 62 (2003): 228–55, here 236.

[40] Magnuson noted this too, but did not see how they were connected to the *curia prima*: *Studies in Roman Quattrocento Architecture*, 139.

[41] A. M. Corbo, *Artisti e artigiani in Roma al tempo di Martino V e di Eugenio IV* (Rome, 1968), 20.

[42] Marder, *Scala Regia*, 52.

just mentioned (33), which is the wing of Nicholas V or perhaps more generally the structures on the crest of the Mons Saccorum, and must be either south or east of it. In general, in Manetti's description of the palace, *inferius* and *superius* reflect topography, as the medieval nomenclature *palatium inferiore* and *palatium superiore* also did. Unlike his description of the walls of Rome and of St. Peter's, there is no indication that Manetti referred to plans of the palace. Because of its multiple levels, such plans are a challenge even to the modern scholar, so perhaps graphics were not attempted or Manetti could not decipher them. Or perhaps the nature of Nicholas's interventions was such that none were needed. In any case, Manetti's descriptive devices concern what one would see or do and seem based primarily on his visual experience of the existing structures. This, in fact, enables us to identify at least some of them.

In this lower part of the palace there was a walled garden of plants and fruits (34). Although there was no garden in the *curia prima* (south), there was one in what would later be the Cortile di San Damaso (east). In the late thirteenth century Nicholas III had established there a *viridarium* — from which the Porta Viridaria was called — part of which was a vineyard and part known in the fifteenth century as the "hortus secretus" probably because it was enclosed by a low wall and towers; there was also a fountain.[43] Whether this is the fountain rebuilt by Eugenius IV in 1437 is not certain.[44] Pius II describes the garden as having domestic and exotic animals and as being used to receive ambassadors or for summer dining: he commissioned a new fountain and pavilion for it.[45] This garden occupied part of the area which began to be called by its present name — the Cortile di San Damaso — in the seventeenth century, when Innocent X restored the so-called Acqua Damasiana and created a new fountain there. However, since Manetti says Nicholas brought the water from the crest of a hill and the Acqua Damasiana is on lower ground outside the Porta Cavalleggeri (south), he refers to conduits from the Acqua Traiana, originally intended to service the Naumachia north/west of Castel Sant'Angelo.[46] These conduits ran down the Mons Saccorum within the Leonine Walls, hence through Nicholas's new wing of the palace, and supplied it with water: all three of the fountains mentioned by Manetti (34–35) seem to have been close to the old walls and probably drew their water from the same source.

Manetti's description seems to move from the *curtis*, where people dismount, to the Cortile di San Damaso, where the visitor, having ascended to the plane

---

[43] Pietrangeli, *Palazzo*, 32, 34–35, 223.

[44] Zippel, "Paolo II," 195.

[45] Zippel, "Paolo II," 96.

[46] See the Commentary at 34 for discussion of the water supply. For the Acqua Damasiana, see R. Funiciello, *La geologia di Roma: Il centro storico* (Rome, 1995), 191. See also G. De Angelis D'Ossat, *La geologia del Monte Vaticano* (Vatican City, 1953).

established for the palace, first apprehends its buildings. But why does he refer to it as the lower part of the palace? This must be a slip. Although all of the space between the upper palace and the new eastern wall was to have been raised as a level platform about 38 m asl, and the northern boundary of the *curia prima* was to have been extended forward to join the new wall, this had not been done by Nicholas's death. Thus Manetti, now describing what he sees and not a plan, is in fact standing at the old level at the foot of the Mons Saccorum, in the old garden, looking up the slope. For once, his literary device of describing how things would look when completed has lapsed.

How were the lower and upper parts of the palace to have been connected? Perhaps through the *turris scalarum* in the north/west corner of the *curtis*, which gave onto the Cortile del Maresciallo. Or perhaps on the site where Manetti was standing, once its level were raised. Here a new staircase for horses (a *cordonata*) could have led from the *curia prima* to the Cortile di San Damaso. This access ramp would have been within the new palace perimeter and could have passed through the wall bounding the *curia prima* at its north. Such a ramp once existed, first recorded in 1551 and shown on Letarouilly's plan of the palace (fig. 20).[47] Although the most recent opinion associates the *cordonata* with Bramante or Giulio Romano,[48] it could have been planned under Nicholas V. It is not shown on Uffizi 287A, but a notation of 1506 seems to refer to it as a "via": "We entered through the gate of the palace where there was a guard post and went up along a street [*via*] that the cardinals use to go up when they arrive at the palace on horseback; the pope gave leave to the more elderly cardinals in front of the stair, yet they went up to the Sala dei Paramenti."[49] Since the *Camera dei Paramenti* was in the east wing, the stairs referred to are not the Scala del Maresciallo in the eponymous courtyard, which led to the main audience hall, but rather stairs in the east wing adjacent to the Cortile di San Damaso. A letter of 1538 also refers to the adjacent Cortile del Maresciallo as where the cardinals dismount, and looks forward to enlarging the stairs to the audience hall which would enable them to go all the way up to it on horseback.[50] Indeed, the main entrance to the upper part of the Vatican Palace, even after the construction of Bernini's Scala

---

[47] Attributed to Pius V (1566–1572) by C. Denker Nesselrath in Pietrangeli, *Palazzo*, 223. See M. Kuntz, "Antonio da Sangallo the Younger's Scala del Maresciallo: A Ceremonial Entrance to the Vatican Palace," in *Pratum Romanum. Richard Krautheimer zum 100. Geburtstag*, ed. R. Colella (Wiesbaden, 1997), 233–45, here 245.

[48] Marder, *Scala Regia*, 47–50.

[49] In Marder, *Scala Regia*, 45, n. 82.

[50] E. Salmi, "Gaspare Contarini alla Dieta di Ratisbona," *Nuovo archivio veneto* 13 (1907): 5–23, 24. The letter is from Nino Sernini to Cardinal Ercole Gonzaga.

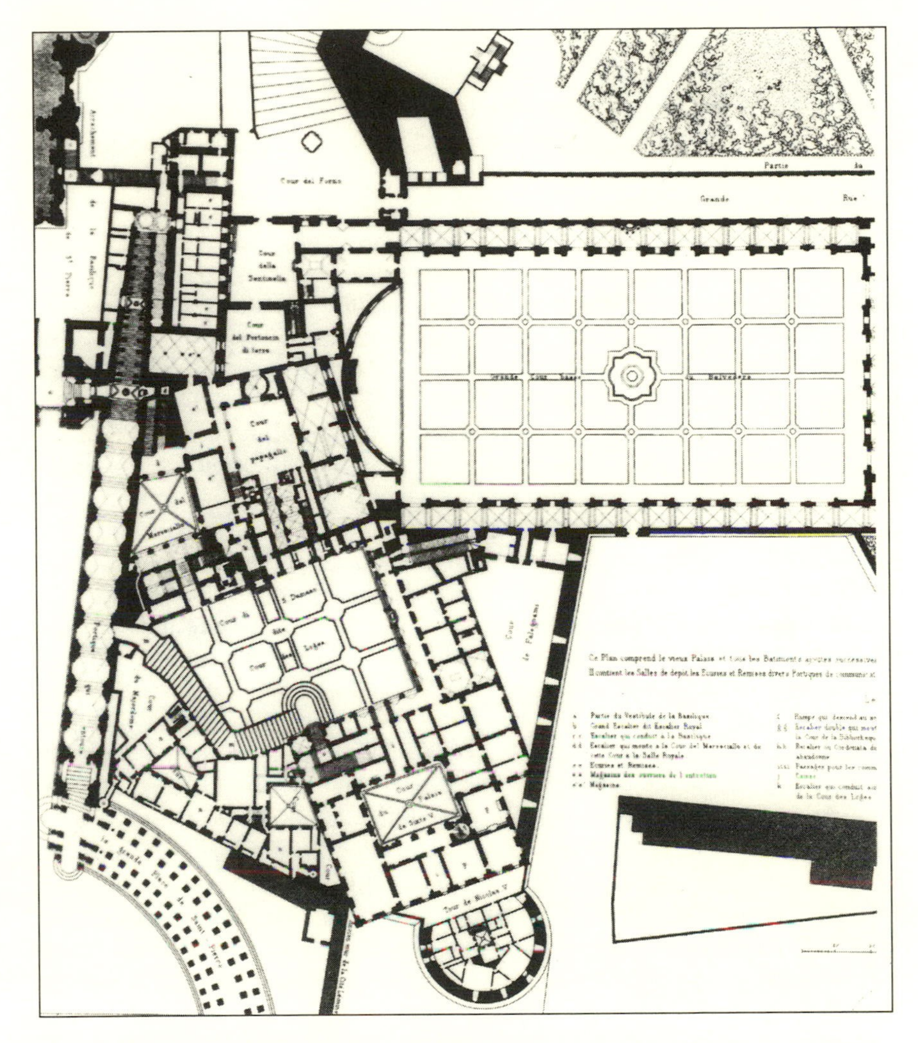

Fig. 20. Plan of the Vatican Palace by P. Letarouilly, showing the *cordonata*. From his *Le Vatican et la Basilique de Saint Pierre* (Paris, 1882; repr. Novara, 1999).

Regia, led into the Cortile di San Damaso, just as Nicholas wished.[51] The purpose of moving the palace's main entrance forward, apart from obtaining larger entrance courts both in the *palatium inferiore* and the *palatium superiore*, might

[51] Marder, *Scala Regia*, 50, shows that this was clearly the main entrance even in the seventeenth century.

have been to improve the ceremonial route to the palace. Although Manetti is vague about staircases (50), it seems that facilitation of access and linkages between parts of the existing fabric were important considerations for Nicholas, in fact the key to understanding his renovation.

The Theater, Atrium, and Chapel

Now we encounter a problem of textual interpretation. Manetti says that three beautiful buildings stood out "in hoc ipso speciosissime paradisi spatio" (34). Virtually all scholars have taken this phrase as designating the garden area, both because that is the subject of the previous sentence and because the word "paradise" means an enclosed garden. Since no such buildings stood on the south/east slope of the Mons Saccorum in the fifteenth century, the conclusion that the theater, atrium, and chapel were new constructions was inevitable. However, the phrase "in hoc ipso speciosissime paradisi spatio" parallels the grammatical construction of the sentence preceding that about the garden, which begins: "in hoc amplo totius edificandi spatio." "Ipso," in other words, refers back to the "spatio" of the building platform just mentioned. In this alternative reading, it is the whole space of the building platform, the perimeter of which Manetti had just defined by tracing its walls, which is a paradise. The garden imagery fleshes out and exemplifies its paradisaical nature rather than designates where the buildings are. That this reading is correct is confirmed by Manetti's summary of the "buildings of this sacred palace" as "a most beautiful paradise" (37). Reading the phrase this way permits an entirely new identification of where and what these buildings were, and renders Manetti's description of them coherent.

The first of the three buildings on the building platform "a parte inferiore" (34) was a theater on arches and columns; the second, to its right, was a vaulted atrium for public ceremonies; connected to the atrium, paired reception or dining halls; and on one side, the Apostolic Treasury (34). Above (*super*) the atrium was an upper story, looking eastward to Ponte Sant'Angelo (Hadrian's Bridge) for papal benedictions. To the left was the third structure, a large vaulted chapel with vestibule (34). Although scholars have consistently interpreted this as left of the theater, Manetti's Latin usage favors the alternate reading of left of the atrium. Both readings need to be considered. Manetti returns to "the main atrium of this palace" at 36, mentioning that on its north side private rooms, reception halls, and a large chapel were being prepared; to its south, rooms for the Apostolic Chamberlain; and west, a garden.

Some of the rooms which Manetti mentions can be positively identified with rooms of the same function in the medieval palace as it was before Nicholas's pontificate: the *capella magna* (probably built in the late fourteenth century and replaced by the Sistine Chapel in 1475) opened from the west side of the *aula prima* and had a very large vestibule, as Manetti notes;[52] and the Apostolic Chamberlain (*Camerarius*) dwelt to the south/west of the *aula prima*, as we saw. Adjoining the *aula prima* to the east were the *aula secunda* and *aula tertia*, reception rooms of similar dimensions, as Manetti suggests ("facing one another back to back" [34]): these are Manetti's "triclinia." The treasury was on the side of (next to) the *aula prima* to its southwest. Since these structures have the relationship to the *aula prima* that Manetti says buildings of the same function were to have to the main atrium of the palace, it would seem that what Manetti calls the atrium is the *aula prima* of the medieval palace.

Atrium

Manetti does not use "atrium" for a courtyard: he prefers "curtis" (33). For Manetti the translator and scriptural scholar, "atrium" and "aula" were equivalents. This association may come from a problematic passage in Scripture, as do other of his terms. Where Jerome translates "et eduxit me ad atrium exterius" and "et aedificavit atrium interius" (*Comm. on Ezekiel*, 12.40.17–19, and cf. Vulgate, 3 Kings 6:36), in the Septuagint we find "aulēn." Jerome meant the inner court of a house. Manetti may also have been confused about what an "atrium" is because in the Gospels the place where Caiaphas interrogated Jesus is called "atrium" meaning "audience hall" (Mark 15:16, John 18:15), but "atrium" is also the place outside the palace where Peter waited (Matthew 26:69, Mark 14:54, 66, 68, and Luke 27:55). In Revelation (11:1–2) the court outside the sanctuary is an "aulēn," again translated by Jerome as "atrium" in the Vulgate. If Manetti had consulted John of Genoa's *Catholicon*, a thirteenth-century dictionary, he would have learned that the word "atrium" derives from "ater" because of the fires that were in them and that the term indicates a "domus ampla et spaciosa" (s.v.). Manetti knew from Ezekiel that the "atrium" or "aula" was the first room behind the vestibule, and from classical sources that the atrium of a house is where the master received clients. Valerius Maximus (another of Manetti's favorite sources) tells the story of Manlius Torquatus being consulted by clients in the atrium of his house, "in prima parte aedium" (5.8). Alberti also used the term (once) to refer to a monarch's council hall: in *Momus*, the gods gather for council "in arcis

[52] During Frederick III's visit in 1452 cardinals met him at the "porta regiarum capella", that is, at the chancel barrier of the *capella magna*, to escort him to his place for Mass. Thus we know that the chapel was divided by its liturgical furniture into a vestibule and a liturgical space: Dykmans, *L'Oeuvre*, 809.

atrium".[53] There is, moreover, precedent for designating the *aula prima* of the Vatican as an "atrium": writing to the Byzantine diplomat Manuel Chrysoloras about the death of Innocent VII (1406), Jacopo Angeli da Scarperia said the conclave was held in a chapel in the Vatican Palace "post quod spatium quoddam in speciem atrii ampli".[54] It may be suggested that for some Quattrocento Humanists who knew both Latin and Greek and were interested in philology, "atrium" was the proper Latin equivalent for the Greek "aulē".[55]

Manetti says that the "great atrium" was suitable for audiences, conclaves, papal coronations, and other rare and worthy ceremonies (34): in fact, these functions took place in the *aula prima*.[56] He describes it as an atrium with two *triclinia*, considering the three *aulae* as a unit. This is also how these rooms were considered by Agostino Patrizi, Master of Ceremonies under Innocent VIII: "In palatio apostolico Sancti Petri tres aulae sunt pontificales."[57] We know that similar functions — receptions of sovereigns and ambassadors, conclaves, public consistories, and canonizations — took place in these rooms, with the *aula prima* reserved for the most solemn and elevated receptions.[58] Remodeled by Julius II and Clement VII, vaulted under Paul III, restructured and decorated by Gregory XIII, the *aula prima* is now the Sala Regia. Since the room seems to have had a flat wooden ceiling, Nicholas's intervention here, according to Manetti, was to be the addition of vaulting (34). Documents show that round windows *a rosette* (with tracery?) were installed in this room in 1450 and that painted glass windows were added to the *aula seconda* and *aula terza* in the same year.[59]

"Above this atrium, a great upper story was being readied," used for anniversaries and ordinary papal benedictions. The grammar suggests that Nicholas intended to add a floor above the *aula prima*. As Manetti rightly says, this would

---

[53] We cite L. B. Alberti, *Momus*, ed. R. Consolo (Genoa, 1986), 194 since the new edition and English translation appeared after our work was at press: L.B. Alberti, *Momus*, ed. S. Knight and V. Brown, trans. S. Knight (Cambridge, MA, 2003).

[54] Voci, *Nord o sud*, 147.

[55] Manetti thus corrects Josephus, who described the open-air court Moses built around the Tabernacle as an "aithrion" (*Jewish Antiquities*, 3.6.2), a grecization of *atrium*.

[56] During conclaves the cardinals discussed the candidates in the *aula prima*, slept in cubicles in the *cappella magna*, and cast their votes in the *cappella parva* or Chapel of St. Nicholas.

[57] Frommel, "Palazzo Vaticano," 118.

[58] Pietrangeli, *Palazzo*, 73, 18; Kuntz, "Antonio da Sangallo," 233; Marder, *Scala Regia*, 34; Redig de Campos, *Palazzi Vaticani*, 29. On the main hall of papal palaces at the Lateran, Viterbo, and the Vatican, see G. Radke, "Form and Function in Thirteenth-Century Papal Palaces," in *Architecture et vie sociale à la Renaissance*, ed. A. Chastel and J. Guillaume (Paris, 1994), 11–24.

[59] Müntz, *Les arts*, 137–38, where the rooms are referred to as "sala de choncestoro", "sichonda sala", and "ultima sala".

have faced east to Hadrian's Bridge. In fact, in the fifteenth century the *aula prima* had a room below it, the *marescalcia*, but nothing above. While it seems that such a room would have been too far away from St. Peter's Square for benedictions — Pius II placed his benediction loggia on St. Peter's facade a few years later — papal elections were announced to the people from a window not much nearer.[60] And it would have been possible for large crowds to be admitted to the *curtis* overlooked by a benediction loggia built out from or into the south/east corner of the upper room. Manetti's term is "cenaculum," which commonly means "upper room," but which literally means dining room. In the fourteenth century, the room referred to as "audientia" ("audience hall") is also called "cenaculum magnum," suggesting that the *aula prima* was also used for state banquets.[61] Nicholas's plan would have separated these two functions, accommodating them in superimposed rooms.

While the identification of Manetti's "atrium" with the *aula prima* seems correct, another location should be considered. Two large rooms in the northern corner of the east wing — the Sala dei Pontefici on the second floor and the Sala di Costantino on the third — were used in the Renaissance for banquets, audiences, and consistories.[62] It might make more sense to use these for benedictions since they were further to the east than the *aula prima*. Magnuson, following Ehrle, believed that the Consistory Hall mentioned in a document of 1450 was, in fact, the Sala dei Pontefici and suggested that Nicholas might have preferred this to the old *aula prima*.[63] However, it faced north/east, away from St. Peter's Square and Hadrian's bridge and does not, moreover, have the relation to identifiable rooms in Manetti's description that the *aula prima* does. Moreover, we know that the *aula consistoriale* in the fifteenth century had at least five windows, whereas the Sala dei Pontifici had only two: how many the *aula prima* had is uncertain.[64] Only

[60] They were announced from a window north of the apse of the Cappella Parva, or Chapel of St. Nicholas, adjoining the *aula prima*. After 1540, with the completion of the Cappella Paolina just south of the *aula prima*, they were announced from there to the crowd in St. Peter's Square: Pietrangeli, *Palazzo*, 33; Kuntz, "Designing," 231.

[61] Kirsch, *Rückkehr*, xxxvi. Unless the "audientia" was the room on the first floor of the south wing mentioned by S. Borsi, F. Quinterio, and C. Vasic Vatovec, *Maestri fiorentini nei cantieri romani del Quattrocento*, ed. S. Danese Squarzina (Rome, 1989), 94. A similar arrangement existed at the papal palace in Avignon, where the first large reception room was called the "tinellum magnum" and from which there was access both to the "cappella parva" and to the guest wing. B. Schimmelpfennig, "Die Einfluss des avignonischen Zeremoniells auf den Vatikanpalast Zeit Nikolaus V," in *Functions and Decorations: Art and Ritual at the Vatican Palace in the Middle Ages and The Renaissance*, ed. T. Weddingen, S. De Blaauw, and B. Kempers (Vatican City, 2003), 41-45, here 45.

[62] Pietrangeli, *Palazzo*, 93; L. Partridge, *The Renaissance in Rome* (London, 1996), 62.

[63] Magnuson, *Studies*, 124.

[64] Corbo, *Artisti e artigiani in Roma al tempo di Martino V e di Eugenio IV*, 22, a payment for five windows in the *aula consistoriali* of the palace in 1421.

if "super" means "in addition to" could Manetti be referring to these rooms, an interpretation not consonant with the other language of the description. If, then, the room for anniversaries and benedictions was to be above the *aula prima*, large-scale public functions would have taken place in the *aula prima* and rooms adjoining it, as had always been the case.

Theatrum

Once again, Manetti's understanding of the term is informed by Scripture. Their income threatened by Paul's preaching against images, the silversmiths' guild of first-century Ephesus caused a riot (Acts 19:23–41). The mob rushed into the theater in order to hold an assembly, but the town clerk dispersed the crowd on the grounds that the assembly had not been regularly called. The account makes it clear that the theater is not only a place for dramatic spectacle, but also the place where issues are discussed by the citizens and town authorities. Manetti's interpretation would also have drawn on his knowledge of Greek, understanding that etymologically, "theatron" comes from the verb meaning "to see" ("theaomai") and means "a place for seeing." This etymological usage was common in the Quattrocento. Lapo da Castiglionchio called the Roman Curia "a theater of all races and nations"; and Poggio referred to knighthood as "a theater of nobility."[65] The connection between rulership and theater is a theme of Poggio's *De infelicitate principum*, dedicated to Nicholas in 1440, in which rulers are compared to actors performing roles and princes are referred to as "homines personati" (101). In reality, Nicholas was performing a role: that of Vicar of Christ.

Westfall realized that in the Middle Ages a theater was not a particular building type but rather whatever accommodated certain activities such as chivalric acts or acts of government, and he cited Quattrocento examples of such terminology.[66] This use of the architectural term, and the Humanists' metaphoric usage, coincided with building practice. Recent research on episcopal palaces shows that, from the thirteenth century, stairs, foyers, and balconies became more important as places where documents were redacted as well as for ceremonial exits and entrances.[67] Interestingly, the notion of a theater as a place for

---

[65] Celenza, *Renaissance Humanism and the Papal Curia*, 21; Poggio Bracciolini, *La vera nobiltà*, ed. D. Canfora (Rome, 1999), 64. The moral, social and political application of "theater" has been traced to John of Salisbury's *Policraticus* by Consolo: Alberti, *Momus*, 13, n. 58.

[66] Westfall, *In This Most Perfect Paradise*, 153–54.

[67] M. Miller, *The Bishop's Palace: Architecture and Authority in Medieval Italy* (Ithaca, 2000), 105.

dramatic performances or game spectacles is entirely absent from Manetti's understanding which, therefore, has nothing to do with Vitruvius or ancient Greek and Roman practice.

If Manetti's "atrium" is the *aula prima*, then the theater was to its left "a parte inferiori" (34). It consisted of marble columns supporting arches or vaulting (34): essentially a portico or loggia. Of course, he will not use the term *loggia*, since it derives from a medieval Latin term ultimately from the Old High German *louba*, meaning porch.[68] It may be that Manetti drew a formal connection between a multi-storied portico and theaters, the Theater of Marcellus in Rome being an example. Left of the Sala Regia today is the Pauline Chapel, occupying an upper floor of the old west wing of the *curia prima*. Thus, perhaps, Manetti returns to his description of the entrance court, which he said was "being built with colonnades and porticoes" (33) (how it appeared on the exterior), now in order to discuss its function (how it related to the interior). The location would be the space between the old *aula prima* and the narthex of St. Peter's, essentially the west wing of the *palatium inferiore*. As we saw, a three-storied portico or loggia on this site in the fourteenth century was replaced by Nicholas's successors: perhaps this is the site of the theater.

The west wing housed the stairs — the old *scala regia* — connecting the palace and the basilica, which is why if the emperor's quarters were on the top floor of this wing, essentially on the site of the Pauline Chapel, they could be described as "above St. Peter's' stairs." A letter of 1452 says Frederick III had four rooms "in the palace of the Apostolic Camera next to St. Peter's, contiguous with the holy pontiff's palace"[69] so the guest quarters must have opened onto the south side of the palace. Julius II created the Via Julia Nova as a replacement or renovation of the old stairs, and Bernini cut through it with his *scala regia*. The *theatrum* could have been built on top, or in front, of the old staircase, as Antonio da Sangallo did in the 1530s in order to support the Cappella Paolina.[70] In order to understand how and why the theater could have been built in the west wing of the *curia prima* we need to make a digression about the stairs themselves.

The old *scala regia*, as we see it on Uffizi 287A (fig. 14), flanked the Sistine Chapel, turned and ran under the *aula prima*, turned again and ended at the narthex of St. Peter's. Its date is unknown, although it must predate the Sistine Chapel. Pagliara's research suggests that in the late fourteenth century the staircase may have gone up one flight on the exterior from the *marescalcia*, ending at the room below the present Sistine Chapel: it did not go up to the *aula prima*, or

---

[68] Miller, *Bishop's Palace*, 63.

[69] A. Hack, *Das Empfangszeremoniell bei mittelalternlichen Papst-Kaiser-Treffen* (Cologne, 1999), 165, also believed this must mean in the west wing of the *palatium inferiore*.

[70] Marder, *Scala Regia*, 53.

if it did, it was not enclosed.[71] Yet before the time of Sixtus IV, a second flight did connect to the south/east corner of the *capella magna*, and this staircase was rebuilt under Julius II as a *cordonata*.[72] This is the state published by Alfarano in the late sixteenth century (fig. 21).

It has escaped scholars that Manetti discusses the old *scala regia* at 50:

> The supreme pontiff, accompanied by a large retinue of prelates, could make his entrance into this temple [St. Peter's] from the palace through many lovely entrances. The procession would move from an entrance [*aditus*] more splendid than the rest along a very beautiful spiral staircase [*cochlea*].

It is hardly likely that Manetti will have understood the term *cochlea* to mean "spiral staircase" (the word means snail, and, from the form of its shell, spiral); the pomp of papal descent would have been complicated rather than ennobled by such a contraption. What he instead means to do is to echo the staircase which 3 Kings records for Solomon's entrance into the temple in the Vulgate and which he quotes at 60: "ostium lateris medii in parte erat domus dexterae et per cochleam ascendebant in medium cenaculum." Thus he does not, as Magnuson thought, refer to the winding *turris scalarum* in the *curia prima*.[73]

Manetti seems to have consulted commentaries like that of Sicardus of Cremona, which defined the biblical form: "cochleae, quarum exemplar a templo sumitur Salomonis, sunt viae muris intervolutae latenter."[74] A similar definition is in Durandus of Mende's *Rationale divinorum officiorum* (1.1.37) where the circular staircases of churches, imitated from Solomon's Temple, are defined as "passages which wind among the walls." Josephus explains that Solomon made a stairway to the upper story "through the thickness of the wall" (*Antiquities* 8.2). What Manetti emphasizes, in fact, is that the staircase connecting palace and church was not exterior, but built within the walls, an important innovation of fifteenth-century palace planning.[75] Indeed, the earliest dated example of an enclosed interior staircase with axial flights in Rome is that of the Palazzo Venezia of 1465, built by

---

[71] P. N. Pagliara, "Nuovi documenti sulla costruzione della Cappella Sistina," in *La Cappella Sistina. La volta restaurata: Il trionfo del colore*, ed. P. De Vecchi (Novara, 1992), 256–65, here 260.

[72] Marder, *Scala Regia*, 35, 45 n. 82: 21 May 1506: "ita quod exivit per portam palatii . . . eo quod scalam, per quam soliti fuerunt pontifices descendere, demoliverant pro nova facienda, tali scilicet quod eques ire posset ex aula regali usque ad S. Petrum."

[73] Magnuson, *Studies in Roman Quattrocento Architecture*, 131.

[74] Sicardus, *Mitrale*, PL 213.22.

[75] MacDougall, review, 72, pointed out this novelty, without connecting it to the term "cochlea".

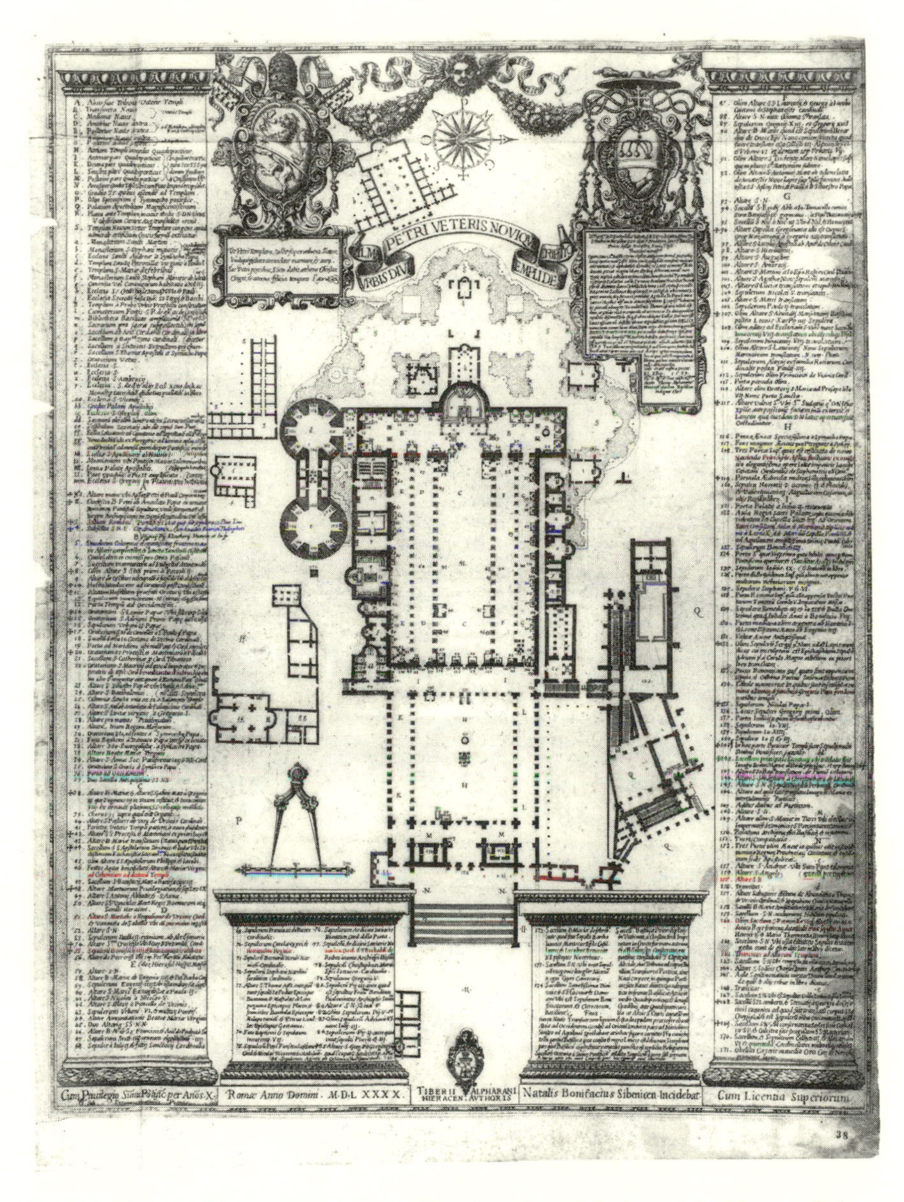

Fig. 21. Tiberio Alfarano, plan of St. Peter's and partial plan of the Vatican Palace, from *De Basilicae Vaticanae antiquissima et nova structura*, Bib. Vat., Chigi P VII, 9, fol. 38r.

one of Nicholas's cardinals.[76] The *cochlea* was not a spiral staircase, nor to be identified with the old *turris scalarum*, [77] but a renovation of the *scala regia*. Manetti mentions it both because it is a term of comparison between Solomon's and Nicholas's buildings and because it was an up-to-date feature of Nicholas's new palace. Very likely, Nicholas added the additional flight bringing the *scala regia* up to the audience hall and enclosed the whole. Dignitaries could be escorted through an entrance to the palace from the already existing landing in the northwest corner of the courtyard behind the *turris scalarum* onto the landing of the *scala regia* in the southern part of the *marescalcia*. From this entrance vestibule they could proceed up to the *aula prima* and be escorted to their quarters in the west wing. The *curia prima* would have had, then, three means of access to the *palatium superiore*: the *cordonata* just behind the entrance which led up to the later Cortile di San Damaso and was used by cardinals and, presumably, other important members of the Curia; the *scala regia*, entered from behind the *turris scalarum* or from the basilica's narthex, and used by those to be received in audience in the *aula prima*; and the old stairs in the *turris scalarum*, which led up to the Cortile del Maresciallo.

If Nicholas's project for the *theatrum* envisioned a loggia in which public acts would be viewed from a guarded outdoor vestibule, it might have been located in the *curia prima*. Alfarano's plan suggests there was a landing in the stairs at the center of the west wing (fig. 21): if this was also a feature of the earlier stairs perhaps Manetti's theater was a balcony in front of it from which the pope and other dignitaries could appear to crowds assembled in the courtyard. Such a balcony would have connected internally to the *aula prima*.

While this solution to the location and nature of Manetti's theater is attractive, another location must also be considered. In the medieval palace, the Cortile del Maresciallo served as an outdoor vestibule and from it a marble staircase, the Scala del Maresciallo, led to the *aula prima*.[78] We suggested that a new main access was being built from the *curtis* into the Cortile di San Damaso. Following this route, the first edifice encountered — and Manetti does say that the theater was the first sight — would have been the loggia facade of the east wing to the arches of which, at some point, a ground level portico was added.[79] We saw above that ambassadors were received in this garden area. And Manetti says that the

---

[76] Marder, *Scala Regia*, 213.

[77] As Magnuson and Marder did: *Studies*, 131; *Scala Regia*, 37, respectively.

[78] Along the south side of this courtyard Paul II erected a travertine loggia the piers of which were reused by Antononio da Sangallo the Younger to create a loggia at the foot of his enlarged Scala del Maresciallo (seen on Uffizi 287 A): Marder, *Scala Regia*, 36, 51, fig. 43; Pietrangeli, *Palazzo*, 38.

[79] Its porticoes and loggias were built by Nicholas III (some attribute them to Urban V [1362–1370]); the northern bays have been attributed to Nicholas V: Pietrangeli, *Palazzo*, 13, 36; Frommel, "Palazzo Vaticano," 121.

Vatican Palace was to have "three marvelous rows of the same number of arches" (61), which suggests that Nicholas intended to complete the loggia facade of the east wing. It could be that the theater was a loggia erected between the south corner of the east wing and the northern boundary of the *curia prima* (effectively a four-bay extension of the east wing's loggia facade): in it, we would suggest, would also be stairs going up to the *Sala dei Paramenti* on the same site as Bramante's. Renovations under Julius II destroyed evidence of earlier structures on this site, but we know that there was access through it to the Cortile del Maresciallo behind.[80] Manetti's theater could have been a free-standing loggia straddling the site, like those in Domenico Veneziano's St. Lucy Altarpiece (1445) and in the Berlin Panel, an anonymous architectural perspective of around 1470 (fig. 22); or the entire, extended three-story facade of the east wing, recalling the Theater of Marcellus; or a loggia attached to a wall like the Piccolomini Loggia in Siena and the Rucellai Loggia in Florence, both dating within a decade of the *Life*.[81] Whatever its exact form, Manetti's language suggests that this may be the right place. He says one encounters the garden "ab inferiori palatii parte" and also the theater "a parte inferiori" (34), so they seem to be in the same place.

But how is the atrium to the right of this theater as he states in 34? It does not seem likely that the *Sala dei Paramenti*, adjacent to the right on the next floor, was the main atrium or audience hall, so near to the papal apartments and serving an entirely different function. The *aula prima* could be said to be to the right of the site in question only by someone standing in the Cortile di San Damaso and looking towards it. From that perspective, view of its left side was blocked by the *turris scalarum*, the *scala del maresciallo*, and the Chapel of St. Nicholas, whereas its right side stood out above the other structures in front of it. Manetti does use right and left in this approximate and relative fashion, as is evident from the relations he establishes between the *atrium* and the Chapel, treasury, and triclinia. Nonetheless, if we imagine Manetti standing at the foot of the Mons Saccorum and looking west at the palace complex, it makes more sense that the theater, left of the *aula prima*, was in the west wing of the lower palace.

Chapel

Manetti's grammatical construction favors the reading that the chapel was to the left of the atrium. After describing the rooms to its right (the two triclinia) to one side (the treasury) and above, he turns our attention to what is on its left. In an alternative reading, he means left of the theater.

---

[80] Pietrangeli, *Palazzo*, 16.

[81] On Pius's loggia, see L. Jenkins, "Pius II and his Loggia in Siena," in *Pratum Romanum*, ed. Colella, 198–214.

Fig. 22. Architectural Perspective (Berlin Panel), Staatliche Museen Preussicher Kulturbesitz Gemäldegalerie, Cat. no.178 c. Bildarchiv Preussischer Kulturbesitz/Art Resource, NY.

During Nicholas's pontificate the Vatican had two chapels adjoining the *aula prima*: the *cappella magna*, built perhaps around 1370 on the site of the future Sistine Chapel, and the small Chapel of St. Nicholas.[82] Manetti says the pope intended to vault the chapel, and indeed Sixtus IV did vault the *cappella magna* when he rebuilt it some twenty years later. In the preferred reading of the Latin, Manetti means the *cappella magna* which, as Manetti says, had a very large vestibule. In this case, the chapel is "left" to someone standing in the *aula prima* facing the throne. However, if he means left of the theater, or left of the atrium in an absolute rather than relative sense, perhaps Nicholas intended to renovate the church of St. Vincent, located between St. Peter's and the palace, connecting it to the Scala Regia through the chapel of St. Gregory, an access Alfarano shows on his plan of the complex. In 1449 Nicholas transferred the priests attached to St. Vincent to the Chapter of Canons: perhaps he appropriated it for his own use, rededicating it to the Holy Sacrament.[83] It could also be that he planned to build a chapel on the site of the later Cappella Paolina, within the west wing, and left of the atrium as well: this is where at least one early source says Nicholas's chapel was.[84] Either Manetti has changed his standpoint in describing the relation of rooms to the atrium, or the chapel was to be in or behind the west wing of the *curia prima*. An argument can be made that the intended site is St. Vincent. One of the functions of the papal sacrament chapel, wherever it was, was as the site of the Easter Sepulcher. We know that in the sixteenth century, when the site was the Cappella Paolina, from Holy Thursday to Good Friday evening crowds of pilgrims venerated the place where the sacrament was reserved and then continued on to St. Peter's basilica.[85] Opening the palace to these crowds posed an evident

---

[82] Pietrangeli, *Palazzo*, 36.

[83] There is some confusion about the location of the Chapel of the Sacrament which Vasari says Nicholas built in the palace and Paul III destroyed (G. Vasari, *Le vite de' più eccellenti pittori scultori e architettori*, P. Della Pergola ed. (Florence, 1967-71), 381–88. Most scholars now believe that it was identical with the *cappella parva*, or Chapel of St. Nicholas, torn down by Paul III to rebuild the Scala del Maresciallo. However, the possibility that it was either in the west wing or on the site of St. Vincent remains, I think, open. Moroni, *Le cappelle*, 10, said Nicholas's chapel of the Sacrament was near the Cappella Paolina. In fact, San Vincenzo is almost directly below it. Writing around 1455, Maffeo Vegio mentions that the door between San Vincenzo and St. Peter's, near the altar of Sts. Philip and James (sixth column, right side) was "newly closed": *De rebus antiquis*, 4.144. Thus its only access was from the *scala regia*. The chapel was later used for storing wine for the Mass, and then, like the *cappella parva*, destroyed under Paul III. See *Tiberii Alpharani de Basilicae Vaticanae antiquissima et nova structura*, ed. M. Cerrati (Rome, 1914), 114; also Grimaldi, *Descrizione*, 281; and Westfall, *In This Most Perfect Paradise*, 118, n. 56.

[84] G. P. Chattard, *Nuova descrizione del Vaticano*, 3 vols. (Rome, 1762–1767), 2:52; in Zippel, "Paolo II," 182 n. 3.

[85] Kuntz, "Designed for Ceremony," 243.

security risk, and we have seen that safety was the key to Nicholas's project. St. Vincent, on ground level, accessed through the part of the palace in any case frequented by visitors and adjacent to St. Peter's, would have been a better place than either of the papal chapels on the upper floor.

Summation

This is the heart of the palace project, and we can suggest that Nicholas intended to retain the original nucleus with the west wing as its center, raising its height by the addition of a third storey, and renovating the connecting wings to the east and to the south. Communication between the upper and lower parts of the palace was a main concern, and much of the work would have involved stairways, a topic which Manetti does not dwell upon but the existence of which is implied by how he describes the pattern of circulation. What was innovative about the project was the rationalization of an existing fabric, the separation of its parts according to their function, and the creation of new routes to access them.

The Northern Section: Three Courtyards, Rooms, the Library, Kitchens, and Stables

Manetti began his description of the ceremonial areas of the palace, clustered around the atrium, as they appeared from the Cortile di San Damaso, and he resumes his account from this location. Across the "wall of the garden," to the west, were rooms (35). The wall is probably the old wall of the secret garden, discernible in contemporary views.[86] The rooms would be in the wing of Nicholas III (the east wing), behind the loggia facade overlooking the Cortile di San Damaso.

To follow the rest of his account, it will be useful to consider the palace as composed of four functional units. The first is the largest and comprises the most public and most ceremonial rooms: the *theatrum*; the *aula prima* with dining hall and benediction loggia above, *aula seconda*, and *aula tertia*; and the *capella magna* (or perhaps St. Vincent). This is the most important unit for Manetti: he begins with it and describes it in the greatest detail. The second unit, the papal suite, occupied the southern and central rooms of the east block and comprised on the second floor the *Sala dei Paramenti*; the *Sala del Pappagallo*;[87] a papal antechamber; and the papal bedroom. Kerscher has shown that the papal palace at Avignon

[86] See Westfall, *In This Most Perfect Paradise*, 148.

[87] We use here the designations from Nicholas's time; later, the *Sala del Pappagallo* was on the floor above.

and other fourteenth-century royal palaces regularly reserve a suite of four rooms located behind the great reception hall for the ruler: the Vatican Palace followed this traditional medieval typology.[88] He suggests that at the Vatican Palace, the *aula seconda* and *aula tertia* were originally called the *Sala dei Paramenti* and *Sala del Pappagallo* (as on fig. 13) (with the antechamber and bedroom behind them), and that the rooms in the east wing acquired these names and their functions in the fifteenth century. Since Manetti tells us that the *aula seconda* and *aula tertia* are part of the ceremonial, not the papal, suite, we may suggest that this change occurred under Nicholas (as on fig. 19). Nicholas retained the medieval typology but shifted the four-room suite to the east wing, thereby freeing up additional ceremonial spaces adjacent to the *aula prima*.

The *Sala dei Paramenti* was where the cardinals vested and where the pope mounted the *sedia gestatoria*: it is where processions into the *cappella magna* or St. Peter's began. But it was also used to receive cardinals and other worthies, to dine, to invest people with offices, and as a waiting room for reception in the *Sala del Pappagallo*. The *Sala del Pappagallo* had similar functions, but with more restricted access: the pope also dressed there. Manetti was made a papal knight by Nicholas in this room in April 1452.[89] Behind this was the antechamber, again for reception, but even more restricted; and finally the papal bedchamber, where the pope might receive visitors seated on a chair in front of his bed. At the Vatican, rooms of decreasing size led one into another from the *aula prima* and could be used for receptions, audiences, and consistories of a more and more intimate character culminating, as it were, with the private meeting in the pope's bedroom. If under Nicholas the four rooms in the east wing became the papal suite, then a stairway leading directly to the *Sala dei Paramenti*, the southernmost room of the east wing, would have been needed and, we suggest, was built. Nicholas's suite also had a study and chapel directly above his second-floor bedroom suite, to which there was presumably access from stairs in the tower in the southeast corner of the Cortile del Pappagallo. All of Nicholas's most private rooms were on the interior of the palace, on a courtyard enclosed on at least three sides and adjacent to or even inside of the old defense tower: the most secure and inaccessible part of the palace.

The third functional unit also has state functions, but is work space, meeting and reception rooms, and living quarters for the papal staff. Because Kerscher

---

[88] G. Kerscher, "Privatraum und Zeremoniell im spätmittelalterlichen Papst- und Königspalast. (Zu den Montefiascone Darstellungen von Carlo Fontana und einem Grundriss des Papstpalastes von Avignon)," *Römisches Jahrbuch der Bibliotheca Hertziana* 26 (1990): 87–134, here 114. See also B. Schimmelpfennig, "*Ad maiorem pape gloriam*. La fonction des pièces dans le palais des Papes d'Avignon," in *Architecture et vie sociale à la Renaissance*, ed. A. Chastel and J. Guillaume (Paris, 1994), 25–46.

[89] Böninger, *Die Ritterwürde in Mittelitalien Zwischen Mittelalter und Früher Neuzeit* (Berlin, 1995), 155.

identified the papal suite at the Vatican, showing that it adhered to a traditional typology, it can no longer be assumed that Nicholas intended his new north wing as his living quarters. It can, instead, be suggested that this idea originated with Alexander VI Borgia in the late fifteenth century and that it reflects a different functional concept. That Julius II took as his bedroom Nicholas's old study on the third floor and used the *Sala dei Palafrenieri* as part of his suite suggests a return to the older spatial configuration, but this is outside the scope of this study. What matters here is that the function of Nicholas's very large new wing requires explanation. This wing can be accessed from stairs in the north corner tower of the east wing leading up from the present Cortile di Belvedere where, we suggested, there would have been a courtyard. Access from the Cortile di San Damaso is also simple. Had the other new northern wing been built between the palace and the Great Tower, these stairs would have been the access route for that too. For what category of person was this route intended? The housing and offices of the financial branch of Nicholas's administration were clustered behind the west wing and the judicial branch in the south wing of the *curia prima*; not only the Chamberlain and the Treasurer-General with him, but also the Auditor, the Depositer, the Datary, the Penitentiary — all those whose work engaged them directly with the public — worked near the *curia prima*. But the third branch of government, the *Cancelleria* or Chancery, needed space. Headed by the Cardinal Vice Chancellor, this office of general administration, previously based at St. John Lateran, employed notaries, abbreviators, correctors, and scribes. In 1431 it met in a palace near San Marco; from the 1460s to 1520 it was housed in what is now the Palazzo Cesarini Sforza, begun by Nicholas's successor Callixtus III in 1458.[90] Room was also needed to keep archives. Some cardinals lived in the palace: Louis Scarampo, Patriarch of Aquileia and Cardinal of San Lorenzo in Damaso, was Nicholas's Chamberlain, resident with his suite behind the *curia prima*; Francesco Condulmer, who had been Chamberlain under Eugenius IV, headed the Chancery until his death in 1453 and was also a resident.[91] So was Bishop Giacomo Vanucci of Perugia, who lived in the treasurer's rooms.[92] Also requiring housing were the Palatine Cardinals, *cubicularii*, the Chamberlain of the Cardinals, Masters of Protocol, other key officials, and some members of the papal *famiglia*. The *famiglia* were those members of the Curia who, as closest collaborators of the pope, sat at his

[90] W. von Hoffman, *Forschungen zur Geschichte der Kurialen Behörden vom Schisma bis zur Reformation* (Rome, 1914), 130.

[91] Hack, *Empfangszeremoniell*, 165.

[92] Giacomo Vanucci, doctor of canon and civil law and bishop of Perugia, became treasurer and vice-chamberlain (i.e. in charge of taxes) in 1451; he lived and had offices in the north wing of the atrium of St. Peter's: Dykmans, *L'Oeuvre*, 799, 803 n. 5; Celenza, *Renaissance Humanism and the Papal Curia*, 57–58.

table: some, but not all, also lived at the palace. Under Eugenius IV the *famiglia* numbered 130 people, under Pius II 230.[93] It seems impossible that the Vatican Palace could have housed all these people: perhaps we should take more seriously Nicholas's statement that he intended to restore the Borgo as "a worthy and secure habitation both for the head [the pope] and for all the members and the whole Curia" (T6); repeated by Manetti: "so that the entire Curia together could live inside [the Borgo] in reasonable security and safety" (25). The Curia consists of the papal *famiglia*, the officers of papal administration (financial, judicial, and administrative — this would include the cardinals), and those who provided for the daily needs of the members of the court. While no figures are available, the Curia surely counted well over one thousand people, counting servants, and would have repopulated the nearly deserted Borgo.[94] It may be suggested, then, that all the new construction projected along the north boundary of the palace would have served as offices for the large staff now either resident or working at the Vatican instead of the Lateran. The north entrance would have been for those who came to work in the offices or who lived in the upper palace: it made it possible to avoid passing through the ceremonial and private papal suites.

The fourth functional unit, actually dispersed topographically, was that of service: food storage, cooking, dining, stabling, gardening, laundry, and sewing.

Manetti's description of the last two functional units (35–36) is summary and therefore permits diverse interpretations, although it clearly leads the reader from east to west along the northern side of the palace and mostly at ground level (i.e. the level of the artificial platform), culminating with the stables. The following interpretation is one possible solution.

Between the wall going west from the Great Tower and the east wing rooms was a court with a fountain. Manetti may mean the Cortile del Pappagallo, which in fact did have a fountain. Nicholas opened a passageway between the garden and this interior courtyard and installed a secondary kitchen, the *cucina diplomatica*, in the north nave of this corridor.[95] The kitchen could have served for banquets in the Sala dei Pontefici above, but also for a refectory for the papal staff, a suggestion taken up below. The location of the library "a bit higher" than the courtyard (35) has never been determined. While some scholars believe

[93] D'Amico, *Renaissance Humanism*, 40.

[94] Although under Eugenius IV the whole papal entourage numbered about 150, by the 1520s it included about 2,000 people. It would have been under Nicholas, the first pope to reside permanently in Rome and at the Vatican since the schism, that the numbers began to increase. See Stinger, *Renaissance in Rome*, 124, and H. Fernandez, "The Papal Court at Rome c.1450–1700," in *The Princely Courts of Europe. Ritual, Politics and Culture under the 'Ancien Régime' 1500–1750*, ed. J. Adamson (London, 1999), 141–64.

[95] Redig de Campos, *Palazzi Vaticani*, 32.

it occupied the rooms of Sixtus IV's library, this is not certain.[96] Recent opinion, however, does suggest that one entered from the Cortile del Pappagallo and looked out on the Cortile del Belvedere.[97] The library would have been in that part of the palace which was open to the staff as well as to all prelates, since Nicholas specified that it was for their use (13, 15). It has not been noticed that Manetti implies that although its location had been chosen, this library was never built: "He determined to found and build a unique and special library at a convenient location in his palace *as soon as* he had arranged all the items that he had collected in their own places with the proper designations" (15) (emphasis added). The books, inventoried immediately after Nicholas's death, were probably still in his study and the room adjacent to it on the third floor of the palace where they were accessible to those working in the new wing.[98]

Beyond the library to the north would be another court with fountains for the papal household: this might have been in the intermediate courtyard (now part of the Cortile del Belvedere), where there is a fountain.[99] In this location, the courtyard and fountain for the household would be outside of the palace although still within the new wall. Alternatively, the courtyard was on the site of the Fontana delle Torri, just north of the Sistine Chapel and again within the new wall to be built at the west. Both of these sites are lower than the palace platform, at about 27 and 17 m asl respectively. This courtyard, to be used by the papal family, supports our suggestion about the intended function of the northern side of the complex.

Kitchens would be next to this court "on the upper part." We know that kitchens stood between the *aula prima* and the western limit of Nicholas V's new wing, hence higher (at 38 m asl) than the just-mentioned courtyard: these were replaced sometime in the third quarter of the century.[100] Since wine and grain were stored in the basement of Nicholas's new wing, the kitchens cannot have been far away from them. Another court behind the kitchens, to the west "a superiori parte," would contain the stables: this would be somewhere between the Sistine Chapel and the Porta Pertusa, perhaps where Bufalini showed them. Stables in this location would be outside the palace walls but within the Leonine circuit: they would be furnished with water from the conduits running in the wall.

---

[96] This was L. Boyle's view in "Sixtus IV and the Vatican Library" in *Rome. Tradition, Innovation and Renewal. A Canadian International Art History Conference* (Victoria, B.C.), 65-73, here 67.

[97] These ground floor rooms have Nicholas V's emblem on their ceilings: Pietrangeli, *Palazzo*, 197.

[98] G. Cornini, "'Domenico Thomasii florentino pro pictura bibliothecae quam inchoavit': Il contributo di Domenico e Davide Ghirlandaio nella Biblioteca di Sisto IV," in *Sisto IV. Le arti a Roma nel primo Rinascimento*, ed. F. Benzi (Rome, 2000), 224–48, here 226, 243 n. 14.

[99] Pietrangeli, *Palazzo*, 251.

[100] Pietrangeli, *Palazzo*, 37.

The Southern Sector

Having arrived at a point west of the palace complex, Manetti returns to the *aula prima*, now observed looking east from the summit of the Vatican Hill, in order to orient his description of the remaining secondary and domestic spaces: "the main hall of this palace [i.e. the *aula prima* or atrium] was being opened in different directions, widely and spaciously" (36). Off one of the sides of the atrium, toward the north, would be bedrooms, reception rooms, and a chapel. He may mean the *cappella magna*, which opens off the north end of the *aula prima*, and its lower story which did in fact have rooms for the Master of Ceremonies and clergy. Or, perhaps more likely, he may be suggesting that the wing with the *aula prima* was to be extended north to meet Nicholas's new wing. This would have enclosed the Cortile del Pappagallo and made the whole upper palace a four-sided, almost square, structure around a courtyard, a typology just becoming popular for urban palaces in Florence. Off the south side of the *aula prima* would be new quarters, offices, and a garden for the Apostolic Chamberlain: these were in fact behind the west wing of the *curia prima* as we saw.

Conclusion

The most fundamental decision Nicholas made was to establish the level of the crest of the Mons Saccorum as that of the "building platform" of the Vatican Palace. This determined his treatment of his new wing, with a fortified basement level facing north over the valley to Mons St. Egidio; it caused him to raise the pavement level in the eastern wing of Nicholas III by eight meters, and it determined the height of the Great Tower as not higher than the building platform. It was really the Mons Saccorum that Nicholas ringed with walls, excluding the northern gardens and vineyards of Nicholas III. Effectively, the old *palatium inferiore* was isolated by walls on four sides and became an intermediate semi-public zone, a guarded and enclosed courtyard, where people dismounted and adjacent to which the financial and judicial branches of government had their offices.

Four staircases were reconceived or rebuilt. A main entrance from the *curia prima* into the Cortile di San Damaso was foreseen, supplementing the older route through the *turris scalarum*. This would be used by cardinals and other members of the household on their way to work, but it would also be a ceremonial route to the *aula prima*. The *scala regia* was either built or modified to connect the upper floor of the palace to the basilica as well as providing ceremonial access from the *curia prima* up to the *aula prima*. Stairs would have been built, unless they already existed, at the south corner of the east wing affording direct access from the Cortile di San Damaso to the *Sala dei Paramenti*; and the stairs in the tower at the north corner of the east wing would have acquired greater importance as an entrance to the upper-level offices from the Cortile di Belvedere and from the Cortile di San Damaso.

The plan was mostly about connections, access, fortification, and beautification. It made the maximum use of existing structures, whether walls or rooms, and added relatively small pieces to an existing fabric. Yet it enormously improved the functioning and security of the palace. The four functional units — ceremonial, papal, governmental, and service — were more clearly separated from one another, more easily accessible to the different groups using them, and provided with services such as water and dining facilities and with amenities such as courtyards and gardens. Access by foot to Castel Sant'Angelo was provided for in case of urgent peril, and the fortress was renovated as a palace annex. The Treasury was made more secure by an additional wall to the west. Visitors of high rank were accommodated in rooms overlooking the *curia prima* where they could be guarded and kept from penetrating further into the palace. The plan also provided new space for offices previously located at the Lateran, like the Chancery, in a kind of office park in the northern sector: the staff had free run of the garden, Cortile del Pappagallo, and Cortile del Belvedere, and perhaps the service of an in-house "cafeteria". This freed the old *curia prima* to be an entrance, reception, and ceremonial space while it defined the relation of staff to the pontiff's inner circle as proximate but separate: they did not have access to the most important and private parts of the palace. More open space and larger stables and kitchen accommodated the increased population working at the palace. All except the most privileged guests were separated from their horses on arrival, a kind of "valet parking" system which also heightened security. While renouncing easy access to the large gardens on Mons St. Egidio, Nicholas enlarged the little garden, the *hortus secretus*, to provide a closer and safer natural park on the site of the future Cortile di San Damaso. It was a plan that achieved a very great deal with a minimum of expense, and its wisdom is confirmed by the fact that so much of it was carried out by Nicholas's successors.

Chapter Seven

Praise and Blame for Nicholas's Patronage: Leon Battista Alberti and Giannozzo Manetti

At the end of Nicholas's life his building program was controversial. That Nicholas (and Manetti) were aware of criticism and intended to address it is shown by the inclusion of the pontiff's deathbed speech, best understood as an *apologia*, in the *Life*. In it, the pope refutes "some objections brought against our diverse building projects, slandered by many, as well as accusations against us personally" (*RIS* 947). The nature of these criticisms is given in the speech itself: it was "not ambition, not pomp, not vainglory, not a lasting propagation of our name" for which he conceived these works (T8). Nicholas, rebutting the personal accusations, does not address the "slanders" directed at the projects themselves. These Manetti defends, for his encomiastic description can be read as a carefully constructed refutation of Nicholas's detractors.[1] His *laudatio* of Nicholas's patronage of architecture in the *Life*, then, seeks not only to persuade his audience that Nicholas's works are worthy of praise, but also to dissuade readers from assigning blame. As a rebuttal to objections which were not developed as a formal *vituperatio*, but which are known from abundant, if fragmentary and sometimes indirect, evidence, Manetti's version of the building program argues for one side of a largely forgotten controversy. Alberti was the most vocal opponent of the building projects; his criticisms illuminate Manetti's defense.

In the older scholarly literature it was supposed that Alberti was Nicholas's chief advisor for the buildings and in some sense their designer.[2] Opinion on his

---

[1] H. Günther has also noted the responsiveness to critics of Manetti's *Life*: "I progetti di ricostruzione della basilica di S. Pietro negli scritti contemporanei: Giustificazioni e scrupoli," in *L'Architettura della Basilica*, ed. Spagnesi, 137–48, here 139–40. Simoncini gives further bibliography for the view that Manetti's *Life* is at least to some degree an apology for the money spent on books and buildings: L. Simoncini, "Roma come Gerusalemme nel Giubileo del 1450. La *renovatio* di Niccolò V e il *Momus* di Leon Battista Alberti," in *Le due Rome del Quattrocento: Melozzo, Antoniazzo e la cultura artistica del '400 romano*, ed. S. Rossi and S. Valeri (Rome, 1997), 322–45, here 336 n. 23.

[2] Alberti is documented as "litterarum apostolicarum scriptor et abbreviator" in the first year of Nicholas's pontificate, 1447 (Arch. Vat. regesto 433, cc.191A–191B), in Pagnotti, "La vita di Nicolò V," 413. Although he does not seem to have been on annual salary,

role evolved only slowly from Dehio's attribution of authorship to him in 1880 to Westfall's more cautious characterization of Alberti as advisor in 1974.[3] But since the mid-1970s it has changed radically. Eugenio Garin first distinguished Alberti's thought from Manetti's (in 1975), contrasting Alberti's pessimism in *Momus* with Manetti's faith in human nature in *De dignitate hominis* and showing how differently the two men responded to the same classical model, Cicero's *De natura deorum*.[4] Then in 1987 Manfredo Tafuri suggested that Alberti opposed, rather than contributed to, Nicholas's building plans. Tafuri's position, recently elaborated by Tavernor and increasingly gaining adherents in the specialized literature, is further supported by the textual evidence presented here.[5] Our position is especially close to that of Borsi's long meditation on Alberti's Roman experience.[6] Since the relevant portions of Alberti's views are in writings which are not securely dated, argument about his role must first address the problem of whether he indeed showed his treatise on architecture, *De re aedificatoria*, to Nicholas around 1452 — something which once seemed certain — and whether his satire *Momus* dates before, during, or after Nicholas's pontificate.

The Date of 'De re aedificatoria'

Until recently, scholars believed that Alberti presented his treatise to Nicholas in 1452 and that the pontiff interrupted his plans for St. Peter's on the architect's advice. However, since we now realize that the treatise surely contains material written after 1452, and most would agree that Alberti revised the work until his death in 1472, the old view about its presentation — and therefore its purpose

---

he received income-producing prebends. Ever since Dehio tried to show that Nicholas V's building project depended on Alberti, Manetti's account of that program has been read, at least by art historians, primarily as a veil through which Albertian ideas might be discerned. See G. Dehio, "Die Bauprojekte Nicolaus des Fünften und Leon Battista Alberti," *Repertorium für Kunstwissenschaft* 3 (1880): 241–57; most recently, Frommel, "Il San Pietro di Nicolò V," 109, with bibliography in n. 38.

[3] Dehio, "Bauprojekte"; Westfall, *In This Most Perfect Paradise*, 179–84.

[4] E. Garin, *Rinascite e rivoluzioni: Movimenti culturali dal XIV al XVII secolo* (Rome, 1975), 161 ff. This comparison was elaborated recently by Borsi, *Momus o del principe*, 58.

[5] Tafuri, "'Cives esse non licere'"; Tavernor, *Art of Building*, 209, n. 23; Borsi et al., *Maestri fiorentini*, 67.

[6] S. Borsi, *Leon Battista Alberti e Roma* (Florence, 2003). The book came out while ours was already at press, and too late to acknowledge each instance in which we have drawn similar conclusions from similar pieces of evidence. The reader should know that our arguments here and in the following chapter were arrived at independently of Borsi's book, and that the many, indeed fundamental, similarities point to some kind of consensus in the present state of Alberti scholarship.

and influence — requires modification.[7] Indeed, the most recent opinions, those of Tavernor, Burroughs, Grafton, and Borsi, propose dates not only after 1452 but as late as 1454 for Alberti's presentation of the work, probably still incomplete, to Pope Nicholas.[8] It will be our suggestion that some short writings on architecture, later incorporated into the treatise (10.1–17; 1.2–6; 8.6), were presented as early as 1452, while other parts of the treatise (2.1–3) respond to events near the end of Nicholas's life.[9]

First, a brief review of the evidence. The chronicle of Mattia Palmieri, which dates to 1475–1483, is the most explicit evidence for the presentation of Alberti's treatise on architecture to Nicholas.[10] Yet although it is invariably cited, its accuracy is uncertain. Not only is Palmieri's information second-hand, written twenty years after the events he reports, but its immediate contexts — Alberti's death and Paul II's resumption of work on the basilica — are entirely different from those in which Manetti wrote just after the pope's death or in which the events Palmieri records took place. There is no contemporaneous evidence that *De re aedificatoria* was ever presented to the pontiff, or even connected with him.[11]

Palmieri mentioned both the new tribune of St. Peter's and its interruption in his entry for the year 1452, an entry centered on another subject, the imperial coronation. He records that work on St. Peter's was interrupted on Alberti's advice:

---

[7] Tavernor, *Art of Building*, 15, with bibliography; Alberti, *Art of Building in Ten Books*, trans. Rykwert, xvii; Alberti, *L'Architettura*, ed. Orlandi, liii–liv.

[8] Tavernor suggested it was presented sometime between 1452 and 1454, perhaps before all ten books were written: *Art of Building*, 15. Burroughs thought it was presented to Nicholas in late 1453 or early 1454: *From Signs to Design*, 241. Grafton suggested that the large number of Greek sources cited in the treatise suggested that he was consulting the Latin translations made for Nicholas between 1451 and 1454: *Alberti*, 28, 279. Borsi, who is preparing a full-length study of the problem, believes that the earliest portions were connected with Ferrara and that the later portions (after 1452) can be dated by tracing the availability of the classical sources cited: *Alberti e Roma*, 227.

[9] V. Zoubov made a similar argument for completely different reasons in "Leon Battista Alberti et les auteurs du Moyen Age," *Medieval and Renaissance Studies* 4 (1958): 245–66.

[10] The Pisan Mattia Palmieri wrote *De temporibus suis* as a continuation of the chronicle by the Florentine Matteo Palmieri, *Liber de temporibus*, which ended in 1449. On the chronicle, see E. Cochrane, *Historians and Historiography in the Italian Renaissance* (Chicago, 1981), 24; and on the passage, Magnuson, *Studies in Roman Quattrocento Architecture*, 89; Tafuri, "'Cives esse non licere'," 63; C. L. Frommel, "'Cappella Iulia'. Die Grabkapelle Papst Julius' II. in Neu-St. Peter," *Zeitschrift für Kunstgeschichte* 40 (1977): 26–62, here 29, 30, 63–64; and Borsi et al., *Maestri fiorentini*, 64.

[11] Modigliani acknowledged this in her recent translation of Manetti's *Life*, yet accepted the conventional dating: *Vita*, 17.

> The pontiff, wishing to build a more ornate basilica to blessed Peter, lays a very deep foundation and erects a wall of 13 *ulnae*, but he first interrupts this great work, one that should be compared to any of the ancients', on the advice of Leon Battista; then his premature death breaks it off completely. This Leon Battista Alberti, a man of sharp and observant talent, refined in the liberal arts and in learning, showed the pontiff very learned books written by him on architecture.[12]

Palmieri tells a whole story in an entry which corresponds chronologically only to one episode, the beginning of the tribune. Alberti had died shortly before (1472) and Palmieri, who was one of the executors of Alberti's will, may have used the entry as an opportunity to commemorate the Humanist.[13] Thus the connections among the project, the treatise, and Alberti's advice may be loosely associative rather than synchronic. Palmieri's version of events, moreover, is at odds with documented facts: since payments for work on the tribune of St. Peter's begun in 1452 were still being made in 1454–1455,[14] it seems clear that the project was not ended on Alberti's advice in 1452; if it was interrupted, that can only have been in 1453 since the new tribune was only begun in the summer of 1452.[15] That Alberti's treatise is not included in the inventory of Nicholas's books at his death is troubling, although it could be supposed that Nicholas threw the work out, as he did Filelfo's biography of him in 1453. Since Nicholas also refused to read George of Trebizond's warnings about the Porcari conspiracy in 1452–1453, this was not untypical. Alberti satirizes the habit in *Momus*.[16] On the other hand,

[12] "Pontifex [Nicholas V] ornatiorem Beato Petro Basilicam condere volens, altissima jacit fundamenta murumque ulnarum tredecim erigit, sed magnus opus, ac cuivis veterum aequandum primo Leonis Baptistae consilio intermittit; mors deinde immatura disrupit. Leo Baptista Albertus vir ingenio praedictus acuto, et perspicaci, bonisque artibus, et doctrina exculto, eruditissimos a se scriptos de architectura libros Pontifici ostendit": *RIS*, 1:241.

[13] As pointed out by F. Caglioti, "Bernardo Rossellino a Roma, II. Tra Giannozzo Manetti e Giorgio Vasari," *Prospettiva* 65 (1992): 31–43, here 37.

[14] In October of 1454 Beltramo di Martino da Varese was paid for digging "passa 600 di fondamento che resta a la tribuna de Santo Pietro": A. M. Corbo, *I mestieri nella vita quotidiana alla corte di Nicolò V (1447–1455)* (Rome, 1998), 57. C. L. Frommel, "Francesco dal Borgo: Architekt Pius' II. und Paul's II.," *Römisches Jahrbuch* 21 (1984): 71–164, here 131.

[15] Borsi also follows this line of reasoning but believes that the payments in 1454–1455 are for work already done and that therefore the suspension of work dates to 1454–1455: Borsi et al., *Maestri fiorentini*, 64.

[16] George of Trebizond had been ordered to leave Rome in April of 1452. From Naples he wrote to Nicholas that the Porcari Conspiracy had been foretold by Joachim of Fiore's *Expositio in Apocalypsim*, but complained the pontiff would not read what he had sent. See G. Coluccia, *Niccolò V. umanista: Papa e riformatore* (Venice, 1998), 227. We cite Alberti,

Palmieri does not say that the treatise was dedicated or presented to Nicholas, only that it was shown to him.

Apart from Palmieri, evidence for the treatise's date is mention of such a work ("miei libri di architettura") in Alberti's dedicatory letter to Meliaduso d'Este (d. 1452) prefacing *Ludi rerum mathematicarum* and reference in that text to what today is the last book of *De re aedificatoria*, Book 10.[17] Flavio Biondo refers to Alberti as the author of books on architecture in his *Italia Illustrata*, begun in 1452 and revised between 1453 and 1455.[18] Another early testimony for Alberti's work is *De viris illustribus* of 1456, in which Bartolomeo Facio referred to "two books" on architecture by Alberti "which he wrote as dinner pieces."[19] Since none of the books in *De re aedificatoria* is as short as the works we know Alberti wrote as dinner pieces, Facio most likely refers to chapters later incorporated into the treatise.[20] The treatise must have existed in some form before 1463 since, as Borsi has recently shown, Francesco Patrizi drew from it in his *De institutione rei publicae*.[21]

In the early 1460s Aeneas Silvius Piccolomini, by then Pius II, wrote that "Alberti the Florentine composed extraordinary volumes on architecture" which "earned the pope's [Nicholas's] gratitude."[22] Although Piccolomini was absent from Rome on diplomatic missions during much of the papacy, he was Nicholas's subdeacon and therefore in the inner circle of the Curia although not yet a cardinal. While his information could have come from Nicholas, it just as likely came from Alberti himself, with whom most assume Piccolomini spoke at the Council of Mantua in 1459 about Vitruvius and his own project to rebuild Corsignano (Pienza). While his comment does not date the treatise (or some part of it) more precisely than to Nicholas's pontificate, it speaks of "volumes" and therefore of a substantial work, as well as supporting Palmieri's claim that these were shown to Nicholas. Piccolomini's testimony, then, is reliable evidence that some of the treatise at least was prepared and known to Nicholas and therefore written before 1455.

Momus, ed. Consolo, 3 (178). Hereafter we give the book and page number from this edition in the text.

[17] Alberti, *L'architettura*, preface, liii. In the dedicatory letter to *Mathematical Games*, Alberti says that he had written on architecture at the request of Leonello d'Este (d.1450). The text is in *Opere volgari*, ed. Grayson, 3:156.

[18] Alberti, *L'architettura*, quoted in preface, liii.

[19] *De viris illustribus*, quoted in F. Borsi, *Leon Battista Alberti* (Milan, 1975), 363.

[20] See L. B. Alberti, *Le intercenali*, ed. I. Garghella (Naples, 1998).

[21] Borsi, *Momus*, 80.

[22] Aeneas Silvius Piccolomini, "De Europa," in *Aeneae Silvii Picolominei Senensis . . . Opera qua extant omnia* (Basle, 1571), 459. Borsi also realized the importance of this testimony which has otherwise been overlooked by scholars: *Alberti e Roma*, 113.

While the treatise in its final form cannot be dated, portions of it reflect Alberti's experience at Nicholas's court and his awareness of Nicholas's building projects. He describes the dilapidated condition of St. Peter's (1.10) and proposes a means of restoring it (10.17). He may also have made a drawing for the restoration of Ponte Sant'Angelo, perhaps in response to the disaster on the bridge of 1450.[23] It has escaped notice that the topic of Book 10, at least some portion of which, we saw, dates before 1452, addresses in a systematic fashion those issues most crucial to Nicholas's renovation of the Vatican area. Under the heading of the correction of faults in buildings and regions Alberti discusses fortification, climate control, health measures, and water supply, and his last chapter, on building restoration, proposes the remedy for St. Peter's. Water supply and water damage receive the longest treatment. While Nicholas's activity in repairing the water supply to St. Peter's and the Vatican and improving the drainage system has received little attention, any project that involved populating the area would have to consider this a priority, and in fact Manetti tells us quite a bit about water supply (34–36, 43–44, 50): we discuss it at some length in the previous chapter and also in the Commentary. It seems plausible that Book 10, at least, was before 1452 and could have been shown to Nicholas.[24]

The first part of Book 1 and Book 10 are complementary, even dialogic. Although the title of Book 1 is "Lineaments of Buildings," chapters 2–6 examine what choices should be made in dealing with a new site, covering many of the same topics treated in Book 10 which examined how an already built site can be ameliorated. Whether to restore what exists or begin anew is dramatized — and satirized — in Alberti's *Momus*: after Jupiter has decided to make a new world he debates whether he ought to remake it on the model of the existing one or proceed by different attempts until chance puts a perfect model before him (3 [214]). This is the issue Alberti considered in a systematic and prescriptive fashion in Books 1 and 10 of *De re aedificatoria*: what conditions need to be considered and provided for in building on a new site as opposed to remedying an existing locale? It seems reasonable to identify Books 1 and 10, or some portion of them, with the two books Facio mentioned in 1456 and with the books on architecture which Palmieri and Piccolomini say were shown to the pope. They represent, in

---

[23] This is Tavernor's suggestion in *Art of Building*, 19. Alberti describes the bridge in his treatise at 8.6.

[24] Borsi also recognized that Book 10 reflects Alberti's Roman experience and does not fit into the structural system of the rest of the treatise. This led him, however, to see it as a later addition: Borsi et al., *Maestri fiorentini*, 46. But in his most recent study, Borsi associates the discussion of water systems and management with problems in the Po valley and thinks this part was written for Leonello d'Este: *Alberti e Roma*, 222–23. Our suggestion is that Alberti presented himself to the pope first as an engineer.

fact, Nicholas's alternative choices in regard to the Borgo, Vatican Palace, and St. Peter's — rebuild, or renovate — and offer a systematic categorization of the choices involved, replete with learned *exempla*.

Book 8, which in the final redaction of the treatise covers the ornament of public secular works, also seems early. It may have started as an antiquarian treatment of ancient building types, consonant with the interests of Flavio Biondo and Poggio Bracciolini, and have been worked on in the 1440s and early 1450s in Rome. In its sixth chapter, Alberti discusses Hadrian's Bridge and the main street in the Borgo.

All three books address Nicholas's interests and concerns and contain material on Nicholas's projects, and they seem to be among the earlier parts written. Book 10 we know existed by 1452: the same date can be proposed for the complementary material in Book 1. If these are Alberti's contributions to framing the scope and nature of the building projects, he appears to have been an eager and optimistic participant in Nicholas's grand project for renewal early on. This suggestion argues against the view that the treatise was to be a critical survey or epitome of Vitruvius or that it can be understood as part of Alberti's scholarly, antiquarian activities.[25] Although its earliest portion, Book 8, might have treated antiquities like Poggio or Biondo (although more technically), what are now the first and tenth books which followed show us, instead, an Alberti quick to realize the possibility of applying his reading and observation to contemporary problems. That other parts of *De re aedificatoria* and other of Alberti's writings which seem to be later criticize Nicholas and his buildings suggests disappointment and even a growing bitterness on Alberti's part. Only in this later phase, we suggest, did he enlarge the scope of his project and increase its scholarly character in order to produce a systematic treatise based on Vitruvius and incorporating his own earlier writings on architecture.

Why did Alberti become disillusioned with Nicholas's building projects? Whereas in 1958 Magnuson suggested that Alberti would not have approved of the design for new St. Peter's because it was old-fashioned, response to Nicholas's building projects by contemporaries suggests that style was never the subject of controversy.[26] This realization is reflected in the more recent literature. Burroughs saw Alberti as opposed to Nicholas on political grounds, evidenced in his depiction of the tyrant in *De re aedificatoria*.[27] This recent tendency to understand the

[25] The view of Grafton, *Alberti*, 273, following the suggestion of R. Krautheimer, "Alberti and Vitruvius," in *The Renaissance and Mannerism. Studies in Western Art: Acts of the Twentieth International Congress of the History of Art* (Princeton, 1963), 2:42–52.

[26] Magnuson, *Studies in Roman Quattrocento Architecture*, 211.

[27] C. Burroughs, "Alberti e Roma," in *Leon Battista Alberti*, ed. J. Rykwert and A. Engel (Milan, 1994), 134–57, here 153. Grafton reviews the literature on whether Alberti was opposed or not in *Alberti*, 302–15.

building projects as expressing the theological, functional, and political thinking of the pope has led to a re-evaluation of the importance of Manetti's theological and cultural contribution to them.[28] Indeed, Borsi went so far as to suggest that Manetti's arrival in 1453 contributed to the decline of Alberti's importance at the court.[29] The shift from seeing Alberti as advisor to casting him as detractor has meant focusing on his response to Nicholas's policies rather than on the proposed architectural forms. Yet, in our view, Alberti was deeply concerned with Nicholas's practice as a building patron. His evaluation of both the projects and politics was not consistent: rather, it changed over time, evolving from initial enthusiastic participation and proffering of advice to criticism and biting sarcasm.

The Date of 'Momus'

While it used to be thought that this satire by Alberti was written around 1444 during the pontificate of Eugenius IV, recent opinion places it as late as 1454.[30] Most of the recent scholarship on *Momus* identifies the target of this satire as Nicholas, with some darts aimed also at Eugenius, in the guise of Jupiter, creator of the world, king of the gods. Those who believe *Momus* to date in Nicholas's reign have suggested that it alludes to Nicholas's building projects, but have disagreed on whether these references are positive or negative. Grayson saw them as positive, observing that one of Alberti's themes is the responsibility of virtuous men to make order from disorder, and loosely connected the work to Nicholas's building projects, as also to Book 4 of the architectural treatise.[31] For Squarzina, instead, Alberti's intent is critical. In *Momus* Jupiter says he is sorry that he did not ask architects for a project to remake the world: Squarzina thought this expressed Alberti's criticism of Nicholas's intention of rebuilding St. Peter's instead

---

[28] Frommel, "San Pietro," 109; Borsi, *Momus*, 85.

[29] Borsi, *Momus*, 85.

[30] Voigt, *Il risorgimento dell'antichità classica*, 2:81, n. 1 (in Rome, 1451); C. Grayson, "Leon Battista Alberti: vita e opere," in *Leon Battista Alberti*, ed. Rykwert and Engel, 28–37, here 36 (before 1450); Tavernor, *Art of Building*, 19–22, with bibliography (1454); Borsi, *Momus*, 92 (after 1450). Borsi's most recent book, *Alberti e Roma*, extends and amplifies his earlier views.

Momus is preserved in a unique fifteenth-century (but not autograph) manuscript in the Vatican Library (MS. Vat. Ottob. 1424, in which *Momus* occupies fols. 65–143v): it seems to have had a very restricted circulation at the time of its composition. It was published in two printed editions in 1520: Alberti, *Momus o del principe*, ed. Martini, xxi.

[31] Grayson, "Leon Battista Alberti," 36.

of repairing it.[32] Tavernor associated the episode in *Momus* when Jupiter visits the theater built in his honor which then collapses with the collapse of the Great Tower in September of 1454, dating the satire to the last six months of Nicholas's life.[33] But the satire seems much more deeply critical of Nicholas's pontificate, so critical that it could hardly have been written while the pope lived and might well be contemporary with Manetti's *Life*, composed within a few months of his death. Indeed, in *Momus* the poor man Peniplusius accuses the tyrant Megalophe of exactly what Nicholas rebutted in his Testament as Manetti reports it:[34]

> Why is it that you boast that you have furnished temples and theaters when these are not for the adornment of the city but for the desire for glory and the silly perpetuation of your name? (4 [286])

In our view, *Momus* was written shortly after Nicholas's death and is therefore contemporary with Manetti's biography. Since Alberti's objections were not unique to him — or there would have been no audience for the satire — it is unclear whether Manetti responds directly to Alberti or more generally to Nicholas's critics.[35] Alberti's attitude towards Nicholas's building projects evolved from optimistic participation around 1452 to condemnation in 1455. We deduce the reasons for this change in Alberti's attitude both from what he praises and from what he condemns in the treatise and in *Momus*. Thus Alberti serves as a foil, explaining the sorts of criticism that Manetti attempts to dispel and bringing into focus some of his arguments.[36] We suppose that Nicholas's critics shared some of Alberti's opinions, and indicate these when evidence permits, but only Alberti wrote sufficiently in detail about architectural patronage and processes to permit a systematic comparison with Manetti's account. To Alberti's condemnation of

---

[32] S. Danese Squarzina, "La Basilica nel Quattrocento," in *La Basilica di San Pietro*, ed. Pietrangeli, 91–113, here 92.

[33] Tavernor, *Art of Building*, 22.

[34] Borsi also recognized this connection: *Momus*, 85.

[35] *Momus* would be an example of what Grafton called "coterie literature" — the ironic or cryptic works that Alberti wrote for a reader or a small group of readers: *Alberti*, 210–11.

[36] Borsi recognized that Manetti's biography is a response to Alberti's criticism, but he saw the 1455 *Life* as a rebuttal to the 1452 treatise on architecture (Borsi et al., *Maestri fiorentini*, 65). We are suggesting instead that in 1452 Alberti supported Nicholas's projects, that his attitude changed in the course of their actualization, and that he became negative only in 1454–1455. Therefore, this means that Manetti is rebutting contemporaneous criticism by Alberti and others at the same time that they are penning their complaints against Nicholas.

works undertaken and left incomplete, revealing the inconstancy, inexperience, and foolish grandiosity of the patron, Manetti will oppose an image of intended wholeness as evidence of Nicholas's diligence, foresight, and virtue. Alberti condemns demolition when it is unnecessary (the patron is incompetent) and because, at St. Peter's, of its historic value (the patron being unable to appreciate its significance for the present and future). Not so in Manetti's account. The past was preventing the present from realization: the patron is God's co-operator in salvation history.

Alberti's Complaint: Incompletion and Inconstancy

Regarding the patron's responsibilities in building, Alberti, especially in Book 2 of *De re aedificatoria*, expresses disapproval of procedures which we know Nicholas followed and for which others also criticized him.[37] Alberti warns against the shame incompletion brings: "We should beware of taking on anything without the resources to bring it to completion" (2.1).[38] Two men who had been close to Nicholas — St. Antoninus, Archbishop of Florence, and Aeneas Silvius Piccolomini, Nicholas's subdeacon — criticized his having begun more building projects than he could complete. St. Antoninus, although he praised Nicholas for the library project and for expenditure on liturgical furnishings, added:

> In enlarging the buildings of the palace and the church of St. Peter he seems to have combined less thought with a costly work, according to what everyone said, so that he validated that Gospel proverb, the mockery of those who fail to weigh their resources: 'This man started to build and could not finish.'[39]

Antoninus's "Gospel proverb" refers to a parable related in Luke:

> Which of you here, intending to build a tower, would not first sit down and work out the cost to see if he had enough to complete it? Otherwise, if he laid the foundation and then found himself unable to finish the work, the onlookers would all start to make fun of him saying 'here is a man who started to build and was unable to finish.' (14:28–30)

---

[37] Tafuri interpreted the presentation of the treatise as Alberti showing his credentials in support of his negative judgment of the project: "'Cives esse non licere'," 63. Borsi also realized that the criticisms of building practice in *De Re aed.* and *Momus* are complementary: *Momus o del principe*, 73.

[38] All quotations are from Alberti, *Art of Building*, trans. Rykwert. Hereafter the citation is given only in the text.

[39] St. Antoninus, *Chronicorum opus*, 3:540.

Piccolomini also complained that more had been attempted than could be completed:

> He wonderfully adorned the city of Rome with many great buildings. If his works had been able to be completed, they seemingly would not yield to any magnificence of the ancient emperors. But the buildings are still lying there like the huge ruins of walls.[40]

Alberti also associates a passion for building great edifices with vice and with the practice of the pagan Roman emperors, themes applied to Nicholas by Piccolomini and Pier Candido Decembrio (see below), saying: "Not everyone would approve of Nero's mania to build, and his passion for completing works of immense size" (2.1). The project was too ambitious to be completed, too expensive, and displayed intemperance.[41]

Alberti deplores inconstancy, urging the patron to prepare models and plans for the whole before beginning work. Nicholas's plans for building and decoration do indeed invite criticism for inconsistency. He paid Fra Angelico to finish the frescoes in the apse of St. Peter's which, three years after the paintings were completed, he decided to tear down. He repaired the windows in the basilica's nave and otherwise embellished it but, before his death, determined to replace the entire structure. In *Momus*, Alberti mocked this lack of foresight. Jupiter sets a day for unveiling his plan for the new world to the gods, but when the day comes, and although the destruction of the old world has begun, has nothing to propose (3 [194]).

Alberti also offers criticisms of Nicholas's procedures not articulated by contemporaries who, perhaps, both cared less and knew less about building, and, since his fuller and more technical discussion fleshes out issues to which others only alluded, Book 2 of *De re aedificatoria* uniquely illuminates Manetti's defense. Alberti repeats, approvingly, Eusebius's story that David and Solomon, building the Temple of Jerusalem — Manetti's paradigm for Nicholas's new St. Peter's — waited until they had gathered all the materials for construction and prepared all the plans before summoning the architect and workmen and beginning work (2.3). This is clearly not what Nicholas had done at the Vatican, having appointed the architects and workmen between 1447 and 1451 (13), that is, before the revenues from the Jubilee made large-scale building possible. Alberti's choice of Solomon's Temple as his exemplar, as it was Manetti's, suggests a dialogical relation between this part of the treatise and the *Life*.[42] Alberti warns

---

[40] Aeneas Silvius Piccolomini, *Europa*, chap. 58: in Müntz, *Les arts à la cour des papes*, 71.

[41] Borsi also realized this: *Alberti e Roma*, 67.

[42] As Borsi suggested, Book 9 especially seems critical of Nicholas for his lack of forethought and seems to reflect a date late in the pontificate or just after Nicholas's death: *Alberti e Roma*, 89.

against undertaking lightly the labor and expense of building, recommending the time-honored custom "practiced by the best builders, of preparing not only drawings and sketches but also models" (2.1). He returns to this subject later in the treatise:

> I must urge you again and again, before embarking on the work, to weigh up the whole matter on your own and discuss it with advisors. Using scale models, re-examine every part of your proposal two, three, four, seven — up to ten times, taking breaks in between, until from the very roots to the uppermost tile there is nothing, concealed or open, large or small, for which you have not thought out, resolved, and determined, thoroughly and at length, the most handsome and effective position, order, and number. (9.9).

And he assures us that this is an integral part of his own practice:

> I have often conceived of projects in the mind that seemed quite commendable at the time; but when I translated them into drawings, I found several errors in the very parts that delighted me most, and quite serious ones; again, when I return to drawings, and measure the dimensions, I recognize and lament my carelessness; finally, when I pass from the drawings to the model, I sometimes notice further mistakes in the individual parts, even over the numbers. (9.10)

Alberti did, in fact, prepare models for the projects on which he was involved: for the Tempio Malatestiano in Rimini, and for San Sebastiano and Sant'Andrea in Mantua. While Nicholas's practice in this regard remains conjectural, Manetti's linguistic practice suggests that he saw a plan of Rome and one of St. Peter's but that he did not have a graphic representation of the Vatican Palace.[43] The sense of Alberti's position, however, is that each part must be perfectly resolved not only in itself but in relation to the whole: one cannot build piecemeal. Concern with precise dimensions is the way in which relation can be evaluated before construction begins. It cannot be said that Manetti shared, or even understood, this view since he gives different units of measurement and even different measurements for the same architectural element (45, 49) (cf. above, 132) — unless, of course, he is accurately reporting drawings which have the careless mistakes Alberti speaks of. Yet if he did not think that the relationship of parts depended on numerical consonance, he understood the core of the criticism — that wholeness was essential to excellence — and responded to it in his version of the story.

[43] See Chapter 5.

Manetti's Version: A Unified Scheme Tragically Interrupted

Manetti's building account projects, retrospectively, a vision of the whole project as a unified, even ideal, program begun early in the pontificate (about 1451), partly realized by 1455, and tragically cut short by Nicholas's untimely death.[44] We should realize at the outset that this was almost certainly not the case. Nicholas's early commissions, for example, seem to have been piecemeal responses to necessity. More likely, the pope's vision of the nature and scope of renewal evolved over the course of his reign, achieving perhaps, and only at the end, the vision Manetti describes. Since, once Nicholas was dead, whatever plan he had in the last year of his life was perforce a culminating vision, Manetti needed only to project this final scheme back in time to an earlier moment in the pontificate in order to claim that earlier works were its constituent parts. Diverse strategies were employed to build up this positive image of Nicholas's patronage. For instance, Manetti created a unified picture of the building program by selecting from many architectural projects a coherent group for his ekphrasis. This meant omitting as many projects as, or more than, he included, as he himself says.

> Clearly, he [Nicholas] built many great buildings. We propose to remark only on the ones both outside and inside the City which the public visits because of their very great cost or unusual magnificence and to lay aside other similar buildings since they are truly countless. (22)

Yet Manetti also acknowledges that the building program was left incomplete. Of the five components of the project within the City, the first two — repair to the walls and of the station churches — were "brought to fulfillment and completely finished" (26); while the remaining three — renovation of the Borgo, fortification and adornment of the Vatican Palace, and the rebuilding of St. Peter's — were not. Manetti says that he will treat the unfinished projects in greatest detail "because the buildings would have been unusual and quite wonderful if they had ever fully come into the light, completed and carried out as he had planned" (26). He takes for his subject, then, Nicholas's plan for the completed state of works left in progress at the pontiff's death. This narrative device is one of the most, if not the most, difficult interpretive problems of the Manettian *Life*.

Scholars have assumed that Manetti describes (or pretends to describe) new buildings which Nicholas intended to build, or at least rebuild. If the structures Manetti mentions in the Borgo, the Palace, and the Basilica were indeed new

---

[44] Borsi recognized Manetti's importance in clarifying the nature and scope of the building projects and presenting them as a unified plan to critics, but he did not analyze the *Life* in detail: *Momus*, 84.

building projects then — as we know from documentary and archeological evidence — very little was actually done. Because of this disparity, scholars have questioned whether Manetti's account is true and if so, in what sense. At one extreme, Mack, who doubted that the pope ever seriously proposed to erect much or any of what Manetti describes, suggested taking the ekphrasis as "just sort of an utopian dream"; Burroughs similarly characterized it as "an ideal and artificial account."[45] At the other pole, Westfall suggested that the deathbed speech was, if not a summary of events, "a review of principles that Nicholas had formulated in 1447 and later executed."[46] Especially troubling for scholars is Manetti's failure to differentiate among "the achieved, the partly achieved, and the merely imagined."[47] Only Westfall attempted a positive interpretation of what others saw as idle dreaming or inflated praise, suggesting that Manetti was indicating "that what Nicholas planned would be built, because what Nicholas planned should be built; therefore, so far as Manetti was concerned, it had been built."[48] And he observed that Manetti "treats intention as accomplishment."[49] We discussed this issue in an earlier chapter, arguing that graphic plans existed: the problem is one of incomplete realization, the gap between intention and accomplishment.

Voluntarism was important for Manetti's understanding of human virtue: free will is posited as one of the three natural potencies of the soul that elevate man above all other animals in the *Oration on the Dignity of Man* (2.47–48). It is also evident in Nicholas's discussion of the sacraments in the Testament, and is integral to that moral virtue which Manetti most closely associates with Nicholas's patronage, namely magnificence (as found in Aristotle, *Nicomachean Ethics* 4.2.1122a19–1123a19). Like other moral virtues, magnificence is in essence an act of the will, not an exterior act such as the building of a building. The will does will the end, e.g. a building; but that the willed building is actually built is incidental to the moral act. The justifications for this are found in three contexts intertwined in Manetti's culture. First, it comes from Aristotle's *Rhetoric*, where we learn that *encomion* deals with achievement and that "achievements, in fact, are signs of moral habit; for we should praise even a man who had not achieved

---

[45] C. Mack, "Nicholas the Fifth and the Rebuilding of Rome: Reality and Legacy," in *Light on the Eternal City: Recent Observations and Discoveries in Roman Art and Architecture*, ed. H. Hager and S. Munshower (University Park, 1987), 31–56, here 39; C. Burroughs, "Below the Angel: An Urbanistic Project in the Rome of Pope Nicholas V," *Journal of the Warburg and Courtauld Institutes* 45 (1982): 94–124, here 123. Most recently, Günther, "I progetti di ricostruzione," 139–40.

[46] Westfall, *In This Most Perfect Paradise*, 18. His opinion was recently reiterated by Frommel, "San Pietro," 105–6.

[47] As Burroughs put it in "Below the Angel," 123.

[48] Westfall, *In This Most Perfect Paradise*, 104.

[49] Westfall, *In This Most Perfect Paradise*, 117.

anything, if we felt confident that he was likely to do so" (1.9.33–34). Second, it comes from Aquinas who considered magnificence connected to the cardinal virtue of fortitude and therefore an act of the will. It is the courage to do great works, not the actual completion of them, that constitutes the virtue (*ST,* 2–2, q. 134 a. 2–4). And finally, it is implicit in the voluntarist theology promoted by Nicholas and ultimately rooted in Augustine, especially in *On Christian Doctrine.* Westfall analyzed this theology in regard to Nicholas's emphasis on the sacrament of penance, and within penance, on confession and contrition;[50] but he neglected to observe that Manetti's approach to virtue is but the obverse of Nicholas's approach to vice, essentially voluntarist. The voluntarist position is expressed succinctly by Bartolomeo della Fonte: "God does not require the work of lips or hands, if we are not able to perform them, but only the will."[51] The same understanding of virtue is expressed by Timoteo Maffei, when he explained that magnificence is a moral disposition and is not defined by the making of large things. Although poor and rich alike may have this disposition, the exercise of magnificence is a gift of fortune.[52] And this is part of Manetti's intellectual solution to the problem of Nicholas's incomplete or unbuilt buildings: because Nicholas clearly planned and desired to build magnificently, and in fact took steps to do so (even in the plague year of 1450, Manetti tells us his building activity did not cease during his absence from the city [20]), his magnificence is on the scale of his plans, not on the scale of what he was able to complete before death interrupted. That was a question of fortune, which determined the exercise of virtue, but not its possession. Manetti insists: Nicholas pursued his projects with steadfastness, care, and precision to the last day of his life (13); and always was greatly concerned to finish projects (21).

Manetti marks the incomplete character of the last three projects through manipulation of verb tense forms. In normal Latin usage "he would have built . . ." conforms to the subjunctive syntax of the contrafactual condition or statement. And Manetti does write three of these when speaking of the potential of these buildings to surpass those of Solomon (55, 57). But for the ekphrasis itself — beginning with the description of the Borgo — he uses the Latin past progressive, not "he would have built . . . ," but "he was in the process of building. . . ." Manetti seems to be consistent throughout in this practice. For work that the pope

[50] Westfall, *In This Most Perfect Paradise*, 23–26. This view of penance proceeds from a conception of sin as "a willful act which could be expiated willfully."

[51] In Trinkaus, *'In Our Image and Likeness'*, 628, from *Donatus seu de poenitentia*, ca. 1468. On the will and ethics more generally, see B. Kent, *Virtues of the Will: The Transformation of Ethics in the Late Thirteenth Century* (Washington, DC, 1995).

[52] Discussed in E. Gombrich, "The Early Medici as Patrons of Art," in idem, *Norm and Form. Studies in the Art of the Renaissance* (London, 1966), 35–57, here 39–40.

completed in regard to his aims, that is, the first two projects (walls and station churches), Manetti uses the perfect tense, while the last three (the Borgo, Palace, and Basilica) are marked by verb tense as being in process.[53]

How Manetti's linguistic practice relates to the content of the ekphrasis is clarified by Aristotle's discussion of motion and potential in the *Physics* (3.1.201a16ff), where the philosopher gives as his example "the buildable":

> The actuality of the buildable as buildable is the process of building. For the actuality must be either this or the house. But when there is a house, the buildable is no longer there. On the other hand, it *is* the buildable which is *being* built. Necessarily, then, the actuality is the process of building. But building is a kind of motion, and the same account will apply to the other kinds [of motion] also.[54]

By using the past progressive tense, Manetti evokes the actuality of the buildable (motion and potential), not the actuality of the built (hypothetical fulfillment), for to describe the latter, he would have used the subjunctive. If he were describing buildings which did not yet exist as actual (fulfilled), he would not have used the past progressive, since motion ends with the fulfillment of potential. Manetti's language signals that the ekphrasis is not to be understood as utopic or ideal. In fact this example alerts us to a reflection on potentiality and actuality also characteristic of his thinking about the Church Militant and Church Triumphant, as we will soon see. For now, let it be enough to establish that Manetti understood there to be two kinds of actuality, one a process (in motion) and the other a final state. He did not view the process as merely the potential for achieving the final state.

Nicholas's aim as patron was, of course, the built (fulfillment), not the buildable (process): this was the final end, the cause for which all other things were done. Put differently (but still in Aristotelian terms), building was not the final cause of Nicholas's patronage. Although this seems obvious, some contemporaries criticized Nicholas's passion for building activity as an end in itself. For instance, Pier Candido Decembrio spoke of his "insatiable thirst for building."[55]

---

[53] Modigliani also realized that the tense distinction corresponds to the status of the project described: *Vita*, 56.

[54] Philoponus's comment on this passage from the *Physics* makes it even more precisely applicable to architecture: "Stones are potentially buildable; when, therefore, they are being built, they acquire the completion which has respect to their potential, their capacity for building being actuated, and this kind of actuation of theirs is called building, and this building is a change": in CAG 16, ed. G. Vitelli (Berlin, 1887), 351; trans. M. J. Edwards (London and Ithaca, 1994), 22. We thank Leslie MacCoull for this source.

[55] M. Borsa, "Pier Candido Decembrio e l'umanesimo in Lombardia," *Archivio storico lombardo* 20 (1893): 5–75, 358–441, here 376. See the discussion in Burroughs, *From Signs to Design*, 20.

And Poggio's biography in the *Liber pontificalis* begins the account of Nicholas's building by saying "in the judgment of many, he exceeded moderation in building" and then criticizes the renovation of Castel Sant'Angelo as "a superfluous work, very little needed."[56] Alberti's criticism of Juno's "lust for building" in *Momus* (3 [184]) is probably also directed at Nicholas.[57]

Did anyone besides Manetti believe that Nicholas pursued an overall, coherent program of building? Certainly the cardinals who attended Nicholas's deathbed speech (assuming it is authentic) knew the motives, aims, and general outline of all the work planned because they were told. Yet discussion of Nicholas's buildings in some of these same cardinals' funeral orations gives no hint of such knowledge. Niccolò Palmieri, who spoke on the first day, said little about buildings in his eulogy, noting only that Nicholas had raised up the temples fallen in the City.[58] Jean de Jouffroy, surely present at the deathbed and probably Manetti's informant, compared Nicholas to Romulus and Remus for his work on the walls of Rome; to Augustus for his public buildings; to Hezekiah and Jeremiah who walled cities; and to Beseleel, the builder of the tabernacle.[59] Yet by choosing disparate historical models he diminishes, rather than enhances, the impression of a unified program. At the funeral, which took place in one of the uncompleted projects, the basilica itself, only completed commissions were mentioned, with no hint that anything more was planned.

Manetti's carefully ordered account, unconfirmed by those as well as or better informed than he, suggests that observers did not understand that what seemed to be a myriad of scattered, even pointless, building interventions were actually integral parts of an overall scheme, the logic of which he sets out in both Book 2 and the Testament. His choice of tense itself implies that Nicholas's goal was not process but result and, by distinguishing as complete or in process the various parts of an overall plan, he rebuts criticisms that Nicholas was a dabbler, or that he expended time and money without having clear goals. In Manetti's

---

[56] *Le Liber pontificalis*, ed. Duchesne, 2:558. Pius II, instead, saw the renovation of Castel Sant'Angelo as part of the strengthening of fortifications of the Leonine City in preparation for the arrival of Frederick III.

[57] A. G. Cassani, "'Libertas, frugalitas, aedificandi libido'. Paradigmi indiziarii per Leon Battista Alberti a Roma," in *Le due Rome del Quattrocento*, ed. Rossi and Valeri, 296–321, here 308.

[58] N. Palmieri, "Oratio funebris per Nicolaum tunc Catazarii nunc Ortanum episcopum et Civitatis castellane in funere Nicolai Pape Quinti prima die exequiarum," Bib. Vat., MS. Vat. lat., 5815, fols. 3r–12v, here 9v. On Palmieri see J. Monfasani, "A Theologian at the Roman Curia in the Mid-Quattrocento. A Bio-bibliographical Study of Niccolò Palmieri," *Analecta Augustiniana* 54 (1991): 321–81 and 55 (1992): 5–98.

[59] Jouffroy, "Oratio Episcopi Atrebatensis," 30v. On Jouffroy, see C. Märtl, *Kardinal Jean Jouffroy (d. 1473). Leben und Werk* (Sigmaringen, 1996).

portrait of Nicholas as builder only the pope knows the reason for which things are done, sees the intended result as if already built, and knows how the parts relate to the whole. In Aristotelian terms (*Metaphysics*, 1.1.981), he is the architect, not the artifex.

Yet Manetti is clear that Nicholas's aim was not to build buildings but rather to win devotion and obedience to the church and glory for himself, and that his own subject is how the buildings would have brought this about. Indeed, he never claimed that Nicholas was concerned with architectural and urban design in the narrower, formal sense, but with fortification, ornamentation, healthy air, and devotion (25). The end, or goal, of the building program was: "that by continually constructing great edifices the honor of the Roman Church and the glory of the Apostolic See as well as the singular and particular loyalty of all Christian peoples might be more abundantly and broadly enlarged"(13). Because these results had not been achieved, Nicholas's program was incomplete. Thus Manetti addresses the criticism of incompletion in terms of unrealized goals, not unfinished buildings. Although St. Antoninus and Piccolomini, knowing that more had been planned than was completed, complained that physical buildings were left unfinished, Manetti emphasizes intention evidenced by the ongoing process.

Manetti presents Nicholas's completed program as a whole of such kind that even if one detail remained incomplete, the whole project could not be said to be *perfecta* and *absoluta*, that is, finished.[60] This is because Nicholas's building plan for the Borgo, palace, and basilica was about the integrity of the whole and the relation of its constituent parts. That is, it concerned coordination, articulation, and enhancement, understood in terms of location, function, and reception. In this total plan, style, or even architectural form, were not the primary bearers of meaning. Although there probably were physical plans of a specifically architectural character that Manetti saw, the plan in Nicholas's mind was something very different.

The pontiff envisioned a built complex accommodating all functions (domestic, official, and religious) and eliciting the desired response from its various audiences. This ideal had nothing to do with design theory, whether architectural or urban. Instead, it exemplified Ptolemy of Lucca's recommendation in *On the Government of Princes* that the king founding a city or a kingdom needs to "distinguish the parts of the chosen place according to the exigencies of those things which the perfection of the City or Kingdom requires" such as where

[60] Unexpectedly, this follows Alberti's definition of the beautiful as a relation of parts to the whole of such kind that nothing could be added or taken away or changed without detriment to the whole (*De re aed.*, 6). But the definition is hardly original with Alberti, and Manetti may instead have in mind Thomas Aquinas's requirement of *integritas* for beauty, itself derived from Aristotle. See Eco, *The Aesthetics of Thomas Aquinas*, 65–66.

study, exercise, and the conduct of business would take place.[61] That is, it was grounded in political theory. For Manetti (although not necessarily for Nicholas), as we will see, it was also theological. Places needed to be designated for sacred matters, for the administration of law, and for artisans. People needed to be assigned suitable places for their duties, and the necessities of each individual, according to his constitution and state, needed to be provided. Manetti covers each and every one of these criteria in his description, especially in that of the Vatican Palace and Borgo. Certainly, this was the first time that the Vatican site had been conceived of in such fashion: it may be the first time that such a diversified urban area had ever been comprehensively conceived.[62] If this is true, the project had little or nothing to do with the rediscovery of Plato's *Republic*, with civic humanism, or with nostalgia for the classical past, and everything to do with Aristotle's *Politics*, and with its Thomist, Scholastic interpreters. Ptolemy's treatise was itself attributed to Thomas and is inventoried as such in Nicholas's library.[63] If, as we suggested, Books 1 and 10 of Alberti's treatise on architecture were originally shorter pieces presenting updated and more technical surveys of what conditions need to be considered in planning a new, or amending an old, site, they would be evidence of how political precepts were applied to the real situation in discussions at the court around 1452. And this would open the possibility that Renaissance urban and architectural theory realized in built form general principles rooted, yes, in classical thought, but interpreted for contemporary life by Scholastic theologians.

The crux of Nicholas's scheme was the re-adaptation, coordination, and selective improvement of a large area which had been developed in a piecemeal fashion over the previous thousand four hundred years. In Manetti's view, Nicholas's main achievement was that he conceived the site as a whole and that its unity would have been apparent to a spectator. This building complex would have had everything it "ought to have" as determined by Nicholas's vision of the Apostolic See and, in broadest terms, by his understanding of the papacy in itself, in its relation to immediate staff and external visitors, to the Petrine legacy, the canons, the city of Rome, and to western Christendom. Instead of offering a verbal

---

[61] Ptolemy of Lucca, *On the Government of Rulers. De regimine principum*, trans. J. Blythe (Philadelphia, 1997), 1.14.4, 97.

[62] C. Thoenes also saw the project as a first attempt to see the Borgo, basilica, and palace urbanistically. However, while we agree that the project was a "piano regolatore" and not utopic, we do not believe that optical or axial design principles were as important as functional considerations: "Studien zur Geschichte des Petersplatz," *Zeitschrift für Kunstgeschichte* 26 (1963): 97–145, here 101.

[63] Müntz and Fabre, *La bibliothèque*, 69; Manfredi, *I codici latini di Niccolò V*, number 246 (now MS. Vat. lat. 774).

definition of the papacy (Nicholas would have said, "of the Church"), his understanding of its nature was exemplified through the building program. Each part of the Vatican project articulates the relationship of a part of the church to its head, exemplifying Cardinal Domenico Capranica's metaphor for the doctrine of papal primacy: "The Pope is the head, and from him goes out the authority to the others as to the members of the body."[64] How the evolving concentration of power in the person of the pope is paralleled by the evolution of the Vatican complex and how the Vatican gives shape to this concept has not been much studied (as Marder, having reviewed the recent literature on the development of the "ecclesiastical monarchy" between 1450 and 1650, observed).[65] Frommel's recent work recognizes this need and begins to address it.[66] Manetti's representation of Nicholas's plans and purposes is pertinent to these very questions.

To achieve the pontiff's aims, a large number of rather small projects would have been going on at the same time at different locations, an hypothesis confirmed by what we know from documents of Nicholas's procedure as a patron of these projects. This helps to understand why, to contemporaries, his building program seemed to be scattered and fragmented. People who did not know the whole of the planned final outcome might well have wondered how work on the Great Tower (31), for example, was related to that at Castel Sant'Angelo (30) or inside the palace (34–37). Manetti's ekphrasis reveals, as does Nicholas's Testament, the relation of the parts to the whole as well as the result that would have been achieved at completion. But his message becomes clear only when we realize that Manetti describes already-existing buildings and that the project's overriding concern, as Nicholas said, was security.

We saw that the palace project foresaw very little new construction and was, instead, about the modification of what already existed.[67] The project had little or nothing to do with creating Renaissance buildings, either in style or in type, but was a modernization initiative involving a large number of small, probably simultaneous, interventions over most of the existing palace and some new construction. Its fundamental wisdom is vindicated by virtually every feature of the project — understood conceptually rather than architecturally — being carried

---

[64] Capranica's *Quedam avisamento* is quoted by R. Colella, "The Cappella Niccolina, or the Chapel of Nicholas V in the Vatican: The History and Significance of its Frescoes," in *Fra Angelico and the Chapel of Nicholas V*, ed. I. Venchi et al. (Vatican City, 1999), 60, n. 134, where it is discussed in relation to Nicholas's Chapel in the Palace.

[65] Marder, *Scala Regia*, 249.

[66] Frommel, "San Pietro," esp. 109.

[67] In Chapter 6. Tafuri recognized that much of the Borgo project re-used the existing medieval fabric, but no one has extended this observation to the Vatican Palace: "'Cives esse non licere'," 48.

out within the next two centuries by Nicholas's successors. Indeed, it is widely agreed that work on the Vatican under Alexander VI, Sixtus IV, and Julius II was indebted to Nicholas's vision.[68]

A word on what we may conclude about Manetti's mind rather than Nicholas's project from his presentation. He does not evaluate architecture in terms of workmanship, taste, proportion, design, style, or materials, and only rarely in terms of sound construction. Rather, his main criterion is function (utility). Yet, within that category, his yardstick is not much different from Alberti's understanding of beauty as "that reasoned harmony of all the parts within a body, so that nothing may be added, taken away, or altered, but for the worse" (*De re aed.* 6.2). This does not mean that he learned it from Alberti, since the criterion of wholeness has a long lineage and diverse applications. It may ultimately be Aristotelian, where the philosopher defines excellence as completeness:

> We call complete that outside of which it is not possible to find even one of the parts proper to it . . . [and] that which in respect of excellence and goodness cannot be excelled in its kind . . . and excellence is completion; for each thing is complete and every substance is complete when in respect of its proper kind of excellence it lacks no part of its natural magnitude. (*Metaphysics* 5.16.1021b)

Manetti used a similar definition of ideal wholeness in his *On the Dignity of Man*, describing the human body as having all necessary and no superfluous parts (1.35). Wholeness as a measure of goodness was accepted as a general principle by many Scholastic theologians, including Aquinas, who included it as the first criterion of beauty (perfection, proportion, and clarity: *ST,* 1, q.39, art.8) and further qualifies all perfection as possessing order (*ST,* 1, q.5 art.5). Indeed, Aquinas's judgment of the goodness of anything depends on its reference to the whole universe in which every part has its own perfectly ordered place (*ST,* 1, q.49, art.3). While Alberti did something quite new in applying this kind of definition to architectural form, Manetti is making something very different of it. For we will see that the "wholeness" of Nicholas's building projects embodied the perfection of the church. But first we need to consider some other objections to them.

---

[68] Frommel, "Palazzo Vaticano," 122; F. Borsi, *Bramante* (Milan, 1989), 291; Pietrangeli, *Palazzo Vaticano*, 217; G. Rocchi Coopmans de Yoldi, "La Fabbrica di San Pietro da Niccolò V a Urbano VIII," in *San Pietro. Arte e storia nella Basilica Vaticana* (Bergamo, 1996), 71–167, here 75; Günther, "Progetti," 142.

Incompetence: Demolition and Historic Preservation

Since renovation entails demolition, Nicholas's project to rebuild St. Peter's calls into question his attitude towards the preservation of the past, for which his translation and library projects have made him famous. In the first months of his pontificate, Nicholas demolished several, but not all, shops in the atrium of St. Peter's.[69] He seems also to have demolished the old church of St. Benedict to clear the entrance court of the Vatican Palace and, before 1451, a large number of churches and houses in Piazza San Pietro.[70] He razed all the houses near Castel Sant'Angelo (28). In 1453 considerable demolition occurred in and near St. Peter's which destroyed or altered some of the old oratories and changed the devotional character and practices of the basilica. In July of 1453, while clearing the site and digging new foundations west of the old apse of St. Peter's, underground chambers with burials were discovered: the mausoleum of the Anicii (the so-called Temple of Probus) was probably demolished about this time ("a" through "e" on our fig. 23, see p. 257).[71] By July of 1453 a chapel dedicated to St. John the Baptist, patronized by the Orsini family, had been demolished to make way for the tribune. This chapel was in the end of the north transept, in the old Baptistery. In 1453, the monastery of San Martino was razed. The oratory of the monastery had recently been restored and embellished by Cardinal Giovanni de Broniaco Vivariense (d. 1426), bishop of Ostia and Vice-Chancellor of St. Peter's, so it was presumably in good repair. Before 1454, the bronze statue of St. Peter, which had been housed in the oratory, was moved to the oratory of SS. Processus and Martinianus in the south transept of the basilica.[72] The oratory of Hadrian I, against the west wall of the south transept, was renovated at the same time in order to accommodate the *cathedra Petri*.[73] Another oratory that was demolished, Sta. Croce, was one of the most privileged in the old basilica because it housed a relic of the True Cross. This oratory, situated against the west wall of the north transept, had been in the charge of the canons and had its own chaplain.

---

[69] Burroughs, *From Signs to Design*, 119. Since one of the canons was given permission to "repair, adorn, and extend" a house in the atrium, it does not seem that Nicholas intended to clear it.

[70] Grimaldi, *Descrizione della basilica*, ed. Niggl, 370.

[71] Vegio, *De rebus antiquis*, 4.106–111. Faltonia Proba, widow of Anicius Sextus Petronius Probus, erected the mausoleum after his death sometime between 383–395 A.D. The sarcophagus was brought to the Chapel of St. Thomas on the south side of the nave and adapted for use as a baptismal font.

[72] P. Réfice, "'Habitatio Sancti Petri': Glosse ad alcune fonti su S. Martino in Vaticano," *Arte medievale* 4 (1990): 13–16, here 15.

[73] Grimaldi, *Descrizione*, 396.

That Nicholas's desire to preserve did not extend to architecture is suggested by projects elsewhere than the Vatican. For the project to widen the street on the other side of the Tiber (Canale di Ponte), Nicholas ordered a nearby triumphal arch torn down and its spoils used for paving.[74] The papal account books are full of payments for the transport of marble and travertine from the Circus Maximus, the Aventine, Sta. Maria Nova, the Forum and the Colosseum.[75] In one year alone, 2,500 cart loads of stone were taken from an amphitheatre.[76] Most of the *spolia* were gathered between 1450 and 1452, but some in 1453 and 1454. By May of 1452 Nikolaus Muffel saw four columns 1.79 m thick and 13.63 m high brought from behind the Pantheon and erected in the choir of St. Peter's (in "Sand Peters Kor").[77]

That the Humanists deplored such destruction is well known.[78] Both Poggio and Biondo, whose ambivalence toward Nicholas's buildings we explored above, were among the most vehement protesters. Poggio lamented the destruction of ancient Rome in *De varietate fortunae*, the work he dedicated to Nicholas in 1447.[79] Biondo, in *Roma instaurata*, deplored the "the shameless hand of those who removed stones and marbles to other very shabby constructions." Of such destruction, he commented, "we see each day so many examples that for this reason alone we sometimes feel disgust at living in Rome" (1.104, 3.8).

Tavernor suggested that Alberti might have made drawings of Old St. Peter's and the Borgo, just as he made a restoration drawing of Ponte Sant'Angelo, either to counter Nicholas's project or to prove his own worth as an architectural advisor.[80] Vasari, who owned Alberti's drawing of the bridge, thought it had been made for Nicholas.[81] If he did this, he would be the first to apply the notion of historic preservation to an entire urban complex. Returning once again to the parallelism between Books 1 and 10 of the architectural treatise, Alberti offered Nicholas an either/or discussion of site planning which may reflect how

---

[74] Burroughs, "Alberti e Roma," 148.

[75] See Corbo, *Mestieri*, 29.

[76] Müntz, *Les arts*, 107.

[77] Nikolaus Muffel, *Beschreibung der Stadt Rom*, ed. W. Vogt (Stuttgart, 1876), 91; and G. Satzinger, "Nikolaus V, Nikolaus Muffel und Bramante: Monumentale Triumphbogensäulen in Alt-St.Peter," *Römisches Jahrbuch der Biblioteca Hertziana* 31 (1996): 92–105. Satzinger argues that they were not in the apse but were used for a triumphal arch between the nave and transept.

[78] See R. Lanciani, *Storia delle scavi di Roma e notizie intorno le collezioni romane di antichità*. vol. 1 *(1000–1530)* (Rome, 1989), passim.

[79] The relevant portion is in R. Valentini and G. Zucchetti, *Codice topografico della città di Roma* (Rome, 1953), 4:230–45.

[80] Tavernor, *Art of Building*, 25.

[81] Vasari, *Vite*, 3:288.

the problem of the Vatican area was framed early in the pontificate. He could have presented these alternatives as *intercoenales*, detailing the consequences of each: would renovation, with isolated and rather small interventions, produce an adequate result for the various functions and papal program, or was it necessary to start over with new structures and a new layout?[82] A recently discovered document assuring us that Alberti was part of the papal *famiglia* in the early years of the pontificate and thus ate at the pope's table confirms that he had such opportunities.[83] Documented work on St. Peter's and our analysis of the Vatican Palace project suggest that Nicholas's initial decision was for renovation. But within that choice lay a wide spectrum of options about what and how much should be retained. Renovation, moreover, inevitably posed difficult engineering problems owing to the dilapidated condition of some structures as well as to the sloping terrain on which they stood. Alberti's proposal for straightening St. Peter's walls (10.17) is an example of a solution which was sure to be costly but less sure to be successful.[84] It was precisely because the problems of renovation were practical ones and therefore required professional competence that Alberti criticized Nicholas's impetuous and amateurish direction of his projects. Alberti's drawing of the bridge, instead, restored to it a covered portico, probably extrapolated from the porticoed street in the Borgo which he also describes. This was based on Alberti's antiquarian studies and likely intended to restore the bridge to an imagined original state: this required not only specialized knowledge but also the assumption that Nicholas should bring back the Vatican area to an earlier condition. There is no evidence that Nicholas shared this archeological interest and — judging from the amount of demolition — much that he did not.

It seems unlikely that Alberti supported the idea of rebuilding St. Peter's from the ground up as Manetti twice says was Nicholas's intention (25 and 27).[85] In his treatise he recommended restoring rather than rebuilding it (1.10 and 10.17).

---

[82] Alberti did in fact write *intercoenales* — dinner pieces — somewhat earlier, most of which are, in the broadest sense, moral philosophy (see note 20). We are suggesting a different kind of conversation at the pope's table, having as its subject the practical problems posed by residence at the Vatican and a learned argumentation for and against solutions carried on in Humanist circles since the beginning of the century.

[83] A document of 1449 refers to Alberti as "decretorum doctore scriptori apostolico et familiarj domine nostrae papae" (ASV reg.Vat. 409, fol. 45r), in H. Burns, "Leon Battista Alberti," in *Storia dell'architettura italiana. Il quattrocento*, ed. F. Fiore (Milan, 1998), 114–65, here 159.

[84] He would have cut out each of the sections of the wall that leaned and replaced them, supporting the roof with a kind of sailing tackle during the operation. The device, which he calls a *capra*, was a weight-lifting mechanism. Alberti's experience in attempting to raise an ancient ship at Nemi (probably in 1446–1447) was of special relevance for this proposal. That attempt was also costly and unsuccessful.

[85] For the view that he did, see for instance Partner, *Renaissance Rome*, 16.

> I have no doubt that eventually some gentle pressure or slight movement will make it collapse . . . I would prefer, however, those whole sections of wall to be strengthened on both sides. (1.10)

In *De re aedificatoria,* Alberti condemns the unnecessary demolition of buildings, warning against beginning work by demolishing existing buildings or laying extensive foundations for the whole: "This is what a foolish or rash man would do" (2.1). But this, instead, is what Nicholas did when he tore down the structures behind the apse of St. Peter's to lay the foundations of the new apse. The old Christian cemetery with the tomb of Pope Leo was dug up and destroyed, and the Mausoleum of the Anicii (or Temple of Probus), believed to be Peter's house, was also demolished. The mausoleum was, as far as we know, directly behind the old apse and not in the way of the new foundations for the tribune project. Why did Nicholas demolish it? The answer seems to be given by Alberti. Before excavating an *area*, he says, you need to mark out its corners and sides, but:

> The inexperienced do not know how to set out these angles without first removing everything within the *area*, leaving the ground clear and absolutely level. Accordingly, they send in demolition men, wielding their mallets with less restraint than they would against their enemies, to ruin and destroy everything. Their mistake must be corrected. Misfortune, unforeseen developments, chance, and stringency may often hamper an undertaking and prevent the completion of what is begun. Moreover, it is not proper to show disrespect to the work of our ancestors, or fail to consider the comfort that citizens draw from their settled ancestral hearths; there will always be time enough to do away with, demolish, and level whatever is standing anywhere. Therefore, I would prefer you to leave all old buildings intact, until such time as it becomes impossible to construct anything without demolishing them. (3.1)

If the inexperienced know how to lay out the perimeter of the building platform only on a perfectly level and leveled site, the expert, instead, knows how to do this without altering what is there. This is a surveying problem, a subject on which Alberti wrote in his *Ludi rerum mathematicarum*.[86] His *Descriptio urbis Romae*, which recent opinion also places before 1453, is itself a demonstration of point-to-point sighting, that is, of surveying techniques. Both works may well date shortly before the demolition of structures behind St. Peter's.[87] The perfectly

[86] Grayson, "Leon Battista Alberti," 34. See also P. Souffrin, "La geometria practica dans les *Ludi rerum mathematicarum*," *Albertiana* 1 (1998): 87–104.

[87] Jacks, noting the close connection between Alberti's knowledge of surveying in *De re aedificatoria* and in the *Descriptio urbis Romae*, dated the works close to each other in 1452–1453: *Antiquarian*, 102.

leveled site would serve for laying out the perimeter of the new building with ropes swung from points on the central axis. In the case of St. Peter's, the structures directly behind the apse would have to have been leveled to clear the main axis and permit ropes to be stretched from it to points defining the perimeter. It would seem that Nicholas demolished structures in places that were not being built on, at least not immediately, in order to obtain a level and leveled site for laying out the new apse.

Manetti's Version

Alberti's criticism of the "inexperienced" who believe that a site has to be leveled and level in order to begin building is directly refuted by Manetti in his account not of St. Peter's, but of the Great Tower:

> He [Nicholas] did not want to have it [the tower] erected higher than was planned for the level platform for building the palace. He did this because he realized from the ancient learning of the proven architects that no building, particularly a large, superior one, could be built well and attractively except on a flat surface [*plana superficie*] and on a platform that had been leveled on all sides [*solo undique adequato*]. In fact, the man who desires to found correctly and, as they say, 'to the rule' and to build magnificently must make all of the new building's places [*loca*] consistent with the level surface of the platform [*equabilem soli superficiem*]. (31)

This, the only passage in the *Life* that addresses Nicholas's knowledge of construction, centers on the importance of clearing and leveling the building platform, exactly what Alberti had said the "inexperienced" think they have to do. And it asserts that Nicholas had consulted the most competent sources for his practice. Manetti's defensive tone, his assurance that Nicholas followed the best experts, and the over-charged informational content of the passage, compared to Manetti's normal usage, as well as its insistence on the importance of obtaining a level plane, suggest that more was at stake here than describing a tower.

Nicholas had reason to be sensitive to criticism about building on sites that had not been perfectly leveled. Stefano Infessura tells us that the pope rebuilt the church of San Teodoro twice: the first time he repaired the existing structure (1450), which then collapsed from the foundations; the second time he rebuilt it entirely.[88] Since the second campaign took place between January of 1453 and April of 1454, the first attempt had failed before the Great Tower fell in September

[88] Infessura, *Diario*, 1132, given also in Müntz, *Les arts*, 145. On the church and its restorations, see F. Fasolo, "San Teodoro al Palatino," *Palladio* 5 (1941): 112–19.

of the latter year.[89] It could be said that San Teodoro fell because the intervention did not take place on a perfectly leveled site.

Alberti condemns those who do not build on a perfectly cleared site:

> All the more to be blamed are those who, without taking the trouble to seek out a naturally solid piece of ground suitable for bearing the weight of a building, find the leftovers of some ancient ruin and rashly use them as the base for a wall of considerable size, without inspecting the dimensions and their state of repair closely enough: greed to reduce costs will be responsible for destroying the whole building. (3.3)

Nicholas's new wing for the Vatican Palace seems to have been built on the remains of the Leonine Walls, rubble from which is also under the present Cortile di San Damaso (figs. 13 and 19). Nicholas faced problems with inadequately level or leveled sites both for the artificial platform beneath St. Peter's, which had eroded to the south, and in the area for the new apse.[90] Manetti claimed that Nicholas intended to "rebuild the sacred church of St. Peter anew, from the foundations up" (27, see Commentary for discussion). That is, he intended to level it. This would have permitted the platform on which it stood to be rebuilt and made level again. Not only is St. Peter's on an artificial platform which uses ancient mausolea as foundations, but Nicholas's new apse also would have stood on the foundations of demolished buildings. The decrepit condition of Old St. Peter's demonstrated that its site was poor, not only because of the ruins and the double slope of the Vatican hill (from west to east and north to south), but also because the soil under it was mostly sand.[91] To build further in this area was risky. About the comparable site of one of the Seven Wonders Alberti says:

> The excellent Cresiphus, who was responsible for the very famous temple of Diana at Ephesus, was not so rash as to lay the foundations of so vast a building on land that was uncertain or insufficiently firm. (3.5)

Manetti rather surprisingly omits comparison of St. Peter's with the temple at Ephesus in the section claiming its superiority to the Seven Wonders (55–56), perhaps because he wished to avoid linking Nicholas's name with that of

---

[89] A. Frutaz, *Il Torrione di Nicolò V in Vaticano* (Vatican City, 1956), 17.

[90] St. Peter's rested on an artificial platform about 240 m long and 90 wide, substantially larger than the church itself (90 m long in the nave and 63 m wide: M. Cecchelli, "Il complesso cultuale Vaticano, dalla fondazione costantiniana ai lavori eseguiti fino al pontificato di Gregorio Magno (anno 604)," in *La basilica di San Pietro*, ed. Pietrangeli, 39–56, here 39.

[91] De Angelis d'Ossat, *Carta geologica della Città del Vaticano.*

Herostratus who burned the Temple so that his name would be remembered. Alberti's example of how a prudent builder would have prepared a solid building platform (taken from Pliny, *HN*, 36.95) also exposed Nicholas's inadequacy.

Manetti's passage about the tower responds to these Albertian criticisms. The Great Tower was one of the only projects that seems to have been built on a fresh, if not entirely level, site and Manetti makes the most of this virtue. We saw that Nicholas decided to ring the palace with walls at the base of the Mons Saccorum, rejecting the circuit of Leonine walls which traversed the sloping topography: the latter had not been built on a level site and required constant repair. However, to remedy this slope, the site of the palace platform, would require enormous quantities of earth fill — an extremely expensive undertaking which we know was never carried out and which itself might well have drawn criticism as unnecessary. Yet Manetti's defense of a perfectly leveled or level site for the Great Tower refers additionally to the undoubtedly more controversial plans to take down the Constantinian basilica in order to rebuild soundly; and it rebuts criticisms regarding the demolition that had already taken place behind the basilica. The Great Tower fell, with loss of human lives, in September of 1454, six months before Nicholas died, as San Teodoro had also fallen. By the time Manetti wrote, not only had Nicholas rebuilt the church and the tower, but he had also leveled the area behind St. Peter's and set his mind to leveling the nave as well.

Who were the ancient and approved architects whose learning made Nicholas understand that to build well and beautifully the platform (*solum*) had to be leveled on all sides? It cannot be Alberti, even if his advice was similar, because he is not an ancient. This intriguing appeal to authority invites consideration of who was considered as such in mid-Quattrocento Rome. Alberti lists as those ancients who wrote useful things about construction: Theophrastus, Aristotle, Cato, Pliny, Varro, and Vitruvius (*De re aedificatoria*, 2.3). Of these, only Vitruvius was a practicing architect, but he is not our source since he speaks of foundations rather than the platform's surface.[92] Whom could Nicholas have considered to be an ancient authority on architecture apart from him? Since Vitruvius's is the only treatise on this art to survive from antiquity, his information must come from some other category of writing. In the library at San Marco in Florence, Vitruvius was shelved with works on human civilization and military engineering (Pliny, Lucretius, Vegetius, Tacitus, and Caesar's *Commentaries*).[93] But Nicholas's procedure is not found in these authors, nor in those cited by Alberti. Nicholas's predecessor, Benedict XIII (1394–1423), had shelved Vitruvius not with ancient authors but with philosophy, where he also placed other works on the mechanical arts (Palladius, *De agricultura*; Frontinus, *De aquis urbis Romae*;

---

[92] See our Commentary at 31.

[93] Schuler, *Vitruv im Mittelalter*, 126.

and Boethius, *De disciplina scolarium*).[94] And in other fifteenth-century libraries Vitruvius was placed near Columella, Cato, and Varro. Of course, there was no section on architecture in any of these libraries because it was not yet considered to be a category of knowledge, nor was there one in the library of Nicholas V. Thus Manetti's evocation of "the ancient learning of the proven architects" could refer to a number of authors only peripherally involved with architectural matters. Yet we have not found the recommendation to build on a perfect level (or leveled) site in any of the above.

Once again the ancient authority turns out to be the Bible, in this case Josephus's retelling of Solomon's construction of the Temple, one of Manetti's main sources for his account in *De illustribus longaevis*. Describing the outmost temple, or Court of the Gentiles, Josephus writes:

> When he had filled up great valleys with earth, which, on account of their immense depth, could not be looked on when you bent down to see them without pain, and had elevated the ground four hundred cubits, he made it to be level with the top of the mountain on which the temple was built, and by this means, the outmost temple, which was exposed to the air, was even with the temple itself. (*Jewish Antiquities*, 8.9.97)

Nicholas's authority is King Solomon as architect/patron and his "proven" architect, Hiram of Tyre. Of course, neither Manetti nor Nicholas realized that the great engineering work that created the vast Temple Mount as Josephus describes it was done by Herod the Great rather than Solomon. In Manetti's comparison, the Vatican Palace is the equivalent of the outmost temple (the Court of the Gentiles), and it has to be on a level platform (level in the sense of having been built up, not leveled meaning excavated). Of course, this does not mean that Nicholas planned to raise the platform of St. Peter's to be equal with the palace. But the biblical model justified the enormous expense of the earthworks necessary to create a level platform for the palace as well as the principle, also applicable to other of Nicholas's projects, that he who wishes to build magnificently has to build on a perfectly level and leveled platform. Manetti chooses the less controversial project of the Great Tower to depict Nicholas as a building patron of great learning and sound judgment.

Josephus's explication of the establishment of the Temple evokes Isaiah's prophecy: "Let every valley be filled in and every mountain and hill laid low, . . . let every cliff become a plain . . . then the glory of God shall be revealed" (Isaiah 40:4, repeated in Luke 3:4–6); but even more closely, Baruch's promise that Jerusalem, which God calls "peace through integrity," will be made a place of safety:

[94] Schuler, *Vitruv im Mittelalter*, 123.

"For God has decreed the flattening of each high mountain, of the everlasting hills, the filling of the valleys to make the ground level [*in aequalitatem terrae*]" (Baruch 5:4–7). In these texts the connection between leveling the ground and the coming of salvation is clear, and that was probably what attracted Nicholas to them; we shall return to this theme in the last chapter.

The Incompetence of the Ignorant and Arrogant

In *De re aedificatoria*, Alberti urges the patron to consult the most competent people:

> In these matters — as I repeatedly advise — be guided by the knowledge of experts and the counsel of those whose advice is honest and impartial. For it is through their opinions and teaching, rather than your own personal whim and feeling, that you will more likely achieve perfection. (2.3)

and again:

> I advise you not to embark on anything without the advice or, better still, the instruction of the greatest experts. (9.11)

We know that Alberti held this view as early as 1454. In a letter of 18 November of that year to the executing architect of the Tempio Malatestiano in Rimini, Alberti praised the patron, Sigismondo Malatesta, for consulting with everyone about his project: "I am extremely pleased that my lord does as I wished, and that is, to take good counsel of all."[95] This was written in Rome four months before Nicholas's death.

In the same letter, Alberti attacked the views of a certain "Manetto." Recent scholarship, taking up Yriate's 1882 proposal, suggests that this "Manetto" was our Giannozzo.[96] The letter records Alberti's rejection of a proposal by "Manetto"

---

[95] C. Grayson, *An Autograph Letter from Leon Battista Alberti to Matteo de'Pasti, November 18, 1454* (New York, 1957). The letter is reprinted in A. Turchini, *Il Tempio Malatestiano, Sigismondo Pandolfo Malatesta e Leon Battista Alberti* (Cesena, 2000), 620. See also A. Calzona, "Leon Battista Alberti e l'immagine di Roma fuori di Roma: Il Tempio Malatestiano," in *Le due Rome del Quattrocento*, ed. Rossi and Valeri, 346–63.

[96] C. Yriate, *Un condottière au XV° siècle. Rimini. Etudes sur les lettres et les arts à la cour des Malatesta d'après les papiers d'état des archives d'Italie* (Paris, 1882), 243; Scapecchi, "*Victoris Imago*," 156, 160; C. Hope, "The Early History of the Tempio Malatestiano," *Journal of the Warburg and Courtauld Institutes* 55 (1992): 51–154, here 104; Turchini, *Tempio*, 273.

regarding the proportions of the dome and criticism of a suggestion about the form of the windows. The letter expresses vehement opposition to round windows (*occhi*).

> As for the matter of the windows (*occhi*), I wish that people who claim to be professionals knew their trade. Tell me why people interrupt the wall and weaken the building in making windows. For the sake of light. If you can get more light with less weakening of the fabric, aren't you acting in the worst possible way in giving me that inconvenience? From the right edge to the left edge of the round window the wall is broken, and the weight above is supported by as much arch as occupies a semicircle. The structure below is in no way strengthened by the fact that the window is round, and that which ought to provide light is obscured. Many arguments could be adduced about this matter, but this alone is enough for me: that never in a building that is praised by those who understood what no one understands now, never, never will you see a round window.[97]

The immediate context of Alberti's remarks is not clear. He may refer to the large circular window in the upper part of the thirteenth-century facade of the Tempio Malatestiano which Alberti had to decide whether to retain or replace.[98] But what is important for us is that round windows were an especially characteristic form for Nicholas's Roman projects being built at exactly this time. Documents

---

[97] As translated by Hope, "The Early History," 114. The Italian is in Grayson, *An Autograph Letter*, 18:

> "Del fatto delli occhi, vorrei chi fa professione intendesse el mestier suo. Dichami perché si squarca el muro et indeboliscono lo edificio in far fenestre? Per necessità del lume. S'tu mi puoi chon men indebolire havere più lume, non fai tu pessime farmi quel incomodo? Da mam dricta a mam mancha dell'occio riman squarciato, et tanto archo quanto el semicircolo sostiene el peso di sopra: di sotto sta nulla più forte el lavoro per essere occio, et è obturato quello che debba darti el lume. Sonci molte ragioni a questo proposito, ma sola questa mi basti, che mai in edificio lodato presso a chi intese quello che niuno intende oggi, mai, mai vederai fattovi occhio."

[98] Turchini, *Tempio*, 148–50. Matteo de'Pasti's medal shows that he intended to cover it over. Hope, instead, thought that Alberti was arguing against a proposal to place round windows in the upper part of the nave walls of the Tempio, the gothic window form of the chapels below having been determined before his involvement with the project. And he observed that the combination of traceried gothic and round windows had precedent in Florentine buildings such as the cathedral and Sta. Maria Novella, San Petronio in Bologna, and the Cathedral of Verona, all large-scale gothic structures: Hope, "The Early History," 114.

report "occhi" being made for Sto. Stefano Rotondo, for S. Teodoro and for the chapels built at Ponte Sant'Angelo.[99] In the *Life*, Manetti singled out the round windows which he says Nicholas planned for the rebuilt St. Peter's as especially beautiful: the new tribune would be "exquisitely adorned on both sides with windows fashioned in the form of great eyes" (46) and "round windows, exquisitely fashioned in the form of great eyes . . . ring the whole circuit most attractively, like a shapely crown of windows" (47). Indeed, Manetti claimed that Nicholas's design for St. Peter's was superior to Solomon's Temple precisely on account of these oculi: "in place of its [the Temple's] oblique windows, transverse and orbicular ones would appear [in St. Peter's]" (59).[100] Thus Alberti's comment in 1454 that "you will never find round windows in a building praised by those who understood such matters" criticizes the architectural style of Nicholas's buildings and specifically that of the proposed new St. Peter's as Manetti describes it. The comment is, in fact, the only certain stylistic criticism of Alberti's which can be applied to Nicholas's buildings. But it is not only a rejection of one window form for another: Alberti argues that round windows do not have any structural advantage, nor are they superior as a source of light. In short, he rejects them as form, as function, and as structure.[101]

In *Momus*, much of Book 3 satirizes Jupiter's consultation with experts on building. Alberti shows us a foolish patron who listens to irrelevant authorities and self-seeking courtiers rather than to qualified professionals and those who would offer disinterested advice. Momus asks whether Jupiter is making a new world for himself or for others — again the implied criticism Nicholas rebutted in his Testament — because, says Momus, if for others, he should take an opinion poll on what kind of a new world the people would like (3 [165]). Of course, neither Jupiter nor Nicholas had any commitment to democracy. Since Jupiter has no vision of the new creation he has decreed, he seeks advice, first from the ancient philosophers, who prove useless. Then he sends Apollo who, wanting to show that he can speculate using the same method as Democritus, engages in a complex exegesis of the meaning of a cut onion, a speculation about the end of time reminiscent of Scholastic theological dispute (3 [213]). Next Jupiter consults the assembled gods about whether anything of the present world should be saved or whether everything should be torn down. The gods all make fools of themselves since they have no ideas and only seek their own interests (3

[99] Müntz, *Les arts*, 142, 146, 152.

[100] St. Peter's already had three oculi in the south transept wall which had been installed in the twelfth century; a drawing of the 1530s by Marten van Heemskerck shows an oculus in the tympanum of the main facade as well: De Blaauw, *Cultus et decor*, 632.

[101] It is difficult to understand why, then, Alberti put round windows in his Mantuan buildings, San Sebastiano and Sant'Andrea.

[196–203]). Jupiter realizes that the good ancient architects are too decrepit to make anything new and that the modern practitioners are inept, so he consults with neither (3 [222]). In the end he abandons the project, but not before causing much damage and receiving great humiliation.

While we do not know with whom Nicholas conversed about his projects (other than Frederick III), Manetti's *Life* provides evidence of how much the projects were framed on the basis of ancient authorities, especially Scripture, and other non-professional sources. His architectural ekphrasis is insistently grounded in literary texts, rather than in experience. Manetti's architectural vocabulary is often derived from scriptural exegesis; his notion of space is closer to Aristotle and Roger Bacon than to recent developments in mathematics, geography, and painting; his understanding of the meaning of buildings depends on St. Paul, St. Augustine, and Durandus of Mende. True, he knows how to read a map and a plan, but he uses these aids conferring credibility on an argument which is really centered on issues of the faith and on politics. Manetti's approach to architecture is like that of Democritus in *Momus* (3 [48–53]), formed by Scholastic logic and concerned with literary abstractions. In Manetti's portrait, Nicholas shares much of this formation. He wanted St. Peter's to be modeled on Noah's Ark, because he had read about this in the authorities; or to be like Solomon's Temple; or the body of Christ: King Solomon is his model of an engineer. While it is easy to imagine Nicholas discussing such ideas with cardinals like Juan de Torquemada, it is inconceivable that Alberti would agree that a patron should model his building on literary images, inherently theological rather than architectural ideas. From Alberti's point of view, as we find it in *De re aedificatoria*, neither Manetti nor Nicholas would count as competent people. But it is not just their literary approach to building that Alberti objected to. To Alberti, it was ridiculous to use Scripture as a handbook for contemporary architectural practice. Architecture, for him, was a branch of knowledge which applied scientific knowledge to practical problems. In *Momus* every new construction collapses almost as soon as it is built: Juno's rainbow-colored and golden arch falls to pieces with a deafening crash (2 [156]); the theater built by humans and admired by Jupiter for its many marble columns is blown apart by wind (4 [272]). Alberti, and at about the same time Filarete, wrote treatises on the principles of architecture for patrons who, like Nicholas, knew so little about the art that they did not realize that they themselves were unqualified to make decisions. Such amateurs had no idea of the body of *exempla*, precedents, and precepts which Alberti assembled in his treatise as the true literary, historical, and intellectual authority for the would-be patron of buildings. Instead, like Jupiter consulting the ancient philosophers in *Momus*, they assumed that authorities in the fields they knew — philosophy and theology above all — possessed the truth in fields they did not know, and in fact did not recognize as fields of knowledge at all. From Alberti's bitter experience with such a patron in Rome arose the first Renaissance treatise on architecture.

Chapter Eight

Magnificence or Tyranny?

The Charge of Tyranny

At his funeral, Nicholas had already been compared with ancient monarchs — favorably, of course.[1] And Manetti also compares him at length and favorably to absolute rulers, to Ptolemy and Solomon (15, 57). But less than a decade later when this same comparison is made it is not clear whether praise or blame is intended. Francesco Griffolini (1462) seems to praise Nicholas for renewing the city of Rome, claiming that "one could boast that he, no less than Augustus, transformed the city from brick to marble."[2] But Pius II's observation that had Nicholas's building program been completed it would have rivaled those of any of the ancient Roman emperors is ambiguous.[3] The first explicit association between the tyranny of ancient monarchs and Nicholas's building projects dates from the 1470s, when Paul II had renewed activity on St. Peter's.[4] Although Vespasiano da Bisticci approved of "that admirable building which Nicholas was having made at St. Peter's, where all the court of Rome could be accommodated," he criticized another, unidentified project: "he built that building which would have been sufficient for one of those Roman emperors who ruled the whole world, rather than for a pope" (*Vite*, 1:70). A building for an emperor, identified as a seat of power, is most likely a palace, hence the Vatican Palace, seen as the seat of world dominance. It seems that Nicholas's reputation as a tyrant developed in

[1] For example in the eulogy by Jouffroy, "Oratio Episcopi Atrebatensis," fol. 30v.

[2] Letter to Cosimo de'Medici, 1462, in R. Black, "Ancients and Moderns in the Renaissance: Rhetoric and History in Accolti's 'Dialogue on the Preeminence of Men of his own Time'," *Journal of the History of Ideas* 43 (1982): 3–32, here 23.

[3] Piccolomini, *Opera . . . omnia*, 458.

[4] A medal of Paul II with the inscription "Tribuna Sancti Petri" and the date 1470 is in G. Hill, "The Medals of Paul II," *Numismatic Chronicle* 10 (1910): 340–69, here 347 and plate XII, no. 22.

proportion to the distance from his reign. Yet the most powerful and detailed accusation of tyranny brought against him was probably composed much earlier, immediately after the pontiff's death, although Alberti does not name Nicholas as the target of *Momus*. Unlike later attacks, the comparison is veiled because, uniquely, Alberti's absolute ruler is not a classical emperor but a classical god. In *Momus*, as we just saw, Alberti criticizes Nicholas's building practices — *Momus* has been described as the comic, satyric, and catastrophic version of theories put forward in *De re aedificatoria*.[5] But his greater subject is Nicholas's conception of the papacy, attacking the core of Manetti's purpose in the *Life*.

Portrait of a Tyrant

The "prince and maker of all things," whose deeds "nothing surpasses and nothing equals" — so Alberti refers to Jupiter in *Momus* (Proem to Book 1 [22] and 1 [40])[6] — hates his job. Everyone, he says, gods and mortals alike, does nothing but complain. Everyone wants something more or different from what he already has. So. Humans do not like the world they have? Very well, says Jupiter, I'll make a new world with a new way of living. Get ready to build! (2 [162]). As maker of all things for whom nothing is impossible (cf. Luke 1:37), Jupiter has the attributes of the first person of the Trinity: to quote the Nicene Creed, the Father almighty is "maker of heaven and earth" and of all that is, "seen and unseen." And God alone can make all things new — "ecce nova facio omnia" (Revelation 21:5). Yet in *Momus*, the Christian God of love and mercy is a petty tyrant thinking only of his own convenience and pleasure. The opposite of omniscient, Jupiter has not an idea in his head. He conceals this by a pretense of rule by consensus and consultation, and acts on the advice of flatterers. Realizing that he has neither the competence nor the ability to make a new world, his vanity prevents him admitting this to the assembled gods. Hercules entreats Jupiter not to punish mortals by destroying their world, but to concede them grace. Jupiter is relieved. Ever the corporate boss, he says he raised the issue only to stimulate productive discussion among the gods. And this discussion has, of course, reached the conclusion that he knew all along: this world is so perfect that it really cannot be improved (3[224]). Can this be an anti-Christian satire?

---

[5] V. Frajese, "Leon Battista Alberti e la *renovatio urbis* di Nicolò V. Congetture per l'interpretazione del *Momus*," *La cultura* 36 (1998): 241–62, here 253.

[6] All references are to Alberti, *Momus*, ed. Consolo.

The Apocalypse Sent Up

While *Momus* is deeply indebted to Lucianic models, its most immediate literary model and the key to its interpretation is the Book of Revelation, or Apocalypse.[7] Like John's revelations, the subject of *Momus* is the end of the world and the creation of a better one. But *Momus* can be read as a send-up of the Apocalypse in which the coming of the new creation is not the longed-for fulfillment of Christian hope, the Heavenly City of peace and justice, but an arbitrary threat by a vain and capricious despot averted only by his inability to bring it about.

The humor of *Momus* depends on reversal of expectation, the expectations of Christian readers familiar with the Bible and more generally with Christian theology, who know that at the end of time God will make all things new. To deny that God is able to do that is to deny God's plan for the salvation of the human race. If the Heavenly Jerusalem does not descend at the end of time, there will be no eternal life; thus, when in *Momus* the project for this new world is abandoned by an impotent God, a central tenet of Christian faith is overturned. Because Christian belief is assumed by Alberti — not an unreasonable expectation for a writer ordained to holy orders and employed by the pope — it is not stated. His silence has misled modern scholars to interpret the classicizing trappings of *Momus* as primary to its content. Instead, *Momus* is a parody of the Apocalypse in classical dress. It is a Humanist modernization of such popular medieval parodies of religious matter as the *Apocalypsis Goliae*,[8] not only employing a classicizing cast and

---

[7] R. Rinaldi, "Parodia come allegoria. Il 'Momus' di Alberti e la parodia classica," *Atti e memorie. Arcadia. Accademia Letteraria italiana* 8 (1986–1987):129–65. More generally, D. Marsh, *Lucian and the Latins: Humor and Humanism in the Early Renaissance* (Ann Arbor, 1998); and idem, "Alberti's *Momus*: Sources and Contexts," in *Acta Conventus Neo-Latini Hofniensis*, ed. R. Schnur et al., MRTS 120 (Binghamton, 1994), 619-32, positing that Jupiter might be Eugenius IV, 630–31. Most recently, Borsi, *Alberti e Roma*, esp. 34–51, noted the "clima apocalittico" of the work, but did not extend the comparison.

For *Momus* and the Apocalypse, see S. Simoncini, "Roma come Gerusalemme nel Giubileo del 1450. La *renovatio* di Nicolò V e il *Momus* di Leon Battista Alberti," in *Le due Rome del Quattrocento*, ed. Rossi and Valeri, 322–45. We arrived independently at some of Simoncini's insights about the apocalyptic character of *Momus*'s plot, Alberti's opposition to Nicholas's politics, and the apologetic character of Manetti's *Life*. However, as will emerge in the text, we do not agree that the best context within which to interpret these is medieval commentary on the Apocalypse and the ideas about Antichrist and Angel pope it developed. A earlier version of our thinking on *Momus*, with a different focus is in C. Smith, "The Apocalypse Sent Up: A Parody of the Papacy by Leon Battista Alberti," *Modern Language Notes* 119 (2004): 162-77.

[8] 68 manuscripts remain of this parody of Revelation which satirized the orders and ranks of clergy: M. Bayless, *Parody in the Middle Ages: The Latin Tradition* (Ann Arbor, 1996), 222.

classical models but, in so far as it also spoofs the last books of Augustine's *City of God*, participating in the patristic revival as well.[9]

Alberti's characterization of the god Momus as he who hates and is hated by all, the architect of every malice, and master of simulation and dissimulation (1 [32]; 2 [99–100]) suggests Momus's identification as Satan, or the devil. St. John's gospel says of the devil: "there is no truth in him at all . . . because he is a liar, and the father of lies" (8:44). In Christian belief, the angel Lucifer was expelled from heaven for claiming to rival the Most High (Isaiah 14:12, alluded to in Revelation 8:10). In Alberti's book, Momus's expulsion follows from his prediction that sooner or later Jupiter will fall from power and he, Momus, will become king (1 [42]).

Alberti suggests the apocalyptic content of *Momus* in the opening lines of each of its four books. The subject of Book 1, he says, is how Momus pushed to the brink of destruction all the gods, heaven itself, and the whole fabric of the universe (32). The subject of Book 2 is, always in the author's words, how Momus found new ways of pushing gods, humans, and the world to destruction (92). Book 3 shows how divine majesty and universal power were dragged to the brink of destruction (170); and Book 4 recounts how Momus brought the majesty of the gods to the brink of destruction (230).

Each of the four books contains apocalyptic imagery of world destruction. In Book 1, Momus predicts that human desire for fame will fill the sea with corpses, bloody the provinces, and obscure the stars with the smoke of flaming cities (86); in Book 2, where Momus recounts his experience on earth, he says un-heard of liquids burst up from rocks; brooks burst into flames; mountains crashed against each other; some rode on a path on the sea, others sailed through forests. The kings of the earth sent their armies against each other, covering heaven with their arrows and blocking waterways with corpses. Everywhere there were farms in flames, devastation, sacking, the roar of collapsing roofs, and the screams of the wounded (126). In Book 3, Heat, Hunger, Fever, and similar gods, having heard that the world was about to end, began to torture humans so that there would be less work of killing later (220). And in Book 4, Charon hurries to visit the world when he learns that the Parcas and Hispiades had already begun to exterminate entire families (246).

Momus is not only modeled on the last book of the Bible; its meaning is infused with a more general theological and ecclesiological content. In Book 4, Charon (elaborating on Genesis 2:7) recounts a parodic version of the Christian story of salvation (256–58). The creator of the world formed humans of mud or

[9] Borsi relates *Momus* to Augustine's treatment of the *pax terrena*: *Alberti e Roma*, 101.

wax shaped in bronze molds. Seeing that some were not content with the form he had given them, the creator gave humans freedom to assume the shape of any other animal, as they chose. Here Alberti alludes to free will, a central theological interest of Nicholas's pontificate.[10] The creator pointed out his palace on the top of a mountain and exhorted humans to climb up to it by the straight and steep path; there they would enjoy all good things in abundance. The palace is the Heavenly Jerusalem: the straight and narrow path (cf. Matthew 7:14), a commonplace that needs no explanation. The humans started up, but along the way some assumed the forms of oxen, asses, and other quadrupeds, while others, led astray by desires, became lost along the crossing alleyways. Finding themselves lost, they transformed themselves into monsters and rejoined the main path but were rejected by the other humans because of their horrible appearance. Alberti refers to the disfigurement of the soul by sin, the result of the misuse of free will. Humans learned to make masks called "fictiones" which they wear until the mist of Acheron dissolves them: "no one has ever passed to the other shore except naked" (258). Here, a reference to the revelation of truth at the Last Judgment (cf. Job 1:21; Ecclesiastes 5:15).

The literary qualities of *Momus* also find their closest counterparts in the Book of Revelation. Like the Apocalypse, the narrative framework of *Momus* does not adequately include or account for all the content. Scholars have noted that *Momus*'s literary structure seems deliberately disorganized, enigmatic, and kaleidoscopic.[11] Not only are the episodes and dialogues fragmented, but a series of allegorical stories interrupts the main narrative without any clear logic or order, and the characters are contradictory.[12] It is as if the persons and events in the text have been fragmented and recomposed as a puzzle, as Balestrini observed.[13] This fragmented literary structure, the abrupt shifts in time and place, unexplained relationships between episodes, and ambiguity regarding literary genre are devices modeled on the Apocalypse. But *Momus* is not merely an exercise in style. Alberti refers to the work as a "historia" (1 [32]) — that is, a narrative — but in the proem says that he has taken the license of poets in its composition (26).[14] These qualities serve, as they do in the Apocalypse, to foster both a historical and an allegorical interpretation.

---

[10] On free will, see Westfall, *In This Most Perfect Paradise*, 25–28; and above, 204.

[11] A. Tenenti, "Il 'Momus' nell'opera di Leon Battista Alberti," in *Credenze, ideologie, libertinismi tra medioevo ed età moderna* (Bologna, 1978), 137–54, here 141.

[12] Tenenti, 'Momus,' 141.

[13] Preface by N. Balestrini to *Momus*, ed. Consolo, viii.

[14] This was pointed out by Rinaldi, "Parodia,"146.

The Target

Alberti's target of ridicule is not ultimately either Jupiter or God. Rather, interpreted historically, *Momus* is a satire of Nicholas V who — by implication — has set himself up as God. Nor does Alberti make fun of the belief that God can and will make all things new. Quite the opposite: the goodness and omnipotence of God are essential "givens" on which the humor turns. But what God is and can do, Nicholas is not and cannot perform. Allegorically, it denounces as blasphemy a new ecclesiology centered on the person of the pope and seeking to elevate the status of the church as a political institution. And ultimately, it affirms a kind of Christian belief which is perfectly orthodox yet different from Manetti's.

Momus is not funny. It is, perhaps, Alberti's most desperately serious and deeply religious work as well as a devastating critique of Nicholas V's pontificate.[15] That it is directed at Nicholas is confirmed by a number of allusions. For instance, Alberti builds on Filelfo's identification of Jupiter and Christ in a letter to Nicholas, writing that he had always wanted to dedicate himself to Christ, "the ruler of Olympus."[16] Jupiter is described in *Momus* as the only one possessing perfect virtue, "uniquely one and uniquely alone" (1, proem), like the papacy: in Antonio da Cannara's words, "the Roman Church alone on its own authority has the power to judge everything, while it is permitted no one to make judgment on her."[17] Jupiter's aim is to strengthen his monarchical power: "suum sibi regnum vellet communire" (1 [36]). These two issues — papal primacy and the person of the pope — go to the heart of Nicholas's vision of the papacy, which we will explore shortly. The difficulty of determining whether the individual in power represents his own interests or those of the institution elicits a greater scrutiny of motives and we know that Nicholas's were widely questioned: the Testament addresses such criticism directly, asserting that it was not for the pontiff's own benefit but for the church that he undertook the building program (T8). Absolute power also raises the question of to whom a ruler is accountable. Alberti depicts Jupiter as handing out offices and riches to the court (1 [36–37]) and manipulating the masses, "ignara et credula" (1 [50]).[18] Again, Nicholas justifies

---

[15] Indeed, we hope to contribute to the elusive subject of Alberti's religious belief, a subject which has only recently begun to be addressed. Grafton intuited that Alberti saw himself as "a passionately devout Christian" in his discussion of the much earlier *Pontifex*: *Alberti*, 194.

[16] Filelfo's comment in von Pastor, *History of the Popes*, 2:203. Simoncini first noticed the connection in "Roma come Gerusalemme," 327.

[17] Antonio da Cannara, *De potestate pape supra concilium generale contra errores Basiliensium*, ed. T. Prügl (Paderborn, 1996), 69.

[18] Borsi also observed the relevance of this to Nicholas: *Momus o del principe*, 15; and *Alberti e Roma*, 34.

himself against this charge in the Testament by arguing that obedience to the church is for the people's welfare (T2, 18). Jupiter is a tyrant (1 [36]), his palace is a fortress: "regiam Jovis arcem" (2 [104]). In the penultimate episode of *Momus,* Peniplusios's denunciation of tyranny (recounted by Charon) is simultaneous with the final scene ("while they were discussing this") of the defeated Jupiter (4 [182–184]) and therefore associated with it. Alberti's tyrant is both inconstant and unjust: Momus, complaining that his advice on how to renovate the world was ignored (Alberti's mouthpiece here), says he hardly knows whether Jupiter's neglect of government or injustice in governing is worse (4 [278]).

Nicholas's devotion to the biblical story of the *navicella* and imagery of the Church as a bark (see Chapter 9 below) is spoofed through Alberti's character Charon, who rows the dead straight to hell, whereas in the Testament the pontiff is the helmsman guiding them to heaven (18). Since the Church is Peter's bark, in *Momus* we can interpret Charon as Peter. Here the identification with Nicholas turns on the formula spoken at papal coronations, "tu es Petrus" (Matthew 16:18), a basis for arguments of papal authority.[19] Through him Alberti mocks Peter's successor, Nicholas. Charon complains that some idiot grabbed his oars and claimed that there were many rowers in his ancestral family (4 [248]). Not so, someone shouted, they never saw the sea but lived in mountains where they did forced labor in quarries. The joke turns on Nicholas's claim to high birth in Pisa, a maritime city, rather than low birth in mountainous Sarzana. In an anecdote on the venality of the Church, perhaps specifically aimed at the revenues from the Jubilee, Charon refuses to transport Gelastos without payment, telling him that he would have done better to hang himself than to be in such poverty that all that sustains him is prayer (4 [250]).

Alberti does not just point out Nicholas's foibles and those of the Roman Curia, as has been said. Instead, *Momus* confronts a new vision of the papacy developed in an abundant apologetic literature under Nicholas V, including Manetti's biography of the pope. Alberti pushes the imagery and claims of this literature to their illogical conclusions. By proclaiming the triumph of folly he hopes to ward it off.

At issue was how the church, which is the mystical body of Christ, could also be a political body, that is, a monarchically and hierarchically structured institution.[20] While Manetti addressed this ecclesiological controversy through the *exempla* of books and buildings in Book 2, it is engaged directly and in professional language in Nicholas's Testament, perhaps an indication of its authenticity. Nicholas associated his building with a particular conception of the Church:

---

[19] On this see B. Tierney, *Foundations of the Conciliar Theory. The Contribution of Medieval Canonists from Gratian to the Great Schism* (Leiden, 1998), 23–32.

[20] We examine this issue in greater detail in the next chapter.

> The only people who know that the authority of the Roman Church is greatest and supreme are the ones who have learned its origin and growth from their knowledge of reading . . . popular respect, founded on information provided by educated men, grows so much stronger and more solid every day through great buildings. (T1–T3)

Nicholas's language in this passage employs technical terms the exact meaning and relevance of which were the subject of theological and legal dispute. There was, for instance, no consensus among the learned about the supreme authority of Rome in the church, nor even on what the term "ecclesia Romana" meant. That the church was the mystical body of Christ in the world was agreed.[21] But how should this be manifest in the church as an institution? Was it consonant with the church as a monarchically and hierarchically structured *corpus politicum*?[22] Is the church the body and Christ the head, in which case all the members, including the bishop of Rome, are equal? Or does the church have a dual nature, invisible and visible, headed respectively by Christ and his vicar? Some aspects of this problem were debated within the conciliar movement. The Council of Constance had decreed (*Haec sancta*, 6 April 1415) that a general council, as representing the Church Militant, held its power directly from Christ and that therefore the pope, as all Christians, was subject to its decisions.[23] Affirmed by the Council of Basel in 1439, this was pronounced to be an article of Christian faith. Other issues were engaged by the Hussite heresy which, by calling for reform of the church, raised the question of who had the power to initiate and implement reform. The recent return of the papacy to Rome — Nicholas was the first to occupy the Roman See continuously in more than a century — and his reconquest of the papal states made the bishop of Rome not only equal, but similar, to the great temporal lords. In what categories and with what kinds of argument could disputes about the nature, and therefore organization and governance, of the church be resolved?

Before the fifteenth century such discussion was dominated by jurists (since the questions involved, literally, jurisdiction as well as rights) and by political theorists, who elaborated the legal basis for papal primacy.[24] As early as the twelfth

---

[21] Izbicki, *Protector of the Faith*, 39, summarizes the development of this formulation. On "ecclesia romana" see also Tierney, *Foundations*, 32–42.

[22] See Colella, "The Cappella Niccolina," 49.

[23] W. Brandmüller, *Das Konzil von Konstanz 1414–1418* (Paderborn, 1991), 244. More generally, C. M. Crowder, *Unity, Heresy and Reform, 1378–1460. The Conciliar Response to the Great Schism* (Great Britain, 1977). Also Celenza, "Renaissance Humanism and the New Testament"; Stinger, *The Renaissance in Rome*, 156–234.

[24] On Conciliarism and the Petrine primacy, see Tierney, *Foundations*, and J. Stieber, *Pope Eugenius IV, the Council of Basel, and the Secular and Ecclesiastical Authorities in the Empire: The Conflict over Supreme Authority and Power in the Church* (Leiden, 1978).

century the pope was said, as vicar, to share Christ's two natures. By 1332 Alvarus Pelagius could claim that "every individual pope participates in a certain manner in Christ's two natures: in the divine nature in what regards spiritual matters, and in the human nature in what regards temporal affairs."[25] In this view, papal authority was not just an abstract attribute of the papacy in general, but was embodied in the person of the reigning pope.[26] It followed that the term "ecclesia Romana" (which Nicholas used) could be said to refer not to the universal church, the diocese of Rome, or the pope and cardinals, but to the person of the reigning pontiff as embodiment of the Roman Church. This is Cannara's sense of the term "Roman Church" in the passage quoted above. Many fifteenth-century professional theologians writing pro-papal apologetic literature continued to argue apodictically through logic and appeal to authority. But unlike the earlier literature, their arguments sought to establish a theological basis for papal primacy.[27] One approach compiled from the writings of Thomas Aquinas all the categories within which to discuss papal authority and all the aspects that needed such discussion: this is what Juan de Torquemada did in his *Most Compendious Tract of Seventy-Three Questions on Papal Power Gathered from the Opinions of Saint Thomas* of 1436.[28] Another method of argument from authority, also Scholastic and encyclopedic, was to assemble evidence from the Gospels, fathers of the church, and early popes: such testimony was marshaled by Antonio da Cannara in his 1443 *On the Power of the Pope over the General Council against the Errors of Basle* which we cited above. Yet another kind of appeal to authority interpreted events as manifestations of divine will, as Michele Canensi did in 1451, asserting that Nicholas had been elected pope by divine rather than human will, a notion repeated by Jean Jouffroy in the funeral oration and evoked by Manetti in the first sentence of Book 2 (1).[29]

Increasingly prominent — and, we will show, essential for Manetti's argument in the *Life* — were general considerations of the nature and goals of government. Such earlier tracts as Ptolemy of Lucca's *De regimine principum*, a response to William of Moerbeke's previous translation of Aristotle's *Politics* and attributed

[25] Paravicini Bagliani, *The Pope's Body*, 70.

[26] See discussion in Colella, "The Cappella Niccolina," 39.

[27] As Stinger first observed in *The Renaissance in Rome*, 163.

[28] Printed as an appendix in Antonio da Cannara, *De potestate pape*, 141 ff.

[29] M. Miglio, "Niccolò V umanista di Cristo," in *Umanesimo e Padri della Chiesa. Manoscritti e incunaboli di testi patristici da Francesco Petrarca al primo Cinquecento*, ed. S. Gentile (Milan, 1997), 77–84, here 80–81; Jouffroy, "Oratio," fol. 30r. Stinger suggests it is more common for newcomers to Rome like Nicholas to be said to be divinely elected than for popes who had already been prominent in the Curia and therefore considered "papabile": *The Renaissance in Rome*, 91.

to Aquinas wholly or in part, had already applied secular political discourse to ecclesiological problems. Leonardo Bruni's new translation of the *Politics* in 1437 and the recovery of Plato's *Republic* supplied new frameworks within which political thought could — and later would — be organized. Nicholas owned two copies of Ptolemy's treatise, attributed to Thomas Aquinas in the inventory of his library, two copies of Aristotle's *Politics*, and Egidio Colonna's (Giles of Rome's) *De regimine principum*.[30] His shelves were well stocked with this literature, in which forms of government are evaluated on the criterion of the common good. Ptolemy, for instance, showed how the king established by God in Deuteronomy for the common good contrasts with the king in 1 Kings, concerned only with his own well-being: the latter is a tyrant and a despot (3.11.1, 9). More explicitly: "One alone who brings about an unjust government by seeking individual profit from the government, and not the good of the multitude subject to that rector, is called a tyrant" (1.2.2). Both Alberti's characterization of Jupiter as a tyrant and Nicholas's self-defense in the Testament as having acted for the benefit of the church assume the common good as the yardstick for their actions. But discussion of the church and its governance can never be exclusively political, for, unlike every other state, the church is ordained by God and is fundamentally a theological institution. Good ecclesiastical governance furthers God's economy of salvation. The common good, then, is consonance with divine purpose. In *Momus* Alberti depicts a tyrant who thwarts God's purpose at every turn and is the source of harm to his subjects. Manetti will need to find an argument for the opposite, and we will see in the next chapter what it is.

Fundamental to any definition of the institutional church is whether the Church Militant precedes or coincides with the millennial reign of Christ and the saints announced in Revelation (19–20:6).[31] Will this last world age end with the beginning of the millennium or with the descent of the Heavenly Jerusalem? Expressed historically, at what stage of salvation history is the present? On this point our protagonists agree. In *Momus*, Alberti assumes that the millennial reign has begun and he looks forward to the coming of the Heavenly Kingdom: hence his focus on its abortion by the tyrant Jupiter/Nicholas. Manetti, too, believed that the millennial reign had begun with, or just after, Jesus's life. He says this explicitly in the first sentence of Book 2, telling us that Nicholas was elected pope: "in the four hundred and forty-seventh year after the millennium of Christian salvation."

---

[30] Müntz and Fabre, *La bibliothèque*, 66, 69, 107, 108. These are now MSS. Vat. lat. 4107 and Vat. lat. 840 (Egidio Colonna); Vat. lat. 2097 and Vat. lat. 2109 (Aristotle); Vat. lat. 807 and Vat. lat. 773 (Ptolemy). For the identifications, see Manfredi, *I codici latini di Niccolò V.*

[31] On this problem, see the summary in C. Smith, *Before and After the End of Time: Architecture and the Year 1000* (New York, 2000), esp. 1–28.

For both it followed that Christ is the head of the church. But does the church's structure prefigure or embody a divine order? Is the Church Militant part of the natural order or is it already in some sense the Kingdom of God? Manetti follows St. Augustine:

> While the devil is bound for a thousand years, the saints reign with Christ, also for a thousand years; which are without a doubt to be understood in the same way: that is, as the period beginning with Christ's first coming . . . Therefore, the Church even now is the kingdom of Christ and the kingdom of heaven. (*City of God*, 22.9)

Ptolemy of Lucca, following Augustine and drawing on Daniel 2:44, interpreted prophecy of the eternal kingdom to be raised up as the kingdom of Christ with the Roman church in his place — that is, as the Church Militant perfected.[32] In *Momus*, Jupiter concludes that this present world is so perfect that it could not be surpassed, justifying why he will make no new world. In fact things are quite dreadful, and Alberti mocks this arrogance. What is he arguing against? Juan de Torquemada had asserted in his 1453 *Summa de Ecclesia* that there were two heads of the mystical body, one invisible — Christ — and one visible, the pontiff (not a new argument, see above). This implied that the pope is in some sense Christ. Indeed, Jean Jouffroy referred to Nicholas as "Prince of Peace," one of Christ's titles (cf. Isaiah 9:6), and Manetti claimed that the princes, kings, Christian peoples and republics sent ambassadors to Nicholas in order "to venerate and worship the new humanity of Christ our Savior now visible on earth and conversing with humans" (2.3). But if Nicholas is Christ made visible, then Christ must be like Nicholas. And this is the starting point for Alberti's satire. What would heaven be like with Nicholas in charge? Why, just like Rome and the Roman Curia. Alberti draws on an old tradition in which the pope is seen as antichrist. In 991, John XV was described as "the Antichrist, seated in God's Temple, behaving as if he were God."[33] And Boniface VIII, whose ecclesiology was important for that of Nicholas, was identified as the angel of the Abyss (Revelation 9:11), the Beast (Revelation 13:1ff), and the mystical Antichrist.[34] Simoncini argued that

---

[32] Ptolemy of Lucca, *On the Government of Rulers. De Regimine principum*, trans. J. Blythe (Philadelphia, 1997), 3.10.9, 176.

[33] A. Paravicini Bagliani, *Il trono di Pietro. L'universalità del papato da Alessandro III a Bonifacio VIII* (Rome, 1996), 38. This was said at the Synod of Reims by Bishop Arnolfo. On the literature more generally, see B. McGinn, "Angel Pope and Papal Antichrist," *Church History* 47 (1978): 155–73; *The Late Medieval Pope Prophecies*, ed. M. H. Fleming, MRTS 204 (Tempe, 1999); and H. Millet, *"Il libro delle immagini dei papi". Storia di un testo profetico medievale* (Rome, 2002).

[34] Paravicini Bagliani, *Trono di Pietro*, 40.

Momus is Alberti's response to the eschatological elements of Nicholas's propaganda, associating himself with the angel pope of the Last Days who would bring peace.[35] Yet it would not seem typical of Alberti to be so receptive to authors like Joachim of Fiore and others — mainly Franciscans — who disseminated these ideas and whose thinking, while certainly political, is contemplative and mystical. This is not Alberti's manner of political thought, as the conclusion of *Momus* makes clear, nor, we will argue in our next chapter, was it Nicholas's. Even so, the argument raises a fundamental issue about how all three of our protagonists — Alberti, Nicholas, and Manetti himself — understood the Church Militant and Church Triumphant. More precisely, it raises an issue about varieties of religious experience.

For Manetti the world has a supernatural dimension perceived by faith, a relationship to divine order which can be seen and known. But not so for Alberti, who finds this presumptuous: the supernatural and the natural are separate realms for him until the end of time. Thus his satire is apocalyptic. But Manetti's mode of religious feeling is not apocalyptic because, like Augustine, he believes the Kingdom of God is already here. Nicholas's faith is more elusive, since Manetti is his spokesman in the *Life*, but from the Testament he seems more doctrinal and sacramental than Manetti. He speaks throughout, not of his personal experience, but about matters he holds to be intellectually right and for the good of the institution he embodies. We see no evidence of eschatological ideology in his pontificate: he espoused a well-established definition of the Church Militant as mirror of the Church Triumphant. That is, he spoke of resemblance between the two, not identity.

Yet the pairing of Christ and the pope as visible and invisible heads of the church in Nicholas's ecclesiology was elaborated with metaphors that blurred distinctions between the earthly and the heavenly church, suggesting that the Church Triumphant — that is, the church after the end of time — could be seen in the Church Militant. Niccolò Palmieri's sermon "De pacis dignitate," perhaps for Nicholas, paraphrased the text from Revelation on the descent of the Heavenly Jerusalem to insist on the unity and monarchical structure that should characterize the Church Militant, constructed "in the likeness of the Heavenly Jerusalem on high, which is our mother"; and Aeneas Silvius Piccolomini, apostolic secretary and subdeacon under Nicholas, wrote that the Roman Curia seen during liturgy resembled the celestial hierarchy on account of its marvelous and stable order.[36] The notion that the Church Triumphant can be seen in the Church Militant under Nicholas is also a theme in Manetti's biography of the pontiff:

---

[35] Simoncini, "Roma come Gerusalemme," 323–24.

[36] Niccolò Palmieri in O'Malley, *Praise and Blame in Renaissance Rome*, 202; Piccolomini, *Opera . . . omnia*, 739.

Palmieri was an Augustinian friar who taught theology at the *studium* at Siena. Since 1448 he was resident in Rome and close to Nicholas. He gave one of the eulogies at the pontiff's funeral. On him, see Monfasani, "A Theologian at the Roman Curia."

> Whenever people witnessed services so splendid and so worthy [as Nicholas's liturgies], they were overcome with such admiration and so great astonishment as well as devotion, that they recognized a kind of image sketched of the Church Triumphant in the midst of this our Church Militant and they clearly and openly glimpsed its sure and explicit outline. (8)[37]

Architectural images in *Momus* satirize this theme. For instance, the Heavenly Jerusalem of Revelation 21:18–23 appears negatively transformed in three different guises. In the Apocalypse the materials of the Heavenly Jerusalem — gold, diamonds, and gemstones — suggest its ideal beauty. In *Momus*, Jupiter adorns the heavens with gold and diamonds because the gods are jealous of the beauty of earth (1 [36]). Then Juno complains that while Jupiter has given all the other gods palaces of gold, with golden doors, roofs, staircases, columns and architraves of gold, and walls of gold and diamonds, she, his wife, has been obliged to live in a house adorned only by its immaculate purity (2 [108–110]). Scholars have interpreted Juno in this episode as representing the church, bride of Christ, who has abandoned the purity of virtue because of greed.[38] But beyond this, the coveted celestial dwellings parody the Heavenly Jerusalem, which is the Church Triumphant. The Heavenly City, a metaphor for that *civitas* which is the church, is a theological concept having little to do with actual architectural form. By taking the image literally and imagining gold staircases and doors, Alberti renders it ridiculous. Just as ridiculous, perhaps, as building a church that imitated Noah's Ark, as Manetti tells us Nicholas intended to do at St. Peter's (52). Moreover, Alberti plays on the Renaissance awareness that value is relative: whether costly things are admirable or vile depends on their moral value.[39] In *Momus*, the ideal architecture of the Heavenly City is vulgar ostentation. Alberti disguises as architectural display the chivalric pomp against which Petrarch wrote in the *Liber sine nomine*, a polemic against the Avignon papacy. Criticizing the "heirs of the fishermen — that is, the cardinals — who have luxurious palaces instead of overturned boats for homes," he gazes on:

> The prancing, snow-white mounts of thieves, bedecked with gold, champing on gold bits, soon to be shod with gold shoes if the Lord does not curtail this debased excess. (59)[40]

---

[37] Manetti's characterization of the Heavenly Jerusalem as visible as a sketch or an outline can be compared to a miniature by Niccolò Polani (1459) in a manuscript of the *City of God* (Bibliothèque Ste. Genevieve, Paris, codex 218, fol. 2r). in Burroughs, *From Signs to Design*, fig. 32.

[38] Frajese, "Alberti," 258.

[39] See Smith, *Architecture in the Culture of Early Humanism*, chap. 3.

[40] *Petrarch's Book Without a Name: A Translation of the 'Liber sine Nomine'*, trans. N. Zacour (Toronto, 1973), 59. Petrarch excerpted this passage from Letter 5, 1352, to Lapo da Castiglionchio in Francesco Petrarca, *Le Familiari*, ed. V. Rossi (Florence, 1933–1942), 12.8.

In a second image related to the Heavenly Jerusalem, Juno wants to use the golden offerings she receives from mortals for home improvements: the hen-pecked Jupiter consents (2 [110–112]). During dinner, a deafening noise is heard at the entrance to heaven. All the gods run to see the enormous triumphal arch revetted in gold and colored with every color which Juno has erected with her votive offerings. Astonishingly, the arch collapses before their eyes. This episode has been linked to the collapse, in 1454, of the Great Tower built by Nicholas V as part of the Vatican Palace's fortification. But Juno's triumphal arch at the entrance to heaven has more than architectural significance, for it is of gold, like the Heavenly Jerusalem, and rainbow-colored, like the light around God's throne in Revelation 4:3, as well as being the gate of heaven, a metaphor for the Church drawn from Genesis 28:17: "How awesome is this place! This is none other than the house of God and the gate of heaven" (the introit sung at church dedications). Juno explains her craze to build ("aedificandi libido" [3 (184–186)], also Pier Candido Decembrio's criticism of Nicholas) as necessary for human salvation, Nicholas's justification exactly.

Again, the military terms "Ecclesia militans" and "Ecclesia triumphans" are metaphors: Alberti, taking them literally, has Juno erect a war memorial the collapse of which disrupts Jupiter's heavenly banquet, itself a parody of Revelation 19:9. Alberti satirizes Nicholas's pretense at creating the image of the Church Triumphant through his building program and his exaggerated claims as Vicar of Christ. Juno's arch, like Nicholas's program, is an *all'antica* fake, creating the appearance but not the substance of the Heavenly Kingdom, and cannot stand.

Yet another imitation of the Heavenly Jerusalem appears in *Momus*. In order to propitiate the angry gods, mortals build a spectacular theater all of gold and diamonds (3 [220]) — once again, the materials of the Heavenly City. Jupiter especially admires the huge columns of Parian marble — perhaps a reference to those which Nicholas had brought from the Baths of Agrippa to the Vatican in 1452.[41] And Jupiter admires the golden awning covering the theater. This awning will be the cause of his final humiliation. As the winds sweep through the theater, the awning blows off and the theater collapses, injuring the gods and sending them scampering back up to heaven (4 [272–276]). The theater of gold and diamonds refers to Nicholas's project for a new St. Peter's, the place of spectacle in which the Church Triumphant is seen on earth. This association is strengthened by Alberti's judgment that the high clerestory walls of St. Peter's, weakened because out of plumb, were vulnerable to wind shear: "I have no doubt that eventually some slight pressure or gentle movement will make it [the basilica]

---

[41] The documents are gathered in M. Gargano, "Niccolò V. La mostra dell'acqua di Trevi," *Archivio della Società Romana di Storia Patria* 111 (1988): 225–66, here 257–58.

collapse" (*De re aedificatoria*, 1.10) and he devised a machine for lifting off its roof while shoring up the walls (10.17).

In the last scene of *Momus*, Jupiter is by himself putting his room in order (4 [288]). He finds a little book Momus had given him and reads with great joy the wise precepts therein and with great sorrow that he had ignored them for so long. Alberti's work closes with a summary of Momus's book. The prince should refrain from radical change: "rebus novandis abstinebit" (4 [290]). Thus Alberti reverses God's declaration at the end of the Apocalypse: "behold, I make all things new" — "ecce nova facio omnia" (Revelation 21:5).

This conclusion has a positive message, interpreted historically, and a negative message, interpreted allegorically. By casting Nicholas as Jupiter, Alberti reveals the ludicrous consequences of confusing God and humankind, the Church Triumphant and the Church Militant. For him, these are separate states, separated precisely by the Last Things (the end of time, the Last Judgment, the descent of the Heavenly Jerusalem, and so on): only when the natural order ends does the supernatural begin. What makes *Momus* such a devastating condemnation of Nicholas's vision of the papacy is that the triumph of ethics is the defeat of divinity. What best regulates human society and institutions is of a totally different order from the nature and action of God. Alberti shows that there is no relation between God's being — omniscient, omnipotent, perfect in love and goodness — and that of human rulers. By raising the papacy to the level of divinity and the Church Militant to the Church Triumphant, Nicholas has blasphemed, for to reduce the divine to human measure is to deny it. By raising man to heaven, Nicholas has made God human. The devil defeats God at the end, because divinity becomes subject to that which is proper for humans: ethics. The ridiculous, unthinkable consequences of this blasphemy are the subject of Alberti's parody of the Apocalypse.

There is also a positive message, although not original with Alberti: the good ruler is guided by an Aristotelian notion of virtue as the mean between extremes (e.g. *Nicomachean Ethics* 2.2.1104a13–27). Alberti's conclusion also suggests that human beings, because they are subject to error and swayed by passions, discern right action through social interaction. In *Momus*, as in the treatise on architecture, Alberti rejects the contemplative in favor of the active life as the path to virtue. And society, the goal and remedy for human frailty, is created by humankind and ordered by that uniquely human creation, ethics. Ultimately, in drawing the distinction between divine and human nature, Alberti celebrates the dignity of man. But Manetti, no less believing in human dignity, having in fact written a treatise on the subject,[42] understands it very differently, as his defense of Nicholas reveals.

---

[42] *De dignitate et excellentia hominis*, ed. Leonard.

Magnanimity

Manetti rebuts criticism of Nicholas's character and deeds throughout the *Life of Nicholas*. Understanding the charge of tyranny to be the most damning, Manetti recasts it in a positive mode, arguing that Nicholas's buildings manifested the virtue of magnanimity. He makes this connection explicitly twice (27, 57), associating magnanimity with piety and boldness, both times in relation to built work. But more frequently (nine occurrences) he evokes the result of this virtue, describing the buildings as magnificent (7, 22, 23 [5 times], 27, 57). In his account of the projects, Manetti goes farther than simply to argue that Nicholas displayed magnificence; he elaborates on both its nature and its effects. Nicholas displayed magnificence in his buildings because of their size (*magnus*, *ingens*) and cost (*impensa*, *sumptus*), the two main features of a building that would most attract people to see them. Because of size and cost, the buildings were out of the ordinary (*egregius*), appealing to the eye (*speciosus*), or beautiful (*pulcher*). This in turn makes them objects of admiration or wonder (*admirabilis*, *mirus*). And because of this, people were drawn to devotion themselves, and rightfully praised their maker for his virtue. This appeal to magnanimity serves not merely to show Nicholas as a good man or a man whose behavior was modeled on the ancients but, further, to justify the appropriation of absolute power by an autocrat. Indeed, the direction of recent scholarship has been, precisely, to see Nicholas as an autocrat at the top of a centralized regime.[43]

Virtue

Undoubtedly Nicholas thought about virtue. In Fra Angelico's "Martyrdom of St. Lawrence" for Nicholas's chapel in the Vatican Palace, behind the suffering saint are fictive statues of the four cardinal virtues, justice, prudence, temperance, and fortitude: a fifth statue represents Hercules, an exemplar from pagan mythology of these virtues applied to action. Fragments of another fresco cycle painted under Nicholas in the palace depict the same virtues with inscriptions detailing aspects of each.[44] Fortitude is qualified with "magnanimitas, magnificentia, perseverantia, constantia, fidutia, pacientia, securitas, tolerantia, firmitas"; justice by "religio, pietas, gratia, observantia, veritas, obedientia, innocentia, [and] concordia"; prudence by "memoria, intelligentia, prudentia, circumspectio, docilitas, caucio [and] ratio"; the representation of temperance is lost. Westfall showed that most of the qualities associated with the virtues come from Macrobius and from Ci-

---

[43] Burroughs, "Alberti e Roma, 143–57, here 153, with bibliography in n. 77.

[44] Westfall, *In This Perfect Paradise*, 136–37, in the Sala Vecchia degli Svizzeri.

cero. Macrobius discusses how they are manifested in rulers of commonwealths so that they may attain blessedness (commentary on Cicero's *Dream of Scipio*, 8.4). Especially relevant for Manetti's *Life* is Macrobius's claim that some people are distinguished by excellence both in the public life and its virtues (e.g. prudence, temperance, courage, and justice) and also in private reflections (e.g. deep thinking, study, introspection, contemplation) (8.4–8). Here we have, essentially, the division that orders Manetti's account of Nicholas's character in the *Life*, especially in Book 1. Macrobius's discussion was repeated by Vincent of Beauvais in his *Speculum doctrinale* (4.9). Thus a first intellectual context for Manetti's biography would seem to be Macrobius's very popular work and, perhaps, Vincent's Scholastic encyclopedia. But we are concerned here with how these virtues relate to the building descriptions in Book 2, and need to look further.

Papal eulogies from the time of Nicholas, as O'Malley has shown, favor what he calls the "courtly virtues," particularly those which Aristotle identified in the *Rhetoric*:

> The components of virtue are justice, courage, self-control, magnificence, magnanimity, liberality, gentleness, practical and speculative wisdom. (*Rhetoric* 1.9.5–6)[45]

Nicholas owned three copies of the *Rhetoric*: one in the old Latin translation, one in Greek, and one in George of Trebizond's new translation.[46] Also widely read was Aristotle's *Nicomachean Ethics* which, it will be remembered, Manetti had re-translated. Indeed, Manetti was something of an expert on this work, having lectured on it in Florence, 1430–1431.[47] Nicholas owned three copies of the work as well as two copies of Eustathius's commentary.[48] Interest in Aristotle's moral theory is further shown by Cyriacus of Ancona's translation into Latin of the pseudo-Aristotle *De Virtutibus* (1433–1436).[49] Leonardo Bruni had dedicated his translation of the *Nicomachean Ethics* to Martin V (1417/18) and of the *Politics* to Eugene IV (1438). In the dedicatory letter of the latter he urges the pontiff not to

---

[45] O'Malley, *Praise and Blame*, 174–75; J. McManamon, "The Ideal Renaissance Pope: Funeral Oratory from the Papal Court," *Archivum Historiae Pontificiae* 14 (1976): 9–70.

[46] Müntz and Fabre, *La bibliothèque*, 107, 336; Vespasiano, *Vite*, 68. See E. Garin, "Le traduzioni umanistiche di Aristotele nel secolo XV," *Atti dell'Accademia fiorentina di scienze morali "La Columbaria"* 16 (1951): 55–104.

[47] Botley, *Latin Translation*, 75.

[48] Müntz and Fabre, *La bibliothèque*, 107–8, 332, 334.

[49] M. Cortesi and E. Maltesi, "Ciriaco d'Ancona e il 'De Virtutibus' pseudoaristotelico," *Studi medievali* 33 (1992): 133–64, here 137. They suggested a connection with Plethon, whom Cyriacus had met in 1437 in Mistra and who wrote "Peri areton", i.e. his own treatise on the virtues (150).

be put off because Aristotle was a philosopher and a pagan; the principles of good government are the same for pagans and Christians: they are justice, temperance, fortitude, and liberality.[50] Scholars have noted how the *Ethics* was re-evaluated in relation to modern life in early Quattrocento Florence.[51] And since Aristotle's virtues in the *Rhetoric* are similar to the four cardinal virtues, some have suggested these latter were, under his influence, reconceived in a classicizing way in relation to public and civic virtue.[52] Yet it cannot be that at the Curia virtue was explored only or even primarily through pagan authors like Macrobius, Cicero, and Aristotle. Surely the Dominicans at the papal court who had responsibility for teaching and preaching read such authors through the lens of the purely theological and tendentially more metaphysical treatment of virtue of Scholastic commentary. For instance, Aquinas repeats Macrobius's list of the parts of fortitude and compares it to Cicero (*ST*, 2/2, q.128 obj.6): his work might well be the direct source for the texts of the Vatican frescoes. Classical sources, no matter how novel and exciting to fifteenth-century thinkers, could modify but not replace the formidable body of Scholastic opinion on virtue, and we need to give it our attention.

Aquinas devotes a considerable amount of discussion to magnanimity and its opposites presumption, ambition, vainglory, and pusillanimity (*ST*, 2/2, qq. 129–133). In his view, magnanimity is a part of the cardinal virtue of fortitude; it has to do with the preparation of the mind that makes it ready to initiate acts of fortitude; the follow-through or execution is related to magnificence. This accords well with Manetti's claim that Nicholas was magnanimous and the buildings, its effects, magnificent. Magnanimity and magnificence have to do with great and difficult undertakings; in less difficult or less great matters, lesser virtues come into play, related as subsidiary virtues to these principal ones. Aquinas argues that magnanimity is a sort of extension of the mind towards great things. Things may be great relatively or absolutely speaking; in the truest sense, magnanimity is a matter of what is truly great, particularly in exterior objects and as different from interior goodness. Manetti in fact uses the buildings to attribute two virtues to Nicholas: one a matter of exterior objects, the moral virtue of magnanimity; the other a matter of interior worth, the theological virtue of charity. (We examine these separately, the lesser being our subject here and the greater in the following chapter.) The result of magnanimity is honor, which is the testimony to virtue. Building on a grand scale reveals the virtue of magnificence, or, as Aquinas explains it, an act of the will to do or make what is great (*ST*, 2/2, q. 134, 1.1–4). In a proper sense, magnificence can be exercised only by those with the capability to do great deeds, i.e. the wealthy

---

[50] *Leonardo Bruni Aretino: Humanistisch-Philosophische Schriften*, ed. Baron, 71.

[51] F. Tateo, "Le virtù sociali e l'immanità nella trattatistica pontaniana," *Rinascimento* 5 (1965): 119–54, here 130–31.

[52] O'Malley, *Praise and Blame*, 174–75.

and powerful (in Manetti, the city of Florence and Pope Nicholas). Magnificence is manifest in great objects which are its product, and their greatness derives from their cost, rarity, or size — exactly the qualities which Manetti mentions as his criteria for inclusion in his account: "we propose to remark only on the [buildings] . . . the public visits because of their very great cost or unusual magnificence" (22).[53] The pursuit of honor according to the rule of reason (rather than passion) is related to magnanimity, because it prompts virtuous action. Because magnificence entails, for example, great men building great buildings, it often results in honor for the magnificent person; such honor, however, does not detract from the virtuous nature of the magnificent act, since it is public recognition of the magnificent person's virtue, and so elevates public morality (*ST*, 2/2, q. 132, a. 2).

In the *Life*, the particular combination of *devotio* (an aspect of justice) and *magnificentia* (an aspect of fortitude) which Manetti attributes to Nicholas's building program assures that his great deeds are motivated by the desire to serve God's cause. This is close to, but not exactly, what Nicholas himself argues in his deathbed apology, citing "the greater authority of the Roman Church, the more complete dignity of the Apostolic See among Christian peoples, and the more sure avoidance of the familiar persecutions" (T8). Whereas Nicholas saw the building project as promoting the stature and security of the institutional Church, Manetti relates it also to *devotio*, a virtue relevant for personal sanctification. Devotion is, to Aquinas, an interior act of religion (as is prayer), as opposed to exterior acts (worship) (*ST* 2/2, q. 82, a. 1–4). It is the special virtue of Nicholas's Testament, in which he thanks God for all good gifts, dwells on the necessity, and his reception of, the sacraments as remedies for original and voluntary sin, and expresses his desire for grace.[54]

Renaissance discussions of magnificence often turn on the suspicion of vainglory. Magnificence, an act of the will, was clearly dependent on motive. For magnificence to be seen as virtue rather than self-promotion, a man's motives must be pure. Great deeds undertaken for the purpose of winning glory or influence are not considered virtuous. Those done to promote good ends, such as the betterment of civic life, are. The highest end magnificence can aim at, according to Aquinas, is

[53] This is why Manetti does not defend the pope by reducing the scale of the projects, as H. Günther wondered in "I progetti di ricostruzione della basilica di S. Pietro negli scritti contemporanei: Giustificazioni e scrupoli," in *L'Architettura della Basilica di S. Pietro,* ed. Spagnesi, 137–48, here 140.

[54] Aquinas describes devotion as a willingness to surrender oneself readily to what suits God's service. It is a special act of the will. Devotion arises from contemplation, specifically of two things: God's goodness and our defects. The first gives delight; the second guards against presumption. Devotion causes a spiritual happiness in the mind — this is its principal effect; secondarily, a sadness, because we are not experiencing God to the fullest.

to bring honor to God and further His plan for human salvation (*ST*, 2/2, q. 134 ad 3); that is the aim of the motives Nicholas named. Aquinas himself had waffled on the relationship between magnificence and the personal glory it brings to the magnificent individual (*ST* 2/2, q. 132, a. 2), concluding that glory rightly comes to the man who is truly magnificent, and is not vainglory, provided the principal motives involve a larger purpose. Yet it is by no means easy to discern the motives of the magnificent, and their very power and wealth is susceptible to envy. In the case of Eugenius IV, the purity of his motives was argued from the asceticism of his private life; he maintained the strict rules of the monastic order he founded, his diet was simple, he wore his monk's habit, and he manifested this inner simplicity in the manner of his death (Vespasiano, *Vite*, 1:22). Manetti uses the affliction of plague, which obliged Nicholas to interrupt his activities in Rome, to counter criticisms of the building projects, his account of which directly follows. Conceding that, in his view, Nicholas sought glory and personal fame, he then needs to assure the reader (and posterity) that this was not vainglory. And so he comments that the removal to Fabriano had been ordained by Divine Providence so that Nicholas, remembering that he was human, would not "slip into the detestable vice of overbearing ambition and unbearable pride" (19). Here his argument becomes subtle, for it is not to ensure in Nicholas the virtue of humility that he is forced to flee, but to make him a more perfect vessel of divine power. Manetti quotes here from Paul: "My power is made perfect in weakness"(2 Corinthians 12:9).

There is nothing original about Thomas's definition of magnificence as an aspect of fortitude. It derives, in part, from Aristotle (*Politics* 1321a.35–40) and had been reiterated by the Florentine Matteo Palmieri in his 1430 *Della vita civile* (3.207–210). Aristotle's discussion of fortitude is also relevant in distinguishing its two kinds: military fortitude, which rests on bodily strength alone, and that which, for the public good, does not yield or flee in the face of danger (*Ethics*, 3.8.1116a.18–b.22, reviewed by Thomas in *ST*, 2.2., q.123 art.5 and 6). The long list of persecuted popes enumerated in the Testament (T9–16) shows that Nicholas felt threatened, as indeed he had been by Stefano Porcari. Whether Nicholas drew from Aristotle, Aquinas, or even Ptolemy of Lucca (4.17.3) for this aspect of fortitude we cannot know. But that he rebuts charges of pomp, ambition, vainglory, and fame — the opposites of magnanimity, according to Aquinas — suggests that we would be misreading his culture and Manetti's were we to omit the Christianization of classical sources in Scholastic theology.

In Roberto Valturio's *De re militare* (ca. 1455) he reviews the virtues of an *imperator* (Book 5). Of the four cardinal virtues which the ruler must possess, the greatest, and only masculine virtue, and that on the basis of which tombs and monuments are erected for rulers, is fortitude.[55] Of course, Valturio refers primarily

[55] The passage is quoted in Turchini, *Il Tempio Malatestiano*, 355.

to courage — his examples are David and Joshua. But magnanimity and magnificence are also reserved for the ruling elite, and we need now to explore their political, rather than moral, dimensions, that is, their connection with rule.

Magnificence and Renaissance Historiography

Fraser Jenkins's often-cited essay on the association of Aristotle's virtue of magnificence with Cosimo de'Medici's building projects implied that the appeal to an impeccable classical authority on virtue to justify great expenditure was an innovation of the early Renaissance; and, indeed, both Giovanni Pontano and Paolo Cortese hailed Cosimo as the first modern exemplar of magnificence.[56] But in reality, as Spilner and Green have recently emphasized, this use of Aristotle can be observed a century earlier.[57] Boccaccio wrote from the Angevin court in 1363:

> Some wish your patronage to be magnificent . . . a virtue not attained through ordinary expenditure . . . indeed, magnificent works are exclusively associated with great expense . . . [such as] to erect buildings intended to endure for a long time, not such as are built by ordinary citizens.[58]

Francesco Filelfo's *Convivia Mediolanensia*, dedicated to Filippo Maria Visconti in 1443, discusses *magnidecentia* (Aristotle's *megaloprepeia*) as a virtue of the rich, although it is not here explicitly connected to building; Pier Candido Decembrio's biography of the same ruler in 1447 includes a chapter "On Buildings Founded by Him" and another "On the Care and Restoration of Sacred Shrines."[59] The use of Aristotle's notion of magnificence in connection with princely building

---

[56] A. Fraser Jenkins, "Cosimo de'Medici's Patronage of Architecture and the Theory of Magnificence," *Journal of the Warburg and Courtauld Institutes* 33 (1970): 162–70; R. Goldthwaite, *Wealth and the Demand for Art in Italy 1300–1600* (Baltimore, 1993), 221.

[57] P. Spilner, "Giovanni di Lapo Ghini and a Magnificent New Addition to the Palazzo Vecchio, Florence," *Journal of the Society of Architectural Historians* 52 (1993): 453–65, here 458–60; L. Green, "Galvano Fiamma, Azzone Visconti and the Revival of the Classical Theory of Magnificence," *Journal of the Warburg and Courtauld Institutes* 53 (1990): 98–113.

[58] "Altri vogliono questo tuo Mecenate essere magnifico . . . la qual virtù non s'aggiugne a popolaresche spese . . . Adunque, con ciò sia cosa che intorno alle cose di grande spesa solamente s'intenda, è cosa del magnifico . . . e per cagione di bene . . . [such as] edifici da durare lungamente, non cittadineschi, in alto porre": cited in Spilner, "Giovanni di Lapo Ghini," 459. The letter is to the Prior of SS. Apostoli in Florence about Niccolò Acciaiuoli, Gran Seneschal of the Kingdom.

[59] Fraser Jenkins, "Cosimo de'Medici," 166, 169; Francesco Filelfo, *Convivia Mediolanensia* (1537), 78f; P. C. Decembrio, *Vita di Filippo Maria Visconti* in *RIS* 20.1, chaps. 36 and 37.

projects can be identified in the history of the Visconti rulers roughly contemporary with Manetti's *Life*: Guarino Veronese praised the buildings of the Ferrarese Lionello d'Este's father as evidence of his greatness of soul: "Very many other buildings proclaim the magnificence of his mind; these he scattered, with great expense and elegance, throughout the land and city of Ferrara."[60] Given this north Italian tradition of praise for tyrants on grounds of Aristotelian magnificence, Timoteo Maffei's 1454–1456 *In magnificentiae Cosmi Medicei Florentini detractores* and Alberto Avogadro's *De religione et munificentia illustris Cosmi Medices Florentini* (1460s) do not seem new.[61] Green responded to Fraser Jenkins, who had presented Maffei's work within the context of Florentine Humanism and the revival of classical literary and ethical models, that justification on the basis of Aristotelian magnificence was a late medieval response to the new political phenomenon of the north Italian regional or territorial state.[62] Further evidence of Maffei's participation in the world of Scholasticism is that, instead of using Aristotle directly, Maffei used Aquinas's discussion of magnificence in the *Summa*.[63] Since Maffei was rector general of the Augustinian Canons from 1454 to 1457, argument from the *Summa* was not surprising. Nor would it be surprising in Manetti, who studied with the Augustinian Canon Luigi Marsigli at Sto. Spirito. The picture that emerges is that the association between large building projects and the virtue of magnificence was developed by professional religious, who arrived at Aristotle through Thomas Aquinas, in order to legitimize power wielded by individuals.

Magnificence and Authority

But how does building deter aggression, as Nicholas claimed in the Testament? The connection between magnificence and control of the masses seems to have begun as an accident of translation in the thirteenth century and, having entered

[60] Guarino Veronese, *Epistolario*, ed. R. Sabbadini (Venice, 1916), 2:416. Giovanni Sabadino degli Arienti's treatise on princely virtues dedicated to Ercole I d'Este in 1497 would devote a third of the entire work to magnificence (37 of 118 folios), drawing his definition both from the *Nicomachean Ethics* (2.7.6 and 4.2.1–19) and Aquinas (*ST* 2.2. q.34). See *Art and Life at the Court of Ercole I d'Este: The "De triumphis religionis" of Giovanni Sabadino degli Arienti*, ed. W. Gundersheimer (Geneva, 1972).

[61] Maffei was published in an inaccurate transcription by G. Lami in *Deliciae eruditorum* (Florence, 1742), 12:150–68 and Avogadro in the same volume, 117–49.

[62] Green, "Galvano Fiamma," 98; Fraser Jenkins, "Cosimo de'Medici."

[63] The sources are given by Fraser Jenkins, "Cosimo de'Medici," 165: MSS. in the Biblioteca Laurenziana, Plut. XLVII, cod. xvii, fols. 78–102; Plut. LXXXX, sup. cod. xlviii, fols. 125v–131v.

commentaries and other kinds of literature, persisted even after accurate translations were available. William of Moerbeke's thirteenth-century translation of Aristotle's discussion of magnificence in *Politics* (6.7.1321a 35–40) read:

> It makes sense, however, that those offering sacrifices make them magnificent and provide something communal so that the people participate in what surrounds the festivities and, looking on the city adorned here with what is suspended above (*sursum suspensis*), there with buildings, they take joy that the state survives.[64]

Now William's mistranslation of Aristotle's "anathemasi" ("votive offerings"; literally "things put up") as "suspensis" ("suspended") led Albertus Magnus to comment on this passage: "that is to say, the people, on seeing magnificence, are suspended in admiration so that they desire such princes to rule."[65] Is it accidental that this earliest discussion of magnificence and politics was initiated by a friend of Thomas Aquinas (William) and developed by the Dominican Albertus? The theme of wonder, then, has a textual history linking it to authority. And this may account for why it is more elaborately developed in Manetti's *Life* (55–56), which has for its subject a head of state, than it is for Florence Cathedral.

Again, this interpretation seems to have entered late medieval Italian historiography in the circle of the Visconti. Galvano Fiamma wrote in his mid-fourteenth-century *Opusculum de rebus gestis ab Azone, Luchino et Johanne vicecomitibus*, paraphrasing Aristotle's *Ethics* (4.2.1–19) and *Politics* (1321a.35–49), that one should have "a handsome home . . . and build magnificent temples" and that "the people, seeing the wonderful dwellings, stand, with their minds suspended because of powerful wonder . . . From this they decide the prince has such power that it is impossible to attack him."[66] Interestingly, Galvano was a Dominican, and therefore perhaps more likely to have approached Aristotle through Aquinas. In his chronological account of Visconti rule, when he reached the year

[64] "Congruit autem sacrificia immitentes facere magnifica, et praeparare aliquid communium ut iis quae circa convivationes, participet populus, et civitatem videns ornatam, haec quidem sursum suspensis, haec autem aedificiis, gaudens videat manentem politiam": ed. F. Susemihl, *Aristotelis Politicorum libri octo; cum vetusta translatione Guilelmi de Moerbeka* (Leipzig, 1872), 494.

[65] The observation is Spilner's, "Giovanni di Lapo Ghini," 458. The quotation is from Albertus Magnus, *Politicorum libri VIII*, ed. B. Geyer, in *Opera omnia* (Münster, 1951), 8:599.

[66] In Spilner, "Giovanni di Lapo Ghini," 458, but the translation is ours; Galvano Fiamma, *Opusculum de rebus gestis ab Azone, Luchino et Johanne vicecomitibus ab anno MCCCXXVIII usque ad annum MCCXLII*, in *RIS* 12.4 (1938), cols. 15–16.

1334–1335, he inserted a chapter "On the Magnificence of Buildings." Green suggested that Azzone Visconti's patronage of architecture did, in fact, begin around 1335 when, with most of his conquests completed, he needed to consolidate his dominions. To confer legitimacy on the new rule he embarked on magnificent building projects.[67] In Green's view, Galvano Fiamma provided the theoretical justification for rule, using Aristotle's theory of magnificence to illustrate the benefits of tyranny.[68]

Manetti already knew this line of argument in 1436, for it appears in the *De pompis* about Florence Cathedral. The building entrances spectators and "holds them as they stare long and often in great bewilderment" (12). In the preceding sentence Manetti reminds us of the "incredible expenses" made for the building; clearly, then, this bewilderment relates to the magnificence of the patrons. The intended effect of this approach on the viewer has been interpreted as "to astonish in order to subjugate" ("stupire per assoggettare").[69] The function of architecture becomes the manifestation of *auctoritas*. Why would Manetti, who knew the *Politics* in Greek and complained at Bruni's funeral of the inadequacy of earlier Aristotle translations, have perpetuated Moerbeke's mistake?[70] Because the error had become embedded in other kinds of literature, not only history but also political science, most importantly in Ptolemy of Lucca's *On the Government of Princes* (2.12.4 [see below]), where it had lost its association with a specific Aristotelian passage.

In her recent study of Cosimo de'Medici's patronage, Dale Kent observed that the development of magnificence as a social virtue is more characteristic of the second half of the fifteenth century, and that earlier the traditional Christian virtues of liberality and charity receive greater attention.[71] But even though Cosimo was a public figure, he was not a head of state in the sense of the northern tyrants or the pope. Her observation points up the difference between the virtue of a private person — no matter how powerful — and that of a ruler whose individuality blends into that of the institution he represents. For we are speaking about overt demonstrations of power permissible only in monarchical or tyrannical forms of government. What is interesting — more than interesting, radically novel — is that Manetti implicitly identifies the church as fitting this political model.

---

[67] Green, "Galvano Fiamma," 101.

[68] Green, "Galvano Fiamma," 112.

[69] Tafuri, "'Cives esse non licere'," 39.

[70] Palla Strozzi had obtained a Greek text of the *Politics* in Constantinople in 1429 which Bruni used for his new translation: Susemihl, *Aristotelis Politicorum libri*, xv. At Bruni's funeral Manetti said that "haec Aristotelica vitio priorum interpretum corrupta": Botley, *Latin Translation*, 75.

[71] D. Kent, *Cosimo de'Medici and the Florentine Renaissance* (New Haven, 2000), 214.

The Rulers and the Ruled

On his deathbed, Nicholas distinguished between works intended for the reading public (the Library project) and those directed at uneducated people (his buildings) because:

> the only people who understand that the authority of the Roman Church is greatest and supreme are the ones who have learned its origin and growth from their knowledge of reading . . . [whereas] popular respect . . . grows so much stronger and more solid day by day through great buildings. (T2–3)

For Onofri, Manetti's differentiation between books and buildings deepened the division between *docti* and *rudes*, using architecture not as an instrument which persuades to consensus but as a demagogic and pedagogic tool for the manipulation of the populace.[72] The idea that the non-reading public required its own (inferior) information media may be traced at least as far back as Gregory the Great's dictum that pictures are the Bible of the unlettered: "what writing does for the literate, a picture does for the illiterate looking at it, because the ignorant see in it what they ought to do."[73] This, of course, was not reciprocal since the educated both read books and looked at pictures. In the fourteenth century, Petrarch had extended the principle that works for one audience are unintelligible to another to include aesthetic appreciation. Having left a painting by Giotto to the lord of Padua in his testament, he drew a distinction between connoisseurs of art and the vulgar crowd and commented that the painting's beauty, incomprehensible to the ignorant, stupefied the master.[74] But the accommodation — or exploitation — of the excluded audience seems to have been a phenomenon of the Quattrocento. One of its earliest manifestations, in 1435, was Alberti's translation of his treatise on painting from Latin into the vernacular so that Brunelleschi could read it. In the treatise he distinguished the responses of the two audiences of painting thus:

> I consider a great appreciation of painting to be the best indication of a most perfect mind, even though this one art is pleasing to the educated and uneducated alike, something which happens in almost no other art in that it gives pleasure to the knowledgeable while it also moves the ignorant. (*Della pittura*, 2.28)

---

[72] Onofri, "La *Vita* di Niccolò ," 66.

[73] *Sancti Gregorii Magni Registrum Epistolarum*, 11.13, PL 77.1128; ed. Norberg, CCSL 140A, 874.

[74] Discussed in E. Castelnuovo, "The Artist," in *The Medieval World*, ed. J. Le Goff (London, 1990), 211–41, here 239.

The distinction between a learned and an unlearned audience also informs Roberto Valturio's characterization of the intended audience for the imagery at the Tempio Malatestiano, in his *De re militari* of 1455, and Manetti's depiction of Nicholas's library and buildings in his *Life of Nicholas* written in that same year. Valturio, after summarizing the iconographic program, observes:

> These representations, not only because of the excellent skill of the stonemason and sculptor, but also because of their knowledge of forms, whose characteristics you, the most intelligent and unquestionably the most distinguished ruler of our time, have taken from the secret depths of philosophy, are especially able to attract learned viewers [*intuentes literarum peritos*] who are almost entirely different from the common run of people [*a vulgo fere penitus alienos*].[75]

At the Tempio Malatestiano, meaning for the educated elite is conveyed mostly through the iconographic program of the figural sculpture, intelligible to those familiar with contemporary (and patristic) theory on the formation of Christian thought (indeed, the iconography of the Sibyls is taken mostly from Lactantius), as Valturio's comment implies, but not to a general public.[76] The imposing dome of the church intended to be visible on the exterior would have spoken to the masses. This is the sense of Valturio's description of the project at Rimini, where the Tempio is said to be the most admirable sight to be seen in the city and near the main square, whereas the sculptural program attracts those who are skilled in understanding philosophy.[77] And it is the organizing principle of Manetti's account of Nicholas's patronage: the library for the learned and buildings, above all the rebuilt St. Peter's, for the masses.

Around 1460, Flavio Biondo distinguished the iconographically skilled and unskilled with specific reference to the apse mosaic at St. Peter's. His argument has to do with how to determine right and left. Educated spectators, he said, know that right is determined by the viewer's position, whereas ignorant people think it is determined by placement within the image. Thus, "in the picture, Paul would appear to God's right and Peter to His left to the unlearned, but not to the experts."[78] The distinction is not so much about the rise of art connoisseurship, whether of form or content, as about knowledge and persuasion.

---

[75] Turchini, *Il Tempio Malatestiano*, 634. See also S. Kokole, "*Cognitio formarum* and Agostino di Duccio's Reliefs for the Chapel of the Planets in the Tempio Malatestiano," in *Quattrocento adriatico: Fifteenth-Century Art of the Adriatic Rim*, ed. C. Dempsey (Bologna, 1996), 177–206.

[76] Turchini, *Il Tempio Malatestiano*, 424.

[77] The whole passage is quoted in Turchini, *Il Tempio Malatestiano*, 634.

[78] Nogara, *Scritti inediti*, 207, letter 20 of 30 September 1461. We discussed the passage in Chapter 5 in another context.

In the High Middle Ages Gregory's distinction between literate and illiterate was assumed to apply to religious and laity, respectively. Duggan has traced this in writers such as Honorius of Autun, Sicardus of Cremona, Albertus Magnus, and Durandus of Mende. For Durandus, "pictures and ornaments in churches are the lessons and the scripture of the laity."[79] The didactic nature of Nicholas's building program, which would have created a "Biblia pauperum" in which one could read the history of the church, has been pointed out by Miglio, and to a lesser extent by Westfall.[80] But seen within the context of Nicholas's professional practice and training as theologian and preacher, his distinction between the audiences for books and buildings reflects the Scholastic *ars predicandi*. In the prologue to his *Sermones vulgares*, the thirteenth-century theologian Jacques de Vitry explained that:

> For the edification of uncultured people and the instruction of rustic folks, you should often present things that seem corporeal and palpable and similar to what they are familiar with through experience; for they are moved more deeply by outward *exempla* than by [the words of] authorities or profound proclamations.[81]

Recently, Jung has discussed the distinction between audiences in regard to the *ad status* sermon developed in the thirteenth century, in which both language and style were aimed at the social class and educational level of the audience. There is evidence that when preaching to laity doctrinal and moral commentary on biblical events was spoken in Latin while the more dramatic parts of the narrative were given in the vernacular.[82] The distinction between Latin and the vernacular also applies to that between *verba* and *exempla* in preaching, appropriate respectively for doctrinal points and what illustrates them.[83]

The Library was for those who understood doctrine and moral philosophy, whereas the buildings were *exempla* accessible to the common people. However, rather than persuading people by what was familiar to them, Nicholas aimed to astonish and amaze. The buildings neither edify nor educate; they impress or even intimidate. Nicholas combines the psychology of a preacher with that of

---

[79] Durandus of Mende, *Rationale*, 1.3.4; translation in W. Tatarkiewicz, *History of Aesthetics* (The Hague, 1970), 106. Also in L. Duggan, "Was Art Really the 'Book of the Illiterate'?" *Word and Image* 5 (1989): 227–51, here 231.

[80] Miglio, *Storiografia pontificia del Quattrocento*, 109; Westfall, *In This Most Perfect Paradise*, 35, 55–57.

[81] Quoted from J. Jung, "Beyond the Barrier: The Unifying Role of the Choir Screen in Gothic Churches," *Art Bulletin* 82 (2000): 622–57, here 647.

[82] Jung, "Beyond the Barrier," 649.

[83] Jung, "Beyond the Barrier," 647.

a politician, drawing on two very different kinds of literature both well represented in his library.[84]

By contrast, it is the persuasive value of art, said to "attract" the expert and strengthen the faith of the ignorant, rather than its didactic or informational function, which Manetti emphasizes. This rhetorical function comes, not from Pope Gregory, but from the passage cited above of Durandus's *Rationale*, which continues:

> For painting seems to move the mind more powerfully than writing. It sets events before the eyes, while writing recalls them to the memory, as it were, through the hearing, which moves the mind less.[85]

Durandus's interpretation probably derives from Horace's comment that people are more moved by what is seen than by what is heard (*Ars poetica* 180–181). And it may reflect the association between laity and carnality on the one hand and professional religious and spirituality on the other made by St. Bernard, who observed that "bishops have a duty towards both wise and foolish. They have to rouse the devotion of the carnal people with material ornament, since they are incapable of spiritual things."[86] Bernard recognized, that is, the connection between affective persuasion and devotion. It is this ability to move the emotions of the ignorant that Manetti referred to in *On the Dignity of Man*:

> Many [Christians] wished to paint God in the image of man in certain basilicas of the apostles and martyrs and other saints in order to help rude and ignorant (*rudibus ignarisque*) men in some way toward divine contemplation.[87]

The difference of opinion between the great Cistercian, Bernard, and the layman, Manetti, about the capacity of the laity for spiritual experience is profoundly revealing. For Manetti's belief that the higher levels of spiritual awareness were accessible to every man, an awareness he himself experiences and recounts at

---

[84] Müntz and Fabre, *La bibliothèque*. The published inventory is organized by *armadii* in which works on similar topics were kept together. Political literature was mostly shelved in the fifth *armadio* on the right; collections of homilies (except for those of the Fathers) in the second on the left.

[85] Durandus, *Rationale*, 1.3.4. This theme is also discussed in E. Dahl, *"Dilexi decorem Domus Dei.* Building to the Glory of God in the Middle Ages," *Acta ad archaeologiam et artium historiam pertinentia* 1 (1981): 157–90, here 182; and G. Constable, "A Living Past. The Historical Environment of the Middle Ages," *Harvard Library Bulletin* n.s. 1 (1990): 49–70, here 52.

[86] In *Cistercians and Cluniacs. St. Bernard's 'Apologia' to Abbot William*, trans. M. Casey (Kalamazoo, 1970), 64.

[87] Trinkaus, *'In Our Image and Likeness'*, 233.

the close of *De pompis*, sets him apart not only from a professional religious like Nicholas but also from many contemporary laypersons like Alberti. Manetti, for instance, believed that God assigns to each person a guardian angel, like a teacher, and that among the duties of angels was to inspire, purge, and perfect human beings (*De dignitate* 3.27, 3.43). For him, the supernatural mingled with the natural and aided every soul, for all were equally created by God *ex nihilo* and in His own image. Paraphrasing Augustine, he writes: "God made man that he might know Him; and, knowing, love Him; and loving, possess Him; and possessing, enjoy Him" (*De dignitate* 3.55).[88] Manetti, then, understood the purpose of Nicholas's buildings to be anagogic rather than educational.

But Nicholas himself, we intuit, had a different aim. The connection between emotional persuasion or, better, intimidation, and architecture comes from the work of another Dominican, Ptolemy of Lucca, in the context of political theory in his *On the Government of Princes*. The people, he says, are

> motivated more by their sensibilities than by reason. When they see the magnificent expenses that kings incur for fortification, their admiration more easily inclines them to obey and submit to the king's mandates, as Aristotle says. (2.12.4)[89]

Fortification was Nicholas's first objective, and he indeed spent enormous sums on it, as we saw in Chapter 6.

To sum up, the distinction in the *Life* between educated and uneducated spectators does not reiterate an early medieval papal justification of images, nor is it primarily concerned with information. Rather, while rooted in Aristotle's *Politics*, it was formed by medieval treatises on rulership like that of Ptolemy of Lucca and enriched by Durandus's *Rationale*, where it had been adapted to the problem of faith.

This distinction is applied differently in Nicholas's own words in the Testament and in how Manetti presents it in the narrative of Book 2. Nicholas, the head of the church, spoke to the cardinals about governance in his Testament: his account of the building project focuses on fortification. For the pontiff, not only would the spectacle of great buildings secure his rule by astonishing the spectator and teaching the unlettered, but it would also imprint the authority of the church in memory for, as he said, "unless they are moved by something extraordinary that they see, all that assent of theirs rests on weak and feeble foundations and will slip bit by bit in the course of time until it lapses to virtually nothing"

[88] Leonard traces the passage to Augustine's *De diligendo Deo* 2, through Peter Lombard, *Sentences* 2.1, 4, 5: *De dignitate et excellentia hominis*, ed. Leonard, 96.

[89] The reference is to Aristotle, *Politics*, 6.7.1321a 35–40, as discussed above.

(T2). Nicholas's psychology rests on Scholastic authority, for it was St. Bonaventure who recognized not only the affective, but also the mnemonic, function of things seen as being retained more than things heard.[90] Manetti, the layman, was concerned with individual religious experience, and his account of Nicholas's architecture in Book 2 dwells on the interior of St. Peter's. He believed that magnificent buildings moved the unlettered spectator to greater devotion. While both the pope and his biographer drew from Scholastic and Thomist, rather than Humanist or classicizing, interpreters in defending the building projects, Nicholas argued within his professional competence as a preacher, theologian, bishop, and monarch, whereas Manetti wrote as a highly educated layman in the light of his personal faith.

Manetti defends Nicholas against the charge of tyranny by casting the building projects as proofs of magnificence. But the sophisticated reader who knew historiography and the incipient political theory developed from Aristotle's works would have understood that magnificence could be a euphemism for manipulation. Alberti was such a reader. Alberti satirized this very notion in *Momus*, mocking the god Stupor whose mouth hangs open, eyes bulge, lips are thrust out, and looks like someone who doesn't even remember who he is. Yet Stupor converts the philosopher Enopre to belief in the gods (4 [238]). In the same work, Jupiter is stupified (*obstupescebat*) that huge columns of Parian marble could have been transported and erected in the theater (4 [234]). Here Alberti associates stupor with uncritical admiration of huge and expensive buildings. Jupiter (Nicholas, that is), who seeks control over gods and humankind through his constructions, falls victim to his own ploy and becomes a fool.

[90] Discussed in Jung, "Beyond the Barrier," 647.

Chapter Nine

"That Admirable and Truly Magnanimous and Most Reverent Plan for the Apostolic Temple"

Manetti's description of St. Peter's, the culmination of his architectural ekphrasis, begins with the physical fabric (39–50) in an account closely tied to the narrative of the coronation of Frederick III that follows (64–68) and serving to present Nicholas as a knowledgeable and responsible — indeed, admirable and praiseworthy — patron of architecture.[1] We have explored the linguistic, literary, political, architectural, and apologetic dimensions of the buildings account up to this point. The description continues, however, with further interpretations of St. Peter's' significance in its own right which are now our subject.

Divided into two main parts, the first proposes a progressive triad of associated images — the human body, the microcosm, and the Ark — defining the basilica as the Church Militant and articulating its historical circumstance. This first section concerns what Nicholas *planned* — "he desired and willed to imitate [the Ark] in his own construction of the divine temple" (52) — and its formal, especially linear and arithmetical but always two-dimensional, analyses seem to describe the building as an idea or sketch. We learn that its "figure," meaning perimeter in plan, is in the shape of the human body (51); and that its proportions are those of both the human body and Noah's Ark (52). The second section (55–62) compares the basilica to the Seven Wonders and to Solomon's Temple, exemplars of gentile and Jewish achievement. This second part, on *spectacula*, takes up how the building would have been responded to by those who saw it. "We would find no sight in the whole world," says Manetti, worth comparing to St. Peter's except the works of Solomon (56). The architectural elements analyzed are those in elevation — walls, windows, vaults, and roofs — as well as optical phenomena like light (58–61). And it explicates what Nicholas *did*, that is, to imitate Solomon's erection of the Jerusalem Temple and to excel its magnificence (57). If the first section exemplifies the mystical significance of what Nicholas decided (as

[1] See Chapters 3 and 7. The specific problems posed by this section of the ekphrasis especially in regard to its terminology and veracity are addressed in Chapter 5 and in the Commentary, passim.

idea or plan), the second puts before the eyes what Nicholas did (as built work), surpassing the greatest achievements of the classical and Jewish traditions. And it explicates the relation of the Church Militant to the Church Triumphant.

As architectural description, the comparative images seem hackneyed and very little architectural. But they resonate with controversial ecclesiological interpretation since all — except for the Seven Wonders — are metaphors used by Scholastic theologians since the thirteenth century in arguments for papal supremacy, many having been included in Boniface VIII's Bull *Unam sanctam* (1303).[2] Only the Seven Wonders, a gentile theme, can be contextualized differently, within Humanist historiography. While it might seem that the first triad — human figure, microcosm, and Ark — is religious or doctrinal and the second group — Wonders and Solomon's Temple — merely cultural, the culminating comparison with Solomon arrives at the kernel of Manetti's argument about Nicholas's historic role in human salvation. As the only topic in the *Life* explicitly elaborated with historical and allegorical allusions, the interpretation of St. Peter's provides the occasion not only for Manetti's fullest display of rhetorical bravura and erudition but also for his exemplification of Nicholas's pontificate. The description is at once the high point and the most complicated argument of the *Life*.

The Human Figure, the Microcosm, and the Ark

The Human Figure and the Microcosm

The ekphrasis begins with Manetti's remark that "this sacred temple's structure . . . strikes me as comparable to the human body" (51), creating the impression that this simile arose purely from his personal observation of built form (fig. 23) rather than its having a long literary heritage. Indeed, Manetti substantiates his (putative) empirical experience with this appeal to the reader's imagination:

> But lest I be thought to have rashly introduced this comparison of mine, such as it is, and that it shrinks far from the truth of the matter, place, I ask you, a man on this temple's upper part, I mean with his whole body prostrate on the ground so that his head points to the west, with his arms stretched sideways in both directions, one pointing north and the other south, and his feet looking to the east, and once you have placed him like so, you cannot hesitate to admit it conforms to and very neatly squares with our comparison. (51)

[2] For *Unam sanctam*, see Paravicini Bagliani, *Il trono di Pietro*, 172. Whether this ecclesiology revives medieval theocratic ideas only or posits a new idea — the monarchy of the church — is not important for our purposes.

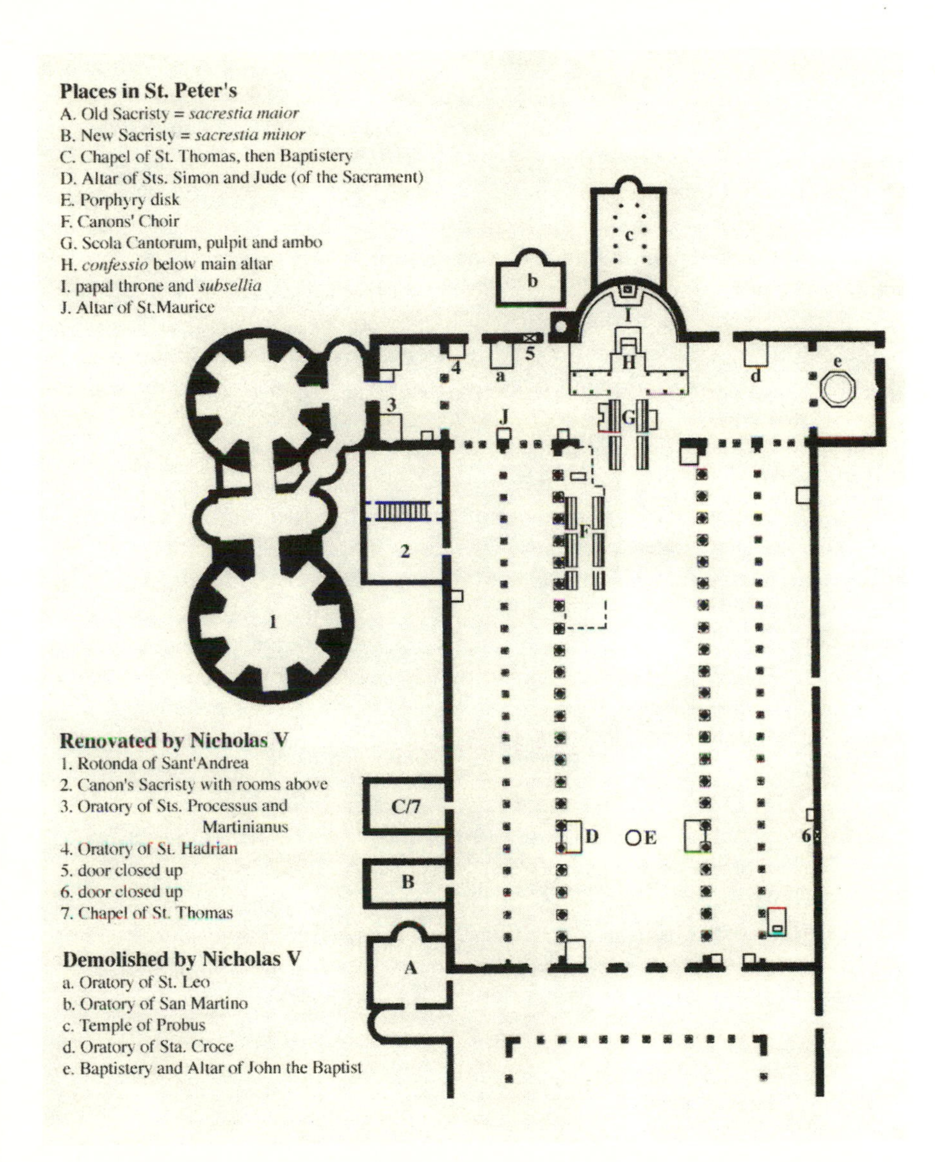

Fig. 23. Plan of St. Peter's with interventions by Nicholas V. Digital image by Steven Wolf, redrawn from S. De Blaauw, *Cultus et Decor: Liturgia e architettura nella Roma tardoantica e medievale: Basilica Salvatoris, Sanctae Mariae, Sancti Petri* (Vatican City, 1994).

The human analogy is, however, as much a literary as a formal figure, recalling biblical passages in which human beings are described as buildings, such as John 2:21: "He spoke of the temple of his body." Paul's conception of the human being as God's temple was important for Manetti: "Didn't you realize that you were God's temple and that the Spirit of God was living among you? . . . the temple of God is sacred and you are that temple" (1 Corinthians 3:16).[3] This temple is the body of Christ in the Pauline message: "You know, surely, that your bodies are members making up the body of Christ" (1 Corinthinas 6:15); and "now you together are Christ's body" (1 Corinthians 12:27). Augustine, elaborating Paul's interpretation, applied it to history and interpreted Haggai 2:9 as foretelling not the restoration of the Jerusalem Temple but the building of the church, whose stones are living stones (*City of God*, 18:48). This, then, is the Church Militant.

The human analogy is also a symbolic figure, ultimately medieval but still current in Scholastic/theological discourse in the fifteenth century, in which the biblical image of person as temple was inverted. Scholars have not failed to note Manetti's probable dependence on Durandus's observation that "the disposition of the material church is in the manner of the human body."[4] Durandus, in turn, may have known Vitruvius's claim that temples "must have an exact proportion worked out after the fashion of the members of a finely-shaped human body" (*De architectura*, 3.1). Onofri thought it odd that Manetti, despite the rediscovery of Vitruvius, did not go beyond the morphology of the human body to develop the geometric implications of man inscribed in the square and the circle,[5] but we will see that this would have been quite foreign to the logic of his argument.

No doubt Durandus was important for Manetti, who drew from the *Rationale* not only terms of description (for instance *cochlea*, 1.1.37), but also ideas about the importance of sight and the distinction between types of audience.[6] Since Nicholas owned two copies of Durandus's *Rationale*, this was a source which also interested the patron.[7] Durandus was especially significant for Nicholas, Burroughs suggested, because of his tomb in S. Maria sopra Minerva, the

---

[3] For this biblical image see R. J. McKelvey, *The New Temple. The Church in the New Testament* (Oxford, 1969), esp. 78.

[4] Durandus of Mende, *Rationale divinorum officiorum*, 1.1.14; Magnuson, *Studies in Roman Quattrocento Architecture*, 207; Burroughs, *From Signs to Design*, 61.

[5] Onofri, "La *Vita* di Niccolò V," 61. See E. De Bruyne, *Etudes d'esthétique médiévale*, 3 vols. (Bruges, 1946), 1:258, for the relationship of Durandus to Vitruvius.

[6] Durandus, *Rationale*, 1.1.37. See Chapters 6 and 8.

[7] Müntz and Fabre, *La bibliothèque*, 93, 95. Manfredi, *I codici latini di Niccolò V*, nos. 559 (lost) and 577, now MS. Vat. lat. 1140.

church of Juan de Torquemada, leading proponent of Nicholas's theories of papal supremacy.[8] And Durandus's metaphor was a source also for Torquemada: Westfall notes similar anthropomorphic imagery used by the cardinal in *De consecratione*.[9] Nonetheless, while Durandus's popularity at mid-century in Rome assured Manetti that his image would be familiar, his use of it in *De pompis* (7) shows that it was not suggested to him by Nicholas but that he culled it from his reading decades earlier while still in Florence. Manetti says that Nicholas chose to imitate the Ark (52), but not the human body, at St. Peter's. Thus this first image, while shared with Nicholas and popular at his court, is Manetti's — we'll see that he draws it initially from Augustine — and he uses it quite differently from Durandus.

Durandus interpreted church buildings which are shaped like a man lying down with the apse as head, transepts as arms extended, and nave as the torso and legs, as signifying by their shape the body of the crucified Christ.[10] This interpretation is both more literal and more allegorical than the apostolic and patristic metaphor. For the Scholastic exegete the historical, or literal, sense was only a beginning, to be followed by the allegorical, the tropologic, and the anagogical senses.[11] For example, summing up how the four senses confer different meanings, Durandus wrote: "Jerusalem is understood historically of that earthly city whither pilgrims journey; allegorically, of the Church Militant; tropologically, of every faithful soul; anagogically, of the celestial Jerusalem, which is our country."[12] But Manetti does not repeat these symbolic interpretations of architectural form, for while his description is laid on the foundations of Scholastic exegesis, this is only his starting point. The definitional character of Durandus's work and its focus on the symbolic, allegorical, and mystical reading of Scripture were not sufficient for Manetti's more visually, historically, and rhetorically oriented approach. In fact, Manetti's order of argument would be better understood as Humanist not only because the subject of the exegesis is a building rather than a text, but also because Manetti begins by placing the building before the spectator's

---

[8] Burroughs, *From Signs to Design*, 256, n. 27. Nicholas's interest in Durandus might well have dated from his student days in Bologna (where the Scholastic had taught law) and have been sparked first by Durandus's *Speculum iudiciale* (a copy of which was in his library) and his *Pontificalis ordinis liber*, which described papal ceremonial: Manfredi, *Codici*, nos. 495 (lost), 496 (Vat. lat. 2635), 502 (Vat. lat. 2636), 506 (Vat. lat. 2629). The Pontifical used for the consecration of Florence Cathedral and for the coronation of Frederick III was essentially that of Durandus (cf. above, Chapter 2).

[9] Westfall, *In This Most Perfect Paradise*, 55.

[10] Durandus, *Rationale*, 1.1.17.

[11] See H. de Lubac, *Medieval Exegesis* 1. *The Four Senses of Scripture* (Edinburgh, 1959, repr. 1998).

[12] Durandus, *Rationale*, 1.12.

eyes, that is, with an ekphrasis, and introduces the scriptural text only at the very last (60). But a more fundamental difference separates him from Scholastic thought. Definitional theology, tending to describe the way things are as a timeless reality, had no need to go beyond the connection between the church and the body of Christ. Manetti, instead, will describe the church in historical time and, more specifically, his own time.

Manetti associates the human *figura* with a second level of symbolic significance: not the cross, or the Crucified, but the cosmos. Some wise men, he says, considered the human body "to have been constructed in the likeness of the whole world, whence they thought man was called by the Greeks 'the microcosm'" (52). Again, the image is not new in Manetti's work, nor especially Roman, for he is essentially repeating what he wrote about the human body in his *Oration on the Dignity of Man* a few years before. Learned and wise men studying the human body, he says in that work, "thought such a fabrication was formed and made in the image of the universe, so they considered that man was called a microcosm by the Greeks, as though a little world" (1.49).

The idea of man as microcosm is so widely diffused in Latin and Greek patristics, the western Middle Ages, and the Renaissance that it is exceptionally difficult to identify Manetti's exact source.[13] In addition to the image being extremely common — this is the kind of image Manetti prefers — in the kinds of literature which Manetti and his readers knew, it was also current. Nicholas of Cusa, for instance, used the image repeatedly in his writings (e.g. *De ludo globi*, 50; *De docta ignorantia*, 2.2, 3.1, and 3.3). St. Antoninus, archbishop of Florence, had just written in his *Summa theologica* that: "Macrocosmos, the great order, is indeed God himself; the medicosmos is the created world, while the *minor mundus*, the microcosmos, is man."[14] And it was an image surely known to both Manetti and Nicholas through Aquinas's use of it in his commentary on Aristotle's *Physics* (8.2.252b.24–28) and the *Summa* (1, q.91, art.1, obj.4), though not one the pope necessarily associated with the basilica.[15]

Manetti did not invent his primary image for Florence Cathedral and St. Peter's, nor did he distinguish these very different buildings from each other by

---

[13] On the image see R. Finckh, *'Minor mundus homo': Studien zur Mikrokosmos-Idee in der mittelalterlichen Literatur* (Göttingen, 1999); H. de Lubac, *Pic de la Mirandole* (Paris, 1974), 160–69; L. Barkan, *Nature's Work of Art: The Human Body as Image of the World* (New Haven, 1975); and R. Allers, "Microcosmus from Anaximandros to Paracelsus," *Traditio* 1 (1943): 319–407.

[14] *Sancti Antonini Summa theologica*, 84.

[15] Aquinas, *In VIII. Phys.*, 1.4, ad 3: "Habet . . . homo similitudinem quandam cum mundo: unde dicitur . . . quod homo sit parvus mundus." Nicholas's copy of this work is in Müntz and Fabre, *La bibliothèque*, 67; Manfredi, *Codici*, nos. 232 (now MS. Vat. lat. 764) and 237.

different images; he associated these specific physical entities with well-established literary and philosophical generalizations. However, the human analogy in the *Life* does not, as it does in *De pompis*, contextualize a personal experience of union. Rather, by qualifying the human figure as a microcosm, Manetti underscores its universality and identifies his subject as a community or even an institution rather than an individual or individuals. This body is the church, as Paul says, evoking the supreme power of Christ "not only in this age but also in the age to come" since God has "made him, as the ruler of everything, the head of the Church, which is his body, the fullness of him who fills the whole creation" (Ephesians 1:21–23). But, for Christian thinkers on government, it is also the body politic which Vincent of Beauvais, quoting from Paul, defined thus: "all of us, in union with Christ, form one body" (Romans 12:5).[16] Vincent's word for the body politic is *corpus*, of which one side is secular, concerned with the necessities of this life, and the other — presided over by the pope — is spiritual. More recently, Nicholas of Cusa had analyzed the imperial and ecclesiastical hierarchies of state and church using analogies of the parts of the body, each containing body and soul.[17] There would be no contradiction, therefore, in Manetti's treatment of the church as both a spiritual and political *corpus*. Yet Manetti's meaning is slightly different. For in order to express the perfection of the human body Manetti writes this particularly tortured sentence:

> If, therefore, the figure of this temple is like the human body, as seemed obvious above, surely it follows that it has acquired the noblest appearance, since we are not unaware that the human form was by far privileged over all the other figures of things animate and inanimate. (51)[18]

What he means is put more clearly by Aquinas, explaining that "the human body has the greatest nobility; since it is perfected by the noblest form, which is the rational soul" (*ST,* 1, q. 91 art.1, obj. 2). Being both corporeal and spiritual, the human body is a microcosm of the twofold nature of the world. But Manetti wants it understood that its *forma* (in the strict sense of organizing pattern), the rational soul, being created *ex nihilo* by God, confers noble appearance on its *figura*. The soul of the human body, he tells us in *De dignitate*, consists of a rational, immortal, and incorruptible *forma* (2.10); and it is divine, rather than human. Because of the soul humans possess the three natural potencies of intellect, memory, and will. While Manetti here says nothing contrary to Christian belief, his thought on the human body owes much to the pagans Cicero (*De natura deorum* 1.27.77;

[16] Vincent of Beauvais, *De morali principis institutione*, ed. R. Schneider (Turnhout, 1995), 1.1.

[17] Discussed in Barkan, *Nature's Work of Art*, 73, citing Nicholas of Cusa's *De concordantia catholica* of ca. 1433.

[18] Compare to the nearly identical sentence in *De pompis* at 7.

1.18.47; 2.37.95) and Aristotle (*De anima* 2.1.412a–413b). And although he acknowledges that physical beauty results from the "sublime and excellent" form (*De dignitate* 3.11), he holds the body itself in high regard. Nothing more beautiful can be imagined than the composition of its members or the symmetrical fashioning of its lineaments, so much so that it is on account of this superlative beauty that the human body is a worthy vessel for the rational soul (*De dignitate* 1.49–52). And the human being is the "only and true image of God" (3.11). Since it is the power of the soul to acquire beatitude, that is, universal and perfect goodness, Manetti not only illustrates the church as a spiritual and secular institution with this image of St. Peter's, but he draws attention to every individual's capacity for sharing in the fullness of Christ. Yet, celebrating the physical, as well as spiritual and symbolic, aspects of the body, he also praises St. Peter's as architectural design. His first image, then, is marked in several ways as drawn from his own reading, experience, and belief, some of which was foreign or at least irrelevant to a purely theological exposition, and Manetti claims this first comparison as his own observation. It would be unlike Manetti to shock his audience by putting forward Cicero's view of humanity as the key to the papal basilica. Because the image is so common, curial readers would, on the basis of other reading, make different associations.

The Ark

From the human body as microcosm, Manetti can move to his comparison with Noah's Ark (as he did also in *De dignitate* 1.50) which, he says, imitated "this most perfect fabric of the human body" and which "saved the human race" (52). Manetti's notion of the Ark is entirely intellectual and literary: it has no relation to the image of Noah's Ark painted on the nave wall of St. Peter's, radically different in shape from what he describes.[19] Nor did he use the image of the Ark for Florence Cathedral: although he says that its nave and side aisles have the form of ships, this is an etymological play on the term *navis* (9).

The description of the Ark in Genesis 6:14–16 had long challenged exegetes. Since it was designed by God, and since His specifications for the structure were almost entirely numerical, it seemed likely that these numbers were not only perfect, but also in some way significant. The practice of interpreting its measurements symbolically goes back at least to Philo, an author whose works Manetti owned in Greek.[20] Just as Noah's Ark in its numerical proportions imitates the

[19] For the fresco, see Grimaldi, *Descrizione della basilica*, ed. Niggl, 140, fols. 106r, 108v–109r.

[20] Giovanni Tortelli used Manetti's Philo manuscripts for the translation project commissioned by Nicholas V at the beginning of his pontificate: Stinger, "Greek Patristics and Christian Antiquity in Renaissance Rome," 155; *Corpus der Orationes*, ed. Wittschier, 42–45 for Manetti's correspondence with Tortelli and Nicholas V in 1448 about the loan.

human body, Manetti says, so does Nicholas's basilica fulfill the same analogy, not in number, but in lineaments ("linear figures," 52). So both are vessels of redemption of the human race. Yet Nicholas's building, as Manetti acknowledges, cannot have the same numerical proportions as the body or the Ark — it would be a short, squat building if it did so. His understanding of "proportion" is not primarily arithmetical and quite innocent of Pythagorean or Platonic number theory. By "proportion" Manetti means "relation", a common classical and medieval use of the term outside of architectural discourse, as in his Ciceronian appreciation of the human figure (above) or in this example from Aquinas: "When we say one thing is in proportion to another we can either mean that they are quantitatively related . . . or else [and this is Manetti's sense] we can mean just any kind of relation ["habitudo"] which one thing may have to another" (*ST*, 1, q. 112 a. 1 ad 4).[21]

It was Augustine who associated the proportions of the Ark with those of the human body, first in *Contra Faustum* (12.5.214–19 or 12.16) and then in *City of God*, the relevant passage of which Manetti quotes almost verbatim in the *Life* (as he had in *De dignitate*) and which is his immediate source for the image. In the *City of God*, Augustine began by defining the meaning of the Ark:

> Without doubt this is a symbol of the City of God on pilgrimage in this world, of the Church which is saved through the wood on which was suspended the mediator between God and men, the man Christ Jesus. (15.26)

Augustine then showed his interpretation to be borne out by the measurement of the Ark, which

> symbolizes the human body, in the reality of which Christ was to come, and did come, to mankind. For the length of the human body from the top of the head to the sole of the foot is six times its breadth from side to side, and ten times its depth, measured on the side from back to belly. I mean that if you have a man lying on his back or on his face, and measure him, his length from head to foot is six times his breadth from right to left, or from left to right, and ten times his altitude from the ground. That is why the Ark was made three hundred cubits in length, fifty cubits in breadth, and thirty in height.

Manetti calls the Ark "a saving ark" and for him the Ark is a metaphor for the church, specifically (following Augustine) the Church Militant. Manetti, then, drew the idea of linking the form of man and the Ark from Augustine, but disassociated his image from Augustinian theology (as also from Durandus's mysticism)

[21] On Aquinas's idea of proportion, see Eco, *The Aesthetics of Thomas Aquinas*, 97–98.

by omitting explicit Christological symbolism.[22] In making the human figure, not the Ark, his primary image Manetti inverted Augustine's exegesis and subordinated Nicholas's stated intention to his own interpretation.

If for Augustine the significance of the Ark was associated with personal salvation, understood as a collectivity of individuals, in medieval texts it more commonly is interpreted ecclesiologically and sacramentally. These follow the interpretation found in 1 Peter:[23]

> Now it was long ago, when Noah was still building that ark which saved only a small group of eight people 'by water', and when God was still waiting patiently, that these spirits refused to believe. That water is a type of the baptism which saves you now. (3:20–22)

Manetti understood the Ark as signifying the church, which floats on the waves of this world and contains all who will be saved, as Bede and Hugh of St. Victor (whose *De arca Noe morali* or *mystica* he owned) had also suggested.[24] And he was aware of contemporary exegeses of the Ark. St. Antoninus, for instance, used the image of the church as a ship in his *Summa* where, commenting on Matthew 8:23–27, he wrote: "What is symbolized is that we are bound to cross over that particular sea of this world, for which a small boat is necessary; for he [Christ] himself used it so that we may reach our homeland, and our city and the mountain of God" (2.1.1. intro., col. 341b): the archbishop wrote a treatise on the spiritual life titled *La nave spirituale* in 1450.[25] While Manetti presents the image in its authoritative Augustinian context, the Ark was a frequent metaphor of the church in theological

---

[22] That Augustine is the source for the linkage of these images was earlier suggested by E. Battisti, *Rinascimento e Barocco* (Turin, 1960), 81. On the uses of Augustine in this period, see P. O. Kristeller, "Augustine and the Early Renaissance," in idem, *Studies in Renaissance Thought and Letters* (Rome, 1969), 355–72.

[23] Discussed in G. Zinn, "Hugh of St.Victor and the Ark of Noah: A New Look," *Church History* 40 (1971): 261–72, here 265.

[24] Bede, *Commentary on Genesis*, PL 91. 221–222; Hugh of St. Victor, *De vanitate mundi*, 3, PL 176.725–726; idem, *De arca Noe mystica*, PL 176.681–704. Manetti's copy of Hugh is in Cagni, "I codici Vaticani," 32. Westfall, who suggested not only Augustine as a possible source but also Hugh of St. Victor, did not distinguish between patristic and medieval interpretations of the image: *In This Most Perfect Paradise*, 121–22. Onofri also pointed out the importance of Hugh's work in "La *Vita* di Niccolò V," 41.

On the Victorine's use of architectural metaphor see L. Bolzoni, "Il 'Colloquio spirituale' di Simone da Cascina. Note su allegoria e immagini della memoria," *Rivista di letteratura italiana* 3 (1985): 9–65, here 42; and G. Beaujouan, "Réflexions sur les rapports entre théorie et pratique au Moyen Age," in *The Cultural Context of Medieval Learning*, ed. J. E. Murdoch and E. D. Sylla (Dordrecht, 1975), 437–84, here 439.

[25] Howard, *Beyond the Written Word*, 20, 196.

and political thinking in Nicholas's circle. Juan de Torquemada explained why the church is called a ship (*navis*) in the *Summa de ecclesia* (1.33). This is, first, because the church, as the treasury of virtue, can intercede for our sins; second, it is the vehicle that keeps us safe from the tempests of our times and brings us to safe port; and third, because being made of the wood which is the cross of Christ, it cannot be shipwrecked. In defining the church as a ship, Torquemada draws a close connection between Noah's Ark and Peter's bark: just as only the ones inside the Ark were saved, so no one outside the church is saved. The argument is not new, and Torquemada cited as his authorities Sts. Jerome, Gregory the Great, and Augustine, omitting recent sources such as Boniface VIII. But it had special relevance to Nicholas's pontificate in relation to schism, heresy, and to union between the Eastern and Western churches. Nicholas followed this interpretation of the church as Ark in 1451 when he told Constantine Paleologus that just as everyone outside the Ark perished, so outside the church's unity there is no salvation.

Nicholas again referred to the church as ship in his discussion of the sacraments in his Testament. The human condition, because of innate frailty, is like the state of shipwreck, he said (*RIS* 3.2:984). The church offers remedies for shipwreck, the first of which is baptism. He evokes here Ambrose's assurance that the wood of the cross is safe from shipwreck (*De Spiritu Sancto* 1.9.110 [PL 16.730C]), recapitulated by Torquemada in his *Summa*. This formulation was also implicit in the nave frescoes of St. Peter's, where the scene of Noah's Ark was directly opposite that of the Baptism of Christ. Penitence is the second remedy from shipwreck, a remedy especially prominent in Nicholas's Jubilee Year during which the treasure of the church was dispensed to heal human frailty (as Torquemada said). Nicholas evoked the image of Peter's bark again toward the end of his Testament:

> [The Church] is that bark of Peter, prince of the Apostles, tossed by the various waves of the stormy deep, as if by the floods of the sea. It is shaken here and there and battered. But since it is continually held up by Christ, her spouse, it can never be in danger of sinking. (*RIS* 3.2:956)

The association of the Ark and Peter's bark evokes Giotto's mosaic of the *Navicella* over the eastern arm of the atrium of St. Peter's. In the mosaic, the storm-tossed boat and terrified apostles contrast with the saving figure of Christ; it is Peter's faith and his cry "Lord! Save me!" which supports him on the waves (Matthew 14:24–33). In the biblical narrative, Jesus then leads him back to the boat, the storm is calmed, and the disciples acknowledge: "Truly you are the Son of God." This story was central for Nicholas's pontificate. Less than three months after his election, Nicholas commissioned two rings with the *Navicella* and the arms of St. Peter.[26] In 1450 he received from the Sienese a set of richly

[26] Müntz, *Les arts*, 168.

embroidered vestments to be worn at the canonization of San Bernardino, on which the scene of the *Navicella* was represented on the chasuble, tunic, stole, and maniple, emphasizing Nicholas's role as Peter's successor, supreme pontiff, and helmsman of Peter's bark, more than his role as bishop of Rome.[27] The *Navicella* also appears on a medal Nicholas struck for the Jubilee of 1450, and on the reverse of the medal commemorating Nicholas's death, the pontiff is depicted as oarsman of a ship inscribed "Ecclesia" (fig. 24).

Nicholas never compares the church to the body of Christ nor refers to the human body as a temple. His concern is with human weakness (the state of shipwreck) and in Book 3 he speaks of the sacraments, "remedies" and "antidotes" for original sin instituted by Christ and the apostles and of the "ineffable grace of merciful God" (*RIS* 948). Just as in the *Navicella* Peter was saved only by crying out to Christ, so Nicholas's last prayer for himself is that, through Christ's passion, he may be saved from the torments of Hell and given a place in heaven (*RIS* 955). For Nicholas the church is the precious Bride of Christ, the seamless garment, and Peter's bark: he speaks of it as an institution quite separate from the individuals who compose it. Instead, the church was born of Christ's blood shed for humankind; Christ maintains it in being. Therefore, he exhorts the cardinals, love it with all your hearts, show your love for it by your works, augment it with all the strength of your spirits, and hold it always in body and in mind: prize it above all human things, whether secular or ecclesiastical (*RIS* 956). Sin occupies a much more prominent place in Nicholas's thought that it seems to in Manetti's; grace is more urgently needed: altogether, it is unlikely that Nicholas saw the Kingdom being built up by men through historic acts. These differences suggest that Manetti's version of Nicholas's life is his own creation. It is Manetti who, in his final lament, attributes the pontiff's achievements to his "extraordinary virtues" and who asks God to grant him a place in heaven on account of his works, that Nicholas whom God had made "divinely perfect through a splendid joining of body and soul" (*RIS* 960). And finally, and most tellingly, Manetti refers not to the church but to his own personal prayer as a "light bark on a great tempestuous sea" in danger of shipwreck (*RIS* 958).

Evidence that the Ark/bark was a key image of the church for Nicholas and the papal apologists is so plentiful that it may well be true, as Manetti says, that "he [Nicholas] willed to imitate it in his own construction of the divine temple" (52). But in Manetti's ekphrasis, where the Ark unites and elides images of the human figure and the microcosm drawn from his own earlier works, it is something different. In part, Manetti expands the connection between Nicholas and Noah drawn in Jean Jouffroy's funeral oration. Although, Jouffroy said, the

---

[27] B. Paolozzi Strozzi, *Il parato di Niccolò V per il Giubileo del 1450* (Florence, 2000); and P. Peti, *Il parato di Niccolò V* (Florence, 1981).

Fig. 24. Nicholas in the bark "eclesia" [*sic*]. Reverse of fig. 4. Bib. Vat., inv. 766.

church has been tossed on waves and flooded with schism, Nicholas guided the church and Ark out of the water and the flood and dried it with the sun of learning and the fire of the Holy Spirit.[28] He speaks of the church not in its doctrinal or sacramental aspect but as a historical institution. The Ark is a dynamic image of the church in historical time, whether one looks to the ship, that is, the institution, to be safeguarded and guided — Nicholas's view — or to its passengers, the pilgrim-citizens of the City of God.

Manetti understood iconography within the most universal interpretive framework available at the time, a *lingua franca* within which the significance

[28] Jouffroy, "Oratio Episcopi Atrebatensis," fol. 35r.

of a building could be explored. Thus he constructs meaning within the established parameters of scriptural exegesis, making the architectural ekphrasis more accessible to an audience which shared this intellectual formation: presenting his interpretive meanings as familiar images enhanced their persuasiveness. These images build a logical argument — again, an accessible way of constructing meaning — which might, in words, be expressed as follows: the church is the body of all the faithful and the body of Christ in the world; as a microcosm, it mirrors the divine order of things; and this body, the Ark, is in a state of constant endangerment. Although individual salvation may depend on being in or out of the Ark, and Nicholas's concern is the salvation of the body which *is* the Ark — that is, the salvation of the church — Manetti's subject extends to the drama of the Church Militant in its progress towards sanctification. What he writes is history, not theology, and the definitional theology of Scholasticism — Durandus's symbolism is static, closed, and entirely cerebral — will not suffice for his purpose. Manetti requires the dynamism of a body which acts, which suffers triumph or defeat, which is endangered but escapes: which will ultimately be united with God. Returning, therefore, to Augustine's understanding of human events as the matter of sacred history, Manetti blurs any distinction between the church and the *res publica*, as Augustine also did in titling his great work *About the City of God Against the Pagans*. For it is within this body, or rather as its head, that Nicholas's historic legacy must be evaluated. Manetti's purpose was to contextualize the achievements of Nicholas's papacy within the broad framework of secular and sacred history; his return to patristic authority is no intellectual pose but an authentic conviction about the need to interpret the church not in the abstract but in its specific historical circumstances.

The Seven Wonders and Solomon's Temple

The Seven Wonders

What, then, was Nicholas's role in the drama of the church? Manetti begins the second part of his interpretation of St. Peter's by expressing "wonder and astonishment" (53). Rather than define or describe, he compares, first with Philo's armory. This example serves to suggest the spiritual arsenal with which the church is fortified and through which Nicholas brought peace, "not by arms, not by upheavals, not with soldiers, but solely by the tranquil and benign agency of the Holy Spirit" (4). Passing from Philo to Hiram of Tyre and Bernardo Rossellino — all architects — Manetti signals transition from discussion of what was intended to what was actually done (meaning, of course, what would actually have been done); from the plan to the building.

Manetti draws the parallel between Solomon and Hiram, who followed the king's designs, and Nicholas and Bernardo Rossellino: as Westfall observed, the point of this is that since Nicholas designed his own buildings they reveal the intelligence of the pope.[29] He thus reminds the reader that, since great buildings perpetuate the memory of their makers, his comparison will eulogize Nicholas. Probably, Manetti subscribed to the conventional classical and medieval view of building according to which the patron is the designer.[30] Having willed the building, the patron is, in Aristotelian terms, its cause. As expressed by Augustine:

> In respect of the form which artists impose upon material things from outside, we speak of Romulus as the founder of Rome, and Alexander of Alexandria, ascribing the foundation of those cities not to the architects and builders, but to the kings at whose will and by whose design and command they were built. (*City of God*, 12.26)

This tradition was succinctly restated in the 1450s by Niccolò Tignosi: "A building does not depend on those who build it but on him who bears the expense."[31] Both Gombrich and Fraser Jenkins have emphasized how commonly the patron is presented as the maker of buildings in the first half of the Quattrocento, especially in biographies. Pier Candido Decembrio described Filippo Maria Visconti's (d. 1447) buildings in his life of the tyrant; the *Cronica di San Marco*, written by its prior, Giuliano Lapaccini (d. 1457), ascribes the buildings of his convent to its "founders, magnificent men, Cosimo and Lorenzo de'Medici"; and around 1462, Filarete listed "Cosimo's buildings" in his treatise on architecture.[32]

---

[29] C. Westfall, "Biblical Typology in the *Vita Nicolai V* by Giannozzo Manetti," in *Acta Conventus Neo-Latini Lovaniensis*, ed. J. IJsewijn and E. Kessler (Munich, 1973), 701–10, here 706.

[30] Although Richard Goldthwaite noted that the idea of the patron as *auctor* of a building is legislated in Justinian's *Digest*, we find only the following relevant passage from the section on public works (*Digest*, 50.10): "It is not lawful for any other name to be inscribed on a public building than that of the emperor or of the man by whose money it was built." See Goldthwaite, *Wealth and the Demand for Art in Italy*, 216; *Digesta Iustiniani*, ed. Mommsen and Krüger, 50.10.3, 2:925.

[31] M. Sensi, "Niccolò Tignosi da Foligno: L'opera e il pensiero," *Annali della Facoltà di Lettere e Filosofia (Università degli Studi di Perugia)* 9 (1971–1972): 359–495, here 456: "Non enim aedificium ab aedificantibus pendet, sed ab eo quem oportet impensam sufficere."

[32] Gombrich, "The Early Medici as Patrons of Art," 40–41; Fraser Jenkins, "Theory of Magnificence," 169; Pier Candido Decembrio, *Vita Philippi Mariae Vicecomitis*, in *RIS*, 20, chaps. 36 and 37; G. Lapaccini, *La Cronica di San Marco*, *Archivio storico italiano* 71 (1913): 11; *Antonio Averlino detto Il Filarete. Trattato di architettura*, ed. Finoli and Grassi, 3.

And now Manetti compares the basilica to the lesser Wonders, those built without divine sanction by the gentiles. Although the explicit comparison with the Seven Wonders is part of the description of St. Peter's (55–56), the building projects which Manetti lingers over in the *Life* also have famous ancient counterparts: thus the engineering feat of moving the obelisk (40) is comparable to that of building the pyramids; the bronze Colossus of Rhodes is the counterpart to the bronze figures of the evangelists and Christ which would have been under and on the obelisk (40). The size and difficulty of the Great Tower (33) parallel those of the Pharos lighthouse tower in Alexandria. The walls of Rome (26) can be compared to those of Thebes and Babylon; the tomb of Hadrian (Castel Sant'Angelo) (26) with the Mausoleum at Halicarnassus; the temple at Cyzicus with St. Peter's (42–49). Manetti does not make these analogies explicit, but the structure of his account of Nicholas's projects is informed by familiarity with the Wonders, if only as suggesting to him qualities and kinds of structures most likely to evoke admiration.[33]

During Nicholas's reign Lorenzo Valla was set the task of translating Herodotus, so this, the fullest account of some of the Wonders (although written before some were created), was especially prominent in Manetti's circle.[34] But the inclusion of Hadrian's Temple and the Capitol warn us that Manetti is not working only from Herodotus or Antipater of Sidon's lists of the Wonders in the recently recovered *Greek Anthology* (8.177, 9.58). Nor does he follow the list of Manuel Chrysoloras in his *Comparison of Old and New Rome*, written in 1411 and widely circulated among the Humanists (the Temple of Artemis at Ephesus; the Colossus of Rhodes; the Mausoleum of Halicarnassus; the Gates of Thebes; the Pyramids; the Lighthouse at Alexandria; and the Walls of Babylon).[35] Instead, Manetti's list exactly agrees with Cyriacus of Ancona's *Septem mundi spectacula*, a Latin translation of a poem long thought (including by Cyriacus and presumably also by Manetti) to be by Gregory of Nazianzus, but which in fact is an anonymous Byzantine work circulated in the Middle Ages.[36]

---

[33] On the Wonders, see P. Clayton and M. Price, *The Seven Wonders of the Ancient World* (London, 1988); G. Brett, "The Seven Wonders of the World in the Renaissance," *Art Quarterly* 12 (1949): 339–58.

[34] *Histories* 1.178–81; 5.184; 2.128. Writing in the fifth century B.C., Herodotus describes the pyramids of Egypt and the city of Babylon. The canon of Seven Wonders, however, is a product of the third century B.C.

[35] The text is translated in G. Cortassa, *Roma parte del cielo. Confronto tra l'Antica e la Nuova Roma di Manuele Crisolora* (Turin, 2000) and in Smith, *Architecture in the Culture of Early Humanism*, 199–216.

[36] Cortesi and Maltesi, "Ciriaco d'Ancona e il 'De virtutibus'," 135 on the poem and its authorship.

Manetti omits the Temple of Diana at Ephesus, the Wonder which is Alberti's very image of classical culture in *Della tranquillità dell'animo* and exemplar of sound building practice in *De re aedificatoria.*[37] Instead, we find him close to Poggio, who wrote that the monumental buildings of Rome used to surpass in size and beauty the pyramids, the basilica of Cyrus, and the other Wonders of the World which Herodotus mentions. Poggio, who opposed Nicholas's buildings and left the Curia in 1453, blames priests for letting ancient things collapse, comparing them to the man who burnt down the Temple of Diana in Ephesus.[38] Poggio referred to Herostratus, who burned the Temple at Ephesus in 368 B.C.; but the temple was condemned by St. Paul (Acts 19:1), finally destroyed by John Chrysostom, and replaced by the martyrium of St. John at Ephesus. The precedent of the Artemision, taken as a whole, provides an additional motive for Manetti's argument that the rebuilt St. Peter's superseded the ancient pagan buildings. In a climate, however, in which the Roman church was frequently accused of the destruction of ancient monuments, in view of Nicholas's own demolitions, and on account of criticisms of his building practices we looked at earlier, Manetti preferred to omit the Temple of Diana at Ephesus from his list.

Solomon's Temple

It was Solomon, Manetti says, "whom our Nicholas closely imitated in magnanimity and boldness"; and had Nicholas's projects been completed, "he either would have equaled the magnificence of the divine temple and the royal house or he would have excelled them by a large margin" (57). The parallel between Solomon's Temple and the Christian *Ecclesia* was a literary *topos* from Augustine on, as Wright has recently shown.[39] Many medieval patrons had been called "Solomon," perhaps referring only to their munificence and social status.[40] Nor was Nicholas the first pope to be seen as the new Solomon; a letter written in 1202 by a member of the court of Innocent III calls him the "third Solomon."[41] Thus Manetti's comparison of Nicholas and Solomon and his culminating image of St. Peter's as surpassing the Jerusalem Temple would seem to be banal, generic, and

---

[37] C. Smith, "Leon Battista Alberti e l'ornamento: rivestimento parietali e pavimentazioni," in *Leon Battista Alberti*, ed. Rykwert and Engel, 196–215, here 197.

[38] Gordon, *Two Renaissance Book Hunters*, 189–90.

[39] Wright, "Dufay's *Nuper rosarum flores*," 408.

[40] W. Cahn, "Solomonic Elements in Romanesque Art," in *The Temple of Solomon: Archeological Fact and Medieval Tradition*, ed. J. Gutmann (Ann Arbor, 1973), 45–72, here 57.

[41] *Federico II. Immagine e potere*, ed. M. Calò Mariani and R. Cassani (Bari, 1995), 150.

trite.[42] But this is not the case: Manetti's images are distinguished not by their originality, but by their contextual aptness. Here, the comparison serves the most telling argument for Nicholas's greatness in Book 2: that he preserved the peace. Manetti notes this as an achievement in the very first year of the pontificate (5, 6, 7); he returns to it near the end (73, 76, 77).

Manetti's comparison was specifically relevant to Nicholas, for the pope himself had initiated the parallel between himself and Solomon which Manetti extended in the *Life*. This parallel was depicted in tapestries (now lost) which the pope himself commissioned. We know of them from an inventory of 1518 where they are described as: "one small one in which David crowns Solomon" and "one small one in which David supplies Nicholas [. . .]."[43] Although their date is unknown, they have to have preceded Manetti's posthumous biography; they may in fact be among those with which he claims Nicholas embellished St. Peter's in the early years of his pontificate (8).[44] The parallel with Solomon was also taken up by Jean Jouffroy in his funeral oration for Nicholas: "Behold a King Solomon and a man wiser than Solomon for he never strayed from God."[45] God chose Nicholas, continued Jouffroy, and he was "a giver of alms, a wonderful builder of temples, the apex of science and learning, an eradicator of schism, a prince of peace." Jouffroy's eulogy owes much to the praise of Solomon in Ecclesiasticus 47:13–16, a source which also nourishes Manetti's eulogistic presentation of the pontiff in our text:

> And God gave him peace all round
> so that he could raise a house to his name
> and prepare an everlasting sanctuary.

---

[42] Manetti's apparent lack of specificity has fostered scholarly interpretations which are equally loose; for instance, the suggestion that the entire building program in the Vatican imitated a model in Jerusalem. Tafuri's idea that the whole complex of Borgo and Old St. Peter's, consisting of a porticoed street, atrium, and colonnades, was meant to parallel Eusebius's description of Constantine's Golgotha basilica compares elements that are too generic to convince: Tafuri, "'Cives esse non licere'," 49. We need to keep in mind that the first Latin translation of Eusebius's *Vita Constantini* (by Jean Porthaise) was published in Antwerp in 1548: *Eusebius' Werke*, ed. F. Winkelmann (Berlin, 1975), xxxiv. While the Greek was not a problem for Manetti, the text was hardly in circulation before its translation.

[43] Müntz, *Les arts*, 182. It is tempting to imagine that the latter image showed David giving Nicholas the plans for the Temple, as he gave them to Solomon (2 Chronicles 28:19). See also H. Smit, "Image Building Through Woven Images. The Tapestry Collection of the Papal Court, 1447–1471," in *The Power of Imagery. Essays on Rome, Italy and Imagination*, ed. P. Van Kessel, (Rome, 1992), 19–30 and 257–64.

[44] Shearman also records five tapestries of the Life of Peter given to the basilica in 1451: *Raphael's Cartoons*, 7.

[45] Jouffroy, "Oratio Episcopi Atrebatensis," fol. 36v.

How wise you were in your youth,
brimming over with understanding like a river!
Your mind ranged the earth,
you filled it with mysterious sayings.
Your name reached the distant islands,
and you were loved for your peace.

Jouffroy added the epithet "Prince of Peace" to his Solomonic comparison, enlarging this relation in a way that shifted its focus and heightened its significance. For the relation previously drawn between Solomon and Christ — "Solomon" means "pacificus" and Jesus is called "Prince of Peace" (fulfilling the prophecy in Isaiah 9:6)[46] — is now extended to Christ's Vicar, "princeps pacis Nicolaus." That Nicholas's pontificate secured the papacy in its seat in Rome after the Avignon exile, importantly through his building projects, and that his policies were distinguished for their furthering of a monarchical papal state, has been recognized by all observers from his own time to the present.[47] That this monarchical ideology was embodied in the person of the pope, in his physical and public being, has also been recognized.[48] As "Prince of Peace," as Jouffroy characterized and Manetti exemplified him, Nicholas was identified more as the Vicar of Christ than Bishop of Rome, an emphasis that was especially controversial.[49] Of course, the role of vicar was not invented by Nicholas, having been extensively discussed in twelfth-century texts.[50] Its theology was fully worked out as early as Petrus Mallius's formulation in that century:

> Blessed Peter himself was made Prince of the Apostles by Christ when the Lord made him vicar of His power with such fullness of authority that whatever the one does on earth, the Other ratifies in heaven.[51]

---

[46] See Theodoret of Cyrrus, *Quaestiones in Librum I Paralipomenon*, PG 80.814.

[47] See also our discussion in Chapters 4 and 8.

[48] Prodi, *The Papal Prince*, 42.

[49] Miglio, "Niccolò V umanista," 80. Miglio discusses the importance in Nicholas's pontificate of the idea of the pope as the Vicar of Christ and the related concepts of the "Sedes Apostolica" and "Cathedra Petri."

[50] Peter Damian may have been the first, in 1057, to apply this title to a pope. Innocent III then adopted it from the writings of Bernard of Clairvaux; one finds it in Durandus's influential *Rationale*: "Being Vicar of Christ, the supreme pontiff is the head of all who live in the Church Militant" (4.54). See Paravicini Bagliani, *The Pope's Body*, 58, 66; Izbicki, *Protector of the Faith*, 83.

[51] Pietro Mallio (Petrus Mallius), "Descriptio Basilicae Vaticanae aucta atque emendata a Romano presbitero," in *Codice topografico della città di Roma*, ed. Valentini and Zucchetti, 3:382–442, here 424. Written in the third quarter of the twelfth century, it was expanded shortly thereafter by Romanus.

And this identity had been embedded in the papal coronation liturgy where, at the crowning with the triple tiara, it was said: "Receive the triple crown and know that you are the father of all Princes and Kings, the guide of the world, and vicar on earth of our Savior Jesus Christ."[52] Gregory X (1271–1276) emphasized the Petrine foundation of power and hence the universality of papal authority by moving the papal coronation to St. Peter's.[53] Peter was both bishop and vicar: the cathedral of Rome, St. John Lateran, preserved the episcopal tradition of apostolic succession and Constantine's transfer of temporal power to the Roman bishop. But at St. Peter's, since earliest times, Peter's authority to bind and to loose, with which he had been invested (so it was argued) by Christ, was central to the cult.[54] Nicholas took as his coat of arms the crossed keys, symbol of this plenitude of power.[55] Responding to the Hussite challenge that the Roman See was only a local part of the universal church and to the conciliarist view that a council represents the Roman church, Torquemada asserted that since Peter alone of the apostles had been granted episcopal powers by Christ the ecclesiastical authority of all prelates was derived from the Roman pontiff.[56] Fra Angelico illustrated Peter's unique authority in the fresco of the ordination of St. Stephen painted in Nicholas's Chapel in the Vatican, where the other apostles are spectators to Peter's action (fig. 7).

The pope alluded to the dual roles as early in his pontificate as his Bull of 1449 decreeing plenary indulgences for the Jubilee: "We conduct matters on earth in the place of Christ and are the successor of Blessed Peter."[57] In a brief of 1451 to Emperor Constantine Paleologus, Nicholas, evoking *Unam sanctam*, asserted that unity, and therefore salvation, depended on acceptance of the pope as vicar:

> A united Church is an impossibility unless there is one visible head to take the place of that Eternal High Priest whose throne is in heaven, and unless all members obey this one head. Where two rulers command there can be no united empire. Outside the Church's unity there is no salvation; he who was not in Noah's Ark perished in the deluge.[58]

---

[52] Quoted from the coronation of Calixtus II in 1455 in von Pastor, *History*, 2:337.

[53] Paravicini Bagliani, *Il trono di Pietro*, 21.

[54] See C. Smith, "Pope Damasus' Baptistery in St. Peter's Reconsidered," *Rivista di archeologia cristiana* 64 (1988): 257–86, for the early importance of penitential pilgrimage to St. Peter's tomb.

[55] Westfall, *In This Most Perfect Paradise*, 20. Westfall noted the importance of this role, but did not connect it to Manetti's text.

[56] *Oratio synodalis*, 21; and *Summa*, 2.55.172v; in Izbicki, *Protector of the Faith*, 146 n. 24; 76.

[57] Coluccia, *Niccolò V. umanista*, 186 n.

[58] von Pastor, *History*, 2:248.

It is in this ecclesiological context that Nicholas spoke of his building projects as demonstrating that "the authority of the Roman Church is greatest and supreme" (T1). Exemplifying the terse theology of Nicholas's Testament in Book 2, Manetti claimed that princes, kings, Christian peoples, and republics sent ambassadors to Nicholas in order "to venerate and worship the new humanity of Christ our Savior now visible on earth and conversing with humans" (3).

Not only were Nicholas's claims challenged by conciliarists, Hussites, and the Eastern Church, but there were other pretenders to the title "Prince of Peace." Gaspar Enenkel records that when Frederick III entered Rome for the coronation:

> Truly it was a glorious sight, and if God himself, made Man, had come down upon earth they [the crowds] could not have reverenced him more, for they had a cross and censers, and they sang with joyous voices: 'Behold! I send my angel to you who will prepare the way before me' (Malachi 3:1, Matthew 11:10).[59]

Nor was Frederick the only competitor; in 1449 Alfonso of Aragon had Pisanello strike a portrait coin with the inscription "Divus Alphonsus Rex Triumphator et Pacificus" — evoking the epithet "princeps pacis" derived from Isaiah and applied to Christ.[60] As so often, Manetti's *Life* comes into focus when seen as a response to unspoken dissent from the truth of what he presents.

By the end of Nicholas's reign it was clear (at least from Manetti's account) that he, personally, had ended the schism, made the French and German princes obedient to the church, and pacified the Italian powers: he had brought peace. But Nicholas's behavior as conciliator and peacemaker was also controversial. In his account of the Porcari conspiracy, Alberti observed that the pope who does not use the sword dies by it.[61] Thus it was important for Manetti to insert prayers into the coronation ceremony which, by reiterating the premises of the Donation of Constantine and the doctrine of the two swords, asserted the emperor's duty to defend the church by military means. Nicholas's military neutrality was severely criticized also in regard to the fall of Constantinople, which he did little to prevent; and rather than being neutral in regard to the Peace of Lodi, Manetti's culminating exemple of Nicholas as peacemaker, Nicholas seems actively to have obstructed its conclusion. Manetti's literary image of Nicholas, however, required the title "Prince of Peace," to relate his comparison of St. Peter's and Solomon's Temple to their purposes within sacred history.

---

[59] von Pastor, *History*, 2:152.

[60] A. Cole, *Virtue and Magnificence. Art of the Italian Renaissance Courts* (New York, 1995), 58.

[61] Alberti, "De coniuratione Porcaria," *RIS* 25.309.

Manetti elaborates both the political and the ecclesiological implications of Jouffroy's themes in Book 2. He does this, typically, by turning to Augustine's *City of God*. Augustine tells us that it was the institution of the monarchy that represented the turning point in the religious and political history of Israel (16.43). The monarchy, with the building of Solomon's Temple and palace, ended the nomadic phase of Jewish experience and made Jerusalem the goal and center of religious life. Nicholas brought peace to the church mostly through astute diplomacy, but peace was evidenced for the masses, so Manetti implies, in the building of the new temple. Manetti's image would seem to be the foundation on which rests the notion of the rebuilding of St. Peter's as a Solomonic enterprise, a topic not mentioned by Jouffroy.[62]

Solomon's Temple is the type and figure of the universal church built by Christ: "the true Solomon, our Lord Jesus Christ, the true bringer of peace (*Pacificus*), built himself a Temple," as Augustine puts it.[63] Augustine's image draws on a biblical text prophesying the rebuilding of Solomon's Temple: "The new glory of this Temple is going to surpass the old, says the Lord of Hosts, and in this place I will give peace" (Haggai 2:8–9). The Temple Mount and the Vatican are seats of princes of peace, historically interpreted. Symbolically, Jerusalem, seat of earthly peace, stands for the Heavenly Jerusalem, seat of true peace ruled by Christ, "verus pacificus" — "What is Jerusalem but the vision of peace?" — in the words of Gregory the Great (*Homilies on Ezechiel* 10.21). It does not follow that Rome is, therefore, the Heavenly Jerusalem; but that it, rather than Jerusalem (or, Nicholas rather than Solomon) has built the new Temple, the place where God gives peace. Even more important than the new Temple's splendor is that its building, or rather rebuilding, signifies the definitive return from exile to the specific and only place where God has promised to give peace. After the exile in Avignon, schism, and forced flight from Rome, Nicholas's building projects at the Vatican are the place of promised peace.

Manetti's argument that Nicholas was a good ruler because he brought peace is as compelling as political theory as theology. Everyone agreed that political society aims to secure the common good and that rulers who act for their own benefit rather than that of the ruled are tyrants, as we saw. But what is the common good? Most Scholastic political theorists argued that the common good lay either in moral goodness (an interior value) or in utility and advantage (exterior

---

[62] By the pontificate of Julius II, the equation Solomon/Temple = pope/St.Peter's was firmly in place, allowing Aegidius of Viterbo to extend the imagery and cast Sixtus IV as David, who abstained from building the Temple: Aegidius of Viterbo, *Historia viginti saeculorum*, quoted in Shearman, *Raphael's Cartoons*, 8.

[63] Augustine, *Enarratio in Psalmum CXXVI*, PL 37.1668; ed. E. Dekkers and J. Fraipont, CCSL 40 (Turnhout, 1956), 1857; see also Wright, "Dufay," 408.

values).[64] But one, the fourteenth-century Dominican Remigio dei Girolami, who lived at Sta. Maria Novella in Florence and whose works had particular influence in that city, identified peace as the true and best good.[65] By peace, he meant harmonious order, quoting from St. Augustine's *City of God*:

> The peace of the body, we conclude, is a tempering of the component parts in duly ordered proportion; the peace of the irrational soul is a duly ordered repose of the appetites; the peace of the rational soul is the duly ordered agreement of cognition and action. The peace of body and soul is the duly ordered life and health of a living creature; peace between mortal man and God is an ordered obedience, in faith, in subjection to an everlasting law; peace between men is an ordered agreement of mind with mind; the peace of a home is the ordered agreement among those who live together about giving and obeying orders; the peace of the Heavenly City is a perfectly ordered and perfectly harmonious fellowship in the enjoyment of God, and a mutual fellowship in God; the peace of the whole universe is the tranquillity of order — and order is the arrangement of things equal and unequal in a pattern which assigns to each its proper position. (19.13)

It is this understanding of peace as harmonious order that informs Manetti's account of Nicholas's deeds and helps explain why architecture — almost by definition the art of arranging equal and unequal things in their proper positions — is the chief exemplar for the pontiff's achievement. Peace, then, is not just the absence of strife, whether military or political, but the presence of divine order in human affairs, and peace, for both Augustine and Aquinas, is the final goal of rational creatures (*City of God* 19.11; *ST*, 2.2, q.29 a.2). Clearly, such peace manifests the moral virtue of justice, which consists in giving to each what is due. But beyond that, peace is motivated by the theological virtue of charity: indeed, Aquinas argued that charity causes peace "precisely because it is love of God and of our neighbor" and "there is no other virtue except charity whose proper act is peace" (*ST*, 2.2, q.29 a.4). By evoking charity as Nicholas's motivating virtue and peace as its outcome Manetti suggests his likeness to God, who is love. Some who, like Alberti, understood this were outraged. But Manetti is careful: he compares Nicholas instead to Solomon. What might have seemed monarchical, not to say tyrannical, in Nicholas's control over the Church, Manetti recasts as the creation of order, and therefore peace. His motive was not power, certainly, nor vainglory, nor ambition, but charity.

Distinguishing the responsibility of the vicar within the rulership of Christ, Torquemada suggested that the state of belief and the state of grace of a Christian

---

[64] See the discussion in M. Kempshall, *The Common Good in Late Medieval Political Thought* (New York, 1997), esp.1–25.

[65] *De bono pacis* quoted in Kempshall, *The Common Good*, 323.

were in the care of the visible church.[66] The main work of the church, he said, was leading sinful believers to the perfection of charity (*Summa de ecclesia* 1.13.16v–18r). The dying Nicholas referred to this responsibility when he urged the cardinals to finish his building projects so that his successors,

> like true shepherds of souls, might have the ability and the strength to nourish the Lord's flock entrusted to them by almighty God more diligently and liberally with saving food and bring them, nourished in this manner, to the life of eternal salvation. (T18)

The metaphor of shepherd and sheep not only alluded to episcopal duty but also evoked Jesus' command to Peter to "feed my sheep" (John 21:17), a text fundamental for arguments of papal supremacy. Nicholas argued, therefore, that the building projects were, no less than the indulgences of the Jubilee or the sacraments (a long discussion of which follows in the Testament), essential for the state of grace of Christians. Since the vicar was said to share the divine nature of Christ in spiritual but not temporal matters, placing the building program in the former category invested it with authority and sanctity, protecting it from the abundant criticism it had provoked as a secular enterprise. Nicholas further justified building by situating it within the duties of the vicar which, as Torquemada defined them, were uniting, ruling, and teaching the faithful.[67] Nicholas argued that the building program was necessary for all three of those purposes, uniting unlettered and lettered in right doctrine, safeguarding the pope's ability to govern, and teaching the masses the right order of the world through "everlasting monuments and almost eternal testimonies, as though built by God" (T3). Thus Nicholas, embodiment of charity, is an exemplary head of the Church and Vicar of Christ — he is, as Jouffroy said, the Prince of Peace.

In his *Roma instaurata* of 1444–1446, Flavio Biondo asserted that:

> The true emperor, Christ, has made Rome the citadel of his eternal religion. From eternal and most glorious Rome now ruled as perpetual dictator not Caesar, but the pope, the successor to the fisherman Peter and vicar of the emperor Christ.[68]

---

[66] Torquemada meant that the pope served the Church's goals of sanctifying souls in this life and securing eternal beatitude for them in the next: Izbicki, *Protector of the Faith*, 38.

[67] Izbicki, *Protector of the Faith*, 84.

[68] *Codice topografico*, ed. Valentini and Zucchetti, 4:318. Trans. by Stinger, "Roma Triumphans," 195.

This is the view argued also by Torquemada when he cited the "Quo vadis?" story to prove that Christ had chosen Rome as seat of the papacy.[69] The long exile of the papacy in France and Eugenius IV's failure to remain in Rome were fresh memories calling into question the necessity of a connection between place and power. Following the Porcari conspiracy (1453), Pietro de Godi presented a dialogue to Nicholas asserting that only Rome could be the seat of the papacy; Giuseppe Brippi's poetic lament on the conspiracy reiterated this point.[70] Some contemporary accounts of the conspiracy suggest that Porcari planned to exile the Curia from Rome, even to northern Europe.[71] As reported in Alberti's account of Porcari's speech to the Romans, the rebel said that there were no Romans in Rome but only *barbari* (that is,"foreigners").[72] Indeed, less than half of Nicholas's cardinalate was Italian, much less Roman. Forced expulsion from Rome was a real danger; Brippi urged Nicholas to complete the fortification of the Vatican and suggested he have three hundred armed men in attendance when he went to St. Peter's.[73] Undoubtedly this is why Nicholas dedicated so much of his Testament to the history of papal persecutions, and reiterated the justification already formulated by Biondo, de Godi, and Brippi, that Rome "had been constituted by almighty God as the perpetual seat of the Supreme Pontiffs and the eternal dwelling of Pontifical holiness" (T5).[74] Nicholas's claim to a divinely sanctioned continuity, contextualized within the temporal framework of the millennial reign, looks both forward to the Church Triumphant and back to the establishment of the Church Militant as the last world empire, succeeding the Roman one: "in this place I will give peace" (Haggai 2:9).

Earlier (in 1438), Nicholas's friend in Bologna, Lapo da Castiglionchio, wrote that no other state — not Athens, Sparta, Carthage, or Rome — could compare with the monarchy of Christ, that is, the Curia Romana.[75] One of the reasons for this, he suggested, was that only the Roman church had never changed over time, preserving instead its ancient institutions pure and integral. This ecclesiological theme of continuity and its corollary, supersession, acquire additional resonance

---

[69] *Commentary on the Decretum*, 2.q7.c37 (2:210) in Izbicki, *Protector of the Faith*, 77.

[70] Pietro de Godis, *De Porcaria coniuratione dialogus*, ed. M. Lehnerd (Leipzig, 1907); von Pastor, *History*, 2:234.

[71] In von Pastor, *History*, 2:231.

[72] Alberti, "De coniuratione Porcaria," 309.

[73] von Pastor, *History*, 2:234.

[74] Manetti also attributes this idea to Eugenius IV in book 1, saying that Eugenius returned to Rome in 1443 because he considered it the true, only, and habitual domicile of Peter, the first pope, and believed it to be the perpetual and eternal seat of the popes: *Vita*, trans. Modigliani, 98.

[75] Celenza, *Renaissance Humanism and the Papal Curia*, 102.

within the context of the Humanist reflection on history. Poggio, for instance, pondered the calamities that had befallen the great ancient cities of Babylon, Carthage, and Rome in *De miseria humanae conditionis* after 1452.[76] The notion that the church under Nicholas was the successor to pagan and Jewish culture, which organizes Manetti's accounts of both the Library and the building projects, is historiographic and political, but fundamentally ecclesiological.

But if Rome was the vicar's seat, did that mean that Roman culture would also rule over the church? Lorenzo Valla believed that Roman culture, rather than the church, was universal, for, he said shortly after Nicholas's death, the universality of Rome was ensured by the universality of Latin.[77] Manetti provides a different answer: the church is Roman in location, but universal in members and in cultural heritage. So we learn that early in Nicholas's pontificate "all the princes, kings, and Christian peoples and republics" sent ambassadors to venerate him (3); that to the Jubilee came "great crowds of Pannonians, Germans, Cimbrians, Britons, Gauls, Spaniards, Celtiberians, Portuguese, Greeks, Dalmatians, Italians, and . . . all the other Christian peoples" (10); and that his aim for general peace included "all Christian princes, republics, and people" (77). Manetti depicts as desirable — indeed, ideal — a universal church embracing diversity. The comparison of St. Peter's to all the Wonders of all the ancient civilizations — Babylonian, Jewish, Egyptian, Greek, and Roman — is part of his contextualization of the theme of universality in Nicholas's papacy.

Universalism, however, is more than a cultural and historical attribute of the church; it is a necessary characteristic of the millennial reign. The fifth monarchy prophesied by Daniel surpasses all previous ones in three ways, according to Ptolemy of Lucca: in universality, for "their sound went out to all the earth and their words to the ends of the globe" (Psalm 18:5 [19:5]); in excellence, in that the pope, both human and divine, has all the temporal virtues of Christ and is the "Prince of Peace"; and in duration, since, having replaced the Roman Empire, it will last until the end of time.[78]

Manetti said that St. Peter's surpassed Solomon's Temple, just as "the new religion of Christ is discernibly to be preferred over and to supersede the old divine law" (62). But the universal church must also confront, include, and surpass the best things built by pagans. Manetti therefore compares St. Peter's to the Seven Wonders: the pyramids, the walls and gates of Thebes and Babylon, the Pharos lighthouse, the Mausoleum at Halicarnassus, and the Temple of Hadrian. That many of these were commissioned by absolute monarchs enhances the development

---

[76] In *Poggius Bracciolini. Opera omnia*, ed. Fubini, Book 2, 118–120.

[77] At the opening lecture at the Studium urbis, 18 October 1455: in Jacks, *Antiquarian*, 111.

[78] Ptolemy of Lucca, *On the Government of Rulers*, trans. Blythe, 3.13.1–5, 185–87.

of this Manettian theme as well. Universal supersession was also a theme of Jouffroy's eulogy which compared Nicholas to Romulus, Augustus, Ezekiel, Jeremiah, and Ioseleel in his buildings: he must be seen as successor to both the Roman and the Jewish biblical heritage.[79] Comparison between the citadel of Rome, site of the state temples; the Seven Wonders; Solomon's Temple, site of the state religion; and St. Peter's, "citadel of eternal religion" all turn on a notion of universal succession that was surely part of Nicholas's vision of the papacy.

Manetti does not exploit in his comparison the Solomonic features associated by his contemporaries with St. Peter's Basilica. Thus he does not mention that the twisted columns of the screen before Peter's tomb were believed to have come from Solomon's Temple,[80] or that Jesus himself had leaned against one of them (the "colonna santa") when he preached in the Temple (in 1438 Cardinal Orsini had it encircled with an inscription to this effect).[81] Nor does Manetti mention that the silver doors of the main portal (replaced by Eugenius IV) had been intended by Pope Honorius to emulate those of the Jerusalem Temple burned by Titus, as Maffeo Vegio tells us (*De rebus antiquis,* 143). And he does not notice, as Paris de Grassis did in the following century, that the lion-headed arms of the papal throne had been intended by Innocent III (1198–1216) to copy the throne of Solomon as described in Scripture.[82] Finally, the physical description of St.

[79] Jouffroy, "Oratio Episcopi Atrebatensis," fol. 30v.

[80] For the columns, Stinger, *Rome in the Renaissance*, 223; Cahn, "Solomonic Elements," 67, n. 29. They seem first to be associated with Solomon's Temple in the *Memoriale de mirabilibus et indulgentiis quae in urbe Romano existunt* of ca. 1360. According to a tradition which Cahn believes to be no earlier than 1360, they had been brought from Jerusalem to the Templum Pacis; Constantine then transferred them to St. Peter's.

[81] C. Krinsky, "Representations of the Temple of Jerusalem Before 1500," *Journal of the Warburg and Courtauld Institutes* 33 (1970): 1–19, here 13. The inscription, partially recorded by John Capgrave with its abbreviations (*Ye Solace of Pilgrims*, ed. C. Mills [London, 1911], 66), is reproduced in extended form in A. Busiri Vici, *La 'Colonna santa' del tempio di Gerusalemme ed il sarcofago di Probo Anicio prefetto di Roma* (Rome, 1888), 8–9. It was the most northern of the exterior row of columns of the pergola before the chancel of St. Peter's, and today is in the Capella della Pietà. For its appearance after 1438 see De Blaauw, *Cultus et decor*, 657. Jean Fouquet, who was in Rome in 1445, included these columns in his representations of the Jerusalem temple in the *Hours* of Etienne Chevalier and in Josephus's *Jewish Antiquities*: Krinsky, "Representations," 13. Filarete, who had worked at St. Peter's in the 1440s, notes of them in his treatise of ca. 1460: "dicono alcuni che vennono di Gerusalem": *Trattato*, 1.8. Stinger suggests that they were important at mid-century because: (1) they were associated with priestly authority, originally conferred on the Temple priesthood; and (2) they underlined the idea that Rome had succeeded Jerusalem as a religious center: Stinger, *Rome in the Renaissance*, 224.

[82] De Blaauw, *Cultus et decor*, 652. The scriptural sources are 1 Kings 10:19 and 2 Chronicles 9:17–19.

Peter's seems to have nothing to do with earlier or contemporary visual depictions of Solomon's Temple, and it shows no relationship to earlier or contemporary accounts by visitors to the Holy Land.[83] Manetti's visual comparison, then, is not nourished by popular tradition, by available images, or by archaeology.

Manetti ends his account with a literal — and rather forced — comparison between the description of Solomon's Temple and palace from 3 Kings (Vulgate), which he quotes in the *Life*, and selected features of St. Peter's and the Vatican Palace, concluding:

> I have been careful to quote these words just as they were found written in Sacred Scripture so that this side-by-side comparison of ours of the four celebrated buildings [Solomon's Temple and palace and Nicholas's church and palace] might be better judged. (60)

His literal approach to the comparison with Solomon's Temple might suggest that the entire description of St. Peter's is an exegesis of the type identified with Scholasticism. Since Manetti was translating the Old Testament for Nicholas, he had a compelling interest in the meaning of the architectural terms in the passage from 3 Kings. Indeed, many of his architectural terms — *porticus*, for instance, *fenestrae obliquae*, and *cochlea* (see Chapters 5 and 6) — find their definition in exegetical works. In interpreting the source text, Manetti could hardly have avoided the *Glossa ordinaria* since it was written on the same page as the text itself in the Renaissance equivalent of a reference Bible. The gloss on Kings, written in the twelfth century, depends on Rhabanus Maurus's ninth-century *Commentaria in Paralipomena*, which in turn compiled patristic exegeses. Here we find that:

> The House of God, which King Solomon built in Jerusalem, became a figure of the holy, universal Church which, from the first elect to the last who will be born at the end of time, is daily being built through the grace of the King who brings peace, that is, her Redeemer. She partly wanders on earth apart from Him, and partly, the hardships of wandering escaped, reigns

[83] See Krinsky, "Representations." One might compare Manetti's account with the illustration by Maso Finiguerra in the *Cronica* of about 1460: *A Florentine Picture Chronicle by Maso Finiguerra*, ed. S. Colvin (London, 1898).

Among the many fifteenth-century Italian visitors to the Holy Land, we mention only Biagio Molino, Latin titular Patriarch of Jerusalem, who consecrated the rotonda at SS. Annunziata in Florence in 1444 and whom Manetti probably met at the consecration of Florence Cathedral in 1436. See F. Quinterio, "Santo Stefano al Celio e la riconsiderazione del 'tempio d'idoli' nella Roma di Niccolò V," in *Roma, centro ideale della cultura dell'Antico nei secoli XV e XVI. Da Martino V al Sacco di Roma*, ed. S. Squarzina (Milan, 1989), 269–79, here 276.

> now with Him in heaven. There, after the Last Judgment, She, whole, will reign with Him (1 Cor. 15). (PL 109.418)[84]

Rhabanus's gloss, which draws heavily on Augustine's *City of God* and retains its historical emphasis in defining the church, summarizes well Manetti's understanding of the Temple image. But while Manetti says nothing different from Rhabanus, he says it differently, interpreting Nicholas's actions in its light. He privileges the standard gloss and through it Augustine over other exegetical aids he might have turned to which were popular and accessible. For example, Nicholas of Lyra's gloss and the *Catholicon* of John of Genoa were both in Nicholas's library.[85] Nicholas of Lyra would seem likely to have interested Manetti since his work was especially influenced by Aristotle, Augustine, and Thomas, and he was a Hebrew scholar.[86] But although Manetti owned part of Nicholas of Lyra's *Postilla*, once again he rejects the unhistorical for the historical source.[87] He would also have consulted his Josephus, *Jewish Antiquities*, which he explicitly cites as a source for his account of the Temple in *De illustribus longaevis* and from which he drew for Solomon's engineering practices (see Chapter 6), but found it devoid of the salvational content he requires here. Philo's works, which Nicholas had in Lilio Tifernate's translation, in part based on manuscripts owned by Manetti, are also possible but rejected sources, perhaps on account of their abstract mysticism.[88]

His adherence to the *Glossa ordinaria* and the historical perspective result in an unexpected affinity between Manetti's interpretation of St. Peter's and a popular source, the thirteenth-century *Bibles moralisées*, where images are inserted next to the text of 3 Kings: as Solomon builds the Temple, so Christ builds the Church.[89] Sometimes the images are contrasted, representing respectively the "status vetustatis" and the "status novitatis" (historically): Manetti makes this point, saying that "these exotic works have been as fully surpassed by ours as the new religion of Christ is discernibly to be preferred over and to supersede that old divine law" (62). In other cases the manuscript images are merged, with

---

[84] Rhabanus repeats this definition word for word in his *Commentaria in libros IV Regum*, PL 109.133–134.

[85] Müntz and Fabre, *La bibliothèque*, 48–49, 100; Manfredi, *Codici*, nos. 7 (lost), 11 (Vat. lat. 68), 18 (lost), 23 (Vat. lat. 70), 25 (Vat. lat. 71), 46 (Vat. lat. 69), 58 (Vat. lat. 160), 635 (Vat. lat. 1472), 636 (Vat. lat. 1473), and 637 (Vat. lat. 1474).

[86] On Nicholas of Lyra, see P. Krey and L. Smith, *Nicholas of Lyra. The Senses of Scripture* (Leiden, 2000), 1–8.

[87] Cagni, "Codici," 32–33.

[88] Müntz and Fabre, *La bibliothèque*, 88.

[89] See G. Guest, *Bible Moralisée. Codex Vindobonensis 2554. Vienna, Österreichische Nationalbibliothek* (London, 1995), 50 recto and verso, with the text translated on 130–31.

Solomon signifying Christ, who symbolically builds the church.[90] Manetti uses the meaning of Solomon's name — "pacificus" — to focus Nicholas's achievement ("princeps pacis") and his relation to Christ ("verus pacificus"). Similarities between the kind of Old Testament exegesis found in illustrated Bibles and in the *Life* are indications that this kind of construction of meaning was both common and popular rather than restricted to a professional audience. They therefore were appropriate for an orator like Manetti and shared in Manetti's concern with the church in history.

Manetti not only locates Nicholas's pontificate within the Church Militant but also, following St. Augustine's *City of God*, articulates its relation to the Church Triumphant.[91] The relationship can be expressed with various images. For Juan de Torquemada, the Tabernacle built by Moses reflects the *status militiae* of present life; it is the church on pilgrimage, living in military tents, whereas "the house of the heavenly church is Jerusalem to which we will go."[92] Manetti drew from this Mosaic example. The biblical references in the 1450 Jubilee account suggest eschatological themes: the freeing of peoples and the bringing of peace. But it is above all in liturgy at St. Peter's that members of the Curia believed, with Manetti, that the Heavenly Jerusalem — that is, the Church Triumphant — was perceived. Manetti writes:

> Whenever people witnessed services so splendid and so worthy [as Nicholas's liturgies], they were overcome with such admiration and so great astonishment as well as devotion, that they recognized a kind of image sketched of the Church Triumphant in the midst of this our Church Militant, and they clearly and openly glimpsed its sure and explicit outline. (8)

Of the three achievements which Poggio Bracciolini selected as truly remarkable about Nicholas's pontificate in the *Liber Pontificalis*, two — the Library and the building projects — have received much attention from scholars. The third, much less studied, is Nicholas's embellishment of liturgy: "in the adornment of vestments designated for liturgical use which he had interwoven

---

[90] R. Hausherr, "Templum Salomonis und Ecclesia Christi: Zu einem Bildvergleich der Bible moralisée," *Zeitschrift für Kunstgeschichte* 31 (1968): 101–21. The textual illustrations sometimes link the Solomon/Christ comparison to Peter and Paul, the guardians of the Church whose bodies, of course, were venerated in St. Peter's: D. Weiss, "Architectural Symbolism and the Decoration of the Ste. Chapelle," *Art Bulletin* 77 (1996): 308–20, here 316 (MS. Oxford, Bod. Lib. 2706).

[91] Miglio, in fact, has suggested that the aim of Book 2 is to make manifest the Church Triumphant in the midst of the Church Militant: "L'Immagine," 322.

[92] *Summa de Ecclesia*, 1.35; published as *The Antiquity of the Church*, ed. W. Maguire (Washington, DC, 1957).

with pearls and various precious stones," he says.[93] Yet the importance of liturgy for Nicholas is well attested by his contemporaries. Manetti assures us that he "was the most exacting and scrupulous observer of ecclesiastical ceremonies" (67). Maffeo Vegio also commented on the magnificence of the liturgy under Nicholas, the splendid liturgical vessels, and the carefully observed and dignified ceremonial.[94]

The Church Triumphant will be manifested in the order and splendor of liturgical ceremony, and expressed through significant human actions. It is a theme Manetti connected in an earlier work with the Temple of Solomon where, describing how the sacrificial instruments were escorted into the Temple, he wrote: "The wonderful order of the processions — as I think about it now and again — always seemed filled with a great divinity."[95] And much of Manetti's interpretation in the *Life* is familiar to the reader, having already appeared in *De pompis*. The suggestion that the Church Triumphant (which is nothing other than the Heavenly Jerusalem) can be seen as an outline or sketch is the organizing principle of the latter and ultimately depends on Paul: "Now we are seeing a dim reflection in a mirror, but then we shall be seeing face to face" (1 Corinthians 13:12) and "the promised, expected, and at the same time already existing city" (Galatians 4:25–26).

But in the context of Nicholas's Rome, the image of the Church Triumphant was current among the court Humanists as it was not in Florence, and for different reasons. For instance, Niccolò Palmieri's sermon *De pacis dignitate* (perhaps for Nicholas) paraphrased the text from Revelation on the descent of the Heavenly Jerusalem in order to insist on the unity and monarchical structure that should characterize the Church Militant, since that Church is constructed "in the likeness of the Heavenly Jerusalem on high, which is our mother."[96] Aeneas Silvius Piccolomini (later Pius II) wrote that the Roman Curia seen during liturgy resembled the celestial hierarchy on account of its marvelous and stable order.[97] Jean Jouffroy, in his funeral oration for Nicholas, said that earth conforms to the Heavenly Jerusalem through the beauty and splendor of the liturgical ceremonies which reflect the beauty and splendor of the heavenly court.[98]

---

[93] *Le Liber Pontificalis*, ed. Duchesne, 2:558.

[94] Vegio, *De rebus antiquis*, 3.105.

[95] G. Manetti, *De illustribus longaevis*, Bib. Vat., MS. Pal. lat. 1603, fol. 73r.

[96] O'Malley, *Praise and Blame*, 202; this may be related to Bernard of Clairvaux's *De consideratione*, a treatise on reform which Nicholas V possessed. See Müntz and Fabre, *La bibliothèque*, 110; Manfredi, *Codici*, nos. 763 (Vat. lat. 658); 764 (Vat. lat. 659); 766 (Vat. lat. 661); and 773 (lost).

[97] *Opera*, 739.

[98] Jouffroy, "Oratio Episcopi Atrebatensis," fols. 32v, 34v, 35v.

Now this Roman, courtly context is that within which Manetti uses the architectural ekphrasis in the *Life*, quite different from its purely liturgical context in the consecration speech. Moreover, in the *Life*, it is the coronation narrative — Roman, courtly, and liturgical — which is the centerpiece of Manetti's argument, a liturgy more political and institutional than personal and salvific.

Understanding the context of the architectural digression as sacred history, and that of the buildings as spiritual rather than temporal, illuminates Manetti's choice of imagery. He compares St. Peter's to a human body with the papal throne at the head in place of Christ; to Noah's Ark, outside of which there is no salvation; to the Seven Wonders, a parallel to the discussion of the Library arguing for the universalism of the church; and to Solomon's Temple, an image of the Church Militant, exemplified in the coronation of the Holy Roman Emperor, but also of the Church Triumphant, as the place where the visible and invisible churches coincide during liturgy.

It is the ecclesiological definition of the unity of the Church, that is, of the invisible mystical body manifest in the visible institution, that permitted the further elision between the present and the future. For the Church Triumphant is the reign of Christ after the end of time ordering and structuring the present.

Ptolemy, Solomon, and Nicholas

Manetti's *exempla* of Nicholas's patronage in Book 2 — the Library and building projects — place the pontiff in historical rivalry with two famous antecedents, both the wealthiest, most powerful, and most intelligent monarchs of their eras. Ptolemy II Philadelphus inaugurated the great Library at Alexandria, paragon of all libraries, and, importantly, the site for the translation from Hebrew to Greek of the Old Testament. As Eusebius had noted and Manetti reaffirmed in his *Apologeticus*, the pagan Ptolemy had thus contributed mightily to the advancement of salvation history.[99] Ptolemy's motives were, seemingly, intellectual and contemplative — the advancement of learning for its own sake, no matter its source. Solomon, endowed by the Lord with great practical wisdom, was a man of affairs, a peacemaker and builder. His enormous resources were channeled into his great Temple project which would center Jewish worship and establish Jerusalem as holy, a special dwelling place for the divine like no other. Thus the

[99] Manetti, *Apologeticus*, ed. De Petris, 2 (32). Manetti quotes Eusebius, *De praep. evang.* 8, where it is argued that as the Savior's time drew nearer, the salvation of the gentiles required that the Scriptures be known in the universal language of Greek, otherwise the Jews would conceal or falsify them. To this purpose, a provident God implanted in Ptolemy a desire to have these books translated.

two historical parallels buttress the two main activities of Nicholas's reign (books and buildings), and elucidate how Nicholas combined the speculative and the practical in service to some grand plan, a theme already developed in Book 1 of the *Life*.

The question then arises whether Manetti is simply drawing on these two parallels as conventional topoi, as part of a rhetorical strategy to eulogize a pope and establish more firmly his place in history. Or alternatively, do the parallels point to some larger contextualization within Nicholas's (and Manetti's) own concept of the historical development of Christian culture? As rhetorical *exempla*, they crystallize issues Manetti raises about the significance of Nicholas's reign. For example, since Ptolemy represents a pinnacle of pagan learning and Solomon the high point of Jewish culture, the comparisons imply an equivalence in cultural and historical importance for the flowering of Christian culture according to the plan of this pope. The fact that Ptolemy engaged in both collecting and translating, and the eclectic, universal scope of his interests add weight to Nicholas's polymath inclusiveness. Solomon's wealth was based on his ability to bring about peace, and from peace and prosperity came the possibility of gracing Jerusalem with new dwelling places both for God and for the king. This closely parallels Manetti's representation of Nicholas's unique historical moment, and the possibilities it created for him to intervene in the pacification of Europe, to provide the resources for great achievements, and to shelter the relic of the Prince of the Apostles and his successors in a magnificent new temple and palace.

While acknowledging that Nicholas was as prone as anyone in his position to be attracted to fame, he sought to influence history because he (and Manetti) took a certain Christian view of exactly what history was about. History is the enactment of a story of human salvation that began with Adam and will end with the "fall of the ages" and the establishment, in the place of temporal kingdoms, of the eternal reign of Christ, the Heavenly Jerusalem — an understanding explicit in Rhabanus's gloss on the Temple. Theologically, this has already taken place, is now taking place, and will take place: its reality is glimpsed as a sketch here and now. The texts we have examined show a constant fascination with temporal Christianity as a "militant" church, organizing itself in its liturgies, in its hierarchies, and in its sacred places as foreshadowings of the "triumphant" church, eternally at peace and praising God in the Heavenly Jerusalem. The visible, in Manetti's words, provides a "sketch" of the invisible, and the present elides with, at certain intense moments, this future. This was his experience at the Eucharist during the consecration of Florence Cathedral. It came to him immediately, through the senses, and it affirmed what he was already convinced of as a matter intellect and faith.

So, too, Nicholas in his apology for his library and his building projects in his dying testament. These were worth doing because they strengthened the faith of people of every station, high and low, and by strengthening and safeguarding the church ensured that the Bride of Christ was made ready for the marriage feast of the Lamb. The essential doctrines of *Unam sanctam* and the scholarly works that immediately preceded it can be found either in Nicholas's Testament (*RIS*), or in Book 2 of the *Life*: the church is the mystical body and Christ is its head, the pope his vicar; there is no salvation outside the Church; Noah's Ark prefigures the unity of the church as a single body with one head. Both swords belong to the power of the church: the temporal sword is wielded for, and the spiritual by, it. These formulations are not evangelical or patristic but Scholastic, and especially associated with Aquinas and other Dominicans.[100] Not surprisingly, they found support and amplification in Ptolemy's treatise on rulership, where papal authority is further illustrated by the pope's sole authority to confer indulgence for all sins and to create emperors — both *exempla* in Book 2 of Manetti's *Life*.[101] And they are substantially repeated in Juan de Torquemada's *Commentary on the Decretum*, for instance: "Whoever is outside the Church of Peter, which is the Church of Christ, is not in the Church."[102] Yet these doctrines reveal papal authority to be essentially pastoral in purpose, enabling the pontiff to unite, rule, and teach the faithful so that not one lamb would be lost (Matthew 18:14).

Both Ptolemy and Solomon, like Nicholas, were players within the drama of salvation. As *exempla*, Ptolemy and Solomon provided the traditional models of unparalleled excellence in two arenas of human endeavor: the promotion of learning and the building of great monuments. Anyone who manifested similar excellences might be compared to them, more convincingly the more these individuals left their mark on history and culture. Thus Cosimo de'Medici can credibly be called a Ptolemy because of his endowment of libraries, or Innocent III a Solomon because of his reputation for effective and practical wisdom. But in the context of salvation history, within which we think both Manetti and Nicholas would view these comparisons, Ptolemy the pagan and Solomon the Jew prefigure an individual like Nicholas because Nicholas strives to imitate them in order to advance the divine agenda and hasten its beatific outcome. Important to this project was the particular way in which Manetti and Nicholas envisioned not just the fusion of, but the supersession of pagan and Jewish accomplishments by, Christian culture. For it is ultimately within Christian culture that the millennial reign has begun and the actual Heavenly Jerusalem will appear.

---

[100] For an analysis of the sources of *Unam Sanctam*, see Izbicki, *Protector of the Faith*, 39.

[101] Ptolemy of Lucca, *On the Government of Rulers*, trans. Blythe, 3.10.7–8 (174–75).

[102] *Commentary on the Decretum*, D 93.C3 (1:68) in Izbicki, *Protector of the Faith*, 37, who notes that this restates *Unam sanctam*.

Nicholas's reenactment of the accomplishments of Ptolemy and Solomon is not and cannot itself be a fulfilment of history or of the process of salvation. Instead, it, in turn, prefigures even as it hopes to advance the coming of the Church Triumphant in the future Heavenly Jerusalem. Great men, both pagans and Jews, form part of God's plan of human history, redeemed by Christ, and brought to completion at history's end. The story is one of both progress and defeat, a continuous striving, nourished by faith and learning, and brought forward by fortitude and diligence. Nicholas's contribution, in Manetti's view, was huge, but tragically incomplete: "Had he been able to complete his plan, he would have . . .". This accounts somewhat for Manetti's urgency in his exhortation to Callixtus at the end of the *Life*, and the dark frustration at his own inability to complete his translation of the Hebrew Scripture. At issue was not simply the material advancement of culture in the city of Rome, or the flowering of learning for its own sake, but a great spiritual leap forward in which the lineaments of the triumph of Christ over history would become clearer, and the New Jerusalem that much closer. The spiritual dimension of the events is exemplified and amplified by comparison of St. Peter's with Solomon's Temple. There are few apocalyptic allusions in Manetti's ekphrasis, since, although the Church Triumphant can be glimpsed in Nicholas's pontificate — peace, security, and the establishment of a capital city for a universal monarch and his court — what we have here below remains the Church Militant. Solomon's Temple is the antetype, in both sacred and secular history, for those achievements. While Manetti's argument seems to look backward in time, comparing St. Peter's to the Jerusalem Temple, the thematic connections thereby established actually look backward from the perspective of the end of time. Manetti knows how history will end. Thus, judging the present by the future, he discerns in St. Peter's the sketch of the True Temple.

Conclusion

"We Shall Be Perfected and Bring About Perfection"

Manetti was a man between two intellectual worlds. He was schooled in the Scholastic view of things, absorbed its dialectic, and accepted its power to define. Evidently, he saw no reason to question its assumptions or advance its arguments. School philosophy seems to be for him a given, an underlying matrix upon which he naturally and unreflectively built ideas drawn from other sources, particularly Scripture, St. Augustine, and Aristotle. His acceptance of and deep acquaintance with Greek and Roman antiquity provided him with an experiential understanding of the issues that interested him. Perhaps because he came to the study of Greek and Latin authors late in life, perhaps because of the perspective and opportunities his early experience in business and of the wealth a lucrative business provided, he read more intently, assimilated more fully, ranged more broadly, and appropriated his studies more personally than all but a few of his contemporaries. His interpretation of history may well be Augustinian and his culture Humanist, but his mind retained its grounding in a Scholastic acceptance of ordered knowledge conforming to an ordered world. Manetti's insistence on order — the order of his narrative, the order of processions, the order produced by renovations to the Borgo and Vatican Palace, in performance of the liturgy — stands out as a defining quality of his mind.

Manetti moved easily between the secular and sacred, and this is truly distinctive about him. These two texts are, ostensibly, a layman's interpretation of their subjects. They draw on and allude to secular writers from antiquity. They do not explicitly develop theological applications or rehearse the traditional allegorical commonplaces. Yet he indirectly addresses theological questions about the nature of the church, interprets the meaning of specific liturgies in the light of his own experience, draws on an unusual familiarity with theological writings and writers not only for his vocabulary but also for his themes, and puts forward his personal faith experience as the criterion by which religious significance is gauged. These practices frame the secular in a coherent and convinced spiritual context. Manetti's contemporary readers would have understood this from the allusions he makes. His discourse does not distance itself from its Christian milieu, as other Humanists might do, but the secular and spiritual are conjoined and somehow dependent in it. One confirmation of this is his prayer over Frederick

III at the coronation. An official emissary of the Florentine Republic, it is already notable that he presumed to pray over the Holy Roman Emperor; but more audacious still, he then placed the very prayer that he himself had uttered into the pontiff's mouth in his account of the coronation in the *Life*. Throughout, he claims a high status for lay spirituality. In the *Life*, discussion of the church as a political and sacramental institution is placed in the mouth of the pontiff—his own engagement with religion is more personal— and his ability to retain Nicholas's own, different, voice may be one of the great achievements of the *Life*. While we can never be sure of the Testament's authenticity, it suggests that Nicholas gave much less importance to lay spiritual experience than Manetti: he speaks as the shepherd of the sheep, concerned that those who have been sealed in Christ be preserved inviolate. Manetti's confidence might be peculiar to himself, yet one wonders if this "democratization" of the spiritual life is not a current in fifteenth-century spirituality which would reward further study. Does it not begin with Coluccio Salutati and with the lay students of Luigi Marsigli and Ambrogio Traversari? Is it not related to the more generally diffused belief in human progress in all endeavors evident at mid-century especially in Florence? Does the greater sophistication of lay spirituality help explain the growing number of paintings of theologically complex mystical subjects commissioned for private devotion in the third quarter of the century?[1]

Manetti was himself a model of what he argued constituted Nicholas V's remarkable character: he was equally contemplative and active in the world. As an ambassador of the Florentine Republic, he was engaged in diplomatic missions where he put his admired oratory to the service of international relations. His contributions to contemporary politics were more practical than theoretical, and much of his scholarly work is encyclopedic and compilatory from sources. Yet he managed to master Hebrew to a level that enabled him to dispute with rabbinical scholars and undertake a new translation of the Old Testament. His philosophical works, such as his *Oration on the Dignity of Man*, show his ability to marshal the details of his reading in the classical authors to construct a treatise that speaks to the intellectual currents of his own time. His *Apologeticus*, defending his proposed translation of the Scriptures, displays his impressive command of philological method and close scholarly reasoning.

Manetti was immersed in his contemporary world. For him, antiquity had not exhausted the fund of human ideas and deeds, but furnished the robust foundation on which modern achievement in words and deeds might build. His impressive library, one of the most extensive assembled by a private citizen, attests

[1] One thinks in the first instance of Filippo Lippi's "Mystical Nativity" for the chapel in the Medici Palace, but also of paintings like Botticelli's "Madonna of the Magnificat."

to his admiration for classical writers, particularly historians, orators, and philosophers. Yet it was quite clear to him that in his own time the deeds of the ancients had been surpassed by the moderns. It is not, however, as if his contemporaries replaced antiquity with something new. Rather they had taken the standards of the classical world and gone farther with them. If Philo's armory was admired by the Athenians for certain values such as size, expense, and beauty, then in size and expense and beauty the Florentines, in building their cathedral, had surpassed them on their own terms, not on new ones.

Manetti was the great articulator of contemporary events. He was not interested in them as historical episodes to be chronicled in detail, but as modern instantiations of ideas and values. They then took on a historic quality as milestones within a process called history, as cultural indicators of the significance of an era. In these two texts, the particular history that Manetti traces is salvation history, imagined not as having been completed with the historical resurrection of Christ, but vigorously building the Kingdom of God on earth, perfecting the Church Militant. Scriptural ideas were important to his concept of the history of his own times, whether the consecration of a monumental building or the restoration and expansion of the authority of the Roman church by a like-minded pope. Much of what history records, as Herodotus and Thucydides argue, are the memorable deeds of men which reveal the causes of the rise and fall of individuals and nations. Manetti is here interested in something else, the men and deeds that continue the great saga of salvation history, building up the material and spiritual edifice of the church and, concurrently, appropriating and surpassing the cultural advances of the ancient world.

Does Manetti have a message? Do his images build an interpretation of either of the buildings he describes? Looking back at his primary image for both Florence Cathedral and St. Peter's, the human body, it may be suggested that his fundamental message is that the True Temple is the body of believers, that is, the church. This is different from Durandus's statement that the church symbolizes the body of Christ, not only because Manetti's context is ethical rather than doctrinal theology, but also because for him the human being is the only and true image of God. St. Peter's, the True Temple, is defined in contradistinction to the Jewish Temple and compared to the Ark of Salvation. Whereas the head of Florence Cathedral was the place of the altar, that is, Christ, at St. Peter's, the head is the place of the papal throne of Christ's vicar. But both buildings have a common significance for Manetti: they represent the new Temple foretold in the Old Testament, the place where God is with men (Revelation 21:3), the Heavenly Jerusalem. This is, at one level, another Manettian commonplace. All churches are, in some way, the Heavenly Jerusalem: that is explicitly conferred on them at their consecration (see Chapter 2). But that Manetti was not aiming at originality in his architectural imagery is by now clear. For him, since this is what all churches represent, the challenge of ekphrasis is to articulate the manner in which this is true for a particular building. In the account of its consecration, the Cathedral of Florence evokes a personal and subjective experience of the glory of God; St. Peter's, by contrast, is understood within the historical unfolding of the institutional church's role in the economy of salvation.

Manetti repeatedly holds up as an ideal completeness, wholeness, and a harmonious relation between the parts. Just as the human body, image of St. Peter's, is a complete and finite system which has "everything that it needs and nothing superfluous,"[2] so the renovated Vatican Palace would have had everything such a complex should have, its parts properly disposed and related to each other; so too the Borgo. When order and wholeness prevail, the outline of the Church Triumphant is seen in the Church Militant. Manetti intuited a continuity between the human and the divine evident in the ordering of things. He certainly knew the writings of Dionysius the Areopagite,[3] whose assertion that "order and rank here below are a sign of the harmonious ordering toward the divine realm" (*The Celestial Hierarchy* 124A) is consonant with his beliefs. This kind of hierocracy, we saw, was also congenial to Nicholas: not surprisingly, he kept a copy of Dionysius in his bedroom, as a nearly apostolic sanction for the monarchical ordering of the church.[4] But Manetti's values are those of a layman, a Florentine, a businessman, and a diplomat — not a pope. Believing in the importance of individual action and that virtue is a matter of right understanding, the purpose of man — the "proprium ipsius solius hominis officium" and that which is "proprie proprium" to human nature (*De dignitate* 3.46) — is to act and to understand. For the purpose of human life is to rule and administer the earth, that earth which God made for man's use and enjoyment (*De dignitate* 3.45, 3.57). Yet, for him, the Kingdom of God is near. Guardian angels inspire, illuminate, purge, and perfect human beings, enabling them to love and enjoy God. Dionysius, speaking of the priesthood, said: "We shall be perfected and bring about perfection."[5] Manetti shared this optimism in regard both to God's operation and to human potentiality with Dionysius, but perhaps less with Nicholas, more concerned with the

[2] The words are Barkan's (in *Nature's Work of Art*, 3), but this is exactly Manetti's meaning in *The Oration on the Dignity of Man*, where the human body is said to have "quoque necessaria quarumdam superfluarum partium carentia" (1.35).

[3] Some of the works had been translated by his teacher Traversari during the period of his study and were in his own and Nicholas's library. Manetti owned essentially all the works of Dionysius in Traversari's translation in a manuscript now Vat. Pal. Lat. 148. Nicholas's copy of *The Celestial Hierarchy* is now MS. Vat. lat. 171, finished in 1437: Cagni, "I codici," 28; Grafton, *Rome Reborn*, 114.

[4] On this, see Stinger, *Renaissance in Rome*, 165; Grafton, *Rome Reborn*, 114.

[5] *The Ecclesiastical Hierarchy* 372B: in *Pseudo-Dionysius*, trans. Luibheid, 196.

assertion and preservation of the church. Manetti was, however, no Platonist but an instinctive Aristotelian. Perfection was the realization of potential, the actualization of *forma* in material being, whether the earthly or the glorified body (*De dignitate* 4.58–70). His view implied the progress, even evolution, of culture, society, and the church, as well as of personal faith. Perfection was not an "out-of-the-body" transport for Manetti, the loss of self, or a merging with universal being. It was particular, indeed, individual; it involved the will, engaged the intellect, and drew on memory. For these reasons Manetti's thinking was nourished by two authors especially. In Aquinas he found Aristotle's understanding of the natural and Dionysius's of the supernatural reconciled and subordinated to a rational, orderly, and Christian account of reality. Augustine's world view was similarly all-inclusive, orderly, and Christian, but more dynamically concerned with history. More than that, Augustine's voice spoke to Manetti across time as a fellow man, saying from his heart those things that lay near Manetti's heart.

Manetti's belief, throughout the texts we have examined, can be summarized in this passage from a work he knew by heart:

> The peace which is our special possession is ours even in this life, a peace with God through faith; and it will be ours for ever, a peace with God through open vision. (*City of God* 19.27)

Part II

Note on the Texts

De secularibus et pontificalibus pompis

Sigla

Biblioteca Vaticana

M	Pal. lat. 1605	fols. 30r-36r
M'	corrector in M, probably Manetti	
P	Pal. lat. 1603	fols. 1r-7v
V1	Vat. lat. 6303	fols. 1r-26r
V2	Vat. lat. 2919	fols. 14r-24r
B	Barber. lat. 120	fols. 36v-41r
U	Urb. lat. 387	fols. 261r-266v
Battisti	E. Battisti, "L'Antichità in Niccolò V e l'iconografia della Cappella Sistina," in *Umanesimo e esoterismo: Atti del V convegno internazionale di studi umanistici*, ed. E. Castelli (Padua, 1960), 207-16, text 310-20.	
van Eck	C. van Eck, "Giannozzo Manetti on Architecture: The *Oratio de secularibus et pontificalibus pompis in consecratione basilicae Florentinae* of 1436," *Renaissance Studies* 12 (1998): 469-75.	

Botley (*Latin Translation*, 71, n.50) omits MS. Vat. lat. 6303 in his list of Vatican manuscripts, but does note a manuscript of the *De pompis* in Paris (MS. BN Lat. 1616, fols. 275v-281v), which attributes the work to Guarino Veronese; the Bibliothèque Nationale catalogue, however, ascribes it to Lapo da Castiglionchio. This manuscipt has not been collated here.

Comparison of the six listed manuscripts favors the readings of M and P, known to have been owned by Manetti. See Cagni, "I codici," esp. 36, items 125 and 126. Of the two, M is less carefully made and contains several instances of haplography, one of which Manetti corrected in his own hand. See A. Campano, "Giannozzo Manetti, Ciriaco e l'arco di Traiano ad Ancona," *Italia medioevale ed umanistica* 2 (1959): 483-504. While made slightly later than M, P is superior to it and serves here as the base text, though in a few instances readings of M have been preferred. A large portion of section 34 is missing in M and was supplied by a corrector. V1 and V2 share a number of errors and can be considered a family, though V1 is closer to M. The Barberini manuscript bears some relation to V2; the Urbino manuscript to P. A full discussion of the manuscripts, based on the longer texts of the *Laudationes Januenses* bound in the same codices as the *De pompis*, and the case for a suggested stemma are to be found in G. Balbi, *Elogi dei Genovesi* (Milan, 1974), 39-54. The patterns found here in the shorter work support Balbi's stemma.

In 1960, Battisti published a transcription of V2, making a text available to scholars, but adding some inaccurate readings of his own to that manuscript's already flawed text. Although the text had previously been published by F. P. Luiso in *Firenze in festa per la consecrazione di Santa Maria del Fiore* (Lucca, 1904), it was wrongly attributed and escaped subsequent scholarly attention. The *De pompis* received very little attention even after Battisti published it, although Westfall (*In This Most Perfect Paradise*, 120-24) compared its technical vocabulary and architectural imagery with Manetti's *Life of Nicholas V*, written around 1455. Van Eck recognized the problems with Battisti's text and transcribed V1, a closely related manuscript. Only V1 and V2 contain an explicit with the date 1436. This, however, does not guarantee that this is the date when the manuscript was made, as van Eck asserts. In fact, the speeches to the Genoese, according to Balbi, were delivered sometime between mid-1437 and December of 1442 (*Elogi*, 26). While it seems likely that Manetti composed the *De pompis* not long after the consecration of the cathedral in 1436, V1 was not made until after both the Genovese orations had been given. Thus V1 cannot be supported as earlier or more reliable than the copies Manetti himself owned (M and P), the readings of which are to be preferred.

We have subdivided the Latin text into paragraphs and numbered them, hoping this system of reference will be simpler and easier for the reader to use than line numbers. The apparatus does not concern itself with slight variations in spelling unless this might indicate affinity among manuscripts. Abbreviations have been silently expanded. As is common practice, no distinction is made between consonantal and vocalic -i-, but consonantal -u- is printed as -v-. Following the manuscripts themselves, the diphthongs -ae- and -oe- are printed as -e-.

Life of Nicholas V

Sigla

Biblioteca Laurenziana

A	Plut. LXVI, 23	fols. 23v-59r
B	Plut. LXVI, 22	fols. 24r-62v
E	Ashburnham 1551	fols. 23r-52v

Biblioteca Vaticana

C	Pal. lat. 868	fols. 24r-36r
C1	Urb. lat. 387	fols. 18r-26v
D	Vat. lat. 2046	fols. 16r-14v

Muratori L. Muratori, *Rerum Italicarum Scriptores*, 3.2 (Milan, 1734).

Pagnotti F. Pagnotti, "La Vita di Niccolò V scritta da Giannozzo Manetti," *Archivio della Società Romana di Storia Patria* 14 (1891): 411-36.

Magnuson T. Magnuson, "The Project of Nicholas V for Rebuilding the Borgo Leonino in Rome," *Art Bulletin* 36 (1954): 89-115.

Frutaz A. Frutaz, *Il Torrione di Nicolò V in Vaticano* (Vatican City, 1956).

The manuscript designations are those of Pagnotti, who published a preliminary study of the *Life* in preparation for a sorely-needed critical edition which was never finished. Pagnotti provides a full description of the manuscripts, as does Modigliani, *Vita*, 62-66. The base text for our edition is A, from the hand of Manetti's son, Agnolo. It is supplemented by B, a Palatine codex owned by Manetti. A and B closely coincide and only in a few instances have B's readings been preferred over A. Magnuson published a text of part of Book 2, inserting Pagnotti's corrections into Muratori's text. Frutaz suggested some unsustainable emendations to the difficult passage on the Great Tower. Our edition is conservative in that it introduces no emendations. We have chosen to present the text which we believe was closest to what Manetti wrote and, through our translation and commentary, to provide explanations of the more difficult Latin passsages.

Two readings we have retained are likely to attract attention. Manetti and his copyists have consistently written various forms of *portendere* "to foretell" where they clearly mean *protendere* "to extend." This verb occurs with some frequency in the architectural descriptions, often with directional or measurement indicators. It seems to be neither a casual error nor a self-conscious implication that, for example, extension implies prediction. It is simply the verb he understands to mean "extend." Muratori corrected these forms; we do not. Similarly, Manetti construes *paradisus* as feminine gender, against common use and the authority of the Vulgate where it is masculine. In both instances (34, 37), Manetti is referring to an area within the papal palace where buildings are situated in a well-irrigated garden, and not to the heavenly or earthly paradise of Scripture. DuCange (s.v. *paradisus*) cites an instance where *paradisus*, referring to a garden, is considered feminine by natural gender. In this case, Manetti can hardly have been unaware of standard use, but chose to depart from it for reasons he does not explain. We have left the text as he wrote it, and taken, as Manetti intended, the adjective *speciosissima* as its modifier in both places.

Since the *Life* has been known mostly through Muratori's edition, we insert in parentheses the numbers of the *RIS* columns and note in the apparatus readings which diverge from the manuscripts. This will allow the reader to note the extent to which Muratori altered the received text. In the architectural portion of Book 2 (22-63), we insert Magnuson's sentence numbers in square brackets at the end of each paragraph, again for comparison. As with the *De pompis*, we have arranged the text in numbered paragraphs and observed the same orthographical conventions with regard to vocalic diphthongs and consonantal and vocalic -i- and -u-.

Note on the Translations

Manetti's Latin style is serviceable, often predictable, and fairly uniform throughout his writings. His vocabulary, however, can sometimes tend towards idiosyncrasy. He was master of three ancient tongues and an innovator; his philology has affected his usage. In addition, where Manetti strives for eloquence, his rhetorical strategies may not equal the refinements of later generations of Latinists or please modern tastes, but they are informed by his broad reading. This aggravates the translator's perennial dilemma. Should his prose be rendered freely and his obscurities expanded so that the reader moves more comfortably through the text? This approach, for the sake of fluency, sacrifices a certain amount of accuracy, interprets through expansion, and perhaps strips his writing of some of its genuine charm. Yet if the translation is too literal, it betrays its author in another way because it fails to communicate the momentum and excitement of his argument by doggedly rendering it word by word. It becomes stilted, lacks flair, and sounds foreign and strange, none of which is true of the original. All translators plead the *via media* and we are no different.

In the period in our study when we were trying to discern Manetti's meaning, we stuck to the doggedly literal until we could tease from the text the specific reference, the action or object described, or the hidden ideology. The translations we provide are perhaps more literal than many because we recognize that readers will probably be more interested in fidelity to meaning than having Manetti be a good read. We have not tried to make Manetti's language more colorful than it is, nor to gloss his Latin by inserting what is not there. When we have a particular take on a worrisome phrase, that will be found in the commentaries or discussed in the chapters. Where we have taken a few liberties, we are consoled that readers now have ready to hand a serviceable Latin text against which to check our renderings.

On the matter of vocabulary, as we note in the commentaries and elsewhere, Manetti's usage is often, but not always, standard fifteenth-century Latin. Sometimes he seems to use words that ordinarily are synonyms to make precise distinctions; at other times, he seems to be merely embellishing his account with pleonasms. We have tended to preserve these and, where we think he has used ordinary words to make distinctions, we have translated them consistently throughout, wherever possible. On the other hand, Manetti uses, as do Latin writers in general, more connective adverbs ("and so," "therefore," "for," "moreover") and referencing words ("aforementioned," "above," "these," "those") than English tolerates; some of these have been omitted.

Manetti favors a type of long sentence which grows through inserted dependent clauses and often trails off into a result clause which itself may contain further subordination. We have made a practice of breaking these sentences into more digestible units in a way we hope preserves the logic but improves the flow. Unlike the Renaissance reader who expected, especially in Latin, to encounter the periodic sentence and who enjoyed its tangled web, we moderns appreciate a more linear presentation. Enough complexity has been left, we hope, to give some idea of Manetti's virtuosity.

There is, however, one important departure from the text which the reader needs to be warned about. In the architectural portion of the *Life of Nicholas*, the verb tenses shift from the Latin perfect, ostensibly to indicate work which had actually been completed by 1455, to the Latin imperfect, seemingly a past progressive for work in progress but not completed. It is not possible on the basis of grammar alone to know what level of actual progress is intended in the verb. Was a project half-done, just started, still being planned? These imperfects are used to describe both work and Nicholas's planning: "the streets were being extended . . . ," "he was deciding . . . ". We have used the English present tense when a building project is described and the simple past for Nicholas's actions: "the streets extend . . . ," "he decided." As justification, it is common in English to describe projects not yet finished, or even not yet begun, in the present tense for vividness. This, in fact, would be how an architect might present a proposal to a client. At section 59, in the comparison of Nicholas's building with Solomon's, though the tenses are still the imperfect, it is clear that Manetti is focusing on their incompleteness, and no longer inviting us to visualize the final result, and so we change modals: "this wonderful temple of ours would spread . . .". Where Manetti actually uses contrafactual clauses, so have we: "he would have equalled . . . ".

Giannozzo Manetti

Prefatio Jannocti Manetti de Secularibus et Pontificalibus Pompis ad Dominum Angelum de Acarolis Incipit Feliciter

Concerning the Secular and Papal Parades: An Introduction by Giannozzo Manetti to Messer Agnolo Acciaiuoli

Prefatio Jannocti Manetti de Secularibus et Pontificalibus Pompis ad Dominum Angelum de Acarolis Incipit Feliciter[1]

1. Rogitanti[2] tibi sepenumero Angele suavissime et tamen verenti ne mihi gravis esses perfacile enim cernebam ut singularissimam omnium nostri temporis ac profecto incredibilem pontificalis magnificentie pompam litteris mandarem quam in florenti urbe nostra cum una forte essemus nuper visebamus denegare non potui ne prestantissimo viro equestrisque ordinis dignissimo fieri videretur iniuria. Quamquam enim mihi magnum opus et arduum iniunxisse videreris, nihil tamen difficile amanti fore putabam; amo nanque et semper amavi generositatem magnitudinemque animi tui.

2. Ad hec accedebat quo facilius tantum dicendi onus assumerem ut hec nostra quecunque gloriosissime pompe adumbratio primum ad ineffabilem immortalis Dei gloriam, ad magnas deinde civitatis nostre laudes pertinere vel maxime videretur. Quandoquidem igitur horum gratia id agimus deus ipse ut spero adiutor noster erit. Nos itaque divino freti auxilio brevius quoad fieri poterit hanc ipsam tam admirabilem nostri temporis pompam adumbrare conabimur ne tibi id petenti si obsequi recusarem ut dixi fieri videretur iniuria.

3. Proinde egregium quendam veterem pictorem in hac nostra adumbratione non inmerito imitabimur qui cum luctuosum immolate Effigenie sacrificium sua pictura exprimere quam maxime vellet ac propterea Calcantem tristem, mestum

---

[1] Prefatio . . . feliciter *M*: PREFATIO IANNOZII MANETTI DE SECULARIBUS ET PONTIFICALIBUS POMPIS AD DOMINUM ANGELUM ACAROLUM INCIPIT FELICITER *P*: Iannozii manetti oratio Ad clarissimum equestris ordinis virum Angelum acciaiolum de secularibus & pontificalibus pompis in consecratione basilice Florentine *V1*: IANNOZII MANETTI ORATIO AD CLARISSIMUM EQUESTRIS ORDINIS VIRUM ANGELUM ACCIAIOLUM DE SECULARIBUS & PONTIFICALIBUS POMPIS IN CONSECRATIONE BASILICE FLORENTINE HABITIS INCIPIT FELICITER *V2* (ET PONTIFICALIBUS *om. B*): PREFATIO IANNOTII MANETTI DE SECULARIBUS ET PONTIFICALIBUS POMPIS AD DOMINUM ANGELUM ASAROLUM *U*

[2] Cogitanti *B*

Concerning the Secular and Papal Parades: An Introduction by Giannozzo Manetti to Messer Agnolo Acciaiuoli

1. Dearest Agnolo, you asked me numerous times, despite your apprehension about being a nuisance, to commit to writing for you the parade of papal magnificence, unparalleled in modern times and absolutely unbelievable, which we witnessed recently when we chanced to be together in our flourishing city. But of course I readily agreed. I could not have refused without it seeming a wrong had been done to a man of distinction, most worthy of knightly rank. Although you might seem to have enjoined on me a great and arduous task, nonetheless I have always thought that "nothing is difficult for one who loves"; for I do love and have always loved your generosity and largeness of soul.

2. Besides, how much more readily would I take on a speaking burden of such importance. Any sketch we make of the most glorious parade would seem especially to relate, first, to the inexpressible glory of immortal God and, next, to the great praise of our city. Inasmuch as I am doing it for these reasons, God himself will, I hope, be our helper (Psalm 61:8). Relying, therefore, on divine help, we shall try to sketch as briefly as we can this very parade, so wondrous in modern times, so that, as I said, an injustice not appear to be done to you the requester, if I should refuse to comply.

3. Accordingly we shall — not without reason — imitate in this sketch of ours a famous ancient painter who wanted to express as strongly as possible in his painting the mournful sacrifice of Iphigenia slain as victim. To this purpose he decided to paint, in front of the altars, Calchas sorrowful, Ulysses desolate,

Ulixem, clamantem Aiacem, lamentantem Menelaum ante aras pinguendo statuisset; ipsius Agamemnonis caput involvendo cooperuit, in quo mea quidem sententia rectissime fecit quod enim sibi per artis lineamenta[3] probe exprimere nullo modo posse videbatur non iniuria intuentis iudicio dereliquit.

4. Sic nos in hac ipsa gloriosissime pompe adumbratione ea duntaxat que verbis apte explicari poterunt, omnibus aliis omissis,[4] vel leviter attingemus. Cetera vero tuo optimo iudicio relinquemus. Sed hec iam satis. Nunc ad ipsam gloriose pompe adumbrationem faustis ominibus accedamus paulo altius pro cognitione rerum ab origine repetentes.

5. Summus igitur pontifex Eugenius quartus quadringentesimo tricesimo[5] sexto supra millesimum christiane salutis anno forte Florentie residebat quo quidem in tempore Florentini altissimam simul atque admirabilissimam cathedralis basilice testudinem per multos antea annos edificari ceptam tandem aliquando expleverant, ex quo factum est ut pro apostolica eiusdem basilice consecratione summis precibus pontificem obsecrarent. At vero ubi acceperunt pontificem sua postulata benigne admodum concessisse atque etiam de constituta consecrationis die certiores ipsi facti sunt, mox perpaucis ante consecrationem diebus omnia que ad se spectabant mirum in modum preparare contenderunt. Pontifex quoque quantum ad se pertinere videbatur ut divine glorie (sic enim arbitror) exemplar quoddam nostris hominibus demonstraret omnes pontificales dignitates suas egregie admodum parare non dubitavit. Adeoque in magnificis apparatibus utrique conabantur ut de pomparum magnificentia certatim inter se agi omnibus videretur.

6. Verum enim vero ut hec nostra quecunque vel descriptio vel potius adumbratio suo quodam ordine incedat, primum admirabiles florentini populi apparatus breviter attingemus; pontificales deinde dignitates pro magnitudine rerum leviter[6] demonstrabimus; postremo in basilica consecranda gesta pontificis parumper ostendemus. Sed antequam hunc dicendi ordinem aggrediamur non alienum visum est pro pleniori rerum notitia basilice nostre interiorem duntaxat situm paucis exponere quo varia ornamentorum genera hinc inde dispersa facilius explicari atque intellegi possint.

7. Admirabile huius sacre basilice edificium mihi diligentius sepenumero intuenti prope instar humani corporis esse videtur. Primum nanque forma humani corporis a thorace[7] ad pedes usque deorsum oblongo basilice nostre spatio quantum a

---

[3] liniamenta *V1V2B*

[4] omnibus aliis amissis *om. PU*

[5] trigesimo *V1V2B*

[6] breviter *V1*

[7] instar . . . a thorace *om. M*: instar humani corporis esse videtur nam a thorace *M' in rasura*

Ajax crying out, and Menelaus lamenting; but he covered up and hid the head of Agamemnon. In my opinion, he acted quite rightly in this. Since it seemed to him he could in no way properly express this through the lineaments of art, he left it to the judgment of the viewer, and rightly so.

4. So too in this sketch of that most glorious parade. Leaving all else aside, we shall lightly touch upon only those things which can be aptly expressed in words. The rest, however, we shall leave to your excellent judgment. But enough of this. Let us now, with good omens, proceed to the sketch itself of the glorious parade, starting a bit earlier, from its beginning, to get acquainted with its circumstances.

5. So then, in the four hundred and thirty-sixth year after the millennium of Christian salvation, the supreme pontiff Eugenius IV happened to be living in Florence. This coincided with the Florentines having at last completed the very high, wonderful east end of the cathedral basilica the construction of which had been begun many years before. So it happened that they implored the pope with the most urgent prayers for an apostolic consecration of this basilica. When they learned that the pope had very graciously granted their request and were likewise informed of the day fixed for the consecration, quickly, in the few days before the consecration, they made an amazing effort to ready everything for which they were responsible. The pope also, in so far as it seemed his task to exhibit to our people an exemplar of divine glory (or so I believe), wasted no time in quite splendidly preparing all his papal dignitaries. Both groups put such effort into their magnificent displays that it seemed to everyone that a competition for the magnificence of the parades was being waged between them.

6. So that this description, or rather, sketch of ours might progress in a proper order, we shall first touch briefly on the wonderful displays of the Florentine people, then highlight a bit the pontifical dignitaries in order of rank, and finally present a quick account of what the pope did in the consecration of the basilica. But before we proceed to this narrative order, it does not seem out of place, for the fuller treatment of the events, to say a few words at least about the interior arrangement of our basilica, so that the different kinds of decorations, distributed here and there, might be more easily displayed and understood.

7. On numerous occasions when I gaze at the wonderful fabric of this sacred basilica carefully, it seems to me nearly the same as the human body. For first of all the form of the human body from the chest down to the feet looks, as one inspects it rather more carefully, very much like the elongated space of our cathedral in its

foribus ad exitum testudinis porrigitur paulo diligentius intuenti persimilis apparet. Reliquum deinde spatium quod ambitu testudinis inferius continetur superiori hominis trunco a capite usque ad thoracem nullatenus dissimile ostenditur. Atque ut hec nostra similitudo recte convenire videatur, constitue aliquem in superiori ecclesie parte cuius universum corpus humi prosternas velim ita ut caput eius ad orientem vergat, brachiis in diversa utrinque extensis, altero ad septentrionem altero vero ad meridiem vergente, pedes autem ad occidentem spectent atque humano corpore per hunc modum abste constituto dubitare non poteris quin hec nostra similitudo omnibus prope modis convenire videatur. Si itaque nostri templi figura humani corporis instar est ut supra patuit nobilissimam omnium atque perfectissimam speciem sortitum esse, quis sanae mentis inficias[8] ibit cum formam hominis ceteris omnibus quaruncumque rerum figuris prestare perfacile constet.

8. Huius igitur templi per hunc modum egregie formati ad ducentos usque sexaginta passus longitudo portenditur; latitudo vero usque ad admirabiles testudinis fornices sexaginta circa sex passus pariter extenta est quamquam superius versus testudinem multo latior appareat. Altitudo autem usque ad eosdem testudinis fornices varia ac diversa est nam intermedium spatium ceteris altius ad septuaginta passus porro elevatur; latera vero huius spatii ad quinquaginta ferme ascendunt. At reliquum quod ambitu testudinis inferius continetur in longum per centum circiter passus porrigitur; in latum[9] vero per centum supra sexaginta extentum est. Altitudo vero testudinis ad centum quinquaginta erecta admirabiliter prominet.

9. Oblongum huius admirabilis delubri nostri curriculum quod truncati hominis capite cum spatulis excepto instar esse diximus in tres partes distinctum esse manifestissime apparet;[10] ingentes et enim quedam saxee columne quadrato lapide utrinque instructe[11] tris velut naves efficere videntur nam singula intercolumnia a suo latere formam navis egregie pre se ferunt. Reliquum vero spatii quod inter ipsas utriusque lateris columnas interiacet tametsi duobus aliis navium lateribus longe latius appareat formam tamen navis quam optime reddit. Ita per hunc modum intercolumnia bifariam structa tres integri spatii dietas speciosissime efficiunt. Ad has basilice dietas per totidem ianuas usque ad testudinis extremum recto tramite intratur. Bine vero fores utrinque a navium lateribus pulcherrime patent.

10. Ceterum quid de admirabili ac pene incredibili ecclesiastice testudinis constructione dicemus, de qua satius esset omnino silere quam pauca dixisse? Nam

---

[8] in inficias *V1*
[9] altum *V1V2B*
[10] appareat *U*
[11] instructe *om. M*

extension from the door to the opening of the east end. The remaining space, enclosed further down by the perimeter of the east end, shows itself in no way unlike the upper body of a human from the head to the thorax. And so that our comparison might be seen to correspond properly, superimpose a person on the church; I would like you to stretch his entire body out on the ground so that his head points east; his arms extend on both sides in opposite directions, one pointing north and the other south; but his feet look to the west. Then you will have no doubt, with a human body so positioned, that this comparison of ours corresponds in nearly every way. And so, if the figure of our temple is the equivalent of the human body, as was obvious above, what person in his right mind would contest that it has acquired the most noble and most perfect appearance, since it is readily apparent that the human form is superior to all other figures of any other things.

8. And so the length of this temple, splendidly formed in this way, extends up to two hundred and sixty paces. The width, although it appears much wider higher up towards the east end, has in fact been uniformly extended about sixty-six paces all the way to the wonderful east end vaults. The height, however, up to these same east end vaults, is varied and not uniform. The space in the middle is higher than the rest and rises up to seventy paces, while the space on the sides ascends to nearly fifty. In contrast, the remaining space contained beneath the circuit of the east end's covering stretches in length about a hundred paces; in width it extends over a hundred and sixty; and the lofty height of the dome actually projects wondrously to a hundred and fifty.

9. The elongated course of our wonderful shrine — which we said to be like a man cut apart, with his head and shoulders missing — gives the very distinct appearance of being divided into three parts, since huge stone columns have been built of stone blocks on both sides and seem to create three naves or "ships," for each intercolumniation splendidly presents from each side the form of a ship. The rest of the space lying in the middle of these same side columns, though obviously far wider than the two side naves, still renders perfectly the form of a ship. And so in this way, the intercolumniations, built as a pair, very attractively create the three chambers of the space as a whole. One enters these chambers of the basilica through an equal number of doors, on a straight path as far as the boundary of the east end. A pair of doors also opens very beautifully from the two sides of the naves.

10. What else shall we say about the wonderful, almost unbelievable fabric of the church's east end? It would be more satisfactory to be totally silent than to say only a few words. For besides its wonderful height, surpassing all the other

preter admirabilem eius altitudinem quae cetera orbis terrarum edificia exuperat inferioris eius spatii figura ad rotundam proxime accedere videtur nisi quod aliquantulo latior quam longior apparet ut formam speciosissime crucis pre se ferat. Hoc itaque tam admirabile testudinis spatium per tres admirabiliores fornices egregie distinctum prominet (vulgo tribunas vocant) quorum unusquisque per quinque ceu cameras distinguitur quas capellas nuncupant. Ita universus testudinei soli ambitus per quindecim capellas speciosissime distinguitur. In medio vero huius inferioris spatii tabulatum quoddam circulare prominet ubi altare ceteris altius collocatum extat.

11. His insuper accedit quod hec tam admirabilis edificii structura ab imo usque ad summum lapide ingenti examussim politissime quadrato deducta videtur esse divinitus nam ab hominibus factum prospicientium oculi ob incredibilem edificii magnitudinem non inmerito suspicantur. At vero universum ambitum superiorem rotunde quedam fenestre in magnorum oculorum formas egregie redacte velut egregia quedam fenestrarum corona speciosissime ambiunt per quas quidem solis radii ita ingrediuntur ut non modo singula testudinis loca luce sua collustrentur sed divine quoque glorie specimen quoddam reddere aspicientibus videantur. In vertice vero testudinis rotunda quedam fenestra ingens mirum in modum prominens omnia condecorat. Sed omissis suis exterioribus magnificentiis ceu miraculis quibusdam et ad nostrum propositum minime pertinentibus de interiori duntaxat huius basilice situ hec dixisse sufficiat.

12. Hoc igitur tam magnificum tam admirabile tam denique incredibile templum inter septem illa orbis terrarum miranda spectacula ob incredibiles magnificentias eius non inmerito commemorandum[12] esse crediderim. Si itaque Athenienses armamentario suo ob id magnopere gloriantur quod fuerit opus ut scriptum est impensa et elegantia visendum et ita gloriantur quod Philonem illius architectum magnis cum laudibus suarum rerum scriptores memorie prodiderunt, nonne Florentini etiam propterea gloriari summopere debent quod opus admirabile construxerunt, usque adeo sumptuosum ut incredibiles impensas ob eius admirabilem constructionem iam factas connumerare difficillimum fuerit, usque adeo insuper elegans ut complures externos quoque homines ad intuendum mirabilem eius elegantiam variis ex locis attraxerit attractosque[13] visentes sepius ac diutius magno cum stupore mentis retinuerit.

13. Hoc itaque gloriosissimum templum (ut ad apparatus tandem aliquando accedamus) Florentini omni ornamentorum genere pulcherrime exornarunt. Ut enim a levioribus incipiam, omnia superiora universi delubri loca integro solo

---

[12] collocandum *V1*

[13] actraxerit actractosque *V2B*

buildings of the world, the figure of the space below seems to come close to being a rotunda, except that its appearance is slightly more wide than long so that it presents the form of a very beautiful cross. This, then, is the wonderful space of the east end; it rises up, splendidly defined by three quite wonderful vaults (in common speech, these are called tribunes) each of which is further defined by five rooms they call chapels. Thus the whole circuit of the east end's platform is attractively defined by fifteen chapels. In the middle of the space below, a circular flooring rises where an altar, placed higher than the others, stands.

11. In addition, the building has such wonderful construction from bottom to top that it seems to have been divinely wrought from a huge stone block which had been precisely and elegantly squared and brought down from heaven. The eyes that look on it suspect — and justifiably so — that it was not made by humans, because of the building's unbelievable size. Indeed, round windows in the form of great eyes, like a splendid crown of windows, attractively encircle the entire upper circuit; through them the rays of the sun actually enter in such a way that they not only illumine with their light the individual places of the east end, but also seem to provide viewers with a specimen of divine glory. In the peak of the east end, a huge round window, wonderfully prominent, adds elegance to everything. We have omitted its exterior magnificences; though wonders, they pertain very little to our present purpose. Let it be enough that we have at least spoken about this basilica's interior arrangement.

12. This temple, so magnificent, so wonderful, and ultimately so unbelievable, I would think should be rightly mentioned among the Seven Wonders of the World because of its unbelievable magnificences. The Athenians take great pride in their armory because, as was written, it was a work that had to be seen for its expense and elegance. They take pride because their history writers, with great praises, passed on the memory of Philo, its architect. Ought not the Florentines, then, also take the highest pride because they have built a wondrous work, and one so sumptuous that it would be difficult to compute the unbelievable expenses already made for its wonderful construction? Moreover, it is so elegant that it attracts many foreigners from all over to gaze on its wondrous elegance. Once they have been attracted, it holds them as they stare long and often in great bewilderment.

13. And so, this most glorious temple (to move on a bit to the displays) the Florentines adorned most beautifully with every sort of decoration. To begin with the less important, once the whole platform had been given a polished surface with

magnis tersisque lateribus perpolito ac velut egregio quodam pavimento effecto lauri, mirti, oleae frondibus multisque aliis arborum atque herbarum floribus varie ut fit distinctis primum referctissima erant.

14. Ordinata deinde insignium drapporum agmina altius a solo suspensa universos basilice parietes magno cum decore circuibant. Per omnes insuper basilice dietas eadem insignium agmina superius appensa circumspiciebantur. Harum quidem tam insignium rerum species aspicientibus iocundissima erat sed pre ceteris ea insignia que in ambitu testudinis altius collocata extabant diversam ab aliis seriem atque inter se variam sortita mirabile profecto spectaculum pre se ferebant. Nam ita collocata erant ut singula agmina se invicem spectantia omnia condecorarent ac propriam testitudinei ambitus figuram mirabiliter exprimere viderentur. Scuta insuper et clipei varie noviterque formata ac pontificalibus armis insignita magno cum decore inter illa insignium agmina pendebant; pontificales quoque mitre altius suspense omnia adornabant. Mille preterea ornamentorum genera singula queque varie atque speciosissime distinguebant.

15. Capelle etiam testudinei ambitus ornatissime erant in quarum prope medio[14] spatio sue queque are extabant ita regaliter ornate ut regie nempe camere apparerent. Altare vero quod in medio testudinei soli collocatum esse diximus quantis ornamentorum generibus condecoratum esset difficile dictu foret nam preter eius egregium opertorium purpura auroque intertextum calices, toreumata, candelabra, variaque vasorum genera aurata, argentea, aurea una cum odoriferis rose pontificalis[15] dignissimis muneribus pretiosissimum altare mirum in modum redimibant. Sacre quoque multorum martirum reliquie margaritis, gemmis, unionibus, ceterisque id genus pretiosis lapidibus multum admodum illustrabant. Astabat preterea in ipso ambitu quo altare pene divinitus ornatum erat regale quinimmo pontificale quoddam solium regie adornatum quod ceteris sedibus universum ambitum circumeuntibus longe altius prominebat.

16. Nec tantis ac tam singularibus ecclesie ornamentis contenti omnem insuper viam qua ab apostolica sede recto tramite ad basilicam ibatur tametsi latis tersisque lapidibus nuperrime strata esset omni tamen ornamentorum genere mirum in modum illustrarunt. Tabulatum quippe admirabile ceu longissimum quendam pontem sublicium altius per ternos fere passus a terra elevatum in hunc modum egregie pre ceteris fabricarunt; a gradibus nanque sedis apostolice incipientes per aream primum per mediam deinde viam omissis utrinque spatiis quibus visens populus deambulare posset ad edem usque dedicandam magnifice simul atque admirabiliter deduxerunt. Hoc tam admirabile tabulatum quod a terra altius per

---

[14] quarum medio prope *V1V2B*

[15] pontificalis rose *V1V2B*

large, smooth bricks and made like a splendid pavement, all the upper places of the entire shrine are first stuffed with boughs of laurel, myrtle, olive, and many other flowers from trees and plants, arranged in patterns, as is done.

14. Then, ordered rows of drapery insignia, suspended rather high above the ground, encircled all the basilica's walls with great dignity. Throughout all the chambers of the basilica identical rows of insignia, suspended higher, could be seen all around. For the spectators, the sights of these banners gave great delight; but, above all, the insignia placed even higher in the circuit of the east end, and with a sequence different from the others and more varied, presented a wonderful spectacle indeed. They were placed so that the individual rows, facing one another, added elegance to everything and seemed wonderfully to copy the exact figure of the east end's circuit. In addition, elongated and round shields, in varied and novel forms and decorated with the papal arms, hung with great dignity among those rows of insignia. Papal tiaras, hung higher up, adorned everything. And then a thousand types of decoration gave various and most attractive definition to each individual item.

15. The chapels of the east end's circuit, too, were highly decorated. In about the middle of each stood its own altar. They were so regally adorned that, without a doubt, they looked like royal rooms. The altar which we said had been placed in the middle of the east end's platform, it would be difficult to say with how many different types of furnishing it was graced. Besides its splendid covering woven with purple, chalices, chased work, candelabra, and various types of vessels — gilded, of silver, or of gold — in wondrous manner encircled the most precious altar, together with the most fragrant and worthy offering of the papal rose. And the sacred relics of many martyrs sparkled with pearls, gems, pearl solitaires, and other similar precious stones. Beyond this, in the very circuit where the altar was most divinely adorned, there stood a royal, or rather, regally adorned pontifical throne, which rose quite a bit higher than the other seats which ringed the entire circuit.

16. Not content with the many extraordinary decorations of the church, they also used every type of decoration to brighten wonderfully the entire street which goes directly from the apostolic residence to the basilica, even though it had been paved quite recently with broad, smooth stones. In fact, they built in a particularly splendid way a platform resembling a very long Sublician Bridge, raised in this manner nearly three paces above the ground. Starting from the steps of the apostolic residence, they conducted it magnificently and wonderfully the entire way to the church that was to be dedicated, first through the open area, then through the middle of the street, leaving spaces on either side where the viewing public could walk. This quite wonderful platform, elevated (as we said) about three paces off

tres fere passus elevatum esse diximus quinque circiter in latitudinem extendebatur; longitudo vero eius usque ad mille ferme passus dignissimum visendarum rerum spectaculum egregie admodum portendebatur.

17. Huius tam admirabilis tamque incredibilis tabulati magne quedam sublicee columne ab utroque latere prominebant odoriferis omnifariam frondibus ita vestite ut preter suavem cuiuspiam viriditatis aspectum variis quoque vaporibus omnia replerent. Columne vero tabulati ita alte erant ut ultra spondas stragulis vestibus mirabiliter ornatas (utrinque enim spondas continebant) varia conspicuaque aulea pontificalibus armis insignita suspendere speciosissime apparerent. Multa insuper egregiorum insignium agmina hec magnifica aulea circumeuntia vehementer condecorabant. Solum autem tabulati quantum eius longitudo portendebatur ornatis perpetuisque tapetis constratum pulcherrime apparebat.

18. Basilica igitur omni ornamentorum genere quemadmodum diximus adornata tabulatoque etiam egregie admodum constructo omnibusque insuper ornamentis accumulatissime predito, quid aliud ad omnes regales, imperiales, pontificalesque denique ac[16] divinos nostri temporis apparatus restare videbatur nisi ut parietibus quoque vie stragule varii generis vestes conspicuaque aulea appenderentur; quod ita egregie factum est ut ad summum ornamentorum omnium cumulum accedere aspicientibus omnibus appareret, ex quo manifeste fieri videbatur ut sive per tabulatum incederent sive per viam deambularent sive denique per basilicam ipsam spatiarentur ut et conspiciendo simul atque olfaciendo variis oblectationibus titillati multiplicibus voluptatibus replerentur.

19. His itaque ornamentis egregie admodum peractis, ecce solemnissima celebratissimaque pre ceteris omnibus ab ecclesia romana[17] institutis angelice annuntiationis dies adventabat quam quidem paucis ante diebus ut supra diximus pontifex opportunum consecrationis tempus fore constituerat. Quocirca Florentinorum presides qui vulgo priores appellantur quique ceu reges ornati cum omnibus pomparum ornamentis ad apostolicam sedem contendebant ut ibi pontificem convenientes concomitarentur. Harum secularium pomparum ingens sane ordo inter pontificales dignitates ex eo aptius connumerabitur quod ubi ad apostolicam sedem per admirabile tabulatum incedentes applicuerunt mox omnes pontificales pompe perpetuo quodam ordine egregie admodum structe versus basilicam per tabulatum ipsum mature ire contenderunt. Pomparum omnium transmissiones bifariam structe[18] erant; quippe ecclesiasticas dignitates omnes seculares pompe antecedebant.

---

[16] pontificalesque ac *V2B*

[17] ad celebrationem *add. M' post* romana

[18] instructe *V1*

the ground, extended about five in width, but its length splendidly extended to about a thousand paces, a sight most worthy of things that must be seen.

17. The great Sublician columns of this wonderful and unbelievable platform jutted out on both sides, so dressed with all manner of fragrant boughs that besides the sweet sight of greenery they all filled everything with various scents. The platform's columns were so tall that on the outside of the frames (for they supported frames on both sides), wonderfully adorned with coverings, varied and eye-catching canopies bearing the papal coat of arms hung, giving a most attractive appearance. Moreover, the many rows of splendid insignia surrounding these magnificent canopies dramatically enhanced them. The floor of the platform, strewn with ornate and continuous carpets, had the most beautiful appearance for its entire length.

18. And so when the basilica had been decorated with every sort of decoration in the manner we described and the platform also had been most splendidly constructed and lavishly endowed with all its other decorations, what else seemed to be left for the royal, imperial, pontifical, and divine displays of our day, except that coverings of various types and eye-catching canopies be also attached to the walls along the route? This was so splendidly done that it was apparent to all who looked at it that it reached the very pinnacle of ornamentation. From then on, what clearly seemed to happen was that, whether they marched along the platform or walked along the street or found themselves a place within the basilica, they were filled with multiple pleasures, titillated by seeing and smelling the variety of delights.

19. And so, with these decorations so splendidly executed, behold! the feast of the Angelic Annunciation arrived, a day most solemn and most celebrated over all others instituted by the Roman Church, which (as we said above) the pope had decided only a few days beforehand would be the fitting date for the consecration. For this reason the Florentine presidents, called "priors" in common speech, adorned like kings, made their way with all the parades' decorations to the apostolic residence to assemble there and join the pope's entourage. From this point on, the huge line of these secular paraders will more appropriately be catalogued along with the pontifical dignitaries because, when they reached the apostolic residence by going along the wonderful platform, all the pontifical paraders, already drawn up most splendidly in a continuous line, began immediately to march briskly along that same platform. The dispatching of all these paraders had been organized in two segments; the secular paraders of course marched in front of the papal dignitaries.

20. Primum nanque tubicinum fidicinumque ac tibicinum[19] ingens ordo erat: singuli quidem tubas, fides, tibias sua manibus instrumenta portantes rutilis vestibus induebantur. Hos multi pretorum famuli adolescentes partim viridioribus partim vero rubeis indumentis vestiti sequebantur. Post istos infinita prope famulorum et quidem adolescentium turba[20] discoloribus vestimentis ibat induta; omnes deinde presidum apparitores cum rutilantibus vestibus prediti tum argenteis quoque baculis a latere pendentibus proficiscebantur; tum nonnulli postea egregii adolescentes magnorum quidem oratorum illustriumque principum assecle[21] comitesque magnifice ac varie pre ceteris antecedentibus ornati continue accedebant. Presides[22] denique una cum urbanis pretoribus multisque quorundam regum imperatorisque augusti egregiis oratoribus ac etiam cum precipuis quibusdam populorum principibus suo quodam ordine permixti magnifice incedebant talaribus togis purpura auroque intertextis usque adeo ornati ut reges quique aspicientibus ob regios ornatus non inmerito viderentur.

21. Has tantas tamque admirabiles secularium pomparum transmissiones multo mirabiliores profecto pontificales dignitates parvo intervallo sequebantur quo facilius a precedentibus dignosci possent. Verum tamen ne quid vacui interesset complures pontificis apparitores singuli suum illum argenteum baculum manibus deferentes hoc ipso parvo intervallo intercedebant.

22. Pontificalium dignitatum non humanus sed divinus prorsus quidem ordo esse videbatur nam magni primum iuris civilis interpretes omnes sua quadam religione prediti ac suis egregiis ornamentis induti ceteros omnes anteibant; prestantes deinde pontificii iuris magistri ac professores variis a prioribus indumentis distincti assequebantur; egregii deinceps pontificis ministri accedebant quos vulgo cubicularios appellant. Ingens preterea turba ecclesie prelatorum incedebat quorum primum locum episcopi obtinebant vestibus albis induti candidisque mitris capita ornati; archiepiscopi deinde non parva hominum multitudo vestibus itidem dealbatis[23] paulo tamen ornatioribus sequebantur; patriarche quoque praedictos episcoporum archiepiscoporumque ordines sectabantur; romane insuper ecclesie cardinales velut veri Christi apostoli ultimo pene loco adventabant.

23. Summus ad extremum pontifex in medio duorum apostolorum gravissime incedebat purpura, auro, gemmisque omnifariam intertextis usque adeo admirabiliter ornatus ut vere supra hominem ac deus ipse pape intuentibus appareret nam subtalaris toga purpura, auro, gemmis affatim ornatissima erat cuius oblongam caudam

---

[19] tibicenum *V1*
[20] turma *U*
[21] a sede *V2B*
[22] Presules *V2B*
[23] dealbatus *U*

20. First came a huge line of trumpeters, lutenists, and reed players, each one carrying his trumpet, lute, or reed in his hands and dressed in costumes of reddish gold. Many young attendants of the praetors followed, dressed in garments of green and red. After them went a virtually endless crowd of attendants and youths dressed in garb of all sorts of colors. Next there set out all the presidents' attendants, outfitted in reddish gold costumes and with silver rods hanging from their sides. Next after them there marched in succession quite a few splendid attendants and companions of the great ambassadors and noble princes, adorned magnificently and in contrast to the ones preceding them. Finally the presidents, intermingled according to each one's rank, with the city praetors, with the splendid ambassadors of kings and of the august emperors, and even with princes of peoples, processed, so adorned with ankle-length togas woven with purple and gold that they seem to the spectators to be kings — and justifiably so, because of their regal trappings.

21. Following at a short distance the great and wondrous dispatching of secular paraders, so they could be more easily distinguished from their predecessors, were the far more wondrous pontifical dignitaries. However, to avoid having an empty space between them, quite a few papal assistants, all of them carrying that silver rod of theirs, bridged this small gap.

22. The line of pontifical dignitaries seemed not human but divine. First all the great interpreters of civil law, each endowed with his own emblem and dressed in their particular splendid trappings, preceded the others. Next the eminent masters and teachers of pontifical law followed, distinguished from the former by their different dress. The splendid ministers, whom they call in common speech "chamberlains," set out. Next a huge crowd of prelates of the church processed, the bishops occupying the first place, dressed in white vestments and wearing gleaming miters on their heads. Next the archbishops, not a small throng of men, followed, also in white vestments, but a bit more ornate. The patriarchs, too, followed these lines of bishops and archbishops. Furthermore, the cardinals of the Roman Church, like Christ's true apostles, came forward in the place next to last.

23. At the end, the supreme pontiff, between two apostles, most gravely processed, so wonderfully adorned with purple, gold, and gems of every sort interwoven that truly to those who looked on the pope he seemed more than a man, God Himself. His toga, reaching to his ankles, was most lavishly ornate with purple, gold, and gems; a distinguished prelate of the church carried its train,

egregius quidam ecclesie prelatus ab humo attollens altiuscule deferebat. Cirotece[24] insuper omni anulorum ac gemmarum genere admirabiliter redimite suas sacratissimas manus speciosissime adornabant. Sanctum denique caput admirabilissima omnium que ullo unquam vise sunt tempore pontificali mitra divinitus tegebatur que quidem tantis gemmarum, margaritarum, unionum, ceterorumque id genus pretiosorum lapidum ornamentis predita esse videbatur ut omnium oculos ad intuendum converteret conversosque in suo admirabili intuitu ita defixos ac demersos continebat ut nihil prorsus aliud prospicere posse viderentur.

24. Huiusmodi militantis ecclesie tam admirabilis tamque divinus ordo tres illas triumphantis militie ierarchias paulo diligentius intuentibus divinitus exprimere videbatur; quod si hec ita se habuerunt ut diximus que unquam romanorum trophea aut qui aliarum quoque gentium ullo tempore triumphi extiterunt ut sint cum huiuscemodi admirabilibus atque incredibilibus[25] pompis comparandi; quippe omnia divina et humana pomparum genera accumulatissime constiterunt. Ad hoc igitur tantum tamque divinum spectaculum incredibilis populorum concursus factus est tantaque utriusque sexus puerorum, mulierum, virorum cuiuscumque etatis multitudo visendi gratia discurrebat ut cuncte urbis vie[26] huiuscemodi hominum capitibus referctissime apparerent.

25. Cum igitur admirabiles Florentinorum pontificisque apparatus ut potuimus verissime pertractarimus, reliquum est ut pontificalia gesta[27] prosequamur. Pontifex itaque cum omni humanarum ac divinarum pomparum genere basilicam ingressus circulare tabulatum in medio testudinei soli spatio astans magna cum gravitate ascendit atque ibi ad altare genibus flexis manibusque pro more orantium ad celum elevatis parum commoratus pontificale solium regalissime ornatum residendi gratia contendit.

26. Quo facto ceteri omnes suis sedibus pro cuiuscumque dignitate consederunt atque paulo post ubi ipse consessum se recepit vexillifer iustitie qui amplissimus apud nos civitatis magistratus est ad pedes eius proxime assedit. Unus deinde postea romane ecclesie cardinalis omnibus sacerdotalibus ornamentis de more preparatus ad altare accessit ut divinum officium celebraret. Interea tantis tamque variis canoris vocibus quandoque concinebatur, tantis etiam symphoniis ad celum usque elatis interdum cantabatur ut angelici ac divini cantus nimirum audientibus apparerent adeoque audientium aures mira variarum vocum suavitate titillabantur ut multum admodum ceu de syrenum cantibus fabulantur obstupescere viderentur

[24] Cirotece *MU*: Cyrotece *P*: Chirothece *V1V2B*

[25] atque incredibilibus *om. V2B*

[26] vie *om. V2B*

[27] parumper *add. M' post* gesta

lifting it slightly off the ground. And gloves, wonderfully encircled with every type of ring and gem, most attractively adorned his most sacred hands. Then his holy head was divinely covered by the most wonderful pontifical miter ever seen. It truly seemed to have been endowed with so much ornamentation of gems, pearls, pearl solitaires, and other similar stones that it made everyone's eyes turn towards it to see. Once their eyes were turned, it held them so firmly fixed and absorbed in their admiring gaze that they seemed completely unable to look at anything else.

24. To those looking a bit more carefully, such a wonderful, such a divine ranking of the church militant seemed divinely to imitate the three hierarchies of a triumphant militia, since, if these events were conducted as I said, what trophies of the Romans and what triumphs of any other people ever existed that should be compared with wonderful, unbelievable parades such as these? And so towards this great and divine spectacle an unbelievable rush of people occurred. Such a great number of children of both sexes and of women and men of all ages dashed about that the streets of the city were visibly and completely stuffed with people's heads.

25. And now, since we have provided as true an account as possible of the wonderful displays of the Florentines and of the pontiff, it remains for us to describe what the pope did. So the pope, after entering the basilica amid every manner of human and divine parade, ascended with great solemnity the circular platform that stands in the east end's middle space. There, after genuflecting to the altar and raising his hands to heaven in the manner of orants and pausing briefly, he then made his way to the most regally adorned pontifical throne to sit.

26. This done, everyone else sat in unison, each seated according to his rank. Shortly after he had seated himself, the standard-bearer of justice, in our city the magistrate with the fullest powers, took a seat by his feet. After that, a cardinal of the Roman Church, furnished with all the normal priestly adornments, approached the altar to celebrate the divine service. Meanwhile, melodies were raised by so many and varied singing voices, alternating with songs made with such symphony lifted up to heaven, that to the audience they appeared for sure angelic and divine. The ears of the hearers were so titillated by the wonderful sweetness of the varied voices that they seemed exceedingly awestruck, as if enchanted by the Sirens' songs. With all due reverence, I could believe this is also

quod in celis etiam quotannis hac ipsa solemnissima die qua principium humane salutis apparuit ab angelis fieri non impie crediderim ut diem festum celebrantes suavissimis cantibus vehementius indulgerent.

27. Interdum vero ubi consuete canendi pause fiebant usque adeo iocunde suaviterque personabatur ut ille mentium stupor iam ex suavissimarum symphoniarum cessatione sedatus rursus vires ob admirabiles sonos resumere videretur; quod nonnulli gravissimi auctores Tymoteum Orpheumque prestantissimos omnium personandi magistros fecisse memorie prodiderunt ut alter sua varia armonia ad quemcunque animi motum homines converteret, alter vero quod mirabilius est ob incredibilem quandam armonie suavitatem lapides et arbores ceteraque id genus omnia partim animata, partim vero inanimata incredibile dictu ad se pertraheret. Ita per hunc modum fieri videbatur ut omnes paulo humaniores sensus nostri partim suavissimos cantus dulcissimosque sonos audientes, partim varios ac redolentes vapores olfacientes, partim denique admirabilia omnia ornamentorum genera conspicientes varie hilarescerent.[28]

28. Dum hec agebantur, ecce magna captivorum turba[29] adventabat quos florentini suis e carceribus eductos summo pontifici condonabant ut eos immortali deo offerret atque a captivitate liberaret eos mox ut ad pedes eius procubuerunt sancta sacrarum manuum benedictione impertitos vinculisque solutos magno cum eorum gaudio dimisit.

29. Iustitie deinde vexillifer quem ad sacros pontificis pedes astare paulo ante demonstravimus opportune iussus assurgit genibusque[30] pro more flexis egregia militie insignia magna cum civitatis gloria atque ingenti sui honore ab ipso pontifice reportavit. Pontifex nanque cupiens hac ipsa solemnissima omnium consecrationis die florentinum nomen multum admodum honestare prestantissimum virum omnium qui in ipsa florentinorum civitate eo tempore reperirentur antea egregiis militie insignibus donare constituerat.

30. Quocirca illustri ariminensium principi atque egregio imperatoris legato dignioribus personis hoc quodcunque officium non indigne commisit quorum alter de more aurata calcaria pedibus immisit, alter vero militarem ensem accinxit quem spatam vulgato[31] nomine appellant. Ita per hunc modum vir prestantissimus militaribus ornamentis honestatus mox equestribus donatus insignibus ad eundem sedis suae locum ad sanctos videlicet pontificis pedes revertitur.

---

[28] ilarescerent *V1V2B*
[29] turma *U*
[30] genibus *V2B*
[31] vulgo *V2BU*

done by angels each year on this most solemn day when the first event of human salvation appeared. In celebrating this feast day, they yield themselves more vigorously to the sweetest song.

27. In between, when the normal pauses in the singing occurred, the instruments played so merrily and sweetly that the bewilderment, relaxed when the sweetest symphonies ended, seemed once again to revive its force because of the wonderful sounds. More than a few very important sources have passed on the tradition that this is what Timotheus and Orpheus did, the most eminent masters of instrumental music. The one with his varied harmony used to turn people to any state of mind; the other (and this is even more wonderful), because of the unbelievable sweetness of his harmony, drew to himself the stones and trees and other like things, both animate and inanimate, incredible to tell! So it seemed to happen the same way. All our slightly more civilized senses grew more joyous, in their separate ways — by hearing the sweetest songs and loveliest sounds, by smelling the varied and redolent fragrances, and by gazing at all the wonderful kinds of decoration.

28. While this was going on, behold! a large gang of captives approached. These the Florentines had brought from prison and released them to the supreme pontiff that he might offer them to God and free them from their captivity. After they had prostrated themselves at his feet, received the holy blessing from his sacred hands, and had their chains removed, he dismissed them, to great rejoicing on their part.

29. Then the standard-bearer of justice (a little while ago we showed him standing at the pontiff's sacred feet) went up to the pope at the appropriate signal and, after the usual genuflection, received from the pontiff himself the splendid insignia of military service, to the great glory of his city and to his enormous personal honor. The pope, desiring on this most solemn day, the day of the consecration, to honor greatly the Florentine name, had decided beforehand to invest with splendid military insignia the most distinguished man that could be found in the city of Florence at that time.

30. To this purpose, he fittingly entrusted this duty to the noble prince of the Riminese and to the eminent ambassador of the emperor, persons of great standing. One of them placed the gilded spurs on his feet in the customary way, while the other girded him with the military sword which they call by the common name "spata". Thus honored with military decorations and invested with knightly insignia in this manner, that most eminent man returned to his seat near the holy feet, the feet of the pope.

31. Dum hec interim agerentur, alter et magnus quidem Romane ecclesie cardinalis alta quadam lectica delatus astante universo populo per sacra basilice loca hinc inde ceteris altius ferebatur ut sanctorum apostolorum imagines basilice parietibus paulo superius depictas consecrationis oleo perungeret ac dignissime consecraret.

32. Pontifex autem ubi satis consederat demum assurgit ut ad altarem assisteret ibique aliquantulum commoratus sacrum consecrationis oleum suis manibus assumpsit quo crebro altare hinc inde perfricuit ac linivit. Has sacras consecrationes sanctissimis suis orationibus ceu quodam divino sale divinitus condiebat. Sanctas deinde martyrum reliquias que super altare ut diximus astabant propriis manibus suscipiebat variisque orationibus velut divino quodam condimento aspersas in altaris dietis dignissime recondebat. His igitur pie admodum peractis, sacratissimas manus suas recentis primum medulla panis pontificali ritu perfricuit; illustri deinde ariminensium principe aquas aureo vasculo religiosissime exhibente perlavit; postremo ad solium reversus consedit.

33. Paulo deinde postquam[32] consedere visus est, ecce maturum dominici consecrandi corporis tempus opportune advenerat quod eucarestiam greci rectissime appellant in cuius quidem sanctissimi[33] corporis[34] elevatione tantis armoniarum symphoniis, tantis insuper diversorum instrumentorum consonationibus omnia basilice loca resonabant ut angelici ac prorsus divini paradisi sonitus cantusque demissi celitus ad nos in terris divinum nescio quid ob incredibilem suavitatem quandam in aures nostras insusurrare non inmerito viderentur. Quocirca eo tempore tantis equidem voluptatibus potitus sum ut beata vita frui hic viderer in terris. Quod utrum ceteris astantibus acciderit non plane scio; de me ipse idoneus testis sum.

34. Perfectis[35] igitur per hunc modum dignissimis universe consecrationis muneribus divinisque officiis omnibus religiosissime celebratis, summus pontifex admirabili quadam pontificali indulgentia basilicam iam consecratam quotannis ea ipsa consecrationis die utpote sanctissimo quodam ablutionis sale condivit. Quo absoluto, e vestigio[36] omnes ille et seculares et pontificales pompe eo ipso quo paulo ante venerant ordine egregium sane ac prorsus mirandum spectaculum ad apostolicam sedem magnificentissime simul atque gravissime contenderunt.[37]

---

[32] postea quam *V2B*

[33] sacratissimi *V2B*

[34] corporis *om. U*

[35] Prefectis *PB*

[36] summus . . . vestigio *om. M*

[37] summus . . . contenderunt *P in manu aliena super rasuram*

31. As this was going on, another great cardinal of the Roman Church, as the entire congregation stood, was lifted in a high litter and carried here and there throughout all the sacred places of the basilica, raised higher than everyone else so that he could anoint with the oil of consecration and most worthily hallow the images of the holy apostles painted a bit higher on the walls.

32. But the pontiff, when he had sat for a sufficient amount of time, at last arose to stand by the altar. Pausing there a moment, he took into his own hands the sacred oil of consecration and with it rubbed and smeared the altar all over repeatedly. He divinely seasoned these sacred consecrations with his most holy prayers as if with a divine salt. Then he took into his own hands the holy relics of the martyrs (we mentioned they were standing on the altar). After they were sprinkled most worthily with various prayers, as if with a divine condiment, he stored them inside the recesses of the altar. When these actions had been devoutly performed, he rubbed his most sacred hands on the inner part of fresh bread in accordance with the pontifical ritual, then washed them as the noble prince of the Riminese most reverently provided water from a golden ewer. Finally he returned to his throne and was seated.

33. Then shortly after he was seen to sit down, behold! the time was ripe and suitably arrived for consecrating the Lord's body, which the Greeks most rightly call the "eucharist". At the elevation of the most sacred body, all the places of the basilica resonated with so many harmonic symphonies with such accompaniment of various instruments that it seemed — justifiably, because of their unbelievable sweetness — that angelic and truly divine sounds and songs of paradise were sent down from heaven to us on earth and whispered something or other divine into our ears. For this reason, at that very moment, I managed to take so many pleasures that I truly seemed to be enjoying the blessed life here on earth. Whether others standing there experienced the same thing, I clearly do not know; about myself, however, I am a competent witness.

34. And so, when all the most solemn rites of the whole consecration service had in this manner been performed and the whole divine service reverently celebrated, the supreme pontiff seasoned, as with the most holy salt of purification, the just-consecrated basilica by granting a wonderful pontifical indulgence annually on the anniversary of its consecration. Immediately after this was done, the secular and pontifical parades in their entirety marched magnificently yet solemnly to the apostolic residence in the same order in which they had arrived a short time before, a splendid and truly wonderful spectacle indeed.

35. Hec habui Angele suavissime que de huiusmodi admirabilibus pompis in presentia ad te scriberem. Et si delicatissimas aures tuas implebunt, mihi profecto gratissimum futurum scias velim; sin minus, tu primum in culpa es cuius gratia hec ipsa litteris mandare adductus sum. Usque adeo deinde admirabilia fuerunt ut venia mihi danda esse videatur si incredibiles tantarum rerum apparatus verbis dignissime explicare non valui. His insuper accedit quod hec ipsa eloquentie minime capacia esse manifestum est. Dabis igitur hanc veniam si tibi viro eloquentissimo minus eloquens vel potius ut verissime dixerim ineptior in hac ipsa nostra adumbratione quam videri soleam apparuero. Finis.[38]

[38] Finis *MPU*: *om. V1V2B*: EXPLICIT DEO GRATIAS. AMEN. ANNO DOMINI MCCCCXXXVI *add. V1V2B*

35. Dearest Agnolo, this is what I have for the present to write to you about these wonderful parades. And if they will satisfy your fastidious ears, I should like you to know that I would find it most welcome. If not, it is, first of all, your fault; for your sake I was coerced into dispatching this in a letter. Second, these events were so wondrous that it seems I deserve to be forgiven if I did not have the power in words to explain worthily the unbelievable displays of things this great. Besides, these are clearly the ones least susceptible to eloquence. Consequently, you will pardon me if I have exposed myself as less eloquent than someone of the greatest eloquence, or rather, to tell the truth, even more inept in this sketch of mine than I usually seem.

The end.

Concerning the Secular and Papal Parades: An Introduction by Giannozzo Manetti

Commentary

title. introduction: The manuscripts closest to Manetti call the work a "prefatio" concerned with the two *pompae*. As a "prefatio" it would parallel the "prefationes" to Tommaso de Campofregosi, Doge of Genoa, that precede the two orations to the Genoese contained in these same two manuscripts, works roughly contemporary with this composition. See Petti Balbi, *Elogi dei Genovesi*, 5–37, for the dating of the delivery and composition of the Genoese orations. The title in the later manuscripts, however, describes the text as an oration, connects the processions with the consecration of the cathedral, and adds Agnolo Acciaiuoli's knightly rank. As is clear, the work is in fact neither a preface nor an oration, but a letter, conforming to epistolary conventions. While it is possible that M. intends his "sketch" to be preliminary to some fuller treatment, the letter is fully developed and, in the usual Manettian manner, rationally organized: Onofri, "La *Vita*," 48, n. 108. For Manetti's rhetorical practice, see Chapter 1.

Agnolo Acciaiuoli: Agnolo Acciaiuoli, who married Manetti's sister-in-law in 1420, was part of a scholarly group that met at Manetti's house in the early 1430s to read Aristotle's *Ethics*. A supporter of the Medici, he had been exiled in 1433 to Cephalonia, captured by Turks in Greece, and escaped a year later. His exile was revoked and he returned to Florence in 1434 when Cosimo de'Medici was restored to power, and began a long and tumultuous political career. In 1436, he was, like Manetti, already involved in complex diplomatic missions for the Republic. Manetti indicates that both were present and together at the ceremony; presumably they marched in their official diplomatic finery among the ambassadors in the secular *pompa* (20). Vespasiano tells us that Agnolo was well known to and trusted by Eugenius IV, who knighted him, and on intimate terms with the pope's closest confidantes: Francesco Condulmer (the papal chamberlain), Cardinal Niccolò Albergati, and the rising star Tommaso Parentucelli who would succeed Eugenius as Nicholas V: Onofri, "La *Vita*," 48; M. E. Cosenza, *Biographical and Bibliographical Dictionary of the Italian Humanists and the World of Classical Scholarship in Italy, 1300–1800* (Boston, 1962), s.v. "Agnolo Acciaiuoli"; *Dizionario biografico degli Italiani*, s.v.; Vespasiano, *Vite*, 2:285–308.

1. ***flourishing city:*** In Latin, a pun on the city's name. But Manetti, now at the beginning of his public career as an orator for the Republic, alludes to the fact that in the 1430s Florentines and others were conscious of the city being "in flower," the common classical usage for *floreo* in reference to material prosperity and culture. The phrase is the first hint of a floral imagery that runs throughout the narrative.

"nothing is difficult for one who loves": a quote from Cicero, *Orator* 9.33

2. ***sketch:*** "adumbratio." Manetti's idea of a "sketch" may reflect awareness of painters' procedures or, as is typical for him, it may have a literary source. For instance, John Chrysostom wrote: "As long as somebody traces the outline as in a drawing, there remains a sort of shadow; but when he paints over it brilliant tints and lays on colors, then an image emerges": *In dictum Pauli . . .* , PG 51.247D; and *Epist. ad Hebraeos*, Homily 17.2, PG 63.130A. Cf. Philostratus, *Life of Apollonius*, 2.28 and 1.2 on *skiagraphia*. Compare to the *Life* at 2.8.

3. ***ancient painter:*** The example is famous in antiquity, concerning a prize-winning painting by Timanthes, noted as much for what it left out as what it included. As a famous topos, it bears a remarkable resemblance to Alberti's account of the same picture in *Della pittura* (Book 2), but it is, in important ways, not identical to it: as Onofri already observed in "La *Vita*," 65; and also van Eck, "Manetti on Architecture," 460. Most recently on Alberti's use of the topos, see Grafton, *Alberti*, 142.

Both men described Timanthes' painting of the event, known from at least four widely-read classical authors (Quintilian, Cicero, Pliny, and Valerius Maximus), and not Euripides' account (*Iphigenia in Aulis*, 1543–1603), which was hardly known in Florence. For the diffusion of Euripides in early Renaissance libraries, see A. Pertusi, "Il Ritorno alle fonti del teatro greco classico: Euripide nell'Umanesimo e nel Rinascimento," *Byzantion* 33 (1963): 391–426, here 400. Although Manetti had a copy of Euripides, his volume did not include the *Iphigenia in Aulis*. Indeed, the only book in Florence that did contain this play seems to be MS. Bib. Laur. conventi soppressi 172, once owned by Antonio Corbinelli (1370/71–1425), which passed to the Badia fiorentina: A. Turyn, *The Byzantine Manuscript Tradition of the Tragedies of Euripides* (Urbana, 1957), 153. The fifteenth century, however, witnessed the revival of interest in the Greek playwright, evidenced not only by the increased number of volumes of his work in circulation, but also by Cyriacus of Ancona's lost *Life* of Euripides: see Cortesi and Maltese, "Ciriaco d'Ancona e il 'De Virtutibus'," 134. Perhaps their interest in the story was sparked by a neo-Attic relief of the sacrifice now in the Uffizi: J. M. Croisille, "Le Sacrifice d'Iphigénie dans l'art romain et la littérature latine," *Latomus* 22 (1963): 209–25.

That both Alberti and Manetti described Timanthes' lost painting in works of 1435–1436 could have been simple coincidence, as Onofri thought ("La *Vita*," 65), but was probably not. This is Alberti's version:

> Timanthes of Cyprus is praised in his panel, the "Immolation of Iphigenia", with which he conquered Kolotes. After he had painted Calchas sad, Ulysses more sad, and in grief-stricken Menelaus expended all his art and talent, with the emotions exhausted, and not finding any dignified way to represent the face of her most sad father, he pulled drapery over his head, and so left for each individual to ponder in his mind more than what he could make out with his sight. *(Della pittura*, trans. J. Spencer [New Haven, 1966], 78.)

The structures of the two descriptions, relying on adjectives of increasing emotional intensity, are the same in Manetti and Alberti. In both instances, the artist's inability or refusal to represent Agamemnon's face leads to a comment about how the viewer must supply the father's emotional state himself. These elements are the core of the ancient *testimonia*. The ultimate model is Cicero (*Orator*, 22.74), in a context of applying painterly concerns to the task of the orator:

> The painter in portraying the sacrifice of Iphigenia, after representing Calchas as sad, Ulysses as still more so, Menelaus as in grief, felt that Agamemnon's head must be veiled, because the supreme sorrow could not be portrayed by his brush.

While *Orator* had been rediscovered in 1421 and was therefore available to both, it is not the direct model for either of our men.

Manetti's version is almost identical to that of Valerius Maximus (*Memorable Doings and Sayings*, 8.11.6), in its turn derived from Cicero:

> But did not that other equally noble painter [Timanthes], in his representation of the sacrifice of Iphigenia immolated, after he had located around the altar Calchas sad, Ulysses desolate, Ajax crying out, Menelaus lamenting, admit, by veiling Agamemnon's head, that the bitterness of his supreme sorrow could not be expressed in art? Thus the picture flows with the tears of augur, friend, and brother, but he leaves the father's weeping to be assessed by the emotional impact on the viewer.

Manetti's copy of Valerius Maximus is now MS. Pal. Lat. 903 in the Vatican Library: Cagni, "I codici," 41. This copy was made in Florence in 1397, according to its explicit, so Manetti could well have owned it by 1435. Manetti drew on Valerius Maximus elsewhere in this same work for his comparison of Florence Cathedral to Philo's great armory in Athens (*De pompis* 12). This second citation taken together with the almost identical wording of the passages on Timanthes permits the identification of Manetti's specific source as Valerius Maximus. This assures us, incidentally, that Lorenzo Ghiberti's use of the same topos in his *Commentarii* (1.8.7) about a decade later is not dependent on Manetti since he draws from Pliny's account (*NH* 35.73).

Alberti, instead, used Quintilian's version (*De Institutione oratoria*, 2.13.13) of the Ciceronian passage:

> Timanthes, who was, I think, a native of Cythnus, provides an example of this [things which cannot be expressed as they deserve] in the picture with which he won the victory over Colotes of Teos. It represented the sacrifice of Iphigenia, and the artist had depicted an expression of grief on the face of Calchas and of still greater grief on that of Ulysses, while he had given Menelaus an agony of sorrow beyond which his art could not go. Having exhausted his powers of emotional expression he was at a loss to portray the father's face as it deserved, and solved the problem by veiling his head and leaving his sorrow to the imagination of the spectator.

Alberti returns to Quintilian on Timanthes several times in *Della pittura*, and so, like Manetti, is appreciative of the apt use of a classical topos in clarifying an argument. Since, like Manetti, he only slightly alters the wording of his classical source, it can securely be identified as Quintilian.

This use of variant sources argues against Manetti's use of the topos as an appropriation of Alberti's insight as van Eck claimed ("Manetti on Architecture," 462). In fact, the two accounts differ in striking ways that point to real differences between the thought of Manetti and Alberti.

First, in Alberti's example, the emotional burden is *tristitia* or "sadness". Timanthes has made Calchas sad, Ulysses sadder, Menelaus grief-stricken, but cannot with dignity represent the girl's father who, of course, would be saddest of all. Menelaus's sorrow was at the limit of his expression. Manetti (and Valerius Maximus), by contrast, see in Timanthes' figures an array of emotions, particular to the individual witnesses of the girl's tragedy; Calchas is sad, but Ulysses is desolate, Ajax is agitated, Menelaus mourning. What emotion would Agamemnon be feeling? Presumably something distinctive to his own treachery and loss.

Second, and more important, Alberti's Timanthes has depleted his artistic resources, both those that came to him from genius and those he acquired by training. His problem is to complete the work without compromising the dignity of his subject or calling attention to the limitations of his painterly range. Manetti's Timanthes, however, makes a decision. Agamemnon's grief is of such a nature that it is outside the realm of the expressible. Some subjects are simply not susceptible to representation either in art or in rhetoric. Thus Manetti forewarns his addressee to expect a similar limit to his description of his own experience in the consecration of the cathedral, and reiterates it once more in his conclusion at 35.

Finally, the task of the spectator is differently explained. In Alberti's version, the spectator is left pondering, with more left unportrayed than represented about Agamemnon's emotional state. With Manetti, the painter expects his viewer to reach a judgment. It may differ from one person to the next, but the participation of the viewer in the construction of the painting's significance is intended by the artist. So it was also with Manetti's description of the cathedral. In the end, his reader was confronted with a decision, personally constructed, and guided only by a "sketch".

5. ***happened to be living:*** There was no chance about it. Eugenius had been forced to flee Rome in disguise, narrowly escaping with his life, as Vespasiano tells us (*Vite*, 1:7–8). On his arrival in Florence on 29 May 1434, he established his court in the Dominican convent of Sta. Maria Novella. He remained there until April of 1436; he returned when the Council of Union was moved to Florence in 1439. Eugenius left for Siena, then Rome in 1443, where he stayed until his death on 23 February 1447. Thus for eight of the sixteen years of this pontificate, the papal court resided in Florence. During this time, Eugenius was rarely seen by the general population of the city, and then only from a distance (Vespasiano, *Vite*, 1:21). His participation in the consecration of the basilica, a matter of enormous civic pride, would have been heightened by his general reclusiveness. Privately, however, he moved in a circle that included Leonardo Bruni, Manetti, Poggio Bracciolini, Carlo Marsuppini, Giovanni Aurispa, and Gaspare Sighicelli da Bologna. In his suite were Tommaso Parentucelli, the future Nicholas V, and Parentucelli's patron, Cardinal Niccolò Albergati, archbishop of Bologna (Vespasiano, *Vite*, 1:42).

east end: That is, Brunelleschi's dome, finished on 12 June 1434: Giovanni di Ser Cambi, in H. Saalman, *Cupola*, 188. However, it was not blessed until 30 August 1436, so that date is sometimes given as its date of completion: Bartolomeo del Corazza, *Diario fiorentino (1435–1439)*, ed. R. Gentile (Anzio, 1991), 36.

In his account, Manetti will consistently refer to the entire east end, rather than specifically to the dome. *Testudo*, therefore, is not accurately translated as "cupola" or "dome". See our analogous comment on the *Life* at 44–45.

This entire area had been blocked to public view since 1380 when a wall was erected at the end of the nave; the liturgy was performed at an altar either in front of this wall or in the second bay of the nave. The consecration ceremony would afford the Florentines their first opportunity to see the east end's interior spaces in use. On 23 August 1435 the *capomaestro* was ordered to demolish this wall, and the question of how to arrange the new choir and high altar was first discussed. We cite doc. 2264 from G. Poggi, *Il Duomo di Firenze. Documenti sulla decorazione della chiesa e del campanile tratti dall'Archivio dell'Opera*, 1 (Berlin, 1909) (docs. 1–1453) and 2, ed. M. Haines (Florence, 1988) (part VII). On 15 November 1435, Nanni Ticcii was commissioned to make an altar mensa of white marble for the new main altar (Poggi, *Il Duomo*, doc. 1175). On 25 November 1435, Brunelleschi's design for the new choir and altar was reviewed by a committee (Poggi, *Il Duomo*, doc. 1176). Since a model of the altar was still being studied in March of 1437, it is unclear what altar was in fact consecrated at the ceremony Manetti describes. The old choir enclosure was demolished only five days before the consecration (Poggi, *Il Duomo*, doc. 2379). A new choir, or rather a kind of rough model of Brunelleschi's proposal made of simple wooden planks, was erected between 1437 and 1439 (Poggi, *Il Duomo*, doc. 1182).

years before: The cathedral had been begun on 8 September, the feast of the Birth of the Virgin, of 1296 or 1298 by Arnolfo di Cambio. Work progressed slowly in the first half of the fourteenth century, and the building was mostly erected between 1357 and 1435. For its chronology, see H. Saalman, "Santa Maria del Fiore, 1294–1418," *Art Bulletin* 46 (1964): 471–500; documents in C. Guasti, *Santa Maria del Fiore. La costruzione della chiesa e del campanile* (Florence, 1887), and Poggi, *Il Duomo*. A database of documents for the cupola period (1417–1436) is being prepared by Margaret Haines. See M. Haines, "Gli anni della cupola. Una bancadati testuale della documentazione dell'Opera di Santa Maria del Fiore," in *Atti del VII centenario del duomo di Firenze*. 1. *La cattedrale e la città*, ed. T. Verdon and A. Innocenti (Florence, 2001), 693–736.

quickly: Manetti may be exact here. On 24 January 1436, the *capomaestro* was instructed to prepare the church so it could be consecrated. But only on 9 March were orders given for the construction of the papal walkway from Santa Maria Novella to the cathedral, and only on 13 March were Lorenzo della Stufa and Nicola de Businis charged with providing all that was necessary for the consecration to be held on 25 March (Poggi, *Il Duomo*, docs. 2367, 2372, 2375).

Whether the date was fixed by the pope or the priors, 25 March was the feast of the Annunciation and the first day of the Florentine calendar year, doubly fitting both the Marian dedication of the church and city pride. 25 March had been chosen as the annual feast day of the cathedral in 1412, although this was subsequently changed (in 1417) to the feast of the Purification of the Virgin: M. Bergstein, "Marian Politics in Quattrocento Florence," *Renaissance Quarterly* 44 (1991): 673–719, here 675.

6. interior arrangement: In 1442, in *Della tranquillità dell'animo*, Alberti composed his own description of the cathedral interior.

> And certainly this temple has in itself grace and majesty; and, as I have often thought, I delight to see joined together here a charming slenderness with a robust and full solidity so that, on the one hand, each of its parts seems designed for pleasure, while on the other, one understands that it has all been built for perpetuity. I would add that here is the constant home of temperateness, as of springtime: outside, wind, ice and frost; here inside one is protected from the wind, here mild air and quiet. Outside, the heat of summer and autumn; inside, coolness. And if, as they say, delight is felt when our senses perceive what, and how much, they require by nature, who could hesitate to

> call this temple the nest of delights? Here, wherever you look, you see the expression of happiness and gaiety; here it is always fragrant; and, that which I prize above all, here you listen to the voices during mass, during that which the ancients called the mysteries, with their marvelous beauty (Leon Battista Alberti, *Opere volgari*, ed. Grayson, 107).

On the passage see Smith, *Architecture in the Culture of Early Humanism*, chaps. 1 and 5.

Whereas Manetti tried to be precise in his account, using much technical terminology, giving measurements, and carefully explaining the relation between parts and the whole, Alberti's account in *Della tranquillità dell'animo* is abstract, characterizing the whole in terms of aesthetic principles; grace and majesty, slenderness and robust solidity, pleasure and utility. The economy of Alberti's language and his poetic tone expose Manetti's prose description of the cathedral as pedestrian, wordy, and devoid of theoretical content. However, it is Manetti who first characterized the experience of the cathedral's interior by evoking senses other than sight: in the consecration account he evokes music heard, both instrumental and vocal (26–27, 33); and the fragrances of plants and incense (13, 27) as acting on the affective response of the spectator.

decorations: Manetti uses "ornamenta" to mean "decorations" such as flowers and banners. For Alberti's very different use of the term and its historical antecedents, see Smith, "Leon Battista Alberti e l'ornamento."

7. ***human body:*** For this image, see Chapter 9.

elongated space: That is, the torso and legs of the human body resemble the nave.

remaining space: Manetti conceives the interior volume of the east end as defined by the multiple vaults of dome and tribunes. Hence he is telling us here that we are to consider the part down below, at pavement level in the *ambitus*, the almost centralized walk-around space of the east end.

8. ***length . . . height . . . width:*** We know from the documents that the cathedral's measurements were worked out in Florentine braccia (1 braccio = 58.36 cm), so Manetti's choice to give the measurements in *passi*, that is, strides, seems odd. Moreover, his measurements are not really in *passi*, each of which equals five Roman feet (*pedes*) but in Roman feet, each approximately equal to 29.5 cm. For the *passus*, see J. Capgrave, *Ye Solace of Pilgrims. A Description of Rome ca. A.D. 1450, by John Capgrave*, ed. C. A. Mills (London, 1911), 61.

Using this unit for conversion, we can compare his measurements to those of the actual building, converting both to meters. Manetti tells us that the nave is 76.7 m long (260 Roman feet) whereas it is 79.37 m (136 br.); he gives its width as 19.5 m (66 Roman feet) whereas it is double that, 39.7 m (68 br.) — he may have meant the central nave alone which in fact equals 19.8 m. The height of the nave is given as 20.6 m (70 Roman feet) whereas it is 42 m (72 br.) high. The height of the side aisles he gives as almost 14.7 m (50 Roman feet). The length of the east end according to Manetti is 29.5 m (100 Roman feet), whereas in reality the diameter of the dome alone is 42 m (72 br.); the width of the east end he gives as 47.2 m (160 Roman feet); and the height of the dome as 44.2 m (150 Roman feet), whereas in fact the dome projects 84 m (144 br.) from the pavement and rises 42 m above its base.

Gregorio Dati, writing some twelve years earlier, gave the dimensions of the cathedral as 240 "passi" long and 66 "passi" wide; evidently, Manetti's "stride" is analogous to Dati's, despite an almost 6 m discrepancy in their stated lengths: C. Gilbert, "The Earliest Guide to Florentine Architecture, 1423," *Mitteilungen des Kunsthistorischen Instituts in Florenz* 40 (1969): 33–46 (appendix). That the cathedral was believed to be 260 — of some unit of measurement — long is suggested by Bartolomeo Scala's claim that it was 260 *cubits* long and Vasari's that it was 260 *braccia* long. Scala believed it to be 150 cubits wide at the transept and 66 in the nave; Vasari gives 166 br. for the transept and 66 for the nave. Since Vasari also gives the height of the dome as 154 br. from the ground, his measurements are close to Manetti's although Manetti measures in strides and Vasari in *braccia*: Vasari, *Le vite*, 2:55; B. Scala, *De historia florentinorum quae extant in Bibliotheca Medicaea*, ed. O. Iacobaeo (Rome, 1677), col. 12. On units of measurement in fifteenth-century architecture, see Tavernor, *Art of Building*, 41, 226 n. 87; Hope, "The Early History of the Tempio Malatestiano," 142. For further discussion of Manetti's units of measurement, see the Commentary on the *Life* at 39 and Chapter 5.

9. columns: Manetti knows only the word "columna" for an architectural support, even when these are not "columns" in our sense. In fact, the nave of Florence Cathedral has compound piers composed of a square core with four attached pilasters on the main faces and polygonal colonnettes on the diagonal axes.

ships: The Latin term "naves" (= "ships") had come in medieval architectural vocabulary to mean naves, and this is the contemporary usage in Florence, as is shown in Poggi, *Il Duomo*, docs. 2190 and 2191. Du Cange, *Glossarium*, 5:579–80, s.v. "navis", pointed out a difference of opinion in the medieval sources about whether the term had derived from the Greek *naos* (= "temple") or from the Latin for ship because its form resembles "navium carina", i.e. the hull of ships.

intercolumniations: Manetti means colonnades. See discussion of this term in Chapter 5.

chambers: "dietas": see below, 14.

boundary: In other words, entering any of the three aisles of the nave through one of the three doors in the west facade you see a kind of tunnel of space before you go up to the crossing. Manetti defines the point where the naves meet the crossing as "extremum", the boundary or edge of the east end; that is, the edge of the east end defines spatial boundaries, not the end of the nave. See Poggi, *Il*

Duomo, doc. 1176 of 26 November 1435, where this tunnel effect is specifically asked for in relation to the choir screen: "le spalliere del detto coro s'alarghi insino al diritto de' pilastri delle navi da lato, ma non se n'escha, sì che chi va per l'andito delle dette navi, l'ochio non sia occupato dal choro, ma seguitisi il diritto de' detti pilastri."

10. few words: Manetti's account of the dome can be seen as a response to Alberti's description of the dome in his letter to Brunelleschi. Alberti had characterized the size and difficulty of the structure in a few pregnant clauses:

> Who could ever be hard or envious enough to fail to praise Pippo the architect on seeing here such a large structure, rising above the skies, ample to cover with its shadow all the Tuscan people, and constructed without the aid of centering or great quantity of wood? (*Della pittura*, trans. Spencer, 40)

But Manetti prefers to leave judgment to the reader rather than to describe what is not susceptible to eloquence. Instead of praising the engineering of the dome as Alberti does, Manetti gives measurements (8), which Alberti does not. He explains the relation of the dome to the interior cathedral space (10), while Alberti praises its exterior appearance and relation to Tuscany. Consequently, whereas Manetti understands the cathedral as a covered space in which people act (he refers to the "circuit of the east end's covering" [8], meaning the ambulatory and tribunes around the choir), Alberti presents the dome as a monument, seen from afar and serving to impress spectators outside the church. Manetti shows how the dome relates to the tribunes (8, 10), which are omitted by Alberti. Indeed, Manetti conceives of the dome as one of several vaults, together with those of the tribunes, defining the volume of the east end (an area which he consistently refers to as the "testudinated platform"), whereas Alberti sees the dome as standing out from the rest of the structure. Manetti will return to Brunelleschi's dome in his treatise *On the Dignity of Man*, where it appears — precisely — as evidence of brilliant engineering and originality, as it does in Alberti's letter (*De dignitate et excellentia hominis*, ed. Leonard, 2.38 and our discussion of the passage in our Introduction). But by then the architect will have died, and Manetti may be responding to the numerous epitaphs by Carlo Marsuppini among others which singled out these qualities for praise. On the epitaphs, see Smith, *Architecture in the Culture of Early Humanism*, 28.

In March or April of 1436 we find Manetti and Alberti engaging similar topics in very different ways: Alberti wrote a letter to the architect of the dome about the importance of the cathedral; Manetti composed a letter on the same subject to a knight. Not only do they differ in the social class of the addressee; Manetti's description is of the cathedral building as a whole, whereas Alberti concentrates on the achievement of a single individual — Brunelleschi — whom Manetti does not even mention. Evidently, Manetti does not believe in "stars", at least not when they are architects. Instead, he supported the interests of the rich and powerful (we recall that at this time he was an ambassador for the Florentine state): much of his account of the consecration ceremony is taken up with description of which dignitaries marched in the parade, what they wore, and how the church was decorated for the occasion. Only eight years earlier the Florentine *catasto* had revealed that Manetti's family was one of the ten richest in Florence; Alberti, the bastard son of an exiled father, could be expected to have a different approach to Florentine society. On Manetti's family, see L. Martines, *The Social World of the Florentine Humanists* (Princeton, 1963), 131–38. Unlike Alberti, whose very different notion of the status of the architect was a novelty in 1435, for Manetti the dome was representative of the intelligence of collective mankind, and of the achievement of the city of Florence, rather than of the creative genius of an individual.

rotonda: Documents of the building project regularly refer to the nave and the east end as separate structures, as does Manetti. One of 1367 differentiates between the "chiesa" and "la croce overo tribuna"; another, of 1429, speaks of "unum modellum totius ecclesie veteris et novi oratorii opere": G. Morolli, "Brunelleschi e l'arredo umanistico di Santa Maria del Fiore," in *Filippo Brunelleschi: La sua opera e il suo tempo* (Florence, 1980), 2:603–23, here 604. In 1431, the "corpus veteris ecclesiae" is differentiated from the "novi edificii" (Saalman, *Cupola*, 270). So also in 1435, the "ecclesiam veterem" is distinguished from the "opus novum" (Poggi, *Il Duomo*, doc. 2264). Manetti's description of the spatial organization, then, projects that understanding of the cathedral's design held by the Opera del Duomo and probably widely shared by Florentines of the time. Timothy Verdon, who seems to be the first to have seen the importance of this terminology, thought it meant that the cathedral was perceived as comprised of two buildings, the nave and octagon: T. Verdon, "'Struttura sì grande, erta sopra e'cieli': La cupola e la città nel 1400," in *Alla riscoperta di Piazza del Duomo di Firenze. 4. La cupola di Santa Maria del Fiore*, ed. idem (Florence, 1995), 9–32, here 15.

cross: Manetti means that if the east end had four tribunes around the crossing and were therefore perfectly centralized, it would be a rotonda; but lacking the western arm it is wider on the transverse than on the longitudinal axis.

11. huge stone block: The image of the church as wrought from a single block dressed by God rather than built up from many blocks by human hands may be an elaboration of Augustine's metaphor for the temple as made of "living stones" (cf. 1 Peter 2:5), meaning the faithful, so bonded by charity as to create a single stone from many: *Enarratio in psalmum xxxix*, PL 36.433; ed. E. Dekkers and J. Fraipont, CCSL 38 (Turnhout, 1990), 424. Alternatively, Manetti may be paraphrasing the description of the tower of faith in the *Shepherd of Hermas* 9.9.4: "it was so built, as if it were all one stone, without a single joint in it, and the stone appeared as if it had been hewn out of rock, for it seemed to me to be a single stone."

not made by humans: Manetti returns to this theme in his *On the Dignity of Man* almost twenty years later: "After that first, new and rude creation of the world, everything seems to have been discovered, constructed, and completed by us out of some singular and outstanding acuteness of the human mind. For those things are ours, that is, they are human, which are seen to be produced by men: all homes, all towns, all cities, finally all buildings in the world, which certainly are so many and of such a nature that they ought rather to be regarded as the works of angels than of men" (3.20). Compare with Manetti's description of the Temple of Solomon, in which the stones were so carefully joined that they seemed "joined by a kind of natural harmony, as is said in myths about the walls of Troy, rather than by any contrivance of tools" in *De illustribus longaevis*, Bib. Vat., MS. Pal. lat. 1603, fol. 72v.

round windows: Florence Cathedral is unusual in possessing nineteen oculi: three on the facade, eight in the tambour of the dome, and eight in the upper part of the nave. Whether "occhi" (round windows) or "fenestre" (oblong, vertical ones) should be in the upper part of the nave had been debated between 1364 and 1367: Saalman, *Cupola*, 44. Although we see "fenestre" in Andrea da Firenze's depiction of the Cathedral in the Spanish Chapel of 1365, an alternative opinion, of 1364, argued that "occhi" would provide more light on the walls of the nave vaults. The question came to committee vote in May of 1367, with eight votes in support of "fenestre" and five for "occhi." But the votes for "fenestre" were conditional on (1) their form being congruent with the structure of the church; (2) their not weakening its fabric; and (3) it being possible to install them without destroying anything except the "occhi" that had already been made: C. Guasti, *La Cupola di Santa Maria del Fiore* (Florence, 1857), doc. 170 (188). The Florentine decision, with its cautions about weakening the wall structure by installing "fenestre," suggests at least that these were seen as more dangerous for the wall than "occhi." Six months later a definitive model of the Cathedral was approved: evidently the conditions of the May vote had not been met, since the building has "occhi": Guasti, *La Cupola*, doc. 193 (208).

The question of "occhi" providing light for the interior was debated again in relation to Brunelleschi's dome. Between 1410 and 1413 the round windows of the drum were built, and Brunelleschi's dome foresaw no additional sources of light except for the central oculus over the cathedral's crossing. A fascinating drawing of 1425 by Giovanni Gherardo da Prato (now in the Archivio di Stato di Firenze) analyzed the consequences of Brunelleschi's design. See F. Gurrieri, *The Cathedral of Santa Maria del Fiore* (Florence, 1994), 1:88, fig. 3. His cross-section of the crossing from pavement to oculus is entirely dark, except for a yellow oculus in the drum, and the light from it is paler yellow lower down on the wall opposite. An even fainter circle of light appears in the upper part of the drum. Next to the drawing Giovanni wrote:

> The function of this eye is that the sun enters through it and is not blocked by glass, but shall hit the opposite part of the pilasters and give light by reflection. Now everybody should consider whether that reflection can be strong enough to go up more than seventy braccia [the height of the dome].

His own common sense, he says, supported by the treatise *De speculis et in prospectivis*, tell him that the dome will be not only dark, but "dim and gloomy." In his opinion, twenty-four windows should have been built on the cornice, by which he must mean the ring of masonry between the drum and cupola proper. Essential to his discussion, and Manetti's, although never actually mentioned by them, is the question of splay. For round windows are set at the interior edge of the wall thickness, with splay towards the exterior, whereas vertical windows are set at the center or towards the exterior, with splay on the interior. This is the sense of Manetti's comment (*Life*, 59) that whereas Solomon's Temple had "oblique" windows (that is, wider on the interior; see Commentary on the *Life*, 59), St. Peter's would have "transverse and orbicular" ones. Evidently, windows placed nearer the outer edge of the wall received more direct light which then illuminated the interior along the splay and thus over a greater area. Round windows, recessed in the wall thickness, received less light. Moreover, as Gherardo's drawing indicates, light from a round window falls as a circle on the interior and illuminates only as much area as the diameter of the window itself. Giovanni seems to have thought of the light from a round window as a kind of spotlight which hit the upper part of the wall and bounced upward. This may also explain why, in 1364, it was believed that round windows would illuminate the vaults. Whereas round windows provide spots of light on the walls and reflect upwards, vertical windows with interior splays create a more diffused radiance reaching to the pavement. This understanding is clear in Rhabanus Maurus's ninth-century Commentary on 3 Kings, where we learn that through windows ("fenestrae"), light fills the deepest recesses of the temple and that "oblique windows" are preferred because they permit everyone in the building to receive this light: PL 109.143. The choice of window shape, then, involved choices about the type, intensity, direction, diffusion, and spectator experience of light.

upper circuit: Manetti means the oculus windows in the drum of the dome and perhaps also those in the nave clerestory. On round windows see Chapter 8.

places: For Manetti's vocabulary of space and place, see Chapter 5.

specimen of divine glory: The image of a crown of lights around the central light of the dome's oculus evokes Canto 10 of Dante's *Paradiso* where the sun, ringed with a rotating crown of lights, provides the poet insight into the divine being.

peak of the east end: Manetti refers to the dome as the "vertex testudinis," precisely the same as in his description of the projected dome of St. Peter's in the *Life* at 45, where the amplification of the inset window into a lantern is made explicit.

huge round window: That is, the oculus at the top, which is actually octagonal. In 1436 the lantern, which reduced the amount of light through this opening, had not yet been begun.

12. Seven Wonders: See *Life*, 55–56 and Chapter 9.

their armory: Manetti paraphrases Valerius Maximus, *Memorable Doings and Sayings*, 8. Compare *Life*, 53 and Chapter 9.

expenses: See Chapter 8 for the relation between cost and the virtue of magnificence.

bewilderment: For the psychology of "wonder" see Chapter 8.

13. pavement: A brick pavement for the new church is first documented in June of 1407; this first campaign, which continued until 1410, was concerned only with the nave. Since the documents include payments for "macigno" (local sandstone) as well as bricks, it may be that quadrants of brick were bordered by strips of grey stone, as was already the case in the pavement of the Piazza della Signoria (Poggi, *Il Duomo*, docs. 2251, 2252, 2253, 2254, 2255, 2256). Manetti refers here to a second campaign, probably for the octagon beneath the dome and, less surely, for the chapels, began on 28 May 1433 and continued until 10 January 1436 (1435 Florentine style): Poggi, *Il Duomo*, docs. 2260, 2265, 2268, 2267. Not until April of 1439, however, was the building entirely paved (Poggi, *Il Duomo*, doc. 2269).

upper places: The location is unclear. For Manetti's use of *superius* and *inferius* see Chapter 5. Since in this case it is linked to a discussion of the east end pavement, he may mean that the floor of that area was strewn with branches and flowers. Alternatively, if "superiora" refers to elevation, he means that bouquets or garlands were hung from the upper parts of the building, perhaps the catwalk (*ballatoio*) that runs below the windows.

boughs: There is a payment of 30 April for laurel and myrtle used at the consecration (Poggi, *Il Duomo*, doc. 2384).

14. chambers: "dietas", a Greek loanword favored by Manetti (cf. 9 above, also translated "chambers"), here referring to the compartments in the naves formed by the vaulting; later in the account, at 32, he applies the same term to the compartments under the high altar where the relics were deposited.

insignia: On 12 January 1435 (Florentine style), the *capomaestro* was ordered to remove all standards and banners hanging in the three naves of the church and reinstall them so that they faced the longitudinal axis in the central nave: at the same time he was to clean the dust from the naves (Poggi, *Il Duomo*, doc. 2190). On 30 January, the *capomaestro* was told to take the banners that were near the main altar and reinstall them in the same way (Poggi, *Il Duomo*, doc. 2191). Among these must have been insignia of the city of Florence (the lily); of the Florentine people (the cross); of the Signoria (the motto "libertas"); of the Opera del Duomo (the Agnus Dei); and of the union of Florence and Fiesole.

exact figure: The reader needs to imagine hangings on the upper walls of the crossing and tribunes which visually enhanced the spectator's perception of the complex shape of that space.

papal arms: There are payments to the painter Piero Chelini for painting a schudo "in tre faccie" with the arms of Eugenius IV (Poggi, *Il Duomo*, docs. 2385, 2386).

15. its own altar: In November of 1435 Brunelleschi and Ghiberti had been commissioned to provide altars for the tribune chapels (Poggi, *Il Duomo*, doc. 1065). On 3 February, with little more than a month until the consecration, Antonio Manetti and Giovanni di Lorenzo were paid for wooden altars ("altaretti") and predellas; Giovanni received a final payment on 30 April and Antonio on 6 June: Poggi, *Il Duomo*, docs. 1066, 1067, 1068. These provided altars for fourteen of the fifteen tribune chapels. The remaining and easternmost chapel, dedicated to San Zenobio, had received an altar commissioned in 1431 (Poggi, *Il Duomo*, doc. 900). Ghiberti's bronze reliquary urn for the remains of San Zenobio, commissioned in 1432, was not finished until 1442 (Poggi, *Il Duomo*, doc. 908). The wooden altars were intended to be temporary, as is clear from contracts given for marble altars for the chapels beginning in 1439. The dedications of the chapels were established in the same years, and frescoes depicting their titular saints were executed on the chapels' walls in 1439–1440: Poggi, *Il Duomo*, docs. 1075, 1082–1084, 1086.

altar . . . in the middle: On the placement and dimensions of the altar, see above at 5 and Poggi, *Il Duomo*, docs. 1172–1185.

chased work: "toreumata", a loanword from Greek, means chased, embossed, or pierced metal vessels; it may refer to censers, which are pierced, or other highly worked furnishings — ciboria, patens, vases, reliquaries, monstrances, and the like.

papal rose: The rose had been delivered by Angelo da Venezia, Bishop of Palermo, on 18 March. Made by Rinaldo Ghini, it weighed 14 ounces and 9 grams: Poggi, *Il Duomo*, doc. 2377. For the earlier history of the papal rose, see A. Paravicini Bagliani, *Le Chiave e la tiara. Immagini e simboli del papato medievale* (Rome, 1998); and E. Cornides, *Rose und Schwert im päpstlichen Zeremoniell: Von den Anfängen bis zum Pontifikat Gregors XIII* (Vienna, 1967).

In 1419 Martin V had also given the city a rose as a sign of his benevolence and gratitude for his reception by the people of Florence while, like Eugenius, he was staying in Santa Maria Novella. The occasion had also been the celebration of the Feast of the Annunciation.

The musical program for the consecration Mass highlights the papal rose in both the Dufay motet for the introit, and the chanted sequence (see Commentary at 26). In these, the connection among the rose, the Virgin, and the city is explicit.

Manetti does not mention the lead inscription for the altar ordered in February but perhaps not executed until after the consecration. Poggi: *Il Duomo*, docs. 2370 and 2371.

pearl solitaires: see below, 23.

the very circuit . . . the entire circuit: A model for the new choir had been presented by Brunelleschi the previous November, but work on this would not begin until 1437 (see Commentary at 5). Evidently a temporary raised wooden platform had been installed for the consecration ceremony. For the cloth on the papal throne, see Commentary at 25.

16. platform: "tabulatum", the same word Manetti used for the raised wooden platform under the dome. Elsewhere he uses this word to mean "floor" or "flooring".

Sublician Bridge: By "Sublician Bridge" Manetti recalls the bridge of that name in Rome, probably destroyed in the fifth century A.D. and known to him through literary sources (Livy, 1.37; 1.33; 2.10; 5.40.7; Seneca, *Vita beata*, 25.1; Pliny, *NH*, 36.15.23; Tacitus, *Histories*, 1.86; Varro, *Lingua Latina*, 5.83, 6.44; Plutarch, *Numa*, 9.2–3): cf. also below, 17. He refers to the bridge either because it, like the one in Florence, was all of wood (in fact it was forbidden to use metal in the Sublician Bridge for religious reasons), or because of its other religious associations. It was under the direct care of the Pontifex Maximus. Since the word "pontifex" (= "pontiff"), which means "bridge-builder", is also a title of the pope, it is especially appropriate that such a bridge was built for the pope to walk on.

magnificently and wonderfully: The "ponte" designed by Brunelleschi was executed by carpenters hired on 9 March (Poggi, *Il Duomo*, doc. 2373). The impact of the *ponte* is clear from other contemporary documents. On 11 August it was decided to commission two inscriptions commemorating the consecration (Poggi, *Il Duomo*, doc. 2388). The two epitaphs were composed. Leonardo Bruni's, still in the cathedral to the left of the north sacristy, reads:

> Because of the unique magnificence of the city and the temple, Pope Eugenius IV, with every solemnity added, dedicated [this church] on 25 March 1436. For the sake of this dedication, a wooden bridge was made with unique munificence and ornament from the church of Santa Maria Novella, where the pope was residing, all the way to this church. On it the pope processed with his cardinals, bishops, and the rest of his court in pontifical garb. A multitude of people gathered to watch so that the overflowing crowd would have blocked the streets had he not been able to pass readily on the bridge.

The other inscription was composed by Andrea di Domenico Fiocchi, a canon of the Cathedral, prior of SS. Apostoli and apostolic secretary to Eugenius IV and, later, to Nicholas V:

> This temple under the title of Santa Maria del Fiore the Lord Pope Eugenius IV dedicated March 25, in the year 1436 of the Lord's Incarnation. To honor him, he came here on a wooden bridge opulently draped, covered, and adorned, from the church of Santa Maria Novella, where he was residing, with papal splendor and entourage, amid the highest devotion and crowd of people.

Both Latin texts are printed in Poggi, *Il Duomo*, doc. 2390 of 1439.

The description of the *ponte* also occupies most of Leonardo Bruni's description of the consecration ceremony in his *Rerum suo tempore gestarum commentarius*, *RIS* 19.3: 423–58, here 453; and Vespasiano begins his account with the *ponte* (*Vite*, 1:15). It is also prominent in St. Antoninus's *Chronicorum opus*, 527. The same point about security is made by Feo Belcari, who says the *ponte* had been provided "to escape the clamor and the crowd" since more than 200,000 people had come into the city from the countryside: in Saalman, *Cupola*, 275.

the entire way: The platform ran from the door of Santa Maria Novella past Santa Maria Maggiore up to the Baptistery, as Vespasiano tells us (*Vite*, 1:15). St. Antoninus agrees that it terminated at the Baptistery, but implies that another short stretch of it went from the Baptistery to the cathedral (*Chronicorum opus*, 10.6 [527]). Giovanni Cambi says the *ponte* went from the stairs of Santa Maria Novella to the stairs of the cathedral, passing through the middle of the Baptistery. He adds that another stretch of it went from the stairs of the cathedral up to the main altar (*Istoria*, 207).

elevated: For the construction of the *ponte*, see Poggi, *Il Duomo*, doc. 2372; it was 2 braccia high and 4 wide. Feo Belcari stated the height accurately, and Giovanni di Ser Cambi and Leonardo Bruni accurately reported its width: Saalman, *Cupola*, 275; Cambi, *Istoria*, 207; Bruni, *Commentarius*, 453; but to others it seemed higher. Antoninus says it was 4 braccia high and that the columnar supports were 7 braccia high (*Chronicorum opus*, 10.6 [527]). Cino Rinuccini said it was 3 braccia high: Filippo di Cino Rinuccini, *Ricordi storici dal 1282 al 1460*, ed. G. Aiazzi (Florence, 1840), 71.

17. Sublician columns: "Sublicius" (cf. above, 16) means "pile"; Manetti, who knows only the word "columna" for "support," attempts with this adjective to describe the actual structural members.

canopies: "aulea": see Horace, *Sat.*, 2.8.54. This is clearly a covered walkway. The classicizing terminology here evokes classical precedents such as the silk awning erected by Julius Caesar for his triumph in 46 B.C., which ran from his residence on the Via Sacra across the whole Roman Forum and up the Capitoline to the Temple of Jupiter Optimus Maximus: Pliny, *NH*, 19.23.

Bruni says that there were awnings on top of the supports:

> The width of the *ponte* was about four braccia, and wooden footings supported the crossbeams. On top of these were the platforms. From the sides, columns, spaced at even intervals, rose to a height of seven feet. These were attached to the beams of the pavement and were bound to more slender beams at its maximum height. On top of these were awnings with which the entire *ponte* was covered, with 'papilionibus' [fringes?] hanging from both sides; the pavement was furnished from each side with draperies all the way to the area where the people were. *(Commentarius*, 453.)

Cambi tells us that it was covered with "panni rovesci turchini, e bianchi," which were the colors of Eugenius IV (*Istoria*, 208). According to Vespasiano, the coverings were "azurri et bianchi" (*Vite* 1:15): in both cases, then, a bright azure or turquoise blue and white.

18. pinnacle: "cumulus": see Cicero, *Pro Roscio Amer.*, 3.8.

19. Florentine presidents . . . called priors: Manetti means the eight priors of the Signoria for March and April of 1436 (1435–1436 Florentine style).

In order to interpret Manetti's Latinized references to the Florentine bureaucracy we can compare accounts of other state processions. Accounts of the arrival in Florence of Martin V (1419) and Pius II (1459) say that the Captains of the Guelf party went to greet them and escorted them to where the Signori waited. When Eugenius left Florence in April of 1436 he was escorted by the Signori, the Collegi, the Sei di Mercatantìa, and the Uffiziali di Monte. Eugenius, mounted, was accompanied by the Gonfaloniere on one side and the Proposto on the other (Corazza, *Diario*, 77). When the Byzantine emperor arrived in 1438 he was met by the Signori, Collegi, Capitani di Parte Guelfa, Dieci di Balìa, the eight Officiali di Monte, the Sei di Mercatantìa, and representatives of the seven major Arti (Corazza, *Diario*, 81). From these examples it seems that the protocol for such processions was not firmly fixed and that the consecration procession departed from that of other state ceremonies. It may have been closer to that for religious ceremonies; in a procession for Corpus Christi in 1425, the Priors marched first, preceded only by the Gonfaloniere di Giustizia. In 1475 the Signoria commissioned the herald, Francesco Filarete, to create a *libro ceremoniale*, which he began by recording how state ceremonies had been conducted since the entrance of Frederick III in 1450; thus there may not have been a standard processional order in 1436. See *Il libro ceremoniale of the Florentine Republic by Francesco Filarete and Angelo Manfredi*, ed. R. Trexler (Geneva, 1978), 11, 75; S. Mantini, *Lo spazio sacro della Firenze medicea: Trasformazioni urbane e cerimoniali pubblici tra Quattrocento e Cinquecento* (Florence, 1995), 84–85, 117.

a huge line: "ordo", a line, but with connotations of hierarchical ranking.

paraders: "pompae", a non-classical usage in the plural; by metonymy refers to the persons who made up the parade.

catalogued: Manetti means that he will not describe the secular parade separately but will include it in his description of the pontifical parade since the two groups, meeting at Santa Maria Novella, proceeded together to the Cathedral.

Chroniclers give the time for the start of the procession as when Eugenius IV appeared: Rinuccini, "in sulla terza" (*Ricordi*, 71); Cambi, "insulle 13. hore" (*Istoria*, 207); Feo Belcari, "in sul ora della terza," in Saalman, *Cupola*, 275. Rinuccini and Belcari are probably referring to the canonical hour of tierce, about 8:00 A.M.; Cambi seems mistaken in giving the time as 1:00 P.M., not only because it conflicts with other testimony but also because he later says that the service of consecration lasted from 9:00 A.M. to 2:00 P.M., which would make sense if the procession took an hour (*Istoria*, 209). We need to remember that Cambi speaks in his own voice in the chronicle from about 1480 on and that for events earlier than this he is copying (or miscopying) earlier authors.

20. trumpeters . . . flautists: There is a payment of 26 March to a horn player and a flute player for proclaiming the consecration of the cathedral (Poggi, *Il Duomo*, doc. 2380). However, the group Manetti describes may have been the *Trombadori* — six large trumpets, one small trumpet, a drum, and a *cenemella* — a group present at all public ceremonies as official representatives of the Florentine commune; together with the *Pifferi*, who played reed instruments such as the bagpipe, tenor shawm, and cornet. See T. McGee, "Dinner Music for the Florentine Signoria, 1350–1450," *Speculum* 74 (1999): 95–114, here 101.

lute: "fides": any stringed instrument; we supply "lute" on the basis of the instruments represented by Luca della Robbia in his *cantoria* of about the same date.

praetors: By "praetors" does Manetti mean the captains of the Guelf party?

presidents: He means the Priors of the Signoria.

intermingled: This must mean that the Signoria and the other urban magistrates did not march as distinct groups, but according to some other protocol of rank. The Capitano del Popolo must have participated in the consecration, as well as representatives of the guilds, but perhaps they were not part of the procession. The account of Francesco Giovanni, who marched in the procession, in fact mentions only the Priors and describes an entirely different order from Manetti's. In his version, the lay dignitaries marched between archbishops in front and cardinals behind: van Eck, "Manetti on Architecture," 454, n. 15. Manetti places all the religious hierarchy together and behind (and therefore above in importance) all the lay representatives. Cambi gives yet another order, with Florentine citizens leading the procession, followed by doctors and knights, with the magistrates bringing up the rear of the Florentine representation (*Istoria*, 208).

The ambassadors included those from the emperor, from the king of France, the king of Aragon, the duke of Milan, and the commune of Venice and of Genoa (Cambi, *Istoria*, 208).

Undoubtedly banners or standards were also carried in procession, as one sees for example in the representation of a St. John's day procession on a cassone, now in the Bargello, by Jacopo Franchi, but Manetti omits them, having finished with his description of decorations: Bergstein, "Marian Politics," 684.
21. far more wondrous: Papal ceremony was far more professional than its civic counterpart at this date. At Eugenius's death, for example, five masters of ceremony were on the payroll: G. Bourgin, "La 'famiglia' pontificia sotto Eugenio IV," *Archivio della Società romana di Storia Patria* 27 (1904): 205–24, here 223. Nonetheless, the participants in the procession for the consecration did not follow the order we know for a procession through a city: Dykmans, *L'oeuvre*, 110.
22. his own emblem: "sua quadam religione." Could this be some sort of religious object as in Cicero, *Verr.* 2.4.43 and Vergil, *Aeneid*, 2.151, and thus crosses or icons? Perhaps it refer to badges of office, or, even "sashes" from the root meaning of *re-ligere* "to tie back."

preceded the others: At the head of the papal parade must have been a crucifer, as Cambi states (*Istoria*, 207), but Manetti does not mention him.

ministers: The various groups of the papal household are not distinguished from one another in other sources. Vespasiano just says "la corte di Roma parata secondo la loro degnità" (*Vite*, 1:15); Cambi mentions only "prelates" in the papal part of the procession; Feo Belcari mentions only cardinals and patriarchs. Vespasiano says apostolic subdeacons accompanied the bishops, cardinals, cardinal bishops, and the pope; if so, they may have carried the epistle and gospel.

prelates: In addition to the Curial officials and assistants and the episcopal hierarchy, it is odd that Manetti does not mention the local clergy, abbots of the great monasteries, or priors of the various Florentine convents. It seems probable that they were included in the procession; the sequence for the Consecration Mass in the great Edili Gradual (cf. below), in fact, explicitly places friars, pastors, and abbots on the *ponte*; and Eugenius, so careful to reform the various religious houses of the city, would hardly have been likely to pass them by. On the sequence, see C. Wright, "A Sequence for the Dedication of the Cathedral of Florence: Dufay's (?) *Nuper almos rose flores*," in *Atti del VII centenario*, 3. *'Cantate Domino'. Musica per il Duomo di Firenze*, ed. Verdon and Innocenti, 55–65. Their omission here may be one more indication of Manetti's selectivity to emphasize papal predominance.

Even more striking is the omission of the archbishop of Florence and the cathedral canons. Bishop Amerigo Corsini had died the previous March and Eugenius had appointed Giovanni Vitelleschi archbishop the following October. Vitelleschi, a condottiere, had also been appointed Prefect of Rome and was likely on campaign outside Florence; the diocese seems to have been run by an Apostolic Administrator, Tommaso Paruta, bishop of Recanati and Macerata: M. Tubbini, "Il Collegio Eugeniano e il Concilio del 1439," in *Firenze e il Concilio del*

1439, ed. P. Viti (Florence, 1994), 175–89, here 180–81. Vitelleschi was also absent from the blessing of the cupola six months later on 30 August 1436; substituting for him was Bishop Benozzo Federighi of Fiesole, senior suffragan bishop (Saalman, *Cupola*, 134). In fact, Vitelleschi made his entrance into Florence only on 25 April 1437 (Corazza, *Diario*, 78).

bishops: Vespasiano says they wore "boccaccino bianco" (*Vite*, 1:15). Since forty-four prelates marched in processional copes and miters, and since seven were cardinals and six were archbishops (Cambi, *Istoria*, 208), thirty-one must have been bishops or patriarchs. Among the bishops must have been Angelo da Venezia, Bishop of Parenzo, who had brought the rose to the cathedral; Benozzo Federighi, Bishop of Fiesole; and the aforementioned Tommaso Paruta, Bishop of Recanati and Apostolic Administrator of Florence.

patriarchs: There were three Latin patriarchs in 1436: Blasio (or Biagio) Molino, Patriarch of Jerusalem; Ludovicus de Teck, Patriarch of Aquileia; and Marco Condulmer, Patriarch of Grado (this patriarchate will be transferred to Venice in 1451): Constantinople and Antioch had no Latin patriarch at the time. Vitelleschi will be appointed Patriarch of Alexandria in 1437. Of these, only one, Biagio Molino, is identified as present in contemporary sources (Feo Belcari in Saalman, *Cupola*, 276). See C. Eubel, *Hierarchia Catholica medii aevi* (Monastir, 1914).

cardinals: There were seven cardinals in the procession (Cambi, *Istoria*, 208). Eubel lists seventeen cardinals under Eugenius, not counting Louis Allemand whose title the pope had revoked. Ten, therefore, were absent.

Of the seventeen, five were cardinal bishops, whose duties would have been primarily curial: Pietro de Fuxo, O.F.M. (Albano); Antonio Correr (as cardinal bishop of Ostia, the dean of the college); Branda Castiglioni (Porto et Santa Rufina); Hugo de Lusignano (Praeneste); and Giordano Orsini (Sabina); these five had all been created cardinals by Martin V, but were promoted by Eugenius on 14 May 1431, three days after his coronation.

In Francesco d'Antonio del Chierico's representation of the ceremony in the Gradual known as Bibl. Laur. MS. Edili 151, fol. 7v, the cardinals are not vested, as are the bishops and archbishops, in copes and miters, but rather in the distinctive scarlet robes and hats of their dignity. However, this miniature was painted perhaps as late as 1477, and Feo Belcari, as well as Vespasiano, said the pope was accompanied by cardinals vested and mitred in white: Belcari in Saalman, *Cupola*, 276; Vespasiano, *Vite*, 1:15.

Because Venice's church of San Marco was well known, our sources sometimes confuse the Cardinal of Venice, Francesco Condulmer (ca. 1410–1453), Eugenius's nephew, chamberlain, and (after 1437) papal pronotary and vice-chancellor, with the titular Cardinal of San Marco in Rome, Agnolotto degli Foschi (Cambi, *Istoria*, 209; Saalman, *Cupola*, 276). It was degli Foschi, not Condulmer, who said the Consecration Mass. Cardinal Giordano Orsini (Rinuccini is mistaken in his identification of him as *Giuliano* Orsini [*Ricordi*, 71]), who was *summo penitenziere*, had done all the preparations for the ceremony, and later anointed the walls of the church. Other likely participants would be Niccolò Albergati, Cardinal of Sta. Croce in Gerusalemme, who had arrived in Florence from Basle in 1434 together with Giovanni Cervantes, Cardinal of S. Pietro in Vincoli; Domenico Capranica, Cardinal of Sta. Maria in Via Lata who had arrived in April of 1435; Branda Castiglione, Cardinal of S. Clemente, arrived in June of that year; Giovanni di Rupescissa, vice chancellor and Cardinal of S. Lorenzo in Lucina, and Prospero Colonna, Cardinal of S. Giorgio, both of whom had come to Florence in December of 1435. Giovanni Casanova, Cardinal of San Sisto, and Lucido de'Conti, Cardinal of Sta. Maria in Cosmedin, had joined Eugenius in Florence in 1434, but Casanova had died on 1 March: C. Bianca, "I Cardinali al Concilio di Firenze," in *Firenze e il Concilio del 1439*, ed. Viti, 147–73, here 162–66. Corazza tells us that when Eugenius left Florence less than a month later he was accompanied by six cardinals: Piacenza, Tricarico, San Marco (degli Foschi), Conti (Lucido de'Conti), Colonna (Prospero Colonna), and the nephew *camerlengo* (Condulmer): *Diario*, 77. Thus we can identify five of the seven cardinals who processed as degli Foschi, de'Conti, Colonna, Orsini, and Condulmer. The procession did not include Antonio Casini, the Cardinal of San Marcello, who met the pope at the cathedral (Saalman, *Cupola*, 276). Casini, appointed bishop of Siena and then transferred to Bologna (later Grosseto), was made cardinal by Martin V in 1426 and died at Florence 1439 (Vespasiano, *Vite*, 1:203).

Some evidence suggests that the initial rites of aspersion, entrance, and writing the Greek and Latin alphabets on the pavement had been carried out before Eugenius arrived, or at least were not performed by him. First, Manetti tells us what the pope did — that is, consecrate the altar. Next, the absence of mention of any singers or cathedral canons and clergy in the procession as well as the absence of some important Florentine magistrates, notably the representatives of the guilds, can be taken to mean that they were engaged at the cathedral with these preparatory rites. The illustration in MS. Edili 151 supports this since it shows Eugenius being met by a cardinal and magistrates at the threshold of the church, in the doorway of which are the choristers. Finally, since the *ponte* ended at the steps of the cathedral, the three circuits around the church with its doors shut would have had to have been done at pavement level, a security risk for the pope.

23. two apostles: Presumably Giordano Orsini, who performed the consecration ceremony or at least anointed the walls, and Agnolotto degli Foschi, who said the Mass. Manetti does not mention it, but since Tommaso Parentucelli, the future Nicholas V, had been made Apostolic Subdeacon by Eugenius in Florence, he may have carried the cross before him in the procession, ministered to him during the consecration, and read the epistle (Vespasiano, *Vite*, 1:49). The notion that the College of Cardinals was founded by Christ in the persons of the apostles was widely discussed in the early fifteenth century. Lapo da Castiglionchio, for instance, refers to the cardinals "qui apostolorum explent ordinem" in *De curiae commodis dialogus*, 3.22: Celenza, *Renaissance Humanism and the Papal Curia*, 131.

God Himself: Lest this seem impious, Honorius of Autun specified that "the dedication of a church is the consummation of a marriage between the Church and Christ. The bishop who consecrates it is Christ who has taken the church as his bride": *Gemma animae* 150, PL 172.590. The tradition is patristic: already in A.D. 115, Ignatius spoke of the bishop as "enthroned as the type of God, and the presbyters as the type of the college of the apostles" ("Epistle to the Magnesians," 6.1 in Dix, *The Shape of the Liturgy*, 28). Since the pope is God's true vicar, and just as human ambassadors will embody in their resplendence the glory of earthly monarchs to the point that they may be mistaken for them, so the pope makes God's presence visible. For discussion of the pope as Vicar of Christ, sharing in divine nature, see Chapters 8 and 9.

His toga: Manetti's romanizing "toga" was the processional cope given to Eugenius by the Florentines on his entrance into the city on 23 June 1434. It was made of "chermixi brocchato d'oro" and cost more than 300 florins (Cambi, *Istoria*, 191).

its train: Although Manetti says it was carried by a prelate, Cambi says it was carried by the emperor's ambassador on the way to the cathedral and that the new papal knight, Giuliano Davanzati, carried the papal train on the pope's return to Santa Maria Novella (*Istoria*, 208–10).

pontifical miter: The triple-crowned papal tiara, also used as a decorative motif in the adornment of the cathedral. The tiara, symbol of the pope's universal power, had replaced the episcopal miter in the Middle Ages and had acquired its definitive three-tiered form by the fourteenth century. Eugenius did not wear the tiara which Ghiberti made for him to celebrate the Union between the Greek and Latin Churches in 1439 and which Ghiberti records in his *Commentarii,* ed. L. Bartoli (Florence, 1998), 94. See also R. Krautheimer, *Lorenzo Ghiberti* (Princeton, 1956), 13; A. Bernareggi, "La tiara pontificia: note di arte liturgica," *Arte cristiana* 11 (1923): 34–50, here 44.

He might have worn the so-called tiara of San Silvestro which Pierre de Foix had acquired from Benedict XIII in 1429 and later gave to Eugenius. It was subsequently used for the coronation of Nicholas V: A. Manfredi, "Da Avignone a Roma. Codici liturgici per la capella papale," in *Liturgia in figura. Codici liturgici rinascimentali della Biblioteca Apostolica Vaticana*, ed. G. Morello and S. Maddalo (Vatican City, 1994), 51–58, here 56. On the symbolism of the papal tiara, see M. Miglio, "'Vidi tiaram Pauli papae secundi'," in idem, *Storiografia pontificia del Quattrocento*, 140; and P. Prodi, *The Papal Prince*, 46.

Compare with Manetti's account of Nicholas's vestments in the *Life* at 8 and our note on it in the Commentary.

pearl solitaires: Isidore of Seville defined "uniones" as a type of pearl: "ex quibus margaritis quidam uniones vocantur, aptum nomen habentes, quod tantum unus, numquam duo vel plures simul reperiantur": *Etymol.*, 16.10. Cf. above, 15 (decorated reliquaries).

unable to look: This sentence parallels the one which concludes Manetti's discussion of the physical church. Both point to magnificence, shown in enormous cost and recognized by the stupefaction of the spectators. See the discussion of magnificence in Chapter 8.

24. church militant: For the Church Militant and Church Triumphant, themes prominent in Manetti's thought, see Chapters 8 and 9. Compare this passage with the analogous one in *Life*, 8. There is another specific association with Eugenius, whose pontificate was vexed with wars in Italy: Guillaume Dufay may have written the motet "Ecclesiae militantis" for his consecration as pope on 11 March 1431 (see further discussion at 26).

wonderful, unbelievable parades: This is clarified by a later passage in Matteo Palmieri:

> Religion makes the city more magnificent when it is solemnly celebrated with admirable observance. This requires the venerable authority of self-controlled priests, more than others helpful and good, and vestments and sacred ornaments of various purples, precious and splendid with gems and gold, so that they appear not only magnificent but as far as is humanly possible celestial and divine. Ecclesiastical solemnities and sacred ceremonies and all priestly displays are worthy of as much reverence as can be observed by mortals. (*Della vita civile*, ed. F. Battaglia [Bologna, 1944], 4:195.)

25. entering the basilica: Manetti omits the rites outside the church and some of the preliminary rites inside. See Commentary at *22* and our analysis of the liturgy in Chapter 2.

east end's middle space: "testudinei soli," i.e. "testudinated platform"; Manetti clearly does not restrict "testudo" to the great dome only; he means the ground area, or the part of the building platform, covered by the domical vaults of the tribunes and crossing, and therefore the east end, as opposed to the nave. Its middle space is, of course, the space beneath Brunelleschi's dome where the choir was. See Commentary at 5.

regally adorned: Vespasiano says that the pontifical throne was covered in "damaschino bianco a oro" (*Vite*, 1:15). There is a payment of 20 April 1436 of 13 gold florins for 8 braccia of "rosato levato da loro" [sic] supplied by Nicholaio di Ugho degli Alessandri, "ritagliatore" to adorn the pope's throne (Poggi, *Duomo*, doc. 2383).

26. sat in unison: "consederunt." "Consedere" is not a classical usage (cf. Tobit 11:12 Vulgate), although there is an instance in Valerius Maximus: "in eo atrio consedisse in quo . . ." (5.8) in the same sentence which formed Manetti's understanding of the term "atrium" (see Chapter 6). Manetti seems to be describing the liturgical action of those located on the raised platform of the choir rising and sitting as the pope rises and sits. His choice of language evokes the Greek term for the place where clerics sit, the "synthronon". The peculiarity of Manetti's account lies in that it is told almost exclusively in terms of standing and sitting rather than as a narrative of the content of the liturgy.

Seats for the Captains of the Guelf Party and for the Consuls of the Wool Guild at the consecration were paid for on 22 February (Poggi, *Duomo*, doc. 2369). See Commentary at 22 for the question of whether they also processed from Sta. Maria Novella. Vespasiano tells us that at the foot of the altar was a platform with benches for the cardinals and prelates. The papal throne was on the gospel (spectators' left) side; the singers on the epistle (right) side. Around the pope was the College of Cardinals and on the other side bishops, archbishops, prelates, and ambassadors, presumably including Manetti and Acciaiuoli (*Vite*, 1:15).

standard-bearer of justice: The Gonfaloniere di Giustizia was Giuliano Davanzati (1390–1446), a Medici supporter. Davanzati had been part of the official Florentine delegation in October 1434 to congratulate Sigismund I on his ascent to the imperial throne: Vespasiano, *Vite* 2:322, n. 2; and *Dizionario biografico degli italiani*, s.v.

a cardinal: It is difficult to piece together from Manetti's account which cardinals performed what parts of the liturgy. He distinguishes here between one cardinal who, vested for Mass, celebrated at the altar and another (at 31) who anointed the walls of the church. Yet a third, identified in the sources as the Cardinal of Venice (Francesco Condulmer) or the Cardinal of San Marco (Agnolotto degli Foschi) but surely the latter, said the first Mass after Eugenius consecrated the altar (32–33). Since other contemporary accounts tell us that Giordano Orsini anointed the walls he must be the "other" cardinal Manetti mentions at 31 and therefore not the one intended here. But if, as other accounts have it, Orsini performed all the consecration liturgy, this first cardinal, celebrating Mass, must have been performing some other liturgy. This Mass, of course, could not have been said on the altar which Eugenius had not yet consecrated. The liturgical texts in MS. Edili 151 may be of help here since the texts for the dedication of the church (fols. 17v–21r) are preceded by the Mass of the Annunciation to the Virgin (fols. 1v–7r); again, the gradual for the dedication of a church (fols. 72r–81v) is preceded by the gradual and tract for the Annunciation (fols. 70r–71v) and followed by the Ordinary of the Mass (fols. 72r–81v). It may therefore be suggested that this first cardinal, perhaps Antonio Casini (see Commentary at 22), celebrated the Mass of the Annunciation on some already-consecrated altar in the cathedral. Indeed, this interpretation clarifies Manetti's comparison, immediately following, of human and angelic singing in celebration of the Annunciation.

melodies: The singing of psalms, antiphons, and hymns is prescribed during the consecration liturgy itself, to say nothing of the music for the Mass which follows and, perhaps, for the Feast of the Annunciation. In addition, other non-liturgical music set to new texts could be inserted, as well as instrumental music.

In 1432 two new organs had been ordered from Matteo da Prato for the organist Antonio Squarcialupi, hired in that year; but since the instruments were not yet ready, the old one had been restored: T. Verdon, "'Ecce homo': Spazio sacro e la vittoria dell'uomo," in idem, *Cupola*, 89–114, here 92. Before the consecration, Eugenius had enlarged the college of clerics who chant in the cathedral with 34 boys "in prima tonsura," i.e. between 10 and 15 years old, and assigned them teachers of grammar and singing. Antoninus says Eugenius did this by using the revenue of the archbishopric during the vacancy of the see (March 1434–October 1435): *Chronicorum opus*, 10.6 (527).

Manetti suggests that the vocal music was of two different styles: "variis vocibus . . . concinebatur" may refer to harmony and polyphony; "symphoniis . . . cantabatur" to singing in unison ("symphonia" = "consonantia" in Latin) and plainsong. On at least one other occasion Manetti distinguished by his terminology between the kinds of music he heard: R. Strohm, *The Rise of European Music, 1380–1500* (Cambridge, 1993), 543. We know that choral polyphony only began to be performed in Italy around 1426 and that in 1436 Florence Cathedral had no more than two polyphonic singers: A. Seay, "The 15th-Century Cappella of Santa Maria del Fiore in Florence," *Journal of the American Musicological Society* 11 (1958): 45–55, here 45.

Guillaume Dufay had been engaged to provide music, among which was the motet "Flos florum," composed for the occasion, whose title reinforced the floral theme that connected the city to the Virgin, patroness of their cathedral, and whose content celebrated the city's cultural flowering under her tutelage:

> Hail! whose fame is spread through all the earth,
> O hail! great glory of the Italian land,
> Hail! happy mother who begets so many learned sons,
> So many by your great counsel and your faith,
> Who begets so many men eminent for wondrous integrity,
> So many men eminent in their religious devotion.
>
> Hail! to you is owed whatever comes from honest art
> Anything of genius, anything that is of eloquence;
> Hail! whose fame is spread through all the earth.
> You come and send your own to the stars.

A second motet by Dufay, "Nuper rosarum flores," was probably sung at the introit which began the Consecration Mass proper, as is suggested by the text of the tenor part "Terribilis est locus iste" — "Awesome is this place! This is none other than the House of God, and this is the Gate of Heaven" (Gen. 28:17) — the scriptural passage used in the Propers for the consecration of a church, although some scholars have suggested other placements in the liturgy for it. See Wright, "Dufay's *Nuper rosarum flores*." The superior voices, however, sang this newly composed modern text:

Anon the flowers of roses
From the pontiff's gift
Though the winter bristled
Adorned without fail
The temple of grand devising
Given with holy devotion
To you, heavenly virgin.

Today the Vicar
Of Christ, Jesus' and Peter's
Successor Eugenius,
Deemed worthy to consecrate
This same most spacious
Temple with his sacred hands
And holy liquids.

And so, devoted parent
And daughter of your Child,
Virgin, glory of virgins,
Your devout people of
Florence pray you
That whoever with clean
Mind and body pleads

By your prayer
And the merits of your
Son's, his Lord's,
Torments in the flesh
May deserve to receive
Welcome blessings
And pardon for sin. Amen.

(In H. Bessler, *Guillelmi Dufay Opera Omnia* [Rome, 1966], 1.3: xxi, 70–75.) (Recorded by Pomerium in the Deutsche Grammophon Archiv 447 773–2, 1997.)

There is a considerable bibliography on possible relations between the structure and/or content of the motet and Florence Cathedral. See especially C. Warren, "Brunelleschi's Dome and Dufay's Motet," *Musical Quarterly* 59 (1973): 92–105; Wright, "Dufay's *Nuper rosarum flores*"; Strohm, *Rise of European Music*, 169; and M. Trachtenberg, "Architecture and Music Reunited: A New Reading of Dufay's 'Nuper Rosarum Flores' and the Cathedral of Florence," *Art Quarterly* 54 (2001): 741–775.

Fallows proposed that Dufay's Sanctus "Papale" (IV/7) and perhaps the Agnus Dei "Custos et pastor ovium" were also composed for the consecration but that "Salve flos Tusce gentis" was for Palm Sunday, which that year fell the week after the consecration: D. Fallows, *Dufay* (London, 1982), 45. Although "Ecclesie militantis" is usually associated with Eugenius's coronation in 1431, its musical similarities with "Nuper rosarum flores," noted by Fallows (*Dufay*, 108), raise the possibility that it also could have been for the consecration day. That the two tenor parts are based on chants associated with the Archangel Gabriel might not only connect the motet with the pope's given name, Gabriele, but would make it especially appropriate for the Feast of the Annunciation. Although Wright and, following him, Tacconi claimed that the sequence "*Nuper almos rose flores*" was written by Dufay for the consecration, in part because it is found in the liturgy for the dedication of a church in MS. Edili 151, it must instead be commemorative and hence for the anniversary of the dedication since it describes the events of the day, the *ponte* and so forth: Wright, "Dufay's Nuper rosarum flores"; Tacconi in *I Libri del Duomo di Firenze*, ed. L. Fabbri and idem, 70; Wright, "A Sequence."
27. Timotheus and Orpheus: For Timotheus of Miletus, see Pliny, *NH,* 7.204; Cicero, *De legibus*, 2.39; and Plutarch, *Agis*, 10. Orpheus is especially described in Ovid, *Metamorphoses* 10.1–85, and Vergil, *Georgics*, 4.454–527. See also Cicero, *De natura deorum*, 1.107; Horace, *Ars poetica*, 391 ff; and Macrobius, *Somnium Scipionis*, 2.3.8.

more civilized senses: Manetti distinguishes between the lower sense of taste and touch and the "more civilized" senses of hearing, smell, and sight. See Manetti's extended discussion of the human senses in Book 1 of his *On the Dignity of Man* (ed. Leonard, 20–45), largely from Cicero, *De natura deorum*, 1.111–112, where he says that man has pleasure (*voluptatem*) from seeing beauty, from hearing sounds and harmony, and from smelling flowers, tasting food and wines, and touching soft substances.
28. captives: This is the first of two ceremonies not actually part of either the consecration liturgy or the Mass. Manetti has placed it out of its actual sequence, as we show in Chapter 2. Cambi reports that after the Creed of the "Messa Grande," the Signoria gave fourteen prisoners to Eugenius; four were returned to prison for private debt; after this the pope returned to Santa Maria Novella (*Istoria*, 210). By placing the freeing of captives as the first action of the pope

after entering the cathedral, Manetti continues his implied analogy between the consecration ceremony and a classical triumphal *adventus*.

29. standing: In fact, Manetti had said that he was seated.

insignia of military service: This is the second ceremony, the knighting of the Gonfaloniere, not part of the consecration or the Mass. Again, the analogy is to an imperial *adventus*: after freeing the captives the faithful followers are rewarded and honored. The ceremony of knighting can be found in the Pontifical of Durandus of Mende. Detailed discussion of Davanzati's knighting are in Böninger, *Ritterwurde*, 148–50; and G. Salvemini, *La dignità cavalleresca nel comune di Firenze* (Florence, 1896), 189, based on the account of the ceremony in ASF, Archivio Notarile Antecosimiano 15200. On 23 March the Priors and Gonfaloniere di Giustizia elected Giuliano di Niccola di Roberto Davanzati to be knighted at the consecration. He was to be honored with the emblem of the people (a red cross on a white ground), banner, man's overcoat, and trappings for his horse, on which the Commune was prepared to spend 50 gold florins, and become Captain of Pisa. Belcari says that the pope pinned a jeweled brooch on Davanzati's breast (Saalman, *Cupola*, 276); elsewhere it is described as a gold cross pin. It would seem that Giuliano was inducted into the *milizia aurata* or *cavalieria aurata*, since that involved the conferring of golden spurs (which Manetti mentions at 50), but the papal equestrian orders were strictly organized only in the sixteenth century: F. Ferri, *Ordini cavallereschi e decorazioni in Italia* (Modena, 1995). For the representation of Palla Strozzi as a knight of this order in Gentile da Fabriano's Strozzi Altarpiece, see R. Jones, "Palla Strozzi e la sagrestia di Santa Trinità," *Rivista d'arte* 37 (1984): 9–106, here 50.

According to Cambi, the knighting occurred after the pope had consecrated the altar and after Cardinal Orsini had anointed the walls; Belcari adds that it was while the Cardinal of San Marco vested to say the Mass: both agree that it happened before the freeing of the captives, after the consecration was finished (Cambi, *Istoria*, 209; Saalman, *Cupola*, 276).

the most distinguished man: This was not the first occasion on which Eugene honored the city's Gonfaloniere di Giustizia. On Christmas Day of 1434 Eugenius had given the sword and the hat — "il chappello di Bavero chon dua armellini appichati da ogni ghota" — to the then Gonfaloniere di Giustizia, Giovanni di Andrea Minerbetti; this was done in the papal chapel of Santa Maria Novella, and received in the name of all the Signori (Cambi, *Istoria*, 202). From then on the hat and the sword were carried before the Signoria when it went to Mass as a group. Minerbetti's investiture with sword and hat, rather than sword and spurs, conforms to the rite of creating a papal gonfaloniere.

30. noble prince: This is Sigismondo Malatesta (1414–1468), who succeeded Pandolfo Malatesta in 1427 and who, since 1428, had been commander of the papal forces in the Romagna and the Marches, and was Vicar of Rimini. Feo Belcari and Cambi agree that Sigismondo placed the sword around Davanzati's waist, but that it was the Podestà of Florence, Count Cecchino di Campello, who put on the spurs, not the imperial ambassador (Cambi, *Istoria*, 209; Saalman, *Cupola*, 276). Manetti mentions only the nobility, although Battista Cigalà of Genoa, the Emperor Sigismond's representative at the Curia, assisted Sigismondo in conferring the sword and Tommaso da Fermo, Capitano del Popolo, helped fasten the spurs.

military sword: The "spata" or "spatha" was a long, double-edged sword. See E. M. Parkinson in *Medieval Latin: An Introduction and Bibliographical Guide*, ed. F. A. C. Mantello and A. G. Rigg (Washington, D.C., 1996), 449.

31. another great cardinal: Cardinal Giordano Orsini, probably the second of the "apostles" who walked next to the pope in procession, climbed a ladder and anointed the crosses of the apostles (see next entry) on the walls, beginning with the San Zenobio chapel (Cambi, *Istoria*, 208). It is Cardinal Orsini to whom the Opera gave marzipan cakes and other confetti (Poggi, *Duomo*, doc. 2382), perhaps because, as Rinuccini says, he had been responsible for all the preparations for the ceremony (*Ricordi*, 71). A breviary owned by Orsini, dating to 1423 and either from or close to the scriptorium of S. Maria degli Angeli in Florence (now Arch. Cap. S. Pietro MS. B.82), contains the service for the dedication of a church: Morello and Maddalo, *Liturgia in figura*, 105. It would be interesting to know if this was the very codex he used for the consecration of the cathedral. Orsini, who had been made a cardinal in 1405, was since 1431 archpriest of St. Peter's; he died in 1438. See V. Saxer, "Trois manuscrits liturgiques de l'Archivio di S. Pietro, dont deux datés aux armes du cardinal Jordan Orsini," *Rivista di storia della chiesa in Italia* 27 (1973): 501–5, here 502. On Orsini, see also E. König, *Kardinal Giordano Orsini +1438. Ein Lebensbild aus der Zeit der grossen Konzilien und des Humanismus* (Freiburg im Breisgau, 1906).

images of the holy apostles: The chrismation of the walls in twelve places, marked with crosses and commemorated by candles, had developed by the high Middle Ages into a decorative program of the twelve apostles and had assumed an allegorical significance: Sicardus of Cremona, *Mitrale* 1.9 (PL 213.54). At Florence Cathedral, frescoes of the apostles had been ordered on 17 February and had been barely finished by Rosello di Jacopo, Bicci di Lorenzo, Lippo d'Andrea, and Giovanni di Marcho in time for the consecration (Poggi, *Duomo*, docs. 2368, 2378). The exact locations of these chrismations in Florence Cathedral can be established today since the frescoes were replaced in the sixteenth century by the twelve statues of the apostles now *in situ*, with candles at their bases. See M. Amy, "The Revised Attributions and Dates of Two Fifteenth-Century Mural Cycles for the Cathedral of Florence," *Mitteilungen des Kunsthistorischen Instituts in Florenz* 42 (1998): 176–89.

The chrismation of the walls would have been preceded by an aspersion with a mixture of water, wine, salt, and ashes, each element of which carried its own symbolism. See Andrieu, *Le pontifical de Guillaume Durand*, 465–71; Honorius of Autun, *Gemma animae*, 3.66–67 (PL 172.592–93); Sicardus, *Mitrale*, 1.7 (PL 213.31–33). Manetti omits all of this. St. Antoninus speaks of making a sign of the cross on the walls, putting candles before them, and anointing them with chrism as the actions performed during a consecration (*Summa*, 6.530).

32. divine salt: Manetti employs the metaphor of seasoning here and later in reference to the indulgences granted; the rite, which could have been completely and efficaciously performed by any bishop, acquired a special pungency from the addition of papal prayers and indulgences. To the medieval liturgical commentators, the actual salt mixed with water in the service signifies the element through which food acquires its savor (cf. Matthew 5:13, Mark 9:50, Luke 14:34), and hence is a figure of divine wisdom and also of healing, since the prophet Elisha had purified the waters by adding salt (4 Kings 2:19–22): Honorius, *Gemma animae*, 3.67 (PL 172.593); Sicardus, *Mitrale*, 1.7 (PL 213.31).

holy relics: (cf. above, 15): Feo Belcari says that Cardinal Orsini consecrated the church up to the point where the relics are to be put into the altar, and then also consecrated the altar and put the relics in (Saalman, *Cupola*, 276). Cambi, on the other hand, says the pope consecrated the altar as soon as he arrived at the church, and that afterwards Cardinal Orsini anointed the walls (*Istoria*, 209).

noble prince of the Riminese: Sigismondo acted as subdeacon during the consecration of the altar.

was seated: Perhaps while the altar was dressed, the ministers vested, and the lights in the church lit as preparation for the Mass.

33. eucharist: "Eucharist" means "thanksgiving" in Greek.

The Cardinal of San Marco, Agnolotto degli Foschi (according to Belcari and Corazza, *Diario*, in van Eck, "Manetti on Architecture," 454), and not the Cardinal of Venice, Francesco Condulmer (as Cambi has it), celebrated the first Mass on the newly consecrated altar (Saalman, *Cupola*, 276; Cambi, *Istoria*, 209). Vespasiano says the pope had already said Mass in the morning "according to their custom" (*Vite*, 1:15). Does this mean that he had celebrated Mass for the papal household at Santa Maria Novella?

At the elevation: The music at the elevation would presumably have been the "Benedictus." Manetti's description clearly indicates not a plainsong setting, but polyphony with orchestral accompaniment.

Compare Manetti's interpretation of the effect of music sung during Mass to Alberti's in *Della Tranquillità dell'animo* of 1442: "that which I prize above all [about being in the cathedral, is that] here you listen to the voices during Mass, during that which the ancients called the mysteries, with their marvelous beauty": *Opere volgari*, ed. Grayson, 107.

St. Augustine compared the well-ordered city or republic to a voice in a melody which, because of its harmony, is delectable to the ears (*City of God* 2.21).

Since his context is political rather than musical (he refers to Cicero, *On the Republic* 2.43, as well as to Sallust) it may be suggested that Manetti's discussion of music has political implications, evoking the civic as well as sacred significance of the cathedral.

34. indulgence: Cambi says the pope blessed the people and gave indulgences of 7 years and 7 *quarantane* (*Istoria*, 209); Feo Belcari says it was 6 years and 6 *quarantane*, but that Cosimo de'Medici begged him to raise it to 7. Cosimo then petitioned the Cardinal of San Marcello (Antonio Casini) who raised it to 10 years and 10 *quarantane* (Saalman, *Cupola*, 276).

marched . . . to the Apostolic residence: According to Cambi, after escorting the pope back to Santa Maria Novella, the Signoria and ambassadors had a reception in the Palazzo Vecchio and, though there was a shortage of fish in the city, dined on "lamprey [eel], fresh sturgeon, fish from the Arno, pike, tench" and then sea fish and "bianchi mangiari" ("white things to eat"). The Signoria paid 250 gold florins for the food (*Istoria*, 210). Francesco Giovanni, a member of the Signoria, set the cost at 92 florins (van Eck, "Manetti on Architecture," 454, n. 15).

Presumably both Agnolo Acciaiuoli and Manetti would have been present at this luncheon. Acciaiuoli had undertaken important diplomatic missions immediately on his recall to Florence in 1434. Manetti himself was the Republic's ambassador in negotiations with Genoa; his praises of Genoa survive, together with prefaces to the Doge, and are in fact preserved in the same manuscripts as this description of the consecration of the Duomo.

Giannozzo Manetti

Iannozzi Manetti
Liber Secundus De Gestis Nicolai Quinti
Summi Pontificis
Incipit Feliciter

Giannozzo Manetti
On the Achievements of Nicholas V,
Supreme Pontiff

Book Two of the Life of Nicholas V

Iannozzi Manetti
Liber Secundus De Gestis Nicolai Quinti Summi Pontificis Incipit Feliciter

1. (921) Cum igitur quadringentesimo quadragesimo septimo supra millesimum christiane salutis, quadragesimo vero octavo etatis sue anno, contra propriam spem ac preter omnium prudentium sanorumque[2] hominum opinionem ad altissimum summi pontificatus apicem divinitus potius quam humanitus sublimaretur, ob memoriam nominis defuncti cardinalis sui Nicolaum appellari et nuncupari voluit atque per hunc modum Nicolaus quintus, quod[3] in ordine Nicolaorum pontificum talis erat, vocatus est, quemadmodum in principio huius operis dixisse meminimus. Hic ut erat alti animi non otio desidieque et inertie se dedere,[4] sed e vestigio cuncta agere et operari ac nihil eorum omittere[5] decrevit que ad rectam et iustam tot tantarumque rerum gubernationem et ad robustam et fortem tante molis sustentationem aliquatenus pertinere arbitraretur.

2. Verum cum romanam[6] ecclesiam pluribus ac continuis bellis, quibus per aliquot Eugenii predecessoris sui annos vexata fuerat, afflictam ac propterea non solum in peculiari[7] erario penitus et omnino bellicis sumptibus exinanitam sed ere quoque alieno onustam inveniret, ac veteris belli reliquias nescio quas, multis oppidis[8] amissis, superesse et preterea per Amadeum quendam[9] Sabaudie ducem, quem concilio basiliensi summum pontificem creaverant Felicemque appellaverant,

---

[1] *ABCE*: Liber secundus. De gestis Nicolai quinti summi pontificis *C*[1]: *post* MANETTI *ins.* *D* F[LORENTINUS]

[2] saniorumque *D*

[3] qui *D*

[4] sedere *D*

[5] obmittere *D*

[6] Romam *D*

[7] inpeculiarii *D*

[8] opibus *D Muratori*

[9] quondam *Muratori*

Giannozzo Manetti
On the Achievements of Nicholas V
Supreme Pontiff

Book Two of the Life of Nicholas V

1. In the four hundred and forty-seventh year after the millennium of Christian salvation, at the age of forty-eight years, to his own surprise and beyond all prudent and rational people's calculations, he was elevated more through divine agency than human to the most high summit of the supreme pontificate. He wished to be addressed and titled as Nicholas in memory of his deceased Cardinal patron's name. Thus he was called Nicholas V, since he was fifth in order of the pontiffs named Nicholas, as we recall having said at the opening of this work. Since he was high-minded, he determined not to surrender himself to a leisure of comfort and idleness, but immediately to become actively engaged in all matters and to overlook nothing which he thought in any way concerned the right and just governance of many important affairs and the robust and courageous shouldering of so great a burden.

2. In fact he discovered that the Roman Church had been weakened by the many unending wars which plagued her for years during his predecessor Eugenius's reign. Because of this the Church had not only thoroughly and completely depleted its own treasury for wartime expenses, but had become burdened with debt. He found too that some traces of the old war survived because many towns had been lost. Furthermore, the church was rent by a vicious and perverse schism because of a certain Amadeus, duke of Savoy, whom they had created supreme pontiff at the Council of Basle and named Felix. He therefore determined straightaway to put

maligno quodam ac perverso scismate discissam reperiret, cum reliquias belli prorsus delere, et es alienum solvere, tum amissas[10] urbes recuperare, et scisma ipsum diluere omnibus corporis et animi, ut dicitur, viribus ac denique omnia pontificalis curie officia priscis ordinibus disponere et[11] ordinare constituit. Quo circa ceteris omnibus posthabitis ad ea curanda et absolvenda animum mentemque convertit.

3. Unde ad hec ipsa celerius citiusque[12] conficienda ut erat suapte natura vehemens et acer ac multarum rerum experientia prudens, nihil utilius fore existimavit quam si initio pontificatus sui singularem quandam et precipuam per generalem humani cuiusdam boni et liberalis pontificis apud principes, reges, populosque Christianos de se opinionem, auctoritatem admirationemque nancisceretur. Proinde omnibus ad eum accedentibus, omissa quin immo neglecta omni proprii corporis cura, se se facilem benignumque prebebat atque cunctis postulantibus et supplicantibus[13] ita respondebat ut benigne gratanterque suscepti et humanis quoque responsionibus contenti et optimis de probitate dexteritateque pontificis opinionibus imbuti, leti alacresque recederent. Ad hec celeris quedam ac liberalis omnium postulatorum per fideles et accuratos ministros suos, nulla intercedente corruptela et simonia, expeditio accedebat. Atque ob hec et huiusmodi tam humana, tam benigna, et[14] tam liberalia pontificatus sui initia, velut certa quedam et expressa totius future gubernationis pignora, tantam et tam admirabilem[15] fama undique increbrescente apud cunctos principes, reges, Christianosque populos ac res publicas auctoritatem (922) consecutus est ut omnes oratores ac legatos ad congratulandum de assumptione sua, ad venerandam, ad[16] adorandam novam Christi salvatoris nostri humanitatem iam in terris existentem et cum hominibus conversantem libenter devoteque transmitterent. Quibus cum publica auditoria de industria preberentur dici non potest quantum sua illa maxima et innata acquisitaque elegantia accommodatis ex tempore responsionibus satisfaciebat; usque adeo enim omnibus satisfacere videbatur ut exinde singularem ingenii et humanitatis famam ac precipuam et generalem cunctarum gentium gratiam consensu omnium compararet.

---

[10] solvendum, amissas *Muratori*

[11] et *om. D*

[12] certiusque *D Muratori*

[13] postulationibus & supplicationibus *Muratori*

[14] humana benignaque, & *Muratori*

[15] tanta & tam admirabili *Muratori*

[16] & quasi ad venerandum ac *Muratori*

an end to the traces of war, pay back the debt, recover the lost cities and, with all the strength of mind and body (as they say) dissolve the schism itself and, finally, dispose and arrange all the offices of the pontifical Curia in their original order. To this purpose, he postponed everything else and turned his mind and attention to tending and resolving these issues.

3. He was forceful and passionate by nature and pragmatic from long experience. So, to produce these results more quickly and sooner, he considered that nothing would prove more useful than acquiring at the beginning of his pontificate a particular and special prestige and admiration by gaining a widespread reputation among princes, kings, and Christian peoples for being a cultured, good, and generous pontiff. Accordingly, setting aside or rather neglecting all concern for his own body, he would make himself accessible and courteous to all those who approached him. He would answer all petitioners and supplicants in a way that made them leave delighted and cheered because they had been welcomed courteously and graciously, pleased with his cultured replies, and filled with the highest regard for the pontiff's decency and willingness to help. Add to this an efficient and generous handling of all petitions by his trustworthy and competent staff, without a hint of corruption and simony. Because his pontificate had such cultured, courteous, and generous beginnings, as though they were sure and explicit guarantees of his entire future governance, he attained a great and wonderful reputation as news of him spread everywhere among all the princes, kings, and Christian peoples and republics. As a result, they all gladly and loyally sent ambassadors and legates to congratulate him on his accession, to venerate and worship the new humanity of Christ our Savior now visible on earth and conversing with humans. Public audiences were purposely held. It is impossible to describe how much his great eloquence, natural and acquired, satisfied them. His remarks were suited to each occasion. He seemed to so satisfy every person that by universal consent he won for himself thereafter a particular reputation for genius and culture and the special and general favor of all the nations.

4. Quid plura? Per hos et huiusmodi admirabilium virtutum suarum rumores hinc inde late ampleque dispersos paulo post factum est ut et veteris belli reliquias non armis, non tumultibus, non militibus sed sola tranquilla ac benigna Sancti Spiritus auctoritate penitus omninoque sedaret; et civitates quoque antea amissas eisdem[17] non militaribus sed pontificalibus potius artibus magnanimiter recuperaret; et commemoratum insuper scisma iamdudum inveteratum, predicto Amadeo illius concilii principe errata sua recognoscente ac confitente et penitente et sanctitati sue ut par erat adherente, dissolveret deleretque. Ipsum enim romane ac catolice ecclesie, ubi veteres perfidie sue errores recognovit, cardinalem sponte creaverat; quod solum, unicum, et certum dissolvendi illius concilii remedium conveniensque et idoneum eiusmodi[18] dissolutionis antidotum fore sua sapientia existimaverat, sicut postea re ipsa comprobante contigisse compertum est. Siquidem ea ipsa tot patrum sinodus post commemoratam predicti Amadei promotionem statim evanuit.

5. Ac preterea erarium apostolicum ab ere alieno celeriter liberavit. Atque hec omnia de reliquiis veteris belli extinctis ac de oppidis romane ecclesie recuperatis et de scismate omnino penitusque deleto, primo sui pontificatus anno quasi celitus agerentur supra humanum modum mirabiliter ac divinitus operatus est. Talibus igitur faustis, fortunatis, ac felicibus sacri pontificatus initiis velut egregiis quibusdam futuri edificii sui fundamentis optime ac pulcherrime iactis paulo post ad conservandam pacem, ad instituendas omnes romane ecclesie terras, ad ordinanda urbis Rome vectigalia, que profecto nervos cuiuscumque principatus et cuiuslibet rei publice semper apud quosque historicos fuisse legerat, ad distinguenda et distribuenda ecclesiastice curie[19] officia ac beneficia animum mentemque convertit.

6. Itaque tribus prioribus membris[20] et de conservatione pacis et de externarum terrarum institutione et de urbanorum vectigalium ordinatione speciosissime ordinatis, cum principale sedis apostolice collegium quod novo et non prisco nomine cardinalatus[21] nuncupatur per mortem quorundam collegarum aliqua reformatione indigere intelligeret, cum ut eum ordinem reformaret tum etiam ut quibusdam excellentibus viris ingentia illa beneficia conferret, octo singulares prestantissimosque homines diversis temporibus ad eam dignitatem (923) non iniuria promovit. Philippum nanque uterinum fratrem suum, ceu antea diximus, Latinum Ursinum, Alanum avinionensem, Antonium hilerdensem, Ioannem eboracensem, Sbigneum cracomensem,[22] Ioannem eduensem, ac Nicolaum cusensem diversorum titulorum cardinales non immerito creavit.

---

[17] idem *Muratori*

[18] illius *D*

[19] curae *Muratori*

[20] mensibus *Muratori*

[21] Cardinalium *Muratori*

[22] Cracoviensem *Muratori*

4. What more? Because word about these and his other admirable virtues spread far and wide from everywhere, after a short time he was able to quell thoroughly and completely the remnants of the old war, not by arms, not by upheavals, not with soldiers, but solely by the tranquil and benign agency of the Holy Spirit, and magnanimously to recover the cities which were lost before, not through military arts, but by the same pontifical ones. And he was able to resolve and annul the schism mentioned above, which had gone on so long, when the aforementioned Amadeus, president of the council, recognized his errors, confessed, did penance, and attached himself to His Holiness, as was right. Once Amadeus recognized the old errors of his disloyalty, Nicholas freely created him a cardinal of the Roman Catholic Church, because he had determined in his wisdom that this alone would be the single sure remedy for dissolving that council and an agreeable and fitting antidote to its dissolution. Afterwards this was found to be what happened and the facts confirm it; that very synod of so many fathers immediately vanished after Amadeus was promoted.

5. In addition he quickly freed the Apostolic Treasury from debt. He accomplished all these things — quenching the remnants of the old war, recovering the towns of the Roman Church, and completely and thoroughly annulling the schism — miraculously and by divine agency in the first year of his pontificate, as if they were brought about by heaven, beyond human means. With such favoring, fortunate, and happy beginnings to his sacred pontificate, as though the remarkable foundations of his future building were most soundly and handsomely laid, he turned his mind and energies shortly thereafter towards preserving the peace, organizing all the lands of the Roman Church, putting in order the taxes of the city of Rome (which indeed he had read in all historians had always been the nerves of every principate and every republic), defining and distributing the offices of the Church's Curia and its privileges.

6. With the three most important elements in place — the preservation of the peace, the organization of the lands outside the city, and the fixing of urban taxation — he understood that the principal college of the Apostolic See, which is called by its new, not original name, the College of Cardinals, required some reformation due to the death of some colleagues. To reform its order as well as to confer those enormous privileges upon men of excellence, he rightly promoted eight singular and most distinguished men at various times to this dignity. On their merits, he made these men cardinals of various titular churches: Philip, his half-brother as we said before, Latino Orsini, Alain of Avignon, Antonio of Ilerda, John of York, Zbigniew of Cracow, Jean of Autun, and Nicholas of Cusa.

7. Quo facto predicta omnia secundo anno ita ordinaverat itaque instituerat ut multo plura ac maiora exinde emolumenta susciperet quam preteritis[23] antea temporibus fieri consueverat. Quod idcirco faciebat ut absque illicitis quamquam iamdudum usitatis sacrorum beneficiorum venundationibus nonnullis maximarum rerum cogitationibus designationibusque suis melius obsequi ac plenius satisfacere valeret. Que quidem magnifica sue mentis proposita sine ingenti cumulande pecunie quantitate exsequi et efficere non poterat, atque duo in primis, pacis conservatio et solida quedam civitatum ecclesiasticarum ordinatio, hec ipsa sibi instrumenta ad predictas eius cogitationes designationesque explendas affatim subministrare posse videbantur. Semper enim omnia cogitabat atque animo et mente volvebat que ad exaugendam romane ecclesie auctoritatem atque ad amplificandam sedis apostolice dignitatem ullatenus pertinere arbitrabatur. Proinde cum statum[24] ecclesie duobus,[25] spiritualibus scilicet et secularibus rebus, maxime contineri et conservari animadverteret, ad illa duo diligenter curanda inter cetera animum adiecit.

8. Itaque spiritualibus tota mente deditus, ecclesiasticas ceremonias mirabiliter et ad unguem maxima cum diligentia et incredibili cura observabat et ut etiam a christianis populis maiori admiratione haberentur atque accuratiori quoque devotione susciperentur, tapetibus, auleis, stragulis vestibus, vasis partim argenteis, partim aureis, et sacerdotalibus indumentis de sirico auroque confectis ac magna unionum et margaritarum multitudine referctis exornabat que communi et vulgato verbo paramenta appellantur. Atque pontificalibus preterea mitris sardiorum, smaragdorum,[26] topatiorum, carbunculorum, saphirorum, iaspidum, liguriorum,[27] acatum, ametistorum, chryssolitorum, onichinorum, berillorum, ac mira quadam huiusmodi gemmarum et pretiosorum[28] lapidum copia exornatis, omnes ecclesiasticas pontificalesque ceremonias preter consuetum et usitatum morem mirabiliter condiebat. Unde ubicunque illa tam speciosa et tam digna officia intuebantur homines, tanta admiratione tantoque stupore simul atque devotione capiebantur ut adumbratam quandam triumphantis ecclesie in hac nostra militante imaginem recognoscerent certamque et expressam umbram plane aperteque conspicerent. Atque hec de sacris ceremoniis dixisse sufficiat.

---

[23] preteritis *A*: plurimis *BCC¹*: primis *D*: predictis *E Muratori*
[24] statim *D*
[25] duabus *Muratori*
[26] smaragolorum *D*
[27] ligurorum *Muratori*
[28] preciosarum *D*

7. This done, in his second year he imposed such order on all the above matters that he took in far more and larger revenues than had been usual in most of the past. This enabled him to pursue better and satisfy more fully his own ideas and the plans he had for his greatest achievements without resorting to the illegal, though previously common, sale of sacred privileges. Indeed, he could not pursue and complete the magnificent projects he envisioned without a huge quantity of ready cash. Two acts in particular, the preservation of peace and the firm organization of the ecclesiastical states, seemed to him to have the potential to serve amply as the very instruments for fulfilling his ideas and plans. He was continually making all sorts of plans and turning in his energetic mind what he thought might somehow enlarge the prestige of the Roman Church and enhance the dignity of the Apostolic See. Accordingly he pondered that the Church's position was best preserved and protected by two factors, the spiritual and the secular, and he applied his mind to the diligent care of both, amid all else.

8. Wholeheartedly committed to spiritual matters, he carried out the ecclesiastical ceremonies in marvelous style and with great and precise diligence and unbelievable care. And so that they might be held in even greater admiration by Christian peoples and might be undertaken with even more scrupulous devotion, he embellished the ceremonies with tapestries, draperies, carpets, vessels of silver and gold, and priestly garments woven of silk and gold and studded with a great crowd of pearl solitaires and seed pearls, items that are in the vernacular called "vestments". Above all, he ornamented the pontifical tiaras with a wondrous abundance of carnelians, emeralds, topaz, carbuncles, sapphires, jaspers, hyacinths, rubies, amethysts, diamonds, onyx, beryl, and other gems and precious stones and so marvelously added a zest to all ecclesiastical and pontifical ceremonies that went beyond the usual, traditional manner. For this reason, whenever people witnessed these splendid and worthy services, they were overcome with such admiration and so great astonishment and devotion, that they recognized a kind of sketched image of the Church Triumphant in the midst of this our Church Militant and they clearly and openly glimpsed its sure and explicit outline. Let this be enough said about sacred ceremonies.

9. Quid vero de secularibus pompis referemus? Hec enim[29] secularia opera multis inter cetera ingentibus et perpetuis edificiis plurimum ornabat que in dies pluribus forensibus oppidis partim extra urbem, partim vero intra moenia reparatis, ita undique augebantur ut in miraculum usque procederet,[30] de quibus quoniam res maxima ac profecto admirabilis est et[31] suo ordine seorsum enarranda, alibi opportunior dabitur dicendi et explicandi[32] locus.

10. Dum igitur pontifex ipse huiusmodi[33] dignis ac memorabilibus operibus mirum in modum primo ad honorem omnipotentis Dei, ad augendam deinde (924) romane ecclesie auctoritatem, ad amplificandam insuper apostolice sedis dignitatem tota mente animoque contenderet, ecce quinquagesimus[34] iubilei annus, sanctus vulgo appellatus, usque a Moysi divine legis latoris temporibus iam dudum[35] institutus ac postea secundum canones ecclesiasticos legitime confirmatus, opportune admodum supervenit, qui fuit quadringentesimus quinquagesimus supra millesimum christiane salutis, tertius vero sui pontificatus annus. Ad hanc celeberrimam sanctissimamque solemnitatem, in qua certa omnium veterum peccatorum remissio atque expressa cunctorum indulgentia delictorum a cunctis cum penitentia ac confessione adventantibus acquirebatur, non solum ob hanc raram divinamque festivitatem, sed etiam ob admirabiles pontificalis persone conditiones que iam per totum pene terrarum orbem fama undique intonante peragraverat,[36] tanta populorum omnium christianorum multitudo concurrisse et confluxisse perhibetur ut, ceteris iubileis hactenus celebratis, quantum coniectura augurari ac consequi valemus,[37] numero et copia hominum utriusque sexus non immerito preferri posse existimetur. Tante enim pannonum, germanorum, cimbrorum, britanorum, gallorum, hispanorum, celtiberorum, portugallensium, grecorum, dalmatum,[38] italorum, ceterorumque christianorum populorum, ut omnes uno verbo summatim comprehendamus, caterve quotidie confluebant ut concurrentium congregatio, cuiuslibet mensis dimidio per arbitrium designato, in stuporem admirationemque procederet. Tante nanque ac tam magne adventantium gentium caterve quotidie concurrebant ut quasi sturnorum apumve et formicarum agmina (mirabile et incredibile[39] dictu) viderentur.

---

[29] etiam *Muratori*
[30] procederent *Muratori*
[31] et *om. Muratori*
[32] explanandi *D*: replicandi *Muratori*
[33] his et huiusmodi *CC¹*
[34] felicissimus *Muratori*
[35] iam dudum *om. Muratori*
[36] peragraverant *CC¹*
[37] valeamus *D*
[38] Dalmatarum *Muratori*
[39] venerabile *E Muratori*

9. What indeed shall we report about secular displays? Among other things, he was greatly embellishing these secular works with many huge, permanent buildings. Day by day they were increased everywhere, with many public places restored both in towns outside the city as well as inside the walls, so that they grew to marvelous proportions. A better opportunity to speak about and describe these will be provided elsewhere, since the topic is very important, utterly amazing, and worth telling by itself in its proper order.

10. He was wonderfully concentrating his mind and energies on worthy and memorable works like this, first to honor almighty God, then to enlarge the prestige of the Roman Church, and expand the dignity of the Apostolic See, when the fiftieth year of Jubilee opportunely arrived in the four hundred and fiftieth year after the millennium of Christian salvation, and the third of his pontificate. This is popularly called the Holy Year, begun long ago in the time of the divine Lawgiver Moses and later confirmed by law in the ecclesiastical canons. At this most solemn and holy celebration, sure remission of all old sins and explicit forgiveness of every fault could be acquired by all who arrived with penance and confession. A great throng of all Christian peoples is reputed to have flocked together and streamed in, not just because this was a rare and divine festivity, but also because the wonderful attributes of the pontifical person and his fame had already traveled through virtually all the world, thundering everywhere. In so far as we can estimate and judge by conjecture, there is every reason to believe it surpassed the other jubilees celebrated up to this time in the number and wealth of persons of both sexes. Great crowds of Pannonians, Germans, Cimbrians, Britons, Gauls, Spaniards, Celtiberians, Portuguese, Greeks, Dalmatians, Italians, and (to include everyone in a single word) all the other Christian peoples streamed together daily. The gathering of those arriving, in any given fortnight, approached astonishing and amazing proportions. So many large crowds of arriving nations would assemble that they seemed like swarms of hornets or bees or ants (marvelous and incredible to tell!).

11. Quid plura? Tantus adventantium populorum concursus factus est ut ad celebratum illum adrianee molis pontem quo ad basilicam Petri apostolorum principis recto tramite hinc inde ibatur redibaturque, ob maximam quandam ac pene innumerabilem euntium revertentiumque multitudinem, quadam die plures utriusque sexus homines diversis oppressionibus variisque suffocationibus interirent. Eorum suffocatorum numerus ad ducentesimum pene pervenisse existimatur et creditur quod profecto in humandis obtritorum et inambulantium pedibus oppressorum cadaveribus postea compertum est. Id ubi pontifex rescivit et satis indoluit et ad perpetuam tanti et tam infortunati casus memoriam duas parvas basilicas in commemorati pontis initio duobus eius lateribus se se invicem e regione respicientes postmodum construxit, ubi ingens predicti casus adversitas antea contigerat, que quidem ab omnibus hinc inde transeuntibus propalam visuntur. Et ne simile infortunium posthac accidere valeret, aream magnam, pluribus tabernis domibusque ad solum dirutis, ibidem effecit,[40] quo caterve hominum in platee latitudinem egrederentur.

12. Pontifex ergo ex hoc[41] tanto et tam immenso ac pene tam incredibili hominum ad hunc iubileum accedentium numero maximam ac fere infinitam argenti et auri copiam cum ob ingentium vectigalium multiplicationem tum ob magnam cunctarum rerum ad victum necessariarum quotidianam consumptionem tum insuper ob generales uniuscuiusque oblationes adeptus est. Unde ad perpetuam huius sacrosancti anni commemorationem plurimos[42] amplos[43] et inusitatos (925) aureos feriri[44] et cudi fecit quos ab effectu ipso iubileos cognominavit; ac tanti ponderis erant ut communi trium usitatorum aureorum pretio suo valore adequarentur. Proinde ex his duabus et obtritorum hominum et iubileorum aureorum causis, cum ea ipsa numquam alias ceteris similibus annis evenisse compererimus[45] ac illa non aliunde quam ob maximam quandam et pene incredibilem adventantium et concurrentium personarum multitudinem profluxisse cognoverimus, hunc de quo loquimur iubileum aliis singulis omnibus hactenus celebratis numero et confluentium populorum copia merito preponere ac preferre non dubitamus.

13. At vero ubi pontifex magnos et ingentes pecuniarum thesauros exinde ad erarium apostolicum provenisse cognovit, quamquam secundo pontificatus sui anno pluribus simul locis et intra[46] et extra urbem non modicis sumptibus construere et

---

[40] efficitur *D*
[41] ex hoc ergo *C¹*
[42] plurimos *om. Muratori*
[43] amplo *D*
[44] ferri *Muratori*
[45] comperimus *D*: comperiamus *Muratori*
[46] intus *Muratori*

11. What more? The congestion of arriving peoples became great. One day, at the famous bridge near the Hadrianic Mass, where direct traffic goes back and forth to the basilica of Peter Prince of the Apostles, because of the very large, almost uncountable crowd of people coming and going, many people of both sexes died, some crushed and others suffocated. Those suffocated are estimated at over two hundred in number. It is believed that this was later discovered while burying the corpses of those crushed under the feet of those who stepped on them and trampled them. When the pontiff learned of this, he expressed due sorrow. For the permanent memory of this large and unfortunate accident, he later built two small basilicas at the beginning of the bridge, on the two sides directly facing one another where the huge disaster of that accident had earlier occurred. These are in plain view of all people crossing in both directions. And so that no similar accident could ever again occur, he razed many inns and houses, making a large open area there so that crowds of people might make their way into the breadth of the platea.

12. So from this great, immense, and nearly unbelievable number of visitors for this Jubilee the Pontiff acquired an almost unlimited supply of gold and silver because tax revenues multiplied hugely, all the necessary provisions were consumed daily on a large scale, and general offerings were made by individuals. From this he had many grand and unusual gold coins struck and minted to permanently commemorate this Most Holy Year. Called "jubilees", they were of such weight that they equaled in worth the common value of three normal gold coins. The people crushed and the jubilee gold coins are two things we have found never before happened in such years. We realized they resulted from nothing other than that a very large, almost unbelievable crowd of people arrived and gathered here. And so we do not hesitate rightly to place and rank this Jubilee of which we speak ahead of each and every other one heretofore celebrated in the number and wealth of peoples streaming here.

13. In the second year of his pontificate he had already begun constructing and building at many places simultaneously both inside and outside the city at not

edificare coepisset, et ingentem quoque latinorum et grecorum codicum congeriem congregare statuisset, atque aliquot insuper doctrine et humanitatis studiis prestantes viros utriusque lingue peritissimos annuis mercedibus et ordinariis[47] salariis ad sese evocasset, ex nova tamen et inopinata predictarum pecuniarum acquisitione ad continuam non modo ceptorum[48] operum prosecutionem sed amplificationem etiam et aliorum huiusmodi innovationem mirum in modum animum applicuit ut ob perpetuam magnorum edificiorum constructionem romane ecclesie honor et apostolice sedis gloria simul cum singulari et precipua christianorum populorum omnium devotione abundantius ac latius amplificaretur et ob assiduam insuper novorum preclarorumque operum cum traductionem tum compilationem presentibus et posteris studiosis hominibus plurimum adiumenti preberetur.[49] Ad id enim duntaxat officium predictos doctissimos viros annuis premiis ad se se accersiverat. Atque huius sue mentalis tam magne ac tam vehementis, cum ad edificandum tum ad traducendum et compilandum et libros congregandum applicationis, etsi duas commemoratas causas in primis fuisse intellexerimus, tertiam nihilominus proprie glorie cuius suapte natura avidissimus erat adeptionem ac sui nominis propagationem non immerito accessisse existimamus[50] et credimus. Nullam enim humanarum rerum memoriam ea ipsa diuturniorem fore animadvertebat que et ingentibus edificiis quodammodo perpetuis et eternis quoque litterarum monumentis mandabatur. His igitur tribus causis[51] adductus dici non potest quantum ad hec tria iam pridem[52] incoepta edificationis ac traductionis compilationis et bibliothece opera, magnorum et inopinatorum thesaurorum opportunitate captata, prosequenda, amplificanda, perficienda, et consumanda animum mentemque converterit. Que quidem tria presertim usque ad ultimum pene vite sue diem tanta diligentia, tanta cura, tanta assiduitate, tantisque impensis prosecutus est ut in magnum miraculum processisse videatur.

14. Tantam enim ut de singulis pauca quedam memoratu digna manifestande veritatis gratia in medium adducantur, grecorum et latinorum librorum[53] in omni doctrinarum genere copiam ab eo, infausta illa ac profecto nobis et ceteris doctis hominibus infelici mortis sue vel potius nostre die, congregatam fuisse novimus, ut (926) supra quinque milia partim grammaticorum, partim poetarum, partim historicorum, partim rhetorum oratorumque, partim dialecticorum,

[47] peritissimos, ardore incredibili, & non ordinariis *Muratori*
[48] acquisitione non modo ad coeptorum *Muratori*
[49] praeberet *Muratori*
[50] existimavimus *D*
[51] de caussis *Muratori*
[52] iam primum *C*
[53] laborum *D*

modest expense, and he had already also resolved to assemble a huge collection of Latin and Greek codices. In addition he had already summoned to himself some of the men most distinguished in erudition and the humanist disciplines and most learned in both tongues, with annual payments and regular wages. Still, when the pontiff understood that great, enormous stores of money had passed into the Apostolic Treasury from this new and unexpected acquisition of funds, he applied his energies in an amazing way not only to continuing to pursue projects already begun but also to expanding and initiating other ones. And so by continually constructing great edifices the honor of the Roman Church and the glory of the Apostolic See as well as the singular and particular loyalty of all Christian peoples was more abundantly and broadly enlarged. And by scrupulously translating and acquiring new and classic texts, much benefit was supplied to present and future scholars. At least for this project, he had already attracted to himself with annual stipends the most learned men. We understand that the two motives mentioned above were foremost to the enormous and vigorous mental energies he expended on building and on translating, composing, and collecting books. Yet we no less firmly believe that there was a third cause that led him on — the acquisition of personal glory, for which he was by nature most eager, and the promotion of his own name. For he recalled that no memory of human affairs lasts longer than that which is committed to enormous permanent buildings and imperishable literary records. Thus attracted by these three motives, it cannot be described how greatly he turned his mind and energies to pursuing, enlarging, perfecting, and completing the three projects already begun — building and translation and the acquisition of a library — seizing the opportunity afforded by great and unexpected fortunes. These are the three special pursuits that occupied him practically to the last day of his life, with such steadfastness, such care, such precision, and such expense that the results seem miraculous.

14. To single out a few items worth recalling to illustrate this truth, we know that he had collected a great stock of Greek and Latin books in every category of learning. By that unlucky day — unhappy for us and for other scholars — when he, or rather we, died, over five thousand volumes were inventoried, codices of grammarians, poets, historians, rhetoricians and orators, dialecticians, cosmographers,

partim cosmographorum, partim architectorum, partim geometrarum, partim musicorum, partim arithmeticorum, partim astrologorum, partim de pictura ac sculptura, et de re militari, et de agricultura, partim moralium, partim physicorum, partim medicorum, partim utriusque iuris et civilis et pontificii consultorum, partim denique theologorum cum plurimis predictorum auctorum commentatoribus et explanatoribus codicum volumina recenserentur. De quo si quis forte miraretur[54] omittende admirationis sue causa consideret, queso, quanta ipse in conducendis rebus ad quas animum applicaverat diligentia utebatur, quanta liberalitate, quanta denique cum esset omnium dominus[55] potestate potiebatur. Quot enim librarios cum grecos tum latinos ad transcribendum et intra et extra urbem annuis[56] mercedibus[57] conduxerat? Quot exploratores doctos homines non per universam Italiam solum, sed usque ad extremos etiam Germanie ac Britannie angulos ad investigandum indagandumque transmiserat? Quot insuper in Greciam ipsam et ante et post deplorandam Constantinopolis captivitatem eruditos viros magnis cum salariis ingentibusque emendorum et perferendorum clarorum[58] codicum commissionibus destinaverat?

15. In quo quidem Ptolemeum Philadelphum inclitum Egypti regem egregie admodum[59] imitatus est, quem in construenda illa sua tam celebrata ac tam admirabili bibliotheca hunc congregandorum librorum modum apud idoneos auctores tenuisse legerat, ubi sexaginta[60] circiter librorum duntaxat grecorum milia (incredibile dictu) collocasse traditur. Quas ob res[61] factum est ut ex toto pene terrarum orbe novi ad eum codices usque ad mortifere egrotationis sue finem quotidie deferrentur.[62] Ex hoc tanto et tam ingenti et grecorum et latinorum librorum numero (quem si diutius vixisset mirum in modum deinceps in dies adauxisset) singularem et precipuam bibliothecam opportuno quodam palatii sui loco condere ac construere decreverat ubi omnes simul congregatos ad communem cunctorum romane ecclesie prelatorum utilitatem et ad perpetuum quoque et eternum[63] sacri palatii ornamentum suis locis propriisque designationibus collocasset; quod predictum Ptolemeum, doctissimo viro ac nobilitato[64] illorum temporum historico

---

[54] miretur *Muratori*

[55] domus *D*

[56] annuis *om. Muratori*

[57] mercibus *A*

[58] carorum *Muratori*

[59] admodum *om. Muratori*

[60] novem *Muratori*

[61] Quamobrem *Muratori*

[62] deferentur *CC¹*: deferuntur *D*

[63] ceterum *D*

[64] nobili *Muratori*

astrologers; on painting and sculpture, and military affairs, and agriculture; of moralists, physical scientists, physicians, experts on both civil and pontifical law, and, finally, theologians together with numerous commentators and explicators of these authors. If anyone is perhaps astonished at this, let him please keep in mind, to dispose of his astonishment, what great steadfastness he employed in conducting those affairs on which he had set his mind, what great liberality, and what great power he possessed when he was the lord of all. For how many copyists, both Greek and Latin, had he employed on annual payments for transcribing, both inside and outside the City? How many learned men had he sent forth as scouts, not only through all of Italy, but to the farthest corners of Germany and Britain to search and track them down? How many scholarly men, both before and after the lamentable capture of Constantinople, had he appointed to Greece itself with large salaries and huge commissions to buy and deliver famous codices?

15. In this he quite remarkably imitated Ptolemy Philadelphus, that renowned king of Egypt. He had read in the pertinent authors that Ptolemy had held to this method of collecting books in building that much celebrated and wondrous library of his, where it is reported he had collected about sixty thousand just of Greek books (unbelievable to tell!). To these ends, new codices were daily delivered to him from practically the whole world up to his final moment from his death-dealing fever. From this huge number of Greek and Latin books (had he lived longer he would have marvelously increased the number day by day), he determined to found and build a unique and special library at a convenient location in his palace where he would have arranged all the items that he had collected in their own places with the proper designations, for the common use of all the prelates of the Roman Church and as a permanent and everlasting ornament to the sacred palace. This is what he recognized Ptolemy had done, to the great

et regio commissario Aristeo procurante, magna cum nominis sui laude fecisse cognoverat. De optimo atque opportuno commemorate bibliothece loco singularem mentionem faciemus cum ad accommodatam urbanorum edificiorum et sacri palatii designationem accedemus.

16. Quid de traductionibus ac diversis[65] novorum operum compilatoribus dicemus? que quidem traductoribus ac propriorum operum scriptoribus quasi[66] certatim agentibus cum suis salariis quisque pro virili parte ad operandum alliceretur, usque adeo creverunt ut quinque ultimis fausti ac felicis pontificatus sui annis longe plura ad hec presertim[67] humanitatis studia quorum amantissimus erat pertinentia quam quinque seculis antea totis centum predecessorum suorum temporibus composita ac traducta fuisse videantur. Etenim ut a grammaticis, poëtis, ac dispersis versibus que (927) sunt leviora[68] incipiamus, quot de orthographia libros, quot poëmata, quot sparsa carmina passim confecta fuisse scimus? Iliados quoque celebratum et decantatum[69] Homeri poëma latinis — difficile sane et arduum opus — versibus a duobus prestantibus viris eodem tempore traducebatur: quod Ioannis Bocacii florentini poete temporibus a Leontio quodam thessalonicensi, illius in grecis litteris preceptore, soluta oratione multo facilius ad traducendum, quam carmine factum fuisse novimus. Nec Strabonis de cosmographia opus silentio obruatur. Ad historicos accedamus. Herodotum, quem greci veteres[70] patrem historie appellare solebant, Thucitidem, Xenophontem, Polibium, Diodorum, Appianum, Philonem iudeum, fortunatis huius summi pontificis temporibus, latini ac grecarum litterarum expertes primum legere ceperunt. Plura insuper egregia Platonis, Aristotelis, Theophrasti, celebratorum philosophorum opera: Platonis celeberrimum illud politie[71] sue vel de republica volumen et alterum de legibus preclarissimum; multa Aristotelis ut posteriora analetica, ut tota physica, problemata, magna moralia, metaphysica, ac plures rhetoricorum et decem et novem illos celebratos de animalibus libros tunc primum conspexerunt que quidem etsi prius traducta fuissent ita tamen traducta reperiebantur ut vix intelligi possent; ac preterea Theophrasti de plantis librum a priscis grecis apprime laudatum eo tempore primum latinum vidimus. Quid de theologis sacrisque codicibus dicemus? Nonne preclarum illud de preparatione evangelica Eusebii cesariensis

---

[65] adversis *D*

[66] quasi *om. Muratori*

[67] plura praesertim ad *Muratori*

[68] quae selectiora *Muratori*

[69] et decantatum *om. D Muratori*

[70] veteres *om. D*

[71] Politicae *Muratori*

praise of his name, under the supervision of Aristeas, a most learned man and famed historian of those times and the royal commissioner. On the excellent and convenient location of this library we shall specially remark when we come to the suitable design of the urban buildings and the sacred palace.

16. What shall we say about the translators and the various composers of new works? Translators and writers of their own books acted as if in competition, since each was enticed by his wages to produce these works to the best of his ability. The works grew in such number that in the five last years of his fortunate and happy pontificate far more seem to have been composed and translated, particularly in the humanistic studies of which he was a great lover, than in the five previous centuries in the times of all his hundred predecessors together. To begin with the grammarians, poets, and scattered verses — which are less serious — how many books on orthography, how many poems, and how many random verses do we know to have been composed? Also the *Iliad*, that celebrated and much-sung poem of Homer, was at the same time translated into Latin verse — a quite difficult and tricky task — by two distinguished gentlemen. (In the time of Giovanni Boccacio the Florentine poet, we recognize that it had been rendered by a certain Leontino of Thessalonike, his Greek teacher, into prose, but that is much easier to translate than poetry.) Nor should Strabo's work on cosmography be silently overlooked. Let us proceed to the historians. During this supreme pontiff's fortunate times, the Latins, even those inexperienced in Greek literature, began to read Herodotus (whom the ancient Greeks called the father of history), Thucydides, Xenophon, Polybius, Diodorus, Appian, Philo Judaeus. In addition, they read more of the remarkable works of the celebrated philosophers Plato, Aristotle, Theophrastus: that most renowned volume of Plato on politics, or *On the Republic*, and a second famous work, *On Laws*. They examined for the first time much of Aristotle, such as the *Posterior Analytics*, the whole of the *Physics*, the *Problems*, the *Great Moralia*, the *Metaphysics*, and many books on the rhetoricians and the nineteen celebrated books *On Animals*. These works had been translated before, but were found to have been translated in such a way that they were scarcely intelligible. In addition, we saw at that time the first Latin version of Theophrastus's book *On Plants*, a work much prized by the ancient Greeks. What shall we say about the theologians and sacred codices? Surely we are not unaware in that fortunate time what was correctly, faithfully, and elegantly converted from Greek into Latin: that extraordinary volume of Eusebius

quatuordecim libris distinctum volumen ac plurima — ne omnium particularem mentionem faciamus — Dionysii ariopagite, magni Basilii, Gregorii nazanzeni, Ioannis chrisostomi, Cirilli hac ipsa temporis felicitate e greca in latinam linguam probe, fideliter, atque eleganter conversa fuisse non ignoramus?

17. Et ut aliquid[72] de nobis captata presertim hoc loco dicendi opportunitate sine arrogantia referamus: nos septimo pontificatus sui anno ab eo e Florentia apostolicis litteris in urbem evocati cum tantam traductorum ac diversorum scriptorum multitudinem undique pro virili sua operantem et in propria, ut dicitur, officina opera cudentem cerneremus, ne forte soli otio marcesceremus neve salarium[73] quod nobis sua benignitate largiri dignabatur omnino deperditum ac penitus amissum fuisse videretur et ut sanctitati sue aliquatenus obsequeremur, duo nova ac magna cepta, profecto humeris nostris imparia, paulo post quam Romam applicueramus[74] invadere atque aggredi decrevimus. Primum erat ingens quoddam viginti librorum volumen quod adversus iudeos et gentes pro catholica Christi salvatoris nostri fide bonis christiane religionis omnibus[75] instituеramus. Nova deinde quedam utriusque et veteris et novi testamenti,[76] partim ex hebreo, partim ex greco idiomate, ut[77] ab origine a propriis scriptoribus suis litteris mandata fuisse constabat, in latinam linguam traductio non iniuria mentem irrepserat. Et nisi importuna ac maligna, quinimmo ut expressius dixerim, importunissima ac procul dubio malignissima eius mors prevenisset preveniensque assiduum operationis nostre cursum non modo[78] impedisset retardassetque sed omnino etiam abstulisset, forsitan divina ope (928) adiuti — quando[79] ea ipsa boni gratia agebamus — utrumque opus omnibus animi et corporis viribus quemadmodum instituеramus prosecuti, non multo post ad finem usque produxissemus. Quod[80] si hic importunus dicendi locus non videretur, nimirum causas quibus et ad traducendum et ad scribendum impellebamur paulisper commemorassemus: quod in prefationibus predictorum operum, si Deus, ut speramus, adiutor noster erit, absque iusta reprehensione non iniuria efficere[81] posse videbimur. Sed ad institutum dicendi ordinem revertamur.

[72] aliquo *D*
[73] salarii *Muratori*
[74] applicuimus *Muratori*
[75] ominibus *B*
[76] testamenta *D*
[77] uti *Muratori*
[78] non modo non *Muratori*
[79] quoniam *Muratori*
[80] quid *D*
[81] afficere *D*

of Caesaria *On the Preparation of the Gospel*, divided into fourteen books, and very many works — not to mention them all specifically — of Dionysius the Areopagite, Basil the Great, Gregory Nazienzus, John Chrysostom, and Cyril.

17. And now I would like to take the opportunity to speak here and refer without arrogance to something that concerns me. In the seventh year of his pontificate I was called by him in an Apostolic letter inviting me to come from Florence to the City. I saw the great mass of translators and diverse writers all over the place working on projects with all their energy and, as the saying goes, forging works in their own workshops. I had no intention that we alone would waste away in idleness or that the wages granted us through his largesse would seem to have been utterly wasted and completely lost. I wanted somehow to provide a service to His Holiness, so I decided, a bit after I had made my way to Rome, to attack and tackle two great new projects, ill-suited to our shoulders. The first, to all good men of Christian religion, was a huge volume in twenty books which we undertook against the Jews and Pagans on behalf of the Catholic faith of Christ our Savior. The second crept into my mind for good reasons, a new translation into Latin of both the Old and New Testaments, made from the original Hebrew and Greek, since their original writers had clearly entrusted them to their own languages. And if that cruel and hateful, or to put it more precisely, that cruellest and most hateful death of his, had not intervened and, intervening, had not blocked and slowed the steady progress of my project or even stolen it completely away, perhaps aided by divine help — as I was engaged in these very activities for a good cause — pursuing each work with all the vigor of mind and body as I planned, I would have brought it to its completion in a timely manner. If this did not seem a cruel place to talk of this, I would have made brief mention of the causes why I was driven to translate and to write. This perhaps I will be able to do properly and without undue criticism in the prefaces of those works, if God, as I hope, will be my helper. Now let us return to the agreed order of discussion.

18. Hoc eodem iubilei anno, ne aliquod ex gestis suis memoratu dignum a nobis pretermissum fuisse videatur, Bernardinum quendam massensem — hoc est Masse natum virum — cum moribus et sanctimonia vite tum multis quoque miraculis celeberrimum, Rome solemni patrum atque prelatorum concilio de more congregato, in catalogo sanctorum non immerito collocavit et posuit.

19. Proinde ad enarranda edificia paulo post accedemus, quando[82] quidem ipsum dominum nostrum cum tota curia pestis gratia ad Fabrianum contulerimus ne inceptum narrandi ordinem pervertamus. Dum igitur pontifex noster et conservande paci et unioni quoque ecclesie romane et ordini etiam gubernandi et congregandis undique et conficiendis codicibus et[83] traducendis insuper operibus et edificiis preterea construendis assiduam operam navaret, factum est ut vehemens et acerba pestilentia civitatem totam et[84] forensem curiam ac finitimum circumquaque agrum romanum ita aggrederetur ut paucis post diebus usque ad palatinos familiares ac domesticos suos maiorem in modum deseviret. Quod ab omnipotenti Deo id circo divina providentia permissum fuisse non iniuria existimamus et credimus ne forte in tanta ac profecto tam admirabili omnium tam secularium quam ecclesiasticarum rerum prosperitate se esse hominem oblivisceretur atque ingentem status sui excellentiam cernens, sic in detestandum nimie ambitionis ac intolerande superbie vitium dilaberetur: quod de se ipso Paulus apostolus ad Corinthios scribens asserere ac testificari non dubitavit. Sic enim ait: ne multitudo[85] revelationum extollat me, datus est mihi stimulus carnis mee angelus Sathane, qui me colaphizet: propter quod ter Dominum rogavi ut discederet a me et dixit mihi, sufficit tibi gratia mea, nam virtus in infirmitate perficitur et reliqua huiusmodi.

20. Unde hac peste in dies crudelius seviente, ex urbe recedere atque Fabrianum, ut diximus, proficisci constituit. Sed cum inter itinerandum Tolentinum applicaret, factum est ut a novo ac molesto ragadiarum morbo vehementer caperetur. Sed paulo post, ut in calce primi libri dixisse meminimus, penitus liberatus atque inceptum iter prosecutus, Fabrianum se contulit. Ubi cum esset, inchoata librorum et commemoratorum edificiorum opera nequaquam deseruit.[86] Nam et antequam e Roma recederet[87] ut continue et sine intermissione edificaretur prefectos et operum conductores instituit et librarios quoque traductores insuper et

---

[82] accedamus, quoniam *Muratori*

[83] et *om. Muratori*

[84] ac *Muratori*

[85] multitudo *codd.*: magnitudo *Vulg* (2 *Cor.* 12:7)

[86] defuit *D*

[87] decederet *B*

18. In this same Jubilee Year (not to pass over any of his achievements worth recalling), he enrolled and placed in the catalogue of saints for his merit Bernardino Massense (that is, a man born at Massa), greatly renowned for his character and the sanctity of his life as well as for many miracles, accompanied by the solemn council of fathers and prelates gathered at Rome according to the custom.

19. We shall shortly proceed to narrating the buildings, but first we will take our lord with all the Curia to Fabriano because of the plague, so as not to distort the narrative order we began. While our Pontiff ceaselessly struggled to preserve the peace, to navigate union and order within the Roman Church, to gather and obtain codices from all over, to have works translated, and also to put up buildings, a raging and bitter plague happened to assault the whole city, the Curia outside the city, and the nearby countryside all around Rome. Within a few days, its raging had especially reached his palace household and domestic staff. This, we firmly believe, almighty God through divine providence had not unjustly permitted, so that amid the great and wonderful prospering of all his secular and ecclesiastical affairs, he might not forget that he was human, and, seeing the mighty superiority of his position, might slip into the detestable vice of overbearing ambition and unbearable pride. The Apostle Paul writing to the Corinthians did not hesitate to claim and testify to the same about himself when he said: "To keep me from being too elated by the abundance of revelations, a thorn was given me in the flesh, a messenger of Satan, to harass me, to keep me from being too elated. Three times I besought the Lord about this, that it should leave me; but he said to me, 'My grace is sufficient for you, for my power is made perfect in weakness'," and so forth (2 Cor. 12:7–9).

20. With this plague raging more cruelly day by day, he decided to withdraw from the city and to make his way to Fabriano, as I said. But on the way to Tolentino, he happened to be vehemently infected with a new and virulent disease called "ragades". Shortly afterwards, however, as I recall having said at the end of the first book, he was completely freed of it, resumed the journey he had begun, and made his way to Fabriano. While there, he never abandoned the projects of books and building which he had begun. For even before he withdrew from Rome, intending that building could proceed continuously without interruption, he appointed foremen and project contractors. He also took to Fabriano with him

compilatores secum ne forte pestilenti contagione[88] arriperentur, Fabrianum usque conduxit. Ibi parum commorati, quisque ad ceptorum operum executionem absolutionemque pro virili sua intendebat.

21. Dum itaque pontifex (929) Fabriani commoraretur, nova edificandi cogitatio ad quod propria natura trahebatur animum suum irrepsit. Proinde tametsi paucis mensibus illic commoraretur, oppidi tamen aream que antea pusilla et angusta erat longe lateque amplificavit, eamque sive ergastulis[89] sive tabernaculis que Greco clariori et tritiori verbo apotece nuncupantur, apprime corroboravit exornavitque.[90] Et beati insuper Francisci basilicam que iam ruinosa videbatur egregiis fundamentis tectisque reparavit. Non multo post, exinanita et extincta peste cuius gratia abiverat, Romam remeavit atque prorsus ad eadem sua[91] bibliothece, traductionis, compilationis, edificationis studia non intermissa sed potius ob eius absentiam parumper impedita, dici non potest quanta diligentia, quanta cura, quanta, ut ita dixerim, solicitudine in predictis operibus partim perficiendis, partim noviter incoandis uteretur. Sed cum de ceteris huiusmodi gestis nonnulla superius retulisse meminerimus, de edificiis duntaxat in presentiarum prosequemur.

22. Multa et quidem magna edificia de quibus solis, pretermissis aliis huiusmodi cum pene infinita sint, verba facere instituimus ab eo fabricata fuisse constat que partim extra, partim vero intra urbem maximis impensis maiorique magnificentia propalam visuntur. Atque ante omnia de exterioribus, postea de interioribus quoad fieri poterit brevius commemorabimus. [1–2]

23. Atque primo ut a levioribus incipiamus, Gualdi principalem oppidi sancti Benedicti basilicam reparavit, amplificavit, novisque edificiis magnifice perpolivit. Assisinatem deinde beati Francisci edem pluribus locis vel iam collapsam vel certe paulo post collapsuram cum egregiis fundamentis stabilivit, tum novis tectis confirmavit. In Civitate quoque que trito et vulgato verbo Vetusta appellatur ingentia quedam magnificaque edificia construxit. In altera etiam Civitate quam Castellanam[92] nuncupant inter cetera maiorem quam tertiam menium partem nuper specioseque[93] refecit. Narniensem insuper arcem novis constructionibus peregregie munivit. In Urbe Veteri ingentem arcem simul cum magnifico quodam palatio maximis fossis undique circundato, opus sane impensa magnificentiaque

[88] contagio *Muratori*
[89] ergastulis sive tabernis *Muratori*
[90] exornavit *D*
[91] suae *Muratori*
[92] Castellarum *Muratori*
[93] spatioseque *D Magnuson Pagnotti*

copyists, as well as translators and compilers, to prevent their being attacked by the plague's contagion. They lingered there a while, each striving as best he could to carry out and complete the projects begun.

21. While the pontiff lingered at Fabriano, a new idea for building entered his mind, something he was drawn to by his own nature. Accordingly, although he lingered there only a few months, he enlarged the length and width of the town's open area which was tiny and cramped before. Then he reinforced and embellished it with workshops and small shops, what are called "stores" in the more elegant and fitting Greek term. He repaired with extraordinary foundations and roofs the basilica of St. Francis which already looked to be in ruins. Not long afterwards, because the plague, dissipating, had died out, he departed, made his way back to Rome and to his same pursuits — the library, translation, composing, building. They had not been interrupted, but only slowed down a bit by his absence. One cannot say what diligence, what care, and what (as I said before) concern he employed in both finishing those projects and beginning new ones. Even though we related above some information about his other accomplishments along this line, let us at least for the moment delve into his buildings.

22. Clearly, he built many great buildings. We propose to remark only on the ones both outside and inside the City which the public visits because of their very great cost or unusual magnificence, and to lay aside other similar buildings since they are truly countless. As briefly as I can, I shall comment first on the ones outside the City, then on those within.

23. To begin with the less important ones, he repaired, enlarged, and magnificently improved with new buildings the principal basilica in the town of Gualdo, that of Saint Benedict. Then, the church of Saint Francis at Assisi, which in many places had already collapsed or was threatening imminent collapse, he stabilized with extraordinary foundations, then strengthened with new roofs. In Civita, too, the one called by the familiar popular title Vecchia, he constructed huge and magnificent buildings. In the other Civita, the one they call Castellana, among other things he attractively rebuilt more than a third of the city walls. He quite splendidly fortified Narnia's citadel with new construction. At Orvieto, he built a very handsome huge citadel with a magnificent palace completely surrounded by very large moats, a work surely worth viewing for its cost and magnificence.

visendum, pulcherrime fabricatus est. Quid preterea de arce spoletana dicemus? nonne tantis sumptibus tantisque et tam egregiis cum atriorum tum cubiculorum edificiis et corroboravit et adauxit atque ita exornavit ut et[94] extrinsecus mirabile opus videatur et intrinsecus eruditis quoruncunque cernentium oculis admirabilius ac magnificentius conspiciatur? Quid denique de balneis viterbiensibus referemus quorum virtutes ad cunctas humani corporis egrotationes et morbos magne mirabilesque ferebantur et cum omnibus idoneis habitationibus pro quotidianis languentibus curandi causa accedentibus privata ac nudata reperirentur, prudenter salubriterque curavit ut plura ac diversa illic opportuna habitacula conderentur? Que quidem tanta magnificentia, tantisque impensis construxit ut non solum idonea ac salubria egrotorum omnium tabernacula sed cunctorum etiam principum accommodata edificia, regalesque regie haberentur. Sed quid nos plura de fabrianensibus, de gualdensibus, assisinatibus, utriusque Civitatis et Vetuste et Castellane, urbevetanis, spoletanis, viterbiensibus et multis aliis novis quorum pene infinitus est numerus vel conditionibus vel extrinsecis reparationibus singillatim colligimus? [3–12]

24. Ad urbana tandem edificia veniamus: quinque singularia et precipua fabricandi et condendi opera ac profecto memoratu laudibusque digna intra urbem partim ad munitionem, partim ad ornamentum, partim ad aeris salubritatem, partim ad devotionem vel maxime pertinentia efficere et consummare cupiebat ac sic[95] in mente sua penitus et omnino proposuerat. [13]

25. Quorum primum erat ut urbis menia pluribus simul locis iam collapsa et confragosa noviter repararet; secundum ut sacras quadraginta mansionum edes a Gregorio primo cognomento magno sancto pontifice primitus institutas novis edificiis et constructionibus reformaret; tertium ut vicum quendam a porta adrianee[96] molis incoandum et usque ad basilicam Petri apostolorum principis porrigendum ita suis stationibus ac munitionibus conderet ut tota simul curia intrinsecus secura tutaque sufficienter habitaret; quartum ut pontificale palatium mirum in modum permuniret[97] atque regaliter exornaret; quintum ut sacram beati Petri edem a fundamentis nuper reedificaret. De quorum duobus prioribus singillatim idcirco pauca dicemus quia iam ea ipsa ad finem suum perducta et omnino consummata fuisse conspicimus. De tribus vero ultimis quoniam edificia inusitata ac profecto mirabilia extitissent si perfecta et absoluta ut ipse instituerat tandem aliquando in lucem apparuissent, paulo latius postea tractabimus. [14–20]

---

[94] et *om. D Muratori Magnuson*

[95] si *D*

[96] *hic et passim* adriane *DBE*: Adrianae *Muratori Magnuson*

[97] praemuniret *Muratori Magnuson*

What besides shall I say of the citadel at Spoleto? Did he not reinforce and expand it at great expense and with many remarkable buildings containing halls and bedrooms and embellish it? From the outside does it not seem a work of wonder and from within present an even more wondrous and magnificent view to the educated eyes of discerning people? What, finally, shall I say of the baths at Viterbo whose great and wonderful powers were being applied to all the afflictions and diseases of the human body? When these baths were found deprived and stripped of all the residences suitable for the sick who came each day for healing, he wisely saw to it that many suitable dwellings of different kinds were founded there to promote health. He built them with such magnificence and at such great expense that they are considered not only suitable and healthful lodgings for all the sick, but buildings congenial to princes, palaces fit for kings. But why go on listing further the many other new works (their number is almost infinite) of construction or repair at places outside the city, at Fabriano, Gualdo, Assisi, the two Civita (Vecchia and Castellana), Orvieto, Spoleto, Viterbo?

24. Let us come now to the urban buildings. Within the City there were five specific special projects of building and founding which he desired to carry out and so he made up his mind completely. Worthy of memory and praise, they particularly related to fortification, ornamentation, healthy air, and devotion.

25. First of these was to repair the city walls to new condition; they had collapsed or crumbled in many places. Second, to reconfigure with new buildings and construction the forty station churches first instituted by Pope Saint Gregory the Great. Third, to found a district beginning at the gate of Hadrian's Mass and extending to the basilica of Peter, prince of the Apostles, with its own guardposts and fortifications so that the entire Curia together could live inside in reasonable security and safety. Fourth, to fortify the papal palace in a wonderful manner and to adorn it regally. Fifth, to rebuild the sacred church of Saint Peter anew, from the foundations up. I shall say only a little about the first two since we see that they are already carried through and completely finished. Then I shall treat the last three somewhat more fully because the buildings would have been unusual and quite wonderful if they had ever fully come into the light, completed and carried out as he had planned.

26. Quippe ut secundum enarratum ordinem procedamus, urbis menia a porta flumentana ex parte inferiori versus orientem per collatinam, per viminalem, per neviam, per latinam, per capenam usque ad trigeminam, ubicumque ruinam minabantur, multis locis continuatis propugnaculis[98] trans piramidem lapideam menibus ipsis astantem aliquot passuum milibus generose[99] admodum et utiliter reparavit. A parte vero superiori versus occidentem prosequens usque ad predictum molis adrianee pontem pulcherrime reformavit. Pontem vero pluribus turribus egregie munivit et molem ipsam extrinsecus crebris[100] propugnaculis corroboravit ac tectoriis dealbavit. Intrinsecus autem aulis et tricliniis ita inter se distinxit ut utroque et arcis et[101] regie officio accommodatissime fungi posse videretur. A ponte vero usque ad portam palatinam nihil innovavit cum[102] quia ibi menia valida et solida apparebant tum etiam quia in constructione vici de quo paulo post dicemus ipsius amplificandi gratia funditus diruere et demoliri constituerat. Ex transverso vero super montem prope quasi ad verticem versus meridiem totam regionem illam novis muris, crebris turribus, frequentibus propugnaculis trans portam vulgato nomine pertusam magnis impensis mirabiliter perfecit atque usque ad regionem Sancti Spiritus xenodochium respicientem absolvit. [21–26]

27. Nunc ad secundum membrum brevius accedamus. Cunctas sanctarum stationum edes carie ac vetustate pene consumptas pontifex magnanimus, atque admodum pius, egregie reparare ac reformare decreverat atque hoc ipsum reformandi et reparandi officium in plurimis[103] minoribus sancte Marie trans Tiberim et beate Praxedis[104] et sancti Theodori ac Petri in vinculis nuncupati plurimumque aliarum huiusmodi basilicarum — ne omnium particularem mentionem faciamus — reparationibus constructionibusque incoavit. Ad maiora deinde conversus in septem celebratiores et principales, ut ita dixerim, totius romane regionis ecclesias animum adiecit. Ioannis enim lateranensis, Marie maioris, Stephani[105] celimontani, sanctorum apostolorum, Pauli exterioris, et Laurentii extra muros basilicas partim munivit, partim reparavit,[106] partim ornavit, partim mirum in modum renovavit. De septem illis maioribus celebratissimisque ceterarum omnium principalissima, mira, ac devota beati Petri edes sola restabat quam quia a fundamentis magnifice

[98] propugnaculis novis *Muratori Magnuson*
[99] generoseque *Magnuson*
[100] crebris *om.* *C¹*
[101] utroque et habitationis et arcis regiae *Muratori Magnuson*
[102] tum *CC1*
[103] pluribus *CC¹*
[104] paraxedis *D*
[105] Stephanam *C*
[106] partim reparavit *om.* *Muratori*

26. To proceed in our announced order, he quite nobly and usefully repaired the city walls from the Porta Flumentana at the bottom moving towards the east through the Porta Collatina, Viminalis, Naevia, Latina, Capena, all the way to the Trigemina, joining many places with battlements wherever they threatened ruin, across the stone pyramid that stands up against the walls, some miles altogether. At the top towards the west moving as far as the bridge of the Hadrianic Mass he had them remodeled very handsomely. The bridge he specially fortified with many towers and on the outside reinforced the Mass itself with frequent battlements and whitened it with stucco. On the inside he divided its spaces between halls and triclinia so that it seemed to serve quite nicely the dual function of citadel and palace. He added nothing new from the bridge to the gate of the palace, not just because the walls there looked stout and solid, but also because in the construction of the District, about which I shall talk in a moment, he had decided to completely raze and demolish them to enlarge it. Going across the hill almost at its peak towards the south he brought, at great expense, that entire region to a wonderful completion with new walls, close towers, and frequent battlements beyond the gate commonly called the Porta Pertusa and finished it all the way to the region that faces the hospital of Sto. Spirito.

27. Let us now briefly proceed to our second point. This magnanimous and very pious pontiff had decided to splendidly repair and remodel all the holy station churches, which had been virtually eaten away by decay and old age. He started this remodeling and repairing project with repairs and construction at most of the minor basilicas — Sta. Maria in Trastevere, Sta. Prassede, S. Teodoro, and S. Pietro called "in Vincoli" and most others of this rank, not to mention them all one by one. Then turning to larger tasks, he concentrated on the seven more celebrated, principal churches, so to speak, throughout greater Rome: the basilicas of S. Giovanni in Laterano, Sta. Maria Maggiore, Sto. Stefano al Celio, SS. Apostoli, S. Paolo fuori le mura, S. Lorenzo fuori le mura. He reinforced some, repaired some, ornamented some, and renewed some in a wonderful manner. Of those seven greatly celebrated major churches, the most important one of all, the wondrous and revered shrine of Saint Peter, alone remained. He had decided to

renovare ac totam usque ad tecta ipsa reedificare constituerat, idcirco ultimo loco post palatinam renovationem de ea partim seorsum, partim vero simul cum palatio idcirco tractabimus quia finitima et contigua edificia futura erant. [27–30]

28. Ad tertium[107] de vico, ut ita dixerim, curiali iuxta nostrum ordinem procedentes, novam huius vici constructionem a porta pontis molis adrianee incoandam fore cognovimus ubi magnam quandam aream,[108] cunctis habitationibus inter menia urbis que tanto ulterius in latitudinem extendebantur ut ad perpendiculum magne turris palatine ab eo ad hoc ipsum edificate dirigerentur et Tiberim[109] consistentibus funditus demolitis, ante predictam Adriani molem instituebat. Ab hac maxima area tres late et ample vie ab invicem distincte, due ab utrisque lateribus, tertia intermedia, derivabantur et ad alteram ingentissimam aream ante apostolicam edem apparentem portendebantur.[110] Per intermediam vero ab area prima usque ad mediam predicte basilice quinque ianuis distincte portam iter per rectam lineam dirigebatur. Per secundam autem que a dextris prominebat recto tramite ad portam palatinam ibatur. At per tertiam a leva versus Tiberim ad eum locum tendebatur ubi nunc ingens ille et altissimus obeliscus exstat et ubi in nova apostolice ecclesie reformatione domestica pro sacerdotibus canonicis cubilia designabantur que vulgo dormitoria appellantur. [31–35]

29. Atque tres commemorate vie diversis habitaculis, variis ergastulis,[111] ac dissimilibus opificum tabernis per hunc modum ab invicem separabantur. Nam a dextris via eisdem propemodum habitaculis pro mediocribus diversorum exercitiorum artificibus se se e regione respicientibus distinguebatur. Intermedia vero usque ad levam similibus nummulariorum, drapporum,[112] pannorumque mensis et huiusmodi maiorum opificum tabernis utrinque institutis ac mutuo se se intuentibus disponebatur. A leva autem usque ad murum super Tiberim edificandum diversorum generum pro infimis opificibus[113] apothece utrisque pariter lateribus ordinabantur. Atque tres predicte vie sex intercolumniis[114] usque adeo muniebantur ut sex continuas porticus, duas a qualibet via se invicem respicientes, pulcherrime simul atque utilissime efficerent.[115] Iuxta enim[116] varie diversorum

---

107 tertiam *Muratori*

108 aream *A*: arcem *B*: arcam *DE*: *om. CC¹*

109 inter Tiberim *Muratori Magnuson*

110 protendebatur *Muratori Magnuson*

111 argasulis *C¹*

112 drapporum *om. Muratori*

113 opicibus *C*

114 intercoluniis *C*: inter Columnas *Muratori*

115 afficerent *D*

116 enim *om. Muratori*

renew it magnificently from its foundations and rebuild it completely to its very roof. For this reason I shall treat it last, after the renovation of the palace, partly in its own right, and partly in conjunction with the palace since the buildings were to be very close, adjoining each other.

28. Following our order we proceed to our third topic, the curial district, if I may call it that. We understand that the new construction of this district would have to begin at the gate of the bridge at the Hadrianic Mass where he created a large open area in front of Hadrian's Mass by completely razing all the houses that stood between the city walls — these were having their width extended so that they would be aligned at right angles to the great palace tower he built for this purpose — and the Tiber. From this great open area three broad and spacious avenues derive, set off from one another, one on either side and the third in the middle, and reach the other enormous open area visible in front of the apostolic church. Along the middle street, the route is arranged on a straight line from that first open area to the middle of the basilica's five doors. Along the second one, projecting to the right, a straight course leads to the door of the palace. But along the third, to the left towards the Tiber, it aligns with the place where that huge, very tall obelisk now stands and where in the new rearrangement of the papal church the bedrooms for the canons are assigned, the ones in vernacular called "dormitories".

29. These three avenues are set off from one another by their varying lodgings, their differing work spaces, and the dissimilar shops of the craftsmen. The avenue on the right is distinguished by almost identical lodgings directly facing one another for modest craftsmen of various trades. The middle street is allotted on its left side to the similar counters of the money-changers, drapers, and cloth merchants, and to shops of such more important tradesmen arranged facing one another on both sides. On the left, however, all the way to the wall to be built above the Tiber, stores of varying sorts for the lowest tradesmen are distributed equally on both sides. These three streets are protected by six colonnades in such a way that they form six continuous porticoes, two facing each other on each street, with great beauty and utility since the miscellaneous shops of the various

opificum taberne supra vero domorum habitacula condebantur. Ac per hunc modum quocunque tempore sub porticibus[117] incedentes homines et voluptate pulcherrimi aspectus capiebantur et omni quoque immoderata et hiemali et estiva tempestate partim ab iugibus pluviis, partim ab intemperie algoris et estus se se tutabantur. Necessaria etiam inferiorum tabernarum ac superiorum domorum habitacula nequaquam suo lumine[118] privabantur. [36–43]

30. Atque hic curialis de quo loquimur vicus a magnis menibus[119] et altis turribus undique cingebatur a quatuor nanque eius lateribus egregiis propugnaculis circundabatur. Si quidem primo a ponte adrianee molis et ab ipsa mole quatuor novis turribus super quatuor angulis permunita;[120] a dextris deinde magnis menibus versus maximam turrim ad palatium vergentibus; a parte vero superiori duobus mirabilibus et dicti palatii et apostolice basilice propugnaculis; et versus occidentem et ex transverso quoque versus meridiem perpetuis muris usque ad predictum adrianee molis pontem continuatis ad orientemque[121] revolutis ita circunquaque muniebatur ut nulla[122] neque rationalia neque etiam[123] rationis expertia animalia nisi volantes duntaxat aves volatibus[124] suis ingredi potuissent. [44–45]

31. Cum igitur in capite huius quem descripsimus vici hoc precipuum et admirandum pontificalis palatii edificium, ut diximus, construere[125] et fabricari[126] vellet, arduum opus, ab ingenti et maxima turri incoavit quam per diametrum septuaginta cubitorum esse voluit cum muri in latitudinem ad sexdecim extenderentur, in altitudinem[127] vero[128] usque ad centum erigerentur, licet altius quam ad trigesimum[129] cubitum[130] non immerito erexerit. Ulterius enim eam elevari noluit[131] quam equabile edificandi palatii solum designaretur; ex veteri nanque approbatorum architectorum disciplina nullum presertim magnum et excellens

---

117 pontificibus *corr. in marg. alt. manu D*
118 homine *C¹*
119 membris *Muratori*
120 praemunita *Muratori Magnuson*
121 et ad Orientem *Muratori Magnuson*
122 nullam *D*
123 enim *D*
124 volatilibus *C¹D*
125 constituere *D*
126 fabricare *Muratori Frutaz*
127 latitudinem *corr. in marg. alt manu D*
128 *om. C¹*
129 trigentesimum *C¹*
130 XXX cubitos *Muratori Frutaz*
131 voluit *Muratori Frutaz*

tradesmen are built near the living quarters of the homes above them. In this way, no matter the season, people going about under the porticoes are captivated by pleasure at their very beautiful appearance and also protect themselves in all inclement weather, winter and summer, from the driving rain or the extremes of cold and heat. Also, the requirements of the shops below and of the living areas of the homes are in no way deprived of their light.

30. Also this curial district which we are discussing is ringed all around with great walls and high towers, for it is surrounded on its four sides with extraordinary battlements. The district is defended, beginning from the bridge at the Hadrianic Mass and from the Mass itself, fortified with four new towers on its four corners; then on the right by great walls sloping towards the very large tower at the palace; then on the upper part by the two amazing battlements of the palace and of the apostolic basilica; towards the west and moving sideways to the south by uninterrupted walls moving on a slant and then looping back towards the east all the way to the bridge of the Hadrianic Mass. The district's defenses on all sides are such that no rational creature nor any animal lacking in reason, except perhaps birds in flight, would be able to get inside.

31. When, therefore, he wished, as I said, to build the papal palace's imposing and marvelous structure at the head of the district I have described, and he wished a steep fortification to be fashioned, he started with the huge great tower, which he wanted to be seventy cubits in diameter, in which case its walls could be extended up to a width of sixteen cubits and could actually be raised in height as much as one hundred, although he rightly raised it to a point higher than the thirty-cubit mark. For he did not want to have it erected higher than was planned for the level platform for building the palace. He did this because he realized from the ancient learning of the proven architects that no building, particularly

edificium nisi in plana superficie et in solo undique adequato bene specioseque construi posse intellexerat.[132] Cuncta quippe novi edificii loca ad equabilem soli superficiem ab eo redigi necessarium est qui probe et, ut dicitur, ad regulam condere ac magnifice edificare concupiscit. [46–48]

32. Hec profecto tam ingens et tam admirabilis turris ad tria officia maxima ac necessaria sibi opportune admodum famulari videbatur. Primo enim ad designatam commemorati vici amplificationem[133] munitionemque, veteribus menibus demolitis novisque ab inde ex parte inferiori usque ad alteram molis adrianee turrim per lineam rectam constructis, speciosissime famulabatur.[134] Secundo ex parte superiori ad alterum murum inserviebat qui altioribus menibus usque ad verticem montis iungebatur. Tertio ad quendam grossissimum[135] parietem aptabatur qui ab uno eius latere incipiebat et ex transverso usque ad apostolici templi scalas[136] portendebatur.[137] Ab extremitate huius parietis ex transverso sursum versus alter murus porrigebatur qui basilicam a palatio separabat. [49–53]

33. In extremitate huius muri qui a turri incipiebat ea parte qua cum illo divisore iungebatur due magne turres erigebantur in quarum meditullio porta cum fornice triumphali condebatur unde in palatium introibatur. Atque primo per accommodatos gradus in quandam ingentem curtem paulatim ascendebatur que pro opportuno quodam generalis descensionis[138] loco cum intercolumniis et porticibus instituebatur; atque hec curtis a muro divisore et ab altero ex una memoratarum turrium incipiente claudebatur. A muro insuper qui a turri incipiebat et ad verticem montis usque portendebatur[139] quando ad supernam palatii partem attingebat, tunc ex transverso alius murus versus meridiem dirigebatur donec cum prenominato divisore coniungeretur. Ac per hunc modum palatium totum a quatuor suis lateribus claudebatur. [54–57]

34. In hoc amplo totius soli edificandi spatio multa ac pulchra diversarum mansionum, variis officiis inservientium, habitacula construebantur.[140] Primo enim ab inferiori palatii parte magnus pulcherrimusque ortus cunctis herbarum atque omnium fructuum generibus referctus ac vivis quoque fontibus irriguus[141] quos e

[132] intellexerat posse *Muratori Magnuson*
[133] applicationem *C¹*
[134] familiariter *D*
[135] gravissimum *C¹*: grossissimam *D*
[136] scolas *D*
[137] protendebatur *C¹ Muratori Magnuson*
[138] dissensionis *D*
[139] protendabatur *Muratori Magnuson*
[140] constituebantur *CC¹*
[141] irriguis *Muratori*

a large, superior one, could be built well and attractively except on a flat surface and on a platform that had been leveled on all sides. In fact, the man who desires to found correctly and, as they say, "to the rule" and to build magnificently must make all the places of the new building consistent with the level surface of the platform.

32. Thus this tower, so huge and wonderful, seems to serve three very great and essential functions quite nicely. First, for the planned enlargement and fortification of that district, once the old walls are down, it quite attractively serves the new walls built from there from the lower part in a straight line all the way to the tower of the Hadrianic Mass. Second, from the upper part it services the other wall which joins the higher walls all the way to the top of the hill. Third, it is fastened to a very thick facade wall which begins from one of its sides and stretches sideways to the steps of the apostolic temple. From the end of this wall, another exterior wall extends sideways and upward and separates the basilica from the palace.

33. At the very end of the wall that begins at the tower, at the place where it joins the dividing wall, two large towers rise, between which a gate is fashioned with a triumphal arch through which one would enter the palace. First one would gradually ascend along accommodating stairs into a huge court built with colonnades and porticoes to provide a convenient place for people to dismount. This court is enclosed by the dividing wall and by a second wall beginning from one of the towers just mentioned. Above, from the wall, which begins at the [great] tower and extends all the way to the crest of the hill where it comes into contact with the upper part of the palace, another wall is positioned sideways to the south until it joins the previously mentioned dividing wall. In this manner the entire palace is enclosed on all four sides.

34. In this space, ample for building the whole platform, many beautiful dwellings with diverse rooms, serving various functions, are arranged. First, from the lower part of the palace, there is a large and very beautiful garden stocked with all varieties of plants and every fruit and irrigated by flowing fountains which

vertice montis per subterraneos meatus usque in commemoratum ortum irrigandi et oblectandi gratia magnis sumptibus maiorique industria traduxerat. Atque in hoc ipso speciosissime[142] paradisi spatio tria pulcherrima atque optima edificia extabant. Primo nanque[143] a parte inferiori nobile quoddam egregiumque theatrum super columnis marmoreis fornicatum in altum elevabatur. A dextera huius theatri magnum quoddam atrium ad conciones, ad conclavia, ad pontificales coronationes, et ad alias huiusmodi raras dignasque celebritates in fornicem accommodatum cum duobus tricliniis,[144] sursum deorsumque se invicem respicientibus, edificabatur in cuius latere apostolicum erarium designabatur ubi ecclesie thesauri condebantur. Super hoc atrium cenaculum magnum anniversariis et ordinariis summi pontificis benedictionibus designatum aptabatur quod versus orientem in pontem molis adrianee respiciebat.[145] A leva autem maxima quedam capella cum ingenti vestibulo a parte superiori in fornicis modum pariter condebatur. [58–64]

35. Trans murum vero orti versus occidentem plurime et maxime ac pulcherrime mansiones accommodabantur. Verum a latere inter murum a magna turri versus summitatem palatii tendentem ac predictas mansiones magna curtis perpetuis fontibus irrigua prominebat. Paulo superius ingens et ampla bibliotheca transversalibus utrinque fenestris ordinabatur. Ultra vero bibliothecam alia curtis continuis fontibus pariter irrigua pro tota familia versus septentrionem designabatur. Iuxta hanc curtem a superiori parte magne ingentesque coquine erant. Trans coquinas deinde alia maxima curtis versus occidentem portendebatur[146] a cuius latere longa quedam lata et ampla ac nobilitata stabula constituebantur. [65–70]

36. A parte vero versus meridiem principale huius palatii atrium hinc inde late ampleque pandebatur atque in uno huius atrii latere versus septentrionem domestica cubicula ac triclinia cum maxima quadam capella parabantur. In altero autem ad meridiem vergente nove mansiones pro camerario apostolico adiacebant. A parte vero superiori versus occidentem alter ortus prospiciebatur ubi diverse a prioribus stationes predicto camerario accommodate coordinabantur.[147] [71–73]

37. Sed quid nos plura huius sacri palatii singillatim edificia conquirimus cum tot tantaque ac tam varia ab illo divino ingenio, maxima presertim magnitudine animi condito, habitacula designarentur ut[148] pulcherrimus quidam et distinctus, et non

---

[142] speciosissimo *Muratori Magnuson*

[143] enim *Muratori*

[144] triclinius *B*

[145] respondebat *Muratori*

[146] protendebatur *Muratori Magnuson*

[147] ordinabantur *Muratori*

[148] et *CC¹*

he conducted from the crest of the hill through underground conduits into this garden to water it and make it lush, at great expense and with greater effort. And in this space of a most lovely paradise, there stand three very beautiful and excellent buildings. First, in the lower part, a noble and exceptional theater, vaulted on marble columns, rises high. To the right of this theater is a great atrium, suitable for meetings, conclaves, papal coronations, and other rare and worthy ceremonies, vaulted, with two triclinia facing one another above and below. To the side is assigned the Apostolic Treasury where the Church's riches are stored. Above this atrium a great upper story is readied, reserved for anniversaries and ordinary papal benedictions; it looks eastward to the bridge at the Hadrianic Mass. To the left a very large chapel with an enormous vestibule is likewise vaulted.

35. Beyond the garden wall to the west very many large and beautiful rooms are arranged. At the side, between the wall running from the great tower towards the top of the palace and these rooms, a great court watered by constant fountains stands out. A bit higher, a huge and spacious library with transverse windows on both sides is situated. Beyond the library, towards the north, another court similarly watered with continuous fountains is reserved for the whole household. Next to this court, on the upper part, are great, enormous kitchens. Beyond the kitchens, another very large court extends towards the west. On its side are situated long and wide stables, spacious and ennobled.

36. In the part towards the south, the main atrium of this palace opens widely and spaciously, this way and that. On one side of this atrium towards the north bedrooms and triclinia with a very large chapel are provided. On the other side as it slopes towards the south lie new quarters for the apostolic chamberlain. In the upper part towards the west another garden is seen where the offices, different from those before, and provided for that chamberlain's convenience, are brought into a coherent order.

37. Why single out more buildings of this sacred palace? Because of his divine genius founded on his exceeding largeness of soul, these dwellings are of such number, quality, and variety that the palace might rightly be seen as a most beautiful and well-marked labyrinth, and not entangled and involved as the poets

intricatus ac involutus ut a poetis fingebatur, laberintus quinimmo potius speciosissima quedam paradisus non immerito videri posset? At vero cum nos duo sola prioribus designationibus suis nuper adiunxerimus, de eo finem dicendi faciemus ut ex his que nostris litteris mandata fuerint reliqua huiusmodi qualia quantaque fore debuissent diligentis lectoris iudicio[149] existimanda relinquamus. [74–75]

38. Hoc de quo loquimur palatium non solum urbanis menibus que profecto maxima et ingentissima erant et a[150] magnis ac pulcherrimis vinetis[151] undique muniebantur et exornabantur sed etiam a propriis muris ita hinc inde cingebatur ut duplicatis etiam longioribus et propioribus[152] menibus circundaretur. In tantum deinde a solo elevabatur ut ad centum usque cubitorum altitudinem extenderetur quousque ingens turris illa erigebatur. Hoc propterea fiebat ut tres pulcherrime mansiones variis anni temporibus accommodate distinguerentur. In superficie[153] nanque soli prima et infima ac[154] ut ita dixerim terrestris habitatio pro estivis duntaxat temporibus opportune designabatur ubi et atria et triclinia ac cubicula[155] et ambulatoria et porticus et capelle et omnia alia huiusmodi edificia ita affatim suppetebant ut exinde in omnibus necessariis ac utilibus et iocundis rebus optime simul atque abundantissime subministraretur. In secunda vero que erat intermedia statio similis priori cum omnibus necessariis,[156] opportunis, commodisque dietis[157] pro hiemalibus tempestatibus tantummodo ordinabatur. Suprema autem duarum antea commemoratarum similis mansio pro vernalibus, autumnalibusque temporibus speciosissime atque utilissime designabatur. Sed hec[158] de sacro palatio hactenus dixisse sufficiat quamquam plura non sicut cetera celebrata a nobis, ne longiores essemus, pretermissa fuisse videantur. [76–82]

39. Nunc vero ad admirabilem[159] ac profecto magnanimam et devotissimam apostolici templi designationem deinceps procedamus. Ante primum igitur huius sacre edis vestibulum super scalas prominens maxima quedam area quingentorum[160] in longitudine, centum in latitudine cubitorum pulcherrime apparebat. A formosis

---

[149] iudiciis *C¹*
[150] e *Muratori*
[151] junctis *Muratori*
[152] proprioribus *Muratori*
[153] Insuper facie *D*
[154] et *Magnuson*
[155] cubitus *Muratori*
[156] ac utilibus . . . necessariis *om. C¹*
[157] dictis *BE Muratori Magnuson*
[158] hoc *Muratori Magnuson*
[159] ad mirabilem *Muratori Magnuson*
[160] ducentorum *Muratori*

imagined, or rather a most lovely paradise. Indeed, as soon as I have added just two more items to its previous specifications, I shall make an end of speaking about it. I will leave it to the careful reader's judgment to assess what the size and quality of the rest would have to be, based on what I have committed to writing.

38. The palace of which I speak is ringed here and there not only by the city walls, which are indeed very grand and huge and reinforced and adorned with large, very beautiful vineyards on all sides, but also by its own walls so that it is surrounded by double walls, farther and nearer. It rises from the platform to such a degree that it reaches a height of one hundred cubits all the way to where the huge tower stands. Because of this three very beautiful lodgings are clearly marked out, suited to the varying weather conditions of the year. On the surface of the platform, the first and lowest, the "earthly dwelling" so to speak, is intended suitably only for summertime. There the halls and triclinia and bedrooms and ambulatories and porticoes and chapels and all other such buildings are so accessible that it can be provided superbly and abundantly with everything necessary, useful, and pleasant. In the second, the middle level, the lodgings, like the previous ones, would be organized with all the necessary, convenient, and comfortable chambers, but for winter weather only. The lodging at the very top, similar to the two just mentioned, is very attractively and usefully set aside for the spring and autumn seasons. Let it suffice to have said this much about the sacred palace, even though I might seem to have neglected too many items which, for the sake of brevity, I have not celebrated as much as the others.

39. Now at last let us proceed to that admirable and truly magnanimous and most reverent plan for the apostolic temple. In front of this sacred shrine's first vestibule which rises at the top of the stairs, a very great open area, five hundred in length and a hundred cubits in width, comes into view most beautifully. To

nanque predicti vestibuli gradibus quos partim marmoreos,[161] partim porphireos,[162] partim smaragdinos diversorum colorum decoris gratia[163] interserebat[164] incipiens usque ad egregia et nobilitata intercolumnia per quingentos,[165] ut diximus, passus in longum extendebatur super quibus tres commemorati vici porticus,[166] speciosorum omnium spectaculorum visu pulcherrimum specimen, sustentabantur. [83–85]

40. In hac amplissima et ornatissima area et, ut greci expressius dicunt, platea ingentissimum illum ac maximum obeliscum in ipso aree meditullio e regione ad intermediam predicti vestibuli portam in hunc modum pulcherrime simul atque devotissime collocabat. Nam pro quatuor pusillis eneisque leonibus quibus colossus ipse nunc pro basibus ac sustentaculis paulo superficie soli altioribus utitur quatuor magnas totidem evangelistarum statuas ex solido liquefactoque ere in staturam humanam fabrefacte conflatis[167] in superficie soli,[168] distantibus inter se proportionibus secundum colossi latitudinem, ponebat super quibus eneis statuis diversis invicem figuris iuxta[169] varias cuiuscunque persone conditiones perpolitissime sculptis, colossea moles sustentabatur. In summitate vero ipsius colossi alteram Iesu Christi Salvatoris nostri statuam, dextera eius manu auream crucem baiulantis, ex ere confectam accommodabat. [86–88]

41. Inter predictas scalas et hoc primum vestibulum magnum quoddam at amplum superficiei solum interiacebat quod[170] maxime hominum multitudinis longitudine ac latitudine sua capacissimum videbatur. In superiori huius ampli soli parte oblongum vestibulum reperiebatur quod quinque egregiis portis equis inter se portionibus distinguebatur et a primo scalarum gradu usque ad predictas primi vestibuli portas septuaginta quinque cubitorum latitudo, longitudo vero ultra centum viginti passus portendebatur.[171] Atque in utraque huius vestibuli extremitate singule turres e pulchris marmoribus in altum ultra centum cubitos erigebantur que quidem et ad munitionem templi et ad opportunam canonicarum horarum pulsationem simul famulabantur. [89–91]

---

161 quos marmoribus *Muratori*
162 porphyreis *Muratori Magnuson*
163 smaragdinorum colorum decoris, gratia *Muratori Magnuson*
164 intersecabat *Muratori*: interferebat *Pagnotti Magnuson*
165 ducentos *Muratori*
166 fornices *CC*[1]
167 conflatas *Muratori Magnuson*
168 sola *Muratori Magnuson*
169 vix *Muratori*
170 quo *D*
171 protendebatur *Muratori Magnuson*

produce the elegance of varied color on the handsome steps of this vestibule, he planned to alternate some of marble, some of porphyry, and some of emerald. Beginning from there, the open area extends, as I said, a full five hundred feet in length all the way to the exceptional and ennobled colonnades, upon which the three porticoes of the district just discussed were supported, an exemplar most beautiful to see of all lovely visual delights.

40. In this most ample and ornamented open area, a "platea" as the Greeks so aptly call it, he intended to position very beautifully and reverently that enormous, grand obelisk in the very center of the area, aligned with the middle door of the vestibule, in the following manner. In place of the four small bronze lions which the colossus itself now uses for its bases and supports, and which are only slightly higher than the surface of the platform, he would place on the surface of the platform four great statues, equal in number to the Evangelists (they are crafted life-sized of pure and molten bronze from items melted down), with the relative distances between them according to the width of the colossus. Above these bronze statues, the colossal mass is supported in turn by diverse figures exquisitely carved to conform to the various attributes of each person. At the very top of this colossus he would fit another statue, wrought in bronze, of our Savior Jesus Christ, bearing a golden cross in his right hand.

41. Between the stairs just discussed and this first vestibule, there lies a great platform with an ample surface which seems to provide plenty of room in its length and breadth for the largest crowd of people. On the upper part of this ample platform an elongated vestibule was devised, which is distinguished by five exquisite doors of equal proportions. From the first step of the stairway to the doors of this first vestibule, the width extends seventy-five cubits, the length more than a hundred and twenty feet. At either end of this vestibule, a single tower of beautiful marbles rises to a height of over one hundred cubits. These serve simultaneously for the temple's defenses and the timely striking of the canonical hours.

42. Ab his duobus campanilibus — sic enim commemorate turres vulgato et trito verbo appellantur — duo longissimi et amplissimi muri utrimque, quisque a latere suo usque ad primum cuiusdam magne crucis principium extendebantur: a dextris nanque unus inter palatium et templum dividens cum exteriori curte; a sinistris vero alter intercedebat a quo retrorsum via publica sternebatur. [92–93]

43. Ab hoc primo vestibulo in alterum simile per quinque egregias portas transibatur et a secundo in magnam curtem ante tertium vestibulum astantem per totidem aditus vadebatur quorum tres patentes porte cum extremis utrinque porticibus apparebant. Sed antequam ad templi ianuas applicaretur, curtis illa ampla interiacebat in cuius meditullio vivum fontem a vertice montis per abstrusos cuniculos derivandum una cum ingenti pino eneo[172] fore designaverat. A lateribus vero utriusque porticus[173] duo intercolumnia se invicem spectantia decoris et utilitatis causa figebantur. A sinistra enim porticu plures commode et opportune pro regularibus presbiteris mansiones construebantur[174] cum ad dexteram murus divisor astaret. Ex transverso vero horum duorum intercolumniorum tertium[175] intercolumnium inter duas predictas porticus porrigebatur super quod ingentes fornices ad tertium templi vestibulum volvebantur quod quinque pulcherrimis portis peregregie fabrefactis mirisque sculpturis adornatis illustrabatur unde in templum ipsum transmittebatur. [94–98]

44. In hoc longo et amplo templi spatio quod usque ad primam crucem magnam centum sexaginta in longitudine, in latitudine vero centum viginti cubitorum extendebatur: a dextris commemorata curtis quo omnes et templi et palatii aque pluvie a predictis locis arcebantur et per cloacas subterraneas emittebantur; a sinistris autem commode et opportune regularium presbiterorum templo ipsi in divinis cultibus continue servientium mansiones construebantur que usque ad illas paulo ante commemoratas contingue ducebantur nisi quod[176] a parte superiori sacrarium quoddam amplum et ingens, pulcrum ac devotum opportune admodum edificabatur. In reliquo vero soli spatio sex pulcra et speciosa[177] intercolumnia ad lineam se se pariter intuentia, tria a singulis lateribus, conspiciebantur que quidem ea quinque latera in formam navis redigebant. Idcirco quinque naves vulgo nuncupabantur quorum medium intercolumnium ideo ceteris lateralibus latius ostendebatur tum quia ambulatorium amplius erat, tum etiam quia exinde

[172] aheneo *Pagnotti Magnuson*: pino eneo *om. Muratori*
[173] porticis *D*
[174] constituebantur *Muratori*
[175] intercolumniorum tertium *om. Muratori*
[176] quia *Muratori*
[177] spatiosa *Muratori*

42. From these two campanili (for that is how the towers are referred to in the common vernacular), two very long, ample walls, one on each side, extend all the way to the beginning of the great crossing. On the right, the one divides the temple from the palace as well as the exterior court; on the left, the other forms a barrier behind which the public road spreads.

43. From this first vestibule, one passes into another similar one through five exquisite doors and from the second one proceeds into a large court standing in front of a third vestibule through the same number of entrances, of which three come into view as exposed portals, with porticoes at both ends. But before one reaches the doors of the temple, that spacious court intervenes. In its middle he arranged that there be a living source of water which would be drawn from the top of the hill through hidden conduits, to connect with the enormous bronze pine-cone. At the sides of each portico two colonnades facing one another were inserted for the sake of elegance and utility. From the left portico many comfortable and convenient rooms for the regular clergy are built, with the dividing wall standing to the right. Intersecting these two colonnades a third colonnade extends between the two porticoes just mentioned. Huge arches are sprung from their tops for the third vestibule of the temple, which are embellished with five very beautiful doors exquisitely fashioned and adorned with marvelous sculptures. From there one passes into the temple itself.

44. This long, ample space of the temple extends one hundred and sixty in length to the beginning of the great crossing, and in width one hundred and twenty cubits. On the right is that court into which is deflected all the rain water from both the temple and the palace, and then carried off through underground drains. On the left are built comfortable and convenient rooms for the regular clergy who serve the temple itself in continuous divine worship; these encroach on the ones mentioned a little earlier, except that on the upper part a sacristy is quite conveniently built, ample and huge, beautiful and reverent. In the platform's remaining space six beautiful and attractive colonnades dominate the view, facing each other in alignment, three on each side, rendering these five lateral spaces into the form of a ship. For this reason, they are popularly called the "Five Ships". Of these, the one produced by the middle colonnade affords a more open view than the ones on the sides both because its walkway is more ample and because from

mirum quoddam totius templi spectaculum liberius apparebat. A dextris in extremitate predicte curtis plurime ac speciose capelle; a sinistris vero totidem per totam longitudinem, illis dexterioribus pariter correspondentes, designabantur. Relique due naves tribus commemoratis speciose admodum suis ordinibus respondebant. [99–105]

45. Ultimo magne crucis intercolumnium octo a dextris versus curtem et totidem a sinistris columnis versus publicam stratam ideo paulum utrinque extendebatur ut maiorem quandam et ampliorem plurium inter se fornicum crucem efficeret. Septem enim cruces inter se invicem involutas fornicatasque in longo centum octuaginta quinque cubitorum spatio — tantum enim per longitudinem portendebantur[178] — pulcherrime speciosissimeque reddebant, quarum intermedia ceterarum maxima in quadraginta; sex vero alie in vinginti quatuor cubitos pariter porrigebantur. Super maximam quadraginta cubitorum crucem altissima centum cubitorum testudo prominebat super quam altera similis viginti quinque cubitorum cum[179] pluribus diversarum formarum cornicibus adiungebatur. Hec parva testudo in summitate sua idcirco patens et aperta relinquebatur ac in modum laterne aptabatur ut lumen undique clarius et apertius per totum spatium diffunderetur. [106–109]

46. Iuxta commemoratam crucem a parte superiori ingens capella in latitudinem quadraginta circiter, in longitudinem vero septuaginta quinque cubitorum portendebatur.[180] Hanc magnam capellam vulgo tribunam vocant. Utraque huius tribune latera ob maiorem personarum capacitatem sedilium gratia hinc inde extendebantur ac utrinque pluribus fenestris in magnorum oculorum formas redactis egregie admodum ornabantur. Atque in eius meditullio ingens ac pulcherrimum et omnibus ornamentorum generibus referctum altare ab extremitate predicte magne crucis astabat. In summitate vero tribune solium pontificale altiuscule eminebat ut et ipse ab omnibus circumstantibus videretur ac pariter omnes astantes sedentesque videret. [110–114]

47. Utraque huius templi latera ab ingentibus fenestris[181] se se mutuo respicientibus ornata singula queque ampli et longi spatii loca cruce illa[182] magna inferiora suis splendoribus illustrabant. At vero universum ambitum superiorem rotunde quedam fenestre in magnorum oculorum formas egregie, ut diximus, redacte velut formosa quedam fenestrarum corona speciosissime ambiebant per quas quidem

---

[178] protendebantur *Muratori Magnuson*

[179] cum *om. Muratori*

[180] protendebatur *Muratori Magnuson*

[181] fenestreis *C*

[182] quaeque ampla, et longi spatii, loca quaeque illa cruce *Muratori Magnuson*

there the marvelous panorama of the whole temple is more freely visible. On the right, at the end of the court just mentioned, many lovely chapels are arranged. Those on the left along the whole length correspond in number exactly to the those on the right. The two remaining naves in their ordering formed very lovely counterparts to the other three.

45. At the farthest reach of the great crossing, a colonnade with eight columns on the right towards the court and the same number on the left towards the public street extends a bit on both sides so that it creates a larger and more ample crossing of more interrelated arches. They produce, most beautifully and attractively, seven crosses made of vaults and arches within a long space of one hundred and eighty-five cubits (for that is how far they extend in length). The largest one in the middle extends forty cubits. The other six all uniformly stretch twenty-four cubits. A very high dome rises one hundred cubits above the great crossing of forty cubits. On top of this is attached another similar one of twenty-five cubits, with many cornices of various shapes. The small dome at its top is left exposed and uncovered and attached like a lantern so that light is diffused more brightly and openly in every direction throughout the whole space.

46. Next to this cross, from the upper part, an enormous chapel extends about forty cubits in width and seventy-five in length. This great chapel they popularly call the "tribune". Both sides of this tribune are expanded in various places for seats to enlarge its capacity for people. It is exquisitely adorned on both sides with windows fashioned the form of great eyes. In its middle, on the edge of that great crossing, stands a huge and very beautiful altar, worked with all manner of ornamentation. At the highest point of the tribune a taller pontifical throne rises, so that all the bystanders can view him and likewise he can view everyone else, whether they are standing or sitting.

47. Both sides of this temple, adorned with huge windows facing one another, illuminate with their splendor every single place of the long and ample space lying below that great crossing. Round windows, exquisitely fashioned in the form of great eyes, as we have said, ring the whole circuit most attractively, like a shapely crown of windows through which the sun's rays enter and not only illuminate the

solares radii ita ingrediebantur ut non modo singula testudinis loca luce sua collustrarent sed divine quoque glorie specimen quoddam cunctis devotis conspectoribus demonstrarent. In vertice vero testudinis rotunda quedam et ingens fenestra ceteris altius prominens in laterne formam, ceu supra commemoravimus, redacta cuncta mirum in modum condecorabat. Ceterum universum totius spatii pavimentum eisdem variis partim marmoreis[183] partim porphireis, partim smaragdinis coloribus ornabatur[184] quibus scalarum gradus condecoratos superius fuisse[185] diximus. [115–118]

48. Et ne tantum, tam pulcrum, tam devotum,[186] tam admirabile, ac denique tam divinum potius quam humanum templum aliquibus defunctorum prelatorum vel[187] pontificum humationibus ullatenus pollueretur, huiusmodi sepulchra a sinistro latere extra templum e regione ad solium pontificale construi condique volebat. [119]

49. Verum cum multa de mira huius templi fabricatione hactenus dixisse videamur, reliquum est ut de dimensionibus suis pauca quedam brevissime subiungamus. Area quingentorum[188] in longitudinem, in latitudinem vero centum cubitorum ante ornatissimas scalas sternebatur. A primo ascensionis gradu usque ad solium pontificale longitudo ultra quingentos[189] cubitos porrigebatur. In latitudinem vero ad[190] centum viginti per totum pene[191] spatium extendebatur nisi ubi a duobus magne illius crucis lateribus brachia utrinque dilatabantur.[192] Ibi enim usque adeo amplificabatur ut ad centum octuaginta mensuraretur. Altitudo vero omnium fornicum ultra octuaginta passus ascendebat cum maxime testudinis sublimitas ad centum supra viginti quinque cubitos attingere videretur. [120–125]

50. A palatio in hoc templum per plures pulcherrimos aditus a summo pontifice, magna prelatorum comitante caterva, incedebatur. Ab uno vero ceteris eminentiori per cocleam quandam speciosissimam[193] vadebatur. Et[194] ne huic tam admirabili et tam digno edificio ullum ornamentorum genus deesse videretur,

---

[183] partim marmoreis] variis marmoribus *Muratori*
[184] ornabat *Muratori*
[185] fuisse superius *Muratori Magnuson*
[186] decorum *Muratori*
[187] ac *Muratori*
[188] ducentorum *Muratori*
[189] ducentos *Muratori*
[190] ab *Muratori*
[191] fere *Muratori*
[192] dilatabatur *Muratori*
[193] spatiosissimam *Muratori*
[194] At *Muratori*

individual places of the dome with their light, but also display to all devout spectators a model of divine glory. At the apex of the dome, a huge round window, towering above the others, fashioned in the form of a lantern, as I mentioned above, beautifies everything in a marvelous manner. All the pavement of the entire space is ornamented in the same varied colors, partly marble, partly porphyry, partly emerald, that we said above was used to decorate the steps of the stairway.

48. And so that a temple so large, so beautiful, so reverent, so admirable, and, in a word, so divine rather than human, might not be in any way polluted by burials of deceased prelates or pontiffs, he wished such tombs to be established and constructed on the left side outside the temple in alignment with the papal throne.

49. While I may seem already to have said much about this temple's marvelous structure, it still remains for me to add a few brief remarks on its dimensions. The open area covers five hundred cubits in length and one hundred in width in front of the highly ornamented stairs. From the first step going up, all the way to the papal throne its length stretches more than five hundred cubits. Its width extends one hundred and twenty cubits for almost the entire space, except where the arms widen in both directions from the two sides of the great crossing. There it expands to measure one hundred and eighty cubits. All the arches rise in height over eighty feet, while the elevation of the great dome seemingly reaches more than one hundred and twenty-five cubits.

50. The supreme pontiff, accompanied by a large retinue of prelates, makes his entrance into this temple from the palace through many very beautiful entrances. The procession moves from an entrance more splendid than the rest along a very lovely spiral staircase. Not wanting so admirable and worthy a building to seem to lack any type of ornament, he adorned the whole circuit of the upper space

universum superioris spatii ambitum plumbeis laminis speciosissime simul atque utilissime adornabat. Verum ut hec ingentia maxime molis edificia facilius construere valeret, Anienis fluvii alveum quo a tiburtino oppido versus Romam navigari consueverat ita mundari atque ita purgari fecit ut ea que ad edificandum necessaria erant[195] aptius a Tibure transmitti ac transferri possent. [126–129]

51. Admirabile et stupendum ac summa christiane religionis devotione venerandum huius sacri templi edificium mihi crebro mecum ipsi animadvertenti ac quale quantumque foret mente et cogitatione volventi instar humani corporis futurum videri solet. Nam a thorace ad pedes usque deorsum oblongo huius basilice spatio[196] quantum a patentibus tertii vestibuli foribus ad magne crucis initium porrigebatur persimile apparebat. Alterum deinde illius crucis spatium brachiis utrinque extensis humanis humeris[197] conforme cunctis diligenter et accurate considerantibus videbitur. Reliquum vero spatium quod ambitu magne tribune continetur nequaquam[198] humano capiti[199] dissimile censebitur. Atqui ne hec, qualiscumque est, similitudo nostra[200] temere a nobis inducta et ab ipsa rei veritate longe abhorrere existimetur, constitue queso hominem in superiori huius templi parte[201] cuius universum corpus humi prosternas velim ita ut caput eius ad occidentem vergat, brachiis in diversa latera utrinque porrectis, altero ad septentrionem, altero vero ad meridiem vergente, pedes autem ad orientem spectent atque, humano corpore per hunc modum abste constituto, dubitare non poteris quin hanc nostram similitudinem undique convenire ac quadrare arbitreris. Si itaque huius templi figura humani corporis[202] instar fuisset, ceu supra patuisse[203] videtur, nimirum ipsam[204] nobilissimam speciem sortiturum fuisse constat cum formam hominis ceteris omnibus et animatarum et inanimatarum rerum figuris longe prelatam[205] esse non ignoremus. [130–135]

52. Eam quippe ad similitudinem totius mundi fabricatam fuisse nonnulli doctissimi viri putaverunt unde hominem a grecis microcosmum appellatum esse existimarunt. Nec defuerunt[206] etiam qui famosissimam illam ac saluberrimam

---

195 sunt *Muratori*

196 spatii *Magnuson*

197 humanis humeris *om. Muratori*

198 nequaquaquam *B*

199 capite *Muratori*

200 nostra *om. Muratori*

201 in superiorem huius templi partem *Muratori*

202 humano corpori *Muratori*

203 potuisse *Muratori*

204 ipsum *Muratori Magnuson*

205 praelatum *Muratori Magnuson*

206 defuerant *Muratori Magnuson*

with lead sheeting, at once very lovely and practical. To facilitate the construction of these huge buildings with their enormous mass, he had the bed of the Anio River, which used to be the navigation channel from the town of Tivoli to Rome, dredged and cleared so that the necessary building materials could be more readily shipped and transported from Tivoli.

51. This sacred temple's edifice, wonderful and astonishing and deserving veneration with Christian religion's highest devotion, as I often consider it and weigh in mind and thought what its nature and size was to be, repeatedly strikes me as comparable to a human body. From the chest to the feet below, the body greatly resembles this basilica's elongated space, extending from the open doors of the third vestibule to the beginning of the great crossing. Then the second expanse, that of the crossing, will seem, to all who think about it closely and accurately, to conform to arms outstretched on either side from human shoulders. Of course, the remaining space, enclosed by the circuit of the great tribune, will be judged not at all unlike the human head. But lest I be thought to have rashly introduced this comparison of mine, such as it is, and it shrinks far from the truth of the matter, place, I ask you, a man on this temple's upper part, I mean with his whole body prostrate on the ground so that his head points to the west, with his arms stretched sideways in both directions, one pointing north and the other south, and his feet looking to the east, and once you have placed him like so, you cannot hesitate to admit it conforms to and very neatly squares with our comparison. If, therefore, the figure of this temple is like the human body, as seemed obvious above, surely it follows that it would have acquired the noblest appearance, since we are not unaware that the human form was by far privileged over all the other figures of things animate and inanimate.

52. Certain very wise men, in fact, considered it to have been constructed in the likeness of the whole world, whence they thought man was called by the Greeks "the microcosm". Nor were there lacking those who affirmed that that most famous

iustissimi illius consolatoris — sic enim Noe nomen hebraice interpretatur — arcam humani generis, quod iam pene totum ex primo et generali diluvio perierat, salvatricem quoniam exinde reparati sumus ad hanc perfectissimam humani corporis fabricam propemodum constructam fuisse autumarent. Etsi enim propria sui ipsius longitudo a vertice usque ad vestigia sexies tantum habeat, quantum latitudo que est ab uno ad alterum latus et decies tantum quantum altitudo[207] cuius mensura in latere a dorso ad ventrem reperiatur, cum huiusmodi dimensionum proportio in templi nostri forma servari non potuerit, in figuris tamen lineamentorum similitudinem tenuit. Nam si iacentem hominem, seu supinum seu pronum metiaris, sexies tantum[208] longus[209] est a capite ad pedes quantum latus est a dextera in sinistram vel a sinistra in dexteram et decies tantum quantum altus[210] a terra. Proinde commemorata arca trecentorum in longitudine cubitorum, quinquaginta in latitudine, triginta in altitudine formata fuisse scribitur. Quippe vir suapte natura prudentissimus et multarum quoque rerum experientia in tanta ac tam diuturna quingentorum annorum vita — nam hac eius etate generale illud diluvium universum terrarum orbem inundasse accepimus — apprime edoctus et divino insuper quodam spiritu afflatus, cum hoc mirabile ac perfectum hominis opificium ab omnipotenti Deo profluxisse et emanasse intelligeret, tale tanti auctoris supremique magistri exemplum sibi, arcam humani, ut diximus, generis salvatricem fabricaturo, non immerito ad construendum imitandumque proposuit. Quod cum Nicolaus apud idoneos auctores legisse meminisset, in hac sua divini templi constructione non iniuria imitari concupivit et voluit. [136–142]

53. In hac nostra huius admirabilis templi descriptione quanto magnificentias ac celebritates suas magis magisque considero tanto amplius admirari et obstupescere cogor atque mihi sic consideranti ac propterea vehementius admiranti plura singularia et precipua celebratorum operum exempla comparandi gratia ante oculos offeruntur.[211] Primo enim si athenienses de armamentario suo a grecis scriptoribus tantopere laudato ob id magnopere gloriati sunt quod fuerit opus impensa et elegantia visendum[212] et ita gloriati sunt ut Philonem illius architectum magnis cum laudibus domestici suarum rerum scriptores memorie prodiderunt,[213] profecto nos tanto magis Nicolaum pontificem huius divini templi architectum eternis litterarum monumentis celebrare debemus. [143–144]

207 que est . . . altitudo *om. Muratori*
208 tamen *Muratori*
209 longum *ABDE*
210 altius *Muratori*
211 offerunt *Muratori*
212 visendi *D*
213 prodiderint *Muratori Magnuson*

and salutary Ark of that most just consoler (for this is how the name Noah is translated from Hebrew) had been built like this most perfect fabric of the human body on behalf of the human race which perished almost entirely during the first universal flood, a saving Ark because from there we were restored. Even if its proper length from its top all the way to its extremities is six times its width, which is from one side to the other and ten times its depth, a measurement taken laterally from the back to the belly, and though the proportion of this kind of dimensions cannot be preserved in the form of our temple, still it kept the resemblance in its linear figures. If you measure a man lying down, whether on his stomach or his back, he is six times as long from the head to the feet as he is wide from right to left or left to right, and ten times as long as his depth from the ground up. Just so, it is written that this Ark had been shaped three hundred cubits in length, fifty in width, and thirty in depth. Indeed, Noah was a man most prudent by his very nature and thoroughly educated by the experience of many things over a great and long lifetime of five hundred years (for we accept that this was his age when the universal flood submerged the entire world), and above all inspired by the divine spirit. He understood that this wondrous and perfect work of man had originated with and emanated from almighty God, so he correctly set before himself this model for construction and imitation from such a great author and teacher when he set about building the Ark which, as I said, saved the human race. When Nicholas remembered he had read this in the pertinent authors, he rightly desired and willed to imitate it in his own building of the divine temple.

53. In my description of this wonderful temple, the more I consider its magnificent and celebrated features, the more fully I am forced to wonder and astonishment. Considering and more strongly than ever marveling at its many features one by one, before my eyes appear choice examples of celebrated works for comparison. First, the Athenians were greatly proud of their armory, so greatly praised by the Greek writers on the grounds that the work had to be seen because of its costliness and elegance. They were so proud of it that the native writers of their history perpetuated the memory of its architect, Philo, with great praise. How much more, then, ought we to celebrate with lasting literary testimonials Pope Nicholas, the architect of this divine temple.

54. Si Hiram quoque tirensem famosissimi templi Salomonis non architectum sed singularem eris magistrum opificemque erarium de sapientia, intelligentia, ac doctrina et de[214] sculpendi arte statuariaque[215] sacris libris apprime laudatum fuisse novimus, quanto nos maiores Nicolao nostro laudes largiri prebereque impellimur qui suopte ingenio suaque industria multos quotidianorum operum variosque prefectos non iniuria constituit atque illis omnibus Bernardum nostrum florentinum peregregium latomorum magistrum unum preesse voluit cui ceteri omnes sive operarii sive baiuli sive opifices et cuiuscumque gradus magistri et professores iuxta pontificias duntaxat designationes ad unguem obtemperarent? Nam cum eo solo omnia ad predictam fabricam pertinentia communicabat. [145–146]

55. Si singuli insuper septem illorum celeberrimorum totius orbis terrarum spectaculorum fabricatores ob sua egregia opera a priscis historicis admodum commendantur; tanto magis Nicolaus noster maximis in celum laudibus extolli et exornari debet, quanto hoc templum, si perfectionem suam, ut institutum erat, consecutum fuisset, singulis operibus, illis duobus duntaxat exceptis, nobilius et excellentius videbatur. Etenim ut de singulis conferendi gratia pauca quedam in medium afferamus, missas facimus Egipti Thebas urbem illam magnam centum egregiis portis — mirabile[216] dictu — menibusque conspicuis illustratam; missos facimus Babilonie urbis itidem maxime[217] muros quos Semiramis Nini assyriorum regis uxor ex coctis lateribus ac bituminibus admirabilibus magnificentiis incredibilibusque impensis construxerat. [147–148]

56. Quod[218] aliud ex quinque reliquis mirandis totius mundi spectaculis cum hoc nostro templo iure comparare poterimus? an illud[219] nobilitatum Mausoli Carie cuiusdam[220] Grecie provincie regis sepulchrum quod Artemisia eius uxor tam amplum, tam magnificum, tam opulentum condidisse fertur ut in omnium intuentium admiratione haberetur? an piramides egiptiacas, edificia ita ingentia itaque magnifica ut a multis scriptoribus mirum in modum laudentur? an nobilissimus ille colossus[221] in quo Rhodi[222] Apollinis idolum colebatur? an celeberrimum illud Adriani imperatoris delubrum in Cizico[223] mirabiliter constitutum?

[214] de *om. D*
[215] staturiaque *D*
[216] mirabili *D*
[217] maximos *Muratori*
[218] Quid *Muratori Magnuson*
[219] illum *ABDE Muratori Magnuson*
[220] Mausolo Cariae cuidam *Muratori*
[221] nobilissimum illum colossum *Muratori Magnuson*
[222] Rhodii *Muratori Magnuson*
[223] Circo *Muratori*

54. We also recognize that Hiram of Tyre (who was not the architect of Solomon's most famous temple, but an unparalleled bronze master and a worker in bronze) has been very greatly praised in sacred scripture for wisdom, intelligence, and learning, as well as for sculptural art and statuary. How much greater the praises we are compelled to shower and bestow on our Nicholas who by his own genius and industry correctly appointed many different men to be in charge of daily operations, and wanted one man, our Bernardo of Florence, the most excellent master of stone masons, to be in charge of them all. He was a man whom all the others, whether workmen or unskilled laborers or craftsmen, and masters and experts of whatever rank would readily obey to the letter according to the Pope's exact instructions. He would confide in him alone all matters pertaining to this construction.

55. Moreover, each one of the crafters of those seven famed Wonders of the World are highly commended by the ancient historians for their exquisite works. Our Nicholas ought to be extolled to the heavens and decorated with the greatest praises in that this temple, if it had reached its completion as it had been begun, would seem more noble and excellent than every single one of those works, with just two exceptions. So in bringing forward a few of these particular cases for the sake of comparison, I omit that great city, Egyptian Thebes, distinguished by its hundred exquisite gates (wonderful to tell!) and its prominent walls. I likewise omit the walls of that greatest city, Babylon, which Semiramis, the wife of Ninus, king of the Assyrians, built of fired bricks and pitch, with wonderful magnificence and unbelievable expense.

56. Which of the five remaining Wonders of the World will we justly compare with this temple of ours? That ennobled tomb of Mausolus, king of Caria, a Greek province, which they say Artemisia his wife built so ample, magnificent, and opulent that it was held in wonder by all who gazed on it? Or the pyramids of Egypt, structures so large and so magnificent that they were wonderfully praised by many writers? Or that most noble colossus in which the idol of Apollo was worshipped at Rhodes? Or that most famous shrine of the emperor Hadrian marvelously built in Cyzicus? Or, finally, the Capitol at Rome, which writers of

an denique Capitolium Rome quod romanarum rerum scriptores tantis in celum laudibus extulerunt? Nullum profecto in toto terrarum orbe, duobus illis duntaxat exceptis, ita dignum spectaculum reperiremus[224] quod cum hoc nostro templo merito, ut diximus, comparare ac conferre valeremus.[225] [149–154]

57. In his duobus ultimis palatii ac templi edificiis Salomonem Hierosolimorum regem, ceterorum omnium qui ullo unquam tempore fuerunt, sunt eruntque hominum sapientissimum, non oraculo Apollinis, ut de Socrate scribitur sed omnipotentis Dei sententia iudicatum, Nicolaus noster magnanimiter animoseque admodum imitatus est quem domum regis ac domum Domini sacris litteris tam laute et tam opulente edificasse legerat. Atque ita egregie imitatus esse videtur ut si vita comite utraque incepta ac pene semiperfecta opera absolvisset vel divini templi regieque domus magnificentias[226] adequasset vel potius maiorem in modum excelluisset. [155–156]

58. Hec enim sacri textus verba sunt ut illa duo Salomonis regis tam laudata et tam celebrata edificia cum his duobus Nicolai pontificis tam commendatis et tam admirabilibus operibus parumper conferamus: Domus quam edificavit rex Salomon Domino habebat sexaginta in longitudine ac viginti in latitudine et triginta cubitos in altitudine et porticus erat ante templum viginti cubitorum longitudinis iuxta mensuram latitudinis templi et habebat viginti cubitos latitudinis ante faciem templi fecitque in templo fenestras obliquas et edificavit super parietem templi tabulata per girum in parietibus domus per circuitum[227] templi et oraculi. Tabulatum quod super[228] erat quinque cubitos habebat latitudinis et medium tabulatum sex cubitorum latitudinis et tertium tabulatum septem habens cubitos latitudinis.[229] Trabes autem posuit in domo forinsecus per circuitum ut non hererent muris templi. Atque hec de templo Salomonis regis tam laudato et tam celebrato verba sacris libris scripta reperiuntur. [157–159]

59. At hoc nostrum admirabile templum ultra quingentos cubitos in longitudinem portendebatur;[230] in latitudinem vero[231] ultra centum viginti extendebatur; in altitudinem[232] ultra octuaginta erigebatur; et pro una sola porticu ante templum

---

[224] reperiemus *Muratori*
[225] valeamus *Muratori*
[226] magnificentia *D*: absolvisset, divini regiaeque domus, vel magnificentius *Muratori Magnuson*
[227] circulum *D*
[228] subter *Vulg*
[229] et tertium . . . latitudinis *om. Muratori*
[230] protendebatur *Muratori Magnuson*
[231] non *Muratori*
[232] latitudinem *D*

Roman history have exalted to the heavens with such great praise? In fact, we would find no sight in the whole world, with just those two exceptions, worth, as I have said, justifiably comparing to and setting beside this temple of ours.

57. Regarding these last two buildings, the palace and the temple, Solomon, king of Jerusalem, was the greatest of all wise men of any era, past, present, or future, judged so not by Apollo's oracle, as was written of Socrates, but in the opinion of almighty God. It was he whom our Nicholas closely imitated in magnanimity and boldness. He had read in the sacred scriptures that he had built a house for a king and a house for God very sumptuously and opulently. And he seems to have imitated him so exquisitely that if he had completed both the projects, which he began and were almost half-finished in his lifetime, he either would have equalled the magnificence of the divine temple and the royal house or he would have excelled them by a large margin.

58. Here are the words of the sacred texts for us to take a moment to compare those two much praised and celebrated buildings of King Solomon with these two much commended and admirable works of Pope Nicholas: "The house which King Solomon built for the Lord was sixty cubits in length, twenty in width, and thirty cubits in height. The portico in front of the temple was twenty cubits long, equal to the measure of the width of the temple, and twenty cubits wide in front of the facade of the temple. And he made in the temple oblique windows. He built storeys upon the wall of the temple, in a ring inside the walls of the house along the circuit of the temple and the throne of mercy. The storey which was above was five cubits wide, the middle storey was six cubits wide, and the third storey was seven cubits wide; but he put beams in the house around the circuit from the outside in so that they would not hang on the temple walls." [1 Kg 6:2–6] And these are the words found written in the sacred books concerning the much-praised and celebrated temple of Solomon.

59. But this wonderful temple of ours would spread more than five hundred cubits in length; its width would extend more than one hundred and twenty; in height it would rise more than eighty. And instead of the one single portico in

Salomonis tria vestibula ante nostrum astabant; et pro obliquis illius fenestris transversales nostre orbicularesque apparebant; pro tribus autem tabulatis multi fornices per septem cruces in se ipsos mirabiliter involuti altissimaque testudo videbantur. [160–165]

60. Ac paulo post de regia ita scribitur: Domus autem cum edificaretur de lapidibus[233] dolatis atque perfectis edificata est et malleus et securis et omne ferramentum non sunt audita in domo cum edificaretur. Ostium lateris medii in pariete[234] erat domus dextere et per cocleam ascendebatur in medium cenaculum et a medio in tertium. Edificavit domum et consummavit eam. Texit quoque domum laquearibus cedrinis et edificavit tabulatum super omnem domum quinque cubitorum latitudinis et operuit domum lignis cedrinis. Atque hec, ut[235] sacris litteris scripta reperiuntur, ad verbum ponere curavi[236] ut ista nostra quatuor celebratorum edificiorum vicissitudinaria comparatio melius discernatur. [166–167]

61. Pro lapidibus dolatis atque perfectis regie illius veteris ingentia saxa quadris instructa ac, ut unico verbo expressius dixerim, quadrata in novo pontificis palatio conspiciebantur; pro ostio vero lateris medii in pariete ingens porta duabus turribus et meditullio permunita[237] astabat; pro tribus cenaculis tres admirabiles totidem fornicum ordines superius inferiusque instituebantur; pro laquearibus cedrinis[238] totius domus coopertoriis ac tegminibus plumbee lamine ponebantur. [168–169]

62. In hac nostra quatuor predictorum admirabilium edificiorum comparatione paria unius cum paribus alterius ordinis ad invicem contulimus. Quod si quedam sacrarum scripturarum veneratio et Salomonis quoque regis debita observatio non me talia conferentem parumper continuisset, profecto reliqua[239] multa silentio pretermissa subdidissem que quidem peregrina illa a nostratibus istis tanto magis superata ostendissent, quanto amplius nova Christi religio veteri illi divine legi preferenda ac preponenda dignoscitur. [170–171]

63. Sed cum de diversis atque procul dubio admirabilibus Nicolai nostri edificiis iam multa superius retulisse videamur, nunc longo quasi postliminio in patriam reversi, ad nostrum dicendi ordinem paulisper redeamus. [172]

---

[233] lapidus *Magnuson*
[234] parte *Vulg*
[235] quae *Muratori*
[236] curavit *Magnuson*
[237] premunita *CC*[1]: praemunita *Muratori Magnuson*
[238] in totius *Muratori Magnuson*
[239] aliqua *Muratori Magnuson*

front of Solomon's temple, three vestibules were to stand in front of ours. And in place of its oblique windows, transverse and orbicular ones would appear in ours. Instead of the three storeys, many vaults would be seen, marvelously folded inward on themselves in seven crosses, and a very high dome.

60. And a little later, this is written of the palace: "But when the house was built, it was built with stones already cut and finished; and neither hammer nor axe nor any tool of iron was heard in the house while it was being built. There was an entrance in the wall in the middle of the side on the right of the house; and one went up by an enclosed staircase to the middle story, and from the middle story to the third. He built the house, and finished it; and he covered the house with cedar ceiling panels, and built a storey above the whole house of five cubits in width and covered it with cedar planks." [3 Kg 6:7–10] I have been careful to quote these words just as they were found written in sacred scripture so that this side-by-side comparison of ours of the four celebrated buildings might be better judged.

61. Instead of the old palace's stones already cut and finished, enormous rocks prepared in squares, and, to express it more clearly in a single word, squared blocks were to dominate the new papal palace. Instead of an entrance in the middle of the side, there would stand in the facade wall a huge portal reinforced with two towers and a midsection. Instead of three storeys, three marvellous rows of the same number of arches were to be furnished above and below. Instead of the cedar ceiling panels, lead sheeting was to be installed on the coverings and roofs throughout the house.

62. In our comparison of these four wonderful buildings, we have contrasted what was equivalent in the order of one with what was equivalent in the order of the other. But if respect for the sacred scriptures and also a certain deference due to King Solomon had not prevented me from continuing with such comparisons, I would have added much more that I now pass by in silence, things which would have shown that those exotic works have been as fully surpassed by ours as the new religion of Christ is discernably to be preferred over and to supersede that old divine law.

63. But since I seem now to have already related in my remarks a great deal about the various and undoubtedly wonderful buildings of our Nicholas, let us now, as if retracing our steps to the fatherland in a long journey home, return quickly to the order of our account.

64. Dum igitur et conservationi pacis et traducendis et componendis novis que quotidie cudebantur operibus sine ulla intermissione vacaret et assiduam magnis diversarum fabricationum constructionibus, ut dictum est, operam navaret, factum est ut Federicus, iam pridem per mortem Alberti predecessoris sui ad imperium iure delectus, eius sanctitatem per litteras prius, per oratores deinde humiliter supplicaret ut legitimam imperii romani coronam ab eo recognoscendi causa susciperet. Cuius quidem rei gratia et ut debitam reverentiam sanctitati sue personaliter exhiberet, e media Germania usque Romam veniendi licentiam humilibus supplicationibus postulabat. Nicolaus vero, supplicibus commemorati Federici postulationibus auditis ac diligenter accurateque consideratis ut debitam et per canonicas leges ordinatam, licet aliquot temporibus intermissam, recognoscendi a summis (941) pontificibus romanum imperium constitutionem atque inveteratam consuetudinem renovaret, benigne faciliterque consensit.

65. Unde Federicus non multo post impetratum veniendi consensum una cum Leonora uxore sua, magna procerum ac principum utriusque sexus comitante caterva, e media, ut diximus, Alamania hiemali tempestate movens, in Italiam venit ubi diversis locis a principibus et dominis regionum ad quas contendebat honorifice susceptus, quinto sui pontificatus anno Romam tandem applicuit ubi in palatio pontificali una cum predicta uxore sua, separatis seorsum habitaculis, magna cum dignitate collocatus, plures dies eo usque commoratus est quoad celebritates pro imperatoriis coronationibus de more usitate et consuete penitus[240] et omnino explerentur.

66. De quibus pauca quedam e multis a nobis tunc visa, cum ad eam celebritatem florentini populi nomine legati simul cum multis aliis totius pene, ut ita dixerim, christianitatis oratoribus conveniremus, memoratu digniora breviter enarrabimus. Ut igitur commemoratus Federicus cognomento tertius in sacrosanctum summi[241] pontificis solio pontificali gravissime simul atque dignissime residentis conspectum, magna undique diversorum prelatorum caterva adornatum, apparuit, primo genibus flexis ipsum veneratus est. Ei[242] deinde ubi propius adhesit, dexterum pedem talemque manum ac similem genam devotissime osculabatur. Atque his et huiusmodi ceremoniis de more habitis, parvam quandam oratiunculam precibus supplicationibusque referctam habuit, grataque et humana responsione recepta, e[243] sancto pontificis conspectu abiit atque ad ordinatam[244] habitationem hilariter[245] rediit. Quod postridie Leonora imperatrix pariter fecit.

---

[240] usitato & consueto, plene *Muratori*

[241] summi *om. CC*[1]

[242] & *Muratori*

[243] a *Muratori*

[244] ordinariam *Muratori*

[245] hilariter *om. Muratori*

64. And so he occupied his time in safeguarding the peace and in the translation and composition of new works, daily being hammered out without interruption, and he dedicated his unflagging efforts, as the expression goes, to large projects of diverse buildings. Meanwhile it happened that Frederick, already through the death of Albert his predecessor lawfully elected to imperial rule, humbly petitioned His Holiness first by letter and later through ambassadors to receive the legitimate crown of the Roman Empire for the sake of being recognized by him. To this purpose and to exhibit in person the respect due to His Holiness, he requested permission through humble petitions to come from the middle of Germany to Rome. Nicholas listened to Frederick's petitions and requests and, after carefully and scrupulously considering that he would renew a practice, prescribed in canon law but unobserved for some time, and a long-standing custom that the rule of the Roman Empire should be confirmed by the supreme pontiffs, he graciously and easily consented.

65. And so Frederick, not long after obtaining permission to come, together with Leonora his wife and accompanied by a large retinue of princes and relatives of both sexes, traveled, as we said, from the middle of Germany in wintry weather, and arrived in Italy. There he was received with honor in various places by the princes and lords of the regions to which he was headed. In the fifth year of Nicholas's pontificate he finally made his way to Rome where he was lodged with great dignity in the papal palace, along with his wife, though in separate accommodations. They stayed there many days, as long as it took for the usual and customary ceremonies for imperial coronations to be thoroughly and completely enacted.

66. I shall now briefly relate a few of the many things I saw when we legates of the people of Florence gathered with many other ambassadors from, so to speak, almost all Christendom. When Frederick, called the Third, made his appearance in the holy sight of the supreme pontiff, arrayed with a large retinue of prelates on all sides as he sat with great gravity and dignity upon the papal throne, he first genuflected and paid him homage. Then he drew closer to him and kissed his right foot and ankle, then his hand and cheek with utmost reverence. These ceremonies being concluded in the customary way, he delivered a short address filled with prayers and petitions. After receiving a kind and cultured reply, he departed the sacred sight of the pontiff and joyfully returned to his appointed lodging. The following day the Empress Leonora performed the same act.

67. His igitur et talibus ceremoniis, velut necessariis quibusdam futurorum ac gloriosorum gestorum preludiis antea institutis, paucis post diebus in basilicam[246] Petri Apostoli ubi prius suscepti fuerant[247] ambo ad suscipiendum coronas suas maxima cum devotione descenderunt.[248] Nicolaus itaque qui ecclesiasticarum ceremoniarum accuratissimus et diligentissimus observator erat, ubi ad ipsum coronationis actum pervenit, antequam ad coronandum progrederetur in solemnibus missarum, pias quasdam devotasque orationes habuit ac Federicum coram sanctitate sua ad altare genibus flexis humiliter procumbentem, ensem aureum incinxit ac paulo post regale sceptrum dextera manu largitus est ac deinde parvo postea temporis intervallo leva pilam auream prebuit. Capiti pretera suo imperatorium diadema ex puro et solido auro confectum ac pluribus insuper margaritarum, unionum gemmarumque, et ceteris pretiosorum lapillorum generibus redimitum solemniter devotissimeque imposuit.

68. Atque cum hec ipsa magna solemnitate eo[249] quo enarravimus ordine peregisset, ad extremum ambabus in celum manibus parumper elevatis in hunc modum altiuscule oravit: Omnipotens et sempiterne Deus qui ad predicandum eterni regni evangelium romanum imperium preparasti, presta quesumus huic Federico tertio novello imperatori fideli famulo tuo arma celestia ut, superatis barbaris et inhumanis gentibus, pacis ac catolice fidei inimicis, secura et intrepida tibi serviat humana libertas. Qua oratione audita, Federicus ita respondens: Exaudi, inquit, quesumus omnipotens et (942) sempiterne Deus, pias et devotas preces Nicolai tui summi pontificis ut cuncti ecclesiastici et seculares populi, prelati, respublice et principes, omnibus christiane fidei hostibus penitus abolitis atque ad ultimam internitionem[250] usque deletis, liberius servire atque efficacius famulari valeant ut[251] per hunc certum ac securum omnium fidelium nostrarum[252] gentium famulatum cuncti christiani homines digna utriusque et presentis et future vite premia consequi mereantur. Quamquam vero Federicus ipse, ut diximus, coronatus esset atque Leonora postea, super capite suo diademate duntaxat suscepto, pariter coronaretur, aliquot tamen dies in Urbe commoratus est.

69. Unde non multo post movens Neapolim cum imperatrice ad visendum Alphonsum clarissimum aragonum regem affinem suum omnibus pomparum generibus contendit atque exinde Romam reversus itineribus terrestribus per Etruriam

[246] Sancti Petri *Muratori*
[247] fuerunt *Muratori*
[248] ascenderunt *Muratori*
[249] & eo *Muratori*
[250] internecionem *Muratori*
[251] & *Muratori*
[252] nostrorum *Muratori*

67. And so, with these and like ceremonies inaugurated beforehand as the required preludes of the more glorious actions to come, a few days later, with the greatest reverence, they both went up into the basilica of the apostle Peter where they had earlier been greeted, to receive their crowns. Nicholas was the most exacting and scrupulous observer of ecclesiastical ceremonies. When he came to the act of coronation, before he proceeded to the crowning during the solemn Mass, he delivered some pious and reverent prayers. Then he invested Frederick, who was humbly kneeling at the altar in His Holiness's presence, with a golden sword, and a bit later he bestowed the royal scepter in his right hand, and finally after a brief interval conveyed to his left hand the golden orb. After that he solemnly and reverently placed on his head the imperial diadem, made of pure and solid gold and embellished on top with many pearls, pearl solitaires, and gems and other kinds of small precious stones.

68. When he had performed all these acts with great solemnity in the order in which I have related them, he concluded by raising both hands to heaven for a short time and praying in a rather high voice the following prayer: "Almighty and eternal God, who provided the Roman Empire for the preaching of the gospel of the everlasting Kingdom, bestow, we pray, the celestial arms on Frederick III here, the new emperor, your faithful servant, so that, with the defeat of the barbarian and uncivilized nations, the enemies of peace and the Catholic faith, human freedom, secure and untroubled, may serve You." After listening to this prayer, Frederick responded: "Hear, we pray, almighty and eternal God, the pious and reverent prayers of Nicholas, Your supreme pontiff, that all ecclesiastics and secular peoples, prelates, republics, and princes, when all enemies of the Christian faith are wiped out and eliminated to their final destruction, may have the strength to more freely serve and more effectively do Your bidding, so that through this sure and secure family of all our faithful nations all Christian people may merit achieving the due rewards both of this life and of the next." Even though Frederick himself, as we said, had been crowned and after him Leonora was likewise crowned by having the diadem placed upon her head, nonetheless they lingered a few days in the city.

69. Then not long afterwards he traveled with the empress to Naples and hastened with all manner of ceremonial to visit Alfonso, the most distinguished king of Aragon, his relative, and then from there, returning to Rome, he made

et Galliam cisalpinam in Germaniam[253] remeavit. At Leonora per mare navigans per Venetias in Alamaniam rediit. Ea vero que ad dignos tantorum dominorum totque principum et satrapum tantarumque et tam extranearum[254] gentium et ab italis moribus longe abhorrentium apparatus exigebantur, singulari quodam ac precipuo ordine a Nicolao nostro ita disposita et instituta sunt ut ne unus et quidem minimus error aut aliqua offensio in non parvo temporis intervallo notaretur neve aliqua dissensio seu contentio inter tam diversas germanorum, pannonum et italorum nationes oriretur.

70. Sexto deinceps felicis pontificatus sui anno cum Alphonsus iam pridem florentinis apprime infensus quod[255] Francisco Sfortie ad acquisitionem ducatus mediolanensis qui sibi a Philippo Maria testamento relictus fuerat anhelanti, non parva nec occulta sed magna ac manifesta equitum peditumque auxilia miserant multasque pecunias ad expeditionem novi belli adversus venetos propterea suscepti atque ob id ipsum cum predicto Alphonso confederatos, Ferrinandum unicum filium suum inclitum Calabrie ducem cum toto eius exercitu in agrum florentinorum[256] populandi, vexandi, ac diripiendi causa destinasset; prudentia sua ita se se gessit ut nec Alphonso ipsi nec venetis nec florentinis nec Francisco ullatenus displiceret atque ecclesiam a bellicis tumultibus militaribusque direptionibus illesam, inviolatam, intactamque servaret. Quemadmodum et primo et secundo sui pontificatus[257] anno antea prudentissime fecerat quando predictus Alphonsus, priusquam ipse ad pontificale fastigium assumeretur, cum infestis gentibus idcirco Tibur venerat ut exinde adversus florentinos hostilibus exercitibus moveret.

71. Ac in eodem deinde conservande et retinende pacis proposito continue perseverans cum per commemorati Philippi Marie mortem tota pene Italia bellicis hinc inde tumultibus confunderetur, solus ipse, Alphonso, venetis, florentinis, senensibus, ac Francisco inter se se[258] contendentibus invicemque belligerantibus, quietem novit, quietem adamavit, quietem et tranquillitatem ceteris omnibus rebus humanis preposuit longeque pretulit tum quia suapte natura a bellis abhorrebat, tum etiam ut preclara illa de componendis traducendisque operibus et de construendis ornandisque et extra et intra urbem edificiis liberius vacare ac studiosius subministrare (943) posset atque omnes insuper subditos suos a bellicis fremitibus et a militaribus direptionibus velut a pestilentibus et contagiosis morbis illesos, inviolatos, intactosque servaret.

---

[253] Galliam *Muratori*
[254] externarum *Muratori*
[255] qui *Muratori*
[256] Florentinum *Muratori*
[257] pontificatus sui *CC¹*
[258] se *B Muratori*

his way back to Germany along the land routes through Tuscany and Cisalpine Gaul. Leonora, however, returned to Germany by sea, sailing via the port of Venice. These arrangements, executed for the dignified accommodation of such great lords and so many princes and governors and of so many foreign nations who diverged greatly from Italian customs, had been so planned and conducted by our Nicholas in an exacting and special order that not a single tiny mistake or any offense was noticed during what was quite a long period of time, nor did there arise any dissension or quarreling among the so very different nations of Germans, Pannonians, and Italians.

70. It was the sixth year of his happy pontificate. Alfonso was already very hostile to the Florentines because they had sent not a small and discreet force of cavalry and infantry but a large and visible one to Francesco Sforza to help him acquire the Duchy of Milan which had been willed to him by Filippo Maria on his deathbed. They had received a great deal of money to mount a war against the Venetians, and the Venetians in turn had aligned themselves with Alfonso. Alfonso then dispatched his only son Ferdinand, the noble duke of Calabria, with his entire army into Florentine territory to pillage, harass, and devastate it. Yet Nicholas conducted himself with such prudence that he in no way fell from favor with Alfonso or the Venetians or the Florentines or Francesco and managed to preserve the church unhurt, unviolated, and intact from the tumult of war and the depredations of armies. In the first and second years of his pontificate he had acted with the same great prudence as he had earlier, before he had assumed the papal dignity, when the same Alfonso had come to Tivoli with aggressive nations to use it against the Florentines as a base of operations for his hostile armies.

71. Finally, he constantly persevered in the same goal of preserving and keeping the peace. When Filippo Maria died, almost all Italy was thrown into confusion by the outbreak of war in various places. Alfonso, the Venetians, the Florentines, the Sienese, and Francesco challenged one another and declared mutual war. He alone knew neutrality, cherished neutrality, valued neutrality and tranquillity above all other human matters and promoted it widely, because he loathed war by his very nature. But he also wanted to devote his time more freely and earnestly to oversee those preeminent projects of collecting and translating works and of constructing and ornamenting buildings within and outside the city, and to protect as well all his subjects unharmed, inviolate, and intact from the upheavals of war and the devastations of armies, as though from pestilential and contagious diseases.

72. Septimo deinde pontificatus sui anno cum predictus Ferrinandus infestis exercitibus per agrum florentinum multa involvisset atque in Gallia quoque cisalpina cuncta pene bellicis perturbationibus, venetis adversus Franciscum iam ducatum mediolani ob predictos florentinorum favores, ut cupiebat, adeptum, omnibus eorum viribus belligerantibus, agitarentur; factum est ut predicti principes, respublice, et populi oratores suos pro componenda inter eos pace Romam[259] transmitterent. Ipse vero dum coram eo de contentionibus ortis ageretur, sapientia sua que profecto in perpendendis et examinandis rebus maxima erat hoc unum conabatur, hoc unum curabat, hoc unum operabatur ut singulis gratificaretur ac nemini suspectus haberetur;[260] quod de industria atque ex proposito ideo faciebat primo ut nullis principibus displiceret, deinde ut ecclesiam suam in pace atque sedem apostolicam extenuatis per continua ac vicissitudinaria inter se bella omnium belligerantium facultatibus maiori auctoritate dignitateque conservaret. Bella enim inter predictos totius pene Italie principes ecclesie sue pacem, concordiam vero eorum versa vice bellum ecclesie non modo verisimilibus coniecturis sed certis etiam[261] et expressis argumentis et experientia quoque magistra rerum[262] intelligebat presagiebatque. Ob has igitur causas cum tepide in hoc ipso pacis concordieque tractatu, ne dicam frigide, se se gereret, contigisse videtur post longam quandam plurium mensium inanem futilemque tractationem ut ea que tractabatur concordia ad nihilum recideret atque propterea oratores, re infecta quinimmo, ut expressius dixerim, confracta, quique[263] in patriam suam remearent.

73. Hoc eodem anno etsi omnes ecclesie romane subditos in summa pace ac maxima tranquillitate continuisset atque Romam ipsam partim menibus apprime munivisset, partim pluribus edificiis circunquaque exornasset, civesque romanos multis privilegiis donasset, factum est tamen ut quidam scelesti homines et perniciosi cives ac proprie patrie proditores in sanctitatis sue caput nefarie nimis coniurassent. Huius coniurationis princeps erat Stephanus quidem Porcarius, vir equestris ordinis nobilis et elegans atque animosus sed parum prudens quem ipse plurimis antea honoribus et similibus emolumentis propterea honestaverat ut magnitudine beneficiorum nature sue perversitatem vel certe superaret vel saltem leniret. Sed ubi ob predicte coniurationis patefactionem rem[264] aliter quam opinabatur evenire conspexit, detecta, ut diximus, conspiratione atque quibusdam eius auctoribus ac principibus ultimo ut merebantur supplicio per suspendium

[259] Romam *om. Muratori*
[260] haberet *D*
[261] etiam *Muratori*
[262] rerum magistra *Muratori*
[263] quoque *Muratori*
[264] vere *Muratori*

72. Finally, in the seventh year of his pontificate, Ferdinand had engulfed much of Florentine territory with his armies of aggression and the entire situation in Cisalpine Gaul was unstable because of warlike disruptions, and the Venetians were waging all-out warfare against Francesco who had already obtained the Duchy of Milan, as he wished, through Florentine favoritism. It happened that these princes, republics, and peoples dispatched their ambassadors to Rome for the purpose of putting together a peace among themselves. The matter of the strife that had arisen was taken up in his presence. Because his wisdom was at its best in sorting out and examining matters, he was aiming at one goal, the one he cared about, the one he worked hard at, that he satisfy each party and that he not be held suspect by anyone. He deliberately acted according to plan: first, not to incur the disfavor of any of the princes; then, to preserve his church and the Apostolic See in peace with greater authority and prestige while the powers of all the belligerents were weakened through constant and reciprocal wars among themselves. For not only through likely inferences, but also with certain and explicit reasoning and from experience, reality's teacher, he understood and knew in advance that wars among those princes of virtually all of Italy meant peace for his Church, while agreement among them in turn was war for the Church. So with this in mind, he conducted himself in a lukewarm, not to say frosty, manner in the negotiations for peace and concord. After a long, empty, and futile negotiation of many months, the outcome seemed to be that the concord under negotiation had come to nothing and the ambassadors returned each to his own country with business unsettled, or more precisely, shattered.

73. During this same year, even though he had prolonged perfect peace and maximum tranquillity for the subjects of the Roman Church and he had greatly fortified Rome itself with walls and adorned her all around with many buildings and had endowed the citizens of Rome with many privileges, it nonetheless happened that some criminal persons and violent citizens and traitors to their own country foully hatched an extravagant plot against the life of His Holiness. The chief of this conspiracy was a certain Stefano Porcari, a man of the noble knightly order, sophisticated and passionate, but with too little sense. Nicholas had previously promoted him with many honors and other advantages, hoping that by the largeness of his kindnesses he might either overcome the defects of his nature, or at least lessen them. But when this conspiracy was exposed, he saw that the matter had turned out differently from what he had hoped. The plot was revealed, as I said, and its instigators and leaders openly condemned to execution by hanging

in mole Adriani propalam damnatis, ipse et civitas tota ac universa prelatorum caterva et reliqua sacerdotum turba in sua solita securitate atque consueta tranquillitate remansit. Hic est Stephanus ille quem sibi dormienti in calce primi libri per quietem apparuisse diximus.

74. Ad extremum octavo et ultimo pontificatus sui anno cum veneti ex ingentibus ac plurimis tam[265] diuturni belli sumptibus vehementer premerentur (944) atque Franciscus ipse facultatibus suis maiorem in modum extenuaretur ac utrique bellicis sumptibus usque adeo onerarentur atque usque adeo[266] exinanirentur ut neutri magnos exercitus suos propriis, ut consueverant, stipendiis ulterius alere et sustentare possent, factum est ut per intercessionem cuiusdam Simonetti religiosi viri ac probitate morum et sanctimonia vite admodum celebrandi, pax et concordia, frustra Rome tam diu antea tractata — mirabile dictu — optatos et concupitos sortiretur effectus. Veneti enim cum Francisco predicto et cum florentinis, inscio et ignorante Alphonso cum quo adversus commemoratos tanquam infensissimos hostes prius confederati erant, acerrimis simultatibus penitus omissis, quibus in se invicem diutius belligeraverant, pacem et concordiam ac confederationem — incredibile dictu — inierunt.

75. Pace itaque mutua confederatione condita per hunc modum, ut diximus, inter se se mirabiliter conclusa, sex legatos suos, clarissimos quidem viros, duos per singula membra ad Alphonsum mittere constituerunt quem moleste et egerrime hanc eorum concordiam laturum non dubitabant; quod idcirco faciebant ut per hanc tam honorificam ac tam gloriosam legatorum suorum transmissionem ipsum ad eam concordiam allicerent atque honestis precibus invitarent et benignis suasionibus traducerent vel saltem mitiorem redderent.[267] Delecti itaque sex oratores Romam ad Nicolaum nostrum, iam pridem magnis non modo podagrarum et cyragrarum et ceterorum[268] arthriticorum[269] dolorum egrotationibus sed lentis quoque[270] febribus apprime oneratum, cum expressis ad sanctitatem suam commissionibus venerant cui cum pacem pro totius Italie salute inter eos factam fuisse significarent, beatitudinem suam suppliciter exhortabantur[271] ut predicte paci pro salute Italie, ceu dicebant, confecte assentiri et adherere dignaretur atque eos ad Alphonsum hac duntaxat causa contendentes, suis sapientibus consiliis, suis devotis suasionibus, suis variis favoribus adiuvaret.

---

[265] plurimis tam *om. Muratori*
[266] onarerentur . . . adeo *om. D*
[267] vel . . . redderent *om. D*
[268] ceterorum *om. Muratori*
[269] arthriticorum *Pagnotti*: arteticorum *codd.*
[270] quidem *Muratori*
[271] cohortabantur *Muratori*

in Hadrian's Mass as they deserved. He and the whole city and the entire entourage of prelates and the remaining crowd of clergy retained their customary security and their usual tranquillity. This is the same Stefano who I said at the end of Book I came to him in an apparition as he slept peacefully.

74. In the end, during the eighth and final year of his pontificate, the Venetians were hard pressed by the many huge expenses of unending war and Francesco himself was even more weakened in his powers, and both sides were so burdened by the costs of war and so drained that neither could any longer nourish and sustain their large armies with the proper salaries to which they had grown accustomed. Then it happened that peace and concord, for such a long time negotiated in vain at Rome — marvelous to tell! — attained its hoped-for and desired effects, through the agency of a certain Simonetti, a religious man with a deserved reputation for the probity of his character and the chasteness of his life. Together with Francesco and the Florentines, the Venetians completely set aside their bitterest feuds for which they had so long warred against each other and entered into peace and concord and — incredible to tell! — alliance. Alfonso meanwhile, with whom previously the Venetians had been allied against those aggressive enemies of his, remained unknowing and uninformed.

75. And so with peace based on mutual alliance, as I have said, remarkably concluded among them, they decided to send six of their legates to Alfonso, men of great distinction, two for each party. They had no doubt that he would receive their agreement with irritation and great reluctance. They did this hoping they might win him over to the agreement through an embassy of their legates which would bring him honor and glory, and hoping that they might attract him with honorable entreaties and change his mind with cordial persuasions, or at least calm him down. And so the six ambassadors selected came to Rome to Nicholas with explicit commissions to His Holiness. He was by now already burdened not only with great afflictions of painful swelling in his feet and hands and pains in his other joints but also with lingering fevers. When they indicated to him that peace had been made among them for the security of all Italy, they humbly urged His Beatitude that he deign to assent to and abide by this peace achieved, as they said, for the security of Italy and that he help them with his wise counsel, his pious persuasions, and his various favors as they hastened to Alfonso for this very purpose.

76. At Nicolaus, oratoribus benigne auditis, cum ipsos inter se pacem ac[272] confederationem inivisse cognovisset et ad prosequendum ulterius totis animis inclinatos esse conspiceret atque se se malignitate morbi in dies vehementius oneratum oppressumque iri[273] coniectura auguraretur, non amplius dissimulandum fore ratus, prudentissime simul atque gratissime in hunc modum respondisse fertur. Pacem nanque semper sibi placuisse, inquit, pro qua componenda multos se labores suscepisse ac tolerasse testatus est. Concordiam deinde simul cum confederatione inter eos initam pluribus elegantibus verbis laudavit atque sibi ipsis ad Alphonsum eadem causa contendentibus persuasionibusque suis uti ab eis postulabatur favere opitularique significavit et ut omnis dubitatio e medio tolleretur atque certa et indubitata pax cum Alphonso Rege conficeretur, cardinalem quendam, preclarissimum ac prudentissimum dominum et multa quoque secularium rerum experientia exercitatum, legatum, ut dicitur, de latere una secum mittere subiunxit; atque talia et tam stricta mandata ei se daturum confirmavit ut vota sua effectibus et operibus penitus et omnino adimplenda esse non dubitaret.

77. Ad extremum ut mentem, inquit, nostram ad pacem Italie semper (945) inclinatissimam extitisse intelligatis, non modo omnibus postulationibus vestris et de adhesione nostra et de exhortationibus erga Alphonsum per nos faciendis libenter assentimur[274] sed legatum etiam de latere ut efficacius et copiosius opitulemur ad eum mittere constituimus quod nequaquam postulabatis ut omnes[275] christiani principes, respublice, et populi plura in hoc vestro generalis pacis desiderio quod itidem nostrum abundantius esse ac videri volumus quam separata et coniuncta totius confederationis vestre membra[276] hactenus postulaverint,[277] facta fuisse intelligant planeque cognoscant. Hoc Nicolai pontificis nostri sapientissimum et efficacissimum responsum quam gratum quamque acceptum predictis oratoribus fuerit, non satis dici explicarive[278] potest, presertim quando[279] Dominicum titulo sancte crucis presbiterum cardinalem, dominum Firmanum, prudentissimum et optimum virum et magne apud omnes mundi principes auctoritatis ac ardentem insuper pacis amatorem, vive vocis oraculo pronuntiatum atque ad id sanctum opus peragendum destinatum designatumque[280] acceperunt.

---

[272] pacem, & concordiam, ac *Muratori*
[273] ita *Muratori*
[274] assentimus *Muratori*
[275] omnes *om. D*
[276] mentibus *Muratori*
[277] postulaverunt *Muratori*
[278] explorarive *Muratori*
[279] quoniam *Muratori*
[280] designatum destinatumque *D*

76. But Nicholas, after politely listening to the ambassadors, realized that they had entered into peace and alliance among themselves and saw that they had been inclined to press further with all their energy and divined by inference that he himself was daily more vehemently burdened with his insidious disease and would continue to be weighed down by it. Judging that the dissimulation could go on no longer, he is reported to have replied most prudently and graciously in the following manner. He said that he had always favored peace; to achieve it he attested that he had undertaken and suffered many labors. Then in much elegant language he praised the agreement arrived at among them, together with the alliance. He indicated that he would favor and assist those who were hurrying to Alfonso for this same purpose and help their persuasions, just as he was asked by them. And so to remove all doubt from the scene and to conclude a sure and unhesitant peace with King Alfonso, he added that he was sending with them a cardinal, a most distinguished and prudent lord trained with much experience in secular affairs, as his legate *a latere*, so to speak. He affirmed that he would give him such specific and strict orders that he would not doubt that his promises were to be fulfilled thoroughly and completely in results and actions.

77. At the end he said, "So that you might know that our mind has always been most intently focused on the peace of Italy, we freely assent not only to all your requests both about our conformity and about exhortations to be made by us for Alfonso's benefit. We have also decided to send to him a legate *a latere* so that we might offer more effective and abundant help, something you were not at all requesting, so that all Christian princes, republics, and people might understand and clearly recognize that more has been done than the parties to your alliance, separate and united, have up to now requested on behalf of your desire for general peace. I wish our role in this to be and seem to be more generous." How welcome and how readily accepted this most wise and useful reply of our Pope Nicholas was to those ambassadors cannot be told in detail. But they received lord Domenico of Fermo, titular cardinal priest of Santa Croce, a most prudent and excellent man with great prestige among all the princes of the world and an ardent lover of peace; his name was announced by proclamation in a loud voice, and he was charged and deputized to accomplish this holy task.

78. Oratores itaque una cum legato Neapolim contendentes post longam quandam et diuturnam preteritarum contentionum agitationem, tandem per efficacem et profecto admirabilem predicti legati intercessionem, pacem ac concordiam preter spem omnium mirabiliter concluserunt. Qua quidem composita ac conclusa, oratores una cum legato ad Nicolaum nostrum, iam morborum gravitate vehementius oppressum, leti et alacres rediere; quos in conspectu suo assistentes magnis ac dignis laudibus sua illa singulari et precipua elegantia plurimum exornavit. Oratores igitur, pace facta, et pontificiis quoque laudibus ornati et nonnullis insuper personarum privilegiis honestati, maximo cum gaudio quique in patriam suam remearunt.

79. Non multo post cum omnia prope morborum genera, quasi agmine facto, in pusillum Nicolai nostri corpusculum concurrissent atque in dies vehementius exaugescerent, ipsum continuis quibusdam diurnis nocturnisque angoribus usque adeo afflixerunt ut extenuatis paulatim viribus personam suam interimerent, personam, inquam, suam omnibus nature muneribus ornatam interimerent atque cunctis quoque ingenuarum facultatum scientiarumque generibus preditam[281] quinquagesimo septimo etatis sue, octavo vero pontificatus anno, indigne admodum ne dicam crudeliter et impie, interimerent, cum id ipsum, qualecumque sit, ab omnipotenti Deo, cuius iudicia velut abyssus multa, singulis hominibus occultissima videntur et sunt[282] provenisse atque emanasse non ignoremus.[283]

---

[281] praeditum *Muratori*
[282] videntur et sunt *om. Muratori*
[283] ignoramus *D Muratori*

78. So the ambassadors, together with the legate, hastened to Naples. After the long and continuous turmoil of their past contentions, finally, through the effective and quite marvelous intercession of that legate, they miraculously concluded the peace and agreement, to everyone's surprise. With this arranged and concluded, the ambassadors together with the legate happily and cheerfully returned to our Nicholas, who was now even more vehemently weighed down with the graveness of his diseases. As they sat in his presence, he graced them lavishly with great and worthy praises by means of his unique and special elegance. And then the ambassadors, with the peace made, adorned with papal praise and honored with a few personal privileges, returned, each to his own country amid great rejoicing.

79. Not long afterwards, almost all types of diseases, as if arrayed in battle, invaded the small, slight body of our Nicholas and grew more violent each day. They afflicted him with continual agony day and night so much that as his strength gradually ebbed they destroyed his very person, his very person, I say, graced with all nature's gifts and endowed with every type of faculty of talent and learning. In his fifty-seventh year, the eighth of his pontificate, they destroyed him unworthily, to say nothing of cruelly and impiously, though we do not fail to realize that this too, whatever it might be, originated with and emanated from almighty God whose judgments, like a great abyss [Ps. 35:6], seem to be and are most hidden from the view of individual men.

Giannozzo Manetti
On the Achievements of Nicholas V
Supreme Pontiff

Book Two of the Life of Nicholas V

Commentary

1. ***in the four hundred and forty-seventh year:*** Nicholas was elected on 6 March 1447. He died during the night between 24 and 25 March 1455. In fifteenth-century Rome, although the civic year began on 1 January, the religious calendar was counted from 1 March, unlike Florence, where the new year began on 25 March. Our dates consider the new year to begin on January 1, but the reader should keep in mind that Manetti's system of counting by the year of the pontificate reckons from 6 March to 6 March, approximately the same as the Roman church calendar.

his deceased Cardinal patron: Niccolò Albergati (1376–1443), Archbishop of Bologna and titular cardinal of Sta. Croce in Gerusalemme. The new pope had managed the cardinal's affairs for over twenty years and was in turn mentored by him in church matters, including diplomacy. Nicholas succeeded Albergati in the see of Bologna: Manetti, *Life*, Book 1, *RIS* 3.2:916, 954; Vespasiano, *Vite*, 1:39–43, 131. Although Manetti says that Nicholas chose his name to honor Albergati, he may also have wished to associate his pontificate with that of Nicholas III (1277–1280) both because the latter was an Orsini, the family to which our Nicholas owed his pontificate, and because the Orsini Nicholas had built up the Vatican Palace and reformed the Canons of St. Peter's: M. Borgolte, *Petrusnachfolge und Kaiserimitation. Die Grablegen der Päpste, ihre Genese unde Traditionsbildung* (Göttingen, 1989), 271. Yet another reason for taking this name is because Nicholas of Tolentino had been canonized in the year preceding his election: J. Nabuco, *Le cérémonial apostolique avant Innocent VIII* (Rome, 1966), 15.

so great a burden: allusion to Vergil, *Aeneid* 1.33, referring to the founding of Rome.

2. ***his predecessor Eugenius:*** Gabriele Condulmer (1383–1447), elected Eugenius IV in 1431.

Amadeus, Duke of Savoy: In 1439 the Council of Basle proclaimed Eugenius IV heretical and deposed him, electing Amadeus VIII (1383–1451) as Felix V (1439–1449). Upon his recognition of Nicholas on 7 April 1449, Nicholas made him a cardinal and appointed him apostolic legate to Savoy, as Manetti relates at 4. ***Council of Basle:*** Convened in 1431 by Martin V in accord with the 1417 decree of the Council of Constance (1414–1418) calling for the regular meeting of such bodies. Constance had also decreed that such general councils, as representative of the Church Militant, held their power directly from Christ and that therefore the pope, like all Christians, was subject to its decisions. This was affirmed at Basle and pronounced an article of Christian faith (1439). On the conciliar movement, see Crowder, *Unity, Heresy and Reform*; W. Brandmüller, *Das Konzil von Konstanz 1414–1418* (Paderborn, 1991); Stieber, *Eugenius IV*; and Tierney, *Foundations of the Conciliar Theory*. For Nicholas's view of the papacy as supreme in the Church, see our Chapters 8 and 9.

3. ***to congratulate him:*** In the case of the Florentine Republic, the delegation was led by Manetti himself, who delivered an oration (MS. Urb. lat. 387, fols. 184v–188r) which, Vespasiano says, Nicholas repeated back verbatim (*Vite*, 1:59). As a cleric attached to the papal court during Eugenius's exile in Florence, Nicholas and Manetti knew one another from the circle of Humanists that gathered for daily disputations: Vespasiano, *Vite*, 1:42–43.

5. ***happy beginnings:*** In 1448 Nicholas signed a concordat between the papacy and the German nation, received the obedience of the Duke of Burgundy, and made a treaty with Francesco Sforza, Duke of Milan: Coluccia, *Niccolò V. umanista*, 180, 189, 195. A more detailed account of the recognition of Nicholas as the legitimate pope from 1447–1448 is in Stieber, *Eugenius IV*, 312–25.

certain historians: Actually, Cicero, *On the Manilian Law*, 7.17.

6. ***College of Cardinals:*** Manetti says that *cardinalatus* or "cardinalate" is the term in use. Since 1150, the corporate entity had been called a *collegium* or "college" (J. B. Sägmüller, s.v., *The Catholic Encyclopedia* [London, 1908], 3:340).

cardinals: These were appointed in 1448: Filippo Parentucelli, half-brother of Nicholas, Bishop of Bologna and Cardinal-Priest of San Lorenzo in Lucina; Latino Orsini, Cardinal of SS. Giovanni e Paolo, then Bishop of Tusculum (d. 1468); Alain de Coetivy, Cardinal of Sta. Prassede, Bishop of Avignon, Bishop of Palestrina, then of Sabina (d. 1474); Antonio de la Cerda, Cardinal of San Crisogono (d. 1458); John Kemp (ca.1380–1454), Cardinal of Sta. Balbina (1439), then Bishop of Sta. Rufina, Archbishop of Canterbury (1452–1454); Zbigniew Olesnicki, Bishop of Cracow, elected 1430, removed by Eugenius IV, reinstated by Nicholas (d. 1455); Jean Rolin, Bishop of Autun, Cardinal of Sto. Stefano Rotondo (d. 1483); and Nicholas of Cusa (1401–1464), Cardinal of S. Pietro in Vinculi, Bishop of Brixen (Bressanone).

Manetti does not mention that in 1449 Nicholas confirmed four cardinals elevated by Felix V: Lodovico Alamandi (d. 1450), Johannes de Arsiis, Lodovico de Varambene, and Guillaume D'Estaing.

Of the cardinals already in office at Nicholas's accession, ten died during his pontificate: one died in 1447 (Henri de Beaufort, Cardinal of S. Eusebius) and two in 1449 (Johannes de Primis, Cardinal of Sta. Sabina, and Giovanni de Tagliacotto, Cardinal of SS. Nereo and Achilleo); two in 1450 (Ludovico Alamandi, Cardinal of Sta. Cecilia, appointed by Felix V, confirmed by Nicholas 1449; and Henricus Rampinus de S. Allosio, Cardinal of San Clemente); two in 1451 (Amadeus, Duke of Savoy, the anti-pope, and Johannes Juvenis); two in 1453 (Johannes Cervantes, Cardinal of San Pietro in Vincoli, then Bishop of Ostia, and Francesco Condulmer, nephew of Eugenius IV, Cardinal-Bishop of Porto, Cardinal of Venice, Vice-Chancellor); one in 1454 (Johannes de Arsiis, appointed by Felix V, confirmed by Nicholas). See Eubel, *Hierarchia catholica medii aevi*, 2 (1431–1503): 3–9.

7. ***sale of sacred benefices:*** for a discussion of simony, see Chapter 3.

8. ***ecclesiastical ceremonies:*** As early as 1437 Eugenius IV had threatened with excommunication clergy entering St. Peter's dressed improperly: C. Reynolds, *Papal Patronage and the Music of St. Peter's, 1380–1513* (Berkeley, 1995), 26. Nicholas ordered all canons and clerics of St. Peter's to wear certain vestments both in and out of the basilica. In the first year of his pontificate he appointed over the canons a vicar charged with both temporal and spiritual reform, and in 1452 he established a committee of bishops to review and reform lapses in the performance of the divine cult in the basilica: L. Martorelli, *Storia del clero vaticano* (Rome, 1792), 228, 110. For further discussion of Nicholas's pontificate and liturgy, see Chapters 5 and 9. Nicholas also reorganized and enlarged the choirs at the Vatican, augmenting the number of singers in the papal choir from 10 to 15 and in St. Peter's choir to 12: Reynolds, *Papal Patronage and the Music of St. Peter's*, 35.

Nicholas's concern with liturgy early in his pontificate is additionally evident from Fra Angelico's frescoes of the ordinations of Saints Stephen and Lawrence in Nicholas's private chapel in the Vatican, begun in May of 1447 and completed in June of 1451 (fig. 7): Redig de Campos, *I Palazzi Vaticani*, 50. St. Lawrence was ordained deacon in Rome by Pope Sixtus II: Fra Angelico might have imagined this taking place either at St. John Lateran or at St. Peter's, although neither had been built. St. Stephen, instead, was ordained by the apostles — Fra Angelico shows Peter himself officiating and six others attending. Since this took place in Jerusalem, the painter might be showing a view of the Temple, although of course this could hardly have been the original site, or a setting that alludes to the Temple. In both scenes, a deacon is being invested with the elements of the Eucharist. Although the action is the same in both frescoes, the persons who assist at the event and the settings are different. St. Peter himself ordains Stephen;

a pope — historically Sixtus II, but represented as Nicholas V — invests Lawrence in the presence of eight clergy, all tonsured. All except the ordinand wear antique garb in the scene of Stephen; modern vestments differentiated by rank are worn in that of Lawrence. Thus we see the greater articulation of the contemporary church in comparison with apostolic times. Continuity in the faith is shown by the presence of an altar with a crucifix and the same chalice and paten in both frescoes; in each, a figure just left of center and facing the spectator holds the Gospels. Historical evolution of the liturgy from the early church to the present is shown in the scene of Lawrence: the chief subdeacon holds a towel, the acolytes an incense boat and censer. The frescoes differentiate the modern from the apostolic church, and they reflect Nicholas's own concerns for proper vestments and liturgical vessels. See I. Venchi, R. Colella, A. Nesselrath, C. Giantomassi, and D. Zari, *Fra Angelico and the Chapel of Nicholas V* (Vatican City, 1999), especially Colella's essay "The Cappella Niccolina, or Chapel of Nicholas V in the Vatican: The History and Significance of its Frescoes," 22–71.

With Nicholas's reforms in mind, the perfect order and decorum of the contemporary liturgy depicted by Fra Angelico acquires specific relevance to the early years of Nicholas's pontificate. Differences between the two scenes, showing the greater order and more articulated ceremonial of the contemporary Roman liturgy, express the view that the Church does and must evolve over time toward a fuller manifestation of the divine plan even while maintaining intact the unchanging faith and sacraments received by the apostles. This theme is explicit in Juan de Torquemada's writings: offices and dignities potentially present in the original church had been fully developed in the modern for the work of saving souls. See Izbicki, *Protector of the Faith*, 38.

he embellished: This activity is confirmed by Aeneas Silvius Piccolomini, who wrote: "Sacrarium apostolicum vasis aureis atque argenteis, sacerdotalibus indumentis mirifice decoravit, altaris ornamenta, aulea quoque ex auro contexta mirandi operis coemit, suppellectilem toto palatio necessariam magnificentissime comparam duplicant triplicavitque": "De Europa," in *Opera*, 459.

Manetti does not mention that Nicholas either acquired or had reliquaries made for relics of St. Andrew (knee); St. Leontius Martyr; and St. Lambert (head): Müntz, *Les arts à la cour des papes*, 167. An inventory of 1454–1455 of the sacristy of St. Peter's lists a silver box with crystals and a silver tabernacle for St. Andrew's knee as having been given by Nicholas. E. Müntz and A. Frothingham, "Il tesoro della basilica di S.Pietro in Vaticano dal XIII al XV secolo, con una scelta di inventari inediti," *Archivio della Società Romana di Storia Patria* 6 (1883): 1–137, here 87.

"vestments": In Latin *paramenta*. A complete set of vestments made for Nicholas in 1450 is conserved in the Museo Nazionale del Bargello in Florence and discussed in Chapter 9. See B. Paolozzi Strozzi, *Il parato di Niccolò V per il Giubileo del 1450* (Florence, 2000).

gems: the enumerated gemstones correspond exactly to the Vulgate description of the pectoral (*rationale*) of Aaron in Exodus 28:18–20. St. Jerome had commented (Letter 64.16–19) that these are the stones of the diadem of the Prince of Tyre and of which the Heavenly Jerusalem is made: *Saint Jérôme, Lettres*, ed. J. Labourt (Paris, 1953), 3:130–31 (PL 22.616–619). In his funeral oration, Jean de Jouffroy calls Nicholas "he who carried Aaron's pectoral on his breast": "Oratio Episcopi Atrebatensis," fol. 33r.

Church Militant . . . Church Triumphant: See Chapters 8 and 9.

9. ***huge, permanent buildings:*** Perhaps Manetti means to include in the category "secular" restoration work on the Capitoline, seat of the Roman government, with renovation of the Palazzo del Senatore and construction of the Palazzo dei Conservatore: Stinger, *The Renaissance in Rome*, 255; Mack, "Nicholas the Fifth and the Rebuilding of Rome," 36; Westfall, *In This Most Perfect Paradise*, 94–99. He may also refer to work on the walls and gates of Rome, and restoration of the Acqua Vergine, finished in 1453, which gave Rome fresh water at the Trevi fountain (Westfall, *In This Most Perfect Paradise*, 106), although C. Burroughs thought that work on the Trevi fountain was due not to Nicholas but to the Colonna family: "Alberti e Roma," in *Alberti*, ed. Rykwert and Engel, 134–57, here 152. See also M. Gargano, "Niccolò V. La mostra dell'acqua di Trevi," *Archivio della Società Romana di Storia Patria* 111 (1988): 225–66, and J. Pinto, *The Trevi Fountain* (New Haven, 1986).

Since his topic is secular displays, Manetti omits many of Nicholas's earliest projects, including early work on churches. For instance, Nicholas restored the Pantheon (Sta. Maria Rotonda or ad Martyres). Work on S. Teodoro, S. Eusebio, and S. Pietro in Vincoli is also early, as is the restoration of the papal palace at Sta. Maria Maggiore; the placement of a new statue of St. Michael on top of Castel Sant'Angelo; and the beginning of the Great Tower, part of the new fortification of the Vatican Palace. See Burroughs, "Below the Angel," 115; idem, "Nicholas V and Rome," 200; idem, *From Signs to Design*, 72–78, 116, 121; Westfall, *In This Most Perfect Paradise*, 105; Fasolo, "San Teodoro al Palatino," 112–19.

Early in the pontificate work is documented on the Vatican Palace, its location rarely specified in the documents and, even when specified, difficult to identify. The stages of work at the palace can hardly be dated (except for the Great Tower which fell in 1454 and the new north wing which bears the inscription 1454), but work was in progress on it virtually throughout the pontificate: we discuss this project in detail in Chapter 6.

10. Jubilee: It began on 24 December 1449. The notion of Jubilee is based on the Mosaic jubilee year where the Law prescribes that slaves be freed and debts forgiven (Lev. 25:8–17). See *La Storia dei Giubilei*, ed. G. Fossi, 1, *1300–1423* (Prato, 1997); 2, *1450–1575* (Prato 1998).

great crowds: The diversity of pilgrims may have amazed Manetti and confirmed in astonishing numbers the church's universality, but it annoyed at least some Romans; Stefano Porcari, for example, complained of the influx of "barbarians" that had made the native populace a minority: L. B. Alberti, "De coniuratione porcaria," *RIS*, 25.310.

bees: Vergilian metaphors for civil life in *Georgics* 4.3, 153–218, repeated by John of Salisbury, *Policraticus* 6.21, PL 199.619–620.

11. Famous bridge: Originally the Pons Aelius, built to connect Hadrian's Mausoleum to the Campus Martius, then Ponte Sant'Angelo after the statue of St. Michael the Archangel atop the mausoleum since the sixth century. See L. Richardson, *A New Topographical Dictionary of Ancient Rome* (Baltimore, 1992), s.v. The disaster at the bridge occurred on 19 December 1450. For Leon Battista Alberti's reconstruction drawing of Hadrian's bridge, see Chapter 7.

two small basilicas: Two oratories where Ponte Sant'Angelo meets Piazza San Celso. For this project, see Burroughs, "Below the Angel," 94–124.

13. personal glory: See Chapter 8 for the place of personal glory within the virtue of magnificence.

14. Greek and Latin books: Inventories of Nicholas's collection are in Manfredi, *Codici*; Müntz and Fabre, *Bibliothèque*; and A. M. Albareda, "Il bibliotecario di Callisto III," in *Miscellanea Giovanni Mercati,* Studi e Testi 124 (Vatican City, 1946), 178-208. For the Library project, see Chapter 4.

15. Ptolemy Philadelphus: See Chapters 4 and 9.

Aristeas: See Chapter 4 and the following entry.

16. translators and composers: Among the works composed for Nicholas were biographies of Nicholas: Michele Canensi's *De laudibus Nicolai pape quinti* of 1451 or 1452; Pietro de'Godi's *Ad laudem Dei et Nicolai papae V*; and one by Francesco Filelfo of 1453 which Nicholas threw into his fireplace and burned. Basinio da Parma's poem of praise is now BAV Vat lat. 1676, fols. 1r–3r. Jacopo Zeno dedicated his biography of their mentor, Cardinal Albergati, to him. Then there were a number of works on ecclesiology and theology: Juan de Torquemada's *Commentaria super decreto* (of which *De consecratione* and *De poenitentia* [1449] are parts); Torquemada's *Summa de ecclesia*, 1449–1453; Domenico Capranica's *Quedam avisamenta super reformatione pape et Romane curie* (1449); Antonio da Cannara's *De potestate papae supra concilium generale*; Lorenzo da Pisa's *Dialogus humilitatis*; Antonio da Bitonto's *Quaestiones in I Sententiarum*; John de Capistrano's *Tractatus de potestate papae et concili* (uncertain) and his *Speculum conscientiae*, probably a gift to the pope; Bernardus de Rosergio's *De sacro statu papalis dignitatis* (a gift in 1441); Pietro de'Monte's *Contra impugnantes sedis apostolicae auctoritatem ad Nicolaum V*; Giovanni Serra's *De controversia trium animae potentiarum inter se de praesentia disputantium*; Maffeo Vegio's *Disputatio inter solem, terram et aurum*; and Antonio degli Agli's *De vitis et gestis sanctorum*. Among secular works were Giovanni

Tortelli's *De orthographia* of 1449; Poggio Bracciolini's *De varietate fortunae* (1447); Flavio Biondo's *Roma instaurata* (originally dedicated to Nicholas in 1453); Gaspare da Verona's *Commentary on Juvenal*; Andrea Fiocco's *Historia ab adolescentia C. Iulii Caesaris*; Bartolomeo Fazio's *De excellentia et praestantia hominis*; and Leonardo Dati's *Jemsale* (*Hiemsal*), a tragedy. Whether Alberti's *De re aedificatoria* was presented to Nicholas is discussed in Chapter 7. See Izbicki, *Protector of the Faith*, 18; *Vita di Nicolò V*, trans. Modigliani, 9; G. Voigt, *Wiederbelebung des classischen*, 2:77; Miglio, *Storiografia pontificia* 16, 77 n. 29, 84; Burroughs, *From Signs to Design Altertums*, 255 n. 17; Colella, "Cappella Niccolina," 60 n. 134; E. Schröter, "Der Vatican als Hügel Apollons und der Musen. Kunst und Panegyrik von Nikolaus V bis Julius II," *Römische Quartalschrift* 75 (1980): 208–40, here 210; and Manfredi, *Codici latini*, nos. 332, 397, 416, 426, 520, 576, 611, 612, 679, 740.

Translation from Greek to Latin was also prolific. In his funeral oration, Niccolò Palmieri mentions mathematical works, the early Fathers, and pagan writers (MS. Vat. lat. 5815, fol. 9v). Jean Jouffroy, in his, enumerates Aristotle, Plato, Theophrastus, Ptolemy, Thucydides, Herodotus, Appian, Diodorus Siculus, Polybius, Chrysostom, Basil, Gregory Nazianzus, and Eusebius ("Oratio," fol. 34 r–v). See Chapter 4; Vespasiano, *Vite*, 1:64–70 ; Voigt, Risorgimento, passim.

16. translated before: He may mean Robert Grosseteste (ca. 1168–1253) and William of Moerbeke (ca. 1215–1286).

On the Preparation of the Gospel: Translated by George of Trebizond, and extremely important to Manetti because it contained a long excerpt from the then-lost "Letter of Aristeas" which described the circumstances in which the Greek Septuagint translation was made from the Hebrew original. Manetti quotes large portions of George of Trebizond's translation of Eusebius in the second book of his *Apologeticus*: *'Apologeticus'*, ed. De Petris; Botley, *Latin Translation*, appendix. The complete "Letter of Aristeas" was translated into Latin in the 1480s by Mattia Palmieri. For Manetti's use of this source see Chapter 4. On George of Trebizond, see Monfasani, *George of Trebizond*.

Dionysius: Translated by Manetti's teacher, Ambrogio Traversari.

17. called by him: Manetti was appointed on 28 July 1451, but came to Rome only in 1453.

huge volume in twenty books: The *Contra Judaeos et gentes* was finished in exile at the court of Alfonso II in Naples, and dedicated to that king. In its final version, it contains only 10 books: De Petris, "*L'Adversus Iudeos et gentes* di Giannozzo Manetti."

Old and New Testaments: Manetti finished the Gospels, the Letters of Paul, and the Book of Revelation of the New Testament, but of the Old Testament only the Psalms appeared, dedicated to King Alfonso. Manetti was bitterly attacked; his response to critics is his *Apologeticus* in ten books. See A. De Petris, "Le teorie umanistiche del tradurre e l'*Apologeticus* di Giannozzo Manetti," *Bibliothèque* *d'humanisme et Renaissance* 37 (1975): 15–32 and *'Apologeticus'*, ed. idem; Botley, *Latin Translation*, chap. 2 and appendix. See Chapter 1.

divine help . . . helper: cf. *De pompis* 2.

18. Bernardino Massense: Saint Bernardino of Siena (actually born at Massa Marittima, as Manetti says), b. 8 Sept. 1380 — d. 20 May 1444; canonized 24 May 1450. The ceremonial for the canonization of S. Bernardino is preserved in a manuscript in the Vatican Library, MS. Barb. lat. 2436, fols. 124–126. On Bernardino, see F. Mormando, *The Preacher's Demons. Bernardino of Siena and the Social Underworld of Early Renaissance Italy* (Chicago, 1999).

19. to Fabriano: 18 June to 25 October 1450. Nicholas had also been there in August of 1449, also because of the plague: von Pastor, *A History of the Popes*, 2:86; R. Sassi, *Documenti sul soggiorno a Fabriano di Nicolò V e della sua corte nel 1449 e nel 1450* (Ancona, 1955).

20. rhagades: Fissures of the skin occurring especially around the mouth or anus (Celsus 6.18.7; Galen 19.446).

foremen and project contractors: Many of these men were probably contractors rather than skilled artisans or intellectuals, but not all. In 1457 Francesco dal Borgo, one of them, commissioned a copy of Archimedes and Euclid with his arms on it: he seems to have been the same kind of Humanist/architect as Alberti: C. Frommel, "Francesco del Borgo: Architekt Pius' II. und Pauls' II.," *Römisches Jahrbuch* 21 (1984): 71–164, here 133–34. And Antonello di Giovanni, who appeared as a "muratore" (waller) in Eugenius IV's account books and worked on the windows of St. Peter's in 1447, was a *beneficiatus* of St. Peter's and in 1448 was made a canon at Tivoli, a post usually reserved for men of good family: Burroughs, *From Signs to Design*, 116–17.

21. building: Manetti's verbs for architectural planning in the *Life* suggest that Nicholas V conceived the overall plan and specific designs for his building projects. We are told that Nicholas "placed" and "arranged" structures, although Manetti might only mean that the pope, as patron, willed buildings to be built and that he paid for them (see Chapter 9). Perhaps, however, as Manetti implies, Nicholas was the designer of his projects in some more direct way. Nicholas's own earlier experience in Bologna and the documented presence of Bolognese architects at work in Rome opens the possibility that at least parts of what Manetti describes were conceived by Nicholas, perhaps with advisors, but without the two men who most interest us, Manetti and Alberti, neither of whom had had any direct experience with construction in the earliest years of the pontificate.

In his Lives both of Niccolò Albergati, Nicholas V's mentor, and of the pontiff himself, Vespasiano da Bisticci tells the story of how Albergati, then bishop of Bologna, entrusted the future pope with a rebuilding project:

> Istava la casa del vescovado come istanno le più case de' preti, che sono male a ordine; giunto maestro Tomaso a Bologna, il cardinale cominciò a ragionare collui dello edificare quella casa del vescovado, et dette la comesione a maestro Tomaso, che facessi lui. In brevissimo tempo fece riedificare la casa del vescovado tutta di novo. (1:43)

> Era la casa del vescovado tutta guasta. Giunto a Bologna, comisse a maestro Tommaso la facessi aconciare e nicistà non a pompa, e fevi edificare grande parte di nuovo, dove ordinò una buona et laudabile stanza per uno vescovo, come si vede infino al presente dì. (1:133)

In addition to renovating the Episcopal Palace in Bologna in 1437, Nicholas may have been responsible for certain improvements to the Cathedral of St. Peter there which took place during Albergati's tenure: a brick pavement was made for its portico; a tabernacle for the host was installed behind the main altar; and the top of the Campanile was renewed in brick and lead. These projects would have familiarized the future pontiff with problems of renovation, including what we would now call "historic preservation", and introduced him to builders.

It would have been in Bologna that Nicholas met the Fioravanti family, members of which worked for him in Rome. In 1444, the year in which Nicholas became bishop of Bologna, the tower of the Palazzo Comunale was built. Most of this structure had been erected by Fioravanti Fioravanti (ca. 1390–1430/47), whose nephew was Aristotele Fioravanti (1415/20–1486). Aristotele's first known work was the installation of a bell in Bologna in 1437. We know that he worked for Nicholas in Rome, since documents of 1451 and 1452 compensate him for transporting four columns from the ruined portico of the Baths of Agrippa (at Sta. Maria sopra Minerva) to St. Peter's. See S. Tugnoli Pattaro, "Le opere Bolognesi di Aristotele Fioravanti architetto e ingegnere del secolo quindicesimo," *Arte Lombarda* 44–45 (1976): 35–70, here 36, note; Gargano, "La Mostra," 257–58 for documents. Nicholas also hired another Bolognese architect, Nello di Bartolomeo da Bologna, who was responsible for the two chapels at the head of Ponte Sant'Angelo, superintended Paolo Romano at the Campidoglio, and worked on the Platea Pontis and the tribune of St. Peter's: Frommel, "Francesco dal Borgo," 131. The documents show, then, that Nicholas was commissioning Bolognese architects (among others) to execute projects early in his pontificate. Some of these had risen to importance by its end.

small shops . . . "stores": *Apothekai* in Greek are places where goods are stored, and Manetti seems to be making a distinction between shops where craftsmen work and shops which sell from a stock of merchandise. Problematic, however, is the Latin *tabernaculis*; both its classical and biblical meanings were clear to Manetti. It means "tents." In ecclesiastical usage, it can refer to the repository where the Eucharist is stored within a church, but Manetti's general rule is to prefer classical or biblical meanings. What Manetti has done in this case is to revive an etymological meaning of *tabernaculum* as the diminutive of *taberna* in the sense of "shop." Thus later he refers in general to the craftsmen of the Borgo as having *habitacula*, *ergastulia*, and *tabernae*, but the lowest craftsmen operate out of *apothecae* (29). The Greek term is clearer and more common because Manetti's substitution of *tabernacula* violates the ordinary meaning of the term. Moreover, the term "apotheca" was current for the shops in the atrium of St. Peter's and near it: P. Paschini, "Banchi e botteghe dinanzi alla Basilica Vaticana nei secoli XIV, XV, e XVI," *Archivi* 18 (1951): 81–23, here 106.

23. less important ones: C. Mack reviews work done on sites outside Rome in Appendix I of "Bernardo Rossellino, L. B. Alberti and the Rome of Pope Nicholas V," *Southeastern College Art Conference Review* 10 (1982): 60–69, here 64–65. See also M. Aurigemma, "Committenze non romane di Niccolò V," in *Niccolò V nel sesto centenario della nascita: Atti del convegno internazionale di studi,* ed. F. Bonatti and A. Manfredi (Vatican City, 2000), 411–39.

Gualdo: Gualdo Tadino. The Cathedral of St. Benedict was begun in 1256.

Assisi: The church of San Francesco, begun in 1228.

Civita . . . vecchia: Probably recovery of the old Roman port, which had been abandoned and which assumed renewed importance after the town became part of the Papal State in 1431.

the other Civita: Pius II recalls the episcopal palace rebuilt and fortified by Nicholas at Civita Castellana: Aeneas Silvius Piccolomini, *The Commentaries of Pius II*, trans. F. Gragg, Smith College Studies in History 22–43, here 25 (New York, 1940), 137 (book 2).

Orvieto: Pius II mentions the papal palace at Orvieto, mostly in ruins and partly restored by Nicholas, as well as a fortress begun in the corner of the city: *Commentaries*, book 4, 30:338. Although the town became definitively part of the Papal State only in 1450, a papal palace (*palazzo dei papi*) had been built in 1297 by Boniface VIII and restored by Eugenius IV in 1443; another palace in the same piazza (*palazzo papale*) also dates from the thirteenth century. The fortress in the northeastern corner of the town, originally of 1364, was restored in 1450–1457.

Spoleto: Manetti refers to the fortress of "La Rocca" outside the town built in the mid-fourteenth century and truly imposing at 80 m in height and 230 in length.

fit for kings: And in fact Frederick III stayed at Viterbo on his way to be crowned emperor (Dykmans, "Le cérémonial," 785). A second reason for Manetti's emphasis on the bath may be that Manetti wished to show that the pope cared for the sick. A less literary motive for the commission, which Tavernor points out, is that Nicholas needed these baths for his chronic gout: Tavernor, *Art of Building*, 248, n. 20 (with bibliography), 193. This bath was commissioned in 1450 and completed around 1454. Now destroyed, the bath had two floors with windows and chimneys to vent steam, towers at either end of the building, and a crenellated roof. See C. Mack, "The Bath Palace of Pope Nicholas V at Viterbo," in *Studies in Architecture Presented to Helmut Hager*, ed. H. Millon and S. Scott Munshower (College Park, 1992), 45–63; and *Il Quattrocento a Viterbo: Viterbo, Museo Civico, 11 Giugno–10 Settembre 1983* (Rome, 1983). In addition to the bath, work was done on a palace at Viterbo (1453–1454), completed by Pius II and destroyed in 1527. It was 20 m tall and fortified with corner towers: it is recorded in a drawing by Lorenzo Danti (GDSU 2003/A). See Borsi et al., *Maestri fiorentini*, 106.

25. ***Hadrian's Mass:*** This is Manetti's consistent way of referring to the Castel Sant'Angelo. In so doing, he permits himself the allusion to its antiquity by recalling the Roman emperor, and to its function as a huge mole, anchoring the structures of the Borgo.

26. ***city walls:*** See our discussions of Manetti's account of the walls of Rome in Chapter 5 and of the Vatican fortifications in Chapter 6.

stone pyramid: The pyramid of Cestius, ca. 20 B.C., abutted by the Aurelian Walls on either side and close to the Porta Ostiensis.

xenodochium: Originally a Greek word, but already in late antique Latin meaning a public building for the reception of strangers or a hospital. Manetti refers to the Hospital of Sto. Spirito in Sassia, founded as part of the *schola saxonum* around 725 and rebuilt under Sixtus IV. See Bianchi, *Il monte di Santo Spirito*, 108.

the bridge: Ponte Sant'Angelo, as in *11*.

27. ***Station churches:*** The stational system which Manetti attributes to Gregory the Great had already begun in Rome in the fifth century. It called for the pope, attended by the papal court, deacons of the seven ecclesiastical regions into which the city was divided, subdeacons, acolytes and priests from these regions, to go to urban churches on set days. The stational system printed in the Roman Missal of 1570 goes back to the *Comes* of Würzburg of about 625, which may represent the arrangements of Gregory the Great. See G. G. Willis, "Roman Stational Liturgy," in idem, *Further Essays in Early Roman Liturgy* (London, 1968), 1–85; idem, *A History of Early Roman Liturgy* (Rochester, 1994), 70. The churches are listed in J. P. Kirsch, *Die Stationskirchen des Missale Romanum* (Freiburg im Breisgau, 1926), 244 ff. See also P. Ugonio, *Historia delle stationi di Roma* (Rome, 1588); and J. F. Baldwin, *The Urban Character of Christian Worship* (Rome, 1987).

The stations were suspended during the Avignon Captivity, although from Pier Paolo Vergerio's letter of 1398 we learn that the Lenten stations were still visited by crowds of the faithful and pilgrims:

> And besides these [relics], there are the Lenten stations which the people call by their ancient name 'statae', and which no longer do the popes, as in

> the old days, but rather the people and crowds of pilgrims frequent in large throngs. (*Epistolario*, ed. L. Smith [Rome, 1934], letter 86)

Moroni believed that after the return to Rome the stations were replaced by the Cappelle Pontificie, involving similar ceremonies but taking place in the papal palace. To this end, he suggested, Nicholas V erected a public papal chapel dedicated to the Holy Sacrament near the present Cappella Paolina where he began to celebrate the Capelle Palatine, in the style of Avignon (Moroni, *Le Cappelle pontificie*, 7). For the location of Nicholas's new chapel, see Chapter 6. It seems, however, that Nicholas did continue the stations, since Stefano Infessura observed that the people in Rome were very impressed with Nicholas's processions in 1447 and 1448 on foot between the churches of Rome, carrying the host in his hands (Infessura, *Diario*, ed. Tommasini, 46–47).

Manetti's list of the seven principal basilicas does not correspond either to the stations or to the seven patriarchal basilicas, since, in defining the latter, he includes Sto. Stefano Rotondo and SS. Apostoli but omits Sta. Croce in Gerusalemme and San Sebastiano. On the other hand, another mid-Quattrocento visitor to Rome, Nikolaus Muffel, also includes Sto. Stefano and SS. Apostoli in his list of stations: *Beschreibung der Stadt Rom*, ed. W. Vogt (Stuttgart, 1876), 79–93. Participants in the 1450 Jubilee, in any case, were required to visit only four churches: St. Peter's, St. John Lateran, S. Paolo flm, and Sta. Maria Maggiore: von Pastor, *History*, 2:83.

28. curial district: Discussed in Chapter 5.

houses: Nicholas's demolition had additional purposes and political implications. A Bull of Leo IX in 1053 had conceded most of the Borgo to the canons. After it was laid waste in 1409, many of the houses in the Borgo stood ruined and empty. Since this affected the revenues of the Chapter, which owned most of them, in 1437 Eugenius IV had fostered the repopulation of the district in response to their complaint. The dilapidation was also dangerous: the rebel Stefano Porcari confessed that he had planned to hide in the uninhabited houses near St. Peter's and from there seize the church. See Martorelli, *Storia del clero*, 227; Voci, *Nord o Sud*, 26; Burroughs, "Below the Angel," 95 and n.5; von Pastor, *History*, 2:229; T. Magnuson, "The Project of Nicholas V for Rebuilding the Borgo Leonino in Rome," *Art Bulletin* 36 (1954): 89–116, here 90.

three . . . avenues: At least three streets ran east/west in the Borgo before the intervention of Sixtus IV (1475). From north to south these were the Via Maggiore, Borgo Vecchio, and Borgo Sto. Spirito. For the urban layout of the Borgo before Nicholas in general, see G. Villetti, "Architetture di Borgo nel medioevo," in *L'Architettura della Basilica*, ed. Spagnesi, 73–90. Since the material is quite complex, we will take up each street in turn, with the relevant bibliography at the end of each.

(1) The center street was the Burgo Veteris or Borgo Vecchio, a name which it acquired after Sixtus I built the Via Alessandrina, known as the Borgo Nuovo. There is disagreement about whether the Borgo Vecchio was identical with a late antique street called La Portica and perhaps also with the ancient Via Cornelia. Since no trace of an ancient road was found during excavation beneath the Vatican, and the earlier hypothesis that the Via Cornelia ran from the river beneath St. Peter's has been abandoned by most scholars, it was probably not identical with La Portica. As for the location of La Portica, Castagnoli's hypothesis — that the porticoed road never existed and that the term refers to porticoes on houses flanking the Via Maggiore — seems contradicted by Alberti's description of it (*De re aedificatoria*, 8.6, quoted below). The same eyewitness evidence refutes Reekmans' and Bianchi's suggestion that the street was flanked, rather than covered, by porticoes since Alberti describes it thus:

> In Rome there are two roads of this type [wide and paved] that I find worthy of the greatest admiration: one runs from the gate as far as the basilica of St. Paul, a distance of roughly five stades, the other from the bridge to the basilica of St. Peter; the latter is 2,500 feet in length and protected by a portico of marble columns and lead roofing. (8.6)

Grimaldi also testifies to La Portica's identity with the Borgo Vecchio, saying that it originally went from the bank of the Tiber in front of Castel Sant'Angelo, and later from S. Maria in Transpontina, to the stairs of St. Peter's following the Burgo Veteris. Not all modern scholars accept this testimony. Bianchi suggested that La Portica was not identical with the Borgo Vecchio but slightly north of it; Tafuri, that it was on the site of the future Via Alessandrina. We, however, agree with Thoenes that La Portica was probably identical with the Borgo Vecchio.

Although Reekmans thought the earliest documentation of the porticoed street was in Procopius's *Gothic Wars* 1.22.21 (mid-sixth century), an inscription in the atrium of Old St. Peter's recorded Pope Simplicius (468–483) as having covered the street leading to the basilica with porticoes to protect the faithful. La Portica may be even earlier if, as Reekmans and Grisar suggested, it dates together with the Porticus Maximae, built around 380 between the Flaminian Circus and the Pons Aelius (Ponte Sant'Angelo). In that case, it may well have been built by Gratian and been connected to the Arch of Gratian, Valentinian, and Theodosius which terminated the Porticus Maximae on the other side of Pons Aelius (Ponte Sant'Angelo). Since Alberti mentions a similarly porticoed street leading to St. Paul's, the basilica constructed around 386, these streets may have been built at the same time. In this case, the covered walkway over Ponte Sant'Angelo which Alberti reconstructs in his treatise and describes as having a roof supported by forty-two marble columns and covered in bronze (*De re aed.*, 8.6) could be considered the first tract of La Portica. The street itself would have been of the same type as the Via Flaminia, planned under Gallienus in the third century A.D. as a porticoed way from the Milvian Bridge to the Capitoline. Reekmans suggested that the medieval portico in the Borgo (which he believed flanked the street) terminated in arches at Piazza San Pietro (perhaps at the hospice of S. Maria in Caput Portici) and near Castel Sant'Angelo (perhaps at the Porta Sancti Petri).

This porticoed street was burnt during the pontificate of Paschal I (817–824) and restored by him, then restored again under Innocent II (1130–1143). It seems to have just been restored by Eugenius IV, who also gave immunity from taxes to inhabitants of the Borgo and built new houses to favor repopulation.

For Manetti's discussion of the street and confusion about whether it was to be covered or flanked by porticoes, see Chapter 5.

See E. Howe, "Alexander VI, Pinturicchio and the Fabrication of the Via Alessandrina in the Vatican Borgo," in *Studies in Architectural History*, ed. Millon and Munshower, 65–93; F. Castagnoli, *Topografia e urbanistica di Roma antica* (Turin, 1980), 241; L. Reekmans, "Le Développement topographique de la région du Vatican à la fin de l'antiquité et au début du Moyen-Age (300–850)," in *Mélanges d'archéologie et d'histoire de l'art offerts au Prof. Jacques Lavalleye* (Louvain, 1970), 197–235, here 206–7; L. Bianchi, *Case e torri medioevali a Roma. Documentazione, storia e sopravivenza di edifici medioevali nel tessuto urbano di Roma* (Rome, 1998), 1:103. All translations from Alberti's treatise are cited from *On the Art of Building*, ed. Ryckwert et al.; also Grimaldi, *Descrizione della basilica*, ed. Niggl, 361; Tafuri, "'Cives esse non licere'," 48; Thoenes, "Geschichte des Petersplatzes," 98–99; Picard, "Le quadriportique de Saint Pierre," 857; H. Grisar, *Roma alla fine del mondo antico* (Rome, 1943), 233–44, esp. 235; Richardson, *A New Topographical Dictionary*, *s.v.* "Arch of Gratian, Theodosius and Valentinian"; A. Moneti, "La grande via colonnata a Roma: Ipotesi sul progetto irrealizzato dell'imperatore Gallieno," *Palladio* 21 (1998): 5–12, here 10.

(2) The Borgo Sto. Spirito (*vicus anglorum*) was to the south, tending toward the Tiber before turning west. Portions of its original basalt pavement still exist. This is the street which Flavio Biondo describes in *Roma instaurata* (1.41) as beginning at the *Pons neronianus* (near the hospital of Sto. Spirito) and ending at the obelisk next to St. Peter's, just as Manetti also says. See *Carta archeologica di Roma* (Florence, 1962), tav. 1.

(3) About streets to the north of the Borgo Vecchio, such as the Via Maggiore, less is known. In 1445 Eugenius IV had imposed a tax "for completing the stone street from the gate of the area of Sant'Angelo to the gate of the Apostolic Palace." If "erea" should be read as "enea" this would refer to the Porta Sancti Petri, also called "aenea" because of its bronze doors (restored by Nicholas in 1454), and would identify a street veering north of the Borgo Vecchio. See Bourgin, "La 'Familia' pontificia sotto Eugenio IV," 208; C. D'Onofrio, *Castel Sant'Angelo e Borgo* (Rome, 1978), 50.

Thus it would seem that Manetti's three streets all pre-existed and at least two of them (Borgo Santo Spirito and La Portica) were late classical or early medieval. Two, La Portica and the street leading to the Vatican Palace, were either initiated or renovated by Nicholas's predecessor, Eugenius IV. The renovation of the Borgo, then, just as that at the Vatican Palace (see Chapter 6), involved little new construction.

dormitories: Around 1200 the four principal monasteries south and west of St. Peter's were abandoned for a large Canonicate with dormitories and refectory. Until the end of the fifteenth century each canon had a right to rooms in it. The new dormitories were financed with 1,774 ducats by Cosimo de'Medici in 1447 and work was overseen by Antonello di Giovanni di Albano, *camerlengo* of the Chapter of St. Peter's. The project is recorded in Stefano Infessura's diary (*Diario*, 49). Very likely the Canonicate would have been a walled compound like that recently completed in Florence: G. Smith, "Gaetano Baccani's 'Systematization' of the Piazza del Duomo in Florence," *Journal of the Society of Architectural Historians* 59 (2000): 454–77, esp. 460. However, by the end of the century most canons had gone to live in the city and the Canonicate seems to have been deserted. See L. Duchesne, "Vaticana, Notes sur la topographie de Rome au Moyen Age X, XI, XII, XIII," *Mélanges d'archéologie et d'histoire* 34 (1914): 307–56, here 323; A. M. Corbo, *I mestieri nella vita quotidiana alla corte di Nicolò V (1447–1455)* (Rome, 1998), 7.

29. dissimilar shops: The division of trades in the three streets closely parallels a 1452 statute of Siena recommending that the more noble trades (bankers, goldsmiths, and cloth merchants) be located in the more public and dignified places in the city and especially on sites frequented by foreign travelers so that they may be encouraged to buy. Butchers, tanners, and sellers of meat, leather, and hay were moved out of Siena's main square, the Campo. See F. Nevola, "'Per ornato della città': Siena's Strada Romana and Fifteenth-Century Urban Renewal," *Art Bulletin* 82 (2000): 26–50, here 31. For the actual shops in the Borgo, especially those closest to St. Peter's, see Paschini, "Banchi e botteghe"; and A. Modigliani, *Mercati, botteghe e spazi di commercio a Roma tra medioevo ed età moderna* (Rome, 1998), 276–84.

six continuous porticoes: Manetti is absolutely clear that each street is flanked by two porticoes, but he contradicts himself at 39, where he says there were only three porticoes. On this problem, see Chapter 5.

Dehio connected Nicholas's plan for porticoed streets in the Borgo with Alberti's recommendation in *De re aed.*: "Apart from being properly paved and thoroughly clean, the roads within a city should be elegantly lined with porticoes of equal lineaments [*lineamentis pariles*]" (*De re aed.*, 8.6, 262). See Dehio, "Die Bauprojekte," 241–57. But see our discussion in Chapter 5 of Manetti's term "intercolumnium" as it relates to porticoes and to Alberti's terminology.

Porticoed streets are an urban amenity praised in ancient accounts: Libanius praised Antioch for its main streets lined with porticoes; Dio Chrysostom spoke of how porticoes enhance the beauty of cities; and Strabo included porticoes in his praise of Rome (Libanius, "On Antioch," 196; Dio Chrysostom, Oration 45.13; Strabo, *Geography*, 33.23, 28). Praise of porticoed streets is also found in Latin medieval texts: for example, Bonvesin della Ripa's late thirteenth-century description of Milan claims that there were more than 60 "coperti" flanking the wider streets: *Bonvesin de la Riva. Grandezza di Milano*, ed. A. Paredi (Milan, 1967), 66 (2.2).

More relevant for Nicholas, however, were probably the modern exemplars he knew beginning with, but hardly limited to, that in the Borgo itself. Between 1407 and 1412 a long portico was built along the side of Piazza del Duomo in Bologna, a city in which both Nicholas and Alberti spent some time: F. Bocchi, *Bologna e i suoi portici: Storia dell'origine e dello sviluppo* (Bologna, 1997). Burroughs suggested this as the model for the porticoed streets of the Borgo project in Rome: Burroughs, "Alberti e Roma," 153. The Bolognese portico may, in turn, have been inspired by a Byzantine portico around St. Mark's Square in Venice. For the Bologna project and its possible connection to Venice, see R. Tuttle, "Vignola's Facciata dei Banchi in Bologna," *Journal of the Society of Architectural Historians* 52 (1993): 68–87, here 79–81.

31. huge great tower: For this passage, see our discussion in Chapter 7.

seventy cubits . . . one hundred: In saying that the diameter of the tower (70) and the width of its walls (16+16=32) made it possible to plan a height of 100, Manetti seems to refer to a rule-of-thumb proportion for the height of a tower in which height equals the diameter plus the thickness of the walls. Nicholas decided not to follow this proportional rule because it would have produced a tower taller than the platform (i.e. the grade level) of the palace. Since he considered the top of the tower as part of the platform of the palace, it was more important to produce a level site than a well-proportioned tower. In *De re aed.*, Alberti gives proportions for circular watchtowers which are entirely different (8.5). Their height should be four times the diameter, he says, or, if a very stout tower, three times the diameter.

platform: Magnuson linked the passage to mention of the collapse of "lo fondamenta de la torre nova" in a document of 4 September 1454 authorizing payment to Niccolo di Lorenzo da Fabriano for meat for the workers who dug out the bodies of men buried when the foundations of the new tower fell: *Studies*, 62–63, 127. The document is in Müntz, *Les arts*, 85.

Magnuson suggested that Beltramo da Varese had been in charge of the Great Tower and was fired when it collapsed (*Studies*, 213). However, since Müntz published a payment of 1452 to Bernardo Rossellino for a "disegno da tirare roba in su la tore" and another of the same year for work on "la tore e del muro grosso," Rossellino may have been in charge of the engineering (*Les arts*, 81). The question of authorship is reviewed in Caglioti, "Bernardo Rossellino," 29–43, here 41 n. 30. See also Borsi et al., *Maestri fiorentini*, 102.

In Magnuson's view, Manetti is telling us that only after work was begun on the great tower, probably in 1447 or 1448, did the pope realize the necessity of strong and well-prepared foundations, and that he therefore reduced the height originally planned since the foundations were too weak to support it. However, the key to interpreting the passage is the word *solum*, which does not mean foundations, for which Manetti uses *fundamenta*. Modigliani, for different reasons, also rejected Magnuson's interpretation of the passage: *Vita*, 135, n.55. *Solum* is used frequently by Manetti to mean "platform," in the sense of a properly prepared and graded building site; an upper surface; or a surface occupied by a building, i.e. in the following occurrences: *De pompis* 10, 15, 17; and in the *Life* at 34, 38, 40, 41, 44. *Spatium* is the extension, composed of places (*loci*), that "adheres to" or bounds the *solum*: or it is the plane of the *solum* (we discuss it at length in Chapter 5). Manetti really means by *solum* a leveled platform for building; the platform on which a building stands. Like Vitruvius, Alberti uses the term "area" for what Manetti means by "solum," that is, "building platform" (*De re aed.*, 1.2).

Although the foundations of the tower might in reality have caused the collapse, that is not Manetti's subject. His defense of Nicholas's plan concerns the necessity of preparing: (1) a flat surface (*plana superficie*); (2) a level or leveled platform (*solo undique adequato*); and (3) fitting the new building onto the level plane of the platform (*equabilem soli superficiem*). None of this has to do with strong foundations.

That Alberti's idea of what is important in building a tower is not related to our passage is suggested from his description of the process in *Della famiglia* where his concern is with firm foundations, not level site:

> Procederemo con quelle ragioni quali fanno gli architetti edificando la torre: prima lasciorono asodare e' fondamonti, ora soprastanno che questi fino a qui levati muri piglino, come e' dicono, dente, poi sicuro sopra edificheranno e renderannola finita, dove, se tutto in un continuato tempo e ininterrutta opera avessero proseguito, non dubito e' prima a terra muramenti fra sé poco insieme tenaci, pel soprapeso si scommetteano, e tutto el lavoro in un tratto avallava ("I libri della famiglia," in *Opere volgari*, ed. Grayson, 317).

flat surface . . . leveled on all sides: Manetti says that Nicholas found out about the importance of a level or leveled platform from the "ancient learning of the proven architects" — who were they? We discuss this in Chapter 7, but address the linguistic and technical aspects of the question here.

The obvious identification would be Vitruvius, since his was the only treatise on architecture to survive from antiquity. Nicholas (and Manetti) owned copies of Vitruvius; a third copy was owned by the Chapter of St. Peter's. But while Vitruvius discusses the importance of a solid site and a solid base for the foundations of temples, he does not say the site must be level. In Vitruvius (*Ten Books on Architecture*, trans. I. Rowland [Cambridge, 1999]), the foundations of works should be "sunk down to solid ground and in solid ground [*ab solida et in solidum*]" (3.4.1). Moreover, the term Vitruvius uses for "level site" is "area planata" (2.8), not "solum adaequatum." In a passage on floors in Faventinus's epitome of Vitruvius he writes: "considerandum erit ut solum firmum sit et aequale": H. Plommer, *Vitruvius and Later Roman Building Manuals* (Cambridge, 1973), 66. This passage in Faventinus should correspond to Vitruvius 7.1, where, however, the phrase does not appear. Although, like Manetti, Faventinus uses *solum* for what Vitruvius and Alberti call *area*, his topic is clearly how to lay a pavement, not how to lay out a platform for building. We find this Vitruvian/Albertian recommendation for level flooring together with Manetti's term "solum" in Pius II's *Commentaries*, describing the Piccolomini Palace in Pienza (ca. 1460). He writes: "the floors were of polished brick and without any unevenness whatever — everywhere the same level surface; in going from room to room and place to place you never had to step up or down" (*Commentaries*, book 9, 35:599). Since Pius uses "solum", he may be reading Faventinus instead of Vitruvius or Alberti, but this brings us no closer to Manetti's understanding of the term.

A passage where Alberti discusses how to prevent the movement of a slope from damaging a building is relevant for the sense of Manetti's comment if not for his terminology. Alberti urges the importance of making the whole "area" at the base of the slope "firmissimam" and making it level. If the building is to be placed on an inclined site it is especially important that "the base of the whole structure be the most solid and best reinforced part of the building" (1.8 [21]). Alberti praises the chapels flanking St. Peter's which sustain its level platform and buttress any earth movement (1.8). In another passage, Alberti says that the entire base of a foundation trench must be absolutely level: "ad libellam plane coaequandum est" (3.3). Alberti's requirement that a flat building platform be prepared, especially at the base of a slope or on top of a hill, corresponds to the sense of what Manetti also says. An important difference, however, is that whereas Alberti recommends flatness for solidity, Manetti adds that a level site is necessary for attractive and magnificent appearance. Although Alberti's requirement of a level site is comparable to Manetti's account of the Great Tower, differences in terminology (*area* rather than *solum*) separate these texts.

Manetti's words for "level" — *adequato* and *equabilem* — have alternate meanings of "leveled"; the Albertian comparison is relevant to only the first of these meanings. Yet Manetti seems to mean by "level" not only perfectly horizontal, but also "leveled", that is, perfectly cleared. This is a common classical usage still current in the Renaissance, for example: Livy 24.47.15, "solo aequata omnia", where a fire at Rome leveled all buildings in a certain area; or Velleius Paterculus, 2.4.2, "aequavit solo", where Scipio Africanus after besieging and destroying Numentia in Spain leveled it to the ground. For the relevance of "level" and "leveled" to Nicholas's building procedure, see Chapter 7.

to the rule: Manetti does not mean only the rod used for measuring or drawing straight lines, but also "rule" or "standard," as in Pliny ("materia ad regulam et libellam erigitur," *NH*, 36.188) or Vitruvius ("si quid parum ad regulam artis grammaticae fuerit," 1.1.18). Thus, although the term is rooted in an architectural instrument, Manetti's metaphorical use of it need not come from an architectural context. Indeed, since in order to lay out a circular building like the great tower only a stake with a line attached for the radius would have been used, "ad regulam" is a purely metaphorical expression here.

32. facade wall: Manetti uses the term *paries* here instead of his usual *murus*, and we have rendered it as "facade wall", since it describes the exterior wall of the Vatican Palace as seen from the piazza. The term may also suggest a difference in finish between this and other stretches of the defensive wall, parts of which were faced or refaced by Bramante. See Magnuson, *Studies*, 117–18. See also 61 where "there was standing in the facade wall a huge portal."

For the walls enclosing the palace, see Chapter 6 and figures 16 and 19.

33. curtis: Manetti never confuses "atrium", the formal reception area, with another sort of enclosed space for which he uses the post-classical term "curtis", meaning "unroofed court". He describes a number of them within the palace complex, and they all serve obvious utilitarian purposes: a place for guests to the palace to dismount on arrival (33), a similar space for staff and employees conveniently located near a fountain (35), a place for drains to carry run-off from the basilica (44), and so forth. For discussion of Manetti's account of the palace, see Chapter 6 and our figs. 13 and 19.

tower: This must be the Great Tower and not one of the towers that flanks the entrance to the papal palace, since Manetti is obviously describing the wall running to the top of the Vatican hill.

beautiful dwellings: The architectural complex of the Vatican Palace, described in 34–38, is analyzed in Chapter 6.

34. very lovely garden: Giovanni Rucellai praised the beauty of the papal gardens, "con una peschiera et fontana d'acqua" which he saw during his visit to Rome in 1450: *Giovanni Rucellai ed il suo Zibaldone*, ed. A. Perosa (London, 1981), 72.

upper story: The primary meaning of "coenaculum" for Manetti is "story", as also at 59. This is another case of how Manetti's architectural terminology derives from his study of the Old Testament, where we find that in Solomon's palace "per cochleam ascendebatur in medium coenaculum, et a medio in tertio" (see Chapter 6 for a discussion of "cochlea"). In classical Latin literature, "coenaculum" means the upper story of a building, a meaning retained throughout the Middle Ages. This upper floor clearly had a benediction loggia, as Magnuson and Westfall agree: Magnuson, *Studies*, 134; Westfall, *In This Most Perfect Paradise*, 151.

"Coenaculum", however, may also be a dining hall. John of Genoa's (Giovanni Balbi's) *Catholicon* derives *cenaculum* from "cena" to mean a place of eating or the upper part of it, recalling Luke 22:12 (*s.v.*). We explore this second association in Chapter 6.

flowing fountains: Most of the water sources in the Vatican were supplied by the Aqua Traiana, built in A.D. 109 and not, as used to be believed, by the Aqua Alsietina. The Aqua Paula (1607–1613), in fact, is a rebuilding of part of this source: H. Bloch, "Aqua Traiana," *American Journal of Archeology* 48 (1944): 337–41, here 337. According to the twelfth-century *Mirabilia urbis Romae* (19), the fountain in the atrium of St. Peter's and the emperor's bath south of the basilica were fed from the Forma Sabbatina (part of the Traiana). Infessura tells us that the water for the fountain in St. Peter's Square was brought from a source "a bit outside the Porta Viridaria," that is, outside the gate leading into St. Peter's Square nearest to the palace (fig. 16). We now know that the *specus* of an aqueduct was enclosed in the stretch of the Leonine Walls from the crest of the Vatican Hill to the palace: we suggest in Chapter 6 that the same source supplied the palace. This is additionally suggested by the location of the Fontana dell'Aquila near the Leonine Wall, commemorating Paul V's restoration of the Aqua Traiana. It may be supposed that the aqueduct continued to the square, especially likely if it originally supplied Hadrian's *naumachia* north/west of Castel Sant'Angelo. This is not, however, to exclude the fact that there are a number of natural springs along the crest of the hill as well which Nicholas might have exploited. The *specus* later incorporated into the Leonine Wall seems, however, to be late classical and may have been laid by Pope Symmachus (498–514) when he installed the fountains in the atrium and open area in front of the basilica. Since Manetti tells us at 43 that Nicholas had brought "living water" from the top of the hill to the pine-cone fountain in the basilica's atrium, this would seem to be part of a quite extensive campaign to restore the conduits of the aqueduct to the whole area. See Infessura, *Diario*, 255; Gibson and Ward Perkins, "The Surviving Remains of the Leonine Wall," 43; Ercadi, "La fontana del Cortile del Belvedere," 239–55.

There was a bath for the poor south of the basilica (near the emperor's bath mentioned in the *Mirabilia*), recorded in the *Liber pontificalis* (Life of Hadrian I), which might also have drawn water from the aqueduct. And this is the area where Nicholas added buildings for the distribution of food by the Apostolic Alms Office; there was a hospice for women next to it established by Eugenius IV (Duchesne, "Vaticana," 343). Likely, then, Nicholas restored water to the area south of the basilica to serve the needs of the canons, whose dormitories he rebuilt, and the poor and sick.

paradise: Nicholas brought the waters flowing from the Aqua Traiana, and these waters are "living," which in one sense means only that they are flowing, but in another recalls the Scriptural figure of "living waters" associated with paradise. But does it relate to the earthly or the heavenly paradise?

Westfall's belief in the importance of this image for the *Life* is evident in the title of his book "*In This Most Perfect Paradise*." He considered Manetti's paradise imagery in relation to chivalric culture and to Juan de Torquemada's analogy between the earthly paradise and the church (155, 159). The earthly paradise, like Nicholas's garden, had every kind of tree and was watered by a river flowing from Eden which from there divided to make four streams (Genesis 2:10). For an overview of the concept of the earthly paradise and its relation to gardens see M. Fagiolo and A. M. Giusti, *Lo specchio del Paradiso: L'immagine del giardino dall'antico al novecento* (Milan, 1996); T. Comito, "Renaissance Gardens and the Discovery of Paradise," *Journal of the History of Ideas* 32 (1971): 483-506; W. McClung, *The Architecture of Paradise: Survivals of Eden and Jerusalem* (Berkeley, 1983).

But Nicholas's garden was unlike the earthly paradise in two ways: it was walled, and it contained the *fons vitae*, both features of the Heavenly Jerusalem, or heavenly paradise. In Revelation 22:1, the angel shows John the "fluvium aquae vitae" rising from the throne of God. The passage is usually related to the vision of Ezekiel (47:1–12) where water flowing from the portal of the temple teems with fish because the water brings health; trees bear fruit of all kinds along the banks. This biblical image corresponds more closely to Manetti's description of Nicholas's garden. However, as we argue in Chapter 6, the term "paradise" refers to the entire palace complex rather than the garden alone, not only at 34 but even more clearly at 37, where the dwellings are said to be a labyrinth and a paradise. Westfall saw the *fons vitae* as a figure for charity, a virtue of Nicholas's government *(In This Most Perfect Paradise*, 160–61). While we agree that charity was central to Manetti's defense of Nicholas' papacy (see Chapter 9), we associate it with right order — its effects — rather than love, its motive. For the same reason we do not agree with Westfall's chivalric associations of love and gardens with the Vatican project. Instead, we see the Vatican Palace complex, signaling by its walls and living water the heavenly paradise, to be interpreted as the place of right order, and therefore peace.

Westfall (117) noted that Manetti does not use the term "paradisus" in his description of the atrium of St. Peter's (43), a term for the church's forecourt not only traditional (most of Du Cange's examples of the rare term in fact refer to this atrium), but current, since Maffeo Vegio used it in 1455 (*De rebus antiquis*, 2.3.72). In this case, then, Manetti rejects common usage, and since this is unusual for him it must be intentional. The atrium had a fountain, and Manetti observes that Nicholas had arranged that "there be a living source of water" there (43). Again, this could mean only that the source was flowing. But if biblical references were intended, they would be not to the topography of the Heavenly Jerusalem but, spiritually, to the "living water" of eternal life for the faithful since the atrium was a place of public gathering outside the church proper. See especially John 7:37–39, "From his breast shall flow fountains of living water"; also Isaiah 55:1–3; Revelation 21:6 and 22:17; Exodus 17:1–7; and 1 Corinthians 10:4.

Especially relevant for the atrium is Revelation 7:4–17: "For the Lamb at the center of the throne will be their shepherd, and he will guide them to springs of the water of life." First, because the fountain in St. Peter's atrium stood before its facade mosaic (originally made under Leo the Great but restored and altered by Gregory IX [1237–1241] and restored again by Nicholas), representing the Lamb. Second, Christ's commission to Peter of John 21:15–17 — "Feed my sheep" — charges the pope to act as shepherd in His stead, leading the faithful of the Church Militant toward beatification in the Church Triumphant, an image evoked in by Nicholas in his Testament (T18).

Thus Manetti's scriptural references when he speaks of living water evoke two related but distinct meanings: on the one hand the Heavenly Jerusalem, mirrored in Nicholas's palace, and on the other the promise of eternal life to the faithful who approach St. Peter's. The first comments on the qualities of Nicholas's reign — he brought order and peace — while the second suggests the benefits of this right order for the faithful, guided and led to eternal life.

35. Library: On its location, see T. Yuen, "The 'Bibliotheca Graeca': Castagno, Alberti and Ancient Sources," *Burlington Magazine* 112 (1970): 725–36; J. Bignami Odier, *La Bibliothèque Vaticane de Sixte IV à Pie XI*, Studi e Testi 272 (Vatican City, 1973), 10; Magnuson, *Studies*, 137; Westfall, *In This Most Perfect Paradise*, 139; Albareda, "Il bibliotecario," 192; F. Carboni and A. Manfredi, "Verso l'edizione del *Convivium scientiarum* di Antonio de Thomeis," in *Sisto IV. Le arti a Roma nel primo Rinascimento*, ed. F. Benzi (Rome, 2000), 60–73, here 68; Boyle, "Sixtus IV," 67–71; and G. Cornini, "'Dominico Thomasii florentino pro pictura bibliotecae quam inchoavit': Il Contributo di Domenico e Davide Ghirlandaio nella Biblioteca di Sisto IV," in *Sisto IV*, ed. Benzi, 224–48. We discuss the location in Chapter 6.

37. labyrinth: Manetti may have known the following negative allusions to labyrinths. Among classical authors, Vergil likens a mock cavalry battle to the confusing Labyrinth in Crete, "whose path runs through blind walls, where craft has hidden / a thousand wandering ways, mistake and error / threading insoluble mazes" (*Aeneid*, 5.588). Onofri also connected Manetti's simile to *Aeneid* 6: "La Vita," 68.

Ovid describes the labyrinth in the *Metamorphoses* as the place of the Minotaur, shameful fruit of adultery:

Daedalus, famously ingenious in the builder's art,

> laid out the work, scrambled the familiar and deflected
> the eyes to wander down complex and devious passages.
> As the Meander sports in Phrygian plains,
> elusively flowing back and forth in doubtful course,
> and, encountering itself, watches its waves coming,
> towards its sources, then towards the open sea,
> it drives its confused waters: so Daedalus filled
> the numberless passages with meandering, and himself
> could barely reach the exit, so deceptive was the building. (8.159–168)

There are also medieval labyrinths, both constructed — for example in the pavement of Reims Cathedral — and described, such as the verse inscription on the twelfth-century pavement at S. Savino in Piacenza which says its labyrinth is an allegory of the unredeemed world: C. Kendall, *The Allegory of the Church* (Toronto, 1998), 103. Onofri also noted that Petrarch, in *Sine nomine*, used the labyrinth as an image with which to accuse the church of Avignon of being a chaos with no way out: "La *Vita*," 681; Petrarch, *Sine nomine*, ed. U. Dotti (Rome, 1974), 580–81.

Onofri saw a connection with Hugh of St. Victor in *De arca Noe morali*, 4.9, a copy of which Manetti owned ("La *Vita*," 68–69):

> Do you think it is a labyrinth? It is not a labyrinth nor is there labor inside, but rest is inside. . . . Because He dwells there who said: "Come to me you who labor and are burdened and I shall restore you and you shall find peace for your souls" (Matthew 11:28–29). For if there is labor where He is, how do those who come to Him find rest? Now indeed His place was made in peace. Where He has broken the powers, the bow, the shield, the sword, and war (Psalm 75:4), all noise and tumult is far from that place; it is where joy and peace and rest are always present. (PL 176.679D–680A).

For Manetti, the simile seems to operate on two levels: first, as architectural criticism, where the negative example of the labyrinth illustrates the desirability of clarity, simplicity, and visual attractiveness over intricacy, illusionism, and ambiguity in buildings; second, it contrasts the moral qualities implied by these two kinds of architecture: purity and peace being associated with the Vatican complex; confusion, deception, and sin with the labyrinth as the poets imagined. Thus this image complements Manetti's evocation of the palace as a paradise.

For an overview of the labyrinth see M. C. Fanelli, *Labirinti: Storia, geografia e interpretazione di un simbolo millenario* (Rimini, 1997); and C. Wright, *The Maze and the Warrior: Symbols in Architecture, Theology and Music* (Cambridge, MA, 2001).

38. varying weather conditions: While Manetti's rooms are differentiated in terms of the amount of light or warmth owing to their location, they are not differentiated in character, all being said to have the same array of functional spaces. It seems unlikely that any inhabitant would have moved lodgings every three months as Manetti says, although it has been suggested that Nicholas spent the summer on the third floor and winter on the second floor: *Il Palazzo Apostolico Vaticano*, ed. Pietrangeli, 107. However, Nicholas's suite was on the second and third floors of a tower facing into the Cortile del Pappagallo (fig. 19), whereas Manetti is here, presumably, referring to the new north wing not surely intended as living quarters for Nicholas and in fact completed only in 1454 (see Chapter 6).

Loosely paralleling the passage in Manetti, Alberti recommends using different parts of a palace for summer and winter:

> Account should also be taken of the seasons, so that rooms intended for summer use should not be the same as those intended for use in winter, in that they should have different sizes and locations; summer rooms should be more open, nor is it amiss if winter ones are more closed in; summer ones require shade and draught, while winter ones need sunlight (*De re aed.*, 1.9 [23])

Magnuson, noting this parallel, suggested that Alberti, but not Manetti, followed Pliny (*Studies*, 155). This does not mean that Manetti, therefore, followed Alberti.

39. apostolic temple: Manetti prefers the word *templum* to describe St. Peter's; the word has a long currency in patristics to mean Christian church. He uses it to the exclusion of *ecclesia*; otherwise he may call it an *aedes* or by its formal shape a *basilica*. His single reference to a pagan temple is that of Hadrian at Cyzicus, which he calls a *delubrum*.

We consider aspects of Manetti's long account of St. Peter's (39–59) in Chapters 3, 5, 7, and especially 9. Here we take up only the architectural project itself. Some of Nicholas's earliest commissions focused on the improvement and restoration of St. Peter's (fig. 21 and especially "1" through "7" in our fig. 23). The basilica was already decrepit by the late thirteenth century, having stood by then almost one thousand years. Between 1271 and 1276 the commission examining its condition was especially concerned about its settling, due to the fact that it had been built on an artificial platform on a hill which sloped both from north to south and from west to east. The commissioners reported that, although the building could be propped up, given the fact that the nave walls inclined as much as 2 1/2 palmi (a little more than half a meter) it would be better to rebuild them from the foundations: De Blaauw, *Cultus et decor*, 633. Alberti gave a similar evaluation of the basilica's nave walls, by his time leaning more than six feet (a little less than two meters) from the vertical, and judged the structure to be on the verge of collapse (*De re aed.*, 1.10). Grimaldi, writing just as the old basilica was demolished in the early seventeenth century, believed it was unstable because its south side rested on the foundations of the circus of Gaius and Nero, itself supported on solid clay resting on unstable earth. Excavation has not supported this hypothesis. The walls, he said, leaned five palmi from the perpendicular (Grimaldi, *Descrizione*, 241–42).

In addition to its structural decrepitude, the appearance of the basilica was deplorable since in the 1430s looters had vandalized tombs and works of art as well as the pontifical throne (Reynolds, *Papal Patronage*, 26). What the condition of the interior was is reported in Raphael Brandolini's sermon addressed to Leo X. Although this account is half a century later, the intervening years were filled with improvements to the basilica so it must have been in even more deplorable a state during Nicholas's pontificate. The sermon described "the ransacked chapels, the stripped altars, the filthy statues of the apostles and martyrs, the tumbled tombs of holy popes, [and] the walls in large part shaken" (O'Malley, *Praise and Blame*, 172, n. 32). Finally, the old basilical mausoleum was poorly suited to the ceremonial functions which now took place in it (see Chapter 3). Nicholas could not avoid addressing these problems of structure, condition, and function.

Nicholas's concern over the structural condition of the Constantinian basilica is first directly stated in 1451, the date of a Bull which describes St. Peter's "with its roof falling in and so full of defects that it threatens ruin," although some work of repair is as early as 1447 (von Pastor, *History*, 2:180). From his accession in 1447 to the coronation of Frederick III in 1452, work entailed repair and improvement only. Some activity was directed to preparing St. Peter's and the Borgo for the Jubilee of 1450 and for the canonization of Bernardino of Siena in that same year. If, as some scholars have thought, proposals for structural intervention in the nave are reflected in the settings of Fra Angelico's "Ordination of St. Stephen" (fig. 7) and "Ordination of St. Lawrence" which date from these early years, as well as in Alberti's *De re aed.*, these were not implemented. See R. Krautheimer, "Fra Angelico and — perhaps — Alberti," in *Studies in Late Medieval and Renaissance Painting in Honor of Millard Meiss*, ed. I. Lavin and J. Plummer (New York, 1977), 290–96. Documents of 1447–1449 for work on St. Peter's refer to the paving of the narthex, and repairing and painting the roof in the nave. A mold for lead roof tiles with Nicholas's arms still exists although the lead roofing was completed only in 1482–1484: Frajese, "Leon Battista Alberti," 241–62, here 260. Payments for glass and marble windows in the nave of St. Peter's began in November of 1447 and continued to 1454 (Müntz, *Les arts*, 112–13, 135). De Blaauw believed that all the tracery windows in the nave, facade, and side aisles were fifteenth-century, and the eyewitness Alfarano in fact attributed the six facade windows to Michelozzo: three carried the arms of their donor, Cosimo de'Medici (*Cultus et Decor*, 637; Alfarano, *Tiberii Alpharani de Basilicae Vaticanae antiquissima et nova structura*, ed. Cerrati, 60, n.2). Other early work included restoration of the facade mosaic, repair to the roof of the atrium portico, continued work on the new sacristy off the south side aisle, and renovation of the doors and portals facing the square (1449): Müntz, *Les arts*, 120; Westfall, *In This Most Perfect Paradise*, 116. For the Sacristy, see our Commentary at 44. Fra Angelico's apse frescoes of the life of St. Peter are documented to 1446–1447 (by May of 1447 money had already been disbursed for scaffolding in the apse of St. Peter's) and seem to have been commissioned by Eugenius IV; they were completed in 1449. See Burroughs, *From Signs to Design*, 117; C. Gilbert, "Fra Angelico's Fresco Cycles in Rome: Their Number and Dates," *Zeitschrift für Kunstgeschichte* 38 (1975): 245–65, here 261; Müntz, *Les arts*, 126.

Despite this refurbishment of the apse area, in June of 1452 payments made to Beltramo da Varese and to Nello da Bologna refer to the digging of a new tribune's foundations: evidently Nicholas had determined to replace the apse: Burroughs, *From Signs to Design*, 111; Müntz, *Les arts*, 122–24. But since payments for nave windows continued from 1451 to 1454, and payments of 1451 and 1453 were for painted decorations in the nave (Müntz, *Les arts*, 130, 131, 135), it does not seem that the nave was to be replaced in the period Manetti designates, that is, 1451–1452. Nicholas had already taken away the canons' rights to the Chapel of S. M. della Febbre in the eponymous rotunda, the whole of which was completely renovated by Beltramo da Varese between 1452 and 1454 (Müntz, *Les arts*, 121). Its new appearance, known from sixteenth-century engravings by N. Bonifacio (1586) and G. Sangerman (1776), was gothic with rib vaults and stained glass windows. See E. Sladek, "I progetti per la sagrestia di San Pietro presentati da Francesco Borromini e Francesco Maria Febei ad Alessandro VII Chigi," *Annali di architettura* 7 (1995): 147–58, figs. 5 and 8. It seems likely that the new apse and transept, being built by the same person and during the same period, would have been in the same gothic idiom as S. M. della Febbre.

At the same time (1452–1453) a considerable amount of demolition took place not only behind the old apse but also along the west and north walls of the old transept ("a" through "e" on our fig. 23). Many of the oratories attached to the west transept wall were razed around 1453. In the north transept only two small chapels near the entrance to the crypt still stood: those further north — the oratory of Sta. Croce, the altar of St. John, and the Baptistery itself — were all razed (Vegio, *De rebus antiquis*, 4.116). The pavement even seems to have been taken up in the Baptistery, since Vegio saw its subterranean water conduits. Along the west wall of the south transept, the door exiting to San Martino was closed up. The oratory of San Sisto, near the stairs to the crypt, was intact (it is not clear that it was attached to the west wall) as was the oratory of San Leo. The oratory of St. Hadrian had been remodeled. And in the south/west corner, the oratory of St. Mary still stood although two papal tombs nearby were destroyed (*De rebus antiquis*, 4.125). Demolition was far advanced, therefore, in the north/west portion of the old church and behind the apse whereas parts of the south transept were being remodeled instead of torn down. The project, then, involved the renovation of the transept as well as a new apse.

Such demolition was completely inappropriate if the new transept wall was to be some meters west of the old one, as shown on Uffizi 20A (fig. 9), since the old wall could have been left standing during construction, but necessary if the new apse or apses were to open out from the old west wall. And in fact, Martino Ferrabosco's plan of the project (fig. 12) shows two deep chapels flanking the main apse, absent in Uffizi 20A. These are labelled "Sacrarium," a term which may mean oratory or chapel as well as sacristy: indeed, altars are shown in them. Yet, although Ferrabosco's plan is thought to be a visualization of Manetti's verbal account in the *Life*, Manetti describes a single, not a triple, apsed east end. Either the two flanking apses are an invention by Ferrabosco, or they depend on a source other than Manetti. The latter seems likely since the flanking apses account for demolition which we know to have taken place. Another problem raised by the west transept wall is its relation to a planned dome. Since the transepts of Old St. Peter's were 1/3 less wide than the nave, a square crossing for a dome could be obtained only by moving the transept wall west. Yet unlike Uffizi 20A, Ferrabosco's plan shows no change in the transept walls, suggesting that the diameter of the dome would have been less than the width of the nave, perhaps aligned with the triumphal arch. Whatever its precise configuration, Nicholas's first plan for St. Peter's was for the replacement of the east end only, a kind of modernization undertaken in many central Italian churches in the first half of the Quattrocento, as in the contemporaneous, or slightly earlier, work on old Florentine churches such as Sta. Trinità, San Lorenzo, and SS. Annunziata.

If there was ever a project to replace the whole building, it must date to after 1453, the date of Flavio Biondo's dedicatory preface to *Italia Illustrata* in which he wrote approvingly of Nicholas's restoration and decoration of the basilica of St. Peter and of the new apse begun above the main altar: "Tu denique beati Petri, cuius a Deo commissas vices in orbe geris, altare suis sacratissimum ossibus abside pergis tanto numini sua celsitudine responsura decorare" (*Scritti inediti*, ed. Nogara, 219–20). A project to rebuild the nave would probably date to after the last payment for windows in the nave of 1454, and therefore in the last year of the pontificate.

Manetti twice says (25 and 27) that Nicholas intended to rebuild St. Peter's completely, from the foundations to the roof. His claim is substantiated in the "Life of Nicholas" from the *Liber pontificalis* which, attributed to Poggio Bracciolini, must date before his death in 1459: C. da Capodimonte, "Poggio Bracciolini autore delle anonime 'vitae quorundam pontificum'," *Rivista di storia della Chiesa* 14 (1960): 27–47, here 36; the Life is in *Le Liber pontificalis*, ed. Duchesne, 2:557–58. Poggio begins the section on building by saying: "He exceeded the mean in building, in the judgment of many" and continues:

> He [Nicholas] began to build from the foundations a *testudinem*, which they call *tribunam*, above the altar of St. Peter: a magnificent work, having walls eight cubits wide, but the work was interrupted by death. He had set his mind on rebuilding the basilica in addition to [or "above"] this *testudinem* in the form of the Baths of Diocletian, having destroyed the earlier stucture.
>
> (Testudinem quoque quam tribunam appellant super altare sancti Petri operis magnificentissimi a fundamentis aedificare aggressus est, muro octo cubitis lato; sed morte intermissa est aedificatio. Basilicam insuper ipsam testudinem in formam thermarum Diocletianorum reducere, destructa priori structura, destinarat animo.)

Manetti's and Poggio's accounts concur that there was a plan to take down St. Peter's *in Nicholas's mind* by 1455, a plan which was prevented by Nicholas's death. While Poggio may have known Manetti's *Life*, he includes information about the St. Peter's design which is not in it, specifically that the nave was to be in the form of the Baths of Diocletian. His testimony, then, depends on a source or sources independent of our text. While Manetti describes the transept in detail (45), his description of the nave is more problematic. Since he tells us that there were to be six rows of columns in the nave (rather than the four which the old basilica had), he evidently includes a new row lining the external walls, perhaps to support vaults: he does not mean that the nave was to have three, rather than two, aisles on each side of the nave since he says the total number of naves was five (44). He does not mention how the nave was to be covered (44). His measurement for the width of the nave, 120 cubits, is nearly four meters wider than the nave of Old St. Peter's if his cubit equals 58 cm, which would mean that the old perimeter wall was to be torn down. Moreover, Manetti says that there were to be round windows in the nave, not possible unless the nave wall clerestory was to be replaced, since it was already pierced with large tracery windows.

The value of Manetti's cubit in the description of St. Peter's is hotly debated in the recent literature. Most scholars believe that Manetti used the Roman or Florentine braccio, between 56 and 58 cm, although Curti argues that Manetti uses the Vitruvian cubit of 47.5 cm ("L''Admirabile Templum'," 111–18). Frommel summarizes the recent arguments in "Il San Pietro di Nicolò V." Frommel's and Curti's reconstructions of Nicholas's St. Peter's are our figs. 10 and 11, and we discuss the problem in Chapter 5.

Poggio tells us that the new nave — not the new apse — was to be in the form of the Baths of Diocletian. What this meant in fifteenth-century Rome, Urban argued (although not in relation to Poggio's text), was groin vaults supported on columns or columns attached to piers, as at S. Onofrio, Sta. Maria sopra Minerva, and Sta. Maria del Popolo: G. Urban, "Zum Neu-bau Projekt von

St. Peter unter Nikolaus V.," in *Festschrift für Harald Keller* (Darmstadt, 1963), 131–73. The same design may be reflected in Alberti's central vault for San Sebastiano in Mantua (begun in 1459), where a groin vault on columns seems to have been planned. If Poggio means that the nave of St. Peter's was to have been renovated or rebuilt with groin vaults on columns, this corresponds to what Manetti says was the design of the transepts at 45. Taking Manetti's description of the transepts together with Poggio's comment about the nave, the two accounts would seem to be complementary: one identifies the classical model, and the other describes the form. Observation of contemporary Roman practice suggests that both texts refer to the same architectural design. Since this design was classicizing rather than gothic, and it involved the entire basilica rather than the apse and transepts only, it was not merely an expansion of the first project but an entirely new design.

open area: Described again at 49. The correct dimension is 500 × 100, not 200 × 100 as Muratori read. Manetti's disparate accounts of Piazza San Pietro (or the "cortina S. Petri") at 49 and 39–40 have received much attention. For the square itself, see H. Millon, "An Early Seventeenth-Century Drawing of Piazza San Pietro," *Art Quarterly* 25 (1962): 229–41. For the fifteenth-century character of this space and the problems of Manetti's measurement, see Magnuson, *Studies*, 73; Westfall, *In This Most Perfect Paradise*, 112 n. 31, 113; and Thoenes, "Studien," 102.

Manetti gives the length first in an unspecified unit of measurement (although arguably in cubits) and then in paces (*passi*). Since the *passus* equals five Roman feet, about 1.5 m, this would mean that the distance from the steps of St. Peter's to the porticoes of the Borgo would be 750 m or over 2,300 feet. By contrast, if the measurement is calculated in cubits, whether ancient, contemporary Roman, or Florentine, the distance would be about a third of that. No passage better illustrates the problems posed by Manetti's inconsistent use of units of measurement than this.

cubits: Despite the awkwardness of this phrase, we have kept the word cubits where it occurs in the text; it would naturally mean that cubits are the measure throughout, but because of the contradiction with paces (*passus*) in the next line, and the scholarly vexation over the size of this space, we followed the line literally.

steps: Alfarano tells us that the thirty-five steps (arranged in five flights of seven each) leading up to St. Peter's were "of marble, in which very ancient mosaic work was visible" (*De Basilicae Vaticanae structura*, 22, 278). Taken together with Manetti's description it would seem that the steps had inlaid porphyry, serpentine, and marble patterns, perhaps therefore cosmatesque and of the twelfth or thirteenth century. These stairs, originally built by Pope Symmachus, were restored and enlarged by Pius II in 1462 with marble from the Colosseum: R. Rubinstein, "Pius II and the Roman Ruins," *Renaissance Studies* 2 (1988): 197–203,

here 199. Manetti is essentially describing what already existed to which Nicholas may have intended a repair or addition, in fact carried out by his successors.
40. obelisk: The obelisk stood on the spine of Nero's circus, then next to the rotonda of Sant'Andrea (Sta. Maria delle Febbre), until in 1586 Sixtus V had Domenico Fontana move it to its present position in the center of St. Peter's Square. See C. D'Onofrio, *Gli Obelischi di Roma* (Rome, 1992), 130–59, with views of it in its original location.

The obelisk and Nicholas's project to move it are recorded in Pier Candido Decembrio's *On Literary Refinement*, begun in the 1440s and dedicated to Pius II in 1462. The most relevant passage is: "Our architects have established the precise nature of the effort or expense needed to raise it. Indeed, some can be found who promise to use devices to move the stone, still standing, either into the entrance of the church of St. Peter or elsewhere in the city" (MS. Vat. Lat. 1794, fol. 55v). Curran and Grafton associated the project with Aristotele Fioravanti, perhaps in 1451–1452 when other work was in progress south of St. Peter's at Sta. Maria delle Febbre and the new Canonicate, and Decembrio's account as part of a site report by Alberti. This last suggestion would be especially interesting support for our hypothesis, in Chapter 7, that some of the earliest parts of Alberti's treatise on architecture also began as site reports for Nicholas in those same years. The word "propyleam" ("entrance" or "gateway") raises the possibility that the obelisk was to be moved into the atrium of the church rather than to the square before it as Manetti says. See B. Curran and A. Grafton, "A Fifteenth-Century Site Report on the Vatican Obelisk," *Journal of the Warburg and Courtauld Institutes* 58 (1995): 234–48.

pure and molten bronze: Rome's first fifteenth-century bronze foundry was established by Filarete ca. 1433 in order to cast the bronze tomb of Martin V begun by Donatello and Michelozzo. He then used this foundry for his own bronze doors for St. Peter's, 1433–1445. See H. Wohl, "Papal Patronage and the Language of Art: The Pontificates of Martin V, Eugene IV and Nicholas V," in *Umanesimo a Roma nel Quattrocento*, ed. P. Brezzi and M. de Panizza Lorch (New York, 1984), 235–46, here 244.
41. platform: For problems arising from Manetti's measurements of this see Thoenes, "Studien," 102.

tower: St. Peter's had only one bell tower at this time, the one erected by Stephen II (752–757) and restored by Leo III (795–816): Reekmans, "Développement," 218.
42. five exquisite doors: The three center doors had been renovated by Nicholas in 1449 with marble surrounds and columns, as shown in a drawing in Grimaldi, *Descrizione*, 195, 278. The four columns of "Egyptian stone" are now part of the Aqua Paula on the Janiculum.

43. similar one: This second vestibule was part of the east portico of the atrium, but divided off by piers. In it was a chapel, Sta. Maria in Turribus (destroyed in 1610).

court: On the atrium of Old St. Peter's, see Egger, "Quadriporticus S. Petri," 101–3; and Picard, "Le Quadriportique," 851–90. In fact, there was no portico on the north side, the wing housing the *auditorium rota*, or on the south.

living water: See 34.

pine cone: The pine-cone fountain was built by Pope Symmachus (498–514) with spoils from classical monuments in the area. The pine cone itself and a bronze peacock are preserved in the Vatican Museums. Symmachus also created the fountain in the center of the piazza in front of the basilica, rebuilt by Innocent VIII (Grisar, *Roma*, 240).

44. all the rain water: Excavation has revealed a ditch 3 meters wide north of the basilica for drainage of water that flowed down the Vatican hill toward the basilica: De Blaauw, *Cultus et decor*, 643; Apollonij-Ghetti et al., *Esplorazioni*, 159. Voci opines that it was excavation in the Vatican Hill to create the original platform for St. Peter's that left a humid depression between the platform and the Mons Saccorum: *Nord o Sud*, 39.

rooms: These rooms for the regular clergy seem not to be identical with the dormitory for the canons mentioned at 28 and which Manetti says was adjacent to them.

sacristy: Although virtually all scholars have assumed the new sacristy Manetti mentions to be the rotonda of Sant'Andrea which Nicholas renovated, this is probably yet another instance in which Manetti gives credit to Nicholas for work begun by his predecessor Eugenius. The new sacristy, in other words, is the one begun in 1444 and still under construction when Manetti wrote. For the traditional view, with bibliography, see Frommel, "Il San Pietro," 105.

St. Peter's had three sacristies (not including the small room south of the apse which occasionally served this function), of which the earliest, in the south end of the narthex, in use until the ninth century, seems to have been rebuilt in the late fifteenth or early sixteenth century, perhaps as a chapel ("DD" on Alfarano's plan, "A" on our fig. 23). A second sacristy, the *sacristia maior*, was off the south aisle of the nave near the chapel of Gregory the Great ("*" on Alfarano's plan at the third column, "B" on our fig. 23). Yet another sacristy was begun in 1444, perhaps on the site of the slightly earlier *sacristia minor*, and completed in 1464. Located at the nineteenth column from the facade off the south aisle ("V" on Alfarano's plan, "2" on our fig. 23), this must be the one Manetti means. It had an upper floor with rooms for clerics and sacristans which Flavio Biondo said were added (like the sacristy itself) by Eugenius IV: "And he improved it by building new rooms in the sacristy" (*Roma instaurata*, 1.57; and Alfarano, *De*

Basilicae Vaticanae structura, 74; mentioned also in a document of 1454–1455 in Müntz and Frothingham, "Il tesoro," 87). It was here in the *sagrestia nuova* or *minor* that the books left to St. Peter's by Giordano Orsini (d. 1438) must have been inventoried in 1454. See Lombardi and Onofri, "La biblioteca di Giordano Orsini," 371–82, here 373; and C. Celenza, "The Will of Cardinal Giordano Orsini," 257–86. Vegio mentions this sacristy at *De rebus antiquis*, 4.131. The sacristy gave access to an oratory restored or founded by Cardinal Antonio de la Cerda, one of the addressees of Manetti's *Life*, who was buried in it at his death in 1459. And in the oratory were stalls in which the canons, beneficiati, and clerics said Matins in the winter. Proximity of the new sacristy to the canons' choir in the southwest part of the main nave, the presence of books left to the basilica in it, and use of the adjoining oratory for the Divine Office suggests that this new sacristy was primarily for the canons' use. However, Vegio designates the sacristy off the south aisle to the east, the *sacristia maior*, as the "secretarium Sancti Petri" (*De rebus antiquis*, 4.142), that is, the main one. On the sacristies, see De Blaauw, *Cultus et decor*, 469, 529, 646, 709.

45. dome: The Latin vocabulary of these elements is not as specific as the term "dome" might suggest. "Testudo"("shell") could refer to any covering. As was the case in his description of Florence Cathedral, Manetti sees this as an interior feature related to the other structural elements on the inside of the basilica, rather than something which defines the building's exterior view.

47. round windows: Since Nicholas V installed gothic windows with tracery in the nave, both types of window would have illuminated St. Peter's if the nave were not replaced. Fra Angelico's fresco of the "Ordination of Saint Stephen" (fig. 7), the architectural setting of which has been thought to depict St. Peter's, also combines both kinds of windows. On the frescoes see Venchi et al., *Fra Angelico and the Chapel of Nicholas V*, 75–80. For further discussion of round windows, see Chapter 7 and Commentary on *De pompis* at 11.

48. polluted by burials: Magnuson thought that the prohibition of burials in St. Peter's was one concrete example of Albertian influence in the Life (*Studies*, 206). The corresponding passage in Alberti is:

> I would not presume to criticize our own custom of having sacred burial grounds within the city, provided the corpses are not brought into the temple, where the elders and magistrates meet to pray in front of the altar, as occasionally this may cause pestilential vapors of decay to defile the purity of the sacrifice. (*De re aed.*, 8.1 [245])

Undoubtedly this view is in contrast with that of Maffeo Vegio, for whom the long roster of papal tombs in St. Peter's was visible proof of the apostolic succession and testimony to the antiquity and sanctity of the basilica (*De rebus antiquis*, passim).

Nicholas's view is no novelty, having been already expressed by Isidore of Seville in the early seventh century. Nicholas owned a copy of Isidore's *Etymologies* (Müntz and Fabre, *La bibliothèque*, 109; Manfredi, *Codici*, no. 757, now MS. Vat. lat. 623). The problem of who, if anyone, should be buried in a Renaissance church has not been much studied by art historians (unlike the attention given to Early Christian practice), although it was clearly a matter of ongoing concern. The relevant legislation has been studied by A. Bernard, *Sépulture en droit canonique* (Paris, 1933). Sicardus of Cremona sums up the canons thus:

> No one ought to be buried inside churches except a person of high position in consideration of merit or of sacramental state; more will be said of this below in the treatise on the dead. (*Mitrale* 4, PL 213.24)

Durandus is more explicit:

> No body should be buried in the church or near the altar where the body and blood of the Lord is made, except for the bodies of the holy fathers who are called 'patrons', that is 'defenders' who by their merits defend the entire country, and bishops and abbots and high-ranking priests and laymen of the highest sanctity. (*Rationale* 1.5.12, ed. Davril and Thibodeau [CCCM 140], 61)

Everyone else is to be buried "circa ecclesiam" in the atrium, portico, and so on, or in a cemetery.

Recent research into policy on burial in Florence Cathedral in the later fourteenth and early fifteenth centuries reveals tension on this issue. For instance, in 1400 the Consuls of the Arte della Lana decreed that there would be no burials in the cathedral and that all bodies already buried there were to be exhumed, except for those of canons and chaplains (Poggi, *Il Duomo*, doc. 2084). But already in 1402 Andrea de'Medici was allowed to be buried (doc. 2085), and in 1409, Francesco de'Bicci de'Medici was interred (doc. 2085). Brunelleschi was also buried in the cathedral in 1446.

Manetti's statement seems to be flatly contradicted by Nicholas's actual practice, since the pope had the tomb of Innocent VII renewed and moved to the Chapel of St. Thomas ("C/7" on our fig. 23), and was himself buried in the south side aisle of St. Peter's near the tomb of Eugenius IV (# 59 on Alfarano) (Borgolte, *Nachfolge*, 272). Eugenius's body had been buried under the floor of St. Peter's in the central nave, but Cardinal Francesco Condulmer (d. 1453) commissioned Isaia di Pisa to make a monument for him which was placed in a chapel in the south side aisle (Borgolte, *Nachfolge*, 269). Although Westfall had argued that Nicholas intended S. Andrea (S. Maria della Febbre) for papal burials, Borgolte has shown that there is really no evidence for this (Westfall, *In This Most Perfect Paradise*, 119; Borgolte, *Nachfolge*, 272).

That many did not agree with the prohibition against tombs is suggested not only by Vegio's positive treatment of the tombs in St. Peter's and by the fact of Nicholas's burial in the basilica, but also by the number of other burials there during Nicholas's pontificate, some of which can be deduced from J. B. Toth's catalogue of the Grotte vaticane (*Grotte vaticane* [Milan, 1955], 42, 52). Other burials during the pontificate are mentioned in the south side aisle by Alfarano, *De Basilicae Vaticanae structura*, 80.

Many of these burials were in the Chapel of St. Thomas, off the south aisle at the sixth column from the facade ("C/7" on our fig. 23), and therefore, strictly speaking, outside the basilica. Alfarano describes the chapel as "built next to and outside the basilica's walls" (*De Basilicae Vaticanae structura*, 82). Thus the tombs created there by Nicholas were in fact outside the basilica, as Manetti says he wished. At least by 1407 the chapel served as the baptistery, and Vegio relates that the sarcophagus of Probus was reused as the font here after his mausoleum behind the apse was torn down, that is, by Nicholas's order in 1453 (*De rebus antiquis,* 4.108). Burials in this chapel are given in Toth, *Grotte*, 90; and O. Panvinio, *De rebus antiquis memoratu dignis basilicae S. Petri in Vaticano*, in *Spicilegium romanum*, ed. A. Mai, 10 vols. (Rome, 1839), 9:289.

The south side aisles of the basilica were especially favored for burials, with some forty-four papal tombs (Alfarano, *De Basilicae Vaticanae structura*, 76–77; Vegio, *De rebus antiquis*, 4.136). Indeed, the south aisle was called the "pontificum porticus" on this account. It corresponded to the southernmost portal on the facade, called the "Porta del Giudizio" because only the dead to be buried were carried through it and on the interior facade wall next to this portal was an altar at which the memorial of all the dead was celebrated annually (Vegio, *De rebus antiquis,* 2.3.60, 69). Manetti is very clear that Nicholas intended a cemetery to be built outside the basilica directly south of the papal throne. The St. Thomas Chapel is in alignment with a papal throne, as Manetti says, but not the one in the apse. Since 1404 there was an altar of the Sacrament at the altar of SS. Simon and Jude in the central nave ("D" on our fig. 23): this is where Fra Angelico depicted Nicholas in the "Ordination of St. Lawrence." Various liturgical ceremonies took place there and it was second in importance only to the high altar of the basilica. Since Nicholas favored the Chapel of St. Thomas, the place where he had placed the tombs of Innocent VII and Giovanni Podio, for burials, and since this was technically outside the basilica and in line with a papal throne, it may be that Manetti describes actual practice rather than future plans.

The issue of burials in churches remained alive in Nicholas's circle: Pius II forbade burials in the new Cathedral of Pienza (1462).

50. cochlea: See discussion in Chapter 6.

51. human body: See Chapter 9.

52. microcosm: See Chapter 9.

linear figures: That is to say, in two, but not three dimensions. Manetti is here thinking of the figures of plane geometry; the building compares with the proportions of the human body in length and width, but not depth.

Noah's Ark: See Chapter 9.

53. ***the Athenians:*** See our Commentary on the *De pompis* at 12.

54. ***Bernardo of Florence:*** Bernardo Gamberelli, called Il Rossellino, 1409–1464. Rossellino is documented in papal payments (from December of 1451 to December 1453), none of which suggests that he was in charge of all the works: Mack, "Bernardo Rossellino," 61; Magnuson, *Studies*, 213; Borsi et al., *Maestri fiorentini*, 100–7. Yet, since Caglioti has shown that Rossellino was still in Rome in the spring of 1455 when Nicholas died, he may have carried out other, undocumented, commissions for the pope. See F. Caglioti, "Bernardo Rossellino a Roma. I. Stralci del carteggio mediceo (con qualche briciola sul Filarete)," *Prospettiva* 64 (1991): 49–59, here 49. The letter Caglioti cites from Giovanni di Cosimo de'Medici to Francesco Sforza (1456) recommending Rossellino as the one who "condusse et ordinò tutte quelle grandi muraglie" that Nicholas made in Rome may, after all, be accurate.

Perhaps Rossellino succeeded Nello da Bologna in 1454 as the man who knew the whole scope of Nicholas's plan and how the various small interventions were to be coordinated. Burroughs described Nello's role at the court as a kind of "minister of the interior," charged with directing the Vatican staff ("Alberti a Roma," 142). His importance is clear from what Pietro da Noceto wrote about him in 1453:

> we had entrusted to you the construction and repair of some churches and other places and various buildings inside the City and outside, as well as the principal management of our affairs and business dealings, together with the care of our family estate and palace (in Tafuri, *Ricerca*, 40).

Burroughs thought that, having worked as assistant to Nello da Bologna, Francesco dal Borgo assumed many of Nello's responsibilities when Nello died in 1454. Born in 1425, as early as 1450 Franceso was working for Nicholas, levying tolls at the harbor. By 1451 he was also receiving payments for architectural work at the Capitoline, Sta. Maria Maggiore, and the Vatican: Frommel, "Francesco dal Borgo," 131; Burroughs, *From Signs to Design*, 113. If, instead, Rossellino succeeded Nello as a superintendent of works he would have only held that office for a few months before Nicholas's death, but Manetti's statement would be accurate since Manetti projects over the whole pontificate the status of the plan in 1455.

55. ***The Seven Wonders:*** see Chapter 9.

57. ***Apollo's oracle:*** The prophecies given at Delphi by the Pythian Apollo, well known in Greek literature, particularly in Herodotus which Nicholas had commissioned Lorenzo Valla to translate. Valla did not finish the translation until after Nicholas's death (Vespasiano, *Vite*, 2:66, n. 3). Manetti would have been aware of Cicero's description of the oracle in *On Divination* 1.37–38, since he drew heavily on that work in his discussion of prophetic dreams in Book 1 of the *Life*. But his immediate source is Plato's *Apology*, 21a, which had been translated by Bruni before 1421 (Voigt, *Risorgimento*, 2:162).

Solomon: See Chapter 9.

60. ***palace:*** In 3 Kings this is still of the temple, not the palace.

oblique windows . . . orbicular ones: See Chapters 2 and 7. Rhabanus Maurus defines "oblique windows" in his *Commentaria in Libros IV Regum*, 3.6, PL 109.143, as "intus fuisse latiores perhibentur." Nicholas of Lyra explains that they are called "oblique" because, being wider on the interior and narrower on the exterior (i.e. splayed), light does not enter at a right angle but obliquely, diffusely, and at an obtuse angle (*Biblia Latina cum postilla* [Venice, 1489], comment on 3 Kings).

many vaults: The transept and crossing of St. Peter's.

61. ***three marvelous rows:*** See Chapter 5.

62. ***new religion . . . old divine law:*** See Chapter 9.

64. ***Frederick:*** Frederick III of Hapsburg, 1440–1493, succeeded Albert II (d. 1439); married Leonora of Portugal.

carefully and scrupulously considering: Nicholas postponed the coronation until after the schism had been resolved. Aeneas Silvius Piccolomini notes Nicholas's reluctance to have Frederick visit Rome since some emperors had used the occasion of coronation to besiege the Leonine City (*Historia Friderici*, 69).

not observed: Actually, Eugenius IV had crowned Sigismund I emperor in Rome on 31 May 1433.

66. ***briefly relate:*** We analyze Manetti's account of the coronation in Chapter 3.

68. ***prayer:*** For the reliability of Manetti's account of the prayers, see Chapter 3.

69. ***Alfonso I of Aragon:*** 1396–1458, King of Sicily, Sardinia, and Naples. The patron of Manetti's *De dignitate et excellentia hominis*. Manetti went to his court after Nicholas's death.

70. ***Francesco Sforza:*** 1401–1466. Became Duke of Milan on 22 March 1450, ending the short-lived Ambrosian Republic established after the death of Filippo Maria Visconti in 1447.

Ferdinand, Duke of Calabria: 1431–1494. Ferrante, Alfonso's natural son, who was made Duke of Calabria in 1443 and became King of Naples in 1458.

71. ***Filippo Maria:*** Filippo Maria Visconti, 1392–1447, Duke of Milan, the last Visconti lord. The succession was bitterly disputed by Alfonso, who claimed it had been left to him in a will, and Francesco, who had married Filippo Maria's daughter and heir Bianca Maria. During the struggle, in which the Florentines, Venetians, and Sienese took sides, the Milanese declared a republic. Francesco

Sforza ended this by a siege and, having assumed power, ended Alfonso's pretensions in northern Italy.
73. ***Stefano Porcari:*** Nicholas, realizing Porcari's republican sentiments, had exiled him to Bologna in 1452 but he escaped to Rome. Before he could act on his plan to seize St. Peter's and the Borgo, he was caught, tortured, and hanged (9 January 1453). On Manetti's account of the Porcari conspiracy, see Chapter 3.
74. ***Simonetti:*** Francesco, called Cicco, 1410–1480, governor of Lodi (1449) and lord of Sartirana, secretary of Francesco Sforza.

alliance: Venice, Milan, and Florence joined in league in August of 1454. Alfonso refused to sign this peace.
75. ***great afflictions:*** Nicholas suffered from gout. He had a severe attack after the Porcari conspiracy, and from late August of 1453 to June of 1454 he was mostly confined to bed. In August of 1454, after another attack, he sought relief at the baths at Viterbo, but in November of 1454 he began to decline from this and other diseases: by the beginning of March 1455, he was very ill (von Pastor, *History*, 2:307).
76. ***a Cardinal:*** This was Cardinal Domenico Capranica (1400–1458), sent on 26 January 1455.
77. ***peace and agreement:*** Alfonso joined the League on 30 December 1454; Nicholas ratified the Italian League on 25 February 1455.

Appendix

FROM

Iannozzi Manetti
Liber Tertius De Testamento Nicolai Quinti

Giannozzo Manetti:
Life of Pope Nicholas V

Book Three: The Testament of Nicholas V

Appendix

FROM

Iannozzi Manetti
Liber Tertius De Testamento Nicolai Quinti

In the third book of the *Life of Nicholas V*, Manetti gives, in the pontiff's own words, a justification for the building program detailed in Book 2. We include a text and translation of that passage here, without commentary.

T1 (949) Nunc ad diluenda edificationum nostrarum obiecta veniamus.[1] In hac parte quamquam omnes cardinales ad audiendum tota mente totisque, ut dicitur, vultibus intentos paratosque videret ut tamen eos ad hauriendum[2] quicquid enarrabatur attentiores redderet: Audite,[3] audite, inquam, venerabiles fratres, rationes causasque considerate quibus adducti ad edificandum construendumque tantopere conversi fuisse videamur. Duas principales edificationum nostrarum causas exstitisse venerationes vestras scire atque intelligere volumus.

T2 Romane nanque ecclesie auctoritatem maximam ac summam esse hi[4] soli intelligunt qui originem et incrementa sua ex litterarum cognitione perceperunt. Ceterorum vero cunctorum populorum turbe litterarum ignare penitusque[5] expertes,[6] quamvis a doctis et eruditis viris qualia et quanta illa sint crebro audire eisque tanquam veris et certis assentiri videantur, nisi tamen egregiis quibusdam visis moveantur, profecto omnis illa eorum assensio debilibus et imbecillis fundamentis innixa, diuturnitate temporis ita paulatim elabitur ut plerumque ad nihilum recidat.

---

[1] venimus *Muratori*
[2] auriendum *D*
[3] ait *ins. Muratori*
[4] ii D *Muratori*
[5] penitus *Muratori*
[6] expartes *C¹*

Appendix

FROM

Giannozzo Manetti: Life of Pope Nicholas V

Book Three: The Testament of Nicholas V

T1 (949) "Now let us come to dissolving the objections to our building projects." At this part [of his speech], although he saw all the Cardinals were intent and ready to listen with full concentration and, as is said, with their whole expressions, still, in order to make them more attentive to draw in what he was about to tell them, he said: "Listen, I say, listen, Venerable Brothers, to the reasons and ponder the causes for which we seem to have been attracted to building and so greatly moved to construction. I wish Your Venerabilities to know and understand that there existed two principal causes of our building projects.

T2 "The only people who understand that the authority of the Roman church is greatest and supreme are the ones who have learned its origin and its growth from their knowledge of reading. In reality, the masses of all the others, ignorant of and thoroughly lacking reading ability, might seem to hear often from educated and learned men the nature and extent of those matters and to assent to their truth and certitude; but still, unless they are moved by something extraordinary that they see, all that assent of theirs rests on weak and feeble foundations and will slip bit by bit in the course of time until it lapses to virtually nothing.

T3 At vero cum illa vulgaris opinio doctorum hominum relationibus fundata magnis edificiis perpetuis quodammodo monumentis ac testimoniis pene sempiternis, quasi a Deo fabricatis, in dies (950) usque adeo corroboratur et confirmatur ut in vivos posterosque illarum admirabilium constructionum conspectores continue traducatur; ac per hunc modum conservatur et augetur atque, sic conservata et aucta, admirabili quadam devotione conditur et capitur.

T4 Ad hanc christianorum populorum erga romanam ecclesiam ac sedem apostolicam devotionem tute quedam habitatoribus ipsis ac terribiles inimicis oppidorum urbiumque munitiones accedunt que nimirum per has magnorum edificiorum constructiones adversus externos[7] hostes ac domesticos novarum rerum cupidos quotidie diripiendi gratia conspirantes et in grave ecclesiasticarum gubernationum damnum insurgentes munitiores redduntur. Quocirca nos et Gualdi — ut a minimis incipiamus — et Fabriani et Assisii[8] et in utraque Civitate et[9] Vetusta et Castellana et Narnia et in Urbe Veteri et Spoleti et Viterbii et multis aliis ecclesie nostre locis plura peregregia ad certum quendam et expressum utriusque devotionis munitionisque effectum edificia condidimus.

T5 Atque eisdem causis abundantius vehementiusque adducti, multa et quidem singularia hic in urbe opera perfecimus; ac plura et longe maiora non immerito incoavimus. Quanto enim hec alma urbs ceteris omnibus maior et dignior habetur, quantoque ampliori cunctorum christianorum populorum devotione[10] magis celebratur et colitur, tanto profecto eam[11] aliis omnibus ornatiorem atque munitiorem fore oportere censebamus; presertim cum perpetuam summorum pontificum sedem atque eternum pontificie sanctitatis habitaculum ab omnipotenti Deo constitutum fuisse non ignoraremus.

T6 Proinde et urbis menia, pluribus hinc inde locis collapsa et confragosa,[12] reparavimus multisque turribus circumquaque munivimus ac nova insuper cum crebris propugnaculis absolvimus. Quadraginta preterea sanctarum stationum[13] basilicas a Gregorio magno predecessore nostro ab orgine institutas pene ad ultimam absolutionem reformavimus; atque ad extremum hoc palatium in quo nunc sumus, idoneum summorum pontificum domicilium, et hoc sacrosanctum Petri apostolorum principis templum, huic nostre domui contiguum, cum magno ac novo vico adiacente, pro digna quadam et secura cum capitis tum omnium membrorum et totius curie habitatione, iam pridem edificare ac reformare incoavimus.

---

[7] hesternos *AD*

[8] Assisi *Muratori*

[9] et *om. Muratori*

[10] cunctorum . . . devotione *om. Muratori*

[11] eam *om. Muratori*

[12] collapsis & confragosis *Muratori*

[13] stationum sanctarum *C¹*

T3 "But actually popular respect, founded on information provided by educated men, grows so much stronger and more solid day by day through great buildings. These are to some extent everlasting monuments and almost eternal testimonies, as though built by God. And then this respect is continually passed on to the living and future viewers of those wonderful constructions and thus preserved and enlarged; it is founded and held fast by a wonderful devotion.

T4 "In addition to the devotion of Christian peoples towards the Roman church and the Apostolic See, there are the fortifications of towns and cities, offering security to the inhabitants and fright to their enemies. By means of constructing these great buildings, these places are rendered more fortified against external enemies and against those at home who desire revolution, daily conspiring to lay waste and arising to do great damage to ecclesiastical governance. This was the reason that we founded many exceptional buildings at Gualdi (to begin with the least), Fabriano, Assisi, in both Civita Vecchia and Civita Castellana, Narnia, Urbino, Spoleto, Viterbo, and many other sites belonging to our church, for the sure and explicit purpose of both goals, devotion and defense.

T5 "And for these same reasons we were led on more fully and strenuously to bring to completion many truly unexampled works here in the City; and we have begun even more and far greater ones, and rightly so. For the greater and more worthy this bounteous City is held to be, the more fully it is celebrated and cherished, then truly the more we judged that it needed to be more ornamented and fortified than all others. This is especially the case since we were hardly unaware that it had been constituted by almighty God as the perpetual seat of the Supreme Pontiffs and the eternal dwelling of Pontifical holiness.

T6 "Accordingly we also repaired the City's walls. In many scattered places they had fallen down and become broken, and we fortified them all around with many towers and finished the new ones with frequent battlements. We have also restored, almost to their final completion, the forty basilicas of the holy stations which were first established by our predecessor Gregory the Great. And finally we have already begun to build and restore this palace, where we now are, as a dwelling place fitting for the Supreme Pontiffs, and this most sacred temple of Peter, Prince of the Apostles, adjoining our house, as well as the great and new district adjacent, for a worthy and secure habitation both for the head and for all the members and the whole Curia.

T7 Que quidem opera antea, ut videtis, incepta, nisi mors a tergo inopinata prevenisset, omnipotentis Dei gratia et sanctorum apostolorum Petri et Pauli de quorum auctoritate et potestate confidebamus opitulationibus adiuti quando ea boni gratia agebamus, ad perfectionem usque perduxissemus. Que quidem si, ut cupiebamus, expleta fuissent aut si, ut institueramus, ullo umquam tempore in posterum absolventur, profecto successores nostri maiori quadam christianorum omnium populorum veneratione adorarentur atque tute ac secure intra urbem commorantes impias et consuetas et externorum hostium et domesticorum quoque inimicorum persecutiones facilius evitarent.

T8 Quibus quidem nos causis, non ambitione, non pompa, non inani gloria, non fama, non diuturniori nominis nostri propagatione, sed maiori quadam romane ecclesie auctoritate et ampliori sedis apostolice apud cunctos christianos populos dignitate ac certiori usitatarum persecutionum evitatione, talia tantaque edificia mente et animo conceperamus.

T9 Nos enim memoria sexcentorum circiter (951) annorum repetita, quo quidem tempore christiana et ortodoxa fides hinc inde late dispersa longeque amplificata — ne forte a primitive ecclesie tempestate ulterius evagati, altius repetamus — multas capitum romanorum persecutiones quondam extitisse accepimus et usque ad tempora nostra profluxisse sensimus. Eugenium nanque secundum, Ioannem nonum, Adrianum tertium, Leonem quintum,[14] Ioannem undecimum, Stephanum octavum, Benedictum quintum, Ioannem tredecimum, Benedictum sextum, Ioannem quatuordecimum, Alexandrum secundum, Gregorium septimum, Urbanum secundum, Pascalem secundum, Gelasium secundum, Innocentium secundum, Alexandrum tertium,[15] Clementem tertium, Ioannem vigesimum tertium, Eugenium quartum, immediatum predecessorem nostrum, et hunc[16] Nicholaum quintum morientem, diversas cum[17] externorum hostium tum domesticorum quoque inimicorum persecutiones non sine maximis romane ecclesie iacturis ac ingenti apostolice sedis dedecore subiisse novimus.

T10 Nam Eugenius, ut de singulis secundum seriem temporum paulo ante commemoratis, pauca quedam exempli gratia referamus, a nonnullis perditis romanis civibus crudeliter captus atque oculis impie admodum privatus, miserabiliter vitam finivit. Ioannes itidem capitur[18] et carceri mancipatur. Adriani temporibus Arnaldus quidam brixiensis heresiarcha, quibusdam romanorum scelestorum

[14] Leonem quintum *om. Mur, sed ins.* Johannem X.

[15] Alexandrum III, Gelasium II, Innocentium II *Muratori*

[16] hinc *Muratori*

[17] tum *Muratori*

[18] captus *Muratori*

T7 "Indeed, we would have brought these works, begun, as you see, beforehand, to full completion if death, sneaking up from behind, had not prevented us, helped by the grace of almighty God and the aid of the holy Apostles Peter and Paul in whose authority and power we trusted as we tried to do these things with good intent. Indeed, if they had been completed as we desired, or if they were to be finished sometime in the future as we planned, our successors would be reverenced with a greater veneration of all Christian peoples. Abiding safely and securely within the City, they would more easily escape the impious and familiar persecutions both of external foes and of enemies at home.

T8 "These are the reasons — not ambition, not pomp, not vainglory, not a longer perpetuation of our name, but the greater authority of the Roman church, the more complete dignity of the Apostolic See among Christian peoples, and the more sure avoidance of the familiar persecutions — why we conceived so many great buildings in our mind and heart.

T9 "Look back in memory over the last six hundred years, a time when the Christian and Orthodox faith was widely dispersed all over and greatly developed — not to go too far back, and excluding the stormy days of the early church — we concluded that many persecutions of Roman heads existed and we perceived that these extended down into modern times. For we know that Eugenius the second, John the ninth, Adrian the third, Leo the fifth, John the eleventh, Stephen the eighth, Benedict the fifth, John the thirteenth, Benedict the sixth, John the fourteenth, Alexander the second, Gregory the seventh, Urban the second, Paschal the second, Gelasius the second, Innocent the second, Alexander the third, Clement the third, John the twenty-third, Eugenius the fourth our immediate predecessor, and Nicholas the fifth dying here, have endured diverse persecutions from external foes as well as enemies at home, accompanied by very great damage to the Roman church and huge embarrassment to the Apostolic See.

T10 "To provide a few details in chronological order about each of those mentioned above, Eugenius was cruelly captured by desperate Roman citizens, then impiously robbed of his eyesight, and ended his life wretchedly. Likewise John was captured and thrown into prison. At the time of Hadrian, the heresiarch Arnold of Brescia, aided by favors from wicked Roman men, entered into the

hominum favoribus adiutus, et urbem intrare et Dominicum tituli sancte Potentiane presbyterum cardinalem ad presentiam summi pontificis de more tendentem in via publica temere aggredi ac nefarie vulnerare sua nimia et intolleranda arrogantia presumpsit.

T11 Leone[19] in carcerem[20] truso, presbiter quidam nomine Christophorus, vi et armis aliquorum romanorum malorum hominum opitulationibus suffultus,[21] pontificatum invasit arripuitque, licet a Sergio postea canonico pastore pontificia dignitate[22] privaretur. Ioannes alter in carcere pariter positus crudelissime suffocatur. Stephanus ab aliquot conspiratoribus romanis per omnia quasi eius membra mutilatus occiditur. Benedictus pontificatu deiectus et in Saxoniam relegatus transmittitur. Ioannes alius a Petro quodam ea tempestate urbis prefecto[23] in ergastulum missus exilio mulctatur. Benedictus alter in carcere similiter collocatus[24] paulo post strangulatur. Ioannes alius, in mole Adriani a populo romano undique obsessus extrema frumenti inopia per sex continuos menses maceratus, tandem fame moritur.

T12 Alexandri tempestate ingens incendium, instar Neronis[25] de industria immissum, magnam urbis partem combussit; eoque facto Catulus[26] parmensis, antipapa per scisma creatus, urbem intravit. Gregorius a Cencio quodam Stephani filio romano ac seditioso cive captivatur ad quem, ubi ex ergastulo in pristinam libertatem restitutus fuit, Henricus illius temporis imperator legatos suos iniquis cum mandatis imparibusque[27] commissionibus misit.

T13 Urbani temporibus moles Adriani a romanis obsidetur et capitur. Paschalis ab Henrico Henrici filio, cum in Etruriam infestis exercitibus venisset Romamque intrasset ac novum scisma concitasset, captivus retinetur. Gelasius predicti Henrici hostilibus cum gentibus ad urbem adventantis pavore perculsus exinde aufugit seque Caietam contulit ac post eius fugam Mauritium quendam bracharum archiepiscopum antipapam creaverunt. Innocentius, magna in urbe contentione orta, ex novo scismate per creationem Petri Leonis suscitato, post fedam et scelestam omnium urbanarum basilicarum direptionem (952) salutis sue causa cum duabus triremibus in Galliam fugere coactus est.

---

[19] Leonem *D*
[20] carcere *C¹*
[21] suffultis *D*
[22] pontifici a dignitate *C¹*
[23] profecto *C¹D*
[24] collocatur *Muratori*
[25] Neroniani *Muratori*
[26] Cadulus *Muratori*
[27] paribusque *Muratori*

City and boldly attacked Dominic, cardinal priest of the titular church of Santa Pudenziana, on a public street as he was making his usual way to the Supreme Pontiff's residence; he had the gall, through his extreme and insufferable arrogance, to wound him horribly .

T11 "When Leo was thrust into prison, a certain priest named Christopher, relying on violence and the armed assistance of some wicked Romans, invaded and seized the pontifical throne, though later Sergius, the canonical shepherd, was able to strip him of the pontifical dignity. Another John was likewise put in prison and cruelly suffocated. Stephen was murdered by Roman conspirators, mutilated over almost his entire body. Benedict was deposed from the papacy, banished, and dispatched to Saxony. Another John was exiled to a workhouse by the prefect of the city at the time, a certain Peter, and was ill used. The other Benedict was likewise imprisoned and shortly thereafter strangled. Another John was besieged on all sides by the Roman populace inside the Hadrianic Mass; through an extreme shortage of food he wasted away for six continuous months and finally died of starvation.

T12 "At the time of Alexander, a huge fire, like the one started through Nero's agency, burned a large part of the City. When that happened, Cadalus of Parma, created antipope in a schism, entered the City. Gregory was taken prisoner by a certain Cencius, son of Stephen and a seditious Roman citizen; after he had been restored from the workhouse to his former freedom, Henry, emperor at the time, sent his emissaries against him with vile orders, and similar plots.

T13 "At the time of Urban, the Hadrianic Mass was besieged by the Romans and captured. Pascal was captured and held by Henry, the son of Henry, who had come into Tuscany amid his jubilant armies, then entered Rome and provoked a new schism. Gelasius, stricken with panic at the same Henry's approach to Rome with hostile tribes, fled and made his way to Gaeta. After his flight they created a certain Maurice, Archbishop of Braca, antipope. Innocent, when a great turmoil arose in the City from new schism stirred up at the election of Pietro Pierleone, after all the urban basilicas had been foully and criminally plundered, was forced to flee to France with two triremes for his own personal safety.

T14 Alexandri tempestate ex ingenti quodam incendio de industria immisso multe urbis partes conflagravere. Hic per suggestionem Octaviani cuiusdam qui ad summum pontificatum aspirabat in basilica Petri apostolorum principis armatis militibus ita obsessus fuit ut fuga saluti sue consulere cogeretur atque Transtiberim clanculum fugiens contendit. Hic a Federico secundo[28] dum in cisalpine Gallie regione infestis exercitibus[29] castrametaretur,[30] per imperatorios legatos ad concilium evocatus est. Quid plura? Hic Alexander ter salutis sue causa urbem reliquit terque unde aufugerat, adiutore Deo, reversus est. Clemens, cum populo romano contentionibus habitis, multas ab eis iniurias diversasque contumelias pertulisse fertur.

T15 Sed quid nos plurima antiqua partim dedecorosa, partim damnosa summorum pontificum[31] nefariarum persecutionum exempla conquirimus? Ad propinquiora ac nostratia veniamus. Nonne temporibus nostris Ladislaus Apulie rex Ioannem vigesimum tertium hic cum tota curia ea tempestate residentem infestis[32] exercitibus suis animose impetere atque hanc almam urbem invadere ita ausus est ut et ipsum et totam curiam e Roma exigeret atque universam insuper civitatem militaribus populationibus diripiendam concederet? Nonne Eugenium predecessorem nostrum quidam sicarii et pessimi patrie sue proditores — de romanis loquimur — et urbe ipsa eiecerunt et molem quoque Adriani armatis militibus obsederunt?

T16 Sed quid plura de nefariis romanorum pontificum persecutionibus dicimus? Nonne his temporibus Stephanus Porcarius nobilis romanus et quidam alii perditi homines paulo ante reperti sunt qui in nos conspirare et in caput nostrum temere et sceleste admodum coniurare presumpserunt? Verum coniuratione opportuno tempore, omnipotentis Dei gratia ac continuis Petri et Pauli favoribus, paulo post detecta, conspiratores ipsi in flagranti crimine deprehensi, capti, et ultimo, ut merebantur, crucis ac suspendii supplicio affecti periere.

T17 Has quidem et veteres ac recentes persecutiones romani pontifices[33] nullo unquam, ut iure existimamus et credimus, tempore pertulissent, si novis et inexpugnabilibus[34] munitionibus se se presertim intra urbem protexissent. Numquam enim neque externi hostes neque domestici inimici, quamquam novarum rerum

---

[28] Primo *Muratori*
[29] exercibus *Muratori*
[30] castrameteretur *Muratori*
[31] pontificum *om.* C^1
[32] infesti *D*
[33] Pontificis *Muratori*
[34] expugnabilibus *Muratori*

T14 "At the time of Alexander, many parts of the City burned from a huge fire, deliberately set. This pope, at the instigation of a certain Octavianus who aspired to the papacy, was so harassed by armed soldiers in the basilica of Peter, Prince of the Apostles, that he was forced to look to his personal safety by fleeing. He escaped in secret and made his way to Trastevere. Frederick II, while he was encamped with his menacing armies in the area of Cisalpine Gaul, summoned him through imperial emissaries to a conference. What more? This Alexander left the City three times for his own safety and three times, with God's help, returned from where he had fled. Clement, when conflicts broke out with the Roman people, is said to have endured many injuries from them and all manner of insults.

T15 "But why do we seek most of our examples of outrageous persecutions — both the shameful and the damaging — in the old days? Let us come to those closer to our own contemporary times. In our own times, did not Ladislaus, king of Apulia, dare viciously to attack John XXIII, who at that time lived here with his whole Curia, and to invade this beneficent City, so as to drive him and the whole Curia from Rome and moreover to give the entire City over to the soldiers and populace to plunder? Did not certain cut-throats and the worst betrayers of their country (I am speaking of the Romans) both expel from this very City our predecessor Eugenius and also besiege the Hadrianic Mass with armed troops?

T16 "But what further should we say about the vile persecutions of Roman pontiffs? Were not, in these times, Stefano Porcari, a Roman nobleman, and certain other detestable men a short while ago exposed? They had presumed to conspire against us and brazenly and wickedly almost carried off an assassination. Indeed, through the grace of God almighty and the constant blessings of Peter and Paul, their conspiracy was detected in the nick of time shortly thereafter, and the conspirators themselves died. They were caught in the very act, captured, and subjected, as they deserved, to the punishment of gibbet and gallows.

T17 "Indeed we are convinced and believe that the Roman pontiffs would never on any of these occasions, in the old days or in recent times, have had to endured these persecutions if they had protected themselves with unassailable fortifications, especially inside the City. Neither external foes nor enemies at home, no

cupidi, usque adeo temerarii insanique fuissent ut ea cum periculo capitis sui aggrederentur que optatos designatosque effectus nequaquam sortiri posse videbantur. At vero, si temeraria audacia allecti et ceca cupiditate raptati fecissent,[35] profecto conatus sui ad nihilum recidissent; ac per hunc modum tuti, quieti, ac securi[36] in continua sedis apostolice tranquillitate cum maxima auctoritate, cum summa potestate, cum immensa denique dignitate semper resedissent.

T18 Quocirca, ut de hac edificationum nostrarum recitatione a principali proposito parumper digredientes aliquem certum et solidum fructum capiamus, venerationes vestras in Domino exhortamur, quatenus predicta constructionum nostrarum opera incoata prosequi ac perficere et absolvere velitis ut successores nostri externorum tumultuum domesticarumque persecutionum penitus omninoque[37] expertes, gregem dominicum[38] sibi ab omnipotenti Deo commissum, tanquam veri animarum pastores, diligentius atque liberius salubribus cibariis alere ac per hunc (953) modum alitum in viam salutis eterne traducere possint[39] et valeant.

---

[35] fuissent *Muratori*

[36] Pontifices *Muratori*

[37] omnino *Muratori*

[38] Dominicum gregem *Muratori*

[39] possunt *C¹*

matter how eager for revolution, would ever have been so bold or insane as to undertake at the risk of their own lives actions that could not possibly achieve their desired and planned results. Instead, even if they had been enticed by rash audacity and seized with blind desire, their attempts actually would have come to nothing. And in this way the pontiffs, safe, undisturbed, and secure, would have always remained in the constant tranquillity of the Apostolic See enjoying the greatest authority, the utmost power, and immense dignity.

T18 "Therefore, so that we, digressing from our main subject, might take some sure and certain fruit from our recital of our buildings, we exhort Your Venerabilities to be willing to finish and complete the construction projects mentioned above that have already been begun. In this way our successors, absolutely and completely untouched by external tumults and persecutions at home, like true shepherds of souls, might have the ability and the strength to nourish the Lord's flock entrusted to them by almighty God more diligently and liberally with saving food, and bring them, nourished in this manner, to the way of eternal salvation."

Bibliography

Primary Sources Before 1500

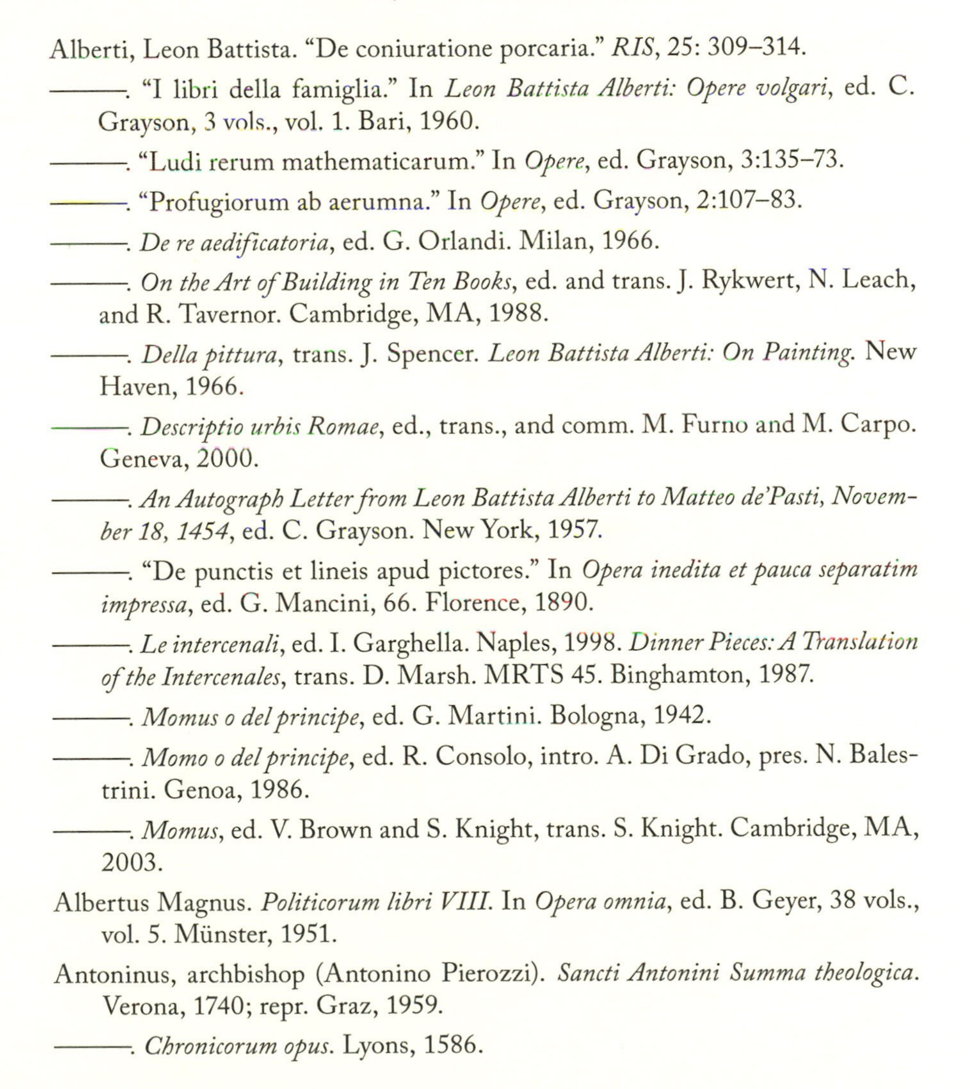

Alberti, Leon Battista. "De coniuratione porcaria." *RIS*, 25: 309–314.

———. "I libri della famiglia." In *Leon Battista Alberti: Opere volgari*, ed. C. Grayson, 3 vols., vol. 1. Bari, 1960.

———. "Ludi rerum mathematicarum." In *Opere*, ed. Grayson, 3:135–73.

———. "Profugiorum ab aerumna." In *Opere*, ed. Grayson, 2:107–83.

———. *De re aedificatoria*, ed. G. Orlandi. Milan, 1966.

———. *On the Art of Building in Ten Books*, ed. and trans. J. Rykwert, N. Leach, and R. Tavernor. Cambridge, MA, 1988.

———. *Della pittura*, trans. J. Spencer. *Leon Battista Alberti: On Painting*. New Haven, 1966.

———. *Descriptio urbis Romae*, ed., trans., and comm. M. Furno and M. Carpo. Geneva, 2000.

———. *An Autograph Letter from Leon Battista Alberti to Matteo de'Pasti, November 18, 1454*, ed. C. Grayson. New York, 1957.

———. "De punctis et lineis apud pictores." In *Opera inedita et pauca separatim impressa*, ed. G. Mancini, 66. Florence, 1890.

———. *Le intercenali*, ed. I. Garghella. Naples, 1998. *Dinner Pieces: A Translation of the Intercenales*, trans. D. Marsh. MRTS 45. Binghamton, 1987.

———. *Momus o del principe*, ed. G. Martini. Bologna, 1942.

———. *Momo o del principe*, ed. R. Consolo, intro. A. Di Grado, pres. N. Balestrini. Genoa, 1986.

———. *Momus*, ed. V. Brown and S. Knight, trans. S. Knight. Cambridge, MA, 2003.

Albertus Magnus. *Politicorum libri VIII*. In *Opera omnia*, ed. B. Geyer, 38 vols., vol. 5. Münster, 1951.

Antoninus, archbishop (Antonino Pierozzi). *Sancti Antonini Summa theologica*. Verona, 1740; repr. Graz, 1959.

———. *Chronicorum opus*. Lyons, 1586.

Antonio da Cannara. *De potestate pape supra concilium generale contra errores Basiliensium*, ed. T. Prügl. Paderborn, 1996.

Aquinas, Thomas. *Summa theologiae*. 5 vols. Madrid, 1959.

———. *Summa theologica*, trans. Fathers of the English Dominican Province. 4th ed. 5 vols. Allen, TX, 1981.

Aristeas. "Letter of Aristeas," trans. R. J. H. Shutt. In *The Old Testament Pseudepigrapha*, ed. J. Charlesworth, 2:7–34. Garden City, 1985.

L'arte della seta in Firenze. Trattato del secolo XV, ed. A. Gargiolli. Florence, 1968.

Avogadro, Alberto. "De religione et magnificentia illustris Cosmi Medices Florentini," ed. G. Lami. In *Deliciae eruditorum*, 12:117–49. Florence, 1742.

Biondo, Flavio. *De Roma triumphante, Romae instauratae, De origine ac gestis venetorum liber.* Basel, 1559.

———. *Scritti inediti e rari di Biondo Flavio*, ed. B. Nogara. Rome, 1927.

Bonvesin della Riva. *De magnalibus Mediolani. Meraviglie di Milano*, ed. P. Chiesa. Milan, 1998.

Bracciolini, Poggio. *Poggius Bracciolini. Opera omnia*, ed. R. Fubini. Turin, 1966.

———. *Poggii epistolae*, ed. T. de Tonellis. Florence, 1832.

———. *De varietate fortunae*, ed. O. Merisalo. Helsinki, 1993.

———. *La vera nobiltà*, ed. D. Canfora. Rome, 1999.

———. *De infelicitate principum*, ed. D. Canfora. Rome, 1998.

———. *De officio principis*. Rome, 1504.

Brewyn, William. *A Fifteenth Century Guidebook to the Principal Churches of Rome, Compiled c. 1470 by William Brewyn*, ed. S. E. Woodruff. London, 1933.

Bruni, Leonardo. *Rerum suo tempore gestarum commentarius*, ed. C. di Pierro. *RIS*, 19.3:1–287.

———. *Leonardo Bruni Aretino: Humanistisch-Philosophische Schriften*, ed. H. Baron. Leipzig, 1928.

Cambi, Giovanni. *Istorie di Giovanni Cambi*, ed. I. di San Luigi. In *Delizie degli eruditi toscani*, vols. 20– 23. Florence, 1785–1786.

Capgrave, John. *Ye Solace of Pilgrims*, ed. C. Mills. London, 1911.

Cavalcanti, Giovanni. *Istorie fiorentine*. Florence, 1839.

Cesariano, Cesare. *De Lucio Vitruvio Pollione de architectura libri decem traducti de latino in volgare*. Como, 1521.

Caesarius of Arles. *Caesarii Arelatensis sermones*, ed. G. Morin. CCSL 104. Turnhout, 1953.

Corazza, Bartolomeo del. *Diario fiorentino (1435–1439)*, ed. R. Gentile. Anzio, 1991.

Cortesi, Paolo. *De hominibus doctis dialogus*, ed. and trans. M. Graziosi. Rome, 1973.

Dati, Gregorio. *Istoria di Firenze*, ed. L. Pratesi. Florence, 1904.

Decembrio, Pier Candido. *Vita di Filippo Maria Visconti. RIS*, 20.1:1–438.

De Godis, Pietro. *De Porcaria coniuratione dialogus*, ed. M. Lehnerdt. Leipzig, 1907.

Durandus, William. *Guillelmi Durantii Rationale divinorum officiorum*, ed. A. Davril and T. Thibodeau. 3 vols. CCCM 140–140A–140B. Turnhout, 1995.

———. *The Symbolism of Churches and their Ornaments. A Translation of the First Book of the 'Rationale divinorum officiorum'*, trans. J. M. Neale and B. Webb. London, 1843.

———. *Le pontifical romain au moyen-age*. vol. 3. *Le pontifical de Guillaume Durand*, ed. M. Andrieu. Studi e Testi 88. Vatican City, 1940.

Fiamma, Galvano. *Opusculum de rebus gestis ab Azone, Luchino et Johanne vicecomitibus ab anno MCCCXXVIII usque ad annum MCCXLII. RIS*, 12.4:1–52.

Filarete, Il. *Antonio Averlino detto il Filarete. Trattato di architettura*, ed. A. Finoli and L. Grassi. Milan, 1972.

Filarete, Francesco, and Manfidi, Angelo. *The Libro Cerimoniale of the Florentine Republic by Francesco Filarete and Angelo Manfidi*, ed. R. Trexler. Geneva, 1978.

Ghiberti, Lorenzo. *I commentarii*, ed. L. Bartoli. Florence, 1998.

Gregory the Great. *Homiliae in Hiezechielem prophetam*, ed. M. Adriaen. CCSL 142. Turnhout, 1971.

Guasti, C. *La Cupola di Santa Maria del Fiore*. Florence, 1857.

———. *Santa Maria del Fiore. La Costruzione della chiesa e del campanile*. Florence, 1887.

Guarino Veronese. *Epistolario*, ed. R. Sabbadini. Venice, 1916.

Guicciardini, Francesco. *Storie fiorentine dal 1378 al 1509*, ed. R. Palmarocchi. Bari, 1931.

Honorius of Autun. *Gemma animae*. PL 172.543–738.

Infessura, Stefano. *Diario della città di Roma*, ed. O. Tommasini. Rome, 1892.

Jerome. *Commentaria in Hiezechielem*, ed. C. Moreschini. CCSL 75. Turnhout, 1975.

John of Genoa (Johannes Balbi). *Catholicon*. Mainz, 1460 (repr. 1971).

John Philoponus. *In Aristotelis Physica*, ed. G. Vitelli. Commentaria in Aristotelem Graeca 16. Berlin, 1887.

———. ———, trans. M. J. Edwards. Ithaca, 1994.

John of Salisbury. *Policraticus. Of the Frivolities of Courtiers and the Footprints of Philosophers*, trans. C. Nederman. Cambridge, 1990.

———. ———, *I–IV*, ed. K. Keats-Rohan. CCCM 118. Turnhout, 1993.

Jouffroy, Jean. "Oratio Episcopi Atrebatensis Habita Rome in Funeralibus Nicolai Pape Quinti." Bibl. Vat., MS. Vat. Lat. 3675, fols. 30r–37r.

Juan de Torquemada. *Summa de Ecclesia*: *The Antiquity of the Church*, ed. W. Maguire. Washington, DC, 1957.

Lapaccini, Giuliano. *La cronica di San Marco. Archivio Storico Italiano* 71 (1913).

Lapo da Castiglionchio. "De curiae commodis." In C. Celenza, *Renaissance Humanism and the Papal Curia. Lapo da Castiglionchio the Younger's 'De curiae commodis'*, 102–227. Ann Arbor, 1999.

Le Liber pontificalis, ed. L. Duchesne. 3 vols. Paris, 1886–1892.

Macrobius. *Commentary on the Dream of Scipio*, trans. W. Stahl. New York, 1952.

Manetti, Giannozzo. *Apologeticus*, ed. and trans. A. De Petris. Rome, 1981.

———. *Biographical Writings*, ed. and trans. S. Baldassarri and R. Bagemihl. Cambridge, MA, 2003.

———. *Contra Judaeos et gentes*. A. De Petris, "L'*Adversus Iudeos et gentes* di Giannozzo Manetti," *Rinascimento* 16 (1976): 193–205.

———. *De dignitate et excellentia hominis*, ed. E. Leonard. Padua, 1975.

———. *De dignitate et excellentia hominis*. Basel, 1532; repr. Frankfurt, 1975.

———. *Giannozzo Manetti. Das Corpus der Orationes*, ed. H. W. Wittschier. Cologne, 1968.

———. *Vita Nicolai summi pontificis*. *RIS*, 3.2: 907–60.

———. *Vita di Nicolò V*, trans., intro., and comm. A. Modigliani, pref. M. Miglio. Rome, 1999.

———. "De secularibus et pontificalibus pompis." In E. Battisti, "L'Antichità in Niccolò V e l'iconografia della Cappella Sistina," in *Umanesimo e esoterismo: Atti del V convegno internazionale di studi umanistici*, ed. E. Castelli, 207–16, 310–20. Padua, 1960.

———. *Giannozzo Manetti: Elogi dei Genovesi*, ed. G. Petti Balbi. Milan, 1974.

———. *De illustribus longaevis*. Bibl. Vat., MS. Pal. Lat. 1603, fols. 42r–112r.

———. "Florentinorum legatorum oratio in fausta ac felici Frederici III Imperatoris coronatione." Frankfurt, 1614.

Muffel, Nikolaus. *Beschreibung der Stadt Rom*, ed. W. Vogt. Stuttgart, 1876.

Naldo Naldi. "Vita Janotii de Manectis." *RIS*, 20: 529–608.

Nicholas of Lyra. *Biblia latina cum postillis.* Venice, 1489.

Palmieri, Mattia. *De Temporibus suis. RIS*, 26.1:1–194.

Palmieri, Matteo. *Della vita civile*, ed. F. Battaglia. Bologna, 1944.

Palmieri, Niccolò. "Oratio funebris per Nicolaum tunc Catazarii nunc Ortanum episcopum et Civitatis castellane in funere Nicolai Pape Quinti prima die exequiarum." Bibl. Vat., MS. Vat. Lat. 5815, fols. 3r–12v.

Petrarch, Francesco. *Sine nomine*, ed. U. Dotti. *Francesco Petrarca. Sine nomine. Lettere polemiche e politiche.* Rome, 1974.

———. *Petrarch's Book Without a Name: A Translation of the 'Liber sine nomine'*, trans. N. Zacour. Toronto, 1973.

Piccolomini, Aeneas Silvius. *The Commentaries of Pius II*, trans. F. Gragg. Smith College Studies in History 22–43. New York, 1936–1957.

———. *Aeneae Sylvii Piccolominei Senensis . . . Opera qua extant omnia.* Basle, 1571; repr. Frankfurt, 1967.

———. *Historia Friderici III imperatoris*, ed. B. Ziliotti. Trieste, 1958.

———. "De morte Eugenii IV creationeque et coronatione Nicolai V." *RIS*, 3.2: 878–98.

Planck, Stephen. *Mirabilia Romae. Rom Stephen Planck 20 Nov. MCCCCLXXXIX: Ein römisches Pilgerbuch des 15. Jahrhunderts in deutscher Sprache.* Berlin, 1925.

Platina, B. *Liber de vita Christi ac omnium pontificum. RIS*, 3.1:1–420; 3.3:1–121.

Poggi, G. *Il Duomo di Firenze. Documenti sulla decorazione della Chiesa e del Campanile tratti dall'archivio dell'Opera*, 1. Berlin, 1909; 2, ed. M. Haines. Florence, 1988.

Pseudo-Dionysius (Dionysius the Areopagite). *The Complete Works*, trans. C. Luibheid. Mahwah, NJ, 1987.

Ptolemy of Lucca. *On the Government of Rulers. De Regimine principum*, trans. J. Blythe. Philadelphia, 1997.

Quaestio de potestate papae (Rex pacificus). An Enquiry into the Power of the Pope, ed. and trans. R. Dyson. Lewiston, NY, 1999.

Rhabanus Maurus. *Commentaria in libros IV Regum.* PL 109.9–280.

Rinuccini, Filippo di Cino. *Ricordi storici dal 1282 al 1460*, ed. G. Aiazzi. Florence, 1840.

Sabadino degli Arienti, Giovanni. "De triumphis religionis." *Art and Life at the Court of Ercole I d'Este: The "De triumphis religionis" of Giovanni Sabadino degli Arienti*, ed. W. L. Gundersheimer. Geneva, 1972.

Scala, Bartolomeo. *De historia florentinorum quae extant in Bibliothecae Medicaea*, ed. O. Iacobaeo. Rome, 1677.

Schiavo, Antonio di Pietro dello. *Il diario romano*, ed. F. Isoldi. *RIS*, n.s. 24.5.

Sicardus of Cremona. *Mitrale*. PL 213.13–454.

Valentini, R., and G. Zucchetti. *Codice topografico della città di Roma*. Rome, 1953.

Valla, Lorenzo. "Elegantiae latinae linguae." In idem, *Opera omnia*, ed. E. Garin, 1:3–234. Basle, 1540; repr. Turin, 1962.

———. *The Treatise of Lorenzo Valla on the Donation of Constantine*, trans. C. B. Coleman. New Haven, 1922.

Vegio, Maffeo. *De Rebus antiquis memorabilibus basilicae S. Petri Romae*. In *Acta Sanctorum* 27 (June 29): 56–76. Brussels, 1965–1970.

Vergerio, Pierpaolo. *P. P. Vergerio Epistolario*, ed. L. Smith. Rome, 1934.

Vespasiano da Bisticci. *Le Vite*, ed. A. Greco. Florence, 1970.

Vincent of Beauvais. *Vincentii Belvacensis De Morali principis institutione*, ed. R. Schneider. CCCM 137. Turnhout, 1995.

Secondary Sources

Acidini Luchinat, C. "The Stained-Glass Windows." In *The Cathedral of Santa Maria del Fiore in Florence*, ed. idem, 273–302. Florence, 1995.

———. "Quarantaquattro vetrate d'artista, un tesoro del Rinascimento nel Duomo." In *Alla riscoperta . . . 6*, ed. Verdon, 40–66. Florence, 1997.

Ackerman, J. *Il Cortile di Belvedere*. Vatican City, 1954.

———. *The Reinvention of Architectural Drawing 1250–1550*. Otley, 1998.

Albareda, A. "Il bibliotecario di Callisto III." In *Miscellanea Giovanni Mercati*, 178–208. Studi e Testi 124. Vatican City, 1946.

Alfarano, T. *Tiberii Alpharani de Basilicae Vaticanae antiquissima et nova structura*, ed. M. Cerrati. Rome, 1914.

Allers, R. "Microcosmus from Anaximander to Paracelsus." *Traditio* 1 (1943): 319–407.

Amati, G. "Inventarium quorundam librorum repertorum in cubiculo Nicolai papae quinti post eius obitam — Notizie di alcuni manoscritti dell'Archivio Segreto Vaticano." *Archivio storico italiano* 13 (1866): 207–12.

Amy, M. "The Revised Attributions and Dates of Two Fifteenth-Century Mural Cycles for the Cathedral of Florence," *Mitteilungen des Kunsthistorischen Instituts in Florenz* 42 (1998): 176–89.

Andrieu, M. *Le pontifical romain au moyen-âge II: Le pontifical de la curie romaine au XIIIe siècle*. Studi e Testi 87. Vatican City, 1940.

———. *Le pontifical romain au moyen-âge III: Le pontifical de Guillaume Durand*. Studi e Testi 88. Vatican City, 1940.

Apollonij-Ghetti, B., A. Ferrua, E. Tosi, and E. Kirschbaum. *Esplorazioni sotto la confessione di San Pietro in Vaticano*. Vatican City, 1951.

Ascani, V. "I disegni architettonici attribuiti ad Antonio di Vincenzo. Caratteristiche tecniche e ruolo degli 'appunti grafici' nella prassi progetturale tardogotica." *Arte medievale* 5 (1991): 105–16.

Aurigemma, M. "Committenze non romane di Niccolò V.' In *Niccolò V nel sesto centenario della nascita: Atti del convegno internazionale di studi*, ed. F. Bonatti and A. Manfredi, 411–39. Vatican City, 2000.

Baldovin, J. *The Urban Character of Christian Worship*. Rome, 1987.

Bandini, A. *Catalogus codicum latinorum Bibliothecae Mediceae Laurentianae*. Florence, 1764.

Barkan, L. *Nature's Work of Art: The Human Body as Image of the World*. New Haven, 1975.

Baron, H. *Humanistic and Political Literature in Florence and Venice*. Cambridge, MA, 1955.

———. "Aulus Gellius in the Renaissance: His Influence and a Manuscript from the School of Guarino." In idem, *From Petrarch to Leonardo Bruni. Studies in Humanistic and Political Literature*, 196–216. Chicago, 1968.

Battisti, E. *Rinascimento e Barocco*. Turin, 1960.

———. "L'Antichità in Niccolò V e l'iconografia della Cappella Sistina." In *Umanesimo e esoterismo: Atti del V convegno internazionale di studi umanistici*, ed. E. Castelli, 207–16, 310–20. Padua, 1960.

———. "Il significato simbolico della Cappella Sistina." *Commentari* 8 (1957): 96–104.

Baxandall, M. *Giotto and the Orators*. New York, 1986.

Bayless, M. *Parody in the Middle Ages: The Latin Tradition*. Ann Arbor, 1996.

Beaujouan, G. "Réflexions sur les rapports entre théorie et pratique au Moyen Age." In *The Cultural Context of Medieval Learning*, ed. J. E. Murdoch and E. D. Sylla, 437–84. Dordrecht, 1975.

Benevolo, L. *Storia dell'architettura del Rinascimento*. Bari, 1977.

Bentivoglio, L. "Il coro di S. Maria del Popolo e il coro detto 'del Rossellino' di S. Pietro." *Mitteilungen des Kunsthistorischen Instituts in Florenz* 20 (1976): 197–204.

Bentley, J. *Humanists and Holy Writ: New Testament Scholarship in the Renaissance.* Princeton, 1983.

Benzi, F., ed. *Sisto IV. Le arti a Roma nel primo Rinascimento.* Rome, 2000.

Bergstein, M. "Marian Politics in Quattrocento Florence." *Renaissance Quarterly* 44 (1991): 673–719.

Bernard, A. *Sépulture en droit canonique.* Paris, 1933.

Bernareggi, A. "La Tiara pontificia: note di arte liturgica." *Arte cristiana* 11 (1923): 34–50.

Bertalot, L. "Cincius Romanus und seine Briefe." *Quellen und Forschungen aus italienischen Archiven und Bibliotheken* 21 (1929–1930): 209–51.

Bertolà, M. *I due primi registri di prestito della Biblioteca Apostolica Vaticana.* Vatican City, 1942.

Besomi, O. "Dai 'Gesta Ferdinandi Regis Aragonum' del Valla al 'De Ortographia' del Tortelli." *Italia medioevale e umanistica* 9 (1966): 75–121.

Bianca, C. "I Cardinali al Concilio di Firenze." In *Firenze e il Concilio del 1439*, ed. P. Viti, 147–73. Florence, 1994.

———. "Il pontificato di Niccolò V e i padri della chiesa." In *Umanesimo e padri della chiesa*, ed. S. Gentile, 85–92. Milan, 1997.

———, P. Farenga, and G. Lombardi. *Scrittura, biblioteche e stampa a Roma nel Quattrocento: Aspetti e Problemi.* Vatican City, 1980.

Bianchi, L. *Case e torri medioevali a Roma. Documentazione, storia e sopravivenza di edifici medioevali nel tessuto urbano di Roma*, 1. Rome, 1998.

———. *Roma. Il Monte di Santo Spirito tra Gianicolo e Vaticano.* Rome, 1999.

Biasiotti, G. "Affreschi di Benozzo Gozzoli in S. Maria Maggiore in Roma." *Bollettino d'arte* 7 (1913): 76–86.

———. "La basilica di S. Maria Maggiore prima delle innovazioni del secolo XVI." *Ecole Française de Rome, Mélanges d'archéologie et d'histoire* 35 (1915): 15–39.

Bignami Odier, J. *La Bibliothèque Vaticane de Sixte IV à Pie XI.* Studi e Testi 272. Vatican City, 1973.

Billanovich, G. "Gli umanisti e le cronache medioevali. Il 'Liber Pontificalis', le 'Decadi' di Tito Livio e il primo umanesimo a Roma." *Italia medioevale e umanistica* 1 (1958): 103–37.

Black, R. "Ancients and Moderns in the Renaissance: Rhetoric and History in Accolti's 'Dialogue on the Preeminence of Men of his own Time'." *Journal of the History of Ideas* 43 (1982): 3–32.

———. "The Donation of Constantine: A New Source for the Concept of the Renaissance?" In *Language and Images of Renaissance Italy*, ed. A. Brown, 51–85. Oxford, 1995.

Blasio, M., C. Lelj, and G. Roselli. "Un contributo al canone bibliografico di Tommaso Parentucelli." In *Le chiavi della memoria. Miscellanea in occasione del I centenario della Scuola Vaticana di Paleografia, Diplomatica e Archivistica*, 125–65. Vatican City, 1984.

Bloch, H. "Aqua Traiana." *American Journal of Archeology* 48 (1944): 337–41.

Boccardi Storoni, P. *Storia della Basilica di San Pietro*. Pavia, 1988.

Bocchi, F. *Bologna e i suoi portici: Storia dell'origine e dello sviluppo*. Bologna, 1997.

Bolzoni, L. "Il 'Colloquio spirituale' di Simone da Cascina. Note su allegoria e immagini della memoria." *Rivista di letteratura italiana* 3 (1985): 9–65.

Bonfil, R. *Jewish Life in Renaissance Italy*. Berkeley, 1994.

Böninger, L. *Die Ritterwürde in Mittelitalien zwischen Mittelalter und Früher Neuzeit*. Berlin, 1995.

Borgolte, M. *Petrus Nachfolge und Kaiserimitation: Die Grablegen der Päpste, ihre Genese und Traditionsbildung*. Göttingen, 1989.

Borsa, M. "Pier Candido Decembrio e l'umanesimo in Lombardia." *Archivio storico lombardo* 20 (1893): 5–75, 358–441.

Borsi, F. *Bramante*. Milan, 1989.

Borsi, S. *Momus o del principe. Leon Battista Alberti, i papi, il giubileo*. Florence, 1999.

———. *Leon Battista Alberti e Roma*. Florence, 2003.

———, F. Quinterio, and C. Vasic Vatovec. *Maestri fiorentini nei cantieri romani del Quattrocento*, ed. S. Danese Squarzina. Rome, 1989.

Botley, P. *Latin Translation in the Renaissance: The Theory and Practice of Leonardo Bruni Giannozzo Manetti, and Desidenius Erasmus*. Cambridge, 2004.

Bourgin, G. "La 'Familia' pontificia sotto Eugenio IV." *Archivio della Società romana di Storia Patria* 27 (1904): 205–24.

Bowen, L. "The Tropology of Mediaeval Dedication Rites." *Speculum* 16 (1941): 469–79.

Boyle, L. "Sixtus IV and the Vatican Library." in *Rome: Tradition, Innovation and Renewal, a Canadian International Art History Conference*, 65–73 Victoria, BC, 1991.

Brandmüller, W. *Das Konzil von Konstanz 1414–1418*. Paderborn, 1991.

Braun, J. *Die liturgische Gewandung in Occident und Orient*. Freiburg im Breisgau, 1907.

Brett, G. "The Seven Wonders of the World in the Renaissance." *Art Quarterly* 12 (1949): 339–58.

Briggs, C. *Giles of Rome's 'De regimine principum'. Reading and Writing Politics at Court and University c. 1275–c. 1525*. New York, 1999.

Brown, A. "The Guelf Party in Fifteenth-Century Florence: The Transition from Communal to Medicean State." *Rinascimento* 20 (1980): 41–86.

Brown, P. "Images as a Substitute for Writing." In *East and West: Modes of Communication*, ed. E. K. Chrysos and I. Wood, 15–34. Leiden, 1999.

Brucker, G. "Florence and its University, 1348–1434." In *Action and Conviction in Early Modern Europe. Essays in Memory of E.H. Harbison*, ed. T. Rabb and J. Siegel, 220–36. Princeton, 1969.

———. *The Society of Renaissance Florence. A Documentary Study*. New York, 1971.

Buddensieg, T. "Gregory the Great, the Destroyer of Pagan Idols." *Journal of the Warburg and Courtauld Institutes* 28 (1965): 44–65.

Burns, H. "Leon Battista Alberti." In *Storia dell'architettura italiana. Il quattrocento*, ed. F. Fiore, 114–65. Milan, 1998.

Burroughs, C. "Below the Angel: An Urbanistic Project in the Rome of Pope Nicholas V." *Journal of the Warburg and Courtauld Institutes* 45 (1982): 94–124.

———. "A Planned Myth and a Myth of Planning: Nicholas V and Rome." In *Rome in the Renaissance: The City and the Myth*, ed. P. Ramsey, 197–207. Binghamton, 1982.

———. *From Signs to Design. Environmental Process and Reform in Early Renaissance Rome*. Cambridge, MA, 1990.

———. "Alberti e Roma." In *Leon Battista Alberti*, ed. J. Rykwert and A. Engel, 134–57. Milan, 1994.

Busink, T. *Der Tempel von Jerusalem von Salomon bis Herodes*. 2 vols. Leiden, 1970–1980.

Busiri Vici, A. *La 'Colonna santa' del tempio di Gerusalemme ed il sarcofago di Probo Anicio prefetto di Roma*. Rome, 1888.

Cadei, A. "Cultura artistica delle cattedrali: due esempi a Milano." *Arte medievale* 5 (1991): 83–104.

Cagiano de Azevedo, M. *Saggio sul labirinto*. Milan, 1958.

Caglioti, F. "Bernardo Rossellino a Roma. I. Stralci del carteggio mediceo (con qualche briciola sul Filarete)." *Prospettiva* 64 (1991): 49–59.

———. "Bernardo Rossellino a Roma. II. Tra Giannozzo Manetti e Giorgio Vasari." *Prospettiva* 65 (1992): 29–43.

Cagni, G. "I Codici Vaticani Palatino-Latini appartenuti alla biblioteca di Giannozzo Manetti." *La Bibliofilia* 62 (1960): 1–43.

———. "Agnolo Manetti e Vespasiano da Bisticci." *Italia medioevale ed umanistica* 14 (1971): 293–312.

Cahn, W. "Solomonic Elements in Romanesque Art." In *The Temple of Solomon: Archeological Fact and Medieval Tradition,* ed. J. Gutmann, 45–72. Ann Arbor, 1973.

Calzona, A. "Leon Battista Alberti e l'immagine di Roma fuori di Roma: Il Tempio Malatestiano." In *Le due Rome del Quattrocento*, ed. S. Rossi and S. Valeri, 346–63. Rome, 1997.

Campana, A. "Giannozzo Manetti, Ciriaco e l'arco di Traiano ad Ancona." *Italia medioevale ed umanistica* 2 (1959): 483–504.

Camporeale, S. *Lorenzo Valla tra medioevo e rinascimento. Encomion S. Thomae, 1457.* Pistoia, 1977.

———. "Lorenzo Valla e il 'De Falsa credita donatione': Retorica, libertà ed ecclesiologia nel '400." *Memorie Domenicane* 19 (1988): 191–293.

———. "Il Problema della *imitatio* nel primo Quattrocento. Differenze e controversia tra Bracciolini e Valla." *Annali di Architettura* 9 (1997): 149–54.

Canfora, L. *The Vanished Library: A Wonder of the Ancient World.* Berkeley, 1990.

———. *Il Viaggio di Aristea.* Bari, 1996.

Cantatore, F. "Tre nuovi documenti sui lavori per San Pietro al tempo di Paolo II." In *L'architettura della basilica di San Pietro,* ed. G. Spagnesi, 119–22. Rome, 1997.

Carboni, F., and A. Manfredi. "Verso l'edizione del *Convivium scientiarum* di Antonio de Thomeis." In *Sisto IV,* ed. Benzi, 60–73.

Cassani, A. "'Libertas, frugalitas, aedificandi libido'. Paradigmi indiziarii per Leon Battista Alberti a Roma." In *Le due Rome,* ed. Rossi and Valeri, 296–321.

Cassirer, E. *The Individual and the Cosmos in Renaissance Philosophy.* Philadelphia, 1927.

Cassuto, U. *Gli Ebrei a Firenze nell'età del Rinascimento.* Florence, 1948.

Castagnoli, F. *Topografia e urbanistica di Roma antica.* Turin, 1980.

Castelnuovo, E. "The Artist." In *The Medieval World,* ed. J. Le Goff, 211–41. London, 1990.

Cavallo, G., ed. *Le biblioteche nel mondo antico e medievale.* Bari, 1993.

Celenza, C. "Renaissance Humanism and the New Testament: Lorenzo Valla's Annotations to the Vulgate." *Journal of Medieval and Renaissance Studies* 24 (1994): 33–52.

———. "The Will of Cardinal Giordano Orsini (ob. 1438)." *Traditio* 51 (1996): 257–86.

Chattard, G. *Nuova descrizione del Vaticano*. Rome, 1762–1767.

Chazelle, C. M. "Pictures, Books, and the Illiterate: Pope Gregory I's Letters to Serenus of Marseille." *Word and Image* 6 (1990): 138–53.

Cherubini, P., A. Esposito, A. Modigliani, and P. Scarcia Piacentini. *Il costo del libro: Scrittura, biblioteche e stampa a Roma nel Quattrocento*. Vatican City, 1983.

Ciappelli, G. "Libri e letture a Firenze nel XV secolo. Le *Ricordanze* e la ricostruzione delle biblioteche private." *Rinascimento* 29 (1989): 267–91.

Ciardi Dupré, M. "Note sulla miniatura fiorentina del quattrocento in particolare su Zanobi Strozzi." *Antichità viva* 12 (1973): 3–10.

Clayton, P., and M. Price. *The Seven Wonders of the Ancient World*. London, 1988.

Cochrane, E. *Historians and Historiography in the Italian Renaissance*. Chicago, 1981.

Cole, A. *Virtue and Magnificence. Art of the Italian Renaissance Courts*. New York, 1995.

Colella, R. "The Cappella Niccolina, or Chapel of Nicholas V in the Vatican: The History and Significance of its Frescoes." In *Fra Angelico and the Chapel of Nicholas V*, ed. I. Venchi et al., 22–71. Vatican City, 1999.

———. ed., *Pratum Romanum. Richard Krautheimer zum 100. Geburtstag*. Wiesbaden, 1997.

Coluccia, G. *Niccolò V. Umanista: papa e riformatore*. Venice, 1998.

Comito, T. "Renaissance Gardens and the Discovery of Paradise." *Journal of the History of Ideas* 32 (1971): 483–506.

Constable, G. "A Living Past. The Historical Environment of the Middle Ages." *Harvard Library Bulletin* n.s. 1 (1990): 49–70.

Corbo, A. *Artisti e artigiani in Roma al tempo di Martino V e di Eugenio IV*. Rome, 1968.

———. *I mestieri nella vita quotidiana alla corte di Nicolò V (1447–1455)*. Rome, 1998.

Cornides, E. *Rose und Schwert im päpstlichen Zeremoniell: Von den Anfängen bis zum Pontifikat Gregors XIII*. Vienna, 1967.

Cornini, G. "'Dominico Thomasii florentino pro pictura bibliotecae quam inchoavit': Il Contributo di Domenico e Davide Ghirlandaio nella Biblioteca di Sisto IV." In *Sisto IV*, ed. Benzi, 224–48.

Cortassa, G. *Roma parte del cielo. Confronto tra l'Antica e la Nuova Roma di Manuele Crisolora*. Turin, 2000.

Cortesi, M., and E. Maltesi. "Ciriaco d'Ancona e il 'De Virtutibus' pseudoaristotelico." *Studi medievali* 33 (1992): 133–64.

Cosenza, M. *Biographical and Bibliographical Dictionary of the Italian Humanists and the World of Classical Scholarship in Italy, 1300–1800*. Boston, 1962.

Coudert, A. P., and J. S. Shoulson, eds. *Hebraica Veritas?: Christian Hebraists and the Study of Judaism in Early Modern Europe*. Philadelphia, 2004.

Croisille, J. "Le Sacrifice d'Iphigénie dans l'art romain et la littérature latine." *Latomus* 22 (1963): 209–25.

Crosby, A. *The Measure of Reality. Quantification and Western Society, 1250–1600*. New York, 1997.

Crowder, C. M. *Unity, Heresy and Reform, 1378–1460. The Conciliar Response to the Great Schism*. London, 1977.

Curran, B., and A. Grafton. "A Fifteenth-Century Site Report on the Vatican Obelisk." *Journal of the Warburg and Courtauld Institutes* 58 (1995): 234–48.

Cullman, O. "L'opposition contre le temple de Jérusalem, motif commun de la théologie Johannique et du monde ambient." *New Testament Studies* 5 (1958–1959): 157–73.

Curti, M. "L''Admirabile Templum' di Giannozzo Manetti alla luce di una ricognizione delle fonti documentarie." In *L'Architettura della basilica*, ed. Spagnesi, 111–18.

Da Capodimonte, C. "Poggio Bracciolini autore delle anonime 'vitae quorundam pontificum'." *Rivista di storia della Chiesa* 14 (1960): 27–47.

Dahl, E. "*Dilexi decorem Domus Dei*. Building to the Glory of God in the Middle Ages." *Acta ad archaeologiam et artium historiam pertinentia* 1 (1981): 157–90.

Dal Nero, D. "L'Insegnamento della teologia in Europa e a Ferrara." In *Rinascita del sapere. Libri e maestri dello studio ferrarese*, ed. P. Castelli, 246–63. Venice, 1991.

D'Amico, J. *Renaissance Humanism in Papal Rome*. Baltimore, 1983.

De Angelis D'Ossat, G. *La geologia del Monte Vaticano*. Vatican City, 1953.

De Blaauw, S. "The Solitary Celebration of the Supreme Pontiff: The Lateran Basilica as the New Temple in the Medieval Liturgy of Maunday Thursday." In *Omnes Circumadstantes: Contributions Towards a History of the Role of the People in the Liturgy Presented to Herman Wegman*, ed. C. Caspers and M. Schneiders, 120–43. Kampen, 1990.

———. *Cultus et Decor: Liturgia e architettura nella Roma tardoantica e medievale: Basilica Salvatoris, Sanctae Mariae, Sancti Petri*. Vatican City, 1994.

De Bruyne, E. *Etudes d'esthétique médiévale.* Bruges, 1946.

De Carlo, L., and P. Quattrini. *Le mura di Roma tra realtà e immagine. La Riscoperta del monumento 'mura' nel suo rapporto con la città dal medioevo all'età moderna.* Rome, 1995.

Dehio, G. "Die Bauprojekte Nicolaus des Fünften und L. B. Alberti." *Repertorium für Kunstwissenschaft* 3 (1880): 241–57.

Del Piano, G. *L'enigma filosofico del Tempio Malatestiano.* Bologna, 1938.

De Lubac, H. *Medieval Exegesis* 1. *The Four Senses of Scripture.* Edinburgh, 1959, repr. 1998.

———. *Pic de la Mirandole.* Paris, 1974.

De Petris, A. "Le Teorie umanistiche del tradurre e l'*Apologeticus* di Giannozzo Manetti." *Bibliothèque d'humanisme et Renaissance* 37 (1975): 15–32.

Des Places, E. "'Des temples faits de main d'homme' (Acts des Apotres XVII.24)." *Biblica* 42 (1961): 217–23.

Devreesse, R. *Le fonds grec de la Bibliothèque Vaticane des origines à Paul V.* Vatican City, 1965.

Dion, R. "Sur l'emploi des mots *ulterior*, *superior*, *inferior*, *infra* dans les passages du *De Bello Gallico* relatifs à la Bretagne et aux expéditions de César en cette île." *Latomus* 22 (1963): 191–208.

Dix, G. *The Shape of the Liturgy.* London, 1945.

D'Onofrio, C. *Gli obelischi di Roma.* Rome, 1992.

———. *Castel Sant'Angelo e Borgo.* Rome, 1978.

———. *Visitiamo Roma mille anni fa. La Città dei Mirabilia.* Rome, 1988.

Dröge, C. *Giannozzo Manetti als Denker und Hebraist.* Frankfurt, 1987.

———. "The Pope's Favorite Humanist in the Land of Reformation: On the Reception of the Works of Giannozzo Manetti in Germany and France." In *Acta Conventus Neo-Latini Barieusis*, ed. R Schnur et al., 217–24. MRTS 184. Tempe, 1998.

Duchesne, L. "Vaticana, Notes sur la topographie de Rome au Moyen Age X, XI, XII, XIII." *Ecole Française de Rome: Mélanges d'archéologie et d'histoire* 34 (1914): 307–56.

Duggan, L. "Was Art Really the 'Book of the Illiterate'?" *Word and Image* 5 (1989): 227–51.

Dunkelman, M. "A New Look at Donatello's St. Peter's Tabernacle." *Gazette des Beaux-Arts* 118 (1991): 1–16.

Dykmans, M. "Le cérémonial de Nicolas V." *Revue d'histoire ecclésiastique* 63 (1968): 780–825.

———. "D'Avignon à Rome. Martin V e le cortège apostolique." *Bulletin de l'Institut historique belge de Rome* 39 (1968): 203–308.

———. *L'Oeuvre de Patrizi Piccolomini. Ou le cérémonial papal de la première Renaissance.* Vatican City, 1980–1982

———. *Le pontifical Romain révisé au XVe siècle.* Studi e Testi 311. Vatican City, 1985.

Eco, U. *The Aesthetics of Thomas Aquinas.* Cambridge, MA, 1988.

Edgerton, S. "Florentine Interest in Ptolemaic Cartography as Background for Renaissance Painting, Architecture, and the Discovery of America." *Journal of the Society of Architectural Historians* 33 (1974): 275–92.

———. *The Renaissance Rediscovery of Linear Perspective.* New York, 1975.

Egger, H. "Quadriporticus S. Petri." *Papers of the British School in Rome* 18 (1950): 101–3.

———. "Das päpstliche Kanzleigebäude im 15. Jahrhundert." In *Festschrift zur Feier des Zweihundertjährigen Bestandes des Haus- Hof- und Staatsarchives,* 487–500. Vienna, 1951.

Ehrle, F., and H. Egger. *Der Vaticanische Palast in seiner Entwicklung bis zur Mitte des XV. Jahrhunderts.* Vatican City, 1935.

———, and H. Stevenson. *Gli Affreschi del Pinturicchio nell'Appartamento Borgia.* Rome, 1897

Eichmann, E. *Die Kaiserkrönung im Abendland. Ein Beitrag zur Geistesgeschichte des Mittelalters.* Würzburg, 1942.

Elkins, J. *The Poetics of Perspective.* Ithaca, 1994.

Ercadi, E. "La fontana del Cortile del Belvedere in Vaticano." *Monumenti, Musei e Gallerie pontifiche: Bollettino* 15 (1995): 239–55.

Ettlinger, L. "A Fifteenth-Century View of Florence." *Burlington Magazine* 94 (1952): 160–7.

Eubel, C. *Hierarchia Catholica medii aevi.* Monastir, 1914.

Fabbri, L., and M. Tacconi. *I Libri del Duomo di Firenze: Codici liturgici e Biblioteca di Santa Maria del Fiore (sec. xi–xvi).* Florence, 1997.

Fagiolo, M., and A. Giusti. *Lo Specchio del Paradiso: L'Immagine del giardino dall'antico al novecento.* Milan, 1996.

Fallows, D. *Dufay.* London, 1982.

Fanelli, M. *Labirinti: Storia, geografia e interpretazione di un simbolo millenario.* Rimini, 1997.

Fasolo, F. "San Teodoro al Palatino." *Palladio* 5 (1941): 112–19.

Favro, D. *The Urban Image of Augustan Rome*. New York, 1996.

Ferber, S. "The Temple of Solomon in Early Christian and Byzantine Art." In *The Temple of Solomon*, ed. Gutmann, 21–43.

Fernandez, H. "The Papal Court at Rome c. 1450–1700." In *The Princely Courts of Europe. Ritual, Politics and Culture under the Ancien Régime*, ed. J. Adamson, 141–64. London, 1999.

Ferri, F. *Ordini cavallereschi e decorazioni in Italia*. Modena, 1995.

Finckh, R. *'Minor mundus homo': Studien zur Mikrokosmos-Idee in der mittelalterlichen Literatur*. Göttingen, 1999.

Fioravanti, G. "L'apologetica anti-giudaica di Giannozzo Manetti." *Rinascimento* 23 (1983): 3–32.

Fleming, M. H. *The Late Medieval Pope Prophecies*. MRTS 204. Tempe, 1999.

Fossi, G. *La storia dei Giubilei*, 1: *1300–1423*; 2: *1450–1575*. Prato, 1997–1998.

Frajese, V. "Leon Battista Alberti e la *renovatio urbis* di Nicolò V. Congetture per l'interpretazione del *Momus*." *La Cultura* 36 (1998): 241–62.

Fraser Jenkins, A. "Cosimo de Medici's Patronage of Architecture and the Theory of Magnificence." *Journal of the Warburg and Courtauld Institutes* 33 (1970): 162–70.

Frommel, C. "Antonio da Sangallos Capella Paolina. Ein Beitrag zur Baugeschichte des Vatikanischen Palastes." *Zeitschrift für Kunstgeschichte* 27 (1964): 1–42.

———. "'Capella Iulia'. Die Grabkapelle Papst Julius' II. in Neu-St.Peter." *Zeitschrift für Kunstgeschichte* 40 (1977): 26–62.

———. "Francesco del Borgo: Architekt Pius' II. und Pauls' II." *Römisches Jahrbuch* 21 (1984): 71–164.

———. "Il Palazzo Vaticano sotto Giulio II e Leone X: Strutture e funzioni." In *Raffaello in Vaticano*, ed. C. Pietrangeli, 118–35. Milan, 1984.

———. "Il San Pietro di Nicolò V." In *L'Architettura della basilica*, ed. Spagnesi, 103–10.

Frutaz, A. *Il torrione di Nicolò V in Vaticano*. Vatican City, 1956.

Funiciello, R. *La geologia di Roma: Il centro storico*. Rome, 1995.

Gandi, G. *Le corporazioni dell'antica Firenze*. Florence, 1928.

Gargano, M. "Niccolò V. La mostra dell'acqua di Trevi." *Archivio della Società Romana di Storia Patria* 111 (1988): 225–66.

Garin, E. "Le traduzioni umanistiche di Aristotele nel secolo XV." *Atti dell'Accademia fiorentina di scienze morali 'La Columbaria'* 16 (1951): 55–104.

———. *Science and Civic Life in the Italian Renaissance.* Garden City, 1969.

———. *Rinascite e rivoluzioni: Movimenti culturali dal XIV al XVII secolo.* Rome, 1975.

———. *La biblioteca di San Marco.* Florence, 1999.

Garofalo, S. "Gli umanisti italiani del secolo XV e la Bibbia." *Biblica* 27 (1946): 338–75.

Gauthier, M. "La cloture émaillée de la confession de Saint Pierre au Vatican, lors du concile de Latran IV, 1215." In *Synthronon. Art et archéologie de la fin d'antiquité et du moyen age. Recueil d'études par André Grabar et un groupe de ses disciples*, 237–46. Paris, 1968.

Gentile, S., ed. *Umanesimo e padri della chiesa. Manoscritti e incunaboli di testi patristici da Francesco Petrarca al primo Cinquecento.* Milan, 1997.

Geymuller, H. *Die Ursprünglichen Entwürfe für Sankt Peter in Rom.* Vienna, 1875.

Gibson, S., and B. Ward-Perkins. "The Surviving Remains of the Leonine Wall." *Papers of the British School at Rome* 47 (1979): 30–57.

———. "The Surviving Remains of the Leonine Wall: Part II. The Passetto." *Papers of the British School at Rome* 51 (1983): 222–39.

Gilbert, C. "The Earliest Guide to Florentine Architecture, 1423." *Mitteilungen des Kunsthistorischen Instituts in Florenz* 40 (1969): 33–46.

———. "Fra Angelico's Fresco Cycles in Rome: Their Number and Dates." *Zeitschrift für Kunstgeschichte* 38 (1975): 245–65.

Gill, M. "'Una simile cosa': Alberti and Harmony in the Roman Facade." In *Pratum Romanum*, ed. Colella, 113–30.

Giuntella, A. "Spazio cristiano e città altomedievale: L'esempio della *civitas* leonina." In *Atti del VI congresso nazionale di archeologia cristiana*, 309–25. Florence, 1985.

Glaap, O. *Untersuchungen zu Giannozzo Manetti 'De Dignitate et excellentia hominis'. Ein Renaissance-Humanist und sein Menschenbild.* Stuttgart, 1994.

Goldbrunner, H. "'Quemcumque elegerit dominus, ipse sanctus erit.' Zur Leichenrede des Jean Jouffroy auf Nikolaus V." *Quellen und Forschungen aus italienischen Archiven* 64 (1984): 385–96.

Goldthwaite, R. *Wealth and the Demand for Art in Italy 1300–1600.* Baltimore, 1993.

Gombrich, E. "The Early Medici as Patrons of Art." In idem, *Norm and Form. Studies in the Art of the Renaissance*, 35–57. London, 1966.

Gordon, P. *Two Renaissance Book Hunters. The Letters of Poggius Bracciolini to Nicholaus de Niccolis*. New York, 1974.

Gow, A. *The Red Jews: Antisemitism in an Apocalyptic Age 1200–1600*. Leiden, 1995.

Grafton, A. *Leon Battista Alberti: Master Builder of the Italian Renaissance*. New York, 2000.

———, ed. *Rome Reborn: The Vatican Library and Renaissance Culture*. Washington, DC, 1993.

Grant, E. "Place and Space in Medieval Physical Thought," In *Motion and Time, Space and Matter*, ed. P. Machamer and R. Turnbull, 137–67. Columbus, 1976.

———, *Much Ado About Nothing: Theories of Space and Vacuum from the Middle Ages to the Scientific Revolution*. London, 1981.

Grayson, C. "Leon Battista Alberti: vita e opere." In *Leon Battista Alberti*, ed. Rykwert and Engel, 28–37.

Greco, A. *La Cappella di Niccolò V del Beato Angelico*. Rome, 1980.

———. "Giannozzo Manetti nella biografia di un contemporaneo." *Res publica litterarum* 6 (1983): 155–70.

Green, L. "Galvano Fiamma, Azzone Visconti and the Revival of the Classical Theory of Magnificence." *Journal of the Warburg and Courtauld Institutes* 53 (1990): 98–113.

Gregory, H. "Palla Strozzi's Patronage and Pre-Medicean Florence." In *Patronage, Art and Society in Renaissance Italy*, ed. F. W. Kent and P. Simons, 201–20. Oxford, 1987.

Grendler, P. *Schooling in Renaissance Italy. Literacy and Learning, 1300–1600*. Baltimore, 1989.

Grimaldi, G. *Descrizione della basilica antica di S. Pietro in Vaticano*, ed. R. Niggl. Vatican City, 1972.

Grisar, H. *Roma alla fine del mondo antico*. Rome, 1943.

Günther, H. "I Progetti di ricostruzione della basilica di S. Pietro negli scritti contemporanei: giustificazioni e scrupoli." In *L'Architettura della basilica*, ed. Spagnesi, 137–48.

Gurrieri, F. *The Cathedral of Santa Maria del Fiore*. Florence, 1994.

Gutmann, J., ed. *The Temple of Solomon*. Ann Arbor, 1973.

Hack, A. *Das Empfangszeremoniell bei mittelalterlichen Papst-Kaiser-Treffen.* Cologne, 1999.

Haines, M. "Gli anni della Cupola. Una bancadati testuale della documentazione dell'Opera di Santa Maria del Fiore." In *Atti del VII centenario del Duomo di Firenze*, ed. T. Verdon and A. Innocenti, 693–736. Florence, 2001.

Hale, J. R. "The Early Development of the Bastion: An Italian Chronology c. 1450–c.1534." In *Europe in the Late Middle Ages*, ed. idem et al., 466–94. London, 1965.

Hartt, F. "'Lucerna ardens et lucens.' Il significato della Porta del Paradiso." In *Lorenzo Ghiberti nel suo tempo*, 1:27–57. Florence, 1980.

Hausherr, R. "Templum Salomonis und Ecclesia Christi: Zu einem Bildvergleich der Bible moralisée." *Zeitschrift für Kunstgeschichte* 31 (1968): 101–21.

———. *Bible moralisée: Faksimile-Ausgabe im Original-Format des Codex Vindobonensis 2554 der Österreichischen Nationalbibliothek.* Graz, 1973.

Heinz-Mohr, G. *Unitas christiana.* Trier, 1958.

Herald, J. *Renaissance Dress in Italy 1400–1500.* London, 1981.

Hill, G. "The Medals of Paul II." *Numismatic Chronicle* 10 (1910): 340–69.

Hoeniger, C. "Cloth of Gold and Silver: Simone Martini's Techniques for Representing Luxury Textiles." *Gesta* 30 (1991): 154–62.

Hoffman, W. von. *Forschungen zur Geschichte der Kurialen Behörden vom Schisma bis zur Reformation.* Rome, 1914.

Holliday, P. "Roman Triumphal Painting: Its Function, Development, and Reception." *Art Bulletin* 79 (1997): 130–47.

Hope, C. "The Early History of the Tempio Malatestiano." *Journal of the Warburg and Courtauld Institutes* 55 (1992): 51–154.

Howard, P. *Beyond the Written Word: Preaching and Theology in the Florence of Archbishop Antoninus 1427–1459.* Florence, 1995.

Howe, E. "Alexander VI, Pinturicchio and the Fabrication of the Via Alessandrina in the Vatican Borgo." In *Studies in Architectural History Presented to Helmut Hager*, ed. H. Millon and S. S. Munshower, 65–93. College Park, 1992.

Izbicki, T. *Protector of the Faith. Cardinal Johannes de Turrecremata and the Defense of the Institutional Church.* Washington, DC, 1981.

Jacks, P. *The Antiquarian and the Myth of Antiquity. The Origins of Rome in Renaissance Thought.* New York, 1993.

Jammer, M. *Concepts of Space.* Cambridge, MA, 1954.

Jenkins, L. "Pius II and his Loggia in Siena." In *Pratum Romanum*, ed. Colella, 198–214.

Jones, R. "Palla Strozzi e la sagrestia di Santa Trinità." *Rivista d'arte* 37 (1984): 9–106.

Jung, J. "Beyond the Barrier: The Unifying Role of the Choir Screen in Gothic Churches." *Art Bulletin* 82 (2000): 622–57.

Jungmann, J. *The Mass of the Roman Rite. Its Origins and Development*. New York, 1951.

Kaufmann, D. "A Rumour about the Ten Tribes in Pope Martin V's Time." *Jewish Quarterly Review* 4 (1892): 503–8.

Kempers, B., and S. De Blaauw. "Jacopo Stefaneschi, Patron and Liturgist. A New Hypothesis Regarding the Date, Iconography, Authorship, and Function of His Altarpiece for Old St. Peter's." *Mededelingen van het Nederlands Institut te Rome* 47 (1987): 83–113.

Kempshall, M. *The Common Good in Late Medieval Political Thought*. New York, 1999.

Kendall, C. *The Allegory of the Church*. Toronto, 1998.

Kennedy, G. *Classical Rhetoric and its Christian and Secular Tradition from Ancient to Modern Times*. Chapel Hill, 1980.

Kent, B. *Virtues of the Will: The Transformation of Ethics in the Late Thirteenth Century*. Washington, DC, 1995.

Kent, D. *Cosimo de'Medici and the Florentine Renaissance*. New Haven, 2000.

Kerscher, G. "Privatraum und Zeremoniell im spätmittelalterlichen Papst-und Königspalast. (Zu den Montefiascone Darstellungen von Carlo Fontana und einem Grundriss des Papstpalastes von Avignon)." *Römisches Jahrbuch der Biblioteca Hertziana* 26 (1990): 87–134.

King, R. *Brunelleschi's Dome*. London, 2000.

Kirsch, J. *Die Rückkehr der Päpste Urban V. und Gregor XI. von Avignon nach Rom*. Paderborn, 1898.

———. *Die Stationskirchen des Missale Romanum*. Freiburg im Breisgau, 1926.

Klauser, T. *A Short History of the Western Liturgy*. London, 1969.

Klijn, A. "Stephen's Speech—Acts 7, 2–55." *New Testament Studies* 4 (1957–1958): 25–31.

Kokole, S. "*Cognitio formarum* and Agostino di Duccio's Reliefs for the Chapel of the Planets in the Tempio Malatestiano." In *Quattrocento adriatico: Fifteenth-Century Art of the Adriatic Rim*, ed. C. Dempsey, 177–206. Bologna, 1996.

Krautheimer, R. "S. Pietro in Vincoli and the Tripartite Transept in the Early Christian Basilicas." *Proceedings of the American Philosophical Society* 83.3 (1941).

———. *Lorenzo Ghiberti*. Princeton, 1956.

———. "Fra Angelico and — perhaps — Alberti." In *Studies in Late Medieval and Renaissance Painting in Honor of Millard Meiss*, ed. I. Lavin and J. Plummer, 290–96. New York, 1977.

Krey, P., and L. Smith. *Nicholas of Lyra. The Senses of Scripture*. Leiden, 2000.

Krinsky, C. "Representations of the Temple of Jerusalem Before 1500." *Journal of the Warburg and Courtauld Institutes* 33 (1970): 1–19.

Kristeller, P. O. "Humanism and Scholasticism in the Italian Renaissance." *Byzantion* 17 (1944–1945): 346–74.

———. *Renaissance Thought II. Papers on Humanism and the Arts*. New York, 1965.

———. "Augustine and the Early Renaissance." In idem, *Studies in Renaissance Thought and Letters*, 355–72. Rome, 1969.

———. "Thomism and the Italian Thought of the Renaissance." In *Medieval Aspects of Renaissance Learning*, ed. E. Mahoney, 29–94. Durham, 1974.

———. *Renaissance Thought and its Sources*. New York, 1979.

Kruft, H. *A History of Architectural Theory from Vitruvius to the Present*. Princeton, 1985; repr. 1994.

Kuntz, M. "Antonio da Sangallo the Younger's Scala del Maresciallo: A Ceremonial Entrance to the Vatican Palace." In *Pratum Romanum*, ed. Colella, 233–45.

———. "Designed for Ceremony. The Cappella Paolina at the Vatican Palace." *Journal of the Society of Architectural Historians* 62 (2003): 228–55.

Lanciani, R. *Storia delle scavi di Roma e notizie intorno le collezioni romane di antichità*, vol. 1 *(1000–1530)*. Rome, 1989.

Lee, E. "Humanists and the 'Studium urbis', 1473–1484." In *Umanesimo a Roma nel Quattrocento*, ed. P. Brezzi and M. De Panizza Lorch, 127–46. Rome, 1984.

Lepik, A. *Das Architekturmodell in Italien 1335–1550*. Worms, 1994.

Letarouilly, P. *Le Vatican et la Basilique de Saint-Pierre de Rome*. Paris, 1882.

Lindberg, D. *Theories of Vision from al-Kindi to Kepler*. Chicago, 1976.

———. *Roger Bacon and the Origins of "Perspectiva" in the Middle Ages*. New York, 1996.

Loerke, W. "'Real Presence' in Early Christian Art." In *Monasticism and the Arts*, ed. T. Verdon, 29–52. Syracuse, NY, 1984.

Lombardi, G. "'Son qui più libri che'n tucto passato'. Aspetti del libro a corte nella Roma del Quattrocento." In *Il libro a corte*, ed. A. Quondam, 39–55. Rome, 1994.

———, and F. Onofri. "La Biblioteca di Giordano Orsini (c. 1360–1438)." In *Scrittura, biblioteche e stampa*, ed. Bianca et al., 371–82.

MacDougall, E. Review of T. Magnuson, *Studies in Roman Quattrocento Architecture. Art Bulletin* 44 (1962): 67–75.

Mack, C. "Bernardo Rossellino, L. B. Alberti and the Rome of Pope Nicholas V." *Southeastern College Art Conference Review* 10 (1982): 60–69.

———. "Nicholas the Fifth and the Rebuilding of Rome: Reality and Legacy." In *Light on the Eternal City: Recent Observations and Discoveries in Roman Art and Architecture*, ed. H. Hager and S. Munshower, 31–56. University Park, 1987.

———. "The Bath Palace of Pope Nicholas V at Viterbo." In *Studies in Architectural History Presented to Helmut Hager*, ed. Millon and Munshower, 45–63.

Maddalo, S. *Appunti per una ricerca iconografica: L'Immagine di Roma nei manoscritti tardomedievali*. Udine, 1987.

———. "I prototipi delle vedute di Roma: Dal maestro del Vat. Lat. 2224 ad Etienne Dupérac." In *Miscellanea Bibliothecae Apostolicae Vaticanae*, 153–86. Studi e Testi 331. Vatican City, 1988.

———. *In Figura Romae. Immagini di Roma nel libro medioevale*. Rome, 1990.

Magnuson, T. "The Project of Nicholas V for Rebuilding the Borgo Leonino in Rome." *Art Bulletin* 36 (1954): 89–116.

———. *Studies in Roman Quattrocento Architecture*. Rome, 1958.

Maltese, C. "Fouquet e Filarete: Un momento della tecnologia dell'imagine nel primo Quattrocento a Roma." In *Roma, centro ideale della cultura dell'antico nei secoli XV e XVI*, ed. S. D. Squarzina, 202–9. Milan, 1989.

Manfredi, A. *I codici latini di Niccolò V: Edizione degli inventari e identificazione dei manoscritti*. Studi e Testi 359. Vatican City, 1994.

———. "Da Avignone a Roma. Codici liturgici per la capella papale." In *Liturgia in Figura. Codici liturgici rinascimentali della Biblioteca Apostolica Vaticana*, ed. G. Morello and S. Maddalo, 51–58. Vatican City, 1994.

Mantini, S. *Lo spazio sacro della Firenze medicea: Trasformazioni urbane e cerimoniali pubblici tra Quattrocento e Cinquecento*. Florence, 1995.

Marder, T. *Bernini's Scala Regia at the Vatican Palace. Architecture, Sculpture and Ritual*. Cambridge, 1997.

Marsh, D. *Lucian and the Latins: Humor and Humanism in the Early Renaissance*. Ann Arbor, 1998.

———. "Alberti's *Momus*: Sources and Contexts." In *Acta Conventus Neo-Latini Hafniensis*, ed. R. Schnur et al., 619–32. MRTS 120. Binghamton, 1994.

Marta, R. *L'architettura del rinascimento a Roma (1417–1503): Tecniche e tipologie*. Rome, 1995.

Martines, L. *The Social World of the Florentine Humanists*. Princeton, 1963.

Martl, C. *Kardinal Jean Jouffroy (d. 1473). Leben und Werk.* Sigmaringen, 1996.

Martorelli, L. *Storia del clero vaticano.* Rome, 1792.

Mazza, A. "L' inventario della 'parva libraria' di Santo Spirito e la biblioteca del Boccaccio." *Italia medioevale ed umanistica* 9 (1966): 1–74.

McClung, W. *The Architecture of Paradise: Survivals of Eden and Jerusalem.* Berkeley, 1983.

McGee, T. "Dinner Music for the Florentine Signoria, 1350–1450." *Speculum* 74 (1999): 95–114.

McGinn, B. "Angel Pope and Papal Antichrist." *Church History* 47 (1978): 155–73.

McKelvey, R. *The New Temple. The Church in the New Testament.* Oxford, 1969.

McManamon, J. "The Ideal Renaissance Pope: Funeral Oratory from the Papal Court." *Archivum Historiae Pontificiae* 14 (1976): 9–70.

———. *Funeral Oratory and the Cultural Ideals of Italian Humanism.* Chapel Hill, 1989.

Meyboom, P. *The Nile Mosaic of Palestrina: Early Evidence of Egyptian Religion in Italy.* Leiden, 1995.

Miglio, M. "Una vocazione in progresso: Michele Canensi, biografo papale." *Studi medievali* 10 (1971): 463–524.

———. *Storiografia pontificia del Quattrocento.* Bologna, 1975.

———. "Immagini di Roma: Babilonia, Gerusalemme, 'cadaver miserabilis urbis'." In *Cultura e società nell'Italia medievale. Studi per Paolo Brezzi*, 509–19. Rome, 1988.

———. "Niccolò V umanista di Cristo." In *Umanesimo a Roma*, ed. Gentile, 77–84.

———. "L'immagine del principe e l'immagine della città." In *Principi e città alla fine del medioevo*, ed. S. Gensini, 315–32. Rome, 1996.

———. "Raccontano le cronache. Curia, corte e municipio." In *Le due Rome*, ed. Rossi and Valeri, 161–71.

Mignanti, F. *Istoria della sacrosancta patriarcale Basilica Vaticana dalla sua fondazione fino al presente.* Rome, 1876.

Miller, M. *The Bishop's Palace: Architecture and Authority in Medieval Italy.* Ithaca, 2000.

Millet, H. *Il libro delle immagini dei papi. Storia di un testo profetico medievale.* Rome, 2002.

Millon, H. "An Early Seventeenth-Century Drawing of Piazza San Pietro." *Art Quarterly* 25 (1962): 229–41.

———. "Da Nicolò V a Giulio II, da Bernardo Rossellino a Donato Bramante: Timori per l'antica basilica e progetti per la nuova." In *San Pietro. Antonio da Sangallo. Antonio Labacco*, ed. P. L. Silvan, 11–13. Milan, 1994.

———, and S. S. Munshower, eds. *An Architectural Progress in the Renaissance and Baroque*. University Park, 1992.

Mitchell, B. *Italian Civic Pageantry in the High Renaissance. A Descriptive Bibliography of Triumphal Entries and Selected Other Festivals for State Occasions*. Florence, 1979.

Mitrovic, B. "Leon Battista Alberti and the Homogeneity of Space." *Journal of the Society of Architectural Historians*. 63 (2004): 425–39.

Mode, R. "The Orsini 'sala theatri' at Monte Giordano in Rome." *Renaissance Quarterly* 24 (1973): 167–72.

Modigliani, A. *Mercati, botteghe e spazi di commercio a Roma tra medioevo ed età moderna*. Rome, 1998.

Moneti, A. "La grande via colonnata a Roma: Ipotesi sul progetto irrealizzato dell'imperatore Gallieno." *Palladio* 21 (1998): 5–12.

Monfasani, J. *George of Trebizond. A Biography and a Study of his Rhetoric and Logic*. Leiden, 1976.

———. "The Fraticelli and Clerical Wealth in Quattrocento Rome." In *Renaissance Society and Culture. Essays in Honor of Eugene Rice, Jr.*, ed. idem and R. Musto, 177–96. New York, 1991.

———. "A Theologian at the Roman Curia in the Mid-Quattrocento. A Bio-bibliographical Study of Niccolò Palmieri." *Analecta Augustiniana* 54 (1991): 321–81; 55 (1992): 5–98.

Mormando, F. *The Preacher's Demons. Bernardino of Siena and the Social Underworld of Early Renaissance Italy*. Chicago, 1999.

Morolli, G. "Brunelleschi e l'arredo umanistico di Santa Maria del Fiore." In *Filippo Brunelleschi: La sua opera e il suo tempo*, 2: 603–23. Florence, 1980.

Moroni, G. *Le cappelle pontificie cardinalizie e prelatizie*. Venice, 1841.

Müntz, E. *Les arts à la cour des papes pendant le XVe et le XVIe siècle*. Paris, 1878.

———, and A. Frothingham. "Il tesoro della basilica di S.Pietro in Vaticano dal XIII al XV secolo, con una scelta di inventari inediti." *Archivio della Società Romana di Storia Patria*. 6 (1883): 1–137.

———, and P. Fabre. *La Bibliothèque du Vatican au XVe siècle*. Paris, 1887.

Nabuco, J. *Le cérémonial Apostolique avant Innocent VIII. Texte du manuscrit Urbinate latin 469 de la Bibliothèque Vaticane*. Rome, 1966.

Nevola, F. "'Per ornato della città': Siena's Strada Romana and Fifteenth-Century Urban Renewal." *Art Bulletin* 82 (2000): 26–50.

O'Malley, J. "Some Renaissance Panegyrics of Aquinas." *Renaissance Quarterly* 27 (1974): 174–92.

———. *Praise and Blame in Renaissance Rome. Rhetoric, Doctrine, and Reform in the Sacred Orators at the Papal Court c.1450–1521.* Durham, NC, 1979.

———. "The Feast of Thomas Aquinas in Renaissance Rome: A Neglected Document and its Import." *Rivista di storia della Chiesa in Italia* 35 (1981): 1–27.

Onofri, L. "Sacralità, immagine e proposte politiche: La *Vita* di Niccolò V di Giannozzo Manetti." *Humanistica Lovaniensia* 28 (1979): 27–77.

———. "'Sicut fremitus leonis ita et regis ira': Temi neoplatonici e culto solare nell'orazione funebre per Niccolò V di Jean Jouffroy." *Humanistica Lovaniensia* 31 (1982): 1–28.

Pagliara, P. "La Roma antica di Fabio Calvi. Note sulla cultura antiquaria e architettonica." *Psicon* 8–9 (1976): 65–88.

———. "Nuovi documenti sulla costruzione della Cappella Sistina." In *La Cappella Sistina. La volta restaurata: Il trionfo del colore*, ed. P. De Vecchi, 256–65. Novara, 1992.

Pagnotti, F. "La Vita di Nicolò V scritta da Giannozzo Manetti. Studio preparatorio alla nuova edizione critica." *Archivio della R. Società Romana di Storia Patria* 14 (1891): 411–36.

Panizza, L. "Pico della Mirandola e il 'De genere dicendi philosophorum' del 1485. L'Encomio paradossale dei 'barbari' e la loro parodia." *I Tatti Studies* 8 (1999): 69–103.

Panofsky, E. *Renaissance and Renascences in Western Art.* New York, 1969.

Panvinio, O. *De rebus antiquis memoratu dignis basilicae S. Petri in Vaticano.* In *Spicilegium romanum*, ed. A. Mai, 9:192–382. 10 vol. Rome, 1839.

Paolozzi Strozzi, B. *Il parato di Niccolò V per il Giubileo del 1450.* Florence, 2000.

Paravicini Bagliani, A. *Il trono di Pietro: L'universalità del papato da Alessandro III a Bonifacio VIII.* Rome, 1996.

———. *Le chiave e la tiara. Immagini e simboli del papato medievale.* Rome, 1998.

———. *The Pope's Body*, Chicago, 1994; repr. 2000.

Parsons, E. *The Alexandrian Library.* New York, 1952.

Partner, P. *The Papal State under Martin V. Administration and Government of the Temporal Power in the Early Fifteenth Century.* London, 1958.

———. *Renaissance Rome 1500–1559.* Berkeley, 1976.

———. *The Pope's Men: The Papal Civil Service in the Renaissance.* Oxford, 1990.

Partridge, L., and R. Starn. "Triumphalism and the Sala Regia in the Vatican." In *'All the World's a Stage.' Art and Pageantry in the Renaissance and Baroque*, ed. B. Wisch and S. Munshower, 22–82. University Park, 1990.

Paschini, P. "Banchi e botteghe dinanzi alla Basilica Vaticana nei secoli XIV, XV, e XVI." *Archivi* 18 (1951): 81–23

Pastor, L. von. *A History of the Popes*. 40 vols. London, 1891.

Pellecchia, L. "Architects Read Vitruvius: Renaissance Interpretations of the Atrium of the Ancient House." *Journal of the Society of Architectural Historians* 51 (1992): 377–416.

Pelletier, A. *Flavius Josèphe adaptateur de la Lettre de Aristée. Une réaction Atticisante contre la koiné*. Paris, 1962.

Pertusi, A. "Il ritorno alle fonti del teatro greco classico: Euripide nell'Umanesimo e nel Rinascimento." *Byzantion* 33 (1963): 391–426.

Peti, P. *Il parato di Niccolò V.* Florence, 1981.

Picard, J. "Le quadriportique de Saint Pierre." *Mélanges de l'Ecole Française de Rome. Antiquité* 86 (1974): 851–90.

Piccolomini, E. "Notize intorno al canone bibliografico di Niccolò V." *Archivio storico italiano* 21 (1876): 207–17.

Pietrangeli, C. *La Basilica di San Pietro*. Florence, 1989.

———. *Il Palazzo Apostolico Vaticano*. Florence, 1992.

Pinelli, A. "Feste e trionfi: Continuità e metamorfosi di un tema." In *Memoria dell'antico nell'arte italiana*, ed. S. Settis, 2:281–349. Turin, 1985.

Plommer, H. *Vitruvius and Later Roman Building Manuals*. Cambridge, 1973.

Pope-Hennessy, J. *Fra Angelico*. London, 1974.

Prandi, A. "La tomba di San Pietro nei pellegrinaggi dell'età medievale." In *Pellegrinaggi e culto dei santi in Europa fino alla prima crociata* (= Convegno del Centro di Studi sulla Spiritualità medievale), 4: 285–447. Todi, 1963.

Prodi, P. *The Papal Prince. One Body and Two Souls: The Papal Monarchy in Early Modern Europe*. Cambridge, 1987.

Quinterio, F. "Santo Stefano al Celio e la riconsiderazione del 'tempio d'idoli' nella Roma di Niccolò V." In *Roma, centro ideale*, ed. Squarzina, 269–79.

Radke, G. "Form and Function in Thirteenth-Century Papal Palaces." In *Architecture et vie sociale à la Renaissance*, ed. A. Chastel and J. Guillaume, 11–24. Paris, 1994.

———. *Viterbo: Profile of a Thirteenth Century Papal Palace*. New York, 1996.

Redig de Campos, D. "Di alcune tracce del palazzo di Niccolò III." *Rendiconti della Pontificia Accademia di Archeologia* 18 (1941–1942): 71–84.

———. "Les constructions d'Innocent III et de Nicholas III sur la colline vaticane." *Ecole Française de Rome: Mélanges d'archéologie et d'histoire* 71 (1959): 359–76.

———. *I Palazzi Vaticani*. Bologna, 1967.

———. "Testimonianze del primo nucleo edilizio de'palazzi Vaticani e restauro delle pitture delle stanze della 'Bibliotheca Latina' e della 'Bibliotheca Graeca'." In *Il Restauro delle aule Niccolò V e di Sisto IV nel Palazzo Apostolico Vaticano*, n.p. Vatican City, 1967.

———. "Bramante e il Palazzo Apostolico Vaticano." *Pontificia Accademia Romana di Archeologia. Rendiconti* 43 (1970–1971): 283–99.

Reekmans, L. "Le développement topographique de la région du Vatican à la fin de l'antiquité et au début du Moyen-Age (300–850)." In *Mélanges d'archéologie et d'histoire de l'art offerts au Prof. Jacques Lavalleye*, 197–235. Louvain, 1970.

Réfice, P. "'Habitatio Sancti Petri': Glosse ad alcune fonti su S. Martino in Vaticano." *Arte medievale* 4 (1990): 13–16.

Reynolds, C. *Papal Patronage and the Music of St. Peter's, 1380–1513*. Berkeley, 1995.

Richardson, L., jr. *A New Topographical Dictionary of Ancient Rome*. Baltimore, 1992.

Rinaldi, R. "Parodia come allegoria. Il 'Momus' di Alberti e la parodia classica." *Atti e memorie. Arcadia. Accademia Letteraria italiana* 8 (1986–1987): 129–65.

Rizzo, S. *Il lessico filologico degli umanisti*. Rome, 1973 .

———. "Per una tipologia delle tradizioni manoscritte di classici latini in età umanistica." In *Formative Stages of Classical Tradition: Latin Texts from Antiquity to the Renaissance*, ed. M. D. Reeve and O. Pecere, 371–407. Spoleto, 1995.

Rocchi Coopmans de Yoldi, G. "La fabbrica di San Pietro da Niccolò V a Urbano VIII." In *San Pietro. Arte e storia nella basilica vaticana*, ed. idem, 71–167. Bergamo, 1996.

Rolfi, G. "Giovanni Vitelleschi, Arcivescovo di Firenze. La sua azione militare all'epoca del concilio." In *Firenze e il Concilio del 1439*, ed. Viti, 121–46.

Ronen, A. "Iscrizione ebraiche nell'arte italiana del Quattrocento." In *Studi de storia dell'arte sul Medioevo e il Rinascimento nel centenario della nascita di Mario Salmi*, 601–24. Florence, 1992.

Rose, P., and S. Drake. "Humanist Culture and Renaissance Mathematics: The Italian Libraries of the Quattrocento." *Studies in the Renaissance* 20 (1973): 46–105.

Rossi, S., and S. Valeri, eds. *Le due Rome del Quattrocento: Melozzo, Antoniazzo e la cultura artistica del '400 romano*. Rome, 1997.

Rubenstein, N. *Florentine Government under the Medici, 1434–1494*. Oxford, 1966.

Rubin, M. *Corpus Christi*. Cambridge, 1991.

Rubinstein, R. "Pius II's Piazza S. Pietro and St. Andrew's Head." In *Enea Silvio Piccolomini. Papa Pio II*, ed. D. Maffei, 221–44. Siena, 1968.

———. "Pius II and the Roman Ruins." *Renaissance Studies* 2 (1988): 197–203.

Rummel, E. *The Humanist-Scholastic Debate in the Renaissance and Reformation*. Cambridge, MA, 1995.

Rykwert, J. *The Dancing Column: On the Orders of Architecture*. Cambridge, 1996.

———, and A. Engel, eds. *Leon Battista Alberti*. Milan, 1994.

Saalman, H. "Santa Maria del Fiore, 1294–1418." *Art Bulletin* 46 (1964): 471–500.

———. *Filippo Brunelleschi: The Cupola of Santa Maria del Fiore*. London, 1980.

Salmi, E. "Gasparo Contarini alla Dieta di Ratisbona." *Nuovo archivio veneto* 13 (1907): 5–33.

Salvemini, G. *La dignità cavalleresca nel comune di Firenze*. Florence, 1896.

Salzberger, G. *Salomons Tempelbau und Thron in der semitischen Sagenliteratur*. Berlin, 1912.

Saperstein, M. *Jewish Preaching 1200–1800. An Anthology*. New Haven, 1989.

Sassi, R. *Documenti sul soggiorno a Fabriano di Nicolò V e della sua corte nel 1449 e nel 1450*. Ancona, 1955.

Satzinger, G. "Nikolaus V., Nikolaus Muffel und Bramante: Monumentale Triumphbogensäulen in Alt-St. Peter." *Römisches Jahrbuch der Biblioteca Hertziana* 31 (1996): 92–105.

Saxer, V. "Trois manuscrits liturgiques de l'Archivio di S. Pietro, dont deux datés aux armes du Cardinal Jordan Orsini." *Rivista di storia della Chiesa in Italia* 27 (1973): 501–5.

Scaglia, G. "The Origin of an Archeological Plan by Alessandro Strozzi." *Journal of the Warburg and Courtauld Institutes* 27 (1964): 137–59.

Scapecchi, P. "*Victoris imago*. Problemi relativi al Tempio Malatestiano." *Arte cristiana* 714 (1986): 155–64.

Scheller, R. *Exemplum: Model-Book Drawings and the Practice of Artistic Transmission in the Middle Ages (ca. 900–ca.1470)*. Amsterdam, 1995.

Schimmelpfennig, B. *Die Zeremonienbücher der römischen Kirche im Mittelalter*. Tübingen, 1973.

———. "*Ad maiorem pape gloriam*. La fonction des pièces dans le palais des Papes d'Avignon." In *Architecture et vie sociale à la Renaissance*, ed. Chastel and Guillaume, 25–46.

———, "Der Einfluss des avignonischen Zeremoniells auf den Vatikanpalast seit Nikolaus V." In *Functions and Decorations*, ed. Weddigen, De Blaauw, and Kempers, 41–45.

Scholz, R. "Eine humanistische Schilderung der Kurie aus dem Jahre 1438." *Quellen und Forschungen aus Italienischen Archiven und Bibliotheken* 14 (1894): 108–53.

Schreckenberg, H. *Die Christlichen Adversus-Judaeos-Texte und ihr literarisches und historisches Umfeld (13.–20. Jh.)*. Frankfurt, 1994.

Schröter, E. "Der Vatican als Hügel Apollons und der Musen. Kunst und Panegyrik von Nikolaus V. bis Julius II." *Römische Quartalschrift*. 75 (1980): 208–40.

Schuler, S. *Vitruv im Mittelalter. Die Rezeption von 'De Architectura' von der Antike bis in die frühe Neuzeit*. Cologne, 1999.

Schulz, J. "Jacopo de'Barbari's View of Venice: Map Making, City Views, and Moralized Geography before the Year 1500." *Art Bulletin* 60 (1978): 425–74.

Scudieri, M., and G. Rosario, eds. *La biblioteca di Michelozzo a San Marco tra recupero e scoperta*. Prato, 2000.

Seay, A. "The 15th-Century Cappella of Santa Maria del Fiore in Florence." *Journal of the American Musicological Society* 11 (1958): 45–55.

Seigel, J. *Rhetoric and Philosophy in Renaissance Humanism*. Princeton, 1968.

Sensi, M. "Niccolò Tignosi da Foligno: L'opera e il pensiero." *Annali della Facoltà di Lettere e Filosofia, Università degli Studi di Perugia* 9 (1971–1972): 359–495.

Sforza, G. *La patria, la famiglia e la giovinezza di Papa Niccolò Quinto*. Lucca, 1884.

Shearman, J. *Raphael's Cartoons in the Collection of Her Majesty the Queen and the Tapestries for the Sistine Chapel*. London, 1972.

Shepherd, R. "Giovanni Sabadino degli Arienti and a Practical Definition of Magnificence in the Context of Renaissance Art." In *Concepts of Beauty in Renaissance Art*, ed. F. Ames Lewis and M. Rogers, 52–65. Burlington, 1998.

Simon, M. "St. Stephen and the Jerusalem Temple." *Journal of Ecclesiastical History* 2 (1951): 127–42.

Simoncini, S. "Roma come Gerusalemme nel Giubileo del 1450. La *renovatio* di Niccolò V e il *Momus* di Leon Battista Alberti." In *Le due Rome*, ed. Rossi and Valeri, 322–45.

Simonetti, M. "Alle origini di una dialettica culturale: I padri della Chiesa e i classici." In *Umanesimo a Roma*, ed. Gentile, 7–20.

Sladek, E. "I progetti per la sagrestia di San Pietro presentati da Francesco Borromini e Francesco Maria Febei ad Alessandro VII Chigi." *Annali di architettura* 7 (1995): 147–58.

Smalley, B. *The Study of the Bible in the Middle Ages*. Notre Dame, 1978.

Smit, H. "Image Building Through Woven Images. The Tapestry Collection of the Papal Court, 1447–1471." In *The Power of Imagery. Essays on Rome, Italy and Imagination*, ed. P. Van Kessel, 19–30, 257–64. Rome, 1992.

Smith, C. "Pope Damasus' Baptistery in St. Peter's Reconsidered." *Rivista di archeologia cristiana* 64 (1988): 257–86.

———. *Architecture in the Culture of Early Humanism. Ethics, Aesthetics and Eloquence 1400–1470*. New York, 1992.

———. "Leon Battista Alberti e l'ornamento: rivestimento parietali e pavimentazioni." In *Leon Battista Alberti*, ed. Rykwert and Engel, 196–215.

———. *Before and After the End of Time: Architecture and the Year 1000*. New York, 2000.

———. "The Apocalypse Sent Up: A Parody of the Papacy by Leon Battista Alberti." *Modern Language Notes* 119 (2004): 162-77.

Smith, G. "Gaetano Baccani's 'Systematization' of the Piazza del Duomo in Florence." *Journal of the Society of Architectural Historians* 59 (2000): 454–77.

Sorabji,R. ed. *Philoponus and the Rejection of Aristotelian Science*. London, 1987.

Souffrin, P. "La geometria practica dans les *Ludi rerum mathematicarum*." *Albertiana* 1 (1998): 87–104.

Spagnesi, G., ed. *L'architettura della basilica di San Pietro: Storia e costruzione*. Rome, 1997.

Spilner, P. "Giovanni di Lapo Ghini and a Magnificent New Addition to the Palazzo Vecchio, Florence." *Journal of the Society of Architectural Historians* 52 (1993): 453–65.

Squarzina, S. Danesi, ed. *Roma, centro ideale della cultura dell'Antico nei secoli XV e XVI. Da Martino V al Sacco di Roma*. Milan, 1989.

———. "La basilica nel Quattrocento." In *La Basilica di San Pietro*, ed. Pietrangeli, 91–113.

Steinke, K. *Die mittelalterlichen Vaticanpaläste und ihre Kapellen: Baugeschichtliche Untersuchung anhand der schriftlichen Quellen*. Vatican City, 1984.

Stieber, J. *Pope Eugenius IV, the Council of Basel, and the Secular and Ecclesiastical Authorities in the Empire: The Conflict over Supreme Authority and Power in the Church*. Leiden, 1978.

Stevenson, H. "Di una pianta di Roma dipinta da Taddeo di Bartolo nella cappella interno del Palazzo del Comune di Siena (1413–1414)." *Bollettino della Commissione archeologica comunale di Roma* 9 (1881): 74–105.

Stinger, C. *Humanism and the Church Fathers. Ambrogio Traversari and Christian Antiquity in the Italian Renaissance.* Albany, 1977.

———. "*Roma Triumphans*: Triumphs in the Thought and Ceremonies of Renaissance Rome." *Medievalia et Humanistica* 10 (1981): 189–201.

———. "Greek Patristics and Christian Antiquity in Renaissance Rome." In *Rome in the Renaissance. The City and the Myth*, ed. P. A. Ramsey, 153–69. Binghamton, 1982.

———. *The Renaissance in Rome.* Bloomington, 1985.

Stookey, L. "The Gothic Cathedral and the Heavenly Jerusalem: Liturgical and Theological Sources." *Gesta* 7 (1969): 35–38.

Stow, K. *Alienated Minority: The Jews of Medieval Latin Europe.* Cambridge, 1992.

Strohm, R. *The Rise of European Music, 1380–1500.* Cambridge, 1993.

Tafuri, M. "'Cives esse non licere'. Niccolò V e Leon Battista Alberti." In idem, *Ricerca del Rinascimento. Principi, città, architetti*, 33–88. Turin, 1992.

Tamburini, F. *Le Cérémonial Apostolique avant Innocent VIII: Texte du manuscrit Urbinate Latin 469 de la Bibliothèque Vaticane.* Rome, 1966.

Tatarkiewicz, W. *History of Aesthetics.* The Hague, 1970.

Tateo, F. "Le virtù sociali e l'immanità nella trattatistica pontaniana." *Rinascimento* 5 (1965): 119–54.

Tavernor, R. *On Alberti and the Art of Building.* New Haven, 1998.

Tenenti, A. "Il 'Momus' nell'opera di Leon Battista Alberti." In idem, *Credenze, ideologie, libertinismi tra medioevo ed età moderna*, 137–54. Bologna, 1978.

Thelen, H. Review of A. Frutaz, *Le piante di Roma. Art Bulletin* 45 (1963): 283–86.

Thoenes, C. "Studien zur Geschichte des Petersplatzes." *Zeitschrift für Kunstgeschichte* 26 (1963): 97–145.

Tierney, B. *Foundations of the Conciliar Theory. The Contribution of Medieval Canonists from Gratian to the Great Schism.* Leiden, 1998.

Toews, J. "Formative Forces in the Pontificate of Nicholas V, 1447–1455." *Catholic Historical Review* 54 (1968–1969): 261–84.

Toth, J. *Grotte vaticane.* Milan, 1955.

Tobin, R. "Leon Battista Alberti. Ancient Sources and Structure in the Treatises on Art." Ph.D. diss., Bryn Mawr College, 1979.

Trachtenberg, M. *Dominion of the Eye. Urbanism, Art, and Power in Early Modern Florence*. New York, 1997.

———, "Architecture and Music Reunited: A New Reading of Dufay's 'Nuper Rosarum Flores' and the Cathedral of Florence." *Art Quarterly* 54 (2001): 741–75.

Trinkaus, C. *'In Our Image and Likeness'. Humanity and Divinity in Italian Humanist Thought*. London, 1970.

———. *The Scope of Renaissance Humanism*. Ann Arbor, 1983.

Tubbini, M. "Il Collegio Eugeniano e il Concilio del 1439." In *Firenze e il Concilio del 1439*, ed. Viti, 175–89.

Tugnoli Pattaro, S. "Le opere bolognesi di Aristotele Fioravanti architetto e ingegnere del secolo quindicesimo." *Arte Lombarda* 44–45 (1976): 35–70.

Turchini, A. *Il Tempio Malatestiano, Sigismondo Pandolfo Malatesta e Leon Battista Alberti*. Cesena, 2000.

Turyn, A. *The Byzantine Manuscript Tradition of the Tragedies of Euripides*. Urbana, 1957.

Tuttle, R. "Vignola's Facciata dei Banchi in Bologna." *Journal of the Society of Architectural Historians* 52 (1993): 68–87.

Tuzzi, S. *Le colonne e il Tempio di Salomone: La storia, la leggenda, la fortuna*. Rome, 2003.

Ullman, B. "A Project for a New Edition of Vincent of Beauvais." *Speculum* 8 (1933): 312–26.

Ullmann, B., and P. Stadter. *The Public Library of Renaissance Florence. Niccolò Niccoli, Cosimo de' Medici and the Library of San Marco*. Padua, 1977.

Urban, G. "Zum Neu-Bau-Projekt von St. Peter unter Nikolaus V." In *Festschrift für Harald Keller*, ed. H. M. von Erffa, 131–73. Darmstadt, 1963.

Vagnetti, L. "Lo Studio di Roma negli scritti albertiani." In *Convegno internazionale indetto nel V centenario di Leon Battista Alberti*, 73–110. Rome, 1974.

Van Dijk, S., and J. Walker. *The Origins of the Modern Roman Liturgy: The Liturgy of the Papal Court and the Franciscan Order in the 13th Century*. London, 1960.

Van Eck, C. "Giannozzo Manetti on Architecture: The 'Oratio de secularibus et pontificalibus pompis in consecratione basilicae Florentinae' of 1436." *Renaissance Studies* 12 (1998): 449–75.

Van Liere, F. "The Literal Sense of the Books of Samuel and Kings; From Andrew of St. Victor to Nicholas of Lyra." In Krey and Smith, *Nicholas of Lyra*, 59–81.

Vasari, G. *Le vite de' più eccellenti pittori scultori e architettori*, ed. P. Della Pergola et al. Vols. 2–3. Florence, 1967–1971.

Venchi, I., R. Colella, A. Nesselrath, C. Giantomassi, and D. Zari. *Fra Angelico and the Chapel of Nicholas V.* Vatican City, 1999.

Verdon, T. "'Struttura sì grande, erta sopra e'cieli': La Cupola e la città nel 1400." In *Alla riscoperta di Piazza del Duomo di Firenze. 4. La Cupola di Santa Maria del Fiore*, ed. idem, 9–32. Florence, 1995.

———. "'Ecce homo': Spazio sacro e la vittoria dell'uomo." In *La Cupola*, ed. idem, 89–114.

———. "L'opera di Santa Maria del Fiore: Sette secoli di laboriosa fedeltà." In *Alla riscoperta di Piazza del Duomo in Firenze. 6. I Tesori di Piazza del Duomo*, ed. idem, 107–30. Florence, 1997.

———, and A. Innocenti, eds. *Atti del VII centenario del Duomo di Firenze.* 5 vols. Florence, 2001.

Villetti, G. "Architetture di Borgo nel medioevo." In *L'Architettura della basilica*, ed. Spagnesi, 73–90.

Viti, P. "Un nuovo testimone dell''Epistola de coronatione Sigismundi imperatoris' di Poggio Bracciolini." In idem, *Forme letterarie umanistiche. Studi e ricerche*, 259–63. Lecce, 1999.

Voci, A. *Nord o sud? Note per la storia del medioevale Palatium Apostolicum apud Sanctum Petrum e delle sue cappelle.* Vatican City, 1992.

Voigt, G. *Il risorgimento dell'antichità classica ovvero il primo secolo dell'umanesimo*, trans. D. Valbusa. Florence, 1859; repr. 1968.

Warren, C. "Brunelleschi's Dome and Dufay's Motet." *Musical Quarterly* 59 (1973): 92–105.

Weddigen, T., S. De Blaauw, and B. Kempers, eds. *Functions and Decorations. Art and Ritual at the Vatican Palace in the Middle Ages and the Renaissance.* Vatican City, 2003.

Weise, G. *L'ideale eroico del rinascimento e le sue premesse umanistiche.* Naples, 1961.

Weiss, D. "Architectural Symbolism and the Decoration of the Ste. Chapelle." *Art Bulletin* 77 (1996): 308–20.

Westfall, C. "Biblical Typology in the 'Vita Nicolai V' by Giannozzo Manetti." In *Acta Conventus Neo-Latini Lovanensis (Proceedings of the First International Congress for Neo-Latin Studies)*, ed. J. IJsewijn and E. Kessler, 701–10. Munich, 1973.

———. *In This Most Perfect Paradise. Alberti, Nicholas V, and the Invention of Conscious Urban Planning in Rome (1447–55).* University Park, 1974.

Williams, A. *Adversus Judaeos: A Bird's-Eye View of Christian 'Apologiae' until the Renaissance*. Cambridge, 1936.

Willis, G. "Roman Stational Liturgy." In idem, *Further Essays in Early Roman Liturgy*, 1–85. London, 1968.

———. *A History of Early Roman Liturgy*. Rochester, 1994.

Wohl, H. *The Aesthetics of Italian Renaissance Art. A Reconsideration of Style*. Cambridge, 1999.

———. "Papal Patronage and the Language of Art: The Pontificates of Martin V, Eugene IV and Nicholas V." In *Umanesimo a Roma*, ed. Brezzi and de Panizza Lorch, 235–46.

Wright, C. "Dufay's *Nuper rosarum flores*, King Solomon's Temple and the Veneration of the Virgin." *Journal of the American Musicological Society* 47 (1994): 395–441.

———. "A Sequence for the Dedication of the Cathedral of Florence: Dufay's (?) *Nuper almos rose flores*." In *Atti del VII centenario*, ed. Verdon and Innocenti, 55–67.

———. *The Maze and the Warrior: Symbols in Architecture, Theology and Music*. Cambridge, MA, 2001.

Wymann, E. "Die Aufzeichnungen des Stadtpfarrers Sebastian Werro von Freiburg i. Br. Über seinen Aufenthalt in Rom vom 10–27. Mai 1581." *Römische Quartalschrift für christliche Altertumskunde und Kirchengeschichte* 33 (1925): 39–71.

Yriate, C. *Un condottière au XVe siècle, Rimini. Etudes sur les lettres et les arts à la cour des Malatesta d'après les papiers d'état des archives d'Italie*. Paris, 1882.

Yuen, T. "The 'Bibliotheca Graeca': Castagno, Alberti and Ancient Sources." *Burlington Magazine* 112 (1970): 725–36.

Zander, G. "Novità sul monumento di Paolo II (1464–71)." In *Studi . . . nel centenario della nascita di Mario Salmi*, 543–54.

Zinn, G. "Hugh of St. Victor and the Ark of Noah: A New Look." *Church History* 40 (1971): 261–72.

———. "'De gradibus ascensionum': The Stages of Contemplative Ascent in Two Treatises on Noah's Ark by Hugh of St. Victor." *Studies in Medieval Culture* 5 (1975): 61–79.

Zippel, G. "Paolo II e l'arte, note e documenti: IV: Gli edifici di San Pietro." *L'Arte* 14 (1911): 181–97.

Zorn, W. *Giannozzo Manetti: Seine Stellung in der Renaissance*. Vienna, 1939.

Zoubov, V. "Leon Battista Alberti et les auteurs du Moyen Age." *Medieval and Renaissance Studies* 4 (1958): 245–66.